Tibet

Bradley Mayhew
John Vincent Bellezza
Tony Wheeler
Chris Taylor

LONELY PLANET PUBLICATIONS
Melbourne • Oakland • London • Paris

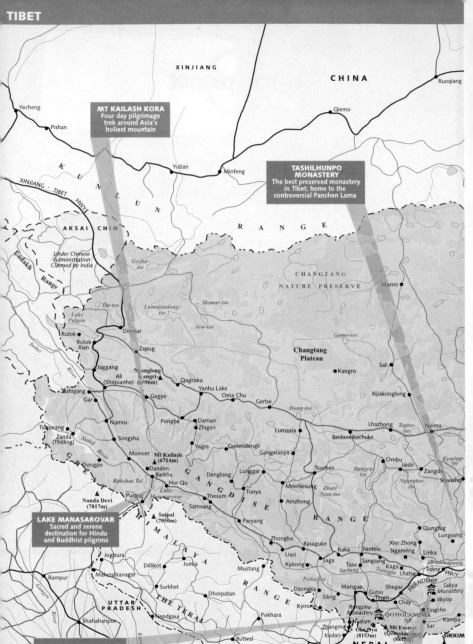

TIBET

XINJIANG

CHINA

Ruoqiang

Yecheng

Pishan

Yutian

Minfeng

Qiemo

MT KAILASH KORA
Four day pilgrimage
trek around Asia's
holiest mountain

TASHILHUNPO MONASTERY
The best preserved monastery
in Tibet; home to the
controversial Panchen Lama

XINJIANG - TIBET HWY

K U N L U N

AKSAI CHIN

Ladakh Range

Under Chinese
Administration
Claimed by India

Gozha-tso

R A N G E

Manni

Tse-tso

CHANGTANG

NATURE PRESERVE

Lumajandong-tso

Memar-tso

Aru-tso

Lake
Palgon

Rutok

Gomo-tso

Changtang
Plateau

Indus

Rutok
Xian

Dormar

Zapug

River

Jaggang

Ngangong
Kangri (6596m)

Kangro

Sali

Ali
(Shiquanhe)

Qagcaka

Yanhu Lake

Xijiakonglong

Tashigang

Gar

Gegye

Oma Chu

Gertse

Dong-tso

Lhazhong

Tagtse-tso

Nyima

Namru

Pongba

Daman

Lumaxia

Kyaring-tso

Tsaparang

Songsha

Zhigon

Beidanekechuke

Shencha

Zanda
(Tholing)

Moincer

Yagra

Gunmidengli

Gongxianya

Ombu

Jaido

Zango

Dongpo

Sutlej River

Mt Kailash
(6714m)

Denglong

Lunggar

Tsochen

Dangra-tso

Ngangtse-tso

Danden
Barkha

Hor Qu

Thesum

Tuoya

Moerkesung

Zhari
Nam-tso

Amzhong

Nanda Devi
(7817m)

Rakshas Tal

Purang

Lake
Manasarovar

Samsang

Paryang

R A N G E

Qungtag

Lungsang

LAKE MANASAROVAR
Sacred and serene
destination for Hindu
and Buddhist pilgrims

Saipal
(7050m)

Zhongba

Basaguke

Raka

Jiaotelo

Xier Zhong

Ngamring

Linka

Jogbura

Dillikot

Jumla

Liasi

Kyirong

Saga

Tase

Sangsang

Kaga

Brahmaputra

Jiding

Rampur

Mahendranagar

Mustang

Yarlung Tsangpo

Lhatse

HWY

Sakya
Monastery

Surkhet

Dhorpatan

Dzongka

Siling

Mangup

Shegar

Gutso Tingri

Chay

Jikyop

Tingche

Ganges River

Nepdgauj

Pokhara

Kyirong

Rongphu
Monastery

Nyalam

Qomolangma NP

FRIENDSHIP

Mt Everest
(8848)

Sar

Kampa

Shahahanpur

UTTAR
PRADESH

THE TERAI

Zhangmu

Kodari

(8153m)

SIKKIM

RONGPHU MONASTERY
Stunning views of
Mt Everest's north face

Butwal

KATHMANDU

SAKYA MONASTERY
Fortress-like monastery
with the most spectacular
assembly hall in Tibet

Kanchenjunga
(8598m)

Lucknow

INDIA

Amiekhganj

Gangtok

Faizabad

Gorakhpur

River

Darjeeling

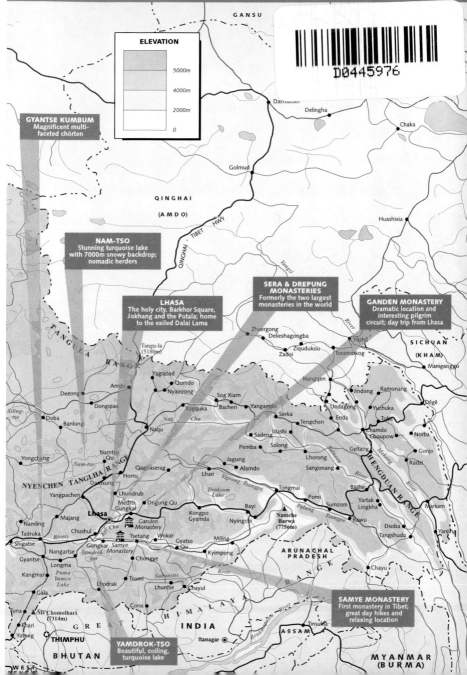

ELEVATION

5000m

4000m

2000m

0

D0445976

GYANTSE KUMBUM
Magnificent multi-faceted chörten

NAM-TSO
Stunning turquoise lake with 7000m snowy backdrop; nomadic herders

LHASA
The holy city, Barkhor Square, Jokhang and the Potala; home to the exiled Dalai Lama

SERA & DREPUNG MONASTERIES
Formerly the two largest monasteries in the world

GANDEN MONASTERY
Dramatic location and interesting pilgrim circuit; day trip from Lhasa

SAMYE MONASTERY
First monastery in Tibet; great day hikes and relaxing location

YAMDROK-TSO
Beautiful, coiling, turquoise lake

GANSU

Dachanman

Delingha

Chaka

Golmud

Huashixia

QINGHAI

(AMDO)

QINGHAI - TIBET HWY

Yangtzi

Zhaergong
Delieshagongba
Ziqudukou
Zadoi

SICHUAN

(KHAM)

Yushu
Toramakog

Maniganggo

Tangu-la
(5180m)

Yagratod

Qumdo
Nyainrong

Sog Xiam
Bachen

Yangamdo

Nangqen

Jindong

Ramonang

Dêgê

Dezong

Amdo

Serka

Undagong

Yuchuka

Tobri

Dongqiao

Xagquka

Chamdo

Norba

Doba

Banlung

Naqu

Nag Chu

Sadeng
Idashi

Tengchen

Enda

Choupow

Gonjo

Yongchang

Pemba

Solong

Jagung
Alamdo

Lhorong

Gyitang

Radzi

Namtso
Qu

Qagbaserag

Lhari

Yigrong Bangpo

Sangonang

Bashe

Horru

Draksum
Lake

Tongmai

Sumzom

Yartak
Lingkha

Markam

NYENCHEN TANGLHA RANGE

Danxung

Lhundrub

Bayi

Pomi

Palung Tsangpo

Rawu

Dsoba

Yangpachen

Medro
Gungkar

Drigung Qu

Kongpo
Gyamda

Nyingchi

Namche
Barwa
(7756m)

Tangshudu

Namling

Majang

Lhasa

Ganden
Monastery

Wokar

Gyatso
Qu

ARUNACHAL
PRADESH

Chayu

Yanjing

Tadruka

Chushul

Tsetang

Miling

Kyimpong

Shigatse

Nangartse

Gongkar

Samye
Monastery

Chongye

Yamdrok-tso

Gyantse

Longma

Kangmar

Lhodrak

Tsomi

Lhuntse

Chayul

Subansiri

INDIA

ASSAM

Gala

Puma
Yumco
Lake

Cona

Tinsuka

Itanagar

Luna

Mt Chomolhari
(7314m)

Phari

Yatung

THIMPHU

BHUTAN

WEST

MYANMAR
(BURMA)

TANGULA RANGE

HENGDUAN RANGE

Mekong River

Salween River

Kyi Chu

Yarlung Tsangpo River

Brahmaputra River

Siling-tso

Nam-tso

GREAT HIMALAYA RANGE

Tibet
4th edition – March 1999
First published – April 1986

Published by
Lonely Planet Publications Pty Ltd A.C.N. 005 607 983
192 Burwood Rd, Hawthorn, Victoria 3122, Australia

Lonely Planet Offices
Australia PO Box 617, Hawthorn, Victoria 3122
USA 150 Linden St, Oakland, CA 94607
UK 10a Spring Place, London NW5 3BH
France 1 rue du Dahomey, 75011 Paris

Photographs
All of the images in this guide are available for licensing from
Lonely Planet Images.
email: lpi@lonelyplanet.com.au

Front cover photograph
Rock painting of Tsongkhapa, founder of the Gelugpa order, Sera
Monastery (Tony Wheeler)

ISBN 0 86442 637 2

text & maps © Lonely Planet 1999
photos © photographers as indicated 1999

Printed by Colorcraft Ltd, Hong Kong

All rights reserved. No part of this publication may be reproduced,
stored in a retrieval system or transmitted in any form by any means,
electronic, mechanical, photocopying, recording or otherwise, except
brief extracts for the purpose of review, without the written permission
of the publisher and copyright owner.

Although the authors
and Lonely Planet try
to make the informa-
tion as accurate as
possible, we accept
no responsibility for
any loss, injury or
inconvenience sus-
tained by anyone
using this book.

Contents – Text

Contents – Maps

MAP LEGEND – SEE BACK PAGE

MAPS

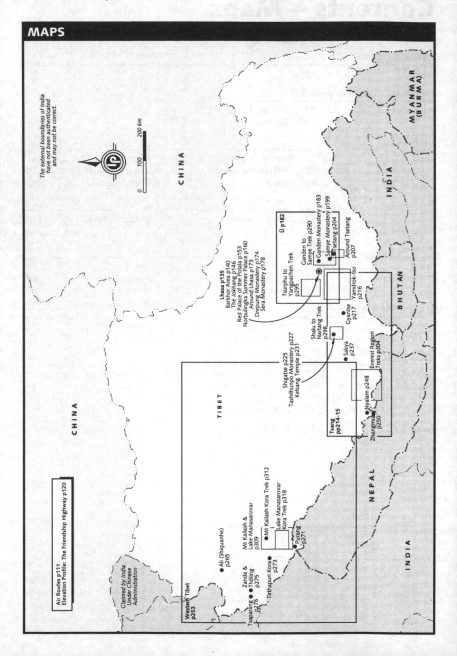

The external boundaries of India have not been authenticated and may not be correct.

0   100   200 km

CHINA

Air Routes p111
Elevation Profile: The Friendship Highway p120

Claimed by India Under Chinese Administration

CHINA

TIBET

Lhasa p135
Barkhor Area p140
The Jokhang p146
Red Palace of the Potala p153
Norbulingka Summer Palace p160
Around Lhasa p173
Drepung Monastery p174
Sera Monastery p178

0 p182

Ganden Monastery p183
Ganden to Samye Trek p290
Samye Monastery p199
Tsetang p204
Around Tsetang p207

Tsurphu to Yangpachen Trek p295

Yamdrok-tso p216

Shalu to Nartang Trek p298

Gyantse p217

Shigatse p225
Tashilhunpo Monastery p227
Kelsang Temple p231

Sakya p237

Everest Region Treks p304

Tsang pp214-15

Nyalam p248

Zhangmu p250

BHUTAN

Western Tibet p253

Ali (Shiquanhe) p265

Mt Kailash & Lake Manasarovar p309

Zanda & Tholing p275

Tsaparang p276

Tirthapuri Kora p273

Mt Kailash Kora Trek p312
Lake Manasarovar Kora Trek p318

Purang p271

NEPAL

INDIA

INDIA

MYANMAR (BURMA)

The Authors

Bradley Mayhew

Bradley started travelling in South-West China, Tibet and northern Pakistan while studying Chinese at Oxford University. Upon graduation he fled to Central America for six months to forget his Chinese and then worked in Beijing in a futile attempt to get it back. Since then he has spent two months in the Silk Road cities of Bukhara and Khiva, two months trekking in Kyrgyzstan and has enjoyed extended trips to Iran, eastern Turkey and Ladakh. He is also the co-author of LP's *South-West China, Pakistan, Karakoram Highway, Indian Himalaya,* and *India* guides.

Bradley is also the co-author and photographer of the *Odyssey Guide to Uzbekistan* and has lectured on Central Asia at the Royal Geographical Society. He splits his time between Sevenoaks in south-east England and Las Vegas, Nevada.

John Vincent Bellezza

John Vincent Bellezza was born in New York City. Suffocating in his comfortable suburban American lifestyle, he left to wander around the mountains and jungles of the Americas for several years before realising his childhood dream of visiting the Himalaya. 'Jungly' John has lived in Tibet and adjoining Himalaya regions for the past 16 years and has covered a great deal of ground on foot. Through much leg-work and study he has become an expert in the indigenous religious traditions of Tibet. His latest book *Divine Dyads: Ancient Civilization in Tibet* examines the history and mythology of sacred mountains and lakes in northern Tibet.

Tony Wheeler

Tony Wheeler was born in England, but grew up in Pakistan, the Bahamas and the USA. He returned to England to do a degree in engineering at Warwick University, worked as an automotive design engineer, returned to London Business School to complete an MBA, then set out on an Asian overland trip with his wife, Maureen. That trip led to Tony and Maureen founding Lonely Planet Publications in Australia in 1973, and they've been travelling, writing and publishing guidebooks ever since.

Chris Taylor

Chris grew up in England and Australia, but has spent much of the past decade in Asia. He has contributed to Lonely Planet's *China; Malaysia, Singapore and Brunei; Indonesia; South-East Asia* and *Japan* guides; *Tokyo* city guide and *Mandarin* phrasebook. He works as a freelance writer out of Taiwan; his stories have appeared in numerous magazines and newspapers.

FROM THE AUTHORS

Bradley Mayhew Thanks to Johannes Belzer and Mandy Ormesher at the Pentoc Guesthouse for allowing me to hijack their computer in Lhasa; Stan Armington at Malla Treks; Sarah Jenkins for mountain biking information; John Bellezza for linguistic advice; David Owen for his letter; Andre Ticheler for excellent information on his Kailash trip and a great trip out to Drigung Til; Kris and Rene for help; Ate Oostra, Dutch Ambassador, for a much-needed lift to Everest Base Camp; Walter Radl for a lift around Shegar; Kelli Hahn for research; and Calum for background info.

John Vincent Bellezza I would like to heartily thank the Tibetan people for making my walks in their beautiful country successful. I would also like to thank my wife Claire and son Eli for all their good energy and for tolerating my wanderlust. A special thanks is also due Stan Armington and his staff at Malla Treks for all their support. I also wish to extend my gratitude to Wendy Brewer Lama of the Mountain Institute and Broughton Coburn of the American Himalayan Foundation.

Tony Wheeler Stan Armington and his staff at Malla Treks in Kathmandu were miracle performers, enabling me to get to some rarely visited corners of Western Tibet and to complete the Kailash kora in, by Tibetan standards, considerable comfort! Bhaktar, Babu Ram and the irrepressible Norbu Lama were prime components of our Nepalese trekking crew. I may have cursed Ngari Travel and their less than scrupulously maintained Land Cruisers but at the end of the day they got us all the way to Lhasa.

This Book

The first edition of this book was researched and written by Michael Buckley and Robert Strauss and the second edition by Robert Strauss. The third edition was rewritten completely by Chris Taylor. Bradley Mayhew was the coordinating author of this edition which features expanded information on visas and permits for individual travellers and redrawn maps. Tony Wheeler updated the Western Tibet chapter, and the new trekking chapter was written by John Bellezza and Tony Wheeler.

From the Publisher

This edition was produced at Lonely Planet's Melbourne office. Lindsay Brown headed the editorial team with assistance from Monique Choy, Thalia Kalkipsakis and Sally Dillon. Paul Piaia coordinated the mapping and book design. The cover was designed by Simon Bracken and the illustrations were drawn by Jenny Bowman and Sarah Jolly. Thanks to Michelle Glynn and Adam McCrow in Melbourne, and to Stan Armington in Kathmandu for their generous assistance throughout the book's production.

THANKS
Many thanks to the travellers who used the last edition and wrote to us with helpful hints, advice and interesting anecdotes. Your names appear in the back of this book.

Foreword

ABOUT LONELY PLANET GUIDEBOOKS

The story begins with a classic travel adventure: Tony and Maureen Wheeler's 1972 journey across Europe and Asia to Australia. Useful information about the overland trail did not exist at that time, so Tony and Maureen published the first Lonely Planet guidebook to meet a growing need.

From a kitchen table, then from a tiny office in Melbourne (Australia), Lonely Planet has become the largest independent travel publisher in the world, an international company with offices in Melbourne, Oakland (USA), London (UK) and Paris (France).

Today Lonely Planet guidebooks cover the globe. There is an ever-growing list of books and there's information in a variety of forms and media. Some things haven't changed. The main aim is still to help make it possible for adventurous travellers to get out there – to explore and better understand the world.

At Lonely Planet we believe travellers can make a positive contribution to the countries they visit – if they respect their host communities and spend their money wisely. Since 1986 a percentage of the income from each book has been donated to aid projects and human rights campaigns.

Updates Lonely Planet thoroughly updates each guidebook as often as possible. This usually means there are around two years between editions, although for more unusual or more stable destinations the gap can be longer. Check the imprint page (following the colour map at the beginning of the book) for publication dates.

Between editions up-to-date information is available in two free newsletters – the paper *Planet Talk* and email *Comet* (to subscribe, contact any Lonely Planet office) – and on our Web site at www.lonelyplanet.com. The *Upgrades* section of the Web site covers a number of important and volatile destinations and is regularly updated by Lonely Planet authors. *Scoop* covers news and current affairs relevant to travellers. And, lastly, the *Thorn Tree* bulletin board and *Postcards* section of the site carry unverified, but fascinating, reports from travellers.

Correspondence The process of creating new editions begins with the letters, postcards and emails received from travellers. This correspondence often includes suggestions, criticisms and comments about the current editions. Interesting excerpts are immediately passed on via newsletters and the Web site, and everything goes to our authors to be verified when they're researching on the road. We're keen to get more feedback from organisations or individuals who represent communities visited by travellers.

Lonely Planet gathers information for everyone who's curious about the planet – and especially for those who explore it first-hand. Through guidebooks, phrasebooks, activity guides, maps, literature, newsletters, image library, TV series and Web site we act as an information exchange for a worldwide community of travellers.

Research Authors aim to gather sufficient practical information to enable travellers to make informed choices and to make the mechanics of a journey run smoothly. They also research historical and cultural background to help enrich the travel experience and allow travellers to understand and respond appropriately to cultural and environmental issues.

Authors don't stay in every hotel because that would mean spending a couple of months in each medium-sized city and, no, they don't eat at every restaurant because that would mean stretching belts beyond capacity. They do visit hotels and restaurants to check standards and prices, but feedback based on readers' direct experiences can be very helpful.

Many of our authors work undercover, others aren't so secretive. None of them accept freebies in exchange for positive write-ups. And none of our guidebooks contain any advertising.

Production Authors submit their raw manuscripts and maps to offices in Australia, USA, UK or France. Editors and cartographers – all experienced travellers themselves – then begin the process of assembling the pieces. When the book finally hits the shops, some things are already out of date, we start getting feedback from readers and the process begins again ...

WARNING & REQUEST

Things change – prices go up, schedules change, good places go bad and bad places go bankrupt – nothing stays the same. So, if you find things better or worse, recently opened or long since closed, please tell us and help make the next edition even more accurate and useful. We genuinely value all the feedback we receive. Julie Young coordinates a well travelled team that reads and acknowledges every letter, postcard and email and ensures that every morsel of information finds its way to the appropriate authors, editors and cartographers for verification.

Everyone who writes to us will find their name in the next edition of the appropriate guidebook. They will also receive the latest issue of *Planet Talk*, our quarterly printed newsletter, or *Comet*, our monthly email newsletter. Subscriptions to both newsletters are free. The very best contributions will be rewarded with a free guidebook.

Excerpts from your correspondence may appear in new editions of Lonely Planet guidebooks, the Lonely Planet Web site, *Planet Talk* or *Comet*, so please let us know if you *don't* want your letter published or your name acknowledged.

Send all correspondence to the Lonely Planet office closest to you:

Australia: PO Box 617, Hawthorn, Victoria 3122
USA: 150 Linden St, Oakland, CA 94607
UK: 10A Spring Place, London NW5 3BH
France: 1 rue du Dahomey, 75011 Paris

Or email us at: talk2us@lonelyplanet.com.au

For news, views and updates see our Web site: www.lonelyplanet.com

HOW TO USE A LONELY PLANET GUIDEBOOK

The best way to use a Lonely Planet guidebook is any way you choose. At Lonely Planet we believe the most memorable travel experiences are often those that are unexpected, and the finest discoveries are those you make yourself. Guidebooks are not intended to be used as if they provide a detailed set of infallible instructions!

Contents All Lonely Planet guidebooks follow the same format. The Facts about the Country chapters or sections give background information ranging from history to weather. Facts for the Visitor gives practical information on issues like visas and health. Getting There & Away gives a brief starting point for researching travel to and from the destination. Getting Around gives an overview of the transport options when you arrive.

The peculiar demands of each destination determine how subsequent chapters are broken up, but some things remain constant. We always start with background, then proceed to sights, places to stay, places to eat, entertainment, getting there and away, and getting around information – in that order.

Heading Hierarchy Lonely Planet headings are used in a strict hierarchical structure that can be visualised as a set of Russian dolls. Each heading (and its following text) is encompassed by any preceding heading that is higher on the hierarchical ladder.

Entry Points We do not assume guidebooks will be read from beginning to end, but that people will dip into them. The traditional entry points are the list of contents and the index. In addition, however, there is a complete list of maps and an index map illustrating map coverage.

There's also a colour map that shows highlights. These highlights are dealt with in greater detail in the Facts for the Visitor chapter, along with planning questions and suggested itineraries. Each chapter covering a geographical region begins with a locator map and another list of highlights. Once you find something of interest in a list of highlights, turn to the index.

Maps Maps play a crucial role in Lonely Planet guidebooks and include a huge amount of information. A legend is printed on the back page. We seek to have complete consistency between maps and text, and to have every important place in the text captured on a map. Map key numbers usually start in the top left corner.

Although inclusion in a guidebook usually implies a recommendation we cannot list every good place. Exclusion does not necessarily imply criticism. In fact there are a number of reasons why we might exclude a place – sometimes it is simply inappropriate to encourage an influx of travellers.

Introduction

Shangri-la, the Land of Snows, the Roof of the World; for centuries the mysterious Buddhist kingdom of Tibet, locked away in its mountain fastness of the Himalaya, has exercised a unique hold on the imagination of the west. The Jesuits, hearing rumours of Tibet in far away Goa, believed it to harbour a long-lost community of Christians, the Land of Prester John. For adventurers and traders it was a land of treasure and riches. Those on a spiritual quest whispered of a lost land steeped in magic and mystery.

But as Tibetans woke to the sound of foreign travellers prying at the closed doors of their kingdom, they slipped the lock and threw away the keys. Lhasa, the ultimate prize for countless proselytisers, adventurers and dreamers, became the 'Forbidden City'. Until recently, very few westerners were privileged to lay eyes on the Holy City.

When the doors finally were flung open in the mid-1980s, Tibet was no longer the hidden hermit kingdom that had so intoxicated early western travellers. In 1950, the newly established People's Republic of China (PRC) decided to make good a long-held but dubious Chinese claim on the strategically important plateau between China and the subcontinent. Between 1950 and 1970, the Chinese 'liberated' the Tibetans of their independence, drove their spiritual leader and some 100,000 of Tibet's finest into exile (admittedly a side-effect rather than a goal of Chinese policy), caused

TIBET

11

some 1.2 million Tibetan deaths (again largely a side-effect) and destroyed most of the Tibetan cultural and historical heritage.

When the Chinese allowed the first tourists into Tibet in the mid-1980s, they came to a devastated country. Most of Tibet's finest monasteries lay in ruins. Monks who, under a recent thaw in Chinese ethnic chauvinism, were once again donning their vestments, cautiously folded them back to display the scars of 'struggle sessions'. The journalist Harrison Salisbury referred to it as a 'dark and sorrowing land'.

Throughout Tibet, Tibetans are rebuilding their world. Some observers have compared this to the Tibetan renaissance of the 11th century, when Buddhism returned to the land after two centuries of persecution. Yet at the turn of the millennium this world is changing faster than at any time in Tibet's history. You can now send emails from Lhasa and get a Pepsi in even the smallest of villages, while modern China-towns continue to sprout up around Tibetan settlements.

And yet the quintessence of Tibet remains remarkably intact. The Jokhang temple is still full of pilgrims murmuring mantras in the golden light of a thousand yak butter lamps. Butter tea remains the most popular beverage by far and strangers will continually invite you to share some tea or a bowl of barley beer. A walk around Lhasa's Barkhor pilgrimage circuit is proof enough that all the efforts of the Chinese to build a Brave New (Roof of the) World have foundered on the remarkable faith of the Tibetan people. Tibet can truly claim to be on a higher plain.

Tibet is without doubt one of the most remarkable places to visit in Asia. It offers fabulous monastery sights, breathtaking high-altitude treks, stunning views of the world's highest mountains and one of the most likeable peoples you will ever meet. But you are never far from the reality of politics. For anyone who travels with their eyes open, a visit to Tibet will be a memorable, fascinating, but a sobering and at times even saddening experience.

Facts about Tibet

HISTORY
Mythological Beginnings

Little is known of the beginnings of the Tibetan people. They originated from the nomadic, warlike tribes known as the Qiang. Chinese records of these tribes, which harried the borders of the great Chinese Empire, date back as far as the 2nd century BC. However, the people of Tibet were not to emerge as a politically united force to be reckoned with until the 7th century AD.

Like all peoples, the Tibetans have a rich corpus of myths concerning the origin of the world and themselves. In the beginning, according to a Tibetan creation myth, the void was filled with a wind that gathered in force until storm clouds brewed and unleashed a torrential rain, forming in time the primeval ocean. After the cessation of the rains, the wind continued to blow over the ocean, churning it like milk, until lands, like butter, came into existence.

According to myth, the Tibetan people owe their existence to the union of an ogress and a monkey on Gangpo Ri mountain at Tsetang (anticipating Darwin by over a millennium!). Another legend tells of how the first Tibetan king descended from heaven on a sky-cord. These early myths are no doubt Bön in origin, but have been appropriated by Buddhism, so that the monkey is seen as a manifestation of Avalokiteshvara (Tibetan: Chenresig), the Bodhisattva of Compassion. The two had six children, who are seen as the ancestors of the six main tribes of Tibet.

Yarlung Valley Dynasty (?-842)

As early myths of the origin of the Tibetan people suggest, the Yarlung valley was the cradle of the civilisation of central Tibet. The early Yarlung kings, though glorified in legend, were probably no more than chieftains whose domains extended not much further than the Yarlung valley area itself. A reconstruction of Tibet's first fortress, Yum-

bulagang, can still be seen in the Yarlung valley, and it is here that the 28th king of Tibet is said to have received Tibet's first Buddhist scriptures in the mid-3rd century. According to legend, they fell on the roof of Yumbulagang.

Credible historical records regarding the Yarlung Valley Dynasty do not emerge until the fledgling kingdom entered the international arena from the 6th century. By this time the Yarlung kings had made significant headway, through conquest and alliances, in unifying much of central Tibet. Namri Songtsen (circa 570-619), the 32nd Tibetan king, continued this trend and extended Tibetan influence into inner Asia, defeating Qiang tribes on China's borders. But the true flowering of Tibet as an important regional power came about with the accession to rule of Namri Songtsen's son, Songtsen Gampo (circa 618-49).

Under Songtsen Gampo, central Tibet entered a new era. Tibetan expansion continued unabated. The armies of Tibet ranged as far afield as northern India and emerged as a threat to the Tang Dynasty in China. Both Nepal and China reacted to the Tibetan incursions by reluctantly agreeing to alliances through marriage. Princess Wencheng, Songtsen Gampo's Chinese bride, and Princess Bhrikuti, his Nepalese bride, became important historical figures for the Tibetans, as it was through their influence that Buddhism first gained royal patronage and a foothold on the Tibetan plateau. The king went as far as passing a law making it illegal *not* to be a Buddhist.

King Songtsen Gampo's reign saw the establishment of the Jokhang and Ramoche temples and the construction of a fort on the site of what much later was to become the Potala palace in Lhasa. Contact with the Chinese led to the introduction of the sciences of astronomy and medicine, and a Tibetan script was developed from Indian sources. It was used in the first translations of Buddhist scriptures, in drafting a code of law and in writing the first histories of Tibet.

For two centuries after the reign of Songtsen Gampo, Tibet continued to grow in power and influence. By the time of King Trisong Detsen (755-97), Tibetan influence extended across Turkestan, northern Pakistan, Nepal and India. In China, Tibetan armies conquered Gansu and Sichuan and controlled the great Buddhist cave complex of Dunhuang. In 783 Tibetan armies overran Chang'an (present day Xi'an), the Chinese capital, forcing the Chinese to conclude a treaty that recognised new borders incorporating most of the Tibetan conquests.

A further Sino-Tibetan treaty was signed during the reign of King Tritsug Detsen Ralpachen (817-36). It was immortalised in stone on three steles: one in Lhasa, outside the Jokhang; one in the Chinese capital of Chang'an; and one on the border of Tibet and China. Only the Lhasa stele still stands (see the 'Barkhor Area' section of the Lhasa chapter). Signatories of the treaty swore that '... the whole region to the east ... being the country of Great China and the whole region to the west being assuredly that of the country of Great Tibet, from either side of that frontier there shall be no warfare, no hostile invasions, and no seizure of territory ...'. The treaty went on to herald a new era in which 'Tibetans shall be happy in Tibet and Chinese shall be happy in China'.

Introduction of Buddhism

By the time Buddhism first arrived in Tibet during the reign of Songtsen Gampo, it had already flourished for some 1100 years and had become the principal faith of all Tibet's neighbouring countries. Buddhism was initially slow to take hold in Tibet.

Early missionaries such as Shantarakshita from the Indian Buddhist centre of Nalanda faced great hostility from the Bön-dominated court. The influence of Songtsen Gampo's Chinese and Nepalese wives was almost certainly limited to the royal court, and priests of the time were probably Indian and Chinese, not Tibetan.

It was not until King Trisong Detsen's reign that Buddhism began to make any real progress. Trisong Detsen was responsible for founding Samye Monastery, the first institution to carry out the systematic translation of Buddhist scriptures and the training of Tibetan monks.

Still, the introduction of Buddhism to Tibet was no simple matter of adopting a proscribed body of precepts. By the 9th century many schools of Buddhism had evolved from the original teachings of Sakyamuni (Tibetan: Sakya Thukpa), and Tibetans were in no way confronted with a coherent unified body of beliefs. On a purely superficial level, Buddhism encompassed the moral precepts and devotional practices of lay followers, the scholastic tradition of the Indian Buddhist universities and a body of mystic Tantric teachings that had a particular appeal to followers of the shamanistic Bön faith.

Contention over the path that Buddhism was to take in Tibet culminated in the Great Debate of Samye, in which King Trisong

Sakyamuni Buddha in Bhumisparsha mudra – calling the earth to witness his enlightenment.

Detsen is said to have adjudicated in favour of Indian teachers who advocated a gradual approach to enlightenment that was founded in scholastic study and moral precepts. There was, however, much opposition to this institutionalised, clerical Buddhism, largely from supporters of the Bön faith. The next Tibetan king, Tritsug Detsen Ralpachen, fell victim to this opposition and was assassinated by his brother, Langdharma, who launched an attack on Buddhism. In 842 Langdharma was himself assassinated during a festival – by a Buddhist monk disguised as a Black Hat dancer – and the Tibetan state quickly collapsed into a number of warring principalities. In the confusion that followed, support for Buddhism dwindled and clerical monastic Buddhism experienced a 150 year hiatus.

Second Diffusion of Buddhism (950-1200)

The collapse of the Tibetan state in 842 put a stop to Tibetan expansion in Asia; Tibet was never again to rise to arms. Overwhelmed initially with local power struggles, Buddhism gradually began to again exert its influence, giving the Tibetan mind a spiritual bent and turning it inward on itself. As the tide of Buddhist faith receded in India, Nepal and China, Tibet slowly emerged as the most devoutly Buddhist nation in the world.

While Tibetan Buddhist tradition holds that the collapse of the Tibetan state corresponds with the systematic persecution of Buddhism, many western scholars hold that this was probably not the case. It is more likely that Buddhist institutions, such as Samye Monastery, which were brought into being by the state, fell into neglect with the collapse of central power. There is evidence that Buddhism survived in pockets and received the patronage of some noble families in the 150 years that passed before the resurgence of monastic Buddhism.

The so-called Second Diffusion of the Dharma (sometimes translated as 'Law'), corresponds with two developments. Firstly, Tibetan teachers who had taken refuge in Kham, to the east, returned to central Tibet

and established new monasteries in the late 10th century. Secondly, and not long after, the kingdom of Guge in Western Tibet invited the Bengali scholar Atisha (982-1054) to Tibet in the mid-11th century. Disciples of Atisha, chiefly Dromton pa, were instrumental in establishing the Kadampa order and monasteries such as Reting in Ü.

This resurgence of Buddhist influence in the 11th century led to many Tibetans travelling to India to study. The new ideas that they brought back with them had a revitalising effect on Tibetan thought and produced other new schools of Tibetan Buddhism. Among them was the Kagyupa order, established by Marpa the translator (1012-93), and his disciple Milarepa (1040-1123). Meanwhile, in Sakya, the Kön family established a monastery in 1073 that was to emerge as the seat of the Sakyapa order.

Sakyapa Order Ascendancy & Mongol Overlordship

With the collapse of a central Tibetan state, Tibet's contacts with China dwindled. By the time the Tang Dynasty reached the end of its days in 907, China had already recovered almost all the territory it had previously lost to the Tibetans. Through the Song Dynasty (960-1276) the two nations had virtually no contact with each other, and Tibet's sole foreign contacts were with its southern Buddhist neighbours.

This was all set to change when Genghis Khan launched a series of conquests in 1206 that led to Mongol supremacy in the form of a vast empire that straddled Central Asia and China. China was not to fall to the Mongols until 1279, but in the meantime the Mongols made short work of Central Asia. Preoccupied with other matters, the Mongols did not give Tibet serious attention until 1239, when they sent a number of raiding parties into the country. Numerous monasteries were razed and the Mongols almost reached Lhasa before turning back.

Tibetan accounts have it that returning Mongol troops related the spiritual eminence of Tibetan lamas to Godan Khan, grandson of Genghis Khan and ruler of the Kokonor region, and in response Godan summoned Sakya Pandita, the head of Sakya Monastery, to his court. The outcome of this meeting was the beginning of a priest-patron relationship between the deeply religious Tibetans and the militarily adventurous Mongols. Tibetan Buddhism became the state religion of the Mongol Empire in east Asia and the head Sakya lama became its spiritual leader, a position that also entailed temporal authority over Tibet.

The Sakyapa ascendancy lasted less than 100 years. It was strife-torn from the start. The Sakyapa relationship with the Mongol court and its rule of Tibet aroused the jealousy of other religious orders. Political intrigue, power struggles and violence were the order of the day. By 1350 Changchub Gyaltsen, a monk who had first trained in Sakya and then returned to his home district in the Yarlung valley as a local official, contrived, through alliances and outright confrontation, to overturn the Sakya hegemony. Just 18 years later, the Mongol Yuan Dynasty in China lost its grip on power and the Chinese Ming Dynasty was established.

Tibetan Independence

Certain Chinese claims on Tibet have looked to the Mongol Yuan Dynasty overlordship of the high plateau, and the priest-patron relationship that existed at the time, as setting a precedent for Chinese sovereignty of Tibet. In fact, Tibetan submission was offered to the Mongols before they conquered China and it ended when the Mongols fell from power in that country. When the Mongol Empire disintegrated, both China and Tibet regained their independence. Sino-Tibetan relations took on the form of regular exchanges of diplomatic courtesies by two independent governments.

After defeating the Sakyapas, Changchub Gyaltsen undertook to remove all traces of the Mongol administration. In this he drew largely on the tradition of the former Yarlung kings: officials were required to dress in the manner of the former royal court; a revised

version of King Songtsen Gampo's code of law was enacted; a new taxation system was enforced; and scrolls depicting the glories of the Yarlung Dynasty were commissioned (though Changchub Gyaltsen claimed they were 'discovered'). The movement was nothing short of a declaration of Tibet's independence from foreign interference and a search for national identity.

Changchub Gyaltsen and his successors ruled Tibet until 1435 from Nedong, near the Yarlung valley. Their rule was succeeded by the princes of Rinpung, an area south-west of Lhasa. In 1565, the kings of Tsang became secular rulers of Tibet from Shigatse. Spiritual authority at this time was vested in the Karmapa, head of a Kagyupa sub-order at Tsurphu Monastery.

Rise of the Gelugpa & the Dalai Lamas

In 1374 a young man named Tsongkhapa set out from his home near Kokonor in eastern Tibet to central Tibet, where he undertook training with all the major schools of Tibetan Buddhism. By the time he was 25 years old, he had already gained a reputation as a teacher and a writer, though he continued to study under eminent lamas of the day.

Tsongkhapa established a monastery at Ganden near Lhasa, and it was here that he had a vision of Atisha, the 11th century Bengali scholar who had been instrumental in the second diffusion of Buddhism in Tibet. At Ganden, Tsongkhapa maintained a course of expounding his thinking, steering clear of political intrigue, and espousing doctrinal purity and monastic discipline. Though it seems unlikely that Tsongkhapa intended to found another school of Buddhism, his teachings attracted many disciples, who found his return to the original teachings of Atisha an exciting alternative to the politically tainted Sakyapa and Kagyupa orders.

Disciples of Tsongkhapa, determined to propagate their master's teachings, established monasteries at Drepung (1416) and at Sera (1419). In 1445 yet another monastery (Tashilhunpo) was established at Shigatse, and the movement came to be known as the Gelugpa (Virtuous) order. The founder of Tashilhunpo, Genden Drup, was a nephew of Tsongkhapa, and shortly before his death he announced that he would be reincarnated in Tibet and gave his followers signs that would enable them to find him. His reincarnation, Genden Gyatso, served as the head of Drepung Monastery, which was now the largest in Tibet, and further consolidated the prestige of the new Gelugpa order.

By the time of the third reincarnated head of the Gelugpa, Sonam Gyatso (1543-88), the Mongols began to take an interest in Tibet's new and increasingly powerful order. In a move that mirrored the 13th century Sakyapa entrance into the political arena, Sonam Gyatso accepted an invitation

Reincarnation Lineages

It is not unusual for an important Tibetan lama to be a *trulku*, or 'incarnate lama'. There are thought to be several thousand of them in contemporary Tibet. The abbots of many monasteries are trulku, and thus abbotship can be traced back through a lineage of rebirths to the original founder of the monastery, or at least to an important figure associated with the founding of the monastery.

Strictly speaking, however, this investiture of power through rebirth is known as *yangsid*, and a trulku is a manifestation of a Tantric deity that repeatedly expresses itself through a series of rebirths. The honorific title *rinpoche*, meaning 'very precious', is a mark of respect and does not necessarily imply that the holder is a trulku.

The most famous manifestation of a deity is of course the Dalai Lama lineage. The Dalai Lamas are manifestations of Avalokiteshvara, the Bodhisattva of Compassion. The Panchen Lama, on the other hand, is a manifestation of Manjushri, the Bodhisattva of Insight. There is no exclusivity in such a manifestation: Tsongkhapa, founder of the Gelugpa order, was also a manifestation of Manjushri, as traditionally were the abbots of the Sakya Monastery.

As a general rule, the reincarnations of high-status lamas tend to be found in aristocratic families (as in the early Dalai Lamas) or in families where trulkus have already been identified. The present Dalai Lama's family, for example, was by no means aristocratic, but his elder brother had already been identified as a trulku and his younger brother was also later recognised as a trulku.

Lamas approaching death often leave behind clues pointing to the location of their reincarnation. The Panchen Lamas have their reincarnation confirmed by lots drawn from a golden urn. Potential candidates are tested by picking out the lama's former possessions from a collection of objects. Disputes over trulku status are not uncommon. A family's fortunes are likely to improve if an incarnate lama is discovered among the children, creating an incentive for fraud.

It is possible to see in the trulku system a substitute for hereditary power (as in western royal lineages) in a society where many of the major players were celibate and unable to produce their own heirs. Not that celibacy was overwhelmingly the case. The abbots of Sakya took wives to produce their own trulku reincarnations, and it is not uncommon for rural trulkus to do the same.

The major flaw with the system is the time needed for the reincarnation to reach adulthood. Regents have traditionally been appointed to run the country but this takes an added dimension in the modern political situation. The Dalai Lama has made it clear that he will not be reincarnated in Chinese-occupied Tibet and may be the last Dalai Lama.

to meet with Altyn Khan near Kokonor in 1578. At the meeting Sonam Gyatso received the title of *Ta-Le* (Dalai), meaning 'Ocean', and implying 'Ocean of Wisdom'. The title was retrospectively bestowed on his previous two reincarnations, and Sonam Gyatso became the third Dalai Lama.

The Gelugpa-Mongol relationship marked the Gelugpa's entry into turbulent waters of worldly affairs. Ties with the Mongols deepened when, at the third Dalai Lama's death in 1588, his next reincarnation was found in a great grandson of the Mongolian Altyn Khan. The boy was brought to Lhasa with great ceremony under the escort of armed Mongol troops.

It is no surprise that the Tsang kings and the Karmapa of Tsurphu Monastery saw this Gelugpa-Mongol alliance as a direct threat to their power. Bickering broke out, and in 1611 the Tsang king attacked Drepung and Sera monasteries. The fourth Dalai Lama fled central Tibet and died at the age of 25 (probably poisoned) in 1616.

The Great Fifth Dalai Lama

A successor to the fourth Dalai Lama was soon discovered, and the boy was brought to Lhasa, again under Mongol escort. In the meantime, Mongol intervention in Tibetan affairs continued in the guise of support for the embattled Gelugpa order.

In 1621 a Mongolian invasion was turned back at the last minute through mediation by the Panchen Lama of Tashilhunpo Monastery, suggesting that there were probably elements of the Gelugpa order which preferred a truce with the kings of Tsang to outright conflict.

Whatever the case, it seems that proponents of Gelugpa domination had the upper hand, and in 1640 Mongol forces intervened on their behalf, defeating the Tsang forces. The Tsang king was taken captive and later executed, probably at the instigation of Tashilhunpo monks.

Unlike the Sakya-Mongol domination of Tibet, under which the head Sakya lama was required to reside in the Mongol court, the fifth Dalai Lama was able to carry out his rule

from within Tibet. With Mongol backing, all of Tibet was pacified by 1656, and the Dalai Lama's control ranged from Kailash in the west to Kham in the east. The fifth Dalai Lama had become both the spiritual and temporal sovereign of a unified Tibet. The new-found political power of the Dalai Lamas is symbolised in wall paintings by the holding of the Wheel of Law (Dharma).

The fifth Dalai Lama is remembered as having ushered in a great new age for Tibet. He made a tour of the monasteries of Tibet, and although he stripped most Kadampa monasteries – his chief rivals for power – of their riches, he allowed them to re-establish afterwards. A new flurry of monastic construction began, the major achievement being Labrang Monastery (now in Gansu Province). In Lhasa, work began on a fitting residence for the head of the Tibetan state: the Potala. He also invited Indian scholars to Tibet, and with Mongol financial support saw to the renovation and expansion of numerous temples and monasteries.

Manchu Intervention

Reincarnation lineages were probably first adopted as a means of maintaining the illusion of a continuous spiritual authority within the various monastic orders of Tibet. With the death of the fifth Dalai Lama, however, the weakness of such a system became apparent when it suddenly extended to the head of the Tibetan state. The great personal prestige and authority of the fifth Dalai Lama himself had played no small part in holding together a newly unified Tibet. When he died in 1682, the Tibetan government was confronted with the prospect of finding his reincarnation and then waiting some 18 years until the boy came of age. The Dalai Lama's regent decided to shroud the Dalai Lama's death in secrecy, announcing that the fifth had entered a long period of meditation (over 10 years!).

In 1695 the secret leaked and the regent was forced to hastily enthrone the sixth Dalai Lama, a boy of his own choosing. The choice was an unfortunate one. The sixth soon proved himself to be more interested in wine and women than meditation and study – he would often sneak out of the Potala to visit the brothels at its base. A resident Jesuit monk who met him noted that 'no good-looking person of either sex was safe from his unbridled licentiousness'. The enthronement of an inept head of state selected by the dubious means of auspicious tokens could not have come at a worse time.

In China the Ming Dynasty had fallen in 1644 and the Manchus from the north swiftly moved in to fill the power vacuum, establishing the Manchu Qing Dynasty (1644-1912). The events which followed are complicated. Basically, Tibet's ineffectual head of state, the Qing perception of the threat of Tibetan relations with the Mongols, disunity within the ranks of Tibet's Mongol allies and Qing ambitions to extend their power into Tibet, led to a Qing intervention that was to have lasting consequences for Tibet.

Tibet's dealings with the new Qing government went awry from the start. Kang Xi, the second Qing emperor, took offence that the death of the fifth Dalai Lama was concealed from him. At the same time, an ambitious Mongol prince named Lhabzang Khan came to the conclusion that earlier Mongol leaders had taken too much of a back-seat position in their relations with the Tibetans and appealed to Emperor Kang Xi for support. It was granted, and in 1705 Mongol forces descended on Lhasa, killed the Tibetan regent and captured the sixth Dalai Lama with the intention of delivering him to Kang Xi in Beijing. The sixth died en route at Litang (probably murdered) and Lhabzang Khan installed a new Dalai Lama in Lhasa.

Lhabzang Khan's machinations backfired. The Mongol removal, possible murder, and replacement of the sixth Dalai Lama aroused intense hostility in Tibet. Worse still, it created enemies among other Mongol tribes, who saw the Dalai Lama as their spiritual leader.

In 1717 the Dzungar Mongols attacked Lhasa, killed Lhabzang Khan and deposed the new Dalai Lama. Not that this solved anything in particular. The seventh Dalai Lama chosen by the Tibetans themselves, who had been discovered according to a prophesy by the sixth in Litang (presentz-day Sichuan), was languishing in Kumbum Monastery under Chinese 'protection'.

The resulting confusion in Tibet was the perfect opportunity for which Emperor Kang Xi had been waiting. He responded by sending a military expedition to Lhasa in 1720. The Chinese troops drove out the Dzungar Mongols and were received as liberators by the Tibetans. It was unlikely they would be received any other way: with them they brought the seventh Dalai Lama.

Emperor Kang Xi wasted no time in declaring Tibet a protectorate of China. Two Chinese representatives, known as *Ambans*, were installed at Lhasa along with a garrison of Chinese troops. It was the thin end of the wedge, leading to two centuries of Manchu overlordship and serving as a convenient historical precedent for the Communist takeover nearly 250 years later.

Manchu Overlordship

The Manchu overlordship was characterised by repeated military intervention in reaction to crises rather than a steady hand in governing Tibetan political affairs. Such interventions typically resulted in a reorganisation of the Tibetan government. The Manchus appointed a king at one stage, but temporal rule reverted to the seventh Dalai Lama in 1750.

The seventh Dalai Lama ruled successfully until his death in 1757. At this point it became clear, however, that another ruler would have to be appointed until the next Dalai Lama reached his majority. The post of regent was created, and it was decided that it should be held by a lama.

It is perhaps a poor reflection on the spiritual attainment of the lamas appointed as regents that few were willing to relinquish their hand on the helm once they had control of the ship. In the 120 years between the death of the seventh Dalai Lama and the majority of the 13th, actual power was wielded by the Dalai Lamas for only seven years.

Three of them died very young and under suspicious circumstances. Only the eighth Dalai Lama survived to his majority, living a quiet, contemplative life until the age of 45.

The last Chinese military intervention took place in reaction to a Gurkha invasion from Nepal in 1788. As usual there was an administrative reshuffle with short-lived consequences, and from this time Manchu influence in Tibet receded, though the post of Amban continued to be filled until the fall of the Qing Dynasty in 1911. Perhaps the one significant outcome of the 1788 intervention was a ban on foreign contact, imposed because of fears of British collusion in the Gurkha invasion.

Barbarians at the Doorstep

Early contacts between Britain and Tibet commenced with a mission to Shigatse headed by a Scotsman, George Bogle, in 1774. Bogle soon ingratiated himself with the Panchen Lama – to the extent of marrying one of his sisters. With the death of the third Panchen Lama in 1780 and the Gurkha invasion of Tibet in 1788, however, Britain lost all official contact with Tibet.

Meanwhile to the north, Britain watched nervously as the Russian Empire swallowed up Central Asia, pushing the borders of its empire 1000km further towards India. The reported arrival of a Russian 'adviser' Agvan Dorjieff in Lhasa merely exacerbated fears that Russia had military designs on Britain's 'jewel in the crown'.

It was against this background that Lord Curzon, viceroy of India, decided to nip Russian designs in the bud. In late 1903, an expedition led by Colonel Francis Younghusband entered Tibet via Sikkim. After several months waiting for a Tibetan delegation the British expedition moved on to

The Missionaries' Position in Early Tibet

The west's earliest contacts with Tibet were via Jesuit missionaries, some of whom were convinced it was the home of a lost Christian community known as the Kingdom of Prester John. Portuguese Jesuits reached the Guge Kingdom of Tsaparang in the 1620s and even managed to set up a church there before it was ransacked by outraged Ladakhis. In 1707 another early Jesuit mission was established in Lhasa. It survived until 1745, when it closed due to lack of funds and local opposition by monks.

One fascinating character was the Italian priest, Ippolito Desideri, who arrived in Tibet in 1716. Not only was he the first westerner to set eyes on Kailash but he also managed to stay five years in Lhasa trying to master the language and customs of Tibet so that he could convert the Tibetans to Catholicism. He even managed to write a refutation of Buddhism in Tibetan, which locals admired and then ignored.

Desideri found that the main obstacle to potential conversion was reincarnation, which he explained away by saying that the Tibetan dead descended into the Pit of Hell and were then sent back to earth possessed by the devil. In the course of his research he writes of one Hell-raiser-style stage of reincarnation, one level below animals, where 'people have a mouth the size of a needle and a neck many miles long, their eyes emit pestiferous gasses and the belly is hideously distended'. During his time in Lhasa he witnessed a Mongol invasion, a massacre of Red Hat monks by Yellow Hats and then a Manchu invasion, before finally being ordered home by the Vatican in 1721.

Neither he nor any of the other missionaries really had much luck in Tibet – after a hundred years of intense proselytising they managed to convert only 13 Tibetans! If you look closely in Lhasa you'll find them still trying to this day.

The Great Game

At the height of the Great Game (the 19th century superpower rivalry between Britain and Russia), some of Asia's most obscure corners rose to vital strategic significance and individuals gained an international importance, even if they weren't aware of it. Tibet was one of those places and Agvan Dorjieff one of those people.

Dorjieff was actually a Buryat Buddhist monk from near Lake Baikal who had studied at Drepung Monastery for 15 years before becoming one of the 13th Dalai Lama's spiritual advisers. As China and Britain began to pressure Tibet's borders, Dorjieff seems to have convinced both himself and the Dalai Lama that the Russian Empire was Shambhala, the mythical kingdom from the north, whose king (or tsar) would come to save Tibet from its enemies.

When Dorjieff led embassies from the Dalai Lama to Tsar Nicholas II in 1898, 1900 and 1901 and British intelligence confirmed that Lhasa had received Russian missions (while similar British advances had been refused) the Raj broke into a cold sweat. There was even wild conjecture that the tsar of Russia was poised to convert to Buddhism. Britain's reaction was swift – the invasion of Tibet.

Lhasa, where it was discovered that the Dalai Lama had fled to Mongolia with Dorjieff. However, an Anglo-Tibetan convention was signed via negotiations with Tri Rinpoche, a lama from Ganden whom the Dalai Lama had appointed as regent in his absence. British forces withdrew after spending just two months in Lhasa (for more on the British invasion see the boxed text 'Bayonets to Gyantse' in the Gyantse section of the Tsang chapter).

The missing link in the Anglo-Tibetan accord was a Manchu signature. In effect the accord implied that Tibet was a sovereign power with the right to make treaties of its own. The Manchus objected and in 1906 the British signed a second accord with the Manchus which recognised China's suzerainty over Tibet. In 1910, with the Manchu Qing Dynasty teetering on the verge of collapse, the Manchus made good on the accord and invaded Tibet, driving the Dalai Lama once again into flight – this time into the arms of the British in India.

Tibetan Independence Revisited

In 1911 a revolution finally toppled the decadent Qing Dynasty in China. The spirit of revolt soon spread to Tibet, which was still under occupation by Manchu troops. In Lhasa, troops mutinied against their officers, and in other parts of the country fighting broke out between Tibetans and Manchu troops. By the end of 1912, the last of the occupying forces were escorted out of Tibet via India and sent back to China. In January 1913 the 13th Dalai Lama returned to Lhasa.

The new Chinese Republican government of Yuan Shikai, anxious to maintain control of former Qing territories, sent a telegram to the Dalai Lama expressing regret at the actions of the Manchu oppressors and announcing that the Dalai Lama was being formally restored to his former rank. The Dalai Lama replied that he was uninterested in ranks bestowed by the Chinese and that he was hereby assuming temporal and spiritual leadership of his country.

This reply has been read as a formal declaration of independence by Tibetans. It certainly was in spirit if not quite in the letter. As for the Chinese, they chose to ignore it, reporting that the Dalai Lama had responded with a letter expressing his great love for the Motherland. Whatever the case, Tibet was to enjoy 30 years free of interference from China. What is more, Tibet was suddenly presented with an opportunity to create a state that was ready to rise to the challenge of the modern world and if needs be protect itself from the territorial ambitions of China. Sadly, the opportunity foundered on Tibet's entrenched theocratic institutions, and Tibetan independence was a short-lived affair.

Attempts to Modernise

During the period of his flight to India, the 13th Dalai Lama had become intimate friends with Sir Charles Bell, a Tibetan scholar and political officer in Sikkim. The relationship was to initiate a warming in Anglo-Tibetan affairs and to see the British playing an increasingly important role as mediators in problems between Tibet and China.

In 1920 Bell was dispatched on a mission to Lhasa, where he renewed his friendship with the Dalai Lama. It was agreed that the British would supply the Tibetans with modern arms providing they agreed only to use them for self defence. The Dalai Lama readily agreed and a supply of arms and ammunition was set up. Tibetan military officers were trained in Gyantse and India, and a telegraph line was set up linking Lhasa and Shigatse. Other developments included the construction of a small hydroelectric station near Lhasa and the establishment of an English school at Gyantse. Four Tibetan boys were sent to public school at Rugby in England. At the invitation of the Dalai Lama, British experts conducted geological surveys of parts of Tibet with a view to gauging mining potential.

It is highly likely that the 13th Dalai Lama's trips away from his country had made him realise that it was imperative that Tibet begin to modernise. At the same time he must also have been aware that the road to modernisation was fraught with difficulties. The biggest problem was the Tibetan social system itself.

Since the rise of the Gelugpa order, Tibet had been ruled as a theocracy. Monks, particularly those in the huge monastic complexes of Drepung and Sera at Lhasa, were accustomed to a high degree of influence in the Tibetan government. And for the monks of Tibet, the principal focus of government was the maintenance of the religious state. Attempts to modernise were seen as inimical to this aim, and before too long they began to meet with intense opposition.

Perhaps as much as anything else, the large monastery complexes of central Tibet feared the increasing empowerment of lay elements in Tibetan society. The establishment of an army, for example, was seen as a direct threat to the monasteries rather than as a means of self defence against external threats to the nation. Most monasteries kept their own small armies of fighting monks, and the presence of a well-equipped state army posed the threat of state intervention in monastic disputes. In fact, such fears proved to be well founded when the Dalai Lama brought the newly established army into action to quell a threatened uprising at Drepung Monastery.

Before too long, the 13th's innovations fell victim to a conservative backlash. Newly trained Tibetan officers were reassigned non-military jobs, causing a rapid deterioration of military discipline; a newly established police force was left to its own devices and soon became ineffective; the English school at Gyantse was closed down; and a motor mail service set up by the British was put to a stop.

Tibet's brief period of independence was troubled by more than just an inability to modernise, however. Conflict sprang up between the Panchen Lama and the Dalai Lama over the autonomy of Tashilhunpo Monastery and its estates. The Panchen Lama, after appealing to the British to mediate, fled to China, where he was kept for 14 years until his death. In 1933 the 13th Dalai Lama died, leaving the running of the country to the regent of Reting. The present 14th Dalai Lama was discovered at the village of Pari Takster near Xining in Amdo, but was only brought to Lhasa after the local Chinese commander had been paid off with a huge 'fee' of 300,000 Chinese dollars. The boy was renamed Tenzin Gyatso and installed as the Dalai Lama on 22 February 1940, aged 4½.

In 1947 an attempted coup d'état, known as the Reting Conspiracy, rocked Lhasa.

And in 1949 the Chinese Nationalist government, against all odds, fell to Mao Zedong and his Communist 'bandits'.

Liberation

When the iron bird flies and horses run on wheels, the Tibetan people will be scattered throughout the world and the Dharma will come to the land of red men.

Guru Rinpoche

Unknown to the Tibetans, the Communist takeover of China was to open what is probably the saddest chapter in Tibetan history. The Chinese 'liberation' of Tibet was eventually to lead to 1.2 million Tibetan deaths, a full-on assault on the Tibetan traditional way of life, the flight of the Dalai Lama to India and the large-scale destruction of almost every historical structure on the plateau. The chief culprits were Chinese ethnic chauvinism and an epidemic of social madness known as the Cultural Revolution.

On 7 October 1950, just a year after the Communist takeover of China, 30,000 battle-hardened Chinese troops attacked central Tibet from six different directions. The Tibetan army, a poorly equipped force of some 4000 men, stood little chance of resisting the Chinese, and any attempt at defence soon collapsed before the onslaught. In Lhasa, the Tibetan government reacted by enthroning the 15-year-old 14th Dalai Lama, an action that brought jubilation and dancing on the streets but did little to protect Tibet from advancing Chinese troops.

An appeal to the United Nations was equally ineffective. To the shame of all involved, only El Salvador sponsored a motion to condemn Chinese aggression, and Britain and India, traditional friends of Tibet, actually managed to convince the UN not to debate the issue for fear of incurring Chinese disapproval.

Presented with this seemingly hopeless situation, the Dalai Lama dispatched a mission to Beijing with orders that they refer all decisions to Lhasa. As it turned out there were no decisions to be made. The Chinese had already drafted an agreement. The Tibet-

ans had two choices: sign on the dotted line or face further Chinese aggression.

The 17 point *Agreement on Measures for the Peaceful Liberation of Tibet* promised a one-country two-systems structure much like that offered later to Hong Kong and Macau, but provided little in the way of guarantees that such a promise would be honoured. The Tibetan delegates protested that they were unauthorised to sign such an agreement and anyway lacked the seal of the Dalai Lama. Thoughtfully, the Chinese had already prepared a forged Dalai Lama seal, and the agreement was ratified.

Initially, the Chinese occupation of central Tibet was carried out in an orderly way, but tensions inevitably mounted. The presence of large numbers of Chinese troops in the Lhasa region soon depleted food stores and gave rise to massive inflation. Rumours of massacres and forced political indoctrination in Kham began to filter through to Lhasa. The Dalai Lama was invited to Beijing in 1954, where, amid cordial discussions with Mao Zedong, he was told that religion was 'poison'.

In 1956 the Preparatory Committee for the Autonomous Region of Tibet (PCART) was established. Although headed by the Dalai Lama, a majority of its seats were filled by Chinese puppets. In any case, real power lay in the hands of the Committee of the Communist Party in Tibet, which claimed no Tibetan representatives at all.

There had been uprisings at Litang and Batang in Kham as early as 1956 and armed revolt started breaking out again in Kham and Amdo (with covert CIA support) and protests started in central Tibet. The Dalai Lama returned to Lhasa from a trip to India to celebrate the 2500th anniversary of the birth of Buddha with a heavy heart. It seemed inevitable that Tibet would explode in revolt and equally inevitable that it would be ruthlessly suppressed by the Chinese.

1959 Uprising

The Tibetan New Year of 1959, like all the New Year celebrations before it, attracted huge crowds to Lhasa, doubling the usual population of the city. In addition to the usual festival activities, the Chinese had added a highlight of their own – a performance by a Chinese dance group at the Lhasa military base. The Dalai Lama's invitation to attend came in the form of a thinly veiled command. The Dalai Lama, wishing to avoid offence, accepted.

As preparations for the performance drew near, however, the Dalai Lama's security chief was surprised to hear that the Dalai Lama was expected to attend in secrecy and without his customary contingent of 25 bodyguards. Despite the Dalai Lama's agreement to these conditions, the news soon leaked, and in no time simmering frustration at Chinese rule came to the boil among the crowds on the streets. It seemed obvious to them that the Chinese were about to kidnap the Dalai Lama. Large numbers of people gathered around the Norbulingka Summer Palace of the Dalai Lama and swore to protect him with their lives.

The Dalai Lama had no choice but to cancel his appointment at the military base. In the meantime the crowds on the streets were swollen by Tibetan soldiers, who changed out of their People's Liberation Army (PLA) uniforms and started to hand out weapons. A group of government ministers announced that the 17 Point Agreement was null and void, and that Tibet renounced the authority of China.

The Dalai Lama was powerless to intervene, managing only to pen some conciliatory letters to the Chinese as his people prepared for battle on the streets of Lhasa. In a last ditch effort to prevent bloodshed, the Dalai Lama even offered himself to the Chinese. His reply came in the sound of two mortar shells exploding in the gardens of the Norbulingka. The attack made it obvious that the only option remaining to the Dalai Lama was flight. On 17 March, the Dalai Lama left the Norbulingka disguised as a soldier. Fourteen days later he was in India.

Bloodshed in Lhasa

With both the Chinese and the Tibetans unaware of the Dalai Lama's departure, tensions continued to mount in Lhasa. Early on the morning of 20 March, the Chinese troops began to shell the Norbulingka and the crowds surrounding it, killing hundreds. Later, searching through the corpses, it became obvious that the Dalai Lama had escaped – 'abducted by a reactionary clique' went the Chinese reports.

The bloodshed continued. Artillery bombed the Potala, Sera Monastery and the medical college on Chagpo Ri. Tibetans armed with petrol bombs were picked off by Chinese snipers, and when a crowd of some 10,000 Tibetans retreated into the sacred precincts of the Jokhang that too was bombed. It is thought that after three days of violence around 10,000 to 15,000 Tibetans lay dead in the streets of Lhasa.

Socialist Paradise on the Roof of the World

The Chinese quickly consolidated on their quelling of the Lhasa uprising by taking control of all the high passes between Tibet and India. Freedom fighters were put out of action by Chinese troops and able-bodied young men were rounded up, shot, incarcerated or put to work on Chinese work teams. As the Chinese themselves put it, they were liberating Tibet of reactionary forces and ushering in a new socialist society. Naturally they did not bother to ask the Tibetans themselves whether they wanted a socialist paradise.

The Chinese abolished the Tibetan government and set about reordering Tibetan society in accordance with their Marxist principles. The educated and aristocratic were put to work on menial jobs and subjected to struggle sessions, known as *thamzing*, which sometimes resulted in death. A ferment of class struggle was whipped up and former feudal exploiters – some of whom the poor of Tibet may have harboured genuine resentment for – were subjected to punishments of awful cruelty.

The Chinese also turned their attention to Tibet's more than 6000 'feudal' monasteries. Tibetans were refused permission to donate food to the monasteries, and monks were compelled to join struggle sessions, discard their robes and marry. Monasteries were stripped of their riches, Buddhist scriptures were burnt and used as toilet paper, and the vast wholesale destruction of Tibet's monastic heritage began in earnest.

Notable in this litany of errors was the Chinese decision to alter Tibetan farming practices. Instead of barley, the Tibetan staple, Tibetan farmers were instructed to grow wheat and rice. Tibetans protested that these crops were unsuited to Tibet's high-altitude conditions. They were right, and mass starvation resulted. By late 1961, it is calculated that 70,000 Tibetans had died or were dying of starvation.

By September 1961, even the Chinese-groomed Panchen Lama began to have a change of heart. He presented Mao Zedong with a 70,000 character report on the hardships his people were suffering and also requested, among other things, religious freedom and an end to the sacking of Tibetan monasteries. Four years later he was to disappear into a high-security prison for a 10 year stay. His removal was for the Chinese the last obstacle to be cleared away in the lead-up to the establishment of the Tibetan Autonomous Region (TAR).

On 1 September 1965 the TAR was formally brought into being with much fanfare and talk of happy Tibetans fighting back tears of gratitude at becoming one with the great Motherland. The tears were set to keep on coming. In China trouble was brewing in the form of a social movement that came to be known as the Great Proletarian Cultural Revolution.

The Cultural Revolution

Among the writings of Mao is a piece entitled 'On Going too Far'. It was a subject on which he was particularly well qualified to write. What started as a power struggle between Mao and Liu Shaoqi in 1965 had become by August 1966 the Great Proletarian Cultural Revolution, a movement that was to shake China to its core, trample all its traditions underfoot, cause countless deaths and give over running of the country to mobs of Red Guards. All of China suffered in Mao's bold experiment to create a new socialist paradise, but it was Tibet that suffered most dearly.

The first Red Guards arrived in Lhasa in July 1966. Two months later, the first rally was organised and Chinese-educated Tibetan youths raided the Jokhang, desecrating whatever religious objects they could get their hands on. It was the beginning of the large-scale destruction of virtually every religious monument in Tibet, and was carried out in the spirit of destroying the 'Four Olds': old thinking, old culture, old habits and old customs. The Buddhist 'om mani padme hum' was replaced by the communist mantra 'Long Live Chairman Mao'. Buddha himself was accused of being a 'reactionary'.

For more than three years the Cultural Revolution went about its destructive business of turning the Tibetan world on its head. Tibetan farmers were forced to collectivise into communes and told what to grow and when to grow it. Merrymaking was declared illegal, women had their jewellery taken from them, and the traditional plaits of Tibetan men were cut off by Red Guards in the street. Anyone objecting was arrested and subjected to thamzing. The Dalai Lama became Enemy of the People Number One and Tibetans were forced to denounce him as a parasite and traitor. The list goes on, a harrowing catalogue of crimes against a people whose only fault was to hold aspirations that differed from those of their Chinese masters.

By late 1969 the PLA had the Red Guards under control. Tibet, however, continued to be the site of outbreaks of violence. Tibetan uprisings were brief and subdued brutally. In 1972 restrictions on Tibetan's freedom of worship were lifted with much fanfare but little in the way of results. In 1975 a group of foreign journalists sympathetic to the Chinese cause were invited to Tibet. The reports they filed gave a sad picture of a land whose people had been battered to their knees by Chinese-imposed policies and atrocities that amounted to nothing less than cultural genocide. In the same year the last

CIA funded Tibetan guerilla bases were closed down in Mustang, in northern Nepal.

The Post-Mao Years

By the time of Mao's death in 1976 even the Chinese themselves must have begun to realise that their rule in Tibet had taken a wrong turn. Rebellion was ever in the wings, and maintaining order on the high plateau was a constant drain on Beijing's coffers. Mao's chosen successor, Hua Guofeng, decided to soften the government's line on Tibet and called for a revival of Tibetan customs. In mid-1977 it was announced that China would welcome the return of the Dalai Lama and other Tibetan refugees, and shortly after the Panchen Lama was released from over 10 years of imprisonment.

The invitation to return to Tibet was taken cautiously by the Tibetan Government in Exile, and the Dalai Lama suggested that he be allowed to send a fact-finding mission to Tibet first. To the surprise of all involved, the Chinese agreed. As the Dalai Lama himself remarks in his autobiography, *Freedom in Exile*, it seemed that the Chinese were of the opinion that the mission would find such happiness in their homeland that 'they would see no point in remaining in exile'. In fact, the results of the mission were so damning that the Dalai Lama decided not to publish them.

Nevertheless, two more missions followed. Their conclusions were despairing. They catalogued 1.2 million deaths, the destruction of 6254 monasteries and nunneries, the absorption of two thirds of Tibet into China, 100,000 Tibetans in labour camps and extensive deforestation. In a mere 30 years, the Chinese had turned Tibet into a land of near unrecognisable desolation.

In China, Hua Guofeng's short-lived political ascendancy had been eclipsed by Deng Xiaoping's rise to power. In 1980, Deng sent Hu Yaobang on a Chinese fact-finding mission that coincided with the visits of those sent by the Tibetan Government in Exile.

Hu's conclusions, while not as damning as those of the Tibetans, painted a grim picture of life on the Roof of the World. A six point plan to improve the living conditions and freedoms of the Tibetans was drawn up, taxes were dropped for two years and limited private enterprise was allowed. The Jokhang was reopened for two days a month in 1978; the Potala opened in 1980. As was the case in the rest of China, the government embarked on a program of extended personal freedoms in concert with authoritarian one party rule.

The Deng Years

The early 1980s saw the return of limited religious freedoms. Monasteries that had not been reduced to piles of rubble began to reopen and some religious artefacts were returned to Tibet from China.

Importantly, there was also a relaxation of the Chinese proscription on pilgrimage. Pictures of the Dalai Lama began to reappear on the streets of Lhasa. Not that any of this pointed to a significant reversal in Chinese thinking on the question of religion, which remained an opiate of the masses. Those who exercised their religious freedoms did so at considerable risk.

Talks aimed at bringing the Dalai Lama back into the ambit of Chinese influence continued, but with little in the way of results. A three person team sent to Beijing from Dharamsala in 1982 heard lectures on how Tibet was part of China and were told in no uncertain terms that the Dalai Lama would be given a desk job in Beijing were he to return. By 1983 talks had broken down and the Chinese decided that they did not want the Dalai Lama to return after all. Tibet became the 'front line of the struggle against splittism'.

Perhaps most dismaying for Tibetans, however, was the emergence of a Chinese policy of Han immigration to the high plateau. Sinicisation had already been successfully carried out in Xinjiang, Inner Mongolia and Qinghai, and now Tibet was targeted for mass immigration. Attractive salaries and interest-free loans were made available to Chinese willing to emigrate to Tibet, and in 1984 alone more than 100,000

Han Chinese took advantage of the incentives to 'modernise' the backward province of Tibet.

In 1986 a new influx of foreigners arrived in Tibet. The Chinese began to loosen restrictions on tourism, and a trickle of tour groups and individual travellers soon became a flood. For the first time since the Chinese takeover, visitors from the west were given the opportunity to see first hand the results of Chinese rule in Tibet.

For the Chinese, the foreigners were a mixed blessing. The tourist dollars were appreciated, but foreigners had an annoying habit of sympathising with Tibetans. They also got to see things that the Chinese would rather they did not see.

When in September 1987 a group of 30 monks from Sera Monastery began circumambulating the Jokhang and crying out 'Independence for Tibet' and 'Long live his Holiness the Dalai Lama', their ranks were swollen by bystanders and arrests followed. Four days later, another group of monks repeated their actions, this time brandishing Tibetan flags.

The monks were beaten and arrested. With western tourists looking on, a crowd of some 2000 to 3000 angry Tibetans gathered. Police vehicles were overturned and Chinese police began firing on the crowd.

The Chinese response was swift. Communications were broken with the outside world and foreigners were evicted from Lhasa. It was still too late, however, to prevent eyewitness accounts of what had happened from reaching newspapers around the world. A crackdown followed in Lhasa, but it failed to prevent further protests in the following months.

The Mönlam festival of March 1988 saw shooting in the streets of Lhasa, and in December of the same year a Dutch traveller was shot in the shoulder; 18 Tibetans died and 150 were wounded.

The Dalai Lama & the Search for Settlement

By the mid-1970s, the Dalai Lama had become a prominent international figure, working tirelessly from his Government in Exile in Dharamsala, India, to make the world more aware of the plight of his people. His visits to the USA led to official condemnation of the Chinese occupation of Tibet. In 1987 he addressed the US Congress and outlined a five point peace plan.

The plan called for Tibet to be established as a 'Zone of Peace'; for the policy of Han immigration to Tibet to be abandoned; for a return to basic human rights and democratic freedoms; for the protection of Tibet's natural heritage and an end to the dumping of nuclear waste on the high plateau; and for joint discussions between the Chinese and the Tibetans on the future of Tibet. The Chinese denounced the plan as an example of 'splittism'. They gave the same response, when, a year later, the Dalai Lama elaborated on the speech before the European Parliament at Strasbourg, conceding any demands for full independence

His Holiness the 14th Dalai Lama.
Born in 1935, enthroned in 1940,
in exile 1959-?

and offering the Chinese the right to govern Tibet's foreign and military affairs.

Protests and crackdowns continued in Tibet through 1989, and despairing elements in the exiled Tibetan community began to talk of the need to take up arms. It was an option that the Dalai Lama had consistently opposed. If there was to be any improvements of the situation in Tibet, he reasoned, they could only be achieved through non-violent means. The Dalai Lama's efforts to achieve peace and freedom for his people were rewarded on 4 October 1989, when he was awarded the Nobel Peace Prize. It must have seemed small consolation for the civilised world's notable failure to put any real pressure on China regarding its activities in Tibet.

Tibet Today

Tibetans have won back many religious freedoms, but at great expense. Monks and nuns, who are often the focus of protests and Tibetan aspirations for independence, are regarded suspiciously by the authorities and are often subject to arrest and beatings. Nuns in particular, considering their small numbers, have been very active, accounting for 55 of 126 independence protests in the mid-1990s according to recent reports. Once arrested and imprisoned, new rules make it impossible for nuns to return to their nunneries.

Religious institutions have recently been the focus of re-education campaigns and have had strict quotas imposed on the numbers of resident monks and nuns. Monks in Drepung were recently forced to sign a form denouncing the Dalai Lama on pain of imprisonment.

The Chinese officially deny any policy of Han immigration to Tibet, but for visitors who have made repeated trips to Tibet the increased numbers of Han Chinese are staggering. The issue of Han immigration to Tibet poses the grave danger that the Tibetans will become a minority in their own country.

It must be said that great effort has been made to curb the worst excesses of the Chinese administration and that a comparatively softened line on minorities has improved conditions for many Tibetans. There are now over 2000 functioning monasteries in Tibet. But the basic problems remain. Protests and government crackdowns have continued into the late 1990s. The Chinese government has in no way relented in its basic position regarding Tibet as a province of China and is no closer to reaching an agreement of any kind with the Dalai Lama.

In 1997, western media interest in Tibet grew with the release of the films *Seven Years in Tibet* and *Kundun*, but in political circles covert sympathy rarely translates into active support.

There have been some positive moves, however. In 1997 the US government appointed a 'Special Coordinator for Tibet' and President Clinton's trip to China in 1998 further shed the spotlight on the Tibetan issue. It is even hoped that talks might begin between the Dalai Lama and Chinese Premier Jiang Zemin in a few years. Don't hold your breath though. In many ways the status quo suits the west; as long as there are no bloody crackdowns in Lhasa foreign countries can continue to trade with China while quietly criticising its human rights status well out of China's earshot.

As the Chinese authorities trumpet rapid advances in industrial and agricultural output (Beijing announced infrastructure projects worth US$286 million in 1995), there is a growing feeling among observers that China has switched from systematic persecution to a second far more sophisticated phase in assimilating Tibet into the Motherland. Foreign investment, Han immigration and an education system that exclusively uses the Chinese language at higher levels ensures that only Sinicised Tibetans will be able to actively participate in Tibet's economic advances. For Tibetans, apart from being crowded out of their home, Chinese economic control coupled with large numbers of Chinese settlers make the Tibetan dream of independence ever harder to realise.

Undercover Monks

Frequent travellers to Tibet will tell you that some of the monks in Tibet's larger monasteries are not what they seem. There is no reason to believe that someone in a monk's or nun's habit is actually a monk or a nun. They may in fact be working for the Chinese government undercover. And if this reeks ever so slightly of paranoia, give some thought to a US couple who brought three taped speeches of the Dalai Lama with them to Tibet and handed one to a monk at Tashilhunpo Monastery in Shigatse.

After being tailed by two plain-clothes Chinese police, they were stopped at a checkpoint and a boy in civilian clothes, whom they recognised as one of the 'monks' from Tashilhunpo, identified them. At the Shigatse police station they were interrogated and then taken back to their hotel room, which was searched; the two remaining cassette tapes and some Dalai Lama pictures were confiscated. They were detained in Shigatse for four days and subject to further interrogations and threats before signing statements to the effect that they were guilty of 'distributing propaganda'. Finally they were escorted to Gongkar airport and deported to Kathmandu.

There are a number of issues at stake in this story. Firstly, it is unreasonable to trust anyone, including monks, when it comes to sensitive issues that might be construed as political. Secondly, even if *you* get away with it, any incriminating material that you hand a Tibetan could have serious consequences for the recipient (such as torture or jail) if it is discovered. And thirdly, never forget that Tibet is a highly politicised issue, and even the simple act of handing out a Dalai Lama picture is significant to the Chinese authorities.

The safest path is to avoid handing out anything 'political' at all times. But in particular be wary of monks who speak English and act as guides at monasteries; even more, do not hand out pictures of the Dalai Lama to those who request them.

GEOGRAPHY

The Tibetan plateau is one of the most isolated regions in the world, bound to the south by the 2500km long Himalaya, to the west by the Karakoram and to the north by the Kunlun and Altyn Tagh ranges. Four of the world's 10 highest mountains straddle its southern border. The north-west in particular is bounded by the most remote and least explored wilderness left on earth, outside of the polar regions. With an average altitude of 4000m and large swathes of the country well above 5000m, the Tibetan plateau (nearly the size of western Europe) deserves the title 'the Roof of the World'.

The Tibetan Autonomous Region (TAR), at 1.23 million sq km, covers only part of this geographical plateau (the rest is parcelled off into Qinghai and Sichuan provinces). It encompasses the traditional Tibetan provinces of Ü (capital, Lhasa), Tsang (capital, Shigatse) and Ngari, or Western Tibet. The TAR shares a 3482km international border with India, Bhutan, Nepal and Myanmar (Burma) and is encircled to the north and east by the Chinese provinces of Xinjiang, Qinghai, Sichuan and Yunnan.

Much of Tibet is a harsh and uncompromising landscape best described as a high-altitude desert. Little of the Indian monsoon makes it over the Himalayan watershed and shifting sand dunes are a common sight along the Samye valley and the road to Kailash.

Regions

Central Tibet, or Ütsang, is the political, historical and agricultural heartland of Tibet. Its relatively fertile valleys enjoy a mild climate and are irrigated by wide rivers such as the Yarlung Tsangpo and Kyi Chu.

To the north of central Tibet are the harsh, high-altitude plains of the Changtang ('northern plateau'), both the highest and largest plateau in the world, occupying an area of over one million sq km. This area has no river systems, and supports little in the way of life. Dead lakes on the plateau are the brackish remnants of the Tethys Sea that found no run-off when the plateau started its ascent skyward.

Ngari, or Western Tibet, is similarly barren, though here river valleys provide grassy tracts that support nomads and their grazing animals. Indeed, the Kailash range in the far west of Tibet is the source of the subcontinent's four greatest rivers: the Ganges, Indus, Sutlej and Brahmaputra. The Ganges, Indus and Sutlej rivers all cascade out of Tibet in its far west, not far from Kailash itself. The Brahmaputra (Yarlung Tsangpo), however, meanders along the northern spine of the Himalaya for 2000km searching for a way south, before coiling back on itself in a dramatic U-turn and draining into India not far from the border with Myanmar.

Kham, or south-eastern Tibet, marks a tempestuous drop in elevations down to the Sichuan plain. The concertina landscape produces some of the most spectacular roller coaster roads in Asia as Himalayan extensions such as the Hengduan Mountains are sliced by the deep gorges of the Yangzi (Jinsha), Salween (Nu Jiang) and Mekong (Lancang) headwaters. The Yarlung Tsangpo itself crashes through a 5km-deep gorge here as it swings around 7756m Namche Barwa. Many parts of this alpine region are lushly forested and support abundant wildlife, largely thanks to the lower altitudes and effects of the Indian monsoon.

Tibet has several thousand lakes, of which the largest are Nam-tso, Yamdrok-tso, Siling-tso, Manasarovar and Palgon, the latter crossing the Indian border into Ladakh.

GEOLOGY

The high plateau of Tibet is the result of prodigious geological upheaval. The time scale is subject to much debate, but at some point in the last 100 million years the entire region lay beneath the Tethys Sea. And that is where it would have stayed, had not the mass of land now known as India broken free from the proto-continent Gondwanaland and drifted off in a collision course with another proto-continent known as Laurasia. The impact of the two land masses sent the Indian plate burrowing under the Laurasian landmass and piled up two vast parallel ridges, over 3000km in length and in places almost 9km high. These ridges, the Himalaya and associated ranges, are still rising at around 10cm a year.

You may well find locals near Shegar selling fossils of marine animals – at an altitude of over 4000m above sea level!

CLIMATE

The high altitudes of the Tibetan plateau make for climatic extremes – temperatures on the Changtang have been known to drop 27°C (80°F) in a single day! At any time of the year, particularly in Western Tibet, it is a good idea to be prepared for sudden drops of temperature at night. But, basically, the Tibetan climate is not as harsh as many people imagine it to be.

The best time of year to be in Tibet is from May to the beginning of November, after which temperatures start to plummet. However, in May and June there is a wind factor to consider, and dust storms are not unusual. These are not pleasant if hitching or trekking but usually come in squalls and can be seen coming. Lhasa and Shigatse generally have very mild weather from May

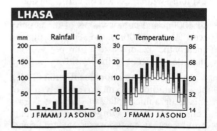

The Big Freeze

A particularly severe winter in 1997/98 caused the greatest natural disaster to hit Tibet in recent years. Consistently low temperatures of -40°C and abnormally large amounts of snow affected over a quarter of a million herdsmen in the Naqu region of Tibet and Yushu region of Qinghai who were moving between pastures when the freeze hit. It is estimated that 20% of all livestock was wiped out – the road up the Largen-la to Nam-tso was littered with yak carcasses in 1998. The disaster went largely unnoticed in the west, though medical agencies, such as Médecins Sans Frontières, joined the PLA in bringing some relief to the more accessible regions.

to November, though July and August can be rainy – these two months usually see around half of Tibet's annual rainfall.

October and November often bring some dazzlingly clear weather and daytime temperatures can be quite comfortable at Tibet's lower altitudes. Trekkers will need suitably warm clothing through these two months, however.

The coldest months are from December to February. It is not impossible to visit Tibet in the winter, but high-altitude trekking becomes almost impossible. High passes sometimes become snowbound, which can make travel difficult. The low-altitude valleys of Tibet (around Lhasa, Shigatse and Tsetang) see very little snow.

Spring does not really get under way until April, though March can have warm sunny days and is not necessarily a bad month to be in Tibet. Again, though, sudden cold snaps can dump snow on passes at this time of the year.

ECOLOGY & ENVIRONMENT

The Tibetan plateau is of global ecological importance, not only as the earth's highest ecosystem and one of its last remaining great wildernesses but also as the source of Asia's greatest rivers; the Ganges, Brahmaputra (Yarlung Tsangpo), Indus, Sutlej, Yangzi, Yellow River, Mekong and Irrawady. Furthermore it is thought that the high plateau affects global jet streams and even influences the Indian monsoon. The Dalai Lama would like to see Tibet turned into a 'zone of peace' and perhaps even the world's largest national park.

The Buddhist view of the environment stresses the intricate and interconnected relationship between the natural world and human beings; a viewpoint closely linked to the concept of death and rebirth. As early as 1642 the fifth Dalai Lama issued an edict protecting animals and the environment. Buddhist practice in general stands for moderation and against overconsumption and forbids hunting, fishing and the taking of animal life. Nomads, in particular, live in a fine balance with their harsh environment.

Modern communist experiments such as collectivisation and the switching of century-old farming patterns (eg from barley to wheat and rice) upset this fragile balance and resulted in a series of great disasters and famines in the 1960s (as indeed they did in the rest of China). By the mid-1970s, the failure of collectivisation was widely recognised and Tibetans have been allowed to return to traditional methods of working the land.

Other resources are less easily renewed. When, in the early 1980s, the Tibetan Government in Exile sent three investigative delegations to Tibet, among the shocking news they returned with was that Tibet had been denuded of its wildlife. Stories of Chinese troops machine gunning herds of wild gazelles circulated with convincing frequency, and it has sadly become necessary to travel to extremely remote locations to see the wildlife that once roamed freely on the plains of Tibet. Commercial trophy hunting, often by foreigners paying tens of thousands of US dollars, has had an effect on the numbers of antelope and argali sheep in particular.

Rapid modernisation threatens to bring industrial pollution, a hitherto almost unknown concept, onto the high plateau. Several cement factories on the edge of Lhasa create huge clouds of noxious smoke, which regularly blankets parts of western Lhasa.

Deforestation is a particularly pressing problem in eastern Tibet as Chinese logging teams continue their relentless advance from Sichuan Province. It has estimated that US$54 billion worth of timber has been felled from the Tibetan region since 1959. Logging trucks in Kham have been described as so regular that 'fifteen fully laden trucks pass by in the time it takes to drink a cup of tea'. The potential effect on sediment and run-off levels for rivers downstream, especially in flood-prone China, is considerable; over half the world's population lives downstream of Tibet.

Energy

Tibet has an enormous potential for hydroelectricity, though current projects at Yamdrok-tso and elsewhere have come in for criticism from both local Tibetans and foreign environmental groups. For more information on this project see the boxed text 'Down the Drain' in the Yamdrok-tso section of the Tsang chapter.

The region also has abundant supplies of geothermal energy thanks to its turbulent geological history. The Yangpachen Geothermal Plant already supplies Lhasa with

Yakety-Yak

Fifty years ago an estimated one million wild yak roamed the Tibetan plateau. Now it is a rare treat to catch a glimpse of this impressive black bovine, weighing up to a tonne, whose shoulder height reaches over 1.8m and whose sharp, slender horns span 1m. Wild yak have reduced in number to 15,000 due to the increased demand in yak meat and a rise in hunting. Although eating yak meat is not sacrilegious in Tibetan culture, hunting wild yak is illegal.

Few, if any, of the yak that travellers see are wild yak or *drong*. Most in fact are not even yak at all but rather *dzo*, a cross between a yak and a bull. A domestic yak rarely exceeds 1.5m in height and unlike its wild relative, it varies in shades of black to grey and, primarily around Kokonor in Qinghai, white. To see only one of a certain colour of yak in a herd is considered a bad omen, while two or more are considered a sign of luck.

Despite their massive size, yak are surprisingly sure-footed and graceful on steep, narrow trails, while burdened by loads of up to 70kg. Yak panic easily and will struggle to stay close together. This gregarious instinct allows herders to drive packs of animals through snow-blocked passes, thus creating a natural snowplow.

Most impressive is the yak's ability to sustain high altitudes. In fact, a descent below 3000m may impair the reproductive cycle and even expose yak to parasites and disease. Cloaked in layers of shaggy, coarse hair and blanketed by a soft undercoat, yak use their square tongues and broad muzzles to forage close to the soil in temperatures that frequently drop to -40°C. With three times more red blood cells than the average cow, yaks thrive in the oxygen-depleted high altitudes. Their curious lung formation, consisting of 14 or 15 pairs of ribs rather than the 13 typical of cattle, allows a large capacity of inhaling and expelling air; thus the Latin name *Bos grunniens*, or the grunting ox.

For centuries the Tibetan nomads have valued the yak. Legends suggest that Guru Rinpoche domesticated the first yak. Tibetans rely on yak milk for cheese, as well as butter for the ubiquitous butter tea and offerings to butter lamps in monasteries. Yak hair is woven into rope and tails are used in both Buddhist and Hindu religious practices. Yak tail hair was the

much of its electricity. Portable solar panelling has also enjoyed some success; the plateau enjoys some of the longest and strongest sunlight outside of the Saharan region. Experimental wind power stations have been set up in northern Tibet.

FLORA

The vast differences in altitude in Tibet give rise to a spread of ecosystems from alpine to subtropical. The high-altitude plains of the Changtang, for example, support little in the way of vegetation beside grasses such as spear grass.

Juniper trees and willows are common in the valleys of central Tibet and it is possible to come across wild flowers such as the pansy and oleander, as well as unique indigenous flowers like the *tsi-tog* (a light pink, high-altitude bloom).

To the south, along the lower-altitude borders with Nepal are forests of pines, firs and spruces. The east of Tibet, which sees higher rainfall than the rest of Tibet, has an amazing range of flora from coniferous forests to deciduous forests with oaks, elms and birches to subtropical plants and flowers such as rhododendrons, azaleas and magnolias.

FAUNA

If you are not trekking in Tibet and your travels are restricted to sights off the Friendship Highway you are unlikely to see

Yakety-Yak

main material used to produce Father Christmas beards in 1950s America! Wool is spun into *chara* felt and used to make bags, blankets and tents. Yak hide is used for the soles of boots and the yak heart is used in Tibetan medicine. Rare, hornless yak are in demand for riding. In the nomadic tradition, no part of the animal is wasted and even yak dung is required as a fundamental fuel, left to dry in little cakes on the walls of most Tibetan houses. Yak are generically referred to as *Nor*, meaning wealth, therefore a man's worth is measured by the size of his herd. So important is the yak to the Tibetans that, like their children, each yak is named.

Just as the yak are instrumental in the continuing salt-grain trade of the nomads, herders take great care to ensure the health and safety of the animals. Relocation three to eight times a year provides adequate grazing. Every spring the thick yak coats are carefully trimmed.

Nomads rely on unique veterinarian skills, which they use to lance abscess, set broken bounds and sear cuts. For some wounds a technique of wrapping in felt and keeping moist via human urine may be used.

Of the 14 million domesticated yak worldwide, five million reside on the Qinghai-Tibetan plateau. The yak, with its extraordinary composition and might, has perhaps been the sole instrument in rendering possible the harsh life of Tibet's nomads, or *drokpa*, and the two coexist in admirable harmony.

anything much in the way of wildlife. On the road out to Kailash, however, it is not unusual to see herds of antelope *(chiru)* and wild asses *(kyang)*.

Marmots are very common, and can often be seen perched up on their hind legs sniffing the air curiously outside their burrows – they make a strange bird-like sound when distressed. Pika, or Himalayan mouse-hares, a relative of the rabbit, are also very common. Those that live on Mt Everest have been observed at 5250m, thus earning the distinction of having the highest habitat of any mammal.

A surprising number of migratory birds make their way up to the lakes of the Tibetan plateau through spring and summer. Tibet has over 30 endemic birds and 480 species have been recorded on the plateau. Birds include the black-necked crane, bar-headed goose and lammergeier, as well as grebes, pheasants, snow cocks and partridges. Two of the best places to go birdwatching in summer are the lakes Yamdrok-tso and Namtso; a section of the latter, on paper at least, has been designated a bird preserve. Flocks of huge vultures can often be seen circling monasteries looking for a sky burial.

Endangered Species

Some species have been listed as protected on the official Chinese government list in recognition of their threat of extinction. These include the snow leopard, white-lipped deer, Tibetan antelope, Tibetan wild ass, bharal (blue sheep), black-necked crane and wild yak (for more on the yak see the boxed text earlier). Omitted from the list is the Tibetan brown bear, a big creature that stands nearly 2m tall. Regarded as a race of the brown bear, it is very rare and can only be found in the forests of southern Tibet and the remote Changtang plateau.

The Tibetan red deer was recently 'discovered' only 75km from Lhasa after a 50 year hiatus, as was a hitherto unknown breed of ancient wild horse in the Riwoche region of eastern Tibet. The horses bear a striking resemblance to stone age paintings.

The illegal trade in antelope cashmere,

bear's paw and other body parts and bones remain a problem. You can often see Tibetan traders huddled on street corners in major Chinese cities selling these and other medicinal cures.

NATIONAL PARKS

Nature reserves officially protect over 20% of the TAR, though many exist on paper only. The highest profile reserve is the Qomolangma Nature Preserve, a 34,000 sq km protected area straddling the 'third pole' of the Everest region. The park promotes the involvement of the local population, which is essential as some 67,000 people live inside the outer ranges of the park. For more information on the park see the boxed text 'Qomolangma Nature Preserve' in the Trekking chapter.

Tibet's newest reserve is the Changtang Nature Preserve, set up in 1993 with the assistance of famous animal behaviourist George Schaller. At 247,120 sq km (larger then Arizona) this is the largest nature reserve in the world after Greenland National Park. Endangered species in the park include bharal, argali sheep, wolf, lynx, gazelle, snow leopards, wild yak, antelope, brown bears and wild asses.

Other reserves include the Medog Nature Reserve on the south side of Namche Barwa, the Zayu Reserve in the far south-east, and the Kyirong and Nyalam reserves. These reserves unfortunately enjoy little protection or policing.

GOVERNMENT & POLITICS

Unfortunately it is necessary to make a distinction between how Tibet is run today by the Chinese and how it might govern itself should it ever have the chance to administer its own affairs.

The Communist State

Since 1965 Tibet has been administered as the Tibetan Autonomous Region (TAR). Not that there is anything particularly autonomous about its government. The Chinese make much of the fact that many high-ranking government positions are filled by Tibetans. One thing is certain, any Tibetan officials are out the minute they stop toeing the Chinese line.

The TAR is made up of the Municipality of Lhasa and six prefectures – Ali (or Ngari), Shigatse, Naqu, Shannan, Nyingchi and Chamdo – divided into 70 counties. The whole affair is presided over by the Communist Party of the Tibetan Autonomous Region, which calls all the shots. There are numerous other working committees and consultative bodies beneath the Communist Party right down to a local village level.

Tibetan Government in Exile

The immediate result of the 1959 Lhasa uprising was the flight of the Dalai Lama and eventually 80,000 Tibetan refugees to India, Nepal and Bhutan. It is estimated that there are now some 120,000 Tibetan refugees in 45 settlements on the subcontinent, and they look to the Dalai Lama's administration in Dharamsala as their government.

The Government in Exile initially consisted of the Dalai Lama's Cabinet, the Kashag, but elections were called in 1960 for the establishment of a new body known as the Commission of People's Deputies. In 1963 a Constitution of Tibet was promulgated. This constitution, which combines the qualities of Buddhism with the needs of modern government is still in a draft form, awaiting the final approval of the people of Tibet, should they ever have the opportunity to vote for their own constitution. The government is supported by voluntary taxes from the exiled Tibetan community and by business interests.

The Dalai Lama continues to be an active voice in the Tibetan struggle for independence. Foreign governments are careful, however, not to receive him in any way that recognises his political status as the head of an exiled government. The Chinese government continues to regularly protest the Dalai Lama's international activities.

In recent years the Dalai Lama has quietly admitted to a growing sense of failure in his dealings with the Chinese and there is a small but growing split among the Tibetan community on the best way forward. In the mid-1990s, a controversy blew up over an obscure protector deity called

Tibet in Exile

Modern political boundaries and history have led to the fracture of the Tibetan nation. Large areas of historical and ethnic Tibet are now incorporated into the Chinese provinces of Qinghai and Gansu (traditionally known as Amdo), and Sichuan and Yunnan (traditionally known as Kham).

Then figure on the 120,000 Tibetans in exile. Pilgrim refugees continue to brave high passes and rapacious border guards to get to Kathmandu, paying as much as Y800 to a guide to help them across. The trek can take up to 25 days with no supplies other than all the dried yak meat and *tsampa* (roast barley flour) they can carry, and no equipment to help them get over the 6000m passes except canvass shoes. Refugees who make it to Mustang, Namche Bazaar or Kathmandu are interviewed by the UN High Commission for Refugees (UNHCR) and then transferred to India. Dharamsala and McLeod Ganj in India's Himachal Pradesh have become de facto Tibetan towns, though the Dalai Lama actively encourages many of the refugees to return to Tibet.

The great monasteries of Tibet have also relocated, many to the south Indian state of Karnataka. Here in the tropical heat not far from the Indian city of Mysore you can find replicas of Sera, Ganden and Drepung monasteries. There are also large communities of Tibetans in mountainous Switzerland and you can even find prayer flags gracing the Scottish glens of Samye Ling Monastery in Dumfrieshire.

Dorge Shugden, with the Dharamsala government accused of heavy-handed tactics in forcing through official orthodoxy. In 1997 several of the Dalai Lamas closest advisers were stabbed to death only 100m from his private residence – perhaps the first ever case of fundamentalist Buddhist terrorism? Meanwhile back in Lhasa, in 1996 a series of small bombs were detonated at night in abandoned buildings, suggesting that at least some Tibetans are moving away from the Dalai Lama's overtly pacifist stand.

ECONOMY

While perhaps not quite matching the juggernaut pace of economic reform elsewhere in China, the economy of Tibet is seeing rapid changes. Communications are being improved and local officials have been encouraging foreign investment. The successes of such reforms are inevitably exaggerated – as in a report which recently claimed that herders could now make direct-dial international calls with cellular phones – but the changes are obvious to anyone who returns to Tibet after being away for a couple of years.

When the Chinese took over Tibet, the local economy had developed little in hundreds of years. It was largely agricultural and self-sufficient in its basic needs. Imports of such things as tea, porcelain, copper and iron from China were compensated by exports of wool and skins. Trading was carried out usually in combination with pilgrimage or by nomads. This movement provided a flow of goods to isolated farming communities that generally harvested barley for *tsampa* (roasted barley flour), the Tibetan staple. Animal husbandry was, and still is extremely important in Tibet and there are around 21 million head of livestock in the region.

Mining

The Chinese have since looked to other methods of developing the high plateau. One of these has been mining, which was traditionally inimical to the Tibetans, who thought it disturbed the sacred essence of the soil.

However, extensive surveys of Tibet's mining potential have been carried out in Tibet, bringing to light rich deposits of gold, zinc, chromium, lithium, copper, silver, boron, uranium and other metals. A single mine in northern Tibet is said to hold over half the world's total deposits of lithium. Reports indicate that over 120 new mining sites have been opened up in recent years to exploit these resources and that mining now accounts for one third of Tibet's industrial output. The Chinese name for Tibet – *Xizang*, or the 'Western Treasure House' – now has a ring of prophetic irony.

Chinese Investment & Migration

The frantic Chinese economic expansion and modernisation of the last 20 years has started to percolate into Tibet and arguably, Tibet today is on the brink of sharing its more recent successes. Tibet, like other outlying regions of China with rich resources and cheap labour, is attracting considerable investment from the booming east coast regions of China. East coast investors are also attracted by favourable terms being offered by the local government to anyone with money to invest in 'opening up wasteland'. Over 30 joint ventures have also been set up with countries such as the USA, Malaysia, Nepal, Hong Kong and Taiwan.

Outside investment has also brought with it a surge in Han immigration to Tibet. Although no figures are available, it is plain that many Chinese people attracted by preferential loans and tax rates, a less strictly enforced one child policy, stipends for a hardship posting and easy business opportunities are setting up shop in urban centres all over Tibet. The government in exile estimates that of Lhasa's 13,000 shopkeepers only 300 or so are Tibetan. Meanwhile standards of living in the countryside remain relatively static with an average annual income of less than Y800 (US$100).

Many Tibetans maintain that Chinese immigrants are the real winners in the race to get rich in Tibet, while China protests that it is simply developing and integrating one of its most backward provinces.

POPULATION & PEOPLE

China's 1996 population change survey put the population of the TAR at 2.44 million, with a natural growth rate of 16.2%, the highest in China. Figures are likely to be higher than this if Han immigrants and PLA troops stationed in Tibet (perhaps up to 200,000) are included, but the Chinese government is very coy about releasing figures that would make it clear just how many Chinese people there are in Tibet.

Official statistics claim 95% of the TAR's population to be Tibetan, a figure that is hotly contested by almost everyone except the government. Chinese figures for the population of Lhasa, for example, indicate it is just over 87% Tibetan and just under 12% Han Chinese, a ratio that stretches the credulity of anyone who has visited the city in recent years. It is more likely that somewhere in the vicinity of 50% of Lhasa's population is Han Chinese. The recent flood of Chinese migrants into Tibet has been termed China's 'second invasion' and ethnic dilution has been pinpointed by the Dalai Lama as probably the gravest threat to the survival of Tibetan culture.

A census conducted in 1990 indicated that there are another 2.5 million ethnic Tibetans in Qinghai, Sichuan and Gansu provinces. There are also thought to be around 120,000 more Tibetans in exile, mainly in India but also in the USA, Canada and Europe (especially Switzerland).

Population Control

Population control is a cornerstone of Chinese government policy but regulations are generally less strictly enforced in Tibet. 'Minority nationalities', as the Tibetans are classified, are allowed two children before they lose certain stipends and housing allowances, as opposed to the stricter one child policy that is applied in the rest of China.

One interesting demographic that goes against world trends is the estimate that there were 12 million Tibetans a millennia ago, four million by the 18th century and barely a million by 1949. The reason for the dramatic decline is neither plague nor invasion, but rather the tendency of families to send at least one son into the monkhood. Ironically the most effective form of birth control in modern Tibet still seems to be to join a monastery.

Ethnic Groups

Like the Han Chinese (and almost all the other ethnic minorities of China), the Tibetans are classified as belonging to the Mongoloid family of peoples. They are probably descended from a variety of nomadic tribes who migrated from the north and settled to sedentary cultivation of Tibet's river valleys. About a quarter of Tibetans, however, are still nomadic. There are considerable variations between regional groups of Tibetans. The most recognisable of these are the Khampas of eastern Tibet who are generally larger and slightly wilder than other Tibetans and who wear red or black tassels in their long hair. Women from Amdo are especially conspicuous because of their elaborate braided hairstyles and jewellery.

There are pockets of other minority groups, such as the Lhoba and Moinba in the extreme south-east of Tibet, though these make up less than 1% of the total population. A more visible ethnic group are the Hui Muslims. Tibet's original Muslim inhabitants were largely traders or butchers (a profession that most Buddhists abhor), though most of the recent migrants are traders and restaurant owners from southern Gansu Province. The Tibetan's closest ethnic cousins are the Qiang who now live mostly in northern Sichuan Province. Tibetans are also closely related to the Sherpas of Nepal and Ladakhis of India.

EDUCATION

Education was once the exclusive domain of the monasteries and the introduction of a secular education system has been a major goal of the Communist government. The number of schools has increased manifold, though literacy rates still hover around 60%.

Much primary school teaching is carried out in Tibetan, though almost all higher education is carried out in Chinese. A knowledge of Chinese is essential for advancement in Tibet, particularly in government jobs.

ARTS

Almost all Tibetan art, with the exception of some folk crafts perhaps, is inspired by Buddhism. Wall hangings, paintings, architecture, literature, even dance, all in some way or another attest to the influence of the Indian religion that found its most secure nesting place in Tibet.

At the same time, the arts of Tibet represent the synthesis of many influences. The Buddhist art and architecture of the Pala and Newari kingdoms of India and Nepal were an important early influence, as were the Central Asian Buddhist culture of Khotan and the 7th to 8th century Buddhist culture of Kashmir. Newari influence is clearly visible in the early woodcarvings of the Jokhang, and Kashmiri influence is particularly strong in the murals of Tsaparang in Western Tibet. As China came to play an increasingly major role in Tibetan affairs, Chinese influences too were assimilated, as is clear at Shalu Monastery near Shigatse. A later, clearly Tibetan style known as Menri was perfected in the monasteries of Drepung, Ganden and Sera.

Tibetan art is deeply conservative and conventional. Personal and innovation expression are not valued and indeed interpretation can actually be an obstacle to art's main purpose, representing the path to enlightenment. Artists generally remain anonymous in Tibet. Colour is decided purely by convention and rigid symbolism.

Much of Tibet's artistic heritage fell victim to the Cultural Revolution. What was not destroyed was in many cases ferreted away to China or onto the Hong Kong art market. Worse still, many of Tibet's traditional artisans were persecuted or fled Tibet. It is only in recent years that remaining artists have again been able to return to their work and start to train young Tibetans in skills that faced the threat of extinction.

The vast amount of newly executed frescoes and statuary in reconstructed Tibetan monasteries and temples is testimony to the remarkable rebound these skills have made.

Dance & Drama

Anyone who is lucky enough to attend a Tibetan festival should have the opportunity to see performances of *cham*, a ritual dance performed over several days by monks and lamas. Although every movement and gesture of cham has significance, the spectacle of the colourful masked dancers no doubt also awed many simple Tibetans who attended the festivals.

Cham is about the suppression of malevolent spirits and is a throwback to the pre-Buddhist Bön faith. It is a solemn masked dance accompanied by long trumpets, drums and cymbals. The chief officiant is a Black Hat (unmasked) lama who is surrounded by a mandalic grouping of masked monks who represent manifestations of various protective deities. The act of exorcism – it might be considered as such – is focused on a human effigy made of dough or perhaps wax or paper in which the evil spirits are thought to reside.

The proceedings of cham can be interpreted on any number of levels. The Black Hat lama is sometimes identified with the monk who slew Langdharma, the anti-Buddhist king of the Yarlung era, and the dance is seen as echoing the suppression of malevolent forces inimical to the establishment of Buddhism in Tibet. Some anthropologists, on the other hand, have seen in cham, a metaphor for the gradual conquering of the ego, which is the aim of Buddhism. The ultimate destruction of the effigy that ends the dance might represent the ego itself. Whatever the case, cham is a splendid, dramatic performance and well worth going out of the way to see.

Performances of cham are most of the time accompanied by other, less significant performances that seem to have evolved as entertainment in festivals. *Lhamo*, not to be confused with cham, is Tibetan opera. it is a largely secular art form and portrays the heroics of kings and the villainy of demons and recounts events in the lives of historical figures. Lhamo was invented by Tangtong Gyalpo, known as 'Tibet's Leonardo da Vinci', as he was also an engineer, a major bridge-builder and physician.

Other festival dances might depict the slaying of Langdharma or the arrival of the Indian teachers to Tibet at the time of the second diffusion of Buddhism. Light relief is provided by masked clowns or children.

Music

Music is one aspect of Tibetan cultural life in which there is a strong secular tradition. In urban centres songs were an important vent for social criticism, news and official lampooning. In Tibetan social life, both work and play are occasions for singing. Even today it is not uncommon to see monastery reconstruction squads pounding on the roofs of buildings and singing in unison. Where there are groups of men and women, the singing alternates between the two groups in the form of rhythmic refrains. Festivals and picnics are also occasions for singing.

Tibet also has a secular tradition of wandering minstrels. It's still possible to see them in Lhasa and Shigatse, where they play on the streets and occasionally (when they are not chased out by the owners) in restaurants.

Generally groups of two or three singers perform heroic epics and short songs to the accompaniment of a Tibetan four stringed guitar and a nifty little shuffle. In times past, groups of such performers travelled around Tibet, providing entertainment for villagers who enjoyed few distractions from the constant round of daily chores. These performers were sometimes accompanied by dancers and acrobats.

While the secular music of Tibet has an instant appeal for foreign listeners, the liturgical chants of Buddhist monks and the music that accompanies cham dances is a lot less accessible. Buddhist chanting creates an eerie haunting effect but soon becomes very monotonous. The music of cham is a discordant cacophony of trumpet blasts and boom-crash drums – atmospheric to the accompaniment of the dancing but not exactly the kind of thing you would want to slip into the CD player. The instruments used include long trumpets known as *dungchen*, human thigh-bone trumpets known as *kangling* and conch shells. Various kinds of cymbals and drums are also employed.

Tibetan Music on Disc Most recordings of Tibetan music have been made in Dharamsala or Dalhousie in India. Tibet's biggest musical export (or rather exile) is Yungchen Lhamo, who sings traditional Tibetans songs, normally a cappella. She also appeared on Nathalie Merchent's *Ophelia*. Another western-based Tibetan singer is Dadon Dawa Dolma. It's all pretty inaccessible stuff but if you fancy a try then the following recordings are available in the west:

Chö Choying Drolma & Steve Tibbets (Hannibal Music Label)
Coming Home Yungchen Lhamo (Real World)
Dhama Suna Tibetan Institute of Performing Arts (Detour)
Freedom Chants From the Roof of the World The Gyuto Monks (Rykodisc)
Kundun Phillip Glass (Nonesuch)
Sacred Tibetan Chants from the Great Prayer Festival Monks of Drepung Loseling Monastery (Music and Arts Program of America)
Seven Years in Tibet John Williams & Yo Yo Ma (Mandalay)
The Gyuto Monks: Tibet Tantric Choir (Windham Hill)
Tibet Incarnations the Meditative Sound of Buddhist Chants (Nascente)
Tibet Tibet Yungchen Lhamo (Real World)

Literature

The development of a written script for Tibetan is credited to a monk by the name of Tonmi Sambhota and corresponds with the early introduction of Buddhism during the reign of Songtsen Gampo. Accordingly, pre-Buddhist traditions were passed down as oral histories which told of the exploits of early kings and the origins of the Tibetan people. Some of these oral traditions were later recorded using the Tibetan script.

But for the most part literature in Tibet was dominated by Buddhism; firstly as a mode of translating Buddhist scriptures from Sanskrit into Tibetan; and secondly, as time went by, to the development of Tibetan Buddhist thought. There is nothing in the nature of a secular literary tradition – least of all novels – such as can be found in China or Japan.

Scholars working in the field point out that one of the great achievements of Tibetan culture was the development of a literary language which could, with remarkable faithfulness, reproduce the concepts of Sanskrit Buddhist texts. In the early 9th century, Tibetan-Sanskrit dictionaries were compiled that ensured a consistent conformity in all subsequent translations.

The alternative to Buddhist scriptures exists in an early tradition of fabulous tales, usually concerning the subjection of malevolent spirits and the taming of Tibet to allow the introduction of Buddhism. Many of these were passed from generation to generation orally, but some were recorded. Examples include the *Gesar* epic and the story of Guru Rinpoche, who is said to have been born in a lotus in the ancient kingdom of Swat before coming to Tibet and performing countless miracles to prepare the land for the diffusion of Buddhism.

Through the 12th and 13th centuries, Tibetan literary endeavour was almost entirely consumed by the monumental task of translating the complete Buddhist canon into Tibetan. The result was the 108 volumes of canonical texts *(Kangyur),* which record the words of the historical Buddha, and 208 volumes of commentary on the Kangyur by Indian masters *(Tengyur)* that make up the basic Buddhist scriptures shared by all Tibetan religious orders. What time was left from this was used in the compilation of biographies and the collection of songs of revered lamas. Perhaps most famous among these is the *Hundred Thousand Songs of Milarepa*, an ascetic who wrote many songs and poems around the theme of his quest for Buddhahood.

Woodblock printing has been in use in Tibet for centuries and is still the most common form of printing in monasteries.

Blocks are carved in mirror image and printers then work in pairs putting strips of paper over the inky block and shuttling an ink roll over it. The pages of the text are kept loose, wrapped in cloth and stored along the walls of monasteries. Tibet's most famous printing presses were in Derge in modern day Sichuan, at Nartang Monastery and at the foot of Lhasa.

Very little of the Tibetan literary tradition has been translated into English. Translations that may be of interest include: *The Tibetan Book of the Dead* (Shambala 1975), a mysterious but fascinating account of the stages and visions that occur between death and rebirth; *The Jewel Ornament of Liberation* (Shambala 1986), which describes the path to enlightenment as seen by the chief disciple of Milarepa and founder of the Kagyupa order; and *The Life of Milarepa* (Shambala 1986), the autobiography of Tibet's most famous ascetic.

Architecture

Probably the most prominent Tibetan architectural motif is the stupa, or *chörten* as it is known in Tibet. See the boxed text 'Chörtens' for more information.

Most early Tibetan architecture – the Jokhang in Lhasa for example – owed much to Indian (Pala) and Nepalese (Newari) influences. Still, a distinctively Tibetan style of architectural design was soon to emerge, which found its greatest expression in the Kumbum of Gyantse, the monasteries of Samye and Tashilhunpo and the Potala. The great American architect Frank Lloyd Wright is said to have had a picture of the Potala on the wall of his office.

Typical features of Tibetan design, which are used to a certain extent in the houses of nobility and even in villages throughout Tibet, are buildings with inward sloping walls made of large tightly fitting stones or sun-baked bricks. Below the roof is a layer of twigs, squashed tight by the roof and painted to give Tibetan houses their characteristic brown band. Roofs are flat, as there is little rain or snow, made from pounded earth and edged with walls.

Chörtens

Chörtens, or stupas, were originally built to house the cremated relics of the historical Buddha Sakyamuni and as such have become a powerful symbol of Buddha and his teachings. Later, chörtens also became reliquaries for lamas and holy men. Larger monumental versions would often hold whole mummified bodies, as is the case with the tombs of the Dalai Lamas in the Potala. And the tradition is very much alive; a stunning gold reliquary chörten was constructed in 1989 at Tashilhunpo Monastery to hold the body of the 10th Panchen Lama.

In the early stages of Buddhism there were no images of Buddha and chörtens became the major symbol of the new faith. Over the next two millennia chörtens have taken many different forms across the Buddhist world, from the sensuous stupas of Burma to the pagodas of China and Japan. Most elaborate of all are the *kumbums,* or '10,000 Buddha images', of which the best remaining example in Tibet is at Gyantse. Many chörtens were built to hold ancient relics and sacred texts and so have been plundered over the years by treasure seekers and vandals.

Chörtens are highly symbolic. The five levels represent the four elements and eternal space: the square base symbolises earth, the dome is water, the spire is fire and the top moon and sun are air and space. The 13 discs of the ceremonial umbrella can represent the branches of the tree of life or the 10 powers and three mindfulnesses of the Buddha. The top seed pinnacle symbolises enlightenment and in fact the chörten as a whole can be seen as a representation of the path to enlightenment. The construction can also physically represent the Buddha, with the base as his seat and the dome as his body.

The Gyantse Kumbum, a massive chörten temple built in the 15th century. Inside are six floors containing chapels whose walls are lined with murals and statuary.

Monastery Layout

Tibetan monasteries are based on a conservative design and share a remarkable continuity of layout. Many are built in spectacular high locations above villages. Most were originally surrounded by an outer wall, built to defend the treasures of the monastery from bands of brigands, Mongolian hordes or even rival monasteries. Most monasteries have a *kora*, or pilgrim path, around the complex, replete with holy rocks and meditation retreats high on the hillside behind.

Inside the gates there is usually a central courtyard used for special ceremonies and festivals. Surrounding buildings usually include a main assembly or prayer hall (*dukhang*) with side protector chapels (*gönkhang*) and subsidiary chapels (*lhakhang*), as well as monks quarters, a library and, in the case of larger monasteries, colleges (*tratsang*), halls of residence (*kangtsang*), kitchens and a printing press (*barkhang*).

The main prayer hall consists of rows of low seats and tables often strewn with cloaks, hats, ritual instruments, drums and huge telescopic horns. There is a small altar with seven bowls of water, butter lamps and offerings of seed mandalas. The main altar houses the main statues, often Sakyamuni (Tibetan: Sakya Thukpa), Maitreya (Jampa) or a trinity of Buddhas and perhaps the founder of the monastery or past lamas. There may be an inner room behind the main hall, whose entrance is flanked by protector gods, one blue, often Vajrapani (Chana Dorje), the other red, often Hayagriva (Tamdrin). There may well be an inner kora of prayer wheels. At the entrance to most buildings are murals of the Four Guardian Kings and perhaps a Wheel of Life or mandala mural. Side stairs lead up from here to higher floors.

Protector chapels are dark and spooky halls which hold wrathful manifestations of deities, often covered with a cloth because of their terrible appearance. Murals are often traced against a black background and walls are decorated with Tantric deities or skeletons. Pillars are decorated with festival masks, weapons and sometimes stuffed animals such as snakes and wolves.

The monastery roof usually has excellent views as well as copper symbols of the Wheel of Dharma flanked by two deer, as well as vases of immortality, victory banners and dragons.

In larger structures, the roof is supported inside by wooden pillars. The exteriors are generally whitewashed brick, though in some areas, such as Sakya in Tsang, other colours may be used. In rural Tibet, homes are often surrounded by walled compounds, and in some areas entrances are protected by painted scorpions.

Nomads, who take their homes with them, live in yak-hair tents (*bar*) which are normally roomy and can accommodate a whole family. An opening at the top of the tent lets out smoke from the fire. White tents (*gur*) with blue embroidery are used by settled town dwellers mainly at festival times.

Painting

Tibetan painting is almost exclusively devotional in nature. With the exception of decorative design, the paintings found in shrines, monasteries and in *thangkas* (wall hangings) always depict Buddhist themes. Early Tibetan painting was heavily influenced by the Buddhist cultures to the south, and in keeping with Indian style generally depicted Buddhist deities.

These usually followed stereotyped forms with a central Buddhist deity surrounded by smaller, lesser deities. Poised above the central figure was often a supreme Buddha figure of which the one below it was an emanation.

This Indian influence soon became subsumed under Tibetan developments, though the underlying forms changed little. The depiction of Buddhist deities, for example, gave way to the depiction of revered Tibetan lamas or Indian spiritual teachers.

In many thangkas and wall frescoes, the central image of a lama is surrounded by incidents from the lama's life. In the case of some mandalas, these surrounding scenes might be replaced by images from the lineage of the particular religious order associated with the lama.

Chinese influence began to manifest itself more frequently in Tibetan painting from around the 15th century. The freer approach of Chinese landscape painting allowed some Tibetan artists to break free from some of the more formalised aspects of Tibetan religious art and employ landscape as a decorative motif in the context of a painting that celebrated a particular religious figure. This is not to say that Chinese art initiated a new movement in Tibetan art. The new, Chinese-influence forms coexisted with older forms, largely due to the fact that painting in Tibet was passed on from artisan to apprentice in much the same way that monastic communities maintained their lineages of teaching.

Thangkas are usually mounted on brocade and rolled up between two sticks making them eminently portable, essential in a land of nomads. Not so portable are the huge thangkas, the size of large buildings, which are unfurled every year during festivals.

Sculpture

Like the painting of Tibet, Tibetan statuary is similarly religious in nature. Ranging from several centimetres to several metres in height, statues usually depict Buddhist deities, protective deities and revered lamas.

The Mandala

The mandala (literally 'circle') is a fascinating concept, as well as often making for quite a beautiful artistic creation in itself. In a sense you might think of a mandala as being like a three-dimensional picture. What on the surface appears as a plain two-dimensional design, with the right visual approach, emerges as a three-dimensional picture. Mandalas can be in the form of paintings, patterns of sand, three-dimensional models or even whole monasteries, as in the case of Samye.

In the case of the two-dimensional mandala the correct visual approach is achieved only through meditation. The mandala is associated with Tantric Buddhism and is chiefly used in a ritual known as *sadhana*, or 'means for attainment'. According to this ritual, the adept meditates on, invokes and identifies with a specific deity, before dissolving into emptiness and re-emerging as the deity itself. The process, in so far as it uses the mandala as an aid, involves a remarkable feat of imaginative concentration.

A typical mandala will figure a central deity surrounded by four or eight other deities who are aspects of the central figure. These surrounding deities are often accompanied by a consort. There may be several circles of these deities, totalling several hundred deities in all. These deities and all other elements of the mandala have to be visualised as the three-dimensional world of the central deity and even as a representation of the universe. One ritual calls for the adept to visualise 722 deities with sufficient clarity to be able to see the 'whites of their eyes' and hold this visualisation for four hours.

The ultimate aim of mandala visualisation, however, is to enter the three-dimensional world of the mandala and to merge with the deity at the centre of that world.

Most of the smaller statues are hollow and are stuffed with paper prayers.

Metal statues are traditionally sculpted in wax and then covered in clay. When the clay is dry it is heated. The wax melts, is removed and you are left with a mould, which can be filled with molten metal.

Sculptures are most commonly made from bronze or stucco mixed with straw but can even be made out of butter and tsampa. Butter sculptures are normally made on a wooden frame and symbolise the impermanence of all things.

SOCIETY & CONDUCT

The Tibetans are such a deeply religious people that at least a basic understanding of Buddhism is essential to making any sense of their world. Buddhism permeates most facets of Tibetan daily life and shapes the aspirations of Tibetans in ways that are often quite alien to the western frame of mind. The idea of accumulating merit, of sending sons to be monks, of undertaking pilgrimages, of devotion to the sanctity and power of natural places are all elements of the unique fusion between Buddhism and the older shamanistic Bön faith.

Although influenced by the cultures of its neighbours, Tibetan culture is markedly different to them. Unlike the subcontinent cultures to the south, Tibet never had a caste system, and the introduction of Buddhism provided a new element of social mobility. Certainly, the Tibetan nobility occupied a privileged position that was perpetuated through heredity; but with the rise of the great monasteries, religious leaders came to play an increasingly important role. Monks and incarnate lamas might come from any level of society, and once entering a monastery could through talent and hard work rise very high indeed.

Traditional Lifestyle

Traditionally there have been at least three distinct segments of Tibetan society: the nomads *(drokpa)*, the farmers of the Tibetan valleys *(rongpa)* and the community of monks and nuns *(sangha)*. Members of these groupings each led very different lives, though all shared a deep faith in Buddhism. For more information on the lifestyle of monastic community see the Religion section later in this chapter. For more information on Tibet's nomads see the boxed text 'Nomads' in the Nam-tso section of the Ü chapter.

Besides Buddhism, one thing that these communities have shared over the centuries is a remarkable resistance to change. While religious orders rose and fell from power and the Mongolians and Chinese jostled for control of the high plateau, the fundamentals of the Tibetan lifestyle remained unchanged and technological innovation of any kind was unheard of. Until the early 20th century, Tibet was a land in which virtually the only use for the wheel was as a device for activating mantras.

Traditional Tibet has changed more in the last 50 years than the previous 500, though many traditional social structures have endured Chinese attempts at iconoclasm.

Farming communities in Tibet usually comprise a cluster of homes surrounded by agricultural lands owned by the nearest large monastery. Most strategic agricultural valleys are protected by the ruins of a *dzong,* or fort, perched on a high outcrop. The farming itself is carried out with the assistance of a dzo, a crossbreed between a bull and a female yak; or, if no cattle are available, by hand. Some wealthier farmers own a small 'walking tractor'. Harvested grain is carried by donkeys to a threshing ground where it is trampled by cattle or threshed with poles. The grain is then cast into the air from a basket and the task of winnowing carried out by the breeze.

Until recently such communities were effectively self-sufficient in their needs, and although it was a hard life it could not be described as grinding poverty. Village families pulled together in times of need, and plots of land were usually graded in terms of their quality and then distributed so that the land of any one family included both good and poorer quality land. This is changing rapidly as many regions become economically more developed and immersed in a cash economy. Most villages have at least one budding entrepreneur who has set up a shop and begun to ship in Chinese goods from the nearest urban centre.

Individual households normally have a shrine in the house or in a small building in the family compound. There might also be several religious texts, held in a place of honour, which are traditionally reserved for occasions when a monk or holy man visited the village. Such visits were not necessarily so uncommon. Monasteries and nunneries were so widespread in old Tibet that most Tibetan villages were reasonably close to a religious institution. It was not unusual for monks to visit villages in their 'parish' and read from religious texts and say prayers for families before sprinkling them with water that dispelled evil. There were also ceremonies for blessing yaks and other livestock to ensure a productive year. At the same time, one of the highlights of the year for rural Tibetans was visiting nearby monasteries at festival times. As traditional life reasserts itself many of these traditions are slowly making a comeback.

Marriage Marriage has traditionally been arranged by the families involved, in consultation with a lama or shaman. In the not-so-distant past many Tibetan farming villages practiced polyandry. When a woman married the eldest son of a family she also married his younger brothers (providing they did not become monks). The children of such marriages referred to all the brothers as their father. The practice was aimed at easing the inheritance of family property (mainly the farming land) and avoiding the break-up of small plots.

Entertainment There is little in the way of entertainment for farming people. Lighting in many places is still only available from gas lamps or yak-butter candles and most people sleep at nightfall and rise with the dawn. Occasionally a wandering band of musicians or a performing troupe might pass through the village and its surrounding area.

Such performing troupes, usually comprising around eight members, but sometimes as many as 40, were once required to perform free in Lhasa once a year as a kind of tax and then allowed to spend the rest of the year touring to generate their own profits.

Other than this, farming communities have to make their own entertainment. It was not unusual for villages to have one or two musicians, though modern entertainment now comes more frequently in the form of Chinese videos and karaoke. In the summer months, picnics and singing are popular activities. Tibetan opera *(lhamo)* is still very popular at festival time.

When demands of work are at a minimum some villagers might elect to go on pilgrimage. It might be a short pilgrimage to a nearby sacred area, a long pilgrimage or a once-in-a-lifetime act of devotion to some particularly sacred area such as Lhasa or an important monastic institution.

Death Ordinary Tibetans have not traditionally buried their dead. The very poor were usually dumped in a river when they died and the very holy were enshrined in a chörten. But in a land where soil is at a premium and wood for cremation is scarcer still, most people were, and still are, disposed of by sky burial.

After death the body is kept for 24 hours in a sitting position while a lama recites prayers from the Tibetan Book of the Dead to help the soul on its journey through the 49 levels of Bardo, the state between death and rebirth. Three days after death the body is blessed, folded up and carried on the back of a close friend to the *dürto* or burial site. Here special body-breakers known as *rogyapas* cut off the deceased's hair, chop up the body and pound the bones together with tsampa for vultures to eat, though as often as not the work might be done by wild dogs.

There is little overt sadness at a sky burial as the soul is considered to have already departed – the burial itself is considered mere disposal. Sky burial is however very much a time to reflect on the impermanence of life.

Sky Burial

It is possible that the dead were disposed of by burial in the early history of Tibet. But at least since the first introduction of Buddhism the most common method has been sky burial. As even sky burial costs money, the dead of the very poor were traditionally dumped in a river. Lamas and senior monks were cremated, and in the case of important lamas their ashes interred in a funerary chörten.

As is famously known now, sky burial involves taking the body to a designated high place, dicing it up and leaving the resulting mess to birds of prey (usually vultures). It is an unusual custom and, as is the case with unusual customs, receives its fair share of interest from foreign visitors.

Naturally, Tibetans are very unhappy about camera-toting foreigners heading up to sky burial sites. The Chinese authorities do not like it either. If Tibetans find you at or near a sky burial ground, they usually respond by throwing rocks and, if you are really unlucky, chasing you away with the corpse knives. The Chinese approach is only slightly less unpleasant. Confiscation of your passport, lengthy scoldings and interrogations, followed by you signing an 'admission of guilt' are the order of the day.

Finally, even if Tibetans offer to take you up to a sky burial site, it is unlikely that other Tibetans present will be very happy about it. A group of Singaporean travellers were taken up to a sky burial site in Shigatse by a Tibetan and then stoned when they got there in mid-'94. And a Swedish traveller who followed in their footsteps alone the next day was arrested by the PSB. Sky burials are funeral services. Nobody invited you. Don't go.

Death is seen as a powerful agent of transformation and spiritual progress. Tibetans are encouraged to witness the disposal of the body and to confront death openly and without fear. This is one of the reasons that Tantric ritual objects like trumpets and bowls are made from human bone.

Dress

Many Tibetans in Lhasa are beginning to wear western, or rather Chinese, clothes but in the countryside traditional dress is still the norm. The Tibetan national dress is a *chuba* or long sleeved sheepskin cloak, tied around the waist with a sash and often worn off the shoulder with great bravado by nomads and Khampas. Chubas from eastern Tibet in particular have super long sleeves, which are tied around the waist. The inner pouch is often used to store money belts, amulets and even lunch. Most wear a long dress with a colourful striped apron over the front. Traditional boots are made of leather strips and have turned up toes.

Women have generally set great store in jewellery and their personal wealth and dowry are often invested in it. Coral is particularly valued so far from the sea, as is amber, turquoise and silver. The Tibetan *zee*, a unique elongated agate stone with black and white markings, is also highly prized. Earrings are common in both men and women and they are normally tied on with a piece of cord. You can see all these goodies for sale around the Barkhor in Lhasa.

Tibetan women traditionally wear their hair in 108 braids, especially those from northern and eastern Tibet. Khampa men plait their hair with red or black tassels and wind the lot around their head. In winter fur hats are common. Most pilgrims carry a *gau*, or amulet, with a picture of the owner's personal deity or the Dalai Lama inside.

Dos & Don'ts

The Tibetans are among the easiest people to get along with in Asia. The smiles are infectious and it is rare for major cultural differences to get in the way of communication. Problems do occur, however and it is worth remembering that there is a lot of anger and long-harboured resentment under the surface in Tibet. Moreover, many Tibetans in business and involved in the region's administration operate within the Chinese scheme of things and some have picked up habits that are encountered all to often by travellers in China: rudeness, overcharging and obstructionism, for example.

In general negotiations it is a good idea to ensure that the person you are dealing with does not lose face, appear to be wrong or be forced to back down in front of others. A negotiated settlement is always preferable and outright confrontation is a last resort. It is best to try to sort out problems with smiling persistence – when one tack fails, try another.

The giving of gifts is a useful way to establish a relationship where there was not one before. If you are a smoker, walking up to someone with a smile and handing them a cigarette is a very effective way of getting business off to a good start. In *rural* Tibet, the selective giving out of gifts (Dalai Lama pictures, chocolates, whatever) is a particularly useful way of making sure you get a thermos of hot water when you stay overnight somewhere – your small act of friendliness will ensure that the recipient will take care of you.

Be aware that Tibetans often gesture with their lips to show a direction, so if a member of the opposite sex pouts at you they are just showing you where to go. Older country folk may stick out their tongue when they meet you, a very traditional form of respect that greeted the very first travellers to Tibet centuries ago. Some sources say that this was traditionally done to prove that the person was not a devil, since devils have green tongues even when they take human form.

The most common hitching gesture is to stick out one or two fingers towards the ground and wave them up or down.

RELIGION

A basic understanding of Buddhism is essential to getting beneath the skin of things

Visiting Monasteries

Most monasteries extend a warm welcome to foreign guests and in remote areas will often offer a place to stay for the night. Maintain this good faith by observing the following courtesies:

- Always circumambulate gompas and other religious objects clockwise, thus keeping shrines and chörtens to your right.
- Don't touch or remove anything on an altar.
- Don't take prayer flags or mani stones.
- Don't take photos during a prayer meeting. At other times always ask permission to take a photo, especially one using flash. The larger monasteries charge photography fees, though some monks will allow you to take a quick picture for free. If they won't there's no point getting angry, you don't know what pressures they may be under.
- Don't wear shorts or short skirts in a monastery.
- Take your hat off when you go into a chapel.
- Don't smoke in a monastery.
- If you have a guide try to ensure that he or she is a Tibetan, as Chinese guides invariably know little about Tibetan Buddhism or monastery history.

in Tibet. Buddhism's values and goals permeate almost everything Tibetan. To explore the monasteries and temples of Tibet, to mix with its people and know nothing of Buddhism is like visiting Rome and knowing nothing of Christianity. To be sure, it might still be an awe-inspiring experience, but much remains hidden and indecipherable.

For those who already do know something of Buddhism, who have read something of Zen, for example, Tibet can be baffling on another level. The grandeur of the temples, the worship of images and fierce protective deities that stand in doorways all seem to belie the basic tenets of an ascetic faith that is basically about the renunciation of the self and following a path of moderation.

Tibetan Buddhism's reaction with existing Bön spirit worship and the Hindu pantheon has created a huge range of deities, both wrathful and benign (though these are all merely aspects of the same entities). Apart from a whole range of different Buddha aspects there are also general protector gods called *dharmapalas* and personal meditational deities called *yidams*, which Tantric students adopt early in their spiritual training. Yet for all its confusing iconography the basic tenets of Buddhism are very much rooted in daily experience. Even high lamas and monks come across as surprisingly down to earth.

Buddhism is perhaps the most tolerant of the world's religions, and wherever it went it adapted to local conditions, like a dividing cell, creating countless new schools of thought. Its basic tenets have remained very much the same and all schools are bound together in their faith in the value of the original teachings of the historical Buddha, Sakyamuni.

Mudras

The six main mudras or hand gestures of Buddha are:

Abhaya Hand lifted to shoulder level with palm turned outward.

Bhumisparsha Also known as 'earth-touching'. The right arm hangs over the right knee with the fingers touching a lotus throne. The left hand lies on the lap with palm upward. This gesture commemorates Sakyamuni's victory over temptation by demons.

Abhaya   Bhumisparsha

Dharmachakra Also known as 'turning the Wheel of Law'. Both hands are held in front of the chest with the thumb and index finger of both hands making circles. Recollects Sakyamuni's first sermon at Sarnath.

Dhyana

Dharmachakra

Dhyana Both hands placed on lap with hands facing upwards. Hands often hold a begging bowl.

Varada Arm is extended all the way down with palm facing outwards.

Vitarka Tips of thumb and index finger form a circle.

Varada   Vitarka

IMPORTANT FIGURES OF TIBETAN BUDDHISM

The following is a brief iconographical guide to some of the gods and goddesses of the vast Tibetan Buddhist pantheon as well as important historical figures. It is neither exhaustive nor scholarly, but it may help you to recognise a few of the statues you encounter during your trip. Sanskrit names are given first (with Tibetan names provided in parentheses) as they are generally more familiar to westerners. Tibetan names only are given for historical figures.

BUDDHAS

Sakyamuni (Sakya Thukpa)

The 'Historical Buddha'. Born in Lumbini in southern Nepal in the 5th century BC with the name Gautama, he attained enlightenment under a bo (peepul) tree and his teachings set in motion the Buddhist faith. In Tibetan-style representations he is always pictured sitting cross-legged on a lotus flower throne. His hair is dark blue with a halo of enlightenment around his head. Buddha is recognised by 32 marks on his body, including a dot between his eyes, a bump on the top of his head and the Dharma wheel on the soles of his feet. In his left hand he holds a begging bowl, his right hand touches the earth in the 'witness' mudra. He is often flanked by two disciples or bodhisattvas.

Sakyamuni

Amitayus (Tsepame)

Buddha of Longevity. Like Amitabha he is red and holds his hands in a meditation gesture but he holds a vase containing the nectar of immortality.

Dipamkara (Marmedze)

The 'Past Buddha', who came immediately before Sakyamuni and spent 100,000 years on earth. His hands are shown in the 'protection' mudra and he is often depicted in a trinity with the Present and Future Buddhas.

Amitabha (Öpagme)

The Buddha of Infinite Light who resides in the Pure Land of the West. The Panchen Lama is considered a reincarnation of this Buddha. He is red, his hands are held together in his lap in a 'meditation' mudra and he holds a begging bow.

Amitayus

Medicine Buddhas (Menlha)

A Medicine Buddha holds a medicine bowl in his left hand and herbs in his right. Often in a group of eight.

Dhyani Buddhas (Gyawa Ri Gna)

A group of five Buddhas, each a different colour with different mudras, symbols and attributes. Amitabha is one of the Dhyani Buddhas.

Maitreya (Jampa)

The 'Future Buddha'. He is passing the life of a bodhisattva until it is time to return to earth in human form 4000 years after the disappearance of Buddha (Sakyamuni). He is normally seated, with a scarf around his waist, his legs hanging down and his hands by his chest in the mudra of 'turning the Wheel of Law'.

Maitreya

BODHISATTVAS

These are beings who have reached the state of enlightenment but vow to save everyone else in the world before they themselves enter Nirvana. Unlike Buddhas they are often shown decorated with crowns and jewels.

Avalokiteshvara (Chenresig)

'Glorious gentle one' – he is the Bodhisattva of Compassion and his name means 'he who gazes upon the world with suffering in his eyes'. The Dalai Lama is considered a reincarnation of Avalokiteshvara and pictures of the two are interchangeable, depending on the political climate. The current Dalai Lama is the 74th manifestation of Avalokiteshvara.

His body is white and he sits on a lotus blossom. He holds rosary beads and a flower of compassion and clutches a gem to his heart. A deer skin is draped over his left shoulder.

There is also a powerful 11 headed, 1000 armed version. His head is said to have exploded when confronted with a myriad of problems to solve. One of his heads is that of wrathful Vajrapani and another (the top one) is of Amitabha, who is said to have reassembled Avalokiteshvara's body after it exploded. Each of the 1000 arms has an eye in the palm. His eight main arms hold a bow and arrow, lotus, rosary, vase, wheel and staff.

Avalokiteshvara

Manjushri (Jampelyang)

The Bodhisattva of Wisdom, is regarded as the first divine teacher of Buddhist doctrine. School children often offer prayers to him. His right hand holds the flaming sword of awareness which cuts through ignorance. His left arm cradles a scripture on a half-opened lotus blossom and his left hand is in the 'teaching' mudra. He is often yellow and may have blue hair or an elaborate crown.

Tara (Drölma)

'The Saviouress' – a female bodhisattva with 21 different manifestations or aspects. She was born from a tear of compassion that fell from Avalokiteshvara's eyes and is thus considered the female version of Avalokiteshvara and a protectress of the Tibetan people. She also symbolises purity and fertility and is believed to be able to fulfil wishes. Images usually represent Green Tara, who is associated with night, or White Tara, who is associated with day. The green version sits in a half-lotus position with her right leg down, resting on a lotus flower. The white version sits in the full lotus position and has seven eyes, including ones in her forehead, both palms and both soles of her feet. She is often seen as part of a longevity triad, along with red Amitayus and three-faced, eight-armed female Vijaya.

Manjushri

Green Tara

White Tara

PROTECTOR DEITIES

Lokpalas (Chokyong)
The Four Guardian Kings are normally seen at the entrance hallway to monasteries and are possibly of Mongol origin. Four kings for each direction; the eastern chief is white with a lute, the southern is blue holding a sword, the western is red holding a thunderbolt. Vaishravana (Namtöse), the Protector of the North, also doubles as the god of wealth and can be seen riding a snow lion and holding a banner of victory and a jewel-spitting mongoose.

Yamantaka (Dorje Jigje)
A wrathful form of Jampelyang. Known as the Destroyer of Yama, the Demon of Death, he is a favourite protector of the Gelugpa order. He is a blue colour with eight heads, the main one of which is the head of a bull. He wears a garland of skulls around his neck, a belt of skulls and holds a skull cup and a flaying knife in his 34 arms. He tramples on eight Hindu gods, eight mammals and eight birds with his 16 feet.

Mahakala (Nagpo Chenpo)
The 'Great Black One'. A wrathful, Tantric deity with connections to the Hindu god Siva. There are many varieties with anything from two to six arms. He is blue with fanged teeth and a tiara of skulls and carries a trident and a skull cup. He is believed by nomads to be the guardian of the tent.

Mahakala

Hayagriva (Tamdrin)

The 'Horse-necked One', a wrathful manifestation of Avalokiteshvara. He has a red body, his right face is white, his left face is green and he has a horse's head in his hair. He wears a tiara of skulls, a necklace of severed heads and a tiger skin around his waist. He holds a skull cup, a lotus, a sword, a snare, an axe, and a club and stands on a sun disc trampling corpses. On his back are the wings of Garuda and the skins of a human and an elephant. Here he embraces a blue consort. He has close connections to the Hindu god Vishnu.

Vajrapani (Chana Dorje)

The name of the wrathful Bodhisattva of Energy means 'thunderbolt in hand'. He holds a thunderbolt (*dorje* or *vajra*) in his right hand, which represents power and is a fundamental symbol of Tantric faith. He is dark blue with a tiger skin around his waist and a snake around his neck. He also has a peaceful, standing aspect.

Hayagriva

Shri Devi (Palden Lhamo)

Special protector of Lhasa, the Dalai Lama and the Gelugpa order and a female counterpart of Mahakala. Her origins probably lie in the Hindu goddess Kali. She is blue, wears clothes of tiger and human skin and has earrings made of a snake and a lion. She carries a club in her right hand and a skull cup full of blood in the left. She holds the moon in her hair, the sun in her belly and a corpse in her mouth and rides a mule with an eye in its rump.

Vajrapani

Shri Devi

HISTORICAL FIGURES

Guru Rinpoche

The 'lotus-born' 8th century master from modern-day Swat in Pakistan who subdued Tibet's evil spirits and helped to establish Buddhism in Tibet. Known in Sanskrit as Padmasambhava, he is regarded by followers of Nyingmapa Buddhism as the second Buddha and wears a red Nyingmapa-style hat. He has a curly moustache, holds a thunderbolt in his right hand, a skull cup in his left hand and a *khatvanga* staff topped with three heads – one shrunken, one severed and one skull – in the crook of his left arm.

Guru Rinpoche

Tsongkhapa (1357-1419)

Founder of the Gelugpa order and a manitestation of Jampelyang. He wears the yellow hat of the Gelugpas and is normally portrayed in a triad with his two main disciples Kedrub Je and Gyatsab Je. His hands are in the teaching mudra and he holds two lotuses. He was the founder and first abbot of Ganden Monastery and many images of him are found there.

Tsongkhapa

Fifth Dalai Lama (Gyawa Gnawa, 1617-82)

The greatest of all the Dalai Lamas, who unified Tibet. Wears the Gelugpa yellow hat and holds a thunderbolt *(dorje)* in his right hand and bell *(drilbu)* in his left. He may also be depicted as holding the Wheel of Law (symbolising the beginning of political control of the Dalai Lamas) and a lotus flower or other sacred objects.

King Songtsen Gampo (618-49)

Early king who unified Tibet and introduced Buddhism to the country. He has a moustache and wears a white turban with a tiny red Amitabha Buddha poking out of the top. He is flanked by his Chinese wife Wencheng on the left and his Nepalese wife Bhrikuti on his right.

Milarepa

A great 11th century Tibetan magician and poet who is believed to have attained the supreme enlightenment of Buddhahood in the course of one lifetime. He became an alchemist in order to poison an uncle who had stolen his family lands and then spent six years meditating in a cave in repentance.

Fifth Dalai Lama

During this time he wore nothing but a cotton robe and so became known as Milarepa or 'Cotton-clad Repa'. Most images of Milarepa picture him smiling, holding his hand to his ear as he sings. He may also be depicted as green because he lived for many years on a diet of nettles.

King Songtsen Gampo   **Milarepa**

Religious Symbols in Tibetan Buddhism

The Eight Auspicious Symbols, *tashi targyel* in Tibetan, are associated with gifts made to Sakyamuni upon his enlightenment and appear as protective motifs throughout Tibet.

Precious Parasol
Usually placed over Buddha images to protect them from evil influences; it is a common Buddhist motif also seen in Thailand and Japan.

Banner of Victory
Heralds the triumph of Buddhist wisdom over ignorance.

White Conch Shell
Blown in celebration of Sakyamuni's enlightenment, and often used to signal prayer time.

Knot of Eternity
Represents the entwined, never-ending passage of time, harmony and love and the unity of all things. Commonly seen on embroidery and tents.

Golden Fishes
Shown leaping from the waters of captivity, they represent liberation from the Wheel of Life. (Once the symbol of Lhasa Beer!)

Lotus Flower
Or *padma*, stands for Sakyamuni's purity and his compassion. The pure lotus rises from the muddy waters of earthly existence.

Vase of Great Treasure
A sacred repository of the jewels of enlightenment or the water of eternity.

Wheel of Dharma
Represents the Holy Eightfold Path to salvation, and is also referred to as the Wheel of Law. The wheel turns twelve times, three times for each of the Four Holy Truths

Bön

In Tibet the establishment of Buddhism was marked by its interaction with the native religion Bön. This shamanistic faith which encompassed gods and spirits, exorcism and the cult of dead kings among other things, almost certainly had a major influence on the direction Buddhism took in Tibet.

Many popular Buddhist practices such as prayer flags, sky burial, the rubbing of holy rocks, the tying of bits of cloth to trees and the construction of spirit traps all have their roots deep in Bön tradition. The traditional blessing of dipping a finger in water or milk and flicking it to the sky derives from Bön and can still be seen today in the shamanistic folk practices of Mongolia.

But it was Bön that was transformed and tamed to the ends of Buddhism and not vice versa. The Bön order, as it survives today, is to all intents and purposes a school of Buddhism. You may see Bönpo pilgrims circumambulating monuments and mountains anti-clockwise and reciting the Bön mantra *om matri muye sale du*. Mt Kailash and Mt Bönri (south-east Tibet) are Bön's holiest mountains.

Sacred Items & Symbols

Swastikas
An ancient symbol of Buddhism often found painted on houses to bring good luck. Swastikas which point clockwise are Buddhist, those which point anti-clockwise are Bön.

Sun & Moon
Another popular protective motif painted on houses. Symbolises complementary opposites, in the form of wisdom and compassion.

Windhorse
Or *Longda*, is the main symbol found on prayer flags. The horse carries the Three Jewels of Buddhism (The Buddha, Dharma and Sangha) on his back and carries prayers to the heavens.

Mani Walls
Mani stones are carved with sutras as an act of merit and placed in long walls often hundreds of metres long at holy sites.

Om Mani Padme Hum
The most common mantra carved on mani stones. The six syllables mean 'Hail to the Jewel in the Lotus' and form the mantra of Avalokiteshvara, the Bodhisattva of Compassion.

Thunderbolt (*dorje*) & Bell (*drilbu*)
These ritual objects symbolise male and female aspects used in Tantric rites and are held in the right and left hands respectively. The indestructible thunderbolt cuts through ignorance.

Ritual Dagger
Or *phurbu*, used during Tantric rituals to drive the invocation on its way.

'om mani padme hum'

Historical Background of Buddhism

Buddhism originated in the north-east of India around the 5th century BC, at a time when the local religion was Brahmanism. Some Brahmin, in preparation for presiding over offerings to their gods, partook of an asceticism that took them to remote places where they fasted, meditated and practiced yogic techniques.

The teachings of some of these ascetic Brahmin have their base in the underlying principle in the cosmos known as *brahman*. This principle had its equivalent in the human mind, and was referred to as *atman*, the universal self. The yogic practitioner who achieved identity with atman achieved liberation from the cycle of death and rebirth and merged into brahman.

Many of the fundamental concepts of Buddhism, then, find their origin in the Brahmin society of this time. The Buddha himself was one of many wandering ascetics whose teachings led to the establishment of rival religious schools. Jainism, a religion that found a basic life principle in all objects and aimed to attain identity with that principle through ascetic practices and even

Sacred Items & Symbols

Skull Drum
Small double sided hand drum traditionally made from two halves of a skull covered in leather or even human skin.

Torma
Small sculptured offerings made of yak butter and tsampa adorned with medallions of butter, often coloured. Most are made during the Shötun festival and remain on display throughout the year.

Tsatsa
Small icons fashioned from clay collected from sacred sites.

Kalachakra Seal
Closely associated with the Kalachakra meditation deity and mandala, and also the Dalai Lama.

Spirit Traps
Series of interlocking threads, often on a tree, which are supposed to ensnare evil spirits and which are burnt after their job is done.

Butter Lamps
Or *chömay* – kept lit continuously in all monasteries and many private homes and topped up continuously by visiting pilgrims equipped with a tub of butter and a spoon.

Rosary Beads
String of beads (traditionally 108) made from dried seeds. Prayers are marked off by each bead, with a second string to mark off higher multiples. British spies or pundits used adapted rosaries to keep record of distances as they secretly mapped large areas of Tibet during the 19th century.

self-mutilation, was one of these schools. Buddhism was another.

Life of the Buddha

The historical dates for the life of the Buddha are much debated, and recent scholarship has put previously long-held beliefs into question. A commonly accepted compromise is something like 480-400 BC, give or take half a century.

The Buddha was born Siddhartha Gautama in the small kingdom of Sakka on the border of contemporary Nepal. The name Sakyamuni, given to him in the Mahayana tradition, has its origin in the kingdom of Gautama's birth, meaning the 'Sage of Sakka'.

Little is known of the life of Sakyamuni. It was probably not until some 200 years after his death that biographies were compiled, and by that time many of the circumstances of his life had merged with legend. It is known that he was born of a noble family and that he

Basic Buddhist Concepts

Rebirth

Life is a cycle of rebirths. The common assumption is that there are many rebirths, but in Buddhist thought they are innumerable. The word *samsara*, literally 'wandering on', is used to describe this cycle, and life is seen as wandering on limitlessly through time, through the birth and extinction and rebirth of galaxies and worlds. There are six levels of rebirth, or realms of existence. It is important to accumulate enough merit to avoid the three lower realms, though in the long cycle of rebirth all beings pass through them at some point. The three lower realms comprise hells of torment, ghost worlds and the world of animals. The three higher realms are human beings, demigods and gods. These six levels are depicted on the Wheel of Life. All beings are fated to tread this wheel continuously until they make a commitment to enlightenment.

Karma

All beings pass through the same cycle of rebirths. Their enemy may once have been their mother, and like all beings they have lived as an insect, as a god and suffered in one of the hell realms. Movement within this cycle, though, is not haphazard. It is governed by karma.

Karma is a slippery concept. It is sometimes translated simply as 'action', but it also implies the consequences of action. Karma might be thought of as an over-arching condition of life. Every action in life leaves a psychic trace that carries over into the next rebirth. It should not be thought of as a reward or punishment, simply a result. In Buddhist thought karma is frequently likened to a seed that ripens into a fruit: thus a human reborn as an insect is harvesting the fruits of a previous immoral existence.

Merit

Given that karma is a kind of accumulated psychic baggage that we must lug through countless rebirths, it is the aim of all practicing Buddhists to try and accumulate as much 'good karma', or merit, as possible. Merit is best achieved through the act of rejoicing in giving, though merit can even be achieved through giving that is purely motivated by will for merit. The giving of alms to the needy and to monks, the relinquishing of a son to monkhood, acts of compassion and understanding are all meritorious and have a positive karmic outcome.

The Four Holy Truths

If belief in rebirth, karma and merit are the basis of lay followers' faith in Buddhism, the Four Holy Truths might be thought of as the deep structure of the faith, its philosophical under-

married and had a son before renouncing a life of comfort on a quest to make sense of the suffering in the world. Traditional Buddhist biographies, however, do not start with the birth of Sakyamuni, but with his early lives '100,000 eons ago'. Thus his striving for Buddhahood passed through countless rebirths before he attained perfection.

Sakyamuni, at the age of 29, left his home, his wife and newly born son. This action is explained as being for the benefit of all sen-

tient beings and set a precedent for the renunciation of domestic life by the members of later monastic communities. He studied with many of the great teachers of the day, passing up opportunities to become a teacher himself. Later he embarked on a course of intense asceticism, before concluding that such a path was too extreme.

At this point, rather than give up his quest, Sakyamuni recalled an earlier meditation state he had once achieved, a state of

Basic Buddhist Concepts

pinning. The Buddha systematised the truths in the manner of medical practice of his time: (1) diagnose the illness, (2) identify its cause, (3) establish a cure, and (4) map a course for the cure. Their equivalents in Buddhism's diagnosis of the human condition are: (1) suffering (dukkha) caused by (2) desire (tanha), which may be cured by (3) cessation of desire (nibbana), which can be achieved by means of (4) the Holy Eightfold Path, or the Middle Way.

The first of the Four Holy Truths, then, is that life is suffering. This suffering extends through all the countless rebirths of beings, and finds its origin in the imperfection of life. Every rebirth brings with it the pain of birth, of ageing, of death, of association with unpleasant things, the loss of things we are attached to, and the failure to achieve the things we desire.

The reason for this suffering is the second Holy Truth, and lies in our dissatisfaction with imperfection, in our desire for things to be other than they are. What is more, this dissatisfaction leads to actions and karmic consequences that prolong the cycle of rebirths and may lead to even more suffering, much like a mouse running endlessly in a wheel.

The third Holy Truth was indicated by the Buddha as nibbana, known in English as Nirvana. It is the cessation of all desire, an end to attachment. With the cessation of desire comes an end to suffering, the achievement of complete nonattachment and an end to the cycle of rebirth – Nirvana, the ultimate goal of Buddhism. Nit-pickers might point out that the will to achieve Nirvana is a desire in itself. Buddhists answer that this desire is tolerated as a useful means to an end, but it is only when this desire too is extinguished that Nirvana is truly achieved.

The Eightfold Path

The Holy Eightfold Path is the fourth of the Holy Truths, and prescribes a course that for the lay practitioner will lead to the accumulation of merit and for the serious devotee may lead to Nirvana. The components of this path are: (1) right understanding, (2) right thought, (3) right speech, (4) right action, (5) right livelihood, (6) right effort, (7) right mindfulness, and (8) right concentration. Needless to say, each of these has a 'wrong' corollary.

The Ten Meritorious Deeds

Do not kill, do not steal, and restrain from inappropriate sexual activity, lying, gossiping, cursing, sowing discord, envy, malice and opinionatedness.

great bliss and peace. In the place now known as Bodhgaya, he sat beneath a bo tree and meditated. Over the course of three moonlit nights he achieved knowledge of the final obstacles to his enlightenment, and at the break of dawn at the end of the third night he became a Buddha.

After achieving enlightenment, Sakyamuni sat for another three or four weeks contemplating his achievement. During this time Brahma Sahampata, the god of compassion, asked Sakyamuni to share his perfect knowledge with those who were ready to hear his teachings. Sakyamuni's compliance with this request is seen as evidence of his compassion, the ideal complement of perfected wisdom.

Early Teachings of Buddhism

The early teachings of Buddhism are based on the original insights of Sakyamuni and form the basis of all further Buddhist thought. The later Mahayana school (to which Tibetan Buddhism belongs) diverged from these early teachings in some respects, but not in their fundamentals.

The Buddha began his teachings by explaining that there was a Middle Way that steered a course between sensual indulgence and ascetic self-torment – of moderation not renunciation. This Middle Way could be followed by taking the Holy Eightfold Path. The philosophical underpinnings of this path were the Four Holy Truths, which addressed the problems of *karma* and rebirth. These basic concepts are the kernel of early Buddhist thought.

Schools of Buddhism

As is the case in all religious movements, not long after Sakyamuni's death, disagreements began to arise among his followers over whose interpretations best captured the true spirit of his teachings. The result was the development of numerous schools of thought and eventually a schism that saw the emergence of two principal schools: Hinayana and Mahayana.

Hinayana, also known as Theravada, might be seen as the more conservative of the two, a school that encouraged scholasticism and close attention to what was considered the original teachings of Sakyamuni. Mahayana, on the other hand, with its elevation of compassion to an all-important idea, took Buddhism in a new direction. It was the Mahayana school that made its way up to the high Tibetan plateau and took root there, at the same time travelling to China, Korea and Japan. Hinayana retreated into southern India and took root in Sri Lanka and Thailand.

Mahayana The claims that Mahayanists made for their faith were many, but the central issue was a change in orientation from individual pursuit of enlightenment to bodhisattvahood. The bodhisattva, rather than striving for complete nonattachment, aims, through compassion and self-sacrifice, to achieve enlightenment for the sake of all beings.

In another development, Sakyamuni began to take on another form altogether. Mahayanists maintained that Sakyamuni had already attained Buddhahood many eons ago and that he was a manifestation of a long-enlightened transcendent being who sent such manifestations to many world systems to assist all beings on the road to enlightenment. There were many such transcendent beings, the argument ran, living in heavens or 'Pure Lands' and all were able to project themselves into the innumerable worlds of the cosmos for the sake of sentient life there.

The philosophical reasoning behind the Mahayana transformation of Buddhism is extremely complex, but it had the effect of allowing Mahayanists to produce new revealed texts that recorded the words of Sakyamuni as they appeared in dreams and visions. It also had the effect of producing a pantheon of transcendent bodhisattvas, a feature that made Mahayana more palatable to cultures which already had gods of their own. In Tibet, China, Korea and Japan the Mahayana pantheon came to be identified with local gods. In Tibet, in particular, many stories of the taming of local gods by their Mahayana equivalents came into being.

Tantrism (Vajrayana) A further Mahayana development that is particularly relevant to Tibet is Tantrism, or Vajrayana. The words of Sakyamuni were recorded in sutras and studied by both students of Hinayana and Mahayana, but according to followers of Vajrayana, a school that emerged from around 600 AD, Sakyamuni left a corpus of esoteric instructions to a select few of his disciples. These were known as *Tantra*.

Tantric adepts claimed that through using unconventional techniques they could jolt themselves towards enlightenment, shortening the long road to bodhisattvahood. The process involved identification with a tute-lary deity invoked through deep meditation and recitation of the deity's mantra. The most famous of these mantras is the *om mani padme hum* mantra of Avalokiteshvara, the patron saint of Tibet. Tantric practice employs Indian yogic techniques to channel energy towards the transformation of enlightenment. Such yogic techniques might even include sexual practices. Tantric techniques are rarely written down but rather passed down verbally from tutor to student.

Most of the ritual objects and images of deities in Tibetan monasteries and temples are Tantric in nature. Together they show the many facets of enlightenment – at times kindly, at times wrathful. Sometimes these deities are pictured at the centre of a mandala, which is a representation of the

Sutra & Tantra

Lurking in the minefield of Buddhist terminology that makes even the briefest of excursions into Tibet so bewildering is the distinction between sutras and Tantras. To understand the difference properly it is useful to go back to the schism in Buddhism that gave rise to the two major schools of Hinayana and Mahayana. The Hinayana school is the older, and is based on the teachings of Sakyamuni, the historical Buddha, which were recorded in the Sutras of the Pali Canon. These sutras can be translated as their Biblical equivalent 'Scriptures'.

So far so good. The situation is complicated, however, with the rise of Mahayana. Mahayanists claimed to have discovered another body of sutras which were entrusted to supernatural beings until sufficiently spiritually advanced human beings appeared in the world to receive them. In this way a second, Mahayana, canon came into being. It also set the precedent that Buddhist practice could be informed not only by the teachings of a living Buddha, but through revelations that came from beyond this world.

As the name suggests Tantras are associated with Tantric Buddhism, also known as Vajrayana. Just as sutras reveal the teachings of Sakyamuni, every Tantra can be traced back to a revelation from a particular deity. Tantra have their origin in Indian devotional cults. They involve practices and rituals that were revealed to an adept by a particular deity and then transmitted by that adept to a disciple and so on through many hundreds of years. In this sense, Tantra need not be written down, and may sometimes be orally transmitted.

The earliest Tibetan Tantra are associated with the Nyingmapa order and came to Tibet via Guru Rinpoche in the 8th century. They are practiced by all Tibetan schools of Buddhism and are called the Old Tantra. The later schools of Tibetan Buddhism – Kagyupa and Sakyapa – supplemented these Tantra with revelations of their own, and these came to be known as the New Tantra. The New Tantra are all associated with places in Tibet visited by Guru Rinpoche, and 'discoverers' *(terton)* of these Tantras are thought to be manifestations of Guru Rinpoche's students.

world they inhabit. The Tantric adept who identifies with a particular deity will visualise the mandala as a three-dimensional world, a feat of meditational concentration that takes many years of training to achieve.

Tibetan Buddhism & Its Schools

The introduction of Buddhism to Tibet is attended by legends of the taming of local gods and spirits and their conversion to Buddhism as protective deities. This panoply of Buddhas, bodhisattvas and sages occupies a mythical world in the Tibetan imagination. Avalokiteshvara is perhaps chief among them, manifesting himself in early Tibetan kings and later in the Dalai Lamas. Guru Rinpoche, the Indian sage who bound the native spirits and gods of Tibet into the service of Buddhism, is another. And there are countless others worshipped in images throughout the land: Tara (Tibetan: Drölma) Manjushri (Jampelyang), Milarepa, Marpa, Tsongkhapa among others. While the clerical side of Buddhism concerns itself largely with textual study and analysis, the Tantric shamanistic-based side seeks revelation through identification with these deified beings and through their 'revealed' words or writings *(terma)*.

It is useful to consider the various schools of Tibetan Buddhism as revealing something of a struggle between these two orientations: shamanism and clericalism. Each school finds its own resolution of the problem. In the case of the last major school to arise, the Gelugpa order, there was a search to return to the doctrinal purity of clerical Buddhism. But even here, the Tantric forms were not discarded altogether; it was merely felt that many years of scholarly work and preparation should precede the more esoteric Tantric practices.

The clerical and shamanistic orientations can also be explained as the difference between state sponsored and popular Buddhism respectively. There was always a tendency for the state to emphasise monastic Buddhism, with its communities of rule-abiding monks. Popular Buddhism, on the other hand, with its long-haired, wild-eyed

ascetic recluses capable of performing great feats of magic, had a great appeal to the ordinary people of Tibet, for whom ghosts and demons and sorcerers were a daily reality.

Nyingmapa Order The Nyingmapa order is the 'Old School', and traces its origins back to the teachings and practices of Guru Rinpoche, who came to Tibet from India and lived in the country in the 8th to 9th centuries. As Buddhism fell into decline until the second diffusion of the faith in the 11th century, the Nyingmapa failed to develop as a powerful, centralised school, and for the most part prospered in villages throughout rural Tibet and was administered by local shaman-like figures.

With the second diffusion of Buddhism in Tibet and the emergence of rival schools, the Nyingmapa order experienced something of a revival through the 'discovery' of hidden texts in the power places of Tibet visited by Guru Rinpoche. In many cases these 'revealed' texts, or terma, were discovered through yogic-inspired visions by spiritually advanced Nyingmapa practitioners, rather than found under a pile of rocks or in a cave. But, however they came about, these terma gave the Nyingmapa a new lease of life.

They gave rise to the *dzogchen*, or Great Perfection teachings. Much maligned by other Tibetan schools, dzogchen postulates a primordial state of purity that pre-exists the duality of samsara and enlightenment, and offered a Tantric short cut to Nirvana. Such ideas were to influence other orders in the 19th century.

The Nyingmapa never had the centralised power of other major Tibetan schools of Buddhism, and can be considered as representing an extreme of the shamanistic orientation.

Its fortunes improved somewhat with the accession of the fifth Dalai Lama, who was born into a Nyingmapa family. He personally saw to the expansion of Mindroling and Dorje Drak monasteries, which became the head Nyingmapa monasteries of Ü and all Tibet.

Kagyupa Order The Kagyupa ('Whispered Transmission') order traces its lineage back to early Indian teachers, but the impetus behind its establishment was Marpa (1012-93), a married Tibetan yogin renowned for his translations and Tantric powers. He took on a disciple, Milarepa, who in turn became a renowned yogin, meditating in high mountain caves and composing songs. Milarepa is a perfect example of the nonmonastic ascetic for whom textual study is less important than Tantric experience, and legends accumulated around him: in particular, he is supposed to have overcome and taught mountain goddesses with the use of Tantric sexual techniques.

The influence of one of Milarepa's disciples, Gampopa, led to the establishment of numerous monasteries that became major teaching centres, eventually overshadowing the ascetic-yogin origins of the Kagyupa. The yogin tradition did not die out completely, however, and Kagyupa monasteries also became important centres for synthesising the clerical and shamanistic orientations of Tibetan Buddhism.

Several sub-orders of the Kagyupa sprung up with time, the most prominent of which was the Karma Kagyupa, also known as the Karmapa. The practice of renowned lamas reincarnating after death probably originated with this sub-order, when the abbot of Tsurphu Monastery, Dusum Khyenpa (1110-93) announced that he would be reincarnated as his own successor. The 16th Karmapa died in 1981, and his successor is resident at Tsurphu Monastery, near Lhasa.

Red Hats Versus Yellow Hats

The terms 'Red Hat' and 'Yellow Hat' have been avoided in this book, though they are widely used elsewhere. The main reason is that they represent a simplification that gives rise to confusion. The old adage, don't judge a Buddhist by his bowler, is a good one to follow in Tibet.

The distinction is actually Chinese. The Chinese differentiated between the yellow-hatted Gelugpa order and the red-hatted Kagyupa order – disputants for religious and political ascendancy until the 17th century Mongol intervention – through their headgear. By extension, the distinction identified the Gelugpa as the Yellow Hats and all other Tibetan schools of Buddhism as Red Hats.

It is a distinction that makes little sense of the complexity of Tibet's religious orders. Confusion also arises due to the fact that the Karmapa, head of the Karma Kagyupa sub-order, is often referred to as the Black Hat lama. It makes a lot more sense to see the major orders of Tibetan Buddhism, not in terms of their dress sense, but in terms of their respective historical rise to power.

The Nyingmapa order, then, is the oldest of the Tibetan schools of Buddhism, tracing its origins back to the early establishment of Buddhism in the reign of King Songtsen Gampo. Tibetans sometimes refer to this school as the Old School. The middle period of the second diffusion of Buddhism in the 11th century saw the rise of the New School Sakyapa and Kagyupa orders. The 15th century search for doctrinal purity gave rise to the Gelugpa order, which by the 17th century had become dominant in Tibet.

Other Kagyupa monasteries include Drigung Til and Talung monasteries in Ü.

Sakyapa Order With the second diffusion of Buddhism in the 11th and 12th centuries, many Tibetan monasteries became centres for the textual study and translation of Indian Buddhist texts. One of the earliest major figures in this movement was Sakya Pandita (literally the 'Scholar from Sakya').

Sakya Pandita's renown as a scholar led to him being recognised as a manifestation of Manjushri, the Bodhisattva of Insight, as were subsequent abbots of Sakya. In the 13th and 14th centuries, the Sakyapa became embroiled in politics and implicated in the Mongol overlordship of Tibet. Nevertheless, at the same time Sakya emerged as a major centre for the scholastic study of Buddhism, and attracted students such as Tsongkhapa, who initiated the Gelugpa order.

Gelugpa Order It may not have been his intention, but Tsongkhapa (1357-1419), a monk who left his home in Kokonor at the age of 17 to study in central Tibet, is regarded as the founder of the Gelugpa order (Virtuous School), which came to dominate Tibetan political and religious affairs.

Tsongkhapa studied with all the major schools of his day, but was particularly influenced by the Sakyapa and the Kadampa orders. The Kadampa order had its head monastery at Netang, near Lhasa, and it was here that the 11th century Bengali sage Atisha spent the last of his days. The Kadampa had sustained the teachings of Atisha, which are a sophisticated synthesis of conventional Mahayana doctrine with the more arcane practices of Tantric Buddhism, and emerged as a major school, emphasising scholastic study. It may never have matched the eminence of the Kagyupa and Sakyapa orders, but in the hands of Tsongkhapa the teachings of the Kadampa order established a renewal in Tibetan Buddhism.

After having a vision of Atisha, Tsongkhapa elaborated on the Bengali sage's clerical-Tantric synthesis in a doctrine known as *lamrim*, or the 'gradual path'. Tsongkhapa basically advocated a return to doctrinal purity and monastic discipline as prerequisites to advanced Tantric studies. He did not, as it is sometimes maintained, advocate a purely clerical approach to Buddhism, but he did reassert the monastic body as the basis of the Buddhist community and maintained that Tantric practices should be reserved for the advanced student.

Tsongkhapa established a monastery at Ganden, which was to become the head of the Gelugpa order. Other monasteries were also established at Drepung, Sera (Lhasa) and at Shigatse. Although the abbot of Drepung was titular head of the order (and is to this day), it was the Dalai Lamas who came to be increasingly identified with the order's growing political and spiritual prestige.

Facts for the Visitor

HIGHLIGHTS

The highlights of Tibet will depend largely on your interests. For trekkers, for example, Tibet offers the opportunity to tread paths in some of the world's highest places. Others will appreciate the rich religious life of the country, while a a few will be satisfied with the wildness of a remote land. For an overview of some of the main highlights of Tibet see the 'Highlights' table on pages 60-1.

It's also worth trying to make it to a couple of sites off the beaten track. Tibet is full of small monasteries and these can be some of the best places to visit. The monks are often very happy to have a foreign visitor and will sit down to share some tea with you and show you around.

The other highlights of a visit to Tibet are harder to define. The joy of hitching on an open-air truck, hiking out to a secluded monastery and spending the night, or following a kora with a happy band of pilgrims all rate highly. But perhaps the memories that remain the longest are those of the Tibetan people: drinking *chang* by the side of the road with complete strangers, the joy a picture of the Dalai Lama can bring and the rare sense of calm and space that emanates from what is one of the most beautiful and unique places on earth. Few people come away unaffected or unimpressed by Tibet.

SUGGESTED ITINERARIES

The chief goal of travellers to Tibet is of course Lhasa itself. Lhasa must rank as one of the most enigmatic cities in the world and it is the focal point and spiritual heart of the nation. There is enough to see in and around the city to keep you busy for at least a week, perhaps 10 days. The monastic institutions of Drepung and Sera are close by, and Ganden and Tsurphu monasteries are easy day trips away.

There are plenty of other excursions to be made from Lhasa. A three day return trip can take you to the stunning lake, Nam-tso.

Highs & Lows of Tibetan Travel

Top Ten

1. The Tibetan people
2. Endlessly wandering the Barkhor circuit, which is different every time
3. Colours and nomads of the Chang-tang at Nam-tso
4. Staring at the views of Everest's north face from Rongphu Monastery
5. Staying the night at a small monastery like Mindroling or Drigung Til
6. Getting a lift on a pilgrim bus
7. Doing a kora with a band of happy pilgrims
8. A hot cup of sweet tea after a hard hike in the hills
9. Old wrinkled pilgrims that wear mountaineering goggles
10. Cheesecake at Tashi I

Pet Peeves

1. Instant noodles (yes, even the expensive ones with *real* vegetables)
2. Hot yak butter tea
3. Cold yak butter tea
4. Karaoke Bars (up to a mile away)
5. Trucks that don't stop (bastards)
6. Checkpoint hassles and permits that nobody checks (unless you don't have one)
7. Truck stops and rabid dogs in Western Tibet
8. Chinese modern architecture (specifically the school of bathroom tiling and blue glass)
9. Tibetan toilets (except those at Samye and Sakya which have the best views!)
10. The dull throb of altitude sickness

Bradley Mayhew

Highlights

	Region	Comments
MONASTERIES & TEMPLES		
Jokhang		
A hushed silence pervades Lhasa's holiest collection of shrines.	Lhasa	The spiritual heart of Tibet and always full of murmuring, shuffling pilgrims.
Drepung & Sera		
Once the largest and second largest monasteries in the world.	Lhasa	Still recovering from the Chinese onslaught but are a highlight of Lhasa.
Ganden		
Stunning location and the scene of frantic rebuilding.	40km east of Lhasa	Take the early morning pilgrim bus from Lhasa for a great day trip.
Samye		
First monastery in Tibet, with a relaxing location beside the Yarlung Tsangpo.	Ü	Good accommodation and base for walks to meditation retreats.
Tashilhunpo		
Traditional seat of the Panchen Lama.	Shigatse, Tsang	Possibly Tibet's best preserved and most spectacular monastery.
Sakya		
An eerie, fortress-like monastery with the most spectacular prayer hall in Tibet.	Tsang	Easy 25km detour off the Friendship Highway and worth an overnight stop.
OTHER BUILDINGS		
Potala Palace		
The focus of travellers for centuries.	Lhasa	Though impressive, the Dalai Lama's palace remains eerily empty.
Kumbum		
The pinnacle of Tibetan architecture.	Gyantse	This multi-layered chörten is well worth visiting en route from Lhasa to Shigatse.
Yumbulagang		
The 'first building in Tibet'.	Yarlung valley	A stunning location in the birthplace of the Tibetan nation.
Shegar Fort		
Spectacularly sited ruins atop the crystal mountain.	Tsang	A good 7km detour off the Friendship Highway.

Highlights

	Region	Comments

NATURAL BEAUTY

Mt Everest

Quite literally the highpoint of Tibet.	Tsang	Views of the mountain from Rongphu Monastery are unsurpassed.

Nam-tso

Stunning turquoise lake set below a snowy range of 7000m peaks.	Changtang plateau	Glimpses of nomadic life and the awesome sense of space.

Yamdrok-tso

The sacred scorpion lake, in between Lhasa and Gyantse.	Tsang	Best views of the coiling lake come from the high pass of Kampa-la.

Lake Manasarovar & Mt Kailash

A true pilgrimage to Tibet's holiest and most compelling mountain.	Western Tibet	It's a rugged two week journey with stunning high-altitude scenery.

PILGRIM CIRCUITS

Barkhor

Lhasa's pilgrim circuit around the Jokhang.	Lhasa	Infinitely interesting, it is worth coming back to again and again.

Ganden

The main seat of the Gelugpa order.	Ü	A high and a low *kora* circuit, with bands of pilgrims.

Lingkhor

Lhasa's 8km pilgrim path has some fascinating spots to see en route.	Lhasa	A good way to see the city's hidden sights.

TREKKING

Ganden to Samye

A classic trek between two of central Tibet's most important monasteries.	Ü	Permits can be a problem in Samye.

Kailash Kora

A three or four day trek around the holy mountain following the other pilgrims.	Western Tibet	Watch in dismay as grannies race past you to the top of 5600m Drölma-la.

Everest

Because it's there! In Qomolangma Nature Preserve.	Tsang	The best way to get to base camp is this three or four day trek from Tingri.

Another three day option is to head up to Drigung Til Monastery and Tidrum Nunnery, both to the east of Lhasa.

From Lhasa, fewer travellers head east towards the Yarlung valley but a visit to Samye Monastery and Yumbulagang are easily fitted into an eight day Land Cruiser trip to the border. Samye Monastery could conceivably be visited as an overnight trip from Lhasa, though it's better to spend a couple of nights there.

The road between Lhasa and Kathmandu is the main travellers' route through Tibet. This route, which basically follows the Friendship Highway from Lhasa to Kathmandu, allows a number of detours to the highlights of Tsang Province. These include Yamdrok-tso, the Kumbum at Gyantse and Shigatse's Tashilhunpo Monastery. Both Gyantse and Shigatse are worth a stop for a day or two to see the sights and get a glimpse of urban life outside of Lhasa. Also en route and a popular destination is Sakya, a small monastery town just 25km off the Friendship Highway.

Closer to the border, and emerging as the most popular trekking destination in Tibet is the Everest region. Many people drive right up to Base Camp and leave the next day but it's much better to fit in an extra day to enjoy the extraordinary views. If you are trekking or hitching, allow a week to get to Rongphu and back from the Friendship Highway, though you could do it in less if you're lucky with lifts.

Much talked about, but little visited, is of course Mt Kailash out in Western Tibet. Those travelling out there are looking at a return journey of around 15 to 20 days by Land Cruiser and up to a month if you're trying to hitch. If heading to Nepal from here you can cut down south on the way back to join the Friendship Highway at Nyalam.

Remember that further is not necessarily better and there are endless remote monasteries, pilgrimage places and lakes that remain off the beaten track just a few kilometres from the main sites. All said and done the biggest constraint to where you go

will be either the time on your visa or the permit situation.

Two Weeks

In two weeks you could see most of the sites of Lhasa and then head down on a seven or eight day Land Cruiser trip to Kathmandu, taking in the sights of Yamdrok-tso, Gyantse, Shigatse, Sakya and possibly Everest Base Camp. If you are not headed to Nepal you could spend the second week travelling on public transport to Shigatse and Gyantse. If you have the money to travel by Land Cruiser you could probably squeeze in an overnight stay at Samye.

One Month

With one month you have more time to add on some excursions to the preceding itinerary, perhaps to Nam-tso or Drigung Til Monastery. You could also extend your trip to the border to take in Samye Monastery. If travelling by public transport you will need this extra time to cover the basic two week itinerary. You could make it out to Western Tibet and back in a month but you wouldn't have enough time to see much more of the country.

Two Months

This is a nice amount of time to be able to enjoy Tibet slowly. In two months you can make a trip to Mt Kailash and back and still have time to see the main highlights of the country. If you are not headed out west you can see most of the other sites covered in this guide in around two months.

PLANNING
When to Go

Climate is not such a major consideration as many people might imagine when visiting Tibet. Certainly, winter is very cold and snowfalls can sometimes make travel difficult; but some travellers swear by the winter months. There are few travellers about at this time and Lhasa, for example, is at its most colourful, crowded with nomads.

Spring, early summer and late autumn are probably the best times to be in Tibet. Prices

Government Travel Advice

The US State Department's Bureau of Consular Affairs issues periodically updated bulletins for travellers. Consular Information Sheets include data such as entry requirements, medical facilities, the crime situation, and areas of general instability. Travel warnings highlight trouble spots with health and safety risks, civil unrest or other dangers. Public announcements may have late-breaking information if there is an imposition of martial law or a ban on travellers to Tibet.

You can receive copies of these by sending a stamped, self-addressed envelope to Overseas Citizens Services, Room 4800, Department of State, Washington DC 20520-4818. You'll also find them on the Internet at travel.state.gov/travel_warnings.html. You can listen to 24 hour travel warnings at ☎ 202-647 5225 on a touch-tone phone, or get information via automated fax by dialling ☎ 202-647 3000 from a fax machine.

British Foreign Office travel advisories are available from the Travel Advice Unit, Consular Division, Foreign and Commonwealth Office (☎ 0171-238 4503/4, fax 238 4545, from 22 April 2000 ☎ 020-7238 4503/4, fax 7238 4545, Web site www.fco.gov.uk/), 1 Palace St, London SW1E 5EH, UK and on BBC2 Ceefax, pp 470ff. It also has a regularly updated recorded travel advice line on ☎ 0374-500900.

Australians can contact the Department of Foreign Affairs advice line in Canberra on ☎ 06-6261 3305 or visit its Web site at www.dfat.gov.au/consular/advice/. Any travel agent linked to the Apollo, Fantasia or Galileo networks can access these directories directly.

---

for accommodation and Land Cruiser rental are generally discounted in May and the weather is good. Everest is particularly clear during this time. From mid-July through to the end of September, the monsoon starts to effect parts of Tibet. Travel to Western Tibet becomes more difficult and the Friendship Highway sometimes becomes impassable on the Nepal side or on the border itself. Trips to Kailash can be undertaken from April to October, though September and October are considered the best times. Lhasa and its environs don't get *really* cold until the end of November.

It's worth trying to coincide your trip with one of Tibet's main festivals. New Year is an excellent (though cold) time to be in Lhasa. Saga Dawa (April or May) is also an excellent time to be in Lhasa or Mt Kailash.

Maps

It shouldn't come as a surprise that good mapping for Tibet is not easy to come by. Most importantly, if good mapping is crucial to you, stock up on maps before you leave.

Maps of Tibet In Lhasa three maps are available: two in Chinese (and possibly also Tibetan) and one in English. The Chinese map, actually a 166 page atlas, *Xizang Zizhiqu Dituceng* is very detailed, shows major roads and towns and has a scale of up to 1:300,000. A fold-out version is available with a scale of 1:2,200,000. Both are of very limited use, however, if you do not read Chinese. Even if you do, most of the place names are known locally in Tibetan only, not Chinese. The English-language map, *China Tibet Tour Map*, by the Mapping Bureau of the Tibet Autonomous Region (1993) is the best local alternative if you are just travelling around Tibet by road.

Road maps to look out for in Kathmandu include *Tibet – South-Central* by Nepa Maps, *Latest Map of Kathmandu to Tibet* by Mandala Maps and the *Namaste Trekking Map*. They are marginally better than the Chinese produced maps but still aren't up to scratch.

Back at home, see if you can get hold of the *Map of the People's Republic of China*, produced jointly by the Cartographic Publishing House of China and Esselte of Sweden. Although this huge fold-out map covers all of China, the section on Tibet and the surrounding provinces of Sichuan and Qinghai is very useful. Along with Pinyin (a standard form of romanised Mandarin), Chinese characters are also included, which is very helpful when organising transport.

Also worth looking out for is the Nelles Verlag *Himalaya* map, which has excellent detail of central Tibet. Geocenter's *Tibet, Nepal, Bhutan* is also good. Bartholomew's *Tibet & the Mountains of Central Asia* is a good geographic overview but shows little detail. A good map if you are doing a lot of travelling is the *Tibet Road Map* by Berndtson & Berndtson. It has a detailed insert of central Tibet and is laminated so it won't rip like all the others.

A specialist map, fascinating but of little practical use, is the *Xizang-Qinghai Plateau Terrain Map*, co-produced by the Chinese Academy of Science and The Mountain Institute. It provides fascinating geographical information in the form of a satellite photo of the Tibetan plateau. You can find it in the top-end hotel gift shops in Lhasa but it's pricey at around US$15 to US$20.

Some of the most detailed maps of China and Tibet available in the west are the aerial survey Operational Navigation Charts (Series ONC). These are prepared and published by the Defense Mapping Agency Aerospace Center, St Louis Air Force Station, Missouri 63118, USA. Cyclists, trekkers and mountaineers have recommended these highly because of their extraordinary detail.

The best maps available for Tibet, published by the US Department of Defense, are the Joint Operations Graphic (JOG) Series 1501 at a scale of 1:250,000. These maps are very difficult to obtain and are semi-classified, but remarkably have been reprinted in Victor Chan's *Tibet Handbook – a pilgrimage guide*, with key additions of religious sites and trekking routes added. For anyone really serious about mapping, this alone should make the book worth buying.

Maps of Lhasa If you intend to explore Lhasa in detail, look out for *Lhasa City* (1:12,500) published by the Amnye Machen Institute in Dharamsala. The detail is awesome and includes many unorthodox sites. It is available from Stanford's Map Centre (see Buying Maps) for UK£10.95.

A less practical but equally fascinating map is *Tibetan Old Buildings and Urban Development in Lhasa 1948-1985-1998*. It shows the development, or rather destruction, of the Tibetan quarter over recent years. The 1948 map of Lhasa is based on the original surveys of Peter Aufschnaiter, Heinrich Harrer's erstwhile companion. Tibet enthusiasts interested in the map can purchase it for Y50 from the Tibet Heritage Fund on the 3rd floor of the Snowlands Hotel in Lhasa. Alternatively, contact the cartographers at Verlag Freie Kultur Aktion (☎ 30-396 4222), Tucholsky Str 15, 10117 Berlin, Germany.

Buying Maps In the UK you can obtain most of these maps from Stanford's Map Centre (☎ 0171-836 1321, from 22 April 2000 ☎ 020-7836 1321), 12-14 Long Acre, London WC2E 9LP or from The Map Shop (☎ 06-846 3146), AT Atkinson & Partner, 15 High St, Upton-on-Severn, Worcestershire, WR8 OHJ.

If travelling from the US you might try Rand McNally in New York (☎ 212-758 7488) or in San Francisco (☎ 415-777 3131). Australians can contact Mapland (☎ 03-9670 4383) 372 Little Bourke St in Melbourne or the Travel Bookshop (☎ 02-9241 3554) at 20 Bridge St in Sydney.

In Paris, France, see Le Vieux Campeur (☎ 01 43 29 12 32) 2 rue de Ltran, 75005; L'Astrolabe (☎ 01 42 85 42 95) 46 rue de Provence, 75009; Ulysse (☎ 01 43 25 17 35) 26 rue Saint Louis en l'ile 75004 or IGN (☎ 01 43 98 80 00) at 107 rue de la Boetie, 75001.

What to Bring

Bring as little as possible to Tibet. It is much better to buy things as you need them than to throw things away because you have too

Lhasa's inspirational skyline – the Potala viewed from the Jokhang roof.

GARRY WEARE

Yumbulagang, site of the oldest building in Tibet.

BRADLEY MAYHEW

The south face of sacred Mt Kailash.

GARRY WEARE

Row of prayer wheels at Sakya Monastery, Tsang.

BRADLEY MAYHEW

BRADLEY MAYHEW

Resting pilgrim, Rongphu Monastery

RICHARD I'ANSON

Gyantse kumbum detail

RICHARD I'ANSON

Prayer flags, Tashilhunpo Monastery

RICHARD I'ANSON

Prayer wheel, Sakya Monastery

BRADLEY MAYHEW

Traditional Tibetan footwear

much to carry. Lightweight and compact are two words that should be etched in your mind when you are deciding what to bring. Having said that, there are some things you will want to bring from home.

Carrying Bags Frameless or internal-frame backpacks are the easiest type of bag to carry. The 'expandable' type are most convenient – a clever arrangement of straps cause these packs to shrink or expand according to how much is inside. Forget suitcases. Packs that close with a zipper can be secured with a padlock. Any pack can be slit open with a razor blade, but a lock will usually prevent pilfering by hotel staff and baggage handlers at airports.

A day-pack is good for hiking and for carrying extra food, books etc on long bus rides. You can even dump your main luggage in a hotel's storage and travel light for a couple of days with a full day-pack. A belt-pack is OK for maps, extra film and other miscellanea, but do not use it for valuables such as travellers cheques, plane tickets and passport – it is an easy target for pickpockets.

Clothes In Tibet, no matter what time of year you are travelling, you should come prepared with some warm clothing. In the summer months, a couple of T-shirts and a good sweater or fleece will do the trick unless you are planning to be trekking at high altitudes or heading out to Western Tibet. At other times of the year, ideally you should have thermal underwear, a down jacket, gloves and even a balaclava to protect your ears.

Some clothing items can be bought in Lhasa or Shigatse, but the selection is limited and the quality poor. It is much better to come prepared. Good walking boots and heavy socks are essential. Items such as a wide-brimmed hat to keep off the sun can be bought in Lhasa very cheaply. Baseball caps are widely available but won't protect your ears.

Shorts are not a very suitable option in Tibet. The days can get pretty hot but wearing shorts in Tibet is akin to walking around with 'TOURIST!' tattooed on your forehead.

The question of whether you need a sleeping bag or not depends entirely on where you plan to go and how you plan to travel. Those who aim to spend time in Lhasa and then head down to Nepal via the sights of Tsang could do without one, though they are always a nice comfort, especially in budget hotels. Anyone planning on trekking or heading out to remoter areas such as Nam-tso, Everest or Western Tibet should definitely bring one along.

Necessities & Accessories A good pair of sunglasses are absolutely essential to block out the UV light and protect your eyes. Also essential is sunscreen (UV) lotion. Hong Kong is a good place to pick up sunscreen with high-protection factors. A compact umbrella is a versatile shelter from rain, sleet, snow and sun.

Some pharmaceutical items are hard to find, examples being shaving cream, decent razor blades, mosquito repellent, deodorant, dental floss, tampons and contact lens cleaning solution. Bring a supply of lip salve. Most travellers' lips start to crack within a few days of arriving in Tibet, and if untreated can become *very* painful. Instant hot drinks like coffee and soup are useful, as boiling water is available everywhere. Water bottles are essential, try to get one that you can use to cool boiled water.

An alarm clock is essential for getting up on time to catch flights and buses – make sure yours is lightweight and bring extra batteries. A strong torch (flashlight) is essential for viewing the inside of most monasteries. Chinese versions are of poor quality. Size AA rechargeable batteries can be bought in China but the rechargers are bulky – bring a portable one and plug adaptors if you cannot live without your Walkman. Following is a checklist of essential and nonessential items to consider packing:

Passport, photocopy of passport, visa, documents (vaccination certificate, student ID card), small emergency stash of cash US currency, money belt or vest, separate list of travellers cheque numbers, air ticket, copy of address book, reading matter, pens, notepad, namecards, visa photos, Swiss army knife, camera and accessories, extra camera battery, radio, padlock, cable lock (to secure luggage on trains), sunglasses, alarm clock, leak-proof water bottle, torch (flashlight) with batteries and bulbs, comb, compass, daypack, long pants, long shirt, T-shirt, nylon jacket, sweater or fleece, razor, razor blades, sewing kit, spoon, sun hat, sunscreen (UV) lotion, compact umbrella, toilet paper, tampons, toothbrush, toothpaste, dental floss, deodorant, shampoo, cord for a laundry line, flip-flops, tweezers, vitamins, laxative, diarrhoea medicine, condoms, contraceptives, special medications you use and medical kit (see Health section later in this chapter).

Gifts It is nice to be able to cement friendships or reward favours with a gift. Pictures of you and your family are good for breaking the ice when no one speaks English. The obvious gift is a photograph of the Dalai Lama, though be aware that these are currently illegal in Tibet. See the 'Dalai Lama Pictures' boxed text, for a discussion of the issues.

RESPONSIBLE TOURISM

Tourism has already affected many areas in Tibet. Most children will automatically stick their hand out for a sweet, a pen or anything. Tibetans in some regions, such as around Everest, have become frustrated to see a stream of rich tourist groups but few tangible economic results. Please try to bear the following in mind as you travel through Tibet:

- Revenues created by organised group tourism go largely into the pockets of the Chinese authorities so try to patronise as many small local Tibetan businesses, restaurants and guest-houses as possible.
- Don't hand out sweets or pens to children – you'll turn them into beggars. Similarly doling out medicines can encourage people not to seek proper medical advice. If you wish to contribute something constructive it's better to give pens directly to schools and medicines to rural clinics.
- Don't buy skins of endangered animals.
- Don't pay to take a photograph of someone and don't take a photo of someone if they don't want you to.

Dalai Lama Pictures

Several Tibetan support networks and some guidebooks (including earlier editions of this one) suggest bringing along Dalai Lama pictures to Tibet. It is actually a good idea, and can sometimes bring the recipient great happiness. The question is when to give.

The most important thing to realise is that, at the time of research at least, pictures of the Dalai Lama are illegal in Tibet and you are committing a crime by bringing them into the country.

Unfortunately, the indiscriminate handing out of Dalai Lama pics by travellers and tour groups has led to a situation (particularly in rural Tibet) where westerners are seen as mobile Dalai Lama picture dispensing machines: say the magic words 'Dalai Lama picture', and out one pops. And if you reply that you don't have any, Tibetans will often point at your bulging backpack as if to say 'what's that full of then?'

We agree with the advice given by Gary McCue, experienced Tibet traveller and author of Trekking in Tibet – a traveler's guide. Firstly, he suggests, never give out Dalai Lama photographs to those who ask for them – this only encourages Tibetans to hassle foreigners. Reserve them for Tibetans who tender some act of kindness. Secondly, be circumspect about handing out Dalai Lama pictures in public places. You can never be too sure who is watching, and it may have repercussions for both you and the recipient. Lastly, bear in mind that pictures of the Dalai Lama with the Tibetan national flag are even 'more' illegal. Handing these out will create serious problems (possibly arrest) for both the recipient and yourself.

- If you agree to send a photograph of someone please follow through on this.
- If you have any pro-Tibetan sympathies be very careful with whom you discuss them. Don't put Tibetans in a difficult or even potentially dangerous situation.
- Always offer to pay for accommodation if it is offered. At monasteries, leave a donation even if no payment is required.

For information on responsible trekking see the Trekking chapter.

TOURIST OFFICES

Tibet is a province of China and does not have tourist offices as such. There are a number of Chinese state-sponsored organisations that provide information on travel in Tibet, but as you might expect they are not particularly forthcoming of information that is useful to individual travellers. They can book domestic train and plane tickets to Chengdu and Golmud, though normally they will only sell tours in Tibet.

Similarly, the Tibetan Government in Exile does not provide information specifically related to travel in Tibet. For a listing of Tibet information services see the Useful Organisations section later in this chapter.

Tourist Offices in China & Tibet

Tibet Tourism Bureau The main function of the state-sponsored Tibet Tourism Bureau (TTB) is to direct travellers into group tours in Tibet. It is this organisation that issues the permits necessary to enter Tibet (see Permits under Visas and Documents later in this chapter), though very few travellers deal with it direct.

The main office outside Tibet is in Shanghai. The address is TTB (☎ 021-6228 8845, fax 6274 8488, email ttbsw@online.sh.cn, Web site www.tibet-tour.com), Block MN 8/F Hong Qiao Office Building, No 179, Zhongshan Xilu, Shanghai. Other contact numbers are found in Beijing (☎ 01-401 8822) and Chengdu (☎ 028-333 3988).

China International Travel Service The China International Travel Service (CITS) deals with China's foreign tourist hordes,

and mainly concerns itself with organising and making travel arrangements for group tours. As an individual traveller in Tibet, you are even less likely to have much contact with this organisation than you are in China. Outside China and Hong Kong, CITS is usually known as the China National Tourist Office.

The main office of CITS in Hong Kong (Tsimshatsui East) can book air tickets to China and has a good collection of English-language pamphlets. The main office and Central branch office are open Monday to Friday from 9 am to 5 pm and Saturday from 9 am to 1 pm; the Mongkok branch office keeps longer hours (Saturday from 9 am to 6.30 pm and half a day on Sunday). Addresses of the main offices are as follows:

Main Office
(☎ 7325888, fax 7217154)
6th floor, Tower Two, South Seas Centre, 75 Mody Rd, Tsimshatsui East, Kowloon
Causeway Bay Branch
(☎ 8363485, fax 5910849)
Room 1104, Causeway Bay Plaza, 489 Hennessy Rd, Causeway Bay
Central Branch
(☎ 8104282, fax 8681657)
Room 1018, Swire House, 11 Chater Rd, Central
Mongkok Branch
(☎ 3881619, fax 3856157)
Room 1102-1104, Bank Centre, 636 Nathan Rd, Mongkok, Kowloon

China Travel Service The China Travel Service (CTS) was originally set up to handle tourists from Hong Kong, Macau and Taiwan, and foreign nationals of Chinese descent (Overseas Chinese). In recent years, it has become a keen competitor with CITS. CITS is trying to cash in on the lucrative Taiwan and Hong Kong markets, while CTS is targeting the western market which was previously the exclusive domain of CITS.

While few travellers use CTS for travel in Tibet, many use the CTS offices in Hong Kong and Macau to obtain visas and book trains, planes, hovercraft and other transport to China. CTS can sometimes get you a better deal on hotels booked through its office than you could obtain on your own (of course, this does not apply to backpackers' dormitories). CTS has 19 branch offices in Hong Kong, and the Kowloon, Mongkok and Wanchai offices are open on Sunday and public holidays. These offices can be crowded – avoid this by arriving at 9 am when the doors open.

CTS offices in Hong Kong include:

Central Branch
(☎ 5217163, fax 5255525)
2nd floor, China Travel Building, 77 Queen's Rd, Central
China Hong Kong City Branch
(☎ 7361863) 10-12 China Hong Kong City complex, 33 Canton Rd, Tsimshatsui, Kowloon
Kowloon Branch
(☎ 7214481, fax 7216251)
1st floor, Alpha House, 27-33 Nathan Rd, Tsimshatsui, Kowloon
Mongkok Branch
(☎ 7895970, fax 3905001)
62-72 Sai Yee St, Mongkok
Wanchai Branch
(☎ 8323888) Ground floor, Southern Centre, 138 Hennessy Rd, Wanchai

Private Agencies in Tibet There are a host of smaller agencies operating in Tibet, mainly out of Lhasa. Most of them are geared to the needs of individual travellers and can help with limited information, the hire of vehicles and so on. See the Lhasa chapter for more details.

VISAS & DOCUMENTS
Passport

A passport is essential, and if yours is within a few months of expiry, get a new one now. Chinese embassies will not issue a visa if your passport has less than six months of validity remaining. Be sure that your passport has at least a few blank pages for visas and entry and exit stamps. It could be embarrassing to run out of blank pages when you are too far away from an embassy to get a new passport issued or extra pages added.

Losing your passport is very bad news indeed. Getting a new one takes time and money, particularly if you are in Tibet. If you lose your passport, you will need to travel to Beijing to apply for a new one. You

will definitely need some ID including your photo – many embassies require this before issuing a new passport. Some embassies will accept a driver's licence but others will not – an expired passport or even a photocopy could save the day.

Visas

Visas for individual travel in China are easy to get from most Chinese embassies. China will even issue visas to individuals from countries that do not have diplomatic relations with the People's Republic of China (PRC). The Chinese government has been known to stop issuing individual visas during summer or the run up to sensitive political events, in an attempt to control the number of tourists.

Most Chinese embassies and consulates will issue a standard 30 day, single-entry visa in three to five working days. Fees vary according to how much your country charges Chinese citizens for a visa. At the time of writing, a standard 30 day visa costs A$30 in Australia, 200FF in France, UK£25 in the UK and US$30 in the USA. Fees must be paid in cash at the time of application and you'll need two passport-sized photos. Express services cost double the normal fee. Your application must be written in English, and you are advised to have one entire blank page in your passport for the visa.

The visa application form asks you a number of questions – your travel itinerary, means of transport, how long you will stay etc – but you can deviate from this as much as you want. You do not have to leave from the place you specify on your visa application form. Whatever you do, however, *do not* let on that you plan to visit Tibet when you fill in this section. When listing your travel itinerary, pick the obvious contenders: Beijing, Shanghai, Guilin and so on. Don't list your occupation as journalist and don't mention bicycles.

Visas valid for more than 30 days can be difficult to obtain anywhere other than Hong Kong, though some embassies abroad (for example the UK) may give you 60 days out of high season if you ask nicely. This saves you the considerable hassle of getting a visa extension in Tibet. Most agencies in Hong Kong should be able to arrange a 60 or even 90 day visa.

A standard single-entry visa is activated on the date you enter China, and must be used within three months from the date of issue. There is some confusion over the validity of Chinese visas. Most Chinese officials look at the 'Valid Until' date, but on most 30-day visas this is actually the date by when you must have *entered* the country, not left. Longer stay visas often start from the day they are issued, not the day you entered the country, so there's no point in getting such a visa far in advance of your planned entry date. Check with the embassy if you are unsure.

If you want more flexibility to enter and leave China several times some Chinese embassies will issue a double-entry visa. Multiple-entry visas are most easily obtained through a travel agency in Hong Kong. These can be very useful if you intend to follow complicated routes in and out of Tibet or China via Hong Kong, Macau, Korea, Laos, Pakistan, Thailand, Mongolia, Russia etc or if you want to head back into Tibet from Nepal. The cheapest multiple-entry visas cost HK$650 and are valid for 90 days; six month multiple-entry visas cost HK$900. Both allow an unlimited number of border crossings during this time but there is a catch – you can only stay in China for 30 days at a time and getting this extended is close to impossible. Another minor catch is that these are in fact business visas, and normally will only be issued if you've been to China at least once before and have a stamp in your passport to prove it.

Most visas are stamped with an 'L' for *lüxing* or travel. Other types of visa include 'F' (business), 'X' (student) or 'Z' (working).

Hong Kong In Hong Kong, the cheapest 30-day visas (HK$100 for next day service, HK$250 for same day) can be obtained from the Visa Office (☎ 2585 1794/1700) at the Ministry of Foreign Affairs of the PRC, 5th floor, Low Block, China Resources Building, 26 Harbour Rd, Wanchai. You'll have to queue and do not expect so much as a smile, but you'll save a few dollars. It is open Monday to Friday, from 9 am to 12.30 pm and 2 to 5 pm, and on Saturday from 9 am to 12.30 pm. From Tsimshatsui on the Kowloon side, the cheapest and easiest way to get there is to take the Star Ferry to Wanchai Pier (not to Central!), one block away from the China Resources Building. Otherwise, it is a rather long hike from either the Wanchai or Causeway Bay MTR (Mass Transit Railway) stations.

There are numerous travel agencies in Hong Kong that issue Chinese visas. Besides saving you the hassle of visiting the visa office and queuing, a few travel agencies can get you more time than the usual 30 days. Two reliable agencies are Phoenix Services (☎ 2722 7378), 6th floor, Milton Mansion, 96 Nathan Rd, Tsimshatsui, Kowloon; and Shoestring Travel (☎ 2723 2306), 4th floor, Block A, Alpha House, 27 Peking Rd, Tsimshatsui, Kowloon.

Kathmandu Try to obtain a Chinese visa before you get to Kathmandu, either at home, in Delhi or in Bangkok. It will save you a whole series of headaches once you get to Tibet. Even if you are planning to whizz through Tibet as quickly as possible and head into China, the Chinese assume that all travellers in Kathmandu are primarily interested in getting into Tibet and for this reason will not issue visas to independent travellers. Even if you turn up with a Chinese visa you're not home dry – you still need to get a Tibet Tourism Bureau permit (see Permits later in this section) – but you will save yourself the hassle of having to split from a group visa and then extending your visa inside Lhasa.

If you do arrive in Kathmandu without a Chinese visa you will have to join a tour in order to get a visa (see the information on Nepal in the Air and Land sections of the Getting There & Away chapter for information). You will be put on a 15 day group visa, which is actually a separate sheet of paper with all the names and passport numbers of the members of your group on it.

Come the end of your tour in Lhasa you will either have to return with the group or split from this group visa. This can only officially be done by the Chinese partner of the Nepalese travel agency that arranged your travel into Tibet and the process is both awkward and pricey. Current fees for splitting from a group visa and then extending your visa are:

country	split a visa	visa extension
Australia	Y400	Y100
Canada	Y620	Y165
France	Y640	Y160
Japan	Y500	Y125
Korea	Y340	Y85
Russia	Y2000	Y500
Sweden	Y430	Y105
UK	Y640	Y160
USA	Y500	Y125
Others	Y200	Y100

Agencies in Lhasa will need your passport and a couple of days for the bureaucracy. If you encounter difficulties arranging this then Shigatse Travels in the Yak Hotel might be able to help you out, for a hefty fee.

Visa Extensions Visa extensions are handled by the Foreign Affairs Section of the local Public Security Bureau (PSB) – the police force. Government travel organisations (like CITS) have nothing to do with extensions so don't bother asking. Extensions of up to a week are usually available in Lhasa if you can produce proof that you are leaving Tibet (a plane ticket to Chengdu will do). It is easier to extend your visa in Chengdu or Xi'an. It may be possible to get a visa extension in Shigatse.

For extensions of longer than a week it's worth going direct to a travel agency (for a list see the Information section of the Lhasa chapter) rather than revealing your plans to the PSB. Travel agencies can arrange a visa extension of up to a month if you book a tour with them to Kailash. Some will sign you onto an imaginary tour to get the ex-

tension and then simply charge you a fee on top of the visa extension fee.

Permits
Tibet Tourism Bureau Permit The official line in the two provinces that border Tibet and are most used by travellers as points of entry – Sichuan and Qinghai – is that a permit is required to visit Tibet full stop. This is partly true. However, even if you fork out whatever local authorities are charging for the 'permit', you will never see anything that looks remotely like a travel permit. You are basically paying a bribe that will allow you to travel to Tibet independently. See the Getting There & Away chapter for more information on buying air and bus tickets into Tibet from Kathmandu, Golmud or Chengdu.

TTB permits are also needed by groups travelling by Land Cruiser but this will be arranged by the travel agency.

Travel Permit Once you have a visa and have managed to wangle a TTB permit you'd think you were home dry. Think again. You'll probably need to arrange a travel permit for much of your travel around Tibet.

Tibet is slightly more complicated than elsewhere in China when it comes to travel permits. An Alien Travel Permit (usually just called a Travel Permit) is granted by the PSB for travel (independent or group) to an area that is officially closed. In Tibet itself there are few areas that fit this category, but requiring travel permits has become something of a bureaucratic institution. For the latest information and travellers' reports check our Lonely Planet's Web site www .lonelyplanet.com.

At the time of research, travel permits were *not* needed for the towns of Lhasa, Shigatse, Tsetang or Naqu, nor for places in Lhasa Prefecture, nor for nonstop travel on the Friendship Highway. Lhasa Prefecture includes such places as Ganden, Tsurphu, Nam-tso, Drigung Til and Reting, giving you quite a lot of scope. Other places, such as Gyantse, Sakya, Samye, the Yarlung valley, the Everest region and Western Tibet all require permits. At the time of research, however, the only places that were actively checking permits were Samye, the Yarlung valley and the road to Kailash, though you could in theory be checked anywhere outside these places.

Lhasa PSB will not issue travel permits to individuals and will direct you to a travel agency. Agencies can arrange a travel permit to almost anywhere but only if you book a Land Cruiser, driver and a guide.

The saving grace in this situation, for the moment at least, is Shigatse PSB (God bless them). For some reason that nobody can quite work out, Shigatse PSB is extremely friendly and will issue permits to individuals for anywhere in Shigatse Prefecture (Sakya, Everest Base Camp, Nangartse, Shalu, Gyantse and anywhere on the Friendship Highway). Permits are issued on the spot for Y50. You are then free to catch a bus or hitch to these places without having to book an expensive tour. If other PSBs find out, this could all change very quickly.

Travel permits for Samye and Tsetang are harder to come by without booking a tour. At the time of research it was possible to 'buy' a permit to Samye for Y50 at the ferry crossing. Permits for the Yarlung valley were only available from Tsetang PSB and only issued when you book transport and a guide with Tsetang CITS.

Permits cost Y50, are valid for as long as your visa and can list any number of destinations. They are well worth getting if you can. If you get caught by the PSB without a permit (most likely when you check into a hotel) you face a fine of between Y200 and Y500.

Travellers flying out of Gongkar airport to Kathmandu are sometimes asked to surrender their travel permit (and sometimes TTB permit). If you don't have one you may well face a fine of around Y100. This is little more than a local money-raising venture.

Beware that the permit situation is subject to rapid and unpredictable change by the Chinese government so it's worth checking the current situation with other travellers in Lhasa. Don't trust the travel agencies on this one as they have a vested interest in booking you on one of their tours.

Other Permits Sensitive border areas such as Kailash and eastern Tibet also require a military permit and a foreign affairs permit. For Thöling and Tsaparang in Western Tibet you will also need a permit from the local Cultural Antiquities Department. All these will be arranged by the tour agency if you book a tour.

Travel Insurance

A travel insurance policy to cover theft, loss and medical problems is a good idea. The policies handled by STA Travel and other student travel organisations are usually good value. There is a wide variety of policies available so check the small print. Some policies specifically exclude 'dangerous activities', which normally includes trekking. Check that the policy covers ambulances or an emergency flight home. Paying for your air ticket with a credit card often provides limited travel accident insurance – ask your credit card company what it covers.

You may prefer a policy that pays doctors or hospitals directly rather than you having to pay on the spot and claim later. If you have to claim later, make sure you keep all documentation. Some policies ask you to call (reverse charges) a centre in your home country where an immediate assessment of your problem is made.

Some policies offer a cheaper plan which covers only medical cover and not baggage loss. This can be worthwhile if you're not carrying any pricey valuables in your grotty 10-year-old backpack. Most policies require you to pay the first US$100 or so anyway and only cover valuables up to a set limit. (Thus if you lose a US$1000 camera you might find yourself only covered for US$400 and having to pay the first US$100!) In case of loss of baggage or valuables, you will almost certainly need a police report to show the insurance company.

Insurance policies can normally be extended while you are on the road by a simple phone call to the insurance company or agent you bought it from. Make sure you do this *before* it expires or you may have to buy a new policy, often at a higher premium.

Student & Youth Cards

International student or youth cards like ISIC or GO 25 cards may get you cheaper fares to China or Nepal but are of little use inside Tibet. The only times you'll use one is for a 50% discount at the few monasteries that don't worry too much about selling you a ticket anyway.

Chinese student cards, bona fide or otherwise, are more useful and can help with discounts in hotels, bus transport and entry fees, despite the fact that the authorities are aware that China is flooded with fakes. Generally, it will help if you can muster together a few phrases of Chinese – at least saying 'I'm a foreign student' in Chinese as you hand over the card will give you a bit more credibility.

Other Documents

Given the Chinese preoccupation with impressive bits of paper, it is worth carrying a few business cards, student cards and anything else that is printed and laminated in plastic.

These additional IDs are useful to leave with bicycle-renters, who often want a deposit or other security for their bikes – sometimes they ask you to leave your passport, but you should insist on leaving another piece of ID or a deposit. Some hotels also require you to hand over your passport as security, even if you've paid in advance – an old expired passport is useful in these situations.

If you are travelling with your spouse, a photocopy of your marriage certificate just might come in handy should you become involved with the law, hospitals or other bureaucratic authorities (especially if one of you is Chinese). Useful, though not essential, is an International Health Certificate to record your vaccinations.

Youth hostel cards, driving licences, senior citizen's cards and the like are all of little use in Tibet.

Foreigners who live, work or study in China will be issued with a number of documents, and some of these can be used to obtain local prices on official bus tickets (not private minibuses) and entry tickets for monasteries and other sights in Tibet. As the dual pricing system is phased out there will be fewer discounts of this type.

Photocopies

All important documents (passport data page, Chinese visa, credit cards, travel insurance policy, air ticket etc) should be photocopied before you leave home. Leave one copy with someone at home and keep another with you, separate from the original. It's also a good idea to keep a list of your travellers cheque numbers separate from the cheques themselves.

EMBASSIES & CONSULATES
Chinese Embassies & Consulates

Some of the addresses of Chinese embassies and consulates in major cities abroad include:

Australia
  (☎ 02-6273 4780, 6273 4781)
  15 Coronation Drive, Yarralumla, ACT 2600
  Consulates: Melbourne, Perth and Sydney
Canada
  (☎ 13-789 3509, 234 2706)
  515 St Patrick St, Ottawa, Ontario KIN 5H3
  Consulates: Toronto, Vancouver
Denmark
  (☎ 039-625806, 611013)
  25 Oregards Alle, 2900 Hellerup, Copenhagen
France
  (☎ 01 47 23 36 77, 01 47 36 77 90)
  11 Ave George V, 75008 Paris
Germany
  (☎ 0228-361095) Kurfürstenallee 12, 5300 Bonn 2 (Bad Godesberg)
  Consulate: Hamburg
Italy
  (☎ 06-3630 8534, 3630 3856)
  Via Della Camilluccia 613, Roma 00135
  Consulate: Milan
Japan
  (☎ 03-3403 3380, 3403 3065)
  3-4-33 Moto-Azabu, Minato-ku, Tokyo 106
  Consulates: Fukuoka, Osaka and Sapporo

Laos
(☎ 021-315103)
Thanon Wat Nak Yai, Vientiane
Nepal
(☎ 01-411740)
Baluwatar, Kathmandu
Netherlands
(☎ 070-355 1515)
Adriaan Goekooplaan 7, 2517 JX, The Hague
New Zealand
(☎ 04-587 0407)
104A Korokoro Rd, Pentone, Wellington
UK
(☎ 0171-636 8845, from 22 April 2000 ☎ 020-7636 8845, visa information 0891-880808)
49-51 Portland Place, London WIN 5AG
Consulate: Manchester
USA
(☎ 202-328 2500, 338 6688, www.chinaembassy.org)
2300 Connecticut Ave NW, Washington DC 20008
Consulates: Chicago, Houston, Los Angeles, New York and San Francisco

Consulates in Tibet

Nepal In Lhasa, the Nepalese consulate (☎ 6822881, fax 6836890) is on a side street just south of the Lhasa Hotel (the former Holiday Inn) and north of the Norbulingka. Visa application hours are Monday to Friday from 10 am to 12.30 pm. Visas are issued in 24 hours. Visa fees change regularly but at the time of research, they are Y135 for a 15 day visa and Y225 for a 30 day visa. A double-entry visa costs Y360 for 30 days or Y540 for 60 days. All visas are valid for six months from the date of issue. Remember to bring one visa photo.

It is also possible to obtain visas for the same costs as above at Kodari, the Nepalese border town, though it would be sensible to check first that this has not changed.

Embassies in Beijing

If you need to contact your embassy while in Tibet you will need to ring or write to Beijing, where all of China's foreign embassies are located. It is not a good idea to send your passport to any of the addresses listed in order to obtain a visa for the next stop of your travels. China's postal service is simply not reliable enough, and some travellers have been left stranded in Lhasa with no passport for weeks on end. Go in person.

There are also consulates for Laos, Myanmar (Burma) and Thailand in Kunming and consulates for Australia, France, Germany, Japan, Thailand and Vietnam in Guangzhou (Canton).

In a real emergency the nearest western diplomatic representation is the US consulate (☎ 028-558 3992) in Chengdu.

In Beijing (☎ code 010) there are two embassy compounds – Jianguomenwai and Sanlitun.

The following embassies are in Jianguomenwai, Beijing:

Ireland
(☎ 6532 1908, fax 6532 2168)
3 Ritan Donglu
Japan
(☎ 6532 2361, fax 6532 4625)
7 Ritan Lu
Mongolia
(☎ 6532 1203)
2 Xiushui Beijie
New Zealand
(☎ 6532 2731, fax 6532 4317)
1 Ritan Dong 2-Jie
Thailand
(☎ 6532 1903, fax 6532 1748)
40 Guanghua Lu
UK
(☎ 6532-1961, fax 6532 1937)
11 Guanghua Lu
USA
(☎ 6532 3831, fax 6532 6057)
3 Xiushui Beijie
Vietnam
(☎ 6532 1155, fax 6532 5720)
32 Guanghua Lu

The Sanlitun compound in Beijing is home to the following embassies:

Australia
(☎ 6532 2331, fax 6532 6957)
21 Dongzhimenwai Dajie
Canada
(☎ 6532 3536, fax 6532 4072)
19 Dongzhimenwai Dajie
Denmark
(☎ 6532 2431, fax 6532 2439)
1 Sanlitun Dong 5-Jie

France
(☎ 6532 1331, fax 6532 4841)
3 Sanlitun Dong 3-Jie
Germany
(☎ 6532 2161, fax 6532 5336)
5 Dongzhimenwai Dajie
Myanmar (Burma)
(☎ 6532 1584, fax 6532 1344)
6 Dongzhimenwai Dajie
Nepal
(☎ 6532 1795, fax 6532 3251)
1 Sanlitun Xi 6-Jie
Netherlands
(☎ 6532 1131, fax 6532 4689)
1-15-2 Tayuan Building, 14 Liangmahe Nanlu
Pakistan
(☎ 6532 2504)
1 Dongzhimenwai Dajie
Russia
(☎ 6532 2051, fax 6532 4853)
4 Dongzhimen Beizhongjie, west of the Sanlitun compound in a separate compound

CUSTOMS

Chinese border crossings have gone from being severely traumatic to exceedingly easy for travellers. Although there seem to be lots of uniformed police around, the third degree at customs seems to be reserved for pornography-smuggling Hong Kongers rather than the stray backpacker.

Note that there are clearly marked 'green channels' and 'red channels', the latter reserved for those with such everyday travel items as refrigerators and colour TV sets.

You are allowed to import 400 cigarettes (or the equivalent in tobacco products), 2L of alcoholic drink and one *pint* of perfume. You are allowed to import a maximum of 72 rolls of film. Importation of fresh fruit is prohibited. It's also officially forbidden to bring more than 20 pieces of underwear into the People's Republic of China (I kid you not).

It is illegal to import any printed material, film, tapes, etc 'detrimental to China's politics, economy, culture and ethics'. This is a particularly sensitive subject in Tibet, but even here it is highly unusual to have Chinese customs officials grilling travellers about their reading matter. Maps and political books printed in Dharamsala could cause a problem, as could a conspicuous bundle of 300 Dalai Lama pictures. Some travellers

have reported being asked whether they have a Tibet guidebook with them when crossing the border from Nepal to Tibet. The appropriate answer is 'no' – again, this is the exception rather than the rule, however.

Anything made in China before 1949 is regarded as a cultural treasure and cannot be taken out of the country.

You can bring in or take out up to Y6000 in Chinese currency and unlimited amounts of foreign currency, though you must declare anything over US$5000 (or its equivalent).

MONEY
Currency

The Chinese currency is known as Renminbi (RMB) or the 'People's Money'. The basic unit of this currency is the *yuan* – designated in this book by a 'Y'. In spoken Chinese, the word *kuai* is almost always substituted for yuan. Ten *jiao* make up one yuan – in spoken Chinese, it is pronounced *mao*. Ten *fen* make up one jiao, but fen are becoming rare because they are worth so little – some people will not accept them.

RMB comes in paper notes issued in denominations of one, two, five, 10, 50 and 100 yuan; one, two and five jiao; and one, two and five fen. Coins are in denominations of one yuan; five jiao; and one, two and five fen.

There are worries that China may devalue its currency soon though there are no signs of this yet.

Exchange Rates

At the time of writing, exchange rates were:

Australia	A$1	=	Y5.03
Canada	C$1	=	Y5.67
Europe	€1	=	Y9.69
France	1FF	=	Y1.39
Germany	DM1	=	Y4.67
Hong Kong	HK$1	=	Y1.06
Japan	¥100	=	Y5.96
Nepal	Rs 100	=	Y13.56
Netherlands	gl	=	Y4.14
New Zealand	NZ$1	=	Y5.70
UK	UK£1	=	Y13.51
USA	US$1	=	Y8.28

Exchanging Money

In Tibet, the only place to change foreign currency and travellers cheques is the Bank of China. The top end hotels in Lhasa have exchange services but they are only available for guests. The sensible thing to do is to change as much money in Lhasa as you think you need. The only other places to change money are in Shigatse, Zhangmu and Purang (and perhaps Ali). If you are travelling up-country, try and get your cash in small denominations: Y100 and Y50 bills are sometimes difficult to get rid of in rural Tibet.

Australian, Canadian, US, UK, Hong Kong, Japanese and most Western European currencies are acceptable at the Bank of China. For cash transactions outside the bank, you will need to have US dollars. The official rate is given at all banks and most hotels so there is little need to shop around for the best deal. A standard commission of 1.5% is charged.

Since the floating of the RMB, there is no problem taking the currency out of the country. It would be sensible to change it back into a more useful currency, however. There are plenty of moneychangers at Zhangmu who will change yuan into rupees and vice versa. Keep some exchange receipts just in case, though you should not need them.

Cash If you don't like the idea of turning up at the border with no Chinese currency you can buy cash RMB from banks in Hong Kong and the Bank of China in large cities like London and New York.

Travellers Cheques Besides the advantage of safety, travellers cheques are useful to carry in Tibet because the exchange rate is more favourable than it is for cash. Cheques from most of the world's leading banks and issuing agencies are now acceptable at the Bank of China – stick to the major companies such as Thomas Cook, Citibank, American Express and Bank of America, and you'll be OK.

Credit Cards You'll get very few opportunities to splurge on the plastic in Tibet unless you spend a few nights in a top end hotel. Flights out of Lhasa can not be paid using a credit card, though this may change in the future. The Lhasa central branch of the Bank of China is the only place in Tibet which provides credit card advances. A 4% commission is usually deducted and the minimum advance is normally Y1200.

International Transfers Getting money sent to you while you are in China is a real drag, and it is even worse if you happen to be in Lhasa – try to avoid it. On average, it takes about five weeks for your money to arrive. If you have high-placed connections in the banking system it can take considerably less time, but most travellers are not so fortunate.

Black Market There is really not much of a black market in Tibet anymore. Money-changers still work the streets of Lhasa, such as outside the main post office, but as they offer almost the same rates as the bank and there is a *big* problem with counterfeit notes in China – you would be foolish to use their services. Change a small amount with them only if you get caught without cash after hours.

Counterfeit Notes Chinese authorities have recently been confronted with a deluge of counterfeit notes. The main culprit is the colour photocopier. Very few Tibetans or Chinese will accept a Y100 or Y50 note without first subjecting it to intense scrutiny, and many will not accept old, tattered notes. If you are having trouble spending older notes, they can be exchanged for small change at the Bank of China – counterfeits, however, will simply be confiscated. Check the watermark when receiving any Y100 note.

Security

A moneybelt or pockets sewn inside your clothes is the safest way to carry money. During the cooler weather, it's more comfortable to wear a vest (waistcoat) with numerous pockets, but you should wear this under a jacket or shirt for security.

Keeping all your eggs in one basket is not advised – you should keep an emergency stash of small denomination cash US dollars separate from your main money belt, along with a record of your travellers cheque serial numbers, emergency contact numbers and your passport number.

Costs

How much will it cost to travel in Tibet? This really depends on how much of Tibet you want to see and how quickly you want to see it. Accommodation is still very economical in Tibet, food is a little more expensive than elsewhere in China, but the major expense – unless you have plenty of time and enjoy rough travelling – is getting around. There is little in the way of public transport in Tibet, hitching can be time-consuming and if you really want to see a lot in a short space of time you will probably have to consider hiring a vehicle (plus driver) at rates of approximately US$0.50 per km.

Of course travel costs can be reduced by sharing transport with other travellers, but even so you will probably spend more money getting around than you would in other parts of China. The per-person cost for a group of six travelling with stops from Lhasa to the Nepalese border, for example, is around US$120. Getting into Tibet is also relatively expensive. Even the bus fare from Golmud has risen to around US$150 and will probably continue to rise as locals see increasing demand and travellers willing to pay continue to turn up. Most hired transport tends to work out at around US$15 to US$20 per person per day.

If you don't hire transport (and it is still perfectly possible to see most of the places covered in this guide if you don't) costs are very reasonable. If you are staying in Lhasa and visiting the surrounding sights you can do it comfortably on around US$15 per day – US$3 for dormitory accommodation, US$5 on food and the rest on transport and entry fees. Outside the main cities of Lhasa, Shigatse and Tsetang, daily costs can drop

drastically, especially if you're hitching or hiking out to remote monasteries and living on instant noodles.

One Country, Two Prices For years in China foreigners have been charged more for most things, and Tibet is no exception. In the last couple of years, dual pricing for things like hotel accommodation, train and plane tickets and entry prices has been phased out in most parts of China but the news has yet to filter through to most parts of Tibet. After years of official encouragement to charge foreigners more, many Chinese (and unfortunately Tibetans too) view upping the price for foreigners as their patriotic duty. Sometimes the charge is just a little bit more, but at other times it is 20 times more than the local price. Interestingly in Tibet, Chinese tourists are feeling the other end of the boot – while Tibetans pay only Y1 to get into the Potala, Chinese tourists have to pay Y40 like everyone else.

There is very little that you can do about this situation. A student card sometimes serves to waive these foreigners' surcharges, and in some situations determined haggling can bring prices down; but in the case of things such as government bus tickets you just have to shut up and pay up.

Tipping & Bargaining

Tibet is one of those wonderful places where tipping is not done and almost no one asks for it.

Basic bargaining skills are essential for travel in Tibet. You can bargain in shops, hotels, street stalls, travel agencies, with pedicab drivers, and with most people – but not everywhere. In large stores where prices are clearly marked, there is usually no latitude for bargaining. In small shops and street stalls, bargaining is expected, but there is one important rule to follow – be polite.

Tibetans are no less adept at driving a hard deal than the Chinese and, like the Chinese, aggressive bargaining will usually only serve to firm their conviction that the original asking price is the one they want. Try to keep smiling and firmly whittle away at the price.

If this does not work, try walking away. They might call you back, and if they don't there is always somewhere else.

POST & COMMUNICATIONS

Tibet is poorly developed when it comes to post and telecommunications but it's catching up with the modern world fast. Get all your postcards sent and make all your telephone calls in Lhasa, Shigatse or Tsetang. Lhasa is the only place in Tibet from where it is possible to send international parcels.

Postal Rates

An air mail letter of up to 20g costs Y6.40 to any country. Postcards cost Y4.20 and aerogrammes Y5.20.

There are cheaper printed matter and small-packet rates but pricing regulations rapidly become complicated. A small packet of 500g will cost around Y50 air mail.

Rates for parcels vary depending on the country of destination and seem quite random. The charge for a 1kg parcel sent by surface mail from China to the UK is Y142, Y81.40 to the USA, and Y88.30 to Australia. The charge for a 1kg parcel sent by air mail to the UK is Y173.20, Y173.50 to the USA, and Y160.20 to Australia. Check at the post office.

Post offices are very picky about how you pack things; do not finalise your packing until the parcel has its last customs clearance. Most countries impose a maximum weight limit (10kg is typical) on packages received – this rate varies from country to country but the Chinese post office should be able to tell you what the limit is. If you have a receipt for the goods, then put it in the box when you are mailing it, since it may be opened again by customs further down the line.

Express Mail Service (EMS) This worldwide priority mail service can courier documents to most foreign countries within a couple of days. Packages up to 500g cost around Y270 to Y300. After this add Y90 for every additional 500g. There are charges

of Y2.30 for recorded delivery and Y6.50 for registered mail.

Sending Mail

The international postal service seems efficient, and air mail letters and postcards will probably take around seven to 10 days to reach their destinations. If possible, write the country of destination in Chinese, as this should speed up the delivery.

Receiving Mail

There is a reliable poste restante service at the Lhasa GPO but it would be foolhardy to risk sending poste restante letters anywhere else in Tibet. All incoming mail is held at window No 12 of the Lhasa main post office. Things are arranged almost alphabetically – check for your first name, surname and even 'M' for Mr, Miss or Mrs. There is a charge of Y1.5 for each item of mail you receive.

Telephone

China's creaky phone system is being overhauled rapidly and domestic direct dialling is available almost everywhere in the main urban areas of Tibet. Major post offices and telecommunications buildings can place long-distance and international calls, though outside Lhasa, Tsetang or Shigatse forget it. Most hotels in Lhasa have international direct-dial telephones.

Domestic long-distance rates from Lhasa vary according to distance, but are cheap. International calls are expensive. Rates for station-to-station calls to most countries in the world are around Y18 to Y20 per minute. Hong Kong is slightly cheaper. There is normally a minimum charge of one minute though it's best to check this before you dial.

Calls are placed by paying a deposit of Y200 and then calling direct from a phone booth. Time the call yourself if you want to limit your call to a certain duration. After you make the call, the cost is deducted from your deposit and the balance returned to you. The time is computer controlled and you are not going to be cheated. Telephone cards are also available at a cost of Y150 for Y100 worth of calls but you might be left with up to US$2 of unusable credits as this is less than the minimum one minute charge. If you get through to an recorded message or fax you will be charged the minimum one minute charge.

Lines are amazingly clear considering where you are. In fact, the biggest problem will probably be the guy yelling in the booth next door.

If you are expecting a call – either international or domestic – try to advise the caller beforehand of your hotel room number. If this cannot be done, then try to inform reception that you are expecting the call and write down your name and room number.

It is still impossible to make collect (reverse charge) calls or to use foreign tele-

phone debit cards. The best you can do is give someone your number and get them to call you back.

Fax

The main telecommunications centre, the business centres in the top-end hotels and the Pentoc and Kyi Chu hotels in Lhasa all offer reliable fax services, though prices vary. Most places charge the basic international rate per minute (around Y20) plus a service charge of Y8 to Y10 per page. The price for receiving a fax ranges from Y3 per page at the Kyi Chu to Y10 at most hotel business centres. Make sure you get a confirmation print out that the fax actually went through.

Email & Internet Access

It is possible to send and receive emails in Lhasa only, at the Barkhor Café and at Jingpa Communications. It costs around Y10 to send and Y5 to receive a message. Internet access is available from the Barkhor Café and should soon be available from other suppliers. This means you can check on Hotmail accounts and, remarkably, surf the Web for, among other things, the Web site of the Office of the Dalai Lama. Charges are Y40 per hour or Y7 for a minimum of 10 minutes.

INTERNET RESOURCES

The World Wide Web is a rich resource for travellers. You can research your trip, hunt down bargain air fares, book hotels, check on weather conditions or chat with locals and other travellers about the best places to visit (or avoid!).

There's no better place to start your Web explorations than the Lonely Planet Web site (www.lonelyplanet.com). Here you'll find succinct summaries on travelling to most places on earth, postcards from other travellers and the Thorn Tree bulletin board, where you can ask questions before you go or dispense advice when you get back. You can also find travel news and updates to many of our most popular guidebooks, and the subWWWay section links you to the

---

Telephone Codes in Tibet

To Phone Out of Tibet
Dial ☎ 010 + country code + local code minus the 0 + local number

To Phone Into Tibet
Dial ☎ international code (usually 00) + 86 + local code minus the 0 + local number

Local telephone codes in Tibet include:

Ali	☎ 0897
Gyantse	☎ 0892
Lhasa	☎ 0891
Naqu	☎ 08064
Nyalam	☎ 08027
Shigatse	☎ 0892
Tingri	☎ 08026
Tsetang	☎ 0893
Zhangmu	☎ 08074

Others useful codes include:

Beijing	☎ 010
Kathmandu	☎ 977-1
Chengdu	☎ 028

most useful travel resources elsewhere on the Web.

For Web sites created by travel companies see the Organised Tours section in the Getting There & Away chapter, and for Tibetan Organisations section later in this chapter. The pick of general Web sites about Tibet are listed here:

Canada Tibet Committee
  www.tibet.ca
  A useful free news gathering service on issues relating to Tibet.
Office of Dalai Lama in London
  www.tibet.com
  Provides lots of background information on Tibet.
Personal Web site
  www.tibetworld.com/
  Lists books and organisations – mostly Europe – concerned with Tibet.
Tibet Information Network
  www.tibetinfo.net
  Another news gathering service with a good rundown of tourism in Tibet.
Tibet Online Resource Gathering
  www.tibet.org
  Has articles on Tibet and good links to other Tibet-related sites.
Tibet Tourism Bureau, Shanghai Branch
  www.tibet-tour.com
  Has mostly pricey tours but a few useful things like flight timetables to Lhasa.
Tibetan Studies WWW Virtual Library
  www.ciolek.com
  Excellent list of Tibet Web sites and general information on the country.

BOOKS

Literature on Tibet is abundant. Quite a bit of it is of the woolly, 'how to find enlightenment in the mysterious Land of Snows' variety, but there is still a lot of very good stuff about.

Bring your own reading material because the only way you will find anything worthwhile to read in Tibet is to swap with other travellers. Bookshops are bad enough in the big cities of China, but in Tibet you'll be lucky to even stumble across a musty copy of *Gulliver's Travels*.

If you are coming in from either Kath-

mandu or Hong Kong, however, both of these cities are excellent places to stock up on reading material. Kathmandu, with its dozens of cheap bookshops simply brimming with novels and books about India, Nepal and Tibet, is the best place to stock up. Not only do they have cheap second-hand books and anything new and current, they also have many expensive and rare books, including Indian reprints of very rare editions. Hong Kong has the disadvantage of being expensive. Still, a few good books are essential for travel and are worth splashing out on.

Most books are published in different editions by different publishers in different countries. As a result, a book might be a hardcover rarity in one country while it's readily available in paperback in another. Fortunately, bookshops and libraries search by title or author, so your local bookshop or library is best placed to advise you on the availability of the following recommendations.

Lonely Planet

If you are headed off into the Tibetan countryside you'll find Lonely Planet's *Tibetan phrasebook* a lifesaver. Guides to neighbouring regions include *China, South-West China, Nepal, Bhutan* and *Indian Himalaya*.

Guidebooks

The market has been flooded with guides to Tibet in recent years, and this is one of them. Interestingly, however, general guides aimed at the first-time visitor to Tibet are sparse on the ground.

The Odyssey Illustrated Guide to Tibet (second edition 1997) is an exception to this rule, and provides good background reading on Tibet and its attractions with an appealing format. Unlike some of the other books around it is also fairly portable. That said, very few independent travellers take it to Tibet.

Books which assume a reasonably deep interest in Tibet and possibly some prior study of the culture include Stephen Batchelor's classic *The Tibet Guide* (second edition 1998), the pick of the pack for serious travellers. Consider getting a copy if you have a strong interest in identifying the myriad of images found in Tibetan monasteries. Unfortunately there's very little practical information along the lines of useful maps or places to stay.

There are a couple of encyclopedic guides to Tibet. Victor Chan's *Tibet Handbook – a pilgrimage guide* (Moon, 1994) is without a doubt the most comprehensive guide (1099 pages) ever written on Tibet and any serious student of the culture should get hold of a copy. Unfortunately, for the average traveller the book is simply too bulky, too baffling in its organisation and simply too comprehensive to be a useful guide. Travellers using the guide complain that there is so much in the book that it is almost impossible to choose an itinerary. A remarkable, fascinating achievement but probably better off on the bookshelf than in your backpack.

A less bulky companion for the serious traveller is the *Tibet Handbook* (Footprint Handbooks, 1996) written by Gyurme Dorje. Like the Moon guide this guide suffers from a baffling organisation (into Chinese counties) and frustrating maps but certainly has a huge amount of scholarly information and covers both Tibet and the Tibetan areas of Sichuan, Qinghai and Gansu provinces.

Finally, the best companion to the book you are holding in your hands is *Trekking in Tibet – a traveler's guide* (1991) by Gary McCue. This well-researched guide has detailed information on treks around Lhasa, Ü, Tsang and Western Tibet, and is indispensable for anyone whose primary interest in Tibet is to explore the country on foot.

Travel

There are a number of books around documenting the exploits of visitors to Tibet. A classic is Heinrich Harrer's *Seven Years in Tibet* translated from German in 1952 and made into a film in 1997. It is an account of Harrer's sojourn in Tibet in the final years before the Chinese takeover. He wrote a less worthy sequel in *Return to Tibet*.

For starry-eyed dreamers of the Land of Snows *Magic & Mystery in Tibet* by Alexandra David-Neel has the lot – flying nuns, enchanted daggers, ghosts and demons, and also some interesting background information on the mystic side of Tibet.

Anyone heading out to Western Tibet simply has to get hold of a copy of *A Mountain in Tibet* by Charles Allen. This superbly crafted book takes a look at the holy mountain of Kailash and the attempts of early European explorers to reach it and to determine its geographical significance. Peter Hopkirk's *Trespassers on the Roof of the World – the race for Lhasa* is another book that is primarily interested in the European assault on Tibet, but again it is a superb read.

An interesting, little known book worth looking out for is *Captured in Tibet* by Robert Ford. This account by a radio operator employed by the Tibetan government and his subsequent incarceration by the Chinese after their takeover deserves more readers. Ford, as a technician is not blind to the inefficiencies that characterised the former lamaist government but at the same time has a great sympathy for the Tibetan people.

A Stranger in Tibet by Scott Berry tells the fascinating story of Kawaguchi Ekai, a young Japanese monk who was one of the first foreigners to reach Lhasa in 1900 and who managed to stay over a year in the capital before his identity was discovered and he was forced to flee the country.

Vikram 'A Suitable Boy' Seth writes of his epic journey to Tibet across China back in the pioneering days of Tibet independent travel in *From Heaven Lake* (1987). It is a straight travel book, and not particularly illuminating on the subject of Tibet, but it is one of the best around all the same.

There are a couple of early travel books around that make for good reads. One of the classics is Robert Byron's *First Russia, then Tibet*. Peter Fleming has written an exciting blow-by-blow account of the British 1904 invasion of Tibet led by Francis Younghusband: *Bayonets to Lhasa* (1961).

Finally, Walt Unsworth has written a 700 page book simply called *Everest*. This is the perfect companion for a trip to Base Camp and further, even if it is a bit hefty to lug around with you. It has fascinating accounts of all the early attempts to reach the peak and some of the key successful later attempts.

For books on Mt Kailash see the Mt Kailash Kora section in the Trekking chapter.

History & Politics

It is difficult to find a general history of Tibet that is worth recommending. The standard text is *Tibet & its History* by Hugh Richardson, a book which is weak on the early history of Tibet and concentrates mainly on the years from the Gelugpa ascendancy to the Chinese takeover. *A Cultural History of Tibet* by David Snellgrove and Hugh Richardson is perhaps a better introduction to the history and culture of Tibet, but is marred for the general reader by the use of a scholarly and at times indecipherable transliteration system of Tibetan – Samye Monastery for example is rendered *bSam-yas*.

The most accessible history of modern Tibet is *Tears of Blood – a cry for Tibet* by Mary Craig. This riveting and distressing account of the Tibetan experience since the Chinese takeover is a catalogue of misery, but should be read by every visitor to Tibet.

An excellent scholarly account of modern Tibet is available in Melvyn Goldstein's *A History of Modern Tibet 1913-1959 – the demise of the lamaist state*. It gives a blow by blow account of the critical years that saw Tibet lose what independence it had to its powerful eastern neighbour. Interestingly, it pulls no punches in showing the intrigues, superstitions and governmental ineptitude that led to the demise of the Lhasa government. For anyone with a serious interest in modern Tibetan history this is the definitive account.

People & Society

Probably the best wide-ranging introduction to Tibet can be found in *Tibet – its history, religion and people* by Thubten Jigme Norbu and Colin Turnbull. As the principal author is Tibetan, it is an account from within Tibet and is perhaps not as objective as it might have been. The book does, however, offer a great deal of insight into how Tibetans perceive and organise their world. Written in 1972, the book can be a little hard to find.

Also highly recommended is John Avedon's *In Exile from the Land of Snows*. This is largely an account of the Tibetan community in Dharamsala, but is an excellent and informative read. For those with an academic bent, look out for *Civilised Shamans – Buddhism in Tibetan Societies* by Geoffrey Samuel, a fascinating anthropological investigation into the nature of Tibetan Buddhism and its relationship with the indigenous Bön faith – heavy but rewarding reading.

Buddhism

A good, lucid exposition of Tibetan Buddhism? Well, they are not that easy to come by. A lot of them seem to assume that you want to practice it rather than just know about it, which of course is a tricky theoretical distinction. But assuming you just want some background to the Buddhist culture of Tibet, the best starting point is a primer on Buddhism in general. The classic for many years now is *Buddhism* by Christmas Humphries. Another good primer is *A Short History of Buddhism* by Edward Conze.

Slightly more academic and not that easy to get hold of is an *Introduction to Buddhism – teachings, history & practices* by Peter Harvey. The fact that Harvey's analysis is rooted both in the theory and practice of Buddhism makes his book particularly interesting, though he spends little time on Tibetan Buddhism. For reading about Mahayana Buddhism in particular, *Mahayana Buddhism* by Beatrice Lane Suzuki is a good reference, though slightly tendentious.

The classic introduction to Tibetan Buddhism – though many of its conclusions and observations are disputed by contemporary Tibetologists – is Charles Bell's *The Religion of Tibet*.

Keith Dowman's new *The Sacred Life of Tibet* builds on his earlier *The Power Places of Central Tibet* and provides an excellent insight into how Tibetans see the spiritual landscape of their land. It also offers a pilgrim's perspective on travelling in Tibet.

Biography

Another illuminating glimpse of the Tibetan experience is provided by *Freedom in Exile – the autobiography of the Dalai Lama*. With great humility the Dalai Lama outlines his personal philosophy, his hope to be reunited with his homeland and the story of his life. *Kundun* by Mary Craig is a recent biography of the family of the Dalai Lama.

Fire Under Snow: Testimony of a Tibetan Prisoner by Palden Gyatso is a moving autobiography which recounts his life as a Buddhist monk imprisoned for 33 years for refusing to denounce the Dalai Lama.

Fiction

The enduring myth of Shangri-la owes much to James Hilton's 1937 classic novel *Lost Horizon*, which tells the story of a group of westerners who crash land into an earthly paradise somewhere in remotest Tibet.

The Third Eye by Lobsang Rampa was a fabulously popular first-hand account of Tibetan mysticism in the 1950s until it came out that the author Lobsang Rampa was actually one Cyril Hoskins, a plumber from Cornwall. It relates, among other things, how the author had an operation in Tibet as a child to stimulate his powers of extra sensory perception. It went on to sell millions of copies. *The Rose of Tibet* by Lionel Davidson is in the Lobsang Rangpa school of Tibetan history but is very readable and suprisingly informative. The novel's Yamdring Monastery is closely based on the Samding Monastery with its female incarnate lama.

One unusual book that might be worth checking out is *Invading Tibet*, a novel by Mark Frutkin based on the story of Edmund Chandler, the journalist who accompanied Younghusband's British invasion of Tibet in 1904. Finally, kids (and most adults) will love Hergé's timeless *Tintin in Tibet*.

FILMS

In 1997 Tibet was Hollywood's flavour of the month (see boxed text Tibet Chic) and two big box office releases focused on Tibet.

Seven Years in Tibet, directed by Jean Jaques Annaud (*The Lover* and *Quest For Fire*), was the big crowd puller. The US$70 million film tells the story of the daring escape of Heinrich Harrer (as portrayed by Brad Pitt) and Peter Aufschnaiter (David Thewlis) from a prisoner of war camp in northern India, their epic trek across Tibet and seven year sojourn in Lhasa as aides to the young Dalai Lama.

A better film is Martin Scorcese's *Kundun* ('Kundun' means 'presence' and is one of the names used to refer to the Dalai Lama). The film features an all Tibetan and Chinese cast, many of them descendants of the original figures they are portraying (the Dalai Lama's mother is played by the Dalai Lama's real life niece). The cinematography in particular is gorgeous.

A Chinese film worth watching out for is acclaimed director Tian Zhuangzhuang's *The Horse Thief*, a documentary-style look at the nomads of east Tibet. Possibly one to miss is the epic Chinese production *Red River Valley*, depicting the Younghusband invasion from a very Chinese perspective (and featuring one of the previous authors of this guide as an extra!).

The Illusion of Tibet

Remember the great sweeping shots of Tibet you saw at the cinema? Think again. *Kundun* was filmed mainly in Quarzate in Morocco (with the Atlas as a backdrop) as well as Casablanca, Marakesh, British Columbia, the Andes and Idaho. *Seven Years in Tibet* was filmed in Mendoza (Argentina), British Columbia, Chile and Austria (and even Leamington Spa!). You'd be forgiven if you never caught on though. Authenticity was apparently so important to director Martin Scorcese that dung from real yaks was scattered over the set to add realism.

Tibet Chic

Volcano movies are passé, Godzilla has come and gone, and Bruce Willis is losing his hair. What's really hip in Hollywood is ... the Dalai Lama.

Hollywood's flirtation with Tibet started way back in 1937 with the film version of James Hilton's classic *Lost Horizon*. The pseudo-Tibet theme continued with such films as *The Golden Child* (1986), apparently inspired by the young Karmapa of Tsurphu Monastery, and Bernardo Bertolucci's *Little Buddha* (1993). But it was the release of *Seven Years in Tibet* and *Kundun* in 1997, two films detailing the Chinese invasion of Tibet, that really made Tibet chic.

Richard Gere remains the most outspoken advocate of Tibetan independence in Tinseltown, using the Academy Awards Ceremony in 1992 as a platform to publicise the cause. But the Hollywood connection doesn't end here. Robert Thurman, the father of actress Uma Thurman, is the Tsongkhapa Professor of Indo-Tibetan Studies at Columbia University. Other stars with an active interest in Tibetan Buddhism include Harrison Ford, Goldie Hawn, Oliver Stone, and Phil Jackson, the coach of the Chicago Bulls. Harrison Ford's wife Melissa Matheson wrote the screenplay for *Kundun* and her husband apparently spent several days reading the script out to the Dalai Lama to gauge his Holiness' reaction. Perhaps most surprising of all was the announcement that Steven Seagal, the pony-tailed kick-boxing movie star, has been discovered to be a reincarnated trulku of the Nyingmapa order of Tibetan Buddhism.

None of this is good PR for China. The Chinese government tried to get *Kundun* scrapped by holding hostage its business deals with Disney (the film's backers) but Disney held firm. *Seven Years in Tibet* was all set to be filmed in northern India until the Indian authorities buckled under Chinese diplomatic pressure. Brad Pitt soon joined Richard Gere on the list of counter-revolutionary actors banned from entering China.

Tibet chic has spread to the music industry. Adam Yauch of the Beastie Boys, a confirmed Tibetan Buddhist, is the organiser of the now annual Tibet Freedom Concert, which has featured such bands as U2, Björk, Alanis Morissette, Radiohead, Blur, De La Soul, the Foo Fighters and Patti Smith. Other Buddhist musicians include Natalie Merchant, Tina Turner and composer Phillip Glass, who composed the soundtrack for *Kundun*. Annie Lennox and Peter Gabriel have also voiced public support for the Tibetan cause.

Back in corporate America, however, Buddhism sells big time. Meditation centres have been popping up all across America and bookings on adventure tours to Tibet are booming. The cosmetic company Impulse named its newest fragrance 'Zen'. You can even get a Kalachakra mandala screensaver for your computer.

Whether all this media fuss is actually helping the Tibetan cause is up for debate. Some argue that the hype merely helps to perpetuate a media myth of Tibet; that somehow Tibet is a remote fantasy, that the suffering isn't real, and doesn't require any hard action. Back in Hollywood they grin knowingly: 'there's no such thing as bad press'.

CD ROMS

A CD Rom titled *The Potala Palace in Tibet* was produced by Tsinghua University. It's in Microsoft Windows format with a game-like interface and has text, photos and video clips describing the history of the Potala and major rooms from a very Chinese perspective. In Lhasa the CD costs Y240 and is sold only in gift shops inside the Potala.

NEWSPAPERS & MAGAZINES

Unless you are fluent in Chinese or Tibetan, you can forget about browsing through newspapers while you are in Tibet. The

Beijing English-language publication *The China Daily* occasionally turns up a couple of weeks late, but is a boring read anyway. Chinese publications like *China's Tibet* (says it all really) are propaganda dedicated to the official line 'the Dalai Lama is a counter-revolutionary splittist' and of little objective interest.

No foreign newspapers or magazines are available in Lhasa, even at the Lhasa Hotel. The lobby of the Pentoc Hotel keeps a print out of world news downloaded from the Internet which is worth a browse if you're feeling cut off from the world.

RADIO & TV

There is unlikely to be anything that you would want to watch or listen to on the television or the radio while you are in Tibet. Tibet has its own TV channel (though most of it is in Chinese) and there are even local stations like Shigatse TV! Broadcasts are made in both Mandarin and Tibetan.

If you have a short-wave radio you can pick up the BBC World Service and Voice of America. Frequencies vary according to the time of day. Both broadcast a Tibetan language service.

VIDEO SYSTEMS

China subscribes to the PAL video standard, the same as Australia, New Zealand, the UK and most of Europe.

PHOTOGRAPHY & VIDEO
Film & Equipment

Tibet is one of the most photogenic countries in the world and you should bring twice as much film as you think you'll need. It is fairly easy to pick up print film in Lhasa and Shigatse – Fuji and Konika film are available, almost always in 100ASA. It is more difficult to find slide film but you can buy Sensia or Ektachrome film in Lhasa for around Y50 for 36 exposures. You won't find any slide film outside of Lhasa.

Technical Tips

Bear in mind, when taking photographs in Tibet, that special conditions prevail. For one, the dust gets into everything – make a point of carefully cleaning your lenses as often as possible. The high altitudes in Tibet also mean that you are dealing with unusual light conditions. The best time to take photographs is when the sun is low in the sky: early in the morning and late in the afternoon. This does not mean that you should not take photographs at other times, but simply that getting a good exposure becomes more difficult – you are likely to end up with a shot full of dark shadows and bright points of light.

One useful accessory to cope with Tibet's harsh light conditions is a polarising filter. When using it, turn the filter until the contrast improves; if there are any clouds in the sky, they will become whiter as the sky itself becomes a deeper shade of blue.

Processing

Believe it or not, it is actually possible to process print film in Lhasa, and with fairly good results. Down in the area of the Potala are a number of shops with the latest Japanese photo processing machines. Photos can be processed in a few hours for around Y25.

Don't even think about processing slide film in Tibet, even if someone in Lhasa claims it is possible. Save your processing for home, Bangkok or Hong Kong. Even in Kathmandu, with the exception of a couple of professional outfits, it is a very risky proposition.

Restrictions

Photography from planes and photographs of airports and military installations are prohibited; bridges may even be a touchy subject, but it is unlikely. Don't take any photos or especially video footage of civil unrest or public demonstrations. The Chinese are paranoid about foreign TV crews filming unauthorised documentaries on Tibet.

Restrictions on photography are also imposed at most monasteries, museums and archaeological sites. This has absolutely nothing to do with religious sensitivity and everything to do with China protecting its inept postcard industry; in the case of flash photography, such restrictions do protect wall murals from damage. Inside the larger monasteries, a fee is often imposed in each room or building for taking a photograph. Generally this is Y50 per shot but you can often negotiate with the monks. Video fees can be up to Y800 (US$100!) in some monasteries. You are free, however, to take photographs of the exteriors of monasteries.

Be aware that these rules are generally enforced. If you want to snap a few photos where you shouldn't, then start with a new roll of film – if it is ripped out of your camera, you won't lose 20 other photos as well.

Photographing People

Tibet is a great place for portraits. Generally, Tibetans do not mind their photographs being taken. Naturally, it is best to ask first. Tibetans, like other asian people, do not like having their photograph taken while they are working (as in monastery restoration crews) and cannot understand why anyone would want to take such a photograph anyway. Be discreet in taking such photographs and try not to upset anyone.

It's not uncommon for Tibetans to ask you to take their photograph. Usually this is because they assume you have a Polaroid camera and can hand them the results immediately. You should try and explain, with sign language if necessary, that you can't give them a photograph on the spot before shooting. If you agree to send them a copy of the photo, please follow through on this.

Video

Properly used, a video camera can give a fascinating record of your holiday. As well as videoing the obvious things – sunsets and spectacular views – remember to record some of the ordinary everyday details of life in the country. Often the most interesting things occur when you're actually intent on filming something else. Remember too that, unlike still photography, video 'flows' – so, for example, you can shoot scenes of countryside rolling past the train window, to give an overall impression that isn't possible with ordinary photos.

Video cameras these days have amazingly sensitive microphones, and you might be surprised how much sound will be picked up. This can also be a problem if there is a lot of ambient noise – filming by the side of a busy road might seem OK when you do it, but viewing it back home might simply give you a deafening cacophony of traffic noise. One good rule for beginners to follow is to try to film in long takes, and don't move the camera around too much. Otherwise, your video could well make your viewers seasick! If your camera has a stabiliser, you can use it to obtain good footage while travelling on various means of transport, even on bumpy roads. And remember, you're on holiday – don't let the video take over your life and turn your trip into a Cecil B de Mille production.

Make sure you keep the batteries charged and have the necessary charger, plugs and transformer (see Electricity below). In most countries, it is possible to obtain video cartridges easily in large towns and cities, but make sure you buy the correct format. It is usually worth buying at least a few cartridges duty-free to start off your trip.

Finally, remember to follow the same rules regarding people's sensitivities as for still photography – having a video camera shoved in their face is probably even more annoying and offensive for locals than a still camera. Always ask permission first.

TIME

Time throughout China – including Tibet – is set to Beijing time, which is eight hours ahead of GMT/UTC. When it is noon in Beijing it is also noon in far-off Lhasa, even if the sun only indicates around 9 or 10 am.

When it is noon in Lhasa it is 8 pm the previous day in Los Angeles, 11 pm the previous day in New York, 4 am in London, 5 am in Paris, 9.45 am in Kathmandu, noon in Hong Kong, 2 pm in Sydney and 4 pm in Wellington.

ELECTRICITY

Electricity is 220V, 50 cycles AC. Plugs come in at least four designs – three-pronged angled pins (like in Australia), three-pronged round pins (like in Hong Kong), two flat pins (US style but without the ground wire) or two narrow round pins (European style) and three rectangular pins (British style). Conversion plugs are easily purchased in Hong Kong but are damn near impossible to find in China. Interestingly, Chinese extension lines often end in a unit that accommodates all the different styles of plug regularly catered for.

Considering the remoteness of Tibet, it is surprising just how many towns and villages are supplied with electricity. Nevertheless, most monasteries are very poorly lit and in Western Tibet there is very little in the way of electricity. Bring a small but good-quality torch (flashlight) from abroad. Chinese torches are awful – 50% of the time they do not work and the bulbs seldom last as long as the batteries.

WEIGHTS & MEASURES
The metric system is widely used in China. However, the traditional Chinese measures are often used for domestic transactions and you may come across them. Chinese traders measure fruit and vegetables by the *jin* (500g). Smaller measurements (eg for dumplings) are measured in *liang* (50g). The following equations may help:

metric	Chinese	imperial
1m	3 *chi*	3.28 feet
1km	2 *li*	0.62 miles
1 hectare	15 *mu*	2.47 acres
1L	1 *gongsheng*	0.22 gallons
1kg	2 *jin*	2.2 pounds

LAUNDRY
The Kirey and Banak Shol hotels in Lhasa offer free laundry, while others like the Pentoc charge around Y15 for a bagful. Upper end hotels charge considerably more. The Tenzin Hotel in Shigatse washes clothes for around Y1 a piece.

Outside of these you are pretty much on your own. All but the crummiest hotel rooms provide a bowl for washing, even if the water supply is less than reliable. Small packets of soap powder can be bought almost anywhere that has a shop.

TOILETS
Chinese toilets might be fairly dismal, but Tibetan toilets make them look like little bowers of heaven. The standard model is a deep hole in the ground that bubbles and gives off noxious vapours. Many people (including women with long skirts) urinate and defecate in the street. On the plus side, Tibetans seem to like doing their business in high places, and there are some fabulous 'toilets with a view' in Tibet. Honours go to the Samye Monastery Guesthouse, the Sakya Guesthouse, the public toilets in the Potala and the small village of Passum en route to Everest Base Camp.

With the exception of the odd hotel here and there, toilets in Tibet are of the squat variety – as the clichés go, good for the digestion and character building too. Stock up on toilet paper in Lhasa and Shigatse. Be warned that toilets are not secure – keep an eye on valuables. And finally, a tip for the boys: if there's nobody about, the women's toilets are always cleaner than the men's.

HEALTH
Tibet poses particular risks to your health, though for the large part these are associated with the high altitude of the plateau. There is no need to be overly worried: very few travellers are adversely affected by the altitude for very long, and greater risks are present in the form of road accidents and dog bites. Infectious and insect-borne diseases are quite rare due to the altitude.

Sensible travellers will rely on their own medical knowledge and supplies when travelling to Tibet. It is a very isolated place, and outside Lhasa there is very little in the way of expert medical care available. Read the following section carefully for information on how to make your trip a safer one.

Pre-departure Planning
Immunisations China does not actually require any immunisations for entry into the

A Fall From Grace

In Lhasa I wanted to use a typical public toilet, so I went to the ones across from the Holiday Inn (now Lhasa Hotel). I have never had problems with toilets in China before and although I read in the Lonely Planet guide that the toilets in Lhasa were particularly disgusting I didn't think it would be a problem. It was bad luck (or perhaps stupidity) that led me to the wrong entrance to the toilet, the entrance from whence the shit is collected. It was like a swimming pool. It was quite dark inside, but I could see it was very dirty and I knew I had to be careful not to fall down. To me it looked like a real floor, I thought the shit was only on the surface. It wasn't.

I took one step, and fell in. I went under (it was really deep – I am 1.8m tall!), swallowed a mouthful, and then I managed to get out. All I could do when I got out was laugh – I could not believe something like that could really happen! There was a Canadian guy waiting for me in the main street and when he saw me I had to laugh again. The only thing I could say was that I was full of shit!

We went to the Holiday Inn, but the staff wouldn't allow me inside. A group of Italians outside the hotel tried to hose me down on the lawn next door. The water was extremely cold. I took my clothes off piece by piece. Fortunately a very nice man from the management of the Holiday Inn sent somebody to take me inside the hotel. I felt quite embarrassed as I walked through the lobby, freezing, almost naked and still very dirty. Everyone was staring at me!

I took a long hot shower. The hotel staff gave me some salt water to make me vomit, and the Canadian guy bought me some underwear and nice Chinese clothes. I went to the doctor because I was concerned that swallowing shit may not be good for your health. The doctor gave me some medicine for worms and to cleanse my insides.

I had to throw away my little backpack and its contents (including Lonely Planet's China and Tibet, both new). Also my money went a funny colour and was very wet and stinky for a few days, so I had some trouble spending it. Neither my passport nor student card looked very nice, I am currently trying to get new ones.

I read in the Lonely Planet that, thank God, no one has ever fallen into a Tibetan toilet! In your new edition you may have to correct that.

Kerstin Knopf

country, but the further off the beaten track you go the more necessary it is to take precautions. The World Health Organisation (WHO) requires travellers who have come from an area infected with yellow fever to have a vaccination before entering the country, see the 'Yellow Fever' entry later in this section. Be aware that there is a greater risk of all kinds of disease with children and in pregnancy.

Plan ahead for getting your vaccinations: some of them require more than one injection, while some vaccinations should not be given together. It is recommended you seek medical advice at least six weeks before travel.

Record all vaccinations on an International Health Certificate, available from your doctor or government health department.

Discuss your requirements with your doctor, but vaccinations you should consider for this trip include:

Hepatitis A Hepatitis A vaccine (eg Avaxim, Havrix 1440 or VAQTA) provides long-term immunity (possibly more than 10 years) after an initial injection and a booster at six to 12 months.

Medical Kit Check List

Following is a list of items you should consider including in your medical kit – consult your phamacist for brands available in your country.

☐ **Aspirin** or **paracetamol** (acetaminophen in the US) – for pain or fever.

☐ **Antihistamine** – for allergies, eg hay fever; to ease the itch from insect bites or stings; and to prevent motion sickness.

☐ **Antibiotics** – consider including these if you're travelling well off the beaten track; see your doctor, as they must be prescribed, and carry the prescription with you.

☐ **Loperamide** or **diphenoxylate** – 'blockers' for diarrhoea; **prochlorperazine** or **metaclopramide** for nausea and vomiting.

☐ **Rehydration mixture** – to prevent dehydration, eg due to severe diarrhoea; particularly important when travelling with children.

☐ **Insect repellent, sunscreen, lip balm** and **eye drops**.

☐ **Calamine lotion, sting relief spray** or **aloe vera** – to ease irritation from sunburn and insect bites or stings.

☐ **Antifungal cream** or **powder** – for fungal skin infections and thrush.

☐ **Antiseptic** (such as povidone-iodine) – for cuts and grazes.

☐ **Bandages, Band-Aids (plasters)** and other wound dressings.

☐ **Water purification tablets** or **iodine**.

☐ **Scissors, tweezers** and a **thermometer** (note that mercury thermometers are prohibited by airlines).

☐ **Syringes** and **needles** – in case you need injections in a country with medical hygine problems. Ask your doctor for a note explaining why you have them.

☐ **Cold** and **flu tablets, throat lozenges** and **nasal decongestant**.

☐ **Multivitamins** – consider for long trips, when dietary vitamin intake may be inadequate.

Alternatively, an injection of gamma globulin can provide short-term protection against hepatitis A – two to six months, depending on the dose given. It is not a vaccine, but is ready-made antibody collected from blood donations. It is reasonably effective and, unlike the vaccine, it is protective immediately, but because it is a blood product, there are current concerns about its long-term safety.

Hepatitis A vaccine is also available in a combined form, Twinrix, with hepatitis B vaccine. Three injections over a six-month period are required, the first two providing substantial protection against hepatitis A.

Typhoid This is an important vaccination to have in Tibet where hygiene standards are low. Available either as an injection or oral capsules.

Diphtheria & Tetanus Diphtheria can be a fatal throat infection and tetanus can be a fatal wound infection. Everyone should have these vaccinations. After an initial course of three injections, boosters are necessary every 10 years.

Hepatitis B China (though not so much Tibet) is one of the world's great reservoirs of hepatitis B infection. This disease is spread by blood or by sexual activity. Vaccination involves three injections, the quickest course being over three weeks with a booster at 12 months.

Polio Polio is a serious, easily transmitted disease, still prevalent in many developing countries, including China. Everyone should keep up to date with this vaccination, which is normally given in childhood. A booster every 10 years maintains immunity.

Yellow Fever Yellow fever is not endemic in China and a vaccine is required only if you are coming from an infected area. You usually have to go to a special yellow fever vaccination centre. Protection lasts 10 years. Vaccination poses some risk during pregnancy but if you must travel to a high-risk area it is advisable; also people allergic to eggs may not be able to have this vaccine. Discuss with your doctor.

Rabies Officially there is no rabies in Tibet. All the same, there are an awful lot of rabid-looking dogs about. If you are bitten, it would be foolish not to get treatment. Recent surveys by the Chinese indicate that incidents of rabies may have been found in Qinghai Province, which borders Tibet.

Vaccination should be considered if you are spending a month or longer in the country, especially if you are cycling, handling animals, caving or travelling to remote areas. Consider vaccinations for children also, as they may not report a bite.

Pretravel rabies vaccination involves having

three injections over 21 to 28 days. The vaccine will not give you 100% immunity, but will greatly extend the time you have for seeking treatment. If someone who has been vaccinated is bitten or scratched by an animal they will require two booster injections of vaccine, those not vaccinated require more.

Tuberculosis TB risk to travellers is usually very low. For those who will be living with or closely associated with local people in high risk areas such as Asia, Africa and some parts of the Americas and Pacific, there may be some risk. As most healthy adults do not develop symptoms, a skin test before and after travel to determine whether exposure has occurred may be considered. A vaccination is recommended for children and young adults living in these areas for three months or more.

Health Insurance Make sure that you have adequate health insurance. See Travel Insurance under Visas & Documents in the Facts for the Visitor chapter for details.

Travel Health Guides If you are planning to be away or travelling in remote areas for a long period of time, you may like to consider taking a more detailed health guide.

CDC's Complete Guide to Healthy Travel, Open Road Publishing, 1997. The US Centers for Disease Control & Prevention recommendations for international travel.
Staying Healthy in Asia, Africa & Latin America, Dirk Schroeder, Moon Publications, 1994. Probably the best all-round guide to carry; it's detailed and well organised.
Travellers' Health, Dr Richard Dawood, Oxford University Press, 1995. Comprehensive, easy to read, authoritative and highly recommended, although it's rather large to lug around.
Where There is No Doctor, David Werner, Macmillan, 1994. A very detailed guide intended for someone, such as a Peace Corps worker, going to work in an underdeveloped country.
Travel with Children, Maureen Wheeler, Lonely Planet Publications, 1995. Includes advice on travel health for younger children.

There are also a number of excellent travel health sites on the Internet. From the Lonely Planet Web site there are links at www.lonelyplanet.com/weblinks/wlprep.htm to the World Health Organization and the US Centers for Disease Control & Prevention.

Other Preparations Make sure you're healthy before you start travelling. If you are going on a long trip make sure your teeth are OK. If you wear glasses, take a spare pair and your prescription.

If you require a particular medication take an adequate supply, as it may not be available locally. Take part of the packaging showing the generic name, rather than the brand, which will make getting replacements easier. It's a good idea to have a legible prescription or letter from your doctor to show that you legally use the medication to avoid any problems.

Basic Rules

Food There is an old colonial adage which says: 'If you can cook it, boil it or peel it you can eat it ... otherwise forget it'. Vegetables

---

Everyday Health

Normal body temperature is up to 37°C or 98.6°F; more than 2°C (4°F) higher indicates a high fever. The normal adult pulse rate is 60 to 100 per minute (children 80 to 100, babies 100 to 140). As a general rule the pulse increases about 20 beats per minute for each 1°C (2°F) rise in fever.

Respiration (breathing) rate is also an indicator of illness. Count the number of breaths per minute: between 12 and 20 is normal for adults and older children (up to 30 for younger children, 40 for babies). People with a high fever or serious respiratory illness breathe more quickly than normal. More than 40 shallow breaths a minute may indicate pneumonia.

and fruit should be washed with purified or bottled water or peeled where possible. Beware of ice cream which is sold in the street or anywhere it might have been melted and refrozen; if there's any doubt (eg a power cut in the last day or two) steer well clear. Undercooked meat should be avoided.

If a place looks clean and well run and the vendor also looks clean and healthy, then the food is probably safe. In general, places that are packed with travellers or locals will be fine, while empty restaurants are questionable. Chinese food in particular is cooked over a high heat, which kills most germs.

Water The number-one rule is *be careful of the water* and especially ice. If you don't know for certain that the water is safe assume the worst. In urban centres Tibetans, like the Chinese, boil their drinking water making it safe to drink hot or cooled. In the country you should boil your own water or treat it with water purification tablets. Soft drinks and beer are always available wherever there is a shop, and these are always safe to drink as is tea. Locally brewed beer, *chang*, however, is another matter. It is often made with contaminated well water and there is always a potential risk with it.

Water Purification The simplest way of purifying water is to boil it thoroughly. At Tibet's high altitude water boils at a lower temperature and germs are less likely to be killed so make sure you boil water for at least 10 minutes.

Consider purchasing a water filter for a long trip. There are two main kinds of filters. Total filters take out all parasites, bacteria and viruses, and make water safe to drink. They are often expensive, but they can be more cost effective than buying bottled water. Simple filters (which can even be a nylon mesh bag) take out dirt and larger foreign bodies from the water so that chemical solutions work much more effectively; if water is dirty, chemical solutions may not work at all. It's very important when buying a filter to read the specifications, so that you know exactly what it removes from the water and what it doesn't. Simple filtering will not remove all dangerous organisms, so if you cannot boil water it should be treated chemically.

Chlorine tablets (Puritabs, Steritabs or other brand names) will kill many pathogens, but not giardia and amoebic cysts. Iodine is more effective in purifying water and is available in tablet form (such as Potable Aqua). Follow the directions carefully and remember that too much iodine can be harmful.

Medical Problems & Treatment

Self-diagnosis and treatment can be risky, so you should always seek medical help. Although we do give drug dosages in this section, they are for emergency use only. Correct diagnosis is vital.

In Tibet the top end hotels can usually recommend a good place to go for advice. In most places in Tibet standards of medical attention are so low that for some ailments the best advice is to go straight to Lhasa and in extreme cases get on a plane to Chengdu or Kathmandu.

Antibiotics should ideally be administered only under medical supervision. Take only the recommended dose at the prescribed intervals and use the whole course, even if the illness seems to be cured earlier. Stop immediately if there are any serious reactions and don't use the antibiotic at all if you are unsure that you have the correct one. Some people are allergic to commonly prescribed antibiotics such as penicillin; carry this information when travelling (eg on a bracelet).

Environmental Hazards

Altitude Sickness Lack of oxygen at high altitudes (over 2500m) affects most people to some extent. The effect may be mild or severe and occurs because less oxygen reaches the muscles and the brain at high altitude, requiring the heart and lungs to compensate by working harder. Acute mountain sickness (AMS) is common at high altitudes, and depends on the elevation, the rate of ascent and individual susceptibility.

The major risk factor in AMS is the speed with which you make your ascent. Any traveller who flies or buses into Lhasa, which is at just over 3600m, is likely to experience some symptoms of AMS. You should take care to acclimatise slowly and take things easy for the first couple of days. On average, one tourist a year dies in Tibet from altitude sickness – make sure it is not you.

AMS is a notoriously fickle affliction and can affect even the most seasoned high-altitude trekker or walker. AMS has been fatal at 3000m, although 3500m to 4500m is the usual range.

Acclimatisation AMS is linked to low atmospheric pressure. Those who travel up to Everest Base Camp, for instance, have reached an altitude where atmospheric pressure is about half that at sea level.

With an increase in altitude the human body needs time to develop physiological mechanisms to cope with the decreased oxygen. This process of acclimatisation is still not fully understood but is known to involve modifications in breathing patterns and heart rate induced by the autonomic nervous system, and an increase in the blood's oxygen-carrying capabilities. These compensatory mechanisms usually take about one to three days to develop at a particular altitude. Once you are acclimatised to a given height you are unlikely to get AMS at that height, but you can still get ill when you travel higher. If the ascent is too high and too fast, these compensatory reactions may not kick into gear fast enough.

Symptoms Mild symptoms of AMS are very common in travellers to high altitudes, and usually develop during the first 24 hours at altitude. Most visitors to Tibet will suffer from at least some symptoms that will generally disappear through acclimatisation in several hours to several days.

Symptoms tend to be worse at night and include headache, dizziness, lethargy, loss of appetite, nausea, breathlessness and irritability. Difficulty sleeping is another common symptom, and many travellers have trouble sleeping for the first few days after arriving in Lhasa.

AMS may become more serious without warning and can be fatal. Symptoms are caused by the accumulation of fluid in the lungs and brain, and include breathlessness at rest, a dry irritative cough (which may progress to the production of pink, frothy sputum), severe headache, lack of coordination (typically leading to a 'drunken walk'), confusion, irrational behaviour, vomiting and eventually unconsciousness.

These signs should be taken very seriously; trekkers should keep an eye on each other as those experiencing symptoms, especially severe symptoms, may not be in a position to recognise them. One thing to note is that while the symptoms of mild AMS often precede those of severe AMS, this is not always the case. Severe AMS can strike with little or no warning.

Prevention The best prevention of AMS is to avoid rapid ascents to high altitudes. If you fly or bus to Lhasa, take it easy for at least three days – for most travellers this is enough to get over any initial ill-effects. At this point you might step up your program by visiting a few sights around town. Within a week you should be ready for something a bit more adventurous, but do not push yourself to do anything that you are not comfortable with. If you are driving up from Kathmandu you will experience rapid altitude gain. An itinerary that takes you straight up to Everest Base Camp is unwise – plan to see it on your way back if possible.

To prevent acute mountain sickness:

• Ascend slowly – have frequent rest days, spending two to three nights at each rise of 1000m. If you reach a high altitude by trekking, acclimatisation takes place gradually and you are less likely to be affected than if you fly directly to high altitude.
• Trekkers should bear in mind the climber's adage: 'climb high, sleep low'. It is always wise to sleep at a lower altitude than the greatest height reached during the day. High day climbs followed by a descent back to lower altitudes for the night are good preparation for high-altitude trekking. Also, once above 3000m, care

should be taken not to increase the sleeping altitude by more than 400m per day. If the terrain won't allow for less than 400m of elevation gain be ready to take an extra day off before tackling the climb.

- Drink extra fluids. The mountain air is dry and cold and moisture is lost as you breathe. Evaporation of sweat may occur unnoticed and result in dehydration.
- Eat light, high-carbohydrate meals for more energy.
- Avoid alcohol as it may increase the risk of dehydration, and don't smoke.
- Avoid sedatives.
- When trekking, take a day off to rest and acclimatise if feeling over-tired. If you or anyone else in your party is having a tough time make allowances for unscheduled stops.
- Don't push yourself when climbing up to passes, rather take plenty of breaks; you can usually get over the pass as easily tomorrow as you can today. Try to plan your itinerary so that long ascents can be divided into two or more days. Given the complexity and unknown variables involved with AMS and acclimatisation, trekkers should always err on the side of caution and ascend mountains slowly.

The symptoms of AMS, however mild, are a warning – take them seriously!

Treatment Treat mild symptoms by resting at the same altitude until recovery, usually a day or two. Take paracetamol or aspirin for headaches. If symptoms persist or become worse, however, *immediate descent* is necessary – even 500m can help.

The most effective treatment for severe AMS is to get down to a lower altitude as quickly as possible. In less severe cases the victim will be able to stagger down with some support; however sufferers may need to be carried down. Whatever the case, do not delay, as any delay could be fatal.

Sufferers may need to be flown out of Tibet as quickly as possible – make sure you have adequate travel insurance.

The drugs acetazolamide (Diamox) and dexamethasone are recommended by some doctors for the prevention of AMS, however their use is controversial. They can reduce the symptoms, but they may also mask warning signs; severe and fatal AMS has occurred in people taking these drugs. Drug treatments should never be used to avoid descent or to enable further ascent. In general we do not recommend them for travellers.

Heat Exhaustion Dehydration and salt deficiency can cause heat exhaustion. Take time to acclimatise to high temperatures, drink sufficient liquids and do not do anything too physically demanding.

Salt deficiency is characterised by fatigue, lethargy, headaches, giddiness and muscle cramps; salt tablets may help, but adding extra salt to your food is better.

Anhydrotic heat exhaustion, caused by an inability to sweat, is quite rare. It is likely to strike people who have been in a hot climate for some time, rather than newcomers.

Heatstroke This serious, occasionally fatal, condition can occur if the body's heat-regulating mechanism breaks down and the body temperature rises to dangerous levels. Long, continuous periods of exposure to high temperatures and insufficient fluids can leave you vulnerable to heatstroke.

The symptoms are feeling unwell, not sweating very much (or at all) and a high body temperature (39°C to 41°C or 102°F to 106°F). Where sweating has ceased the skin becomes flushed and red. Severe, throbbing headaches and lack of coordination will also occur, and the sufferer may be confused or aggressive. Eventually the victim will become delirious or convulse. Hospitalisation is essential, but in the interim get victims out of the sun, remove their clothing, cover them with a wet sheet or towel and then fan continually. Give fluids if they are conscious.

Hypothermia Winter in Tibet is not to be taken lightly. You should always be prepared for cold, wet or windy conditions especially if you're out walking, hitching or trekking at high altitudes or even taking a long bus trip over mountains (particularly at night).

Hypothermia occurs when the body loses heat faster than it can produce it and the core temperature of the body falls. It is surprisingly easy to progress from very cold to dangerously cold due to a combination of wind, wet clothing, fatigue and hunger, even if the air temperature is above freezing.

It is best to dress in layers; silk, wool and some of the new artificial fibres are all good insulating materials. A hat is important, as a lot of heat is lost through the head. A strong, waterproof outer layer and a 'space' blanket for emergencies are essential. Carry basic supplies, including food that contains simple sugars to generate heat quickly, and fluid to drink.

Symptoms of hypothermia are exhaustion, numb skin (particularly toes and fingers), shivering, slurred speech, irrational or violent behaviour, lethargy, stumbling, dizzy spells, muscle cramps and violent bursts of energy. Irrationality may take the form of sufferers claiming they are warm and trying to take off their clothes.

To treat mild hypothermia, first get the person out of the wind and/or rain, remove their clothing if it's wet and replace it with dry, warm clothing. Give them hot liquids – not alcohol – and some high-kilojoule, easily digestible food. Do not rub victims, instead allow them to slowly warm themselves. This should be enough to treat the early stages of hypothermia. The early recognition and treatment of mild hypothermia is the only way to prevent severe hypothermia, which is a critical condition.

Frostbite Frostbite refers to the freezing of extremities, including fingers, toes and nose. Signs and symptoms of frostbite include a whitish or waxy cast to the skin, or even crystals on the surface, plus itching, numbness and pain. Warm the affected areas by immersion in warm (not hot) water or with blankets or clothes, only until the skin becomes flushed. Frostbitten parts should not be rubbed. Pain and swelling are inevitable. Blisters should not be broken. Get medical attention right away.

Motion Sickness Eating lightly before and during a trip will reduce the chances of motion sickness. If you are prone to motion sickness try to find a place that minimises movement – near the wing on aircraft, near the centre on buses. Fresh air usually helps; reading and cigarette smoke don't. Commercial motion-sickness preparations, which can cause drowsiness, have to be taken before the trip commences. Ginger (available in capsule form) and peppermint (including mint-flavoured sweets) are natural preventatives. At the end of the day your Chinese and Tibetan neighbours on buses and trucks are far more likely to succumb – if they start looking green, be ready to jump out of the way

Sunburn It is very easy to get sunburnt in Tibet. Sunburn can be more than just uncomfortable. Among the undesirable effects are premature skin ageing and possible skin cancer in later years. Sunscreen (UV lotion) with a high sun protection factor (SPF), good quality sunglasses and a wide-brimmed hat are good means of protection. Calamine lotion is good for mild sunburn.

Those with fair complexions should bring reflective sunscreen (containing zinc oxide or titanium oxide) with them. Apply the sunscreen to your nose and lips (and the tops of your ears if you are not wearing a hat).

Infectious Diseases

Respiratory Infection Upper respiratory tract infections (common cold) or the China Syndrome are a common ailment all over China, including Tibet. Why is it such a serious problem in China? Respiratory infections are aggravated by cold weather, air pollution, chain-smoking and overcrowded conditions which increase the opportunity for infection. But the main reason is that Chinese people spit a lot, thereby spreading the disease. It is a vicious circle: they are sick because they spit and they spit because they are sick.

Symptoms of influenza include fever, weakness and sore throat. Any upper respiratory tract infection, including influenza, can lead to complications such as bronchitis and pneumonia which may need to be treated with antibiotics. Seek medical help in this situation.

The Chinese treat bronchitis, which can be a complication of flu, with a powder made from the gall bladder of snakes – a treatment of questionable value, but there is probably no harm in trying it.

No vaccine offers complete protection, but there are vaccines against influenza and pneumococcal pneumonia which might help. The influenza vaccine is good for no more than a year.

Diarrhoea Simple things like a change of water, food or climate can all cause a mild bout of diarrhoea (*la duzi* or 'spicy stomach' in Chinese), but a few rushed toilet trips with no other symptoms is not indicative of a major problem. Even Marco Polo got the runs.

Dehydration is the main danger with any diarrhoea, particularly in children or the elderly as dehydration can occur quite quickly. Under all circumstances fluid replacement (at least equal to the volume being lost) is the most important thing to remember. Weak black tea with a little sugar, soda water, or soft drinks allowed to go flat and diluted 50% with clean water are all good. With severe diarrhoea a rehydrating solution is preferable to replace minerals and salts lost. Commercially available oral rehydration salts (ORS) are very useful; add them to boiled or bottled water. In an emergency you can make up a solution of six teaspoons of sugar and a half teaspoon of salt to a litre of boiled or bottled water. You need to drink at least the same volume of fluid that you are losing in bowel movements and vomiting. Urine is the best guide to the adequacy of replacement – if you have small amounts of concentrated urine, you need to drink more. Keep drinking small amounts often. Stick to a bland diet as you recover.

Loperamide or diphenoxylate can be used to bring relief from the symptoms, although they do not actually cure the problem. However, neither is available in China – a good Chinese equivalent is berberine hydro-chloride (*huang lian su*). Only use these drugs if you do not have access to toilets eg if you *must* travel. For children under 12 years these drugs are not recommended. Do not use these drugs if you have a high fever or are severely dehydrated.

In certain situations antibiotics may be required: diarrhoea with blood or mucus (dysentery), any diarrhoea with fever, profuse watery diarrhoea, persistent diarrhoea not improving after 48 hours and severe diarrhoea. These suggest a more serious cause of diarrhoea and in these situations gut-paralysing drugs should be avoided.

In these situations, a stool test may be necessary to diagnose what bug is causing your diarrhoea, so you should seek medical help urgently. Where this is not possible the recommended drugs for bacterial diarrhoea (the most likely cause of severe diarrhoea in travellers) are norfloxacin 400mg twice daily for three days or ciprofloxacin 500mg twice daily for five days. These are not recommended for children or pregnant women. The drug of choice for children would be co-trimoxazole (Bactrim, Septrin or Resprim) with dosage dependent on weight. A five day course is given. Ampicillin or amoxycillin may be given in pregnancy, but medical care is necessary.

Two other causes of persistent diarrhoea in travellers are giardiasis and amoebic dysentery.

Giardiasis (commonly known as giardia) is caused by a common parasite, *Giardia lamblia*. It is a type of diarrhoea that is relatively common in Tibet. Mountaineers often suffer from this problem. The parasite causing this intestinal disorder is present in contaminated water. Many kinds of mammals harbour this parasite, so you can get it easily from drinking 'pure mountain water' unless the area is devoid of animals. Just brushing your teeth using contaminated water is sufficient to make you get giardiasis, or any other gut bug. Symptoms include stomach cramps, nausea, a bloated stomach, watery, foul-smelling diarrhoea and frequent gas. Giardiasis can appear several weeks after you have been exposed to the parasite. The symptoms may disappear for a few days and then return; this can go on for several weeks.

Amoebic dysentery caused by the protozoan *Entamoeba histolytica*, is characterised by a gradual onset of low-grade diarrhoea, often with blood and mucus. Cramping abdominal pain and vomiting are less likely than in other types of diarrhoea, and fever may not be present. It will persist until treated and can recur and cause other health problems. You should seek medical advice if you think you have giardiasis or amoebic dysentery, but where this is not possible, tindazole or metronidazole are the recommended drugs. Treatment is a 2g single dose of tindazole or 250mg of metronidazole three times daily for five to 10 days.

Metronidazole is not easily obtained in Tibet, though equivalent drugs are available in Lhasa. If you are going to be travelling in high mountain areas, it might be prudent to keep your own stock of metronidazole with you.

Hepatitis Hepatitis is a general term for inflammation of the liver. It is a common disease worldwide. There are several different viruses that cause hepatitis, and they differ in the way that they are transmitted. The symptoms are similar in all forms of the illness, and include fever, chills, headache, fatigue, feelings of weakness and aches and pains, followed by loss of appetite, nausea, vomiting, abdominal pain, dark urine, light-coloured faeces, jaundiced (yellow) skin and yellowing of the whites of the eyes. People who have had hepatitis should avoid alcohol for some time after the illness, as the liver needs time to recover.

Hepatitis A is transmitted by contaminated food and drinking water. You should seek medical advice, but there is not much you can do apart from resting, drinking lots of fluids, eating lightly and avoiding fatty foods.

Hepatitis A is most often spread in China and Tibet due to the custom of sharing food from a single dish rather than using separate plates and a serving spoon. It is a wise decision to use the disposable chopsticks now freely available in most restaurants in Tibet, or else buy your own chopsticks and spoon.

Hepatitis E is transmitted in the same way as hepatitis A; it can be particularly serious in pregnant women.

There are almost 300 million chronic carriers of **Hepatitis B** in the world, and China has more cases than any other country – almost 20% of the population are believed to be carriers. It is spread through contact with infected blood, blood products or body fluids, for example through sexual contact, unsterilised needles and blood transfusions, or contact with blood via small breaks in the skin. Other risk situations include having a shave, tattoo, or body piercing with contaminated equipment. The symptoms of hepatitis B may be more severe than type A and the disease can lead to long term problems such as chronic liver damage, liver cancer or a long term carrier state.

Hepatitis C and **D** are spread in the same way as hepatitis B and can also lead to long term complications.

There are vaccines against hepatitis A and B, but there are currently no vaccines against the other types of hepatitis. Following the basic rules about food and water (hepatitis A and E) and avoiding risk situations (hepatitis B, C and D) are important preventative measures.

HIV & AIDS Infection with the human immunodeficiency virus (HIV) may lead to acquired immune deficiency syndrome (AIDS), which is a fatal disease. Any exposure to blood, blood products or body fluids may put the individual at risk. The disease is often transmitted through sexual contact or dirty needles – vaccinations, acupuncture, tattooing and body piercing can be potentially as dangerous as intravenous drug use. HIV/AIDS can also be spread through infected blood transfusions; some developing countries cannot afford to screen blood used for transfusions.

HIV is not thought to be a major problem in Tibet, though anyone who intends to work or study in Tibet for longer than 12 months is required by the Chinese authorities to undergo an AIDS test.

If you do need an injection, ask to see the syringe unwrapped in front of you, or take a needle and syringe pack with you. Fear of HIV infection should never preclude treatment for serious medical conditions.

Sexually Transmitted Diseases Gonorrhoea, herpes and syphilis are among these diseases; sores, blisters or rashes around the genitals and discharges or pain when urinating are common symptoms. In some STDs, such as wart virus or chlamydia, symptoms may be less marked or not observed at all, especially in women. Syphilis symptoms eventually disappear completely but the disease continues and can cause severe problems in later years. While abstinence from sexual contact is the only 100% effective prevention, using condoms is also effective. The treatment of gonorrhoea and syphilis is with antibiotics. The different STDs each require specific antibiotics. There is no cure for herpes or AIDS.

Condoms are available in China – the word is *batào* which literally translates as 'insurance glove'.

Typhoid Typhoid fever is a dangerous gut infection caused by contaminated water and food. Medical help must be sought.

In its early stages, sufferers may feel they have a bad cold or flu on the way, as early symptoms are a headache, body aches and a fever which rises a little each day until it is around 40°C (104°F) or more. The victim's pulse is often slow relative to the degree of fever present – unlike a normal fever where the pulse increases. There may also be vomiting, abdominal pain, diarrhoea or constipation.

In the second week the high fever and slow pulse continue and a few pink spots may appear on the body; trembling, delirium, weakness, weight loss and dehydration may occur. Complications such as pneumonia, perforated bowel or meningitis may occur.

Cuts, Bites & Stings

See Less Common Diseases for details of rabies, which is passed through animal bites.

Bedbugs & Lice Bedbugs live in various places, but particularly in dirty mattresses and bedding, evidenced by spots of blood on bedclothes or on the wall. Bedbugs leave itchy bites in neat rows. Calamine lotion or a sting relief spray may help.

All lice cause itching and discomfort. They make themselves at home in your hair (head lice), your clothing (body lice) or in your pubic hair (crabs). You catch lice through direct contact with infected people or by sharing combs, clothing and the like. Powder or shampoo treatment will kill the lice and infected clothing should then be washed in very hot, soapy water and left in the sun to dry.

Bites & Stings Bee and wasp stings are usually painful rather than dangerous. However, people who are allergic to them may have severe breathing difficulties and require urgent medical care. Calamine lotion or a sting relief spray will give relief and ice packs will reduce the pain and swelling.

Cuts & Scratches Wash well and treat any cut with an antiseptic such as povidone-iodine. Where possible avoid bandages and Band-Aids, which can keep wounds wet.

Less Common Diseases

The following diseases pose a small risk to travellers, and so are only mentioned in passing. Seek medical advice if you think you may have any of these diseases.

Cholera This is the worst of the watery diarrhoeas and medical help should be sought. Outbreaks of cholera are generally widely reported, so you can avoid such problem areas. *Fluid replacement is the most vital treatment* – the risk of dehydration is severe as you may lose up to 20L a day. If there is a delay in getting to hospital, then begin taking tetracycline. The adult dose is 250mg four times daily. It is not

MANDALA OF AVALOKITESHVARA

This mandala portrays the eight-armed Avalokiteshvara (Tibetan: Chenresig) as the central deity surrounded by the four directional guardians sitting at the gates. This mandala would be used for meditation during retreat and initiation and may be found in Gelugpa monasteries as well as in private homes.

Artist: Andy Weber

WHEEL OF LIFE

The Wheel of Life, most commonly seen at monastery entrances, is essentially a pictorial representation of how desire chains us to *samsara*, the endless cycle of birth, death and rebirth.

The Wheel is held in the mouth of Yama, the Lord of Death. The inner circle of desire shows a cockerel (desire) biting a pig (ignorance) biting a snake (hatred or anger). A second ring is divided into figures ascending through the realms on the left and descending on the right.

The six inner sectors of the Wheel symbolise the six realms of rebirth – gods, battling titans and humans (the upper realms) and hungry ghosts, hell and animals (the lower realms). All beings are reborn through this cycle dependent upon their *karma*. In each realm Buddha attempts to convey his teachings (the *dharma*).

The 12 outer segments depict the 12 experiences of life.

recommended for children under nine years nor for pregnant women. Tetracycline may help shorten the illness, but adequate fluids are required to save lives.

Rabies This fatal viral infection is found in many countries. Many animals can be infected (such as dogs, cats, bats and monkeys) and it is their saliva which is infectious. Any bite, scratch or even lick from an animal should be cleaned immediately and thoroughly. Scrub with soap and running water, and then apply alcohol or iodine solution. Medical help should be sought promptly to receive a course of injections to prevent the onset of symptoms and death.

At the time of writing, treatment for rabies was not available anywhere in Tibet and it was necessary to fly to Kathmandu or Chengdu. If you think you've been infected, get to Lhasa as quickly as you can and seek medical advice.

Tetanus This disease is caused by a germ which lives in soil and in the faeces of horses and other animals. It enters the body via breaks in the skin. The first symptom may be discomfort in swallowing, or stiffening of the jaw and neck; this is followed by painful convulsions of the jaw and whole body. The disease can be fatal. It can be prevented by vaccination.

Tuberculosis (TB) TB is a bacterial infection usually transmitted from person to person by coughing but which may be transmitted through consumption of unpasteurised milk. Milk that has been boiled is safe to drink, and the souring of milk to make yoghurt or cheese also kills the bacilli. Travellers are usually not at great risk as close household contact with the infected person is usually required before the disease is passed on. You may need to have a TB test before you travel as this can help diagnose the disease later if you become ill.

Women's Health
Gynaecological Problems Antibiotic use, synthetic underwear, sweating and con-

traceptive pills can lead to fungal vaginal infections, especially when travelling in hot climates. Fungal infections are characterised by a rash, itch and discharge and can be treated with a vinegar or lemon-juice douche, or with yoghurt. Nystatin, miconazole or clotrimazole pessaries or vaginal cream are the usual treatment. Maintaining good personal hygiene and wearing loose-fitting clothes and cotton underwear may help prevent these infections.

Sexually transmitted diseases are a major cause of vaginal problems. Symptoms include a smelly discharge, painful intercourse and sometimes a burning sensation when urinating. Medical attention should be sought and sexual partners must also be treated. Remember that in addition to these diseases HIV or hepatitis B may also be acquired during exposure. Besides abstinence, the best thing is to practise safe sex using condoms.

Pregnancy It is not advisable to travel to some places while pregnant as some vaccinations normally used to prevent serious diseases are not advisable during pregnancy (eg yellow fever). In addition, some diseases are much more serious for the mother (and may increase the risk of a stillborn child) in pregnancy.

Most miscarriages occur during the first three months of pregnancy. Miscarriage is not uncommon and can occasionally lead to severe bleeding. The last three months should also be spent within reasonable distance of good medical care. A baby born as early as 24 weeks stands a chance of survival, but only in a good modern hospital. Pregnant women should avoid all unnecessary medication, vaccinations should still be taken where needed. Additional care should be taken to prevent illness and particular attention should be paid to diet and nutrition. Alcohol and nicotine, for example, should be avoided.

WOMEN TRAVELLERS
Sexual harassment is extremely rare in Tibet and foreign women seem to be able to travel

with no risks. Naturally, it is worth noticing what local women are wearing and how they are behaving, and making a bit of an effort to fit in, as you would in any other foreign country. Tibetan women dress (probably because of the harsh climate) in bulky layers of clothing that mask their femininity. It would be wise to follow their example and dress modestly, especially when visiting a monastery.

Women may be forbidden to enter the *gönkhang* (protector chapel) of some monasteries.

GAY & LESBIAN TRAVELLERS

The official attitude to gays and lesbians in China is ambiguous, with responses ranging from draconian penalties to tacit acceptance. Travellers are advised to act with discretion. Chinese men routinely hold hands and drape their arms around each other without any sexual overtones.

DISABLED TRAVELLERS

Tibet can be a hard place for disabled travellers. The high altitudes, rough roads and lack of access can make travel difficult. Monasteries in particular often involve a hike up a hillside or steep, very narrow steps. Few hotels offer any facilities for the disabled.

The following organisations offer general travel advice but have no specific information on Tibet:

Australia
NICAN
(☎ 02-6285 3713, fax 6285-3714)
PO Box 407, Curtin, ACT 2605

UK
RADAR (Royal Association for Disability & Rehabilitation)
(☎ 0171-250 3222, fax 250 0212, from 22 April 2000 ☎ 020-7250 3222, fax 7250 0212)
12 City Forum, 250 City Rd, London EC1V 8AF. Produces three holiday fact packs.
Holiday Care Service
(☎ 01293-774535, fax 784647)
Imperial Buildings, Victoria Rd, Horley, Surrey RH6 7PZ.

Travelcare
(☎ 0181-295 1797, fax 467 2467, from 22 April 2000 ☎ 0120-8295 1797, fax 8467 2467)
35A High St, Chislehurst, Kent BR7 QAE. Specialises in travel insurance for the disabled.

USA
SATH (Society for the Advancement of Travel for the Handicapped)
(☎ 212-447 7284)
347 Fifth Ave No 610, New York, NY 10016.
Access (The Foundation for Accessibility by the Disabled)
(☎ 516-887 5798)
PO Box 356, Malverne, NY 11565.
Mobility International
(email info@miusa.org, PO Box 10767, Eugene, OR 97440,). Publishes *You Want to Go Where? A Guide to China for Persons with Disabilities & Anyone Else Interested in Disability Issues*, with travel tips and information on the Chinese disability-rights movement (US$9).

Two Web sites for and by disabled travellers are www.travelhealth.com/disab.htm and www.access-able.com/.

SENIOR TRAVELLERS

The main risks to senior travellers in Tibet are the altitude and the prevalence of China Syndrome or chronic bronchitis. See the Health section for more details. When planning a trip try not to pack in too much in a short time.

TRAVEL WITH CHILDREN

Once again altitude is the major problem in Tibet. Be especially careful with children as they won't be on the lookout for the signs of altitude sickness. Children don't get on with Tibetan food or toilets any better than grown ups. They also tire more easily from an endless round of monasteries. Bring along *Tintin in Tibet* for when morale flags.

On the upside children can be a great icebreaker and generally generate a lot of interest. Many hotels have family rooms which normally have three or four beds arranged in two connected rooms.

Tibet is probably not a great place to bring a very small child. You should bring all supplies (including nappies and medicines) with you. Small spoons can be useful as most places have only chopsticks. There's plenty of boiling water to sterilise bottles etc. It's possible to make a cot from the copious amounts of duvets supplied with most hotel rooms.

USEFUL ORGANISATIONS

There are numerous Tibet information services scattered around the world and for some travellers these may be worth contacting for background information and the latest developments in Tibet. Most advocate some form of independence for Tibet. Some of these offices are as follows:

Australia
Australian Tibetan Society
  (☎ 02-9489 0353, fax 9489 8563)
  PO Box 347, Killara, NSW 2071
Tibet Information Office
  (☎ 02-6285 4046, fax 6282 4301)
  3 Weld St, Yarralumla, Canberra ACT 2600

Canada
Canada Tibet Committee
  (☎ 514-487 0665, fax 487 7825, email cantibet@tibet.ca, Web site www.tibet.ca)
  4675 Coolbrook Avenue, Montreal, Quebec H3X 247 plus branches throughout Canada.

France
Foundation of Alexandra David-Neel
  (☎ 04 92 31 32 38) Samten Dzong, 27 Avenue du Marachel Juin, Digne, 04000

India
Library of Tibetan Works & Archives
  (☎ 01892-22467) Gangchen Kyishong, Dharamsala, HP, 176215
Tibet House
  (☎ 011-611 515) 1 Institutional House, Lodhi Rd, New Delhi, 11000
Tibetan Government in Exile
  (☎ 01892-22457, email diir@tcrclinux.tibdsala.org.in, Web site www.tibet.com)
  Office of Information: Gangchen Kyishong, Dharamsala, 176215

Nepal
Office of Tibet
  (☎ 01-419240, email tiboff@tibetnet.mos.com.np)
  PO Box 310, Lazimpat, Kathmandu

UK
Free Tibet Campaign
  (☎ 0171-359 7573, fax 354 1026, from 22 April 2000 ☎ 020-7359 7573, fax 7354 1026, email tibetsupport@gn.apc.org; Web site www.free tibet.org)
  9 Islington Green, London N1 2XH
Tibet Foundation
  (☎ 0171-404 2889, fax 404 2366, from 22 April 2000 ☎ 020-7404 2889, fax 7404 2366, email getza @gn.apc.org, Web site www.gn.apc.org/tibetgetza)
  11 Bloomsbury Way, London WC1A 25H
Tibet House
  (☎ 0171-722 5378, fax 722 0362, from 22 April 2000 ☎ 020-7722 5378, fax 7722 0326, email tibetlondon@gn.apc.org)
  1 Culworth St, London NW8 7AF
Tibet Information Network
  (☎ 0171-814 9011, fax 814 9015, from 22 April 2000 ☎ 020-7814 9011, fax 7814 9015, email tin@gn.apc.org)
  188-196 Old St, London EC1 9FR UK
Tibet Society
  (☎ 0171-383 7533, from 22 April 2000 ☎ 020-7383 7533, email members@tibet-society.org.uk, Web site www.tibet-society.org.uk)
  114 Tottenham Court Road, London W1P 9HL

USA
The International Campaign for Tibet
  (☎ 202-785 1515, email ict@peacenet.org)
  1825 K St NW Suite 520 Washington DC 20006
Tibet House Cultural Centre
  (☎ 212-807 0563, fax 807 0565, email mail@tibethouse.org, www.tibethouse.org)
  22 West 15th St, New York, NY 10011
Tibetan Cultural Centre
  (☎ 0812-855 8222) 3655 South Snoddy Rd, Bloomington, Indiana, 47401

DANGERS & ANNOYANCES
Theft
Tibet is very poor and it is to be expected that there will be a risk of theft when travelling here. That said, Tibet is safer than most other provinces of China and indeed other countries in the region. Trekkers in the Everest region have reported problems with petty theft, and pickpockets work parts of Lhasa.

Pick-pocketing is the most common form of theft. The best protection is attentiveness to your surroundings and avoiding situations where you are caught up in crowds. The big cities of China are far more dangerous in this respect than Lhasa and the rest of Tibet.

Be careful in public toilets – quite a few foreigners have laid aside their valuables, squatted down to business, and then straightened up again to discover that someone had absconded with the lot.

Do not leave anything valuable in hotel rooms, particularly dormitories. There are at least a few people who subsidise their journey by ripping off their fellow travellers. Other things of little or no apparent value to the thief – things like film – should also be safeguarded, since to lose them would be a real heartbreak to you.

Small padlocks are useful for backpacks and some dodgy hotel rooms. Bicycle chain locks come in handy not only for hired bikes but for attaching backpacks to railings or luggage racks.

Loss Reports If something of yours is stolen, you should report it immediately to the nearest Foreign Affairs Branch of the PSB. They will ask you to fill in a loss report before investigating the case and they sometimes even recover the stolen goods.

If you have travel insurance (recommended), it is essential to obtain a loss report so you can claim compensation.

Staring Squads

It is very unusual to be surrounded by staring Tibetans and Chinese in Lhasa, unlike other remote parts of China, but up-country is another affair. Trekkers will soon discover that it is not a good idea to camp beside Tibetan villages. The spectacle of a few foreigners putting up tents is probably the closest such people will ever come to TV and the whole village will come out in force to watch. It is not unusual to get up in the morning and find half the village still sitting and watching.

Beggars

Being a devout Buddhist region, Tibet has a long tradition of begging for alms. It is unusual to sit down in a restaurant in Tibet without being pestered by women with babies in their arms, wizened old men, urchins dressed in rags, boy monks and even itinerant musicians. Generally, they approach with thumbs up and mumble *guchi guchi* – 'please, please' (not a request for Italian designer clothes). Only the monks are occasionally pushy. Often it is food that is being sought and restaurant owners seem to tolerate this – the instant you push your plate to one side (or get up to leave) anything remaining on it is likely to disappear instantly.

Tibetans with money are generally very generous with beggars and usually hand out a couple of mao to anyone who requests it.

If you do give (and the choice is entirely yours), give the same amount Tibetans do; do not encourage beggars to make foreigners a special target by handing out large denominations. In this case it's worth keeping all your small change in one pocket – there's nothing worse than pulling out a Y100 note! Banks will swap a Y10 note for a wad of one mao notes and these will go a long way. The giving of pens and Dalai Lama pictures to whomever asks for them is not advised.

Bookjacking

Tibetans are a very curious and devout people and so the slightest glimpse of a photo of a monastery or whiff of a Dalai Lama picture will result in the temporary confiscation of your Lonely Planet guide. For many Tibetans this is the only chance to see other parts of their country so try to be patient, even after the 10th time in five minutes. A good deed like this can often open hitherto locked doors (literally) in the place you are visiting.

Dogs

Lhasa used to be infested with packs of mangy, rabid-looking dogs that made catching a pre-dawn bus a life-threatening experience. In recent years however a series of clean-up campaigns by the Chinese has largely done away with these. Dogs can still be a problem in other towns though, and you should be especially vigilant when exploring backstreets or seeking out an obscure monastery. Hurling a few rocks in their direction will let them know you are not in the mood for company, while a hefty stick is good for action at close quarters. Do not underestimate the ones asleep in the shadows; they can spring into action at any moment and give you a nasty bite. The most dangerous dogs belong to remote homesteads or nomad encampments and these should be given an extremely wide berth. See the Rabies entry of the Health section earlier in this chapter for more information on what to do if you are bitten.

LEGAL MATTERS

Only the most serious cases are tried in front of a judge (never a jury). Most lesser crimes are handled administratively by the PSB, who act as police, judge and executioner.

China takes a particularly dim view of opium and all its derivatives. It's difficult to say what attitude the Chinese police will take towards foreigners caught using marijuana – they often don't care what foreigners do if it's not political and if Chinese aren't involved. Then again the Chinese are fond of making examples of wrong-doings and you don't want to be the example.

Public Security Bureau

The Public Security Bureau (PSB) is the name given to China's police, both uniformed and plain-clothed. Its responsibilities include suppression of political dissidence, crime detection, preventing foreigners and Chinese or Tibetans from having sex with each other (no joke), mediating family quarrels and directing traffic. The Foreign Affairs Branch of the PSB deals with foreigners. This branch (also known as the 'entry-exit' branch) is responsible for issuing visa extensions and Alien Travel Permits.

The PSB is responsible for introducing and enforcing regulations that concern foreigners. So, for example, they bear responsibility for exclusion of foreigners from certain hotels. If this means you get stuck for a place to stay, they can offer advice. Do not pester them with trivia or try to 'use' them to bully a point with a local street vendor.

Do turn to them for mediation in serious disputes with hotels, restaurants, taxi drivers etc. This often works since the PSB wields god-like power – especially in remote areas.

In Tibet it is fairly unusual for foreigners to have problems with the PSB. It does of course depend on what you get up to when you are there. Making an obvious display of your political sympathies (assuming they are pro-Tibetan) is guaranteed to lead to problems. Photographing Tibetan protests will lead to confiscation of your film and possibly a brief detention. Attempting to travel into or out of Tibet on any of the closed routes (mainly to Sichuan or Yunnan) is likely to end in an unpleasant encounter somewhere en route. If you are caught in a closed area without a permit you face a fine of Y200 to Y500, which can often be bargained down. Some officers have been known to offer a 'student discount' on fines!

If you do have a run-in with the PSB, you may have to write a confession of your guilt and pay a fine. In more serious cases, you can be expelled from China (at your own expense). But in general, if you are not doing anything particularly nasty like smuggling suitcases of dope through customs, the PSB will probably not throw you in prison.

BUSINESS HOURS

Banks, offices, government departments and the PSB are open from Monday to Friday, with perhaps a half day Saturday. As a rough guide only, they open around 8 to 9 am, close for two hours in the middle of the day (often one hour in winter or three during a heat wave in summer), then reopen until 5 or 6 pm. Saturday and Sunday are public holidays.

Many of Lhasa's main tourist attractions are only open in the morning. Most smaller monasteries have no set opening hours and will open up chapels for you once you've tracked someone down. Others like Samye are notorious for only opening up certain rooms at certain times. In general try to tag along with a group of tourists or pilgrims.

HOLIDAYS

The PRC has nine national holidays during the year. These are mainly Chinese holidays and mean little to many Tibetans but are still a good opportunity to catch a Tibetan opera or join families picnicking in a local park.

New Year's Day	1 January
Chinese New Year	Usually February
International Working Women's Day	8 March
International Labour Day	1 May
Youth Day	4 May
Children's Day	1 June
Anniversary of the founding of the Communist Party of China	1 July
Anniversary of the founding of the Chinese PLA	1 August
National Day	1 October

The Chinese New Year, otherwise known as the Spring Festival, starts on the first day of the old lunar calendar. Although officially lasting only three days, many people take a week off from work. Be warned: this is China's only three day holiday and this is definitely not the time to cross borders (especially the Hong Kong one) or to run out of money. In general though, Spring Festival has a minor effect in Tibet compared to the chaos engendered in the rest of China.

Be aware also that 10 March is not a holiday but it is a politically sensitive date as it is the anniversary of the 1959 Tibetan uprising. Also, 1 September marks the founding of the TAR. Other politically sensitive dates are 5 March and 1 October. It may be impossible for travellers to fly into Tibet a few days before these dates.

CULTURAL EVENTS

The Tibetan cultural heritage took such a hammering during the Cultural Revolution that traditional festivals, once important highlights of the Tibetan year, are only now starting to revive. Tibetan festivals are held according to the Tibetan lunar calendar, which usually lags at least a month behind our Gregorian calendar. You will need to ask around for the exact dates of festivals, which are often only fixed by monasteries a few months in advance.

The following are some of the more important festivals your trip might coincide with:

January
Shigatse New Year Festival
    The Shigatse New Year Festival is held in the first week of the 12th lunar month.

February–March
Year End Festival
    Dancing monks can be seen on the 29th of the 12th lunar month in this festival held to dispel the evil of the old year and auspiciously usher in the new one.
New Year Festival (Losar)
    Taking place in the first week of the first lunar month, Losar is a colourful week of activities; Lhasa is probably the best place to be. There are performances of Tibetan drama, pilgrims making incense offerings and the streets are thronged with Tibetans dressed in their finest.
Lantern Festival
    Held on the 15th of the first lunar month; huge yak-butter sculptures are placed around Lhasa's Barkhor circuit.
Mönlam
    Known also as the Great Prayer Festival, this is held mid-way through the first lunar month (officially culminating on the 25th). An image of Maitreya from Lhasa's Jokhang is borne around the Barkhor circuit, attracting enthusiastic crowds of locals and pilgrims.

May–June
Birth of Sakyamuni
    This is not exactly a festival, but the seventh day of the fourth lunar month is an important pilgrimage date and sees large numbers of pilgrims in the Holy City of Lhasa and other sacred areas in Tibet. Festivals are held at this time at Tsurphu (see below), Ganden, Reting and Samye monasteries.
Tsurphu Festival
    Cham dancing and chang drinking are the order of the day at this festival on the 10th day of the fourth lunar month. The highlight is the dance of the Karmapa.

Saga Dawa (Sakyamuni's Enlightenment)
The 15th day of the fourth lunar month (full moon) is an occasion for outdoor operas and also sees large numbers of pilgrims at Lhasa's Jokhang and on the Barkhor circuit. Many pilgrims climb Gephel Ri, the peak behind Drepung Monastery, to burn juniper incense. Saga Dawa is also a particularly good time to be at Mt Kailash.

June–July
World Incense Day
Incense burning and picnicking.

Gyantse Horse Racing Festival
A traditional festival whose date authorities are trying to fix to boost the number of tourists. June 8th to 14th is rumoured to be the future date, though check locally. Fun and games include dances, picnics, archery and equestrian events.

Tashilhunpo Festival
During the second week of the fifth lunar month, Shigatse's Tashilhunpo Monastery becomes the scene of a festival, and a huge *thangka* is hung.

Worship of the Buddha
During the second week of the fifth lunar month, the parks of Lhasa, in particular the Norbulingka, are crowded with picnickers.

Samye Festival
Held on the 15th of the fifth lunar month (full moon).

August–September
Chökor Duchen Festival
Held in Lhasa on the fourth day of the sixth lunar month, this festival celebrates Buddha's first sermon at Sarnath near Varanasi.

Guru Rinpoche's Birthday
On the 10th day of the sixth lunar month.

Drepung Festival
The 30th day of the sixth lunar month is celebrated with the hanging of a huge thangka at Drepung Monastery. Lamas and monks do masked dances.

Shötun
The Yoghurt Festival is held in the first week of the seventh lunar month. It starts at Drepung and moves down to the Norbulingka. Operas and masked dances are held, and locals take the occasion as another excuse for more picnics.

September–October
Bathing Festival
The end of the seventh and beginning of the eighth lunar months sees locals washing away the grime of the previous year in rivers.

Horse Racing Festival
In the first week of the eighth lunar month a festival with horse racing, archery and other traditional nomad sports is held in Damxung and Nam-tso. A similar event is held in Naqu a few weeks earlier.

Onkor
In the first week of the eighth lunar month Tibetans get together and party in celebration of this traditional Harvest Festival.

November–December
Lhabab Düchen
Commemorating Buddha's descent from heaven, the 22nd day of the ninth lunar month sees large numbers of pilgrims in Lhasa.

Palden Lhamo
The 15th day of the 10th lunar month has a procession in Lhasa around the Barkhor bearing Palden Lhamo, protective deity of the Jokhang.

Tsongkhapa Festival
Respect is shown to Tsongkhapa, the founder of Gelugpa order, on the anniversary of his death on the 25th of the 10th lunar month; monasteries light fires and carry images of Tsongkhapa in procession.

ACTIVITIES
Adventure Sports
Tibet offers the type of topography to entice mountaineers, white-water rafters, hang-gliding enthusiasts, and others who want to pursue their adventurous hobbies in the world's highest mountains.

The problem, as always, are those faceless, sombre figures known collectively as 'the authorities'. High-ranking cadres, the PSB, the military, CITS and others in China with the power to extort money know a good business opportunity when they see it. Foreigners have been asked for as much as US$1 million for mountaineering and rafting permits.

In many cases, it is doubtful that the law really requires a permit. A Chinese person may climb the same mountain as you without having any authorisation at all, and it may be perfectly legal. But many local governments simply make up the law as they go along. In general, when foreigners do something which is deemed unusual – and hang-gliding, bungy jumping, kayaking etc, are unusual in China – a permit will be required and a fee will be charged. The more unusual the activity, the higher the fee demanded.

Cycling

Tibet offers some of the most extreme and exhilarating mountain biking in the world. If you are fit and well-equipped it's possible to visit most places in this book by bike, though the most popular route follows the Friendship Highway from Shigatse down to Kathmandu. For more information on cycling see the Bicycle section in the Getting Around chapter.

Trekking

One of the remarkable things about Tibet, considering the difficulties placed in the way of those heading up there by Chinese authorities, is that once you are up on the high plateau there is considerable freedom to strike off on foot and explore the Tibetan valleys and ranges. Of course no one at CITS or any other Chinese organisation will tell you this, but nevertheless it is the case. Experienced and hardy trekkers have the opportunity to visit places that are almost impossible to reach any other way, and are unlikely to find any official obstacles. For information on trekking routes see the Trekking chapter.

Mountaineering

There are some huge peaks in Tibet, including the 8000m plus giants of Cho Oyu, Shisha Pangma and, of course Everest, which are enough to send a quiver of excitement through vertically inclined explorers. Unfortunately, the Chinese government charges exorbitant fees for mountaineering permits, which puts mountaineering in Tibet out of the range of most individuals or groups devoid of commercial sponsorship.

For more information on mountaineering in Tibet you could contact Tibet International Sports Travel (☎ 633 1421, fax 633 4855), Himalaya Hotel, Lhasa or the Chinese Mountaineering Association, 9 Tiyuguan Lu, Beijing.

Horseback Riding

The idea of riding a horse across Tibet may be an admirably romantic one but there are a few snags. Firstly, there are no set places to hire a horse – you would have to find a local who would be prepared to hire you his horse (and probably travel with you) or you would have to buy one. Secondly, the logistics of finding or transporting enough fodder would be a problem in most areas of Tibet. This is probably only an option for serious explorer types.

COURSES

It might be possible to enrol in a Tibetan language course at Lhasa University but you would have to negotiate the considerable bureaucratic hurdles placed in your way. Most people, however, find it more convenient to study at Dharamsala in India, seat of the Tibetan Government in Exile. Courses offered here include Tibetan Buddhist philosophy, Tibetan language and Tibetan performing arts.

The various Tibetan organisations around the world (see Useful Organisations earlier in this chapter) offer courses and meditation retreats. Contact them for details. The Tibet Foundation (☎ 0171-404 2889) in London, for example, offers a 10 week Tibetan language course for UK£130.

WORK

It might be possible to get work as an English teacher at Lhasa University, though it's a long shot. US citizens are currently not allowed to teach in Tibet.

ACCOMMODATION

Outside Lhasa, Shigatse and Tsetang, the traveller in Tibet is not going to be overwhelmed with accommodation options. The standard hotel in rural Tibet is a dirt floor truck stop with a row of rooms each containing four or five beds. Hot water is provided in thermoses and usually a basin is provided for washing. Electricity and running water are luxuries that cannot be expected. At least such places are cheap – from around Y8 to Y15 on average – and bedding is provided.

In urban centres such as Lhasa, Shigatse, Gyantse, Tsetang and Zhangmu, there is more choice and conditions are better. Due to demand, hot showers are becoming more common in such hotels. Accommodation along the Friendship Highway is also getting increasingly developed.

In the towns, the Chinese government keeps a pretty tight lid on which places can and cannot accept foreigners. Most tourists will only come up against this problem in Tsetang, where the bottom-end hotels are not permitted to accept foreigners, and Gyantse, where foreigners are occasionally forced to stay at the Y400 a night Gyantse Hotel rather than the Y20 a night local hotels.

Camping

A large proportion of the Tibetan population is nomadic, and there is a strong tradition of making your home wherever you can hammer in a tent peg. You probably run the risk of an unpleasant run-in with the PSB if you attempt to set up a tent in Lhasa, but get 20km or so out of town and the nearest patch of turf is yours for the picking.

Truck Stops

Travellers making their way out to Mt Kailash will probably get to sample quite a few truck stops. They are basically just places to crash out after a long day of travelling. The bedding is usually filthy (it is good to have a sleeping bag or an inner sheet) and you may have to pay to get your thermos of hot water. If you value your privacy it is a good idea to pay for a whole room (usually four or five beds), because the staff at truck stops like to fill rooms up before they open up another room. Some truck stops will have an attached restaurant, but this is less likely to be so in remote parts of Western Tibet.

Army Camps

An increased number of privately run guesthouses and truck stops in Tibet means that travellers rarely have to stay in army camps anymore – a frequent occurrence, even on the road between Lhasa and the Nepal border, back in the early days of individual travel.

Cyclists, however, might have to make use of road-maintenance camps, recognisable by the steering wheel symbol. In free-market China these camps are normally open to foreigners and go under such glamorous names as the '22nd Team Road Maintenance Division Guesthouse'. Rates are usually around Y15 per bed and there is usually food available.

Homestays

It is sometimes possible for trekkers to stay with Tibetan families. Some families living on popular trekking routes have a room that they hire out to foreign trekkers. Food is sometimes available, but if not they can usually offer you hot water. Sometimes a charge of Y1 is asked for hot water – it is not a lot of money considering the effort involved in producing the stuff. Be careful not to force any hospitality as it is technically illegal for foreigners to stay in a Tibetan home without the host first registering with the PSB.

Guesthouses & Hotels

Most of the accommodation used by foreigners in Tibet could be classed as guesthouse accommodation. In Lhasa there are a few clean, well-run Tibetan-style guesthouses and similar set-ups can be found in Gyantse, Shigatse, Sakya and Tingri. Some monasteries, such as Samye, Ganden, Drigung Til, Tidrum and Rongphu also have guesthouses which charge a standard Y15, though monastery guesthouses are always more basic than those in the towns. Remoter monasteries often have a spare room which they may be willing to let out. If no fee is asked, leave a Y15 donation in the prayer hall.

Tibetan-style guesthouses tend to be much more friendly and homey than Chinese guesthouses; prices are also lower. In Lhasa, Tibetan guesthouses have dorms for around Y25 per person. Accommodation elsewhere in Tibet is cheaper – around Y15 – but standards are not as high as those in Lhasa.

Outside Lhasa and Shigatse, you cannot expect to find budget guesthouses with running water, though all guesthouses will provide hot water for drinking; if there is enough, you can use it for a quick wash. The only place conspicuously lacking in budget accommodation is Tsetang, where the cheapest rooms currently cost around Y100.

There is comfortable hotel-style accommodation in Lhasa, Shigatse, Gyantse, Tsetang and Zhangmu. Choice and range has increased dramatically in the last couple of years, especially in Lhasa where there are now at least 20 hotels rated at two star or above. Most of these are Chinese-style and Chinese-managed. They are all pretty much anonymous but share several traits: plumbing is often very dodgy, the carpets are dotted with a mosaic of cigarette burns and all offer a ratty pair of flip flops so you don't have to touch the bathroom floor. Hotel rates range from Y60 to Y400 for a double room. Few of the upper-end hotels have single room rates.

All hotels and guesthouses offer plentiful thermoses of boiled water for making your own tea or coffee.

FOOD

The food situation can get a bit depressing if you are in Tibet for an extended stay. Nevertheless, the situation has improved vastly over the last five or six years. Fresh vegetables are more widely available than they once were, and there are now a lot more (mainly Chinese) restaurants around.

Tibetan

Tellingly, the basic Tibetan meal is *tsampa*, a kind of dough made with roasted barley flour and yak butter (if available) with water, tea or beer – something wet. It has a certain novelty value the first time you try it, but only a Tibetan can eat it every day and still look forward to the next meal.

No, Tibetan cuisine is not going to win any prizes. In Lhasa there are a few restaurants about that have elevated a subsistence diet into the beginnings of a cuisine, notably the Tashi restaurants. But outside Lhasa,

Tibetan food is limited mainly to *momos* and *thugpa*.

Momos are small dumplings filled with meat and/or vegetables. They are actually pretty good, but it's rare to come across them outside Lhasa and Shigatse.

More common is thugpa, a noodle soup with meat and/or vegetables. Thugpa is often served at restaurants associated with monasteries. In more remote towns, if there is a restaurant, it is likely to be thugpa that they are serving.

Other varieties on the theme include *hipdu* (squares of noodles and yak meat in a soup), *thanthuk* (more noodles) and *shemdre* (potatoes and yak meat on a bed of rice).

Also popular among nomads is dried yak (*yaksha*) or lamb meat. It is normally cut into strips and left to dry on tent lines and is pretty chewy stuff. Sometimes you will see bowls of little white lumps drying in the sun which even the flies leave alone – it is dried yak cheese and is eaten as a sweet. For the first half-hour it is like having a small rock in your mouth, but eventually it starts to soften up and taste like old, dried yak cheese.

Chinese

Han immigration into Tibet may be a threat to the very essence of Tibetan culture but it's done wonders for the restaurant scene. Even most Tibetans have to admit that Chinese food is better than tsampa, momos and thugpa. All of the Tibetan urban centres have Chinese restaurants these days, and they can also be found on major roads, even on the road out to Kailash. Chinese restaurants in Tibet are generally around 50% more expensive than Chinese restaurants in the rest of China.

Chinese food in Tibet is almost exclusively Sichuanese. This is the hottest of the Chinese regional cuisines, but in Tibet it is rarely made with as many spices as it is in Sichuan. You may find some dishes include *huajiao* (flower pepper), a curious mouth-numbing spice which tastes a bit like washing detergent. Another interesting sauce is *yuxiang*, a spicy, piquant sauce that is supposed to resemble the taste of fish (probably the closest thing you'll get to fish in Tibet). Dishes are usually stir-fried quickly over a high flame and so are generally more hygienic than their Tibetan counterparts.

Very few Chinese restaurants have English menus. Usually the dishes on offer are written on a board, and if you do not read Chinese the only thing you'll gather from it are the range of prices. This is rarely a problem, as in most restaurants you can wander out into the kitchen and point to the vegetables and meats that you want fried up. The main snag with this method is that you'll miss out on many of the most interesting sauces and styles and be stuck with the same dishes over and over.

Chinese snacks are excellent and worth trying. The most common are ravioli-style dumplings called *shuijiao*, ordered by the bowl or weight (half a jin is enough for one person) and steamed dumplings similar to momo, called *baozi*, normally ordered by the steamer. You can usually get a bowl of noodles anywhere for around Y5. Fried noodles (*chaomian*) are not as popular as in the west but you can get them in many Chinese and backpacker restaurants.

For a list of the most common dishes see the Language chapter.

Muslim

An interesting alternative to Chinese or Tibetan food are the Muslim restaurants found in Lhasa, Tsetang and Gyantse. These are normally recognisable by a green flag hanging outside or Arabic script on the restaurant sign. Most chefs come from the Linxia area of Gansu Province. Food is heavily noodle based and of course there's no pork.

Dishes worth trying include *ganpian*, a kind of stir-fried spaghetti bolognaise made with beef (or yak) and sometimes green peppers. Muslim restaurants also offer good breads and excellent tea, made with dried raisins, plums and rock sugar, and which only releases its true flavour after several cups. Most restaurants sell take-away packets of the tea if you really like it. You can

often go into the kitchen and see your noodles being hand made.

Breakfasts

You can get decent breakfasts of muesli and toast at backpacker hotels in Lhasa and Shigatse but elsewhere you are more likely to be confronted by Chinese-style dumplings, fried bread sticks and rice porridge. One good breakfasty type food that is widely available is scrambled eggs and tomato (*fanqie chaojidan* in Chinese).

Self-Catering

There will be a time when you need to be self-sufficient, whether you're staying overnight at a monastery, arriving at a town late at night or heading off on a trip to Kailash or Nam-tso. Unless you have a stove, your main saviour will be instant noodles. After a long trip to Kailash and back you will know the relative tastes of every kind of packet noodle sold in Tibet. Your body will also likely be deeply addicted to MSG. Even the faintest smell of noodles will leave you gagging.

Fortunately the range of foods available in most towns has improved greatly in the last couple of years. Instant options now include fruit (dried, fresh and in jars), vegetables, puffed rice, cans of tuna, soup mixes, peanuts, sweets (White Rabbit is the best brand), pink sausages, biscuits and many others.

Vegetables such as onions, carrots, tomatoes and bok choy can save even the cheapest pack of noodles from culinary oblivion. Other things available include 531 biscuits, high-glucose bricks used by the Chinese army but inedible to most people. You can also find a type of red fruit roll in Lhasa which travels well. Even Tashi Restaurant's take-away fried apple momos travel quite well.

DRINKS
Nonalcoholic Drinks

The local beverage that every traveller ends up trying at least once is yak butter tea (see the boxed text over the page).

The more palatable alternative to yak butter tea is sweet milk tea. It is similar to the tea drunk in neighbouring Pakistan. Chinese tea is also widely available. Tibetans do not drink coffee and you will not find any outside Lhasa. Soft drinks and mineral water are widely available throughout Tibet. The most popular Chinese soft drink is Jianlibao, a honey and orange drink sometimes translated on restaurant menus as 'Jellybowl'!

In many remote areas, even if there is nothing else available to drink, there will at least be beer on sale.

Alcoholic Drinks

The Tibetan brew is known as *chang* a fermented barley beer. It has a rich, fruity taste, and ranges from disgusting to pretty good. It is normally served out of a jerry can. Those trekking in the Everest region should try the local variety, which is served in a big pot. Hot water is poured into the fermenting barley and the liquid is drunk through a wooden straw – it is very good.

The main brand of beer available in Tibet is Wuquan, a Sichuan brew that is pretty good. Huanghe (Yellow River) is a bit

chemically, but Lhasa Beer is OK. Pabst Blue Ribbon (*landai* in Chinese) is a US beer brewed in Sichuan under franchise; no one admits to drinking it in the US but out in Tibet it tastes pretty good. In Lhasa you can get Heinekin, Carlsburg etc but at a higher cost. Out in Western Tibet Xinjiang Beer is available. Some travellers swear by Chinese brandy (*bailandi*), which at around Y10 per bottle is remarkably cheap.

ENTERTAINMENT

Hopefully entertainment is not high on your list of priorities. If it is, go somewhere else. The Tibetan idea of fun is having a picnic and getting sloshed on chang. In general, foreigners make their own entertainment in Tibet, and evenings in the hotels of Lhasa and Shigatse often see groups of travellers knocking back a couple of beers and swapping tall stories while someone strums *Tears from Heaven* or *Knocking on Heaven's Door* (not *again*!) in the background.

Lhasa has a burgeoning nightlife scene, but very little in the way of cultural entertainment. Like the rest of China, karaoke bars have taken off in a big way in urban

Yak Butter Tea

Bö cha, literally Tibetan tea, is unlikely to be a highlight of your trip to Tibet. Made from yak butter mixed with salt, milk, soda, tea leaves and hot water all churned up in a wooden tube, the soupy mixture has more the consistency of bouillon than tea. When mixed with tsampa it becomes the staple meal of most Tibetans and you may well be offered it at monasteries, people's houses and even while waiting for a bus by the side of the road. Most Tibetans mix it in a small wooden bowl and knead the mixture into small balls, which they pop into their mouths – not as easy as it looks!

At most restaurants you mercifully have the option to drink *cha ngamo* (sweet, milky tea) but there will be times when you just have to be polite and down a cupful of bö cha (without gagging). Most nomads think nothing of drinking up to 40 cups of the stuff a day. At least it stops your lips from cracking.

Most distressing for those not sold on the delights of butter tea is the fact that your cup will constantly be refilled every time you take even the smallest sip, as a mark of the host's respect. There's a pragmatic reason for this as well; there's only one thing worse than hot yak butter tea – cold yak butter tea.

centres. Lhasa is the karaoke capital of Tibet, but you will also find bars in Shigatse, Gyantse, Tsetang and even far away Ali. It is worth dropping into one of them once, but you would have to be weird to make a habit of it.

A karaoke bar will have drinks available at slightly inflated prices (from Y10 to Y15 or more for a beer) and customers have to pay to sing a song – the price depends on the bar. Some bars in Lhasa alternate between karaoke sessions and dancing, and can be innocent, good fun. Be aware, however, that some karaoke bars are a front for prostitution.

The PSB does not look too kindly on foreigners seeking out night-time entertainment in venues frequented by locals. Some travellers have been warned off from dancing and chatting with locals. Proceed with caution.

Those seeking out cultural entertainment will probably have to wait for a festival. Festivals often include performances of *cham* (monk dancing) and Tibetan opera, but unfortunately such times represent your only opportunity to see them.

Tibetans are not big on sports. Festivals like the Gyantse Horse Festival (see Cultural Events earlier in this chapter) are probably your only chance to see any sporting action.

SHOPPING

Tibet is not a bad place for souvenir hunting, though much of the stuff you see in markets, particularly the bronzes, has been humped over the high passes from Nepal and can probably be bought cheaper in Kathmandu, where you will have a better selection of quality goods.

Some travellers buy a Tibetan carpet and send it home. There are carpet factories in Lhasa and Shigatse producing new carpets of average quality. Good quality traditional carpets, on the other hand, are harder to come by. A small contingent of frequent travellers to Tibet have made carpets their business and if you fall in with some of them they may give you some tips for finding one for yourself.

For an overview of possible purchases in Tibet, the best place to look is the Barkhor in Lhasa. The entire Barkhor circuit is lined with stalls selling all kinds of oddities. Prayer flags and shawls, prayer wheels and daggers are all popular buys. Itinerant pilgrims may also come up to you with things to sell – the proceeds will often finance their trip home.

Be prepared to bargain for any purchase. You can probably reckon on at least halving the price, but there are no hard-and-fast rules. If you look like a sucker, you might be quoted a price that is 10 times the real value of what you want to buy. Shop around for a while and get a feel for prices; asking other travellers what they paid for their souvenirs is also a good approach.

Other possible buys are Tibetan ceiling drapes and thangkas. Some of the ceiling drapes and door curtains are very tasteful and can be bought in Lhasa and Shigatse. Most of the thangkas for sale are gaudy – good ones do not come cheap. There are a couple of workshops in Lhasa where you can see thangkas being painted.

Getting There & Away

Tibet is not the most accessible of destinations, but then getting there is half the fun. There are only five flights to Tibet. Four are to Lhasa's airport at Gongkar: from Chengdu, Chongqing and Xi'an in China, and Kathmandu in Nepal. The fifth is to the eastern town of Chamdo from Chengdu in China, although this flight is not currently open to foreigners.

Overland routes into Tibet involve days of gruelling travel from either Nepal or China. The only officially sanctioned overland routes into Tibet are via the Qinghai-Tibet Highway, which runs between Lhasa and Golmud or the Friendship Highway, which runs from Kathmandu to Lhasa.

At the time of writing, bureaucratic obstacles to entering Tibet – a potentially more insurmountable barrier than the Himalaya – had loosened enough to make entry relatively easy, from China at least. Travellers headed from Nepal still have to join a nominal tour in order to get into Lhasa but after that you can break off on your own.

All present indications suggest that this will remain the case, with the Chinese government announcing that it hopes tourist figures will dramatically increase in the next decade. Such hopes, however, rest squarely on the assumption that Chinese development of the high plateau will proceed unhindered by Tibetan resentment and protest.

It is to be expected that if major protests emerge, there will be restrictions – probably temporary – on access to Tibet by foreign travellers and tourists. Political events heavily affect entry regulations; for a few months in 1997 American citizens faced difficulties in getting travel permits in reaction to an undercover visit to Tibet by a US senator. It would be wise to check on the latest developments in Tibet before setting out. See the Useful Organisations section in the Facts for the Visitor chapter.

Warning

The information in this chapter is particularly vulnerable to change: prices for international travel are volatile, routes are introduced and cancelled, schedules change, special deals come and go, and rules and visa requirements are amended. Airlines and governments seem to take a perverse pleasure in making price structures and regulations as complicated as possible. You should check directly with the airline or a travel agent to make sure you understand how a fare (and ticket you may buy) works. In addition, the travel industry is highly competitive and there are many lurks and perks.

The upshot of this is that you should get opinions, quotes and advice from as many airlines and travel agents as possible before you part with your hard-earned cash. The details given in this chapter should be regarded as pointers and are not a substitute for your own careful, up-to-date research.

AIR
Airports & Airlines

Air travel is complicated by the fact that there are no direct long-haul flights to Tibet. You will probably have to stop over in Kathmandu, Beijing or Hong Kong if you are making a direct beeline for Lhasa. There are also direct flights from South-East Asia to Chengdu and Kunming (Yunnan Province).

Once you are in the region, direct air access to Lhasa is basically limited to flights from either Kathmandu in Nepal or Chengdu in China. There are other connections but they involve considerably more bureaucratic hassle. In general, it is easiest and most cost-effective to fly into Lhasa from Chengdu. It *is* currently possible to fly from

Kathmandu but you must temporarily join a group in order to get a ticket.

The only airline which flies into Tibet is China Southwest Airlines, based in Chengdu. All Chinese airlines come under the jurisdiction of the Civil Aviation Authority of China (CAAC).

Flights to and from Lhasa are frequently cancelled or delayed in the winter months so if you are flying at this time give yourself a couple of days leeway in Chengdu if you have a connecting flight. If you miss a flight out of Chengdu, you will be hard pressed to get a refund of any kind and will probably have to buy a new ticket.

Buying Tickets

For budget travellers, buying a plane ticket is a major outlay and can eat into savings that might otherwise be spent on the road. It is worth spending some time looking into the various routings and airlines that fly into China or Nepal and their comparative costs.

If you want to get to Tibet as quickly as possible (perhaps to get the maximum use from your visa) consider buying a domestic Air China ticket to Chengdu as part of your international ticket. Some Air China offices will give you a discount of up to 50% on the domestic leg if you buy the long-haul leg through them, making this the cheapest way to get to Chengdu.

Another ticket worth looking into is an open jaw ticket. This involves, for example, flying into Hong Kong and flying out of Kathmandu, allowing you to travel overland across Tibet. If there are no open jaw tickets available then consider buying two one-way tickets. Travel agencies may have trouble booking a one-way inbound ticket but can normally manage something if you book the outbound ticket at the same time.

Start early: some of the cheapest tickets have to be bought months in advance, and some popular flights sell out early. Find out the fare, the route and the duration of the flight (and the stop over if there is one) and, importantly, check for any restrictions on the ticket (see Restrictions in the boxed text 'Air Travel Glossary' later in this chapter).

Be wary of impossibly cheap flights advertised in newspapers. It is often the case

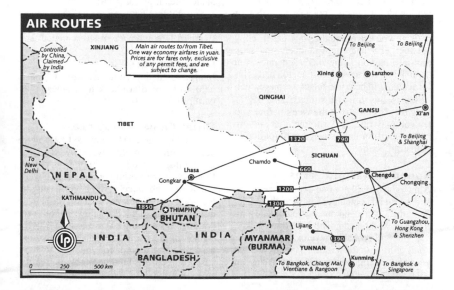

that they are booked out ... 'but a slightly more expensive ticket is available'; before you know it you are booked on an inconvenient routing and paying more than you want to. Another common ploy is to tell you that just a couple of seats are still available and you will have to pay up before 5 pm. Do not fall into these traps. Take your time. It always pays off to be a bit cautious.

In the UK and the USA many of the cheapest flights are offered by small 'bucket shops' whose names have not yet reached the phone directory. There is no need to assume that such agencies are in the business of ripping travellers off, but again they should be approached with caution. Standard procedure in buying plane tickets is to pay a deposit of around 20% and the balance upon issue of the ticket. Avoid agencies which demand you pay the full price in advance. Always demand a receipt for any money you fork out and once you have the ticket, ring the airline to confirm that you are actually booked on the flight.

An alternative to these risks is to pay a little more and make your bookings with a reputable, well-established agency. Firms such as Trailfinders, STA Travel (with offices worldwide), Council Travel in the USA or Travel CUTS in Canada are all good options.

Once you have bought your ticket, copy out the ticket and flight numbers and keep this information somewhere separate from the ticket. If the ticket is lost or stolen, this information will help you to get a replacement.

Try to buy travel insurance as early as possible. If you buy it the week before you fly you may find, for example, that you are not covered for delays to your flight due to industrial action.

Round-the-World Fares

Although you will not find a round-the-world (RTW) fare that includes Lhasa, it should not be so difficult to find one that includes Hong Kong or Kathmandu. The only drawback is that you will probably have to return to your point of origin after visiting Tibet to pick up your onward flight unless you can arrange an overland sector in the ticket.

There are basically two types of RTW tickets: airline tickets and agent tickets. Airline tickets are usually put together by two or more airlines, which combine their routes to provide a RTW flight. Agent tickets are usually cheaper, representing a collection of cheap fares strung together by a travel agency. The latter probably will not offer as many route options as the former, and there will be various ticket limitations to bear in mind – check to see if you get a refund if you miss a flight for example.

Travellers with Special Needs

Most international airlines can cater for special needs – travellers with disabilities, people with young children and even children travelling alone. They can also cater for special dietary preferences (vegetarian, kosher, low-fat) with advance notice. Contact the airline directly.

Airlines usually carry babies up to two years of age at 10% of the adult fare, though a few carry them free of charge. Reputable international airlines usually provide nappies (diapers), tissues, talcum powder and all the other paraphernalia needed to keep babies clean, dry and half-happy.

For children between the ages of two and 12, international fares are usually 50% of the standard fare and 67% of a discounted fare.

Departure Tax

International departure tax from China is Y90, to be paid at check in. Domestic departure tax is Y50.

Other Chinese Provinces

From China there are flights to Lhasa twice daily from Chengdu, twice weekly from Chongqing and once weekly from Xi'an. Flights to/from Beijing operate once a week via Xi'an and once a week via Chengdu. Rumours of a Guangzhou-Lhasa flight have circulated for some years now without ever coming to anything. There is also a twice weekly flight from Chengdu to Chamdo in eastern Tibet though foreigners may have troubles getting on this flight. In reality, 99% of travellers flying from China into

Lhasa go from Chengdu as arranging a permit is so much easier from here. For information on getting to Chengdu from Hong Kong, now a part of China, see the Getting To/From China and Nepal section later in this chapter.

Chengdu Flights between Chengdu and Lhasa currently cost Y1200, but you'll be very lucky if this is all you end up paying for the flight. Both in Chengdu and other cities, China Southwest Airlines will normally not sell you a ticket to Lhasa unless you already have a Tibet Tourism Bureau (TTB) permit (see Permits in the Facts for the Visitor chapter).

To get around this, many travel agencies, especially those around the Traffic Hotel in Chengdu, will sell you a 'tour' which allows them to arrange a ticket for you. What the tour consists of depends largely upon the political climate in Lhasa. Out of the high tourist season (July to September) you can normally book a ticket-only deal but at the height of summer, agencies may have to book you transport from Gongkar airport to Lhasa and possibly a couple of nights accommodation in one of Lhasa's budget hotels.

In May 1998 a standard Tibet package, consisting of the flights only, cost Y1750 (Y1200 for the ticket and Y550 for the TTB permit). By August this had risen to Y1980 and included airport transfers. Sometimes travellers must travel in groups of five, though the agencies can normally rustle up enough individual travellers to form a small group. Everyone goes their own way once in Lhasa. Agencies normally need 24 hours to process the mythical TTB permit.

Whether your TTB permit actually exists is up to debate. You will certainly never see it, though your travel agency will wave something at airport security to allow you through. As long as it works, who cares? This is still the most cost-effective way to enter Tibet.

With some advanced planning it is sometimes possible to buy a Chengdu-Lhasa ticket from Air China offices abroad. The price for this is normally higher than Y1200 but you won't have to pay for any permits. The main problem arises when you try to board the plane in Chengdu without a TTB permit. You might be able to bluff your way through but it's a bit of a gamble. Unless restrictions tighten up in Chengdu this is probably not a worthwhile option.

For information on stopping over in Chengdu see the boxed text 'Stopover Survival Details'.

Nepal

Flights between Kathmandu and Lhasa operate twice weekly in the low season (departing Tuesday and Saturday) and three times a week in the high season.

As with Chengdu, individual travellers cannot buy air tickets from the China Southwest Airlines office without a TTB permit. Your only option is to buy a three to eight day package tour through a travel agency (see the boxed text 'Stopover Survival Details').

At the time of research, the cheapest of these tours was a three day tour for around US$360. This included the flight ticket (US$228), airport transfer to Kathmandu and Lhasa, TTB permits and dormitory accommodation for three nights in Lhasa.

The Chinese embassy in Kathmandu is not in the habit of giving Chinese visas to individual travellers so it is important that you arrive in Kathmandu with a Chinese visa in your passport. See the Visas & Documents section in the Facts for the Visitor chapter for more details on visas in Kathmandu. If you arrive in Lhasa on an individual visa (as opposed to a group visa) you may face a fine of around Y100. The same applies when flying from Lhasa to Kathmandu.

Flights between Kathmandu and Lhasa may be cancelled at the slightest whiff of trouble in Lhasa and may also be shut down during the winter months.

Getting To/From China & Nepal

Whether you are flying or travelling overland to Lhasa by bus you will probably still need to get to Nepal or China in the first place.

Air Travel Glossary

Baggage Allowance This will be written on your ticket and usually includes one 20kg item to go in the hold, plus one item of hand luggage.

Bucket Shops These are unbonded travel agencies specialising in discounted airline tickets.

Bumped Just because you have a confirmed seat doesn't mean you're going to get on the plane – see Overbooking.

Cancellation Penalties If you have to cancel or change an Apex or other discounted ticket, there are often heavy penalties involved; insurance can sometimes be taken out against these penalties. Some airlines impose penalties on regular tickets as well, particularly against 'no-show' passengers.

Check-In Airlines ask you to check in a certain time ahead of the flight departure (usually one to two hours on international flights). If you fail to check in on time and the flight is overbooked, the airline can cancel your booking and give your seat to somebody else.

Confirmation Having a ticket with the flight and date you want doesn't mean you have a seat until the agent has checked with the airline that your status is 'OK' or confirmed. Meanwhile you could just be 'on request'.

Courier Fares Businesses often need to send urgent documents or freight securely and quickly. Courier companies hire people to accompany the package through customs and, in return, offer a discount ticket which is sometimes a phenomenal bargain. In effect, what the companies do is ship their freight as your luggage on the regular commercial flights. This is a legitimate operation, but there are two shortcomings – the short turnaround time of the ticket (usually not longer than a month) and the limitation on your luggage allowance. You may have to surrender all your allowance and take only carry-on luggage.

Full Fares Airlines traditionally offer 1st class (coded F), business class (coded J) and economy class (coded Y) tickets. These days there are so many promotional and discounted fares available that few passengers pay full economy fare.

ITX An ITX, or 'independent inclusive tour excursion', is often available on tickets to popular holiday destinations. Officially it's a package deal combined with hotel accommodation, but many agents will sell you one of these for the flight only and give you phoney hotel vouchers in the unlikely event that you're challenged at the airport.

Lost Tickets If you lose your airline ticket an airline will usually treat it like a travellers cheque and, after inquiries, issue you with another one. Legally, however, an airline is entitled to treat it like cash and if you lose it then it's gone forever. Take good care of your tickets.

MCO An MCO, or 'miscellaneous charge order', is a voucher that looks like an airline ticket but carries no destination or date. It can be exchanged through any IATA (International Association of Travel Agents) airline for a ticket on a specific flight. It's a useful alternative to an onward ticket in those countries that demand one, and is more flexible than an ordinary ticket if you're unsure of your route.

Air Travel Glossary

No-Shows No-shows are passengers who fail to show up for their flight. Full-fare passengers who fail to turn up are sometimes entitled to travel on a later flight. The rest are penalised (see Cancellation Penalties).

On Request This is an unconfirmed booking for a flight.

Onward Tickets Some (though few) Chinese embassies ask for proof that you have a ticket out of the country. If you're unsure of your next move, the easiest solution is to buy the cheapest onward ticket to a neighbouring country or a ticket from a reliable airline which can later be refunded if you do not use it.

Open Jaw Tickets These are return tickets where you fly out to one place but return from another. If available, this can save you backtracking to your arrival point.

Overbooking Airlines hate to fly empty seats and since every flight has some passengers who fail to show up, airlines often book more passengers than they have seats. Usually any excess passengers can fly due to the no-shows, but occasionally somebody gets bumped. Guess who it is most likely to be? The passengers who check in late.

Point-to-Point Tickets These are discount tickets that can be bought on some routes in return for passengers waiving their rights to a stop over.

Reconfirmation At least 72 hours prior to departure of an onward or return flight, you must contact the airline and 'reconfirm' that you intend to be on the flight. If you don't do this the airline can delete your name from the passenger list and you could lose your seat.

Restrictions Discounted tickets often have various restrictions on them – such as needing to be paid for in advance and incurring a penalty to be altered. Others are restrictions on the minimum and maximum period you must be away, such as a minimum of 14 days or a maximum of one year.

Round-the-World Tickets RTW tickets give you a limited period (usually a year) in which to circumnavigate the globe. You can go anywhere the carrying airlines go, as long as you always travel in the same direction (either west or east). The number of stop overs or total number of separate flights is decided before you set off and these tickets usually cost a bit more than a basic return flight.

Stand-by This is a discounted ticket where you only fly if there is a seat free at the last moment. Stand-by fares are usually only available on domestic routes.

Transferred Tickets Airline tickets cannot be transferred from one person to another. Travellers sometimes try to sell the return half of their ticket, but officials can ask you to prove that you are the person named on the ticket. This is less likely to happen on domestic flights, but on an international flight, tickets may be compared with passports.

Travel Periods Some officially discounted fares, Apex fares in particular, vary with the time of year. There is often a low (off-peak) season and a high (peak) season. Sometimes there's an intermediate or shoulder season as well. Usually the fare depends on your outward flight – if you depart in the high season and return in the low season, you pay the high-season fare.

Flights to Kathmandu are generally not all that cheap as there are a limited number of carriers operating out of the capital. Depending on where you are coming from, it may be cheaper to fly to Delhi and make your way overland from there.

To China, you generally have the choice of flying first to Beijing or Hong Kong, though there are a small number of flights direct to Chengdu or Kunming from South-East Asia. Hong Kong has traditionally enjoyed the cheapest flights but this is not so often the case these days. If there's not much difference in the fares then it's just a choice of which city you would prefer to visit. It is generally cheaper to fly to Chengdu from Beijing than from Hong Kong, though Hong Kong is the easier place to get a 60 or 90 day Chinese visa.

Those travelling first to either India, Nepal, Hong Kong or elsewhere in China should consult Lonely Planet's travel guides for these countries. Below is some basic information on getting into the region.

The USA & Canada It is far cheaper to fly to Hong Kong from the USA or Canada than it is to fly to India. This might work out quite well if your ultimate destination is India. Overland travel from Hong Kong to Nepal and India via Tibet is reasonably time consuming – but what a trip!

The cheapest prices of tickets to Hong Kong are offered by bucket shops run by ethnic Chinese. The highest concentration of these is in San Francisco, though Los Angeles and New York are also good places to check them out. Good deals are also available at more reliable long-running agencies: try Council Travel (☎ 800-226 8624, www.ciee.org), Overseas Tours (☎ 415-692 4892, www.overseastours.com) in Milbrae, California and Gateway Travel (☎ 800-441 1183).

One good Web site with information on international and domestic airfares in China is www.flychina.com.

From the US west coast, bottom-end fares one way/return to Hong Kong start at around US$385/660. From New York to

---

Stopover Survival Details

As there are no direct long-haul flights into Tibet, air travellers will have to stopover in either Chengdu or Kathmandu to arrange air tickets and permits. The following information should be of help.

Chengdu

Most budget travellers stay at the *Traffic Hotel* on the southern side of the Jinjiang River. Dorm beds are Y40. Other options include *Sam's Backpacker Guesthouse* in the north-east part of town which has beds from Y25.

China Southwest Airlines, opposite the Jinjiang Hotel, will not sell air tickets to Lhasa so you'll have to try the agencies around the Traffic Hotel. These include Tibet Budget Tour (☎ 554 1376) and Traffic Travel Service (☎ 553 1285). Other agencies like those at the Highfly Café (☎ 550 1572) and Sam's Backpacker Guesthouse (☎ 777 2593) can also arrange an air ticket. Costs are pretty standard and include transfer to Chengdu airport. Check whether other transfers are included.

It normally takes a day or two to arrange a ticket so to fill the time you might like to take a taxi or cycle out to the **Panda Research Centre**, 12km to the north-east of town. Other recommended things to do include visiting the teahouse in Renmin Park and the Wenshu Monastery, plus grabbing a few beers in the street of Chinese pubs south of the Traffic Hotel.

In an emergency, Chengdu has a US consulate (☎ 558 3992) at 4 Lingshiguan Lu in the south of town. See Lonely Planet's *South-West China* guide for more details.

Hong Kong one way/return fares start at around US$410/770. Fares may be higher at the peak of summer.

Tickets from the west coast cost around US$1350 return to New Delhi or Bombay, US$1500 return to Kathmandu. Kathmandu is pretty much on the other side of the globe so it doesn't matter much whether you fly east or west. From the east coast you are looking at around US$1000 return to Delhi.

Canadian prices are similar to those in the USA. Try Travel CUTS (☎ 416-977 5228, www.travelcuts.com) for good deals on tickets to Asia. Canadian Airlines and Korean Air have the cheapest flights to Hong Kong.

Australia & New Zealand Check major newspapers such as the *Age* and the *Sydney Morning Herald* and the travel agents section of the Yellow Pages for information on agencies dealing with tickets to China, India and Nepal. Both STA Travel (www .sta-travel-group.com) and Flight Centre (www.flightcentre.com.au) are reliable agents

that are represented in most Australian and New Zealand cities.

Those flying to China from this region should bear in mind that it is cheaper to fly to Hong Kong than other parts of China. The cheapest fares will be advance purchase fares, which vary in cost seasonally, and will probably be with airlines that stop in another South-East Asian capital en route. The cheapest one-way (low season) tickets from Australia to Hong Kong cost around A$840; return tickets will cost at least A$1100. Flights from New Zealand cost around NZ$990/1345 for a single/return.

Return advance purchase fares to the Indian subcontinent from the east coast of Australia range from around A$1275 to A$1575 depending on the season and the destination. Prices for return flights from New Zealand range from around NZ$1820 to NZ$2170.

The UK There are some very good deals available in London's bucket shops for

---

Stopover Survival Details

Kathmandu

China Southwest Airlines (☎ 411302) is a 10 minute walk east of the backpacker mecca of Thamel, but they won't sell you a ticket to Lhasa without a TTB permit. Agencies which offer tours to Tibet include:

Royal Mt Trekking
    (☎ 241452, fax 245318) Durbar Marg. Has three day overland tours for US$240, one-way flight packages for US$360.
Explore Nepal Richa Tours
    (☎ 423064, email explore@enrtt.mos.com.np) Thamel. Has a wide range of tours.
Green Hill Tours
    (☎ 424968, email ghill@wlink.com.np) Thamel. Has eight day fixed departure minibus tours to Lhasa for US$370, plus other tours.
Yeti Travels
    (☎ 221234) Durbar Marg.

The Thamel district of Kathmandu is the place to get a yak steak, repair a sleeping bag, buy a backpack, shop for souvenirs or purchase hard-to-find books on Tibet. Pilgrim's Bookstore has the best selection.

There are dozens of things to do in Kathmandu, though during the June to August monsoon it is hot, humid and rainy. See Lonely Planet's *Nepal* guide for more details.

flights to Beijing, Hong Kong and major Indian cities, mainly New Delhi. Check the travel sections of newspapers and 'what's on' magazines like *Time Out*. Travel Agencies like Trailfinders, STA Travel, Campus Travel, Flight Bookers and Council Travel are all reliable.

Most British travel agencies are registered with the Association of British Travel Agencies (ABTA). If you have paid for your flight with an ABTA-registered agent which then goes out of business, ABTA will provide either a refund or an alternative.

Those looking at travelling via the subcontinent and shaving costs wherever possible will undoubtedly find it cheapest to fly to New Delhi and then travel overland to Nepal. Fares to India generally start from around UK£220 one way or from UK£325 to UK£440 return. The cheapest return fares to Kathmandu are around UK£500. It pays to shop around.

There are sometimes some great offers to Beijing on Air China (☎ 0171-630 7678, from 22 April 2000 ☎ 020-7630 7678) or British Airways (☎ 0345-222 111). Several specialist agencies in London can book both international and Chinese domestic tickets. China Travel Service and Information Service (☎ 0171-388 8838), 124 Euston Rd, London NW1 2AL, offers some of the lowest fares to China and offers a 50% discount on any domestic Air China ticket booked in conjunction with an international Air China ticket.

Summer peak season fares to Beijing run at around UK£300 one way and UK£500 return. Cheap flights (often with Middle Eastern Airlines) to Hong Kong will work out a little more expensive but not much more.

Continental Europe Those flying from Europe have the option of flying to Beijing with Air China and bypassing Hong Kong. This would be the best option for travellers looking at getting to Tibet as quickly as possible. Numerous other airlines fly to Hong Kong, which should work out around the same price as flying to Beijing.

In France try OTU (☎ 01 43 36 80 47) or Council Travel (☎ 01 42 66 20 87). In the Netherlands, NBBS is a reliable agency. Airfares to the Indian subcontinent are much cheaper in the UK than they are in the rest of Europe – about half-price if you shop around.

Hong Kong Hong Kong is the main entry point for China and it is now formally part of the People's Republic of China (PRC). Most travellers make their way from Hong Kong into China by train or ferry, but for those with limited time there are daily direct flights from Hong Kong to Chengdu with Dragonair and China Southwest Airlines for around HK$2400.

Hong Kong agents do not deal with China Southwest Airlines flights and you will need to go to one of Hong Kong's CAAC offices. The Central office (☎ 2739 0022), is on the ground floor, 10 Queen's Rd Central, while the Kowloon office (☎ 2739 0022) is at 1 Mody Rd, Tsim Sha Tsui. Dragonair tickets can be booked through travel agencies.

A final point worth making with regard to

The Hong Kong Special Administrative Region

Though Hong Kong was handed back to China on 1 July 1997, the ex-colony still functions much like an independent country. Most nationalities do not need a visa for a short visit to Hong Kong but visa regulations for longer stays have changed recently so you should check with your nearest Chinese embassy. The important thing to remember is that if you travel from China to Hong Kong and want to go back into China again you will need a new (or double entry) Chinese visa since immigration formalities remain firmly in position at the 'border'.

Hong Kong is that it is considerably cheaper to fly from Shenzhen or Guangzhou (Canton) to Chengdu than from Hong Kong. Shenzhen in particular is just a hop, skip and a jump from Hong Kong, and tickets from Shenzhen to other parts of China are half the price of tickets from Hong Kong. Tickets from Shenzhen and Guangzhou can be booked in Hong Kong at CAAC offices.

A flight from Hong Kong to Kathmandu costs around US$320 one way.

South-East Asia There are direct flights from Bangkok and Singapore to Chengdu and from Bangkok, Chiang Mai, Yangon, Vientiane and Singapore to Kunming in China's Yunnan Province. From Kunming there is a road into Tibet, but unfortunately it is currently closed. Check the Yunnan-Tibet Highway section later in this chapter for more information.

Bangkok is a popular place to pick up air tickets, and prices are generally very competitive. The best place to shop around is Kao San Rd, the Bangkok backpacker ghetto. Flights with China Southwest Airlines from Bangkok to Chengdu/Kunming cost around US$300/200 one way. Flights to Kathmandu can be picked up for around US$300. (Don't forget to organise your Chinese visa in Bangkok too.)

STA Travel has branches in Singapore, Bangkok and Kuala Lumpur.

LAND

Many individual travellers make their way to Tibet as part of a grand overland trip through China, Nepal, India and onwards. In many ways, land travel to Tibet is the best way to go, not only for the scenery en route but also because it can help spread the altitude gain over a few days.

In theory there are a number of land routes into Tibet. In practice, however, most travellers only use one of two officially sanctioned routes: Kathmandu to Lhasa via the Friendship Highway or Golmud to Lhasa via the Qinghai-Tibet Highway. Other possible routes (as yet officially closed) are the Sichuan-Tibet Highway, the Yunnan-Tibet Highway and the Xinjiang-Tibet Highway. Of these the Yunnan-Tibet Highway is the 'most closed' (ie very few travellers are getting through to Tibet this way); the 'least closed' is the Xinjiang-Tibet Highway.

Friendship Highway (Nepal to Tibet)

The 920km stretch of road between Kathmandu and Lhasa is known as the Friendship Highway. The journey is without a doubt one of the most spectacular in the world.

From Kathmandu the road travels gently up to Kodari (1873m), before leaving Nepal to make a steep switch-back ascent to Zhangmu (2300m), the Tibetan border town. From here the road climbs and climbs, past Nyalam (3750m) to the top of the Tong-la pass (5120m), where travellers from Kathmandu are likely to feel decidedly weak and wobbly due to the altitude. Tingri (4390m) provides fabulous views of Mt Everest and the Himalaya Range and is where many travellers spend the night before travelling on. It is essential to watch out for the effects of altitude sickness during the early stages of this trip (see the Health section in the Facts for the Visitor chapter). Try to slip in a rest day at Tingri or Nyalam if you are heading up to Everest Base Camp at 5200m. See the Tsang chapter for details of sights and landmarks en route.

This highway is very well travelled nowadays and is a pleasant journey except for one big fat problem. The Chinese authorities will not let individual travellers leave the Chinese border town of Zhangmu without a TTB permit, which means hiring a Land Cruiser, and sometimes a guide, for the entire trip to Lhasa.

Because of this, several of Kathmandu's travel agencies offer 'budget' tours of Tibet to get you in to Lhasa. At the time of research the cheapest of these tours cost US$240 per person for a three day Land Cruiser trip to Lhasa, stopping in Zhangmu, Lhatse and Lhasa. Prices include transport and all permits but no accommodation. Eight-day minibus tours also depart every Saturday from various agencies in

ELEVATION PROFILE: THE FRIENDSHIP HIGHWAY

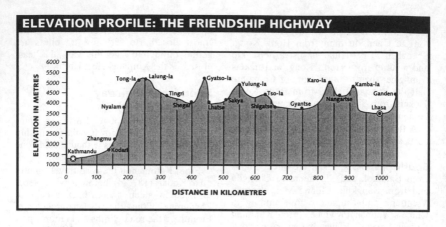

Kathmandu's Thamel district. The cost, from US$350 to US$400, includes transport, accommodation, permits and entrance fees. The tour stops in Nyalam, Lhatse, Sakya, Shigatse and Gyantse. It is recommended that you obtain an individual Chinese visa before arriving in Kathmandu and ensure that you are not put on a group visa. For more information on potential visa snags see the Visas & Documents section of the Facts for the Visitor chapter.

At the time of writing, there was nothing stopping travellers (providing they had a valid Chinese visa) heading up to the border and crossing over into Tibet as far as Zhangmu. There are daily buses from Kathmandu's City Bus Station to Kodari (five hours, Rs 64) and Barabise along the Friendship (Arniko) Highway. There are several hotels at Kodari with beds for around Rs 80. China is 2¼ hours ahead of Nepalese time.

Individual travellers are normally referred to the China International Travel Service (CITS) in the next major town of Zhangmu, who will not let you leave until you have hired a Land Cruiser and guide to Lhasa, normally for around US$150 to US$200 per person. If you are travelling on your own you will have to wait around for other travellers and share the cost. A checkpoint high above Zhangmu ensures that travellers don't leave Zhangmu without a valid TTB permit

from CITS. It's a good idea to confirm this with other travellers, though, as immigration officials have been known to turn away travellers with a valid visa.

Qinghai-Tibet Highway

The 1115km journey between Golmud and Lhasa is actually the subject of an ancient Chinese curse: 'may you travel by Chinese bus from Golmud to Lhasa'. Actually, I made that one up – but it deserves to be.

Golmud (3200m), the drab little Chinese town where the journey begins, is approached by rail or bus or even plane from Xining (capital of Qinghai Province). If Golmud were not one of the most utterly depressing places in China, it would probably serve as a good place to hang out for a few days and acclimatise to the altitude. But it *is* one of the most utterly depressing places in China and consequently most people jump on a Lhasa-bound bus quicker than a CITS official can say 'give us your cash'.

If Golmud did not exist, CITS would have to invent it. It is a perfect bottleneck to capture Lhasa-bound individual travellers and screw them for every yuan possible. CITS officials make it their job to form welcoming parties for all incoming buses and trains, and then start laying down the law: thou shalt only stay at the Golmud Guesthouse, thou shalt not hitch nor even stand on public thoroughfares with thine thumb extended, thou shalt pay extortionate sums to sit in a clapped-out Chinese bus for 30 hours, and so on.

Buses for Lhasa leave from Golmud's Tibet bus station but you'll be lucky to buy a ticket there. Foreigners are required to buy their tickets from CITS on the 1st floor of the Golmud Hotel at a massive mark up. Tickets cost Y1180 for a clapped-out Chinese bus or Y1380 for a clapped-out sleeper bus; locals pay Y132 for the Chinese bus. The justification for this price gouging used to be the inclusion of a three-day tour of Lhasa on arrival, but now you don't even get that! Travellers making their way from Lhasa to Golmud by bus pay Y414.

There's not much you can do about this except fly at a higher cost (but better value) from Chengdu. The main checkpoint lies 25km south of Golmud and your ticket will be checked. If you decide to try and hitch, bear in mind that some travellers have been sent back from Naqu, about three quarters of the way to Lhasa!

The Qinghai-Tibet Highway is cold and bleak and almost devoid of interesting sights. Before setting off you should stock up on munchies and drinks and, if you have not already done so, buy some warm clothing. Xining is a better place to buy the latter than Golmud. Golmud has several markets

---

Tibetan Tasters

If you're going overland from China to Tibet there are several excellent detours you can make to give you an idea of what you are in for. **Labrang Monastery**, around 100km south of Lanzhou in Gansu Province, is one of the six major monasteries of the Gelugpa Buddhist order and is well worth a visit. Another of the six is **Ta'ersi (Kumbum) Monastery**, 26km south-east of Xining in Qinghai Province. Both are easily visited on the way from Xi'an to Golmud.

---

and numerous shops where you can buy food and drinks.

The trip itself takes anywhere between 30 and 50 hours, longer if there is a serious breakdown. Even in summer it can get bitterly cold, especially up on the high passes, the highest of which is Tangu-la (5180m). It is one of those once in a lifetime trips.

Sichuan-Tibet Highway

The road between Chengdu and Lhasa is either around 2400km or around 2100km, depending on whether you take the northern route or the southern route.

While the occasional intrepid traveller still manages to make it through on this road, if your destination is Lhasa, this is not the most sensible of routes to take. It is currently closed to individual travellers, though the occasional tour group and renegade explorer passes along it. Be prepared for a difficult trip that might end with a fine and an abrupt return to sender. The following brief description is not a recommendation that you try it.

There is very little in the way of public transport. Truck drivers face fines of up to Y2000 and the loss of their licence for carrying foreigners in their trucks, and it is a dangerous trip – numerous accidents have occurred on it. Perhaps your best chance is to hook up with a truck that is itself slightly illegal and therefore inclined to drive through the checkpoints at night. Outside of checkpoints the likeliest place to be caught is at a hotel.

Food and accommodation is of a better standard and more widely available than on the Qinghai-Tibet Highway (where there is basically nothing) or in Western Tibet.

The early sections of the Sichuan-Tibet Highway have been open to foreigners for several years now. For details see Lonely Planet's *South-West China* guide. There are daily sleeper buses from Chengdu's Xinanmen bus station to Kangding, which is the last real town before the road divides into northern and southern routes.

From Kangding onwards the risk of being caught, fined and then sent back increases

Mission Impossible

Chinese engineers and bureaucrats love to prove the dominance of Chinese technology and mass mobilisation over Mother Nature – just look at the Three Gorges Dam or even the Great Wall of China. But there's one project that still stumps China's finest technocrats: how to build a railway line to China's most 'backward' province, the only one today without a rail connection.

Since 1958 there have been repeated investigations into building a railway line from Golmud to Lhasa, a project that would involve drilling dozens of ice tunnels through the Tangulashan mountains. Finally, in 1979, it was declared impossible.

The latest feasibility study was inaugurated in August 1998 to investigate a potential 1654km routing from Dali in Yunnan Province to Lhasa. Almost half of the line, some 710km, would have to consist of tunnels or bridges at an estimated cost of US$8 billion. If it can be done the line will eventually link Lhasa to South-East Asia along another line from Kunming to Thailand.

Fancy the train ride from Bangkok to Lhasa? Watch this space ... but don't hold your breath.

considerably. It is not a good idea to tell anyone that your destination is Lhasa. It should be possible to get a bus to Litang (4700m), the next town on the southern route, which is around 250km west of Kangding and then Batang, a further 167km west. Onward travel from Batang, over the Jinsha (Yangzi) river and Tibetan border to Markam, a further 275km west of Litang, is likely to be more difficult. Markam is where the Yunnan-Tibet Highway joins the Sichuan-Tibet Highway and so the local PSB is particularly scrupulous about making sure that no travellers continue on to Lhasa.

The stretch of road between Markam and Bayi, a nondescript town that no one has a good word for, covers over 780km of amazing changes in scenery but is likely to be the biggest hurdle for travellers en route to Lhasa. From Markam it is 158km to Yougong and a further 201km to Bashe. During this stretch, the road crosses a concertina landscape, crossing the upper reaches of the Mekong (Lancang) and Salween (Nu Jiang).

From Bashe the road swings south 90km to Rawu and then follows the river valley 129km to Pomi, where there is a checkpoint, and then Tongmai, a further 89km away. By

now the scenery is lush, forested and alpine and the drive from Tongmai to Nyingchi is the most beautiful one of the trip, passing frozen waterfalls and crossing several 5000m plus passes, with views of the 7756m Namche Barwa to the south-east.

If you make it as far as Bayi, you will have to deal with the Bayi PSB. Many travellers have had problems with these people, and the best advice is to tell them you have come from Lhasa and let them have the pleasure of sending you back. Be patient and not belligerent. From Bayi it is just 401km to Lhasa, passing the turn-off to Draksum Lake after 79km and the town of Kongpo Gyamda after 128km. If you have made it this far, you will probably make it all the way.

The northern route involves a detour off the southern road just west of Kangding, travelling via Dêgê and Chamdo and rejoining the southern route around Bashe. From Kangding there are daily buses running the 305km north-west to Ganzi, a monastery town. From here it is 207km west, past the 6168m Chola Shan, to Dêgê, the next major town and site of one of Tibet's most famous printing presses. It is 339km from Dêgê to the large town of Chamdo, and a further 171km from Chamdo south to the southern route. A little-trafficked route heads due east from Chamdo to Naqu.

Yunnan-Tibet Highway

The Yunnan-Tibet Highway would be a wonderful way to approach Tibet were it ever to open. From Dali a road heads up to Zhongdian, an open town, and from Zhongdian a road continues north to Deqin, for which you can get a permit in Zhongdian. From here there are public buses north across the Tibetan border and checkpoint, 112km to Yanjing and on another 111km to Markam on the Sichuan southern route.

Unfortunately the Yunnan route is most definitely closed. I met one guy who had made it from Dali to Lhasa non-stop in six days but the vast majority are fined and sent back to Dali. Check the latest gossip in Dali if you are particularly interested in taking this route, but bear in mind that you may be given a nasty fine once you get out of Deqin.

Xinjiang-Tibet Highway

The Xinjiang-Tibet Highway is officially off limits, but interestingly, at the time of research, quite a large number of travellers were managing to get through, even on bicycles. Approximately 1350km of road separates Kashgar from Ali in Western Tibet and for the adventurous this can form an extension to a trip along the Karakoram Highway (for information on travelling between Ali and Lhasa or Zhangmu see the Getting There & Away section of the Western Tibet chapter).

With at least two passes over 5400m, the Xinjiang-Tibet Highway is the highest road in the world. It can be bitterly cold and closes down for the winter months from December to February. The whole trip takes around four days of travel, depending of course on how lucky you are with lifts.

From Kashgar it is now possible to travel around 250km by bus to Yecheng (Kargilik), or a day's travel, to the south. Try to get a travel permit for Yecheng in Kashgar.

There is no onward public transport from Yecheng to Ali but some travellers have successfully hitched lifts with trucks for a few

hundred yuan. Be prepared for some serious haggling and checkpoint shenanigans just outside Yecheng. The trip from Yecheng to Ali consists of around three days of travel that passes through Aksai Chin, a large area of land so remote that it took several years for India to realise that China had seized it and built a road through it.

Other Routes into Tibet

Since 1994 another route into Tibet has been open, to tour groups only, passing through Purang (Taklakot in Nepali). Special visas are required for this trip. (See Lonely Planet's *Trekking in the Nepal Himalaya* for more information.)

Overland Routes into China

There are countless ways to cross overland into China. There's the Karakoram Highway from Pakistan, the Torugart Pass from Kyrgyzstan, the Eurasian rail link from Kazakhstan, the Trans-Siberian railway from Russia and Mongolia, and the subtropical crossings from Vietnam, Laos and even Myanmar if you are lucky.

For more information on these crossings see Lonely Planet's *Karakoram Highway*, *China* or *South-West China*, or more specialist publications such as *The Trans-Siberian Rail Guide* by Robert Strauss or the *Trans-Siberian Handbook* by Bryn Thomas.

The Karakoram Highway in particular provides travellers with the opportunity to do a subcontinental circuit through Tibet, Nepal, India and Pakistan and back into China (in any order you like).

ORGANISED TOURS

The following companies all lead group tours to Tibet. If you only have three weeks holiday each year, they can be a useful way to see a lot in a short time, though most are pretty exhausting on the wallet. Most lead standard tours along the Friendship Highway but some offer adventurous exploratory trips into the back of beyond. Short tour description are given but be aware that most companies change their programs every couple of years.

USA

Adventure Center
(☎ 510-654 1879)
1311 63rd St, STE 200, Emeryville, CA 94608,
USA. Information and booking agent for a
wide variety of adventure travel companies. US
agent for Explore Worldwide (see UK listing).

Asian Pacific Adventures
(☎ 800-825 1680, 213-935 3156, fax 935 2691)
826 S Sierra Bonita Ave, Los Angeles, CA
90036, USA

Boojum Expeditions
(☎ 800-287 0125, 406-587 0125, fax 585
3474, email boojum@boojumx.com, Web site
www.boojumx.com)
14543 Kelly Canyon Rd, Bozeman MT 59715,
USA. Horse treks in Chinese parts of eastern
Tibet.

High Asia
(☎/fax 800-809 0034, email travel@highasia
.com, Web site www.highasia.com)
PO Box 2438, Basalt, Colorado 81621, USA.
Groundbreaking and environment-aware touring, trekking and mountaineering trips to
Kham and the Changtang.

Himalayan High Treks
(☎ 800-455 8735, 415-861 2391, fax 415-861
2391)
241 Dolores St, San Francisco, CA 94103,
USA. Humla-Kailash trek.

InnerAsia Expeditions
(☎ 800-777 8183, 415-922 0448, fax 415-346
5535, email info@geoex.com)
2627 Lombard St, San Francisco, CA 94123,
USA. Specialises in itineraries it has often
pioneered.

Journeys
(☎ 800-255 8735)
4011 Jackson, Ann Arbor, MI 48103, USA.

Latitudes, Expeditions East
(☎ 800-580 4883, fax 415-680 1522, email
info@weblatitudes.com)
870 Market St, Suite 482, San Francisco, CA
94102, USA. Standard tour of Tibet with a trek
to Kharta.

Mountain Travel-Sobek
(☎ 800-227 2384, 415-527 8100, fax 525 7710)
6420 Fairmount Ave, El Cerrito, CA 94530,
USA. Trekking.

Snowlion Travels
(☎ 800-525 TREK)
Small group (max eight) tours and treks, plus
a pricey 30 day mountain biking trip.

Wilderness Travels
(☎ 800-368 2794, 415-548 0420, fax 548 0347)
801 Allston Way, Berkeley, CA 94710, USA.
Trekking.

UK

China International Travel Service (CITS)
(☎ 0171-836 9911, from 22 April 2000 ☎ 020-
7836 9911)
7 Upper St Martin's Lane, London, UK. Pricey
tours of four days to one week from Chengdu
or Kathmandu.

Exodus
(☎ 0181-675 5550, fax 673 0779, from 22
April 2000 ☎ 020-8675 5550, fax 8673 0779)
9 Weir Rd, London SW12 0LT, UK. Interesting tours through Kham, plus treks and
overland trips.

Explore Worldwide
(☎ 01252-319448, fax 343170, email info
@explore.co.uk, Web site www.explore.co.uk)
1 Frederick St, Aldershot, Hants GU11 1LQ,
UK. Offers a standard 15 day tour covering all
the main highlights.

Himalayan Kingdoms
(☎ 0117-923 7163, fax 974 4993)
20 The Mall, Clifton, Bristol, BS8 4DR, UK.
Trekking and mountaineering.

KE Adventure Travel
(☎ 017687-73966, 72267, fax 74693, email
keadventure@enterprise.net, Web site www.ke
adventure.com)
32 Lake Rd, Keswick, Cumbria CA12 5DQ,
UK. Tours, treks to Mt Kailash, mountaineering on Mt Shisha Pangma and mountain bike
trips from Lhasa to Kathmandu.

OTT Expeditions
(☎ 0114-258 8508, fax 255 1603, email andy
@ottexpd.demon.co.uk, Web site www.ott
expeditions.co.uk)
Unit 5b, Southwest Centre, Troutbeck Rd,
Sheffield S7 2QA, UK. Hard-core mountaineering including an ascent of 8201m Cho Oyu!

Regent Holidays
(☎ 0117-921 1711)
15 John St, Bristol BS1 2HR, UK. Tours and do-
it-yourself pre-booked trips.

Sherpa Expeditions
(☎ 0181-577 2717, fax 572 9788, from 22
April 2000 ☎ 020-8577 2717, fax 8572 9788;
email sherpa.sales@dial.pipex.com)
131a, Hounslow, Middlesex TW5 0RD, UK.
A 19 day tour from Lhasa to Kathmandu including a trek from Tingri to Everest Base
Camp.

Steppes East
(☎ 01285-810267, fax 810693, email sales
@steppeseast.co.uk, Web site www.steppe-
seast.co.uk)
Castle Eaton, Cricklade, Swindon, Wiltshire
SN6 6JU, UK. Standard tour of Tibet with a
well-respected company.

Trans-Himalaya
  (☎ 0181-459 7944, 459 8017, from 22 April
  2000 ☎ 020-8459 7944, fax 8459 8017)
  30 Hanover Rd, London, NW10 3DS, UK.
  Specialist in exploratory trips throughout the
  Tibetan region.
Voyages Jules Verne
  (☎ 0171-616 1000, fax 723 8629, from 22
  April 2000 ☎ 020-7616 1000, fax 7723 8629,
  email sales@vjv.co.uk, Web site www.vjv.co.uk)
  21 Dorset Square, London NW1 6QG, UK.
  Luxury short tours to Tibet with add-ons to
  other parts of China.
World Expeditions
  (☎ 01753-581808, fax 581809)
  101c Slough Rd, Datchet, Berkshire SL3 9AQ,
  UK

Australia
Adventure World
  (☎ 02-9956 7766, fax 9956 7707)
  3rd floor, 73 Walker Street, North Sydney,
  NSW 2059
Everest Trekking
  (☎ 03-9249 9504)
  832 High St, Kew, Vic 3102

Exodus
  (☎ 1-800-800724, 02-9925 5439, fax 9251 5432)
  Suite 5, 1 York St, Sydney, NSW 2000
Peregrine Adventures
  (☎ 03-9663 8611)
  258 Lonsdale St, Melbourne, Vic 3000
  (☎ 02-9290 2770)
  5th Floor, 38 York St, Sydney, NSW 2000
World Expeditions
  (☎ 02-9264 3366)
  441 Kent St, Sydney, NSW 2000

France
Allibert
  (☎ 01 48 06 16 61, fax 01 48 06 47 22)
  14 rue de l'Asile Popincourt, 75011 Paris
  (☎ 76 45 22 26, fax 76 45 27 28)
  route de Grenoble, 38530 Chapareillan

New Zealand
Adventure World
  (☎ 0800-652 954, 09-524 5118, fax 520 6629,
  email discover@adventureworld.co.nz)
  101 Great South Road, Remeura, Auckland,
  New Zealand. Australasian agent for Explore
  Worldwide (see UK listing).

Getting Around

Tibet's transport infrastructure is poorly developed and, with the exception of the Friendship Highway and the Qinghai-Tibet Highway, most of the roads are in very poor condition. Some work is being undertaken to improve this situation – a vital condition in Chinese plans to develop Tibet – but it is unlikely that travel in Tibet will become comfortable or easy in the near future.

The main problem for travellers who do not have oodles of time to trek across Tibet is that there is very little in the way of public transport in the country. There are no flights (except those in or out of Tibet), no rail system and only a handful of buses and minibuses plying the roads between Lhasa and other major Tibetan towns such as Shigatse and Tsetang. So-called public 'pilgrim buses' to monastery attractions have become more widespread in recent years, but are generally restricted to the major monastic sites in the Lhasa region.

For those who would like to tour Tibet by driving a car or motorcycle, the news is bleak – basically it's impossible unless you have a Chinese driver's licence. It's not like India, where you can simply buy a motorcycle and head off on your own.

Foreign residents may drive in China after obtaining a Chinese driver's licence or are in an international car rally. However, there are often restrictions on how far you can drive from your place of residence – the local Public Security Bureau (PSB) can inform you of the latest half-baked regulations.

This situation leaves many travellers in the position of having to band together to hire 4WDs and drivers to get around Tibet. The availability of such vehicles has increased recently, but in the peak summer months of August and September there can still be a squeeze and prices can rise. Travellers should bear in mind that, if they have limited time and want to see as much of Tibet as possible, they are probably going to end up spending quite a bit of money renting vehicles.

The other main option is to hitch. If you can get the necessary travel permits (see Permits in the Facts for the Visitor chapter) and you have enough time to stand by the side of the road this isn't a bad idea. You will still have to pay but it will cost a fraction of the amount for a Land Cruiser. You'll need to be much more self-sufficient, though, and be prepared to wait for hours, if not days, for a truck driver willing to take you. It can be very frustrating.

Those with more time can, of course, trek or cycle their way around the high plateau.

BUS

Bus travel in Tibet is slow and gruelling. Most bus services originate in Lhasa and connect the capital with Shigatse, Tsetang and local sites like Ganden Monastery. There are also public buses from Shigatse to Gyantse and Sakya. Schedules tend to be slightly erratic. A further annoyance is the fact that all public bus services exact a 100% surcharge from foreign travellers. Many bus routes go to places off limits to foreigners like Yatung or Bayi and you'll be lucky to be allowed on.

The usual rules concerning bus travel apply in Tibet. Try to avoid sitting in the back of the bus. The combination of bad suspension and shocking roads make for very bumpy bus journeys, and the back of the bus is the worst place to be. You will almost certainly be required to stow your baggage on the roof if you have a bulky backpack. If possible, check that it is tied down properly – bus drivers normally do a good job of checking such details – and lock your pack as a precaution against theft. Try to see what everyone else is paying before you hand over your cash.

For long journeys it is a good idea to stock up on some snacks. Meal stops are usually infrequent and often yield fairly inedible fare.

Minibus

Private entrepreneurs are taking to the roads in increasing numbers, and minibus services are now available to many areas that are not served by buses, for example Lhatse and Tsurphu. Minibuses are cheaper than public buses in that foreigners are only charged local prices. How long it will remain this way is anyone's guess.

Local authorities occasionally fine minibus services between Lhasa and Shigatse and taxis running between Tsetang and Lhasa because they don't have government permission (and insurance) to take foreigners. Given that minibuses are more comfortable, quicker and a third of the price of public buses, there is little surprise that foreigners are deserting the public services in droves.

Minibuses operate out of Lhasa to monastic sites such as Drepung, Tsurphu, Ganden and Samye, and to Tsetang and Shigatse. From Shigatse, minibuses run to Gyantse and Lhatse. Ticket prices are cheap but you can expect to spend a lot of time sitting around waiting for the minibus to fill up.

It is often possible to get a ride from Lhasa to the Nepalese border (with an overnight stop in Shigatse) on minibuses which head down to pick up groups arriving from Kathmandu. Most of the budget travel agencies in Lhasa can book you a seat to Zhangmu (or anywhere else on the route) for anything between Y250 and Y350 but be warned that if the group doesn't run, neither does the minibus and the agency won't bother to tell you. Minibuses normally depart on Thursdays but can leave at any time – check the noticeboards in Lhasa. There are no discounts if you are only going to Tingri or Lhatse.

VEHICLE RENTAL

Vehicle rental has become the most popular way of getting around in Tibet. Tourists are not yet permitted to drive rental vehicles in

Contracts

It has become standard practice among foreign travellers hiring vehicles to draw up a contract with the driver. The exact value of these contracts is somewhat dubious. They certainly do not mean a great deal to the average Tibetan or Chinese driver. And in the case of a one-way trip to the Nepalese border, for example, how long are you prepared to hang around on the border waving the contract in the air and poring over it with your driver and local PSB officials?

This is not to say that you shouldn't bother with a contract. Draw one up by all means. But try and keep it short and to the point. List your exact itinerary, the price and method of payment. Clauses that prevent the driver from picking up 'friends' and 'relatives' en route are useful if you do not want to be squeezed by freeloaders. But above all get together with the driver before the trip and go through the main points of the contract verbally. Both Chinese and Tibetans find the idea of a contract-based relationship cold and businesslike. You are likely to have much fewer problems on your trip if you can get on friendly terms with your driver by treating him with respect – give him some cigarettes or some kind of small gift – than by waving a contract in his face.

When I was last in town, a group of travellers heading out to the Nepalese border were proudly showing around a contract of mind-numbing complexity they had put together. Loaded with Draconian articles, it forbade the driver from picking up hitchers or smoking, from seeking freebie meals from his passengers, and finally from playing his own music on the tape deck – the poor bastard. It was unlikely that they made any friends on that trip, and it is also an invitation to vengeful obstructionism.

China, however on Tibet's roads you're not likely to mind. Rental agencies will organise one or more drivers (who also act as guides) and a vehicle for you.

There are numerous agencies dealing with the rental of Land Cruisers, jeeps and minibuses in Lhasa (see the Travel Agencies section in the Lhasa chapter) and a few are also based in Shigatse. Costs are calculated on a per kilometre basis, and if you are making a one-way trip (from Lhasa to the Nepalese border for example) the cost will include a charge for returning to Lhasa (normally 50% of the outbound charge). The going price at the time of writing was between Y2.50 and Y3.50 per kilometre. Cheaper rates are available for clapped-out minibuses and Beijing jeeps.

Toyota Land Cruisers are probably the most widely seen rented vehicles plying the

Dealing with an Agency

When dealing with an agency to rent a vehicle, you need to establish a few ground rules. Firstly work out an itinerary for your trip. You'll need to fix the rate for any extra days that may need to be tacked onto an itinerary. For delays caused by bad weather, blocked passes, swollen river crossings etc the cost for extra days should be split 50% between your group and the agency. For delays caused by vehicle breakdowns, driver illness etc then the agency should cover 100% of the costs and provide a backup vehicle if necessary.

Secondly ask the agency about its policy on refunds for an uncompleted trip. Some agencies refuse any kind of refund, others are more open to negotiation.

Thirdly, make sure that the trip price covers all permit costs and establish which costs are not covered in the tour price.

Finally, be aware that the vehicle you receive has probably been subcontracted from outside the agency. You should ensure that the vehicle and driver have the necessary permits and insurance required to carry foreigners. Also, more importantly, you should verify that the agency will take responsibility in the event of vehicle breakdown. Some reputable agencies will calmly refuse to take any role in disputes between you and the owner of the vehicle. Find out where you stand in advance.

Once you are sorted with the agency it's a good idea to organise a meeting between your group and the driver(s) and guide a day or two before departure. Make sure the drivers are aware of your itinerary (it may be the first time they have seen it!). Ensure that the guide speaks fluent Tibetan, good Chinese and useable English. Strong personality clashes would suggest a change of personnel.

Unless you are qualified mechanic, inspecting the soundness of the vehicles may prove to be difficult but you should carry out the following basic checks. First make sure that the 4WD can at least be engaged (not just that the stick moves!) and that the 'diff lock' can be locked and unlocked (this is usually done via tabs on the front wheel hubs). Then, for the truck, make sure that at least two shovels are supplied and that it carries a long steel tow cable (rope cables are useless). Snow chains are apparently available for trucks but not for Land Cruisers. Tyres and spares on both vehicles should be in reasonable condition (by Tibetan standards).

The only other pre-departure issues to consider for long trips are warm clothing, a good sleeping bag, plenty of food and perhaps a small stove. A tent is an excellent backup. A few plastic barrels (available in most markets) are useful to protect your gear from the thrashing it will get in the back of the truck. Jerry cans to carry water (and even chang!) are a good idea.

Andre Ticheler

high plateau loaded with backpackers. They have room for six or seven people and their luggage, though five is more comfortable. Four can go in the back, one can sit comfortably (two uncomfortably) in the front and there is often a fold-down seat in the boot.

Beijing jeeps are cheaper but can only hold around four people with their luggage, which ends up making them more expensive per person. Naturally, renting a minibus with 20 or more seats really spreads the costs around – but who can be bothered looking for 19 other travel companions?

The best place to hire vehicles is Lhasa. Before going ahead and organising a vehicle, check the notice boards at the main budget hotels. There are usually dozens of notes there advertising seats on trips to all quarters of Tibet. The most popular options are to the Nepalese border, Nam-tso and Mt Kailash. Day trips to places such as Ganden Monastery are also popular, and there are likely to be a few notices advertising places on trips to more obscure destinations.

Actually hiring a vehicle is subject to all kinds of pitfalls. Drawing up a contract in English and Tibetan or Chinese is a good idea, but carries much less weight in Tibet than it would elsewhere in the world. It is not unusual for drivers to flaunt the conditions of a contract and in the end there is little that can be done about it (see the boxed text 'Contracts'). It is a good idea to reach an agreement that payment be delivered in two instalments: one before setting off and one on successful completion of the trip. The fact that you are holding back some of the payment gives you far more leverage in negotiating problems with drivers.

Approximate rates for the most popular itineraries are given in the boxed text 'Land Cruiser Rates in Lhasa' in the Lhasa chapter.

BICYCLE

Long-distance cyclists are once again appearing on the roads of Tibet. Some buy mountain bikes in China and bring them up to Lhasa; others cycle all the way up from Kathmandu. Some travellers even buy their bikes in Lhasa. Any of these options is cur-

rently feasible, and local authorities appear to be turning a blind eye to the phenomenon.

Bringing a Bicycle into Tibet

There don't seem to be any regulations on bringing a bike into Tibet from Kathmandu or elsewhere. If you enter from Nepal, however, you will not be allowed to ride on from Zhangmu. You will have to put your bike on the roof of a Land Cruiser, drive all the way to Lhasa and then cycle back!

Rental

At present the only place in Tibet that you can easily rent bicycles is Lhasa. Rates of Y2 per hour or Y20 per day prevail, and the bikes are usually clunky, Chinese Flying Pigeons, useless on anything other than (downhill) tarmac. Test the brakes and tyres before taking the bike out onto the streets of Lhasa. An extra padlock might be a good idea, as there is a problem with bicycle theft in the capital. The Pentoc Guesthouse in Lhasa rents out mountain bikes for around Y60 per day.

Purchase

It is possible nowadays to buy a Chinese-made or Taiwanese-made (better) mountain bike in Lhasa for about Y500. Shop around in the area near the Potala on Dekyi Nub Lam. Standards aren't all that bad, though you should check the gears in particular. Do not expect the quality of such bikes to be equal to those you might buy at home – bring plenty of spare parts. Bikes have a relatively high resale value in Kathmandu and you might even make a profit if the bike's in good shape (unlikely after a trip across Tibet!).

Touring

Most PSB officials have no idea whether foreigners are allowed to cycle around Tibet, which means that most will leave you alone as long as you have a valid Chinese visa and a travel permit.

Despite the official ambivalence, Tibet still poses unique challenges to the individual cyclist. The roads are generally very bad even though there's not much traffic, wind squalls and dust storms can make your work particularly arduous, the warm summer months can bring flash flooding, and then there is the question of your fitness. Tibet's high-altitude mountainous terrain is sure to test the determination of all cyclists who set out on its roads.

Whether you bring a bike with you or buy one in China or Tibet, you will need to be prepared to do your own repairs. A full bicycle repair kit, several spare inner tubes and a spare tyre and chain are essential. Preferably bring an extra rim and some spare spokes. Extra brake wire and brake pads are useful (you'll be descending 3000m from Lhasa to Kathmandu!). Other useful equipment includes reflective clothing, a helmet, goggles, gloves, a dust mask and padded trousers.

You will also need to be prepared with supplies: food, water purifying tablets and camping equipment as if you were trekking. Most long-distance cyclists will probably find formal accommodation and restaurants only available at intervals of two or three days of cycling. It may be possible to stay with army and road repair camps in remote places. See the boxed text 'Kilometre Markers on the Friendship Highway' in the Tsang chapter and 'Kilometre Markers along the Yarlung Tsangpo' in the Ü chapter.

Obviously you need to be in good physical condition to undertake road touring in Tibet. Experienced cyclists recommend a program of training before heading off. Spend some time acclimatising to the altitude and taking leisurely rides around Lhasa (for example) before setting off on a long trip.

On the plus side, while Tibet has some of the highest altitude roads in the world, gradients are usually quite manageable. Tibetan roads are designed for low-powered Chinese trucks, and tackle the many high passes of the region with low-gradient switch-back roads. Most cyclists report that there are few occasions when it is necessary to get off their bikes and push.

Touring Routes The most popular touring route at present is Lhasa-Kathmandu, along the Friendship Highway. It is an ideal route in that it takes in most of Tibet's main sights, offers you superb scenery and (for those travelling from Lhasa) features a spectacular roller-coaster ride down from high La Lung-la into the Kathmandu valley. The trip takes a minimum of two weeks, though to do it justice and include stop overs at Gyantse, Shigatse and Sakya, it will expand into 20 days. The entire trip is just over 940km, though most people start from Shigatse. Watch for the km markers, as these can be a very useful way of knowing exactly how far you have gone and still have to go. See the Tsang chapter for more information about this route.

It is also possible to cycle to Everest Base Camp, though very few travellers have been attempting this tour. Keen cyclists with good mountain bikes might want to consider this option as a side trip on the Lhasa-Kathmandu route. The trip would have to be tackled from the Shegar turn-off, and it would take around two days to Rongphu Monastery.

Other possibilities are endless. Tsurphu and Ganden monasteries are relatively easy (though uphill) trips. Drigung Til also makes a good destination. Cycling in the Yarlung valley region would be a wonderful option if it were not for the permit problems. Some cyclists even tackle Nam-tso, though the nomad's dogs can be a real problem here.

Hazards

Cycling in Tibet is not to be taken lightly. Traffic on Tibetan roads is relatively light, but cyclists do have to be prepared for some very erratic driving. Some cyclists have also complained of deliberate offensive driving by Chinese troop convoys, for whom driving a couple of foreign cyclists off the road is a brief escape from the tedium of soldiering up on the high plateau. It would be wise to pull off the road and wait for such convoys to pass.

Dirt roads prevail in Tibet, and these present particular problems. Cyclists who pick up too much speed on downhill stretches run the grave risk of slipping on gravel.

Numerous cycling trips have been brought to an abrupt conclusion by such a misadventure. Be sensible. Wear a cycling helmet and lightweight leather gloves and, weather permitting, try to keep as much of your body covered with protective clothing as possible. A denim jacket, jeans, gloves and a helmet will protect you from the worst of gravel rash and head injuries if you take a tumble. It goes without saying that cyclists should also be prepared with a comprehensive medical kit. See the boxed text 'Medical Kit Check List' under Health in the Facts for the Visitor chapter for details.

Dogs are a major problem for cyclists in Tibet especially in more remote areas. You may have to pedal like mad to outpace them. Children have also been known to throw stones at cyclists.

HITCHING

Hitching is never entirely safe in any country in the world, and we don't recommend it. Travellers who decide to hitch should understand that they are taking a small but potentially serious risk. However, in Tibet hitching is often the only alternative to hiring an expensive Land Cruiser and so has become a fairly established practice. The advice that follows should help to make journeys as fast and safe as possible.

With the exception of travellers hitching out to Western Tibet or those making their way illegally from Chengdu to Lhasa, few foreigners travel long distances by truck these days. The main reason is that the authorities impose heavy fines on truck drivers caught transporting foreign travellers and may even confiscate their licence. This is particularly the case on the Lhasa-Chengdu route, where fines of Y2000 prevail, plus whatever local officials demand in bribes. There seems to be little stopping truck drivers picking up travellers off the main highways, however, especially if there are no checkpoints en route. Sometimes you can get a lift on a pilgrim truck or an organised passenger truck.

The most frequently seen truck in Tibet is the Dongfeng (East Wind), a sturdy and basic Chinese-made vehicle with a carrying capacity of around 10 tonnes. It comes in a variety of models. The occasional Japanese-made truck also turns up.

If you hitch by truck in Tibet, be prepared to share the hardships of a trucker's life. You will probably end up helping to drag your vehicle out of rivers and sand drifts, and assisting in repairs. Particularly in Western Tibet, the roads are atrocious and accidents, breakdowns and delays are par for the course. If you are headed out to fairly remote destinations you should be equipped to camp out for the night if you don't get a ride.

Trucks aren't the only transport on the roads. There are also plenty of half-empty Land Cruisers which are headed down the Friendship Highway to pick up a group, or returning after having dropped one off. It's a wonderful feeling to get a lift in an empty Land Cruiser after being rejected all day by a stream of dilapidated trucks travelling at 30km/h.

Finally, it's worth investing in a face mask (readily available in Lhasa) as the roads in Tibet are very dusty.

Getting a Lift

Back in the early days of travelling in Tibet, truck depots were good places to organise lifts with trucks. Nowadays you will be drawing unwanted attention to yourself and your intentions by popping into depots in Tibet's urban centres. It is a far better course of action to get out on the road. Those planning on hitching along the Friendship Highway, from Lhasa for example, should at least get as far as Shigatse, preferably Lhatse before 'extending a thumb'. See the 'Routes to Western Tibet' section in the Western Tibet chapter for information on hitching out to Mt Kailash.

It's a good idea to start hitching a few kilometres out of town because then you know that traffic is going in your direction and is not about to turn off after 400m. This is especially important if there is a checkpoint nearby. It's best to walk through the checkpoint yourself and wait for a lift a couple of kilometres on the other side.

One thing you do have to bear in mind is that it is very unusual nowadays to hear of people getting free lifts in Tibet. It does occur occasionally, but more often than not you will be expected to pay for your lift. The amount is entirely negotiable, but in areas where traffic is minimal, drivers will often demand quite large sums.

TREKKING

Tibet offers excellent, though tough trekking. There are none of the foreigner-friendly trekking agencies and lodges that you find in Nepal and the rigours of high-altitude trekking are not to be taken lightly, but trekking in Tibet offers experienced walkers unrivalled freedom to explore the country.

For a detailed look at seven of the most popular treks in Tibet and general information for anyone planning a trek on the roof of the world, see the Trekking chapter.

LOCAL TRANSPORT

Local transport is only available in Lhasa and Shigatse. In some parts of Tibet it is possible to get short lifts with tractors, an extremely uncomfortable way to travel.

Bus

Minibuses ply the streets of Lhasa these days and it is possible to get quickly from one end of town to the other for Y2. It is the only service of its kind in Tibet.

Pedicab

Pedicabs are available in Lhasa, Gyantse and Shigatse. They are a slow and expensive way to get around. In Lhasa, for example, it costs a minimum of Y10 to go from one end of town to the other and is much more time consuming than travelling by minibus. Serious haggling is required for hiring pedicabs.

Tractor

In Shigatse, tractors serve as the town's public transport system and rides cost around Y2 or Y3. Elsewhere in Tibet the tractor can be a good option for short distance trips. For a few yuan, drivers are normally quite happy to have some passengers in the back. Rides of anything over 10 minutes quickly become excruciatingly painful.

Taxis

One result of China's economic infusion into Tibet is the large number of taxis now available in Lhasa, Shigatse and even Ali in Western Tibet. Taxis in all three towns charge a standard Y10 anywhere in the city. Fixed route passenger taxis also run between Lhasa, Gongkar airport and Tsetang and you need only pay for your seat.

Lhasa

HIGHLIGHTS

- **Barkhor circuit** – Lhasa's fascinating medieval pilgrim circuit, chock-a-block with religious artefacts and prostrating pilgrims

- **Jokhang Temple** – the spiritual heart of Tibet, this network of shrines hums with shuffling, murmuring pilgrims

- **The Potala** – deserted home of the Dalai Lama

- **Sera & Drepung** – two of the largest and most intact of Tibet's great monasteries

- **Pilgrim circuits** – fascinating ways to explore Lhasa while also rubbing shoulders with pilgrims

Lhasa, the heart and soul of Tibet, centuries-long abode of the Dalai Lamas and object of devout pilgrimage, is still a city of wonders, despite the large-scale encroachments of Chinese influence.

As you enter the Kyi Chu valley, either on the long haul from Golmud or from Gongkar airport, your first hint that Lhasa is close at hand is the sight of the Potala, a vast white and ochre fortress soaring head and shoulders over this, one of the world's highest cities. It is a sight that has heralded the marvels of the holy city to travellers for close to four centuries.

While the Potala dominates the Lhasa skyline and, as the residence of the Dalai Lamas, serves as a symbolic focus for Tibetan hopes of self-government, it is the Jokhang, some 2km to the east of the Potala, that is the spiritual heart of the city. A curious mix of sombre darkness, wafting incense and prostrating pilgrims, the Jokhang, is the most sacred and active of Tibet's temples. Encircling it is the Barkhor, the holiest of Lhasa's devotional circumam-

bulation circuits. It is here that most visitors first fall in love with Tibet. The medieval push and shove of crowds from another time and place, the street performers, the stalls hawking everything from prayer flags to jewel-encrusted yak skulls, and the devout tapping their foreheads to the ground at every step is an exotic brew that few newcomers can resist.

However, the Potala and the Jokhang, though prominent, are just two of the sights that Lhasa has to offer. Close to the Jokhang are a number of smaller active temples that are little visited by foreign travellers. The alleys running off the Barkhor circuit are cluttered with pool tables, market stalls and milling crowds from all over Tibet. The Norbulingka, summer palace of the Dalai Lamas, is a short distance away in the western part of town; and in Lhasa's low-lying surrounding hills are the important Gelugpa monasteries of Sera and Drepung.

And just a word of warning: it's not uncommon to feel breathless, suffer from headaches and sleep poorly if you fly straight into Lhasa. Take things easy for the first few days and try to drink lots of fluids. For detailed information on AMS (altitude sickness), its symptoms and treatment see the Health section in the Facts for the Visitor chapter.

HISTORY

Lhasa rose to prominence as an important centre of administrative power in the 7th century AD, when Songtsen Gampo (618-49), a local ruler in the Yarlung valley, continued the task initiated by his father of unifying Tibet in concert with other local chieftains. Songtsen Gampo moved his capital to Lhasa and built a palace on the site that is now occupied by the Potala. At this time the temples of Ramoche and the Jokhang were also established to house Buddha images brought as the dowries of Songtsen Gampo's Chinese and Nepalese wives. Both of the temples still stand in Lhasa, though little evidence of their 7th century origins remains.

The rule of the Yarlung kings from their new capital, Lhasa, lasted some 250 years. Despite the founding of the Jokhang, Buddhism seems initially to have been a courtly affair. Tibet's first monastic community, Samye, was not established until the rule of a later Lhasa king, Trisong Detsen (755-97). More energy was expended in waging war on Tibet's neighbours, China, Nepal and India, than in propagating the new faith. Eventually Buddhism came into increasing conflict with Bön, the native shamanistic faith of Tibet, and the two religions became the focus of courtly intrigues that led to the break-up of the Lhasa regime into a number of competing fiefdoms in the early 10th century.

There is little to draw on in imagining the kind of capital Lhasa might have been in the time of the Lhasa kings. Chinese records from Dunhuang state that the capital of Lhasa was a walled city with flat-roofed houses and refer to the 'king and his nobles' as living 'in felt tents'. The same records refer to an aversion to washing, the eating of *tsampa* (made with roasted barley flour) and the plaited hair of Tibetan women – customs that persist to the present day.

With the break-up of the early Lhasa state, Buddhism enjoyed a gradual resurgence at various monastic centres, notably Samye and Sakya. It was at the latter that the next large-scale Tibetan regime emerged with Mongol support in the 13th century. Subsequent Tibetan governments were located in Nedong (Ü) and Shigatse (Tsang). Lhasa languished in the back waters of Tibetan history until the fifth Dalai Lama (1617-82) defeated the Shigatse Tsang kings with Mongol support.

The fifth Dalai Lama moved his capital to Lhasa. He built his palace, the Potala, on the site of the ruins of Songtsen Gampo's 7th century palace. Lhasa has remained Tibet's capital since 1642, and most of the city's historical sights date from this second stage of the city's development. Very little remains of Lhasa's 7th century origins.

Modern Lhasa in many ways provides the visitor with both the best and the worst of contemporary Tibet. After all, despite the city's rich historical associations and colourful Tibetan population, it is here that Chinese control is at its most trigger-happy, and much of the city's charm has fallen prey to Chinese 'modernisation'.

Photographs of the city prior to 1951 reveal a small town nestled at the foot of the Potala and linked by an avenue to another cluster of residences in the area of the Jokhang. The population of the city prior to the Chinese takeover is thought to have been between 20,000 and 30,000. Today the city has a population of over 150,000, and it is likely that Chinese residents outnumber Tibetans.

Shöl, the village at the foot of the Potala, has all but disappeared and the old West Gate, though which most people entered the holy city, has been torn down to be replaced by a smaller, modern version. The area in front of the Potala has been made into a Tiananmen-style public square and Gumolingka Island, one a traditional picnic spot for Tibetans, has been renamed 'Dream Island' and replaced by a Chinese-style shopping and karaoke complex. The Tibetan quarter is now an isolated enclave in the eastern end of town, comprising only around 4% of the total area of contemporary Lhasa. Even these lingering enclaves of tradition are under threat despite official protection. Lhasa has probably changed more in the last twenty years than in the thousand years before.

ORIENTATION

While Lhasa has emerged as a surprisingly sprawling city in recent years, orientation is still a relatively simple affair. The city divides clearly into a western (Chinese) section and an eastern (Tibetan) section. The Chinese section holds Lhasa's few upmarket accommodation options, along with Chinese restaurants, karaoke bars and the Nepalese consulate. The Tibetan eastern

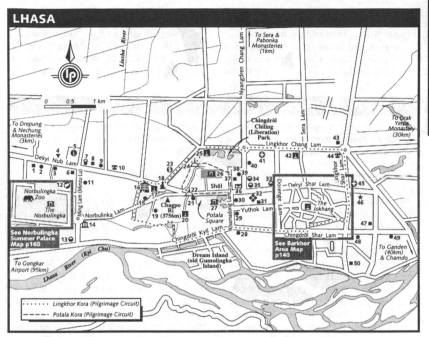

LHASA

See Norbulingka
Summer Palace
Map p160

See Barkhor
Area Map
p140

······· Lingkhor Kora (Pilgrimage Circuit)
––––– Potala Kora (Pilgrimage Circuit)

LHASA

PLACES TO STAY
1 Tibet Hotel
6 Lhasa Hotel
8 Grand Hotel
28 Tibet Royal Hotel
31 Gold Grain Hotel
37 Airway Hotel
43 Yinqiao Hotel
47 Sunlight Hotel
50 Himalaya Hotel

PLACES TO EAT
4 Yeti Café

OTHER
2 Xinhua Bookstore
3 Tibet International Worker
   Travel Service
5 CITS
7 Gleckes Fresh Beer
9 Lhasa Foreign Trade Building
10 Main Telecom Building

11 Tibetan Dance & Drama
   Theatre
12 Nepalese Consulate
13 Main Bus Station
   (Long Distance)
14 Tibet Museum
15 Tibet Tourism Bureau (TTB)
16 Kunde Ling Monastery
17 Gesar Ling Temple
18 Yak Statues
19 Rock Carvings
20 Palha Lupuk Temple
21 Yeti Mountaineering Shop
22 Chörten (Former City Gate)
23 Main Bank of China
   (Main Branch)
24 Three Chörtens
25 Lukhang Temple
26 The Potala
27 Workers' Cultural Palace
29 Xinhua Bookstore
30 Photographic Shops

32 New Century Department
   Store
33 Minibus No 3 to Drepung
34 Minibuses to Chushul
   & Yangpachen
35 Minibus No 5 to Sera
   Monastery
36 Main Post Office &
   Telecommunications Building
   (Branch)
38 Vegetable Market
39 Civil Aviation Authority of
   China (CAAC)
40 Bakery & Shop
41 People's Hospital
42 Ramoche Temple; Tsepak
   Lhakhang
44 Telecom Building (Branch)
45 People's Hospital
46 PSB
48 Carpet Factory
49 Tibet University

end of town is altogether more colourful and has all the lower-end accommodation popular with individual travellers.

The principal thoroughfare for orientation is Dekyi Nub Lam, which becomes Dekyi Shar Lam in the east of town (*nub* means west in Tibetan, *shar* means east). This road, known as Beijing Dong Lu in Chinese, runs from west to east past the Tibet Hotel, the Lhasa Hotel (former Holiday Inn), the Yak statues, the Potala, the main post office and into the Tibetan part of town, passing the

Lhasa's Pilgrim Circuits

For Tibetan pilgrims, who approach the holy city with somewhat different priorities to those of the average western visitor, the principal points of orientation are Lhasa's three *koras* (pilgrimage circuits): the Nangkhor, Barkhor and Lingkhor.

The Nangkhor This kora encircles the inner precincts of the Jokhang.

The Barkhor This traces the outskirts of the Jokhang in a circuit of approximately 800m. It is the most famous of Lhasa's pilgrimage circuits and probably the best introduction to the old town for newcomers. See the Barkhor Area section for more details.

The Lingkhor This is the devotional route that traditionally encompassed the entirety of the old city. Nowadays the Lingkhor includes a great deal of scenery that is of a decidedly secular and modern nature, but it is still used by pilgrims. The route is marked on the Lhasa and Barkhor Area maps. You can join the circuit anywhere. One option is to walk south of Barkhor Square onto Chingdröl Shar Lam and head west. After about 1½km a small alley turns north (look out for the stonecarvers) and then west to the excellent rock carvings of Chagpo Ri. From here the trail continues west and then north up to the Kunde Ling Temple. Head east along Dekyi Nub Lam, past the Gesar Ling Temple, and turn left at the golden yak statue up to the chörtens near the Lukhang Temple. From here follow the main road east along Lingkhor Chang Lam and then south down Lingkhor Shar Lam. Turn right towards the main city mosque and head west past the Ani Sangkhung Nunnery and a second smaller mosque until you reach the Lho Rigsum Lhakhang, one of four chapels surrounding the Jokhang at cardinal points and with connections to Ganden Monastery. The chapel, which is almost completely ignored by tourists, houses a central statue of Amitayus (Tibetan: Tsepame) flanked by the four main bodhisattvas and has its own inner kora. From here the Lingkhor turns south onto Chingdröl Shar Lam, taking you back to where you started. The whole kora is around 8km and takes most of the morning, longer if you make many stops en route.

The Potala Kora Another popular kora encircles the holy Potala Palace and follows an almost continuous circuit of prayer wheels. The route leads past teahouses, chörtens, stonecarvers, rock paintings and often buskers and is worth a visit, especially if you wish to visit the Lukhang Temple.

Others There are also koras around both Drepung and Sera monasteries.

All the koras are well worth following, especially during festivals such as Saga Dawa, when the distance between tourist and pilgrim can become very fine. Remember always to proceed clockwise.

Yak and Banak Shol hotels, two of the most popular budget accommodation options.

The Barkhor circuit and the Jokhang, at the centre of the Tibetan quarter, are about five minutes walk south-east of the Yak Hotel. There is a small Muslim quarter with a couple of operating mosques south-east of the Barkhor area.

The Jokhang and Barkhor Square are between Dekyi Shar Lam and Chingdröl Shar Lam (Jinzhu Donglu) and are connected to these two main roads by a web of winding alleyways lined with the white-washed façades of traditional Tibetan homes. This Tibetan area is not particularly extensive. Rather than worry about orientation it is more fun to simply slip away from the Barkhor circuit at some point and aimlessly wander the alleys. You won't stay lost for long.

'The Jewels of the Plateau'

The Golden Yaks that dominate Lhasa's main crossroads were unveiled on 26 May 1991 in celebration of the 40th anniversary of the 'liberation' of Tibet. It is difficult not to wonder whether the Chinese authorities were aware of the irony of having to call a temporary state of martial law, ban all foreign journalists and restrict all foreign tourists to their hotel rooms during the celebrations. At all events, the result is a depressingly uninspiring civic monument.

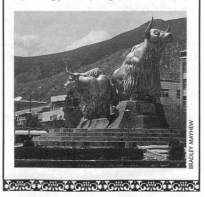

BRADLEY MAYHEW

Maps

Lhasa Tour Map is a relatively useful English-language map of the city produced by the Mapping Bureau of Tibet Autonomous Region. This and other local maps are available at the Xinhua Bookstores, some of the travel agencies around town and in the gift shops of the top end hotels.

For other maps of Lhasa available abroad see the Maps section in the Facts for the Visitor chapter.

INFORMATION

Useful information is scarce in Lhasa. Most travellers find out more about what is going on and how things work by sitting around chatting among themselves in the courtyard of the Yak Hotel or at Tashi I or II restaurants than they do by calling in to travel agents or government organisations like CITS. The information boards at the Pentoc Guesthouse and the Yak, Banak Shol, Snowlands and Kirey hotels can be very useful if you are looking for travel partners, a ride on a Land Cruiser, or even a second hand Lonely Planet guide. If you post up a question, someone will probably scribble up an answer before too long.

Money

The Bank of China sub-branch on Dekyi Shar Lam, between the Banak Shol and Kirey hotels, changes cash and travellers cheques without fuss and is the most conveniently located option. Opening hours are from 9.30 am to 6 pm, Monday to Friday only. It's also open at the weekend but won't change money then.

For credit card advances and foreign exchange during the weekend go to the main Bank of China office just north of Dekyi Nub Lam west of the Potala. Visa, MasterCard, Diners Club and American Express cards are accepted. Opening hours are from 9.30 am to 12.30 pm and 2 to 5.30 pm weekdays, 9.30 am to 12.30 pm Saturday, and closed on Sunday.

There is a small black market for US dollars in Lhasa but, given that rates are almost the same as those at the bank, the risks involved (there are a lot of counterfeit Y100 notes floating about) make such transactions rather silly unless you are caught cashless after hours.

The top end hotels all have an exchange service, but this is normally only available for hotel guests.

Post

The main post office is on Dekyi Shar Lam, about 15 minutes walk west of the Yak Hotel. It is open from 9 am to 8 pm Monday to Saturday, 10 am to 6 pm on Sunday. Buy stamps from the counter immediately on the left as you walk through the main doors.

All poste restante is thrown into a drawer at counter No 12 and a collection charge of Y1.50 is required for each letter. In practice, however, as there seldom seems to be any staff on duty, most travellers grab the bundle of letters and take what they want.

You will need to organise your own packaging for parcels. It is also a good idea to leave the parcel unsealed until you get to the post office. The staff (again at counter No 12) will probably want to check the contents.

Telephone & Fax

The main telecom building is on Dekyi Nub Lam, east of the Grand Hotel. There is no service charge to make calls here and off-peak discounts of 20% and 40% are given at weekends and from 11 pm to midnight respectively. Opening hours run from 8 am to midnight, seven days a week.

There is a smaller telecom building at the northern end of Lingkhor Shar Lam in the east of town (near the Yinqiao Hotel) and a third more conveniently located in the main post office building. Both follow the same opening hours as the main post office and provide international phone and fax services.

International calls require a deposit of Y200. Change is provided after the cost of the call is deducted. It is refunded in total if you don't get through. Prepaid cards are also available (card phones can be used until 11.30 pm). They cost Y150 for Y100 worth of calls. The same deal is also available in

the foyer of the Lhasa Hotel, where phones are available 24 hours a day.

Jingpa Communications (☎/fax 6321532) and the Pentoc Guesthouse Business Centre (see the Barkhor Area map), both in the Tibetan quarter, are more conveniently located, though both levy a Y10 service charge on top of standard China Telecom rates. Jingpa means 'generosity' in Tibetan, which fits as all profits from the company go to alleviating poverty in the Tibetan village of Nangchen in Qinghai province.

Faxes can be sent reliably and easily from the Kyi Chu Hotel for Y30 a page and received for Y3.

Email & Internet Access

The Barkhor Café provides Internet (and therefore Hotmail) access at Y40 per hour (minimum Y7 for 10 minutes) and you can send and receive emails for Y10 and Y5 respectively. The Pentoc will no doubt offer a similar service before long. Jingpa Communications used to offer an email service and might do so once again.

Travel Agencies

Most travellers use the budget agencies scattered around the old Tibetan part of town around the Yak and Banak Shol hotels. All can provide limited information and offer reasonably cheap deals on vehicle rental, but most are fairly disorganised and are dedicated more to relieving you of the contents of your wallet than to providing reasonable levels of service.

When finding out information bear in mind that almost all local travel agencies are self-serving and geared to misinforming individual travellers. Difficulties are always exaggerated and you will most likely be encouraged to apply for unnecessary permits and to join costly tours. None of the agencies listed below are especially recommended and travellers have made complaints about all of them at some time or other:

CITS Shigatse Travels
(☎ 6330489, fax 6330482, email potala@usa .net) at the Yak Hotel. This is a popular first stop, partly due to the fact that it has the only

foreign travel consultants in Lhasa. It's not the cheapest, nor is it much more reliable than most of the other agencies but it has had a lot of experience in arranging transport, tours and visa extensions. They are probably the best people to contact if you need to split from a group visa or extend an existing visa. Services can be arranged in advance through their partners in Kathmandu, Royal Mt Trekking (see the Kathmandu Stopover information in the Getting There & Away chapter). If you need to split from a group visa but didn't book your tour through Royal Mt Trekking then you face an additional service fee of around Y300 on top of the government fee to split the visa (see Visas in Kathmandu in the Facts for the Visitor chapter for more information).

Tibet Niwei International Travel
(☎ 6321239, fax 6330700), next to the Pentoc Guesthouse and run by Alex Chundak. Prices are generally quite cheap, though misinformation can be a problem here.

Tibet Nyingchi Tour Corporation
(☎ 6333871, fax 6333563) This place is under Tashi I Restaurant, friendly and helpful, though their fixed departure minibuses to the Nepalese border aren't always as fixed as they seem.

Snowland Travel Service
(☎ 9001376, fax 6332675) based at the Grand Hotel with an office at the Kirey Hotel.

Most of Lhasa's budget hotels have agency branches on the premises which range from competent (Lhasa Travel Agency at the Banak Shol) to hopeless (Naqu Travels at the Snowlands Hotel).

A final word on budget travel agencies, while there are many operations functioning under different names, many of them are in cohorts. Some travellers give up on one agency and move to another, only to find themselves dealing with the same people.

More reliable (and expensive) agencies located in the western part of town include:

Tibet Holiday International Travel Service
(☎ 6824305, fax 6834957) ground floor, Lhasa Hotel

Tibet Wind-Horse Adventure
(☎ 6833009, fax 6836793) Rm 1120, Lhasa Hotel

China Tibet Travel & Tours (CTTT)
(☎ 6824305) Rm 1688, Lhasa Hotel

Tibet International Worker Travel Service
(☎ 6814304, fax 6834472) No 215 Dekyi Nub Lam

The CITS office (☎ 6833787), at 208 Dekyi Shar Lam, is almost derelict and rarely seems to actually do anything.

Public Security Bureau

The Lhasa Prefecture PSB is on Dekyi Shar Lam and is open from 9 am to 1 pm and 4 to 6.30 pm Monday to Saturday. It is not a good place for visa extensions, but then no PSB offices in Tibet are. Extensions of up to a week are normally given if you can conjure up some evidence such as a flight ticket out of Tibet. If you're looking for a longer extension then it's wiser to enquire at one of the private travel agencies before revealing your plans to the PSB.

Travel permits are rarely given to individual travellers in Lhasa and you're better off trying in Shigatse.

Bookshops

There is very little in the way of decent mapping or non-Chinese reading material available in Lhasa. The Xinhua Bookstore has three locations. The small branch on the south-eastern corner of the Barkhor circuit has some posters of Buddhist deities but little else. The larger branch on Yuthok Lam (about 10 minutes walk west of Barkhor Square) has some maps, postcards and photo books but there's a better selection available at the branch on Dekyi Nub Lam, east of the Tibet Hotel.

The only English reading material available is a number of locally produced coffee-table publications with photographs and text on Tibet. None of them are of particularly good quality, but they are generally cheap and might be worth sending home as souvenirs. The gift shops at the Lhasa Hotel, Himalaya Hotel, the Potala and the Norbulingka are also good places to track down these books, though prices are more expensive than at Xinhua.

Libraries

The Makye Amye Restaurant on the Barkhor circuit has a small library of books on Tibet which you can borrow after leaving a small deposit.

LHASA

Laundry

The Banak Shol and Kirey hotels offer free laundry to guests. Snowlands' Laundry charges Y2 per piece. The Pentoc charges Y15 for a bagfull.

Medical Services

In the case of an emergency you will probably be taken or directed to the People's Hospital on Lingkhor Shar Lam. Expect minimal hygiene standards, but the staff are competent. Official policy, or so we were told, is to charge foreigners six times the local price. Don't be surprised when you get your bill, though there is some latitude for bargaining.

BARKHOR AREA

The first stop for most newcomers to Lhasa is the Jokhang in the heart of the old Tibetan part of town. But before even venturing into the Jokhang it is worth taking a stroll around the Barkhor, Lhasa's pilgrimage circuit (*kora*), a quadrangle of streets that surrounds the Jokhang and some of the old buildings adjoining it. It is an area unrivalled in Tibet for its fascinating combination of deep religiosity and push-and-shove market economics. This is both the spiritual heart of the holy city and the main commercial district for Tibetans.

For your first visit, enter from Barkhor Square (at the eastern end of Yuthok Lam), a large plaza that was cleared in 1985. The square receives a of criticism from western commentators as being 'ill-conceived' and so on, but it is a popular meeting area for Tibetans. It certainly does have its moments of incongruity, but at least the Chinese gracefully resisted the temptation to plunk a Mao statue in the middle of it all. No doubt, for the Chinese, the clearing of a plaza in the centre of Lhasa makes it easier to keep an

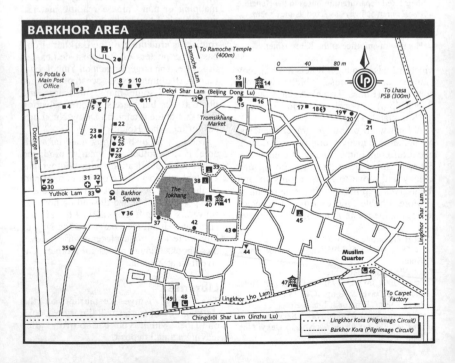

BARKHOR AREA

To Ramoche Temple (400m)
Ramoche Lam
To Potala & Main Post Office
Dekyi Shar Lam (Beijing Dong Lu)
To Lhasa PSB (300m)
Dosenge Lam
Tromsikhang Market
Yuthok Lam
Barkhor Square
The Jokhang
Lingkhor Shar Lam
Muslim Quarter
To Carpet Factory
Lingkhor Uho Lam
Chingdröl Shar Lam (Jinzhu Lu)

········· Lingkhor Kora (Pilgrimage Circuit)
--------- Barkhor Kora (Pilgrimage Circuit)

eye on the activities of locals (watch out for video cameras on the roofs above the square), but the square has still become a focus for protest and has been the scene of pitched battles between Chinese and Tibetans on several occasions.

Protest is the exception rather than the norm, however, and visitors entering Barkhor Square are much more likely to be confronted with crowds of devout Tibetans filing past the magnificent Jokhang than with monks dodging tear-gas canisters.

Close to the entrance to the Jokhang is a constant stream of Tibetans following the Barkhor circumambulation route in a clockwise direction. Look for the two pot-bellied, stone *sangkang* (incense burners) in front of the Jokhang. There are four altogether, the other two are positioned at the rear of the Jokhang, comprising the four extremities of the Barkhor circuit. Behind the first two sangkang are two enclosures. The larger one harbours the stump of an ancient willow tree (allegedly planted by Songtsen Gampo's Chinese wife, Princess Wencheng) and a stele inscribed with the terms of the Sino-

Tibetan treaty of 822. The inscription guarantees mutual respect of the borders of the two nations – an irony seemingly lost on the Chinese authorities. It is simply amazing that the stele was not hauled away in the Cultural Revolution.

For your first few visits to the Barkhor circuit, it's best to let yourself be dragged along by the centrifugal force of the pilgrims but there are also several small, often fascinating temples to pop into en route.

Walking Tour of the Barkhor

As you follow the flow of pilgrims past sellers of religious photos, suspect antiques and horse tackle you will see a couple of narrow alleys leading off to the north that are worth exploring. The alley that heads up to Dekyi Shar Lam just east of the Yak Hotel is notable for its outdoor pool tables where Khampas from the east of Tibet huddle over weathered felts and rarely pot a ball. Alleys also head north-east to the bustling market area of the **Tromsikhang**. One busy alley heads south from here back down to the Barkhor.

BARKHOR AREA

PLACES TO STAY		OTHER		30	No 2 Minibus Stand
4	Hotel Kyi Chu	36	Barkhor Café		(to Norbulingka)
9	Yak Hotel; Shigatse Travels	44	Makye Amye Restaurant	31	Tibetan Traditional Hospital
16	Kirey Hotel; Tashi II				(Mentsikhang)
	Restaurant	**OTHER**		33	Minibuses to Drepung
17	Gang Gyen Hotel	1	Tsomeling		Monastery
21	Banak Shol Hotel;	2	Tent Workshop	34	Minibuses to Tsurphu
	Kailash Restaurant	5	Mount Green Trekking;		Monastery; Buses to Ganden,
22	Tashi Targyel Hotel		Jingpa Communications		Samye & Tsetang
23	Pentoc Guesthouse	7	Tibet Nyingchi Tour	35	City Bus Station
27	Snowlands Hotel		Corporation	37	Ticket Office for Bus
		11	Buy & Sell Antiques Shop		to Ganden
PLACES TO EAT		12	Minibuses to Shigatse,	38	Jamkang Temple
3	Friend's Corner Restaurant		Samye & Naqu	39	Mani Lhakhang
6	Tashi I Restaurant	13	Gyüme (Lower Tantric	40	Gongkar Chöde Chapel
8	Third Eye Restaurant		College)	41	Meru Nyingba Monastery
10	Crazy Yak Saloon	14	Meru Sarpa Monastery	42	Thangka Workshops
19	Muslim Restaurant	15	Discount Shops	43	Xinhua Bookstore (Branch)
25	Dumpling Restaurant		(Wholesale Food)	45	Karmashar Temple
28	Snowlands Restaurant	18	Bank of China	46	Main Mosque
29	Alougang Restaurant		(Branch Office)	47	Ani Sangkhung Nunnery
	(Pink Curtain)	20	Cinema	48	Mosque
32	Welcome Restaurant	24	Niwei Travel	49	Lho Rigsum Lhakhang
		26	Snowlands Laundry		

Continuing around the Barkhor clockwise you'll soon see a small building on the right, set off from the main path but very much part of the pilgrim circuit. This is the **Mani Lhakhang**, a small chapel which houses a huge prayer wheel set almost continuously in motion. To the right of the building is the grandiose entrance of the old city jail.

If you head south from here, after about 10m you will see the entrance to the **Jamkhang** on the right. The ground floor of this small temple has a two storey statue of Maitreya (Tibetan: Miwang Jampa) the Future Buddha, flanked by rows of various protector gods. Pilgrims ascend to the upper floor to be blessed with a sprinkling of holy water (the temple is also known as the Water Blessing Temple) and the touch of a holy *dorje* (thunderbolt).

Continue down the alley following the prayer wheels, then pass through a doorway into the old **Meru Nyingba Monastery**. This small monastery is a delight. The main attraction is less the chapel than the courtyard

area, which is invariably crowded with Tibetans thumbing prayer beads or lazily swinging prayer wheels and chanting under their breath. Sit quietly among them for a while with a camera in your hand and someone will invariably invite you to take their picture. The chapel itself is administered by Nechung Monastery and so has several images of the Nechung oracle inside. The building, like the adjoining Jokhang, originally dates back to the 7th century but most of what you see today is of very recent construction. On the west side of the courtyard up some narrow stairs is the small **Gongkar Chöde** chapel.

From here you can return north or head east to join up with the Barkhor circuit. The eastern side of the circuit has more shops and even a couple of small department stores on the right side specialising in turquoise. The southern stretch has several *thangka* (religious painting) workshops, where you can watch the artists at work. The circuit finally turns north up to Barkhor Square and the entrance to the Jokhang.

Adorning the roof of the Jokhang, two deer flank the Wheel of Dharma symbolising Buddha's historic sermon in a deer park.

THE JOKHANG

Also known in Tibetan as the Tsuglhakhang, the Jokhang is the most revered religious structure in Tibet. Although little remains of its 7th century origins and most of the sculptures that adorn its interior post-date the Cultural Revolution, the Jokhang, bustling with worshippers and redolent with mystery, is an unrivalled Tibetan experience.

Entry is free (except for tour groups, people with guides, etc who pay Y25). The inner chapels are open daily except Sunday from around 8 am to midday and sometimes from 3 to 5.30 pm, though the outer halls and the roof are effectively open daily from sunrise to sundown if you enter by the side door to the right of the main entrance.

History

Estimated dates for the Jokhang's founding range from 639 to 647. Construction was initiated by King Songtsen Gampo to house a Buddha image, Akshobhya (Tibetan: Mikyöba), brought to Tibet as part of the dowry of his Nepalese wife Princess Bhrikuti. At the same time the Ramoche Temple was also constructed to house another Buddha image, Jowo Sakyamuni (Tibetan: Sakya Thukpa) brought to Tibet by his Chinese wife Princess Wencheng. It is thought that after the death of Songtsen Gampo, Jowo Sakyamuni was moved from Ramoche for its protection and hidden in the Jokhang by Princess Wencheng. The image has remained in the Jokhang ever since (Jokhang, or Jowokhang, means 'chapel of the Jowo'), and is the most revered Buddha image in all of Tibet.

Princess Wencheng is said to have chosen the site of the Jokhang, and just to be difficult she chose Lake Wothang. The lake had to be filled in, but it is said that a well in the precincts of the Jokhang still draws its waters from those of the old lake. Over the years, many legends have emerged around the task of filling in Lake Wothang. The most prominent of these is the story of how the lake was filled by a sacred goat (the Tibetan word for 'goat', ra is etymologically connected with the original name for Lhasa – Rasa). A small carving of the goat can be seen in the Chapel of Maitreya on the south wall of the Jokhang's ground floor inner sanctum.

Over the centuries, the Jokhang has undergone many renovations, but the basic layout is ancient and differs from many other Tibetan religious structures – one crucial difference is the east-west orientation of the building, said to face towards Nepal to honour Queen Bhrikuti. Alterations were undoubtedly undertaken during the many centuries that Lhasa fell from prominence but the most drastic renovations took place during the reign of the fifth Dalai Lama in the 17th century. Lhasa returned to the centre stage of Tibetan affairs at this time and the Jokhang was enlarged accordingly. Only a few carved pillars and entrance arches remain from the original 7th century work of Newari artisans from Nepal's Kathmandu valley.

In the early days of the Cultural Revolution, much of the interior of the Jokhang was desecrated by Red Guards and many objects are thought to have been removed. At one stage the monks' quarters were renamed Guesthouse No 5 and it is claimed that part of the Jokhang was utilised as a pigsty. Since 1980 the Jokhang has been restored and, without the aid of an expert eye, there is little sign of the misfortunes that have befallen the temple in recent years.

Inside the Jokhang

In front of the entrance to the Jokhang is a forecourt generally crowded with prostrating pilgrims. Take a look at the paving stones worn smooth by centuries of devotion.

Just inside the entrance to the Jokhang are the **Four Guardian Kings** (Tibetan: Chokyong; Jokhang map key No 4), two on either side. Beyond this point is the **main assembly hall** (6) or *dukhang*, a paved courtyard that is open to the sky. There is not a lot to see here, except during festivals, when the hall is often the focus of ceremonies. At the end of the courtyard and just before the entrance to the interior of the Jokhang itself is a long altar marked by a row of flickering butter lamps.

Demoness Subduing Temples

Buddhism's interaction with Bön – a shamanistic folk religion of ghosts and demons – combined with the inhospitable high places of the Tibetan plateau has led to many fables about Buddhism's taming and domestication of Tibet. Along with Guru Rinpoche's fabulous exploits, the early introduction of Buddhism to Tibet is attended by the story of a vast, supine demoness whose body straddled all the high plateau.

It was Princess Wencheng, the Chinese wife of King Songtsen Gampo, who divined the presence of this demoness. Through Chinese geomantic calculations she established that the heart of the demoness lay beneath a lake in the centre of Lhasa, while her torso and limbs lay far away in the outer dominions of the high plateau. As in all such fables, the demoness can be seen as symbolic of the inhospitableness of Tibet and its need to be tamed before Buddhism could take root there. It was decided that the demoness would have to be pinned down.

The first task was to drain the lake in Lhasa of its water (read life-blood of the demoness) and build a central temple that would replace the heart of the demoness with a Buddhist heart. The temple built there was the Jokhang. A stake through the heart was not enough to put a demoness of this size out of action, however, and a series of lesser temples, in three concentric rings, were conceived to pin the extremities of the demoness.

There were four temples in each of these rings. The first are known as the *runo* temples and form a protective circle around Lhasa, pinning down the demoness' hips and shoulders. One of them is Tandruk Monastery in the Yarlung valley. The second group, known as the *tandrul* temples, pin the knees and elbows of the demoness. And the final group, known as *yandrul* temples, pin the hands and feet. These last temples are found as far away as Bhutan and Kham (Sichuan), though the location of two of them is unknown.

The Potala, Lhasa, is an inspiring architectural wonder to all and a symbol of hope for the Tibetan people.

RICHARD I'ANSON

RICHARD I'ANSON

RICHARD I'ANSON

THE BARKHOR

Following the crowds into the Barkhor circuit, there is a curious sensation of having slipped through time into a medieval carnival. This is one part of Lhasa that has resisted any invasion of the modern world. Pilgrims from Kham, Amdo and farther afield, step blithely around a prostrating monk and stop briefly to finger a jewel-encrusted dagger at a street stall; children dressed like bit players in a stage production of Oliver Twist tug at the legs of a foreign visitor and beg for Dalai Lama pictures; a line of monks sit cross-legged on the paving stones before their alms bowls muttering mantras.

The whole circuit is lined with stalls selling everything a Tibetan or visiting tourist could possibly need. Some of the stalls sport a wide variety of souvenir items of dubious quality (be prepared to bargain hard), others specialise: some in hats, others in carpets, some in *kathak* (prayer scarves) and prayer flags,

Right: Pilgrim's produce – dried fruit stall on the Barkhor circuit.

Bottom: Barkhor Square and distant Potala, as viewed from the roof of the Jokhang.

some in clothes – great browsing even if you are not in the mood for a purchase. One curiosity worth noting is that many of the stall keepers these days are Chinese. How times change. From razing monasteries to the ground and stripping monks of their vestments, the Chinese have moved to cashing in on the booming market for Tibetan religious items.

Souvenirs on sale in the colourful pilgrim's market around the Barkhor circuit.

Clockwise from top: Handwoven carpets, thangkas, decorated yak and sheep skulls, and vibrant textiles.

BRADLEY MAYHEW

TONY WHEELER

TONY WHEELER

TONY WHEELER

GARRY WEARE

BRADLEY MAYHEW

TONY WHEELER

TONY WHEELER

The Jokhang's golden roof ornaments and ornately carved eaves brackets bear silent witness to ritual and barter in the pilgrim's market on Barkhor Square.

Entry to the Jokhang proper is via a short, dark corridor punctuated midway by a chapel on either side. The chapel to the right (7) houses Naga, and the chapel to the left (8), fierce, red-faced Nojin, benign subterranean dragon-like creatures. Together they serve as protective deities.

The inner sanctum of the Jokhang houses its most important images and chapels. Most prominent are six larger-than-life statues that dominate the central area. In the foreground and to the left (9) is a 6m statue of Guru Rinpoche. The statue opposite it, to the right (11), is of Maitreya, the Future Buddha. At the centre of the hall, between and to the rear of these two statues is a 1000 armed Avalokiteshvara (Tibetan: Chenresig; 10). At the far right are two more Maitreya statues, one behind the other (12, 13), and to the far rear, behind Avalokiteshvara, is another statue of Guru Rinpoche encased in a cabinet (14).

Encircling this enclosed area of statues is a collection of chapels. Tibetan pilgrims circle the central area of statuary in a clockwise direction visiting the chapels en route. There are generally queues for the holiest chapels, particularly the Chapel of Jowo Sakyamuni.

The chapels, following a clockwise route, are as follows:

Chapel of Tsongkhapa & His Disciples (15) Tsongkhapa was the founder of the Gelugpa order, and you can see him seated centre, flanked by his eight disciples.

Chapel of the Buddha of Infinite Light (16) Currently closed. Just outside is a large chörten (17).

Chapel of the Eight Medicine Buddhas (18) The Eight Medicine Buddhas are recent and not of great interest.

Chapel of Avalokiteshvara (19) This chapel contains the Jokhang's most important image after the Jowo Sakyamuni. Legend has it that the 1000 armed statue of Avalokiteshvara sprang spontaneously into being and combines aspects of King Songtsen Gampo, his wives and two wrathful protective deities. The doors of the chapel are one of the few remnants of the Jokhang's 7th century origins and were fashioned by Nepalese artisans.

Chapel of Maitreya (20) Inside are statues of Maitreya and four smaller bodhisattvas: Manjushri (Tibetan: Jampelyang), Avalokiteshvara, Vajrapani (Chana Dorje) and Tara (Drölma); Amitabha (Öpagme) and Tsongkhapa.

Chapel of Tsongkhapa (21) This chapel's image of Tsongkhapa, founder of the Gelugpa order, was commissioned by the subject himself and is said to be a precise resemblance. It is the central image to the left of the raised chapel.

THE JOKHANG

UPPER FLOOR

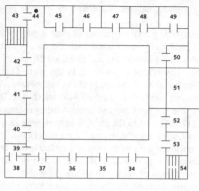

0   5   10 m
Approximate Scale

GROUND FLOOR

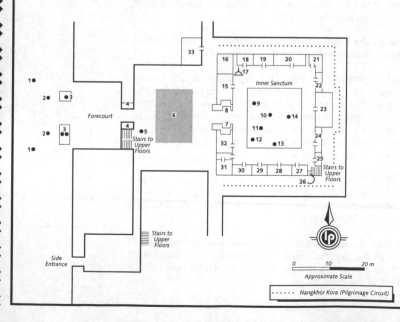

Forecourt

Inner Sanctum

Stairs to Upper Floors

Stairs to Upper Floors

Side Entrance

Stairs to Upper Floors

0   10   20 m
Approximate Scale

· · · · · Nangkhor Kora (Pilgrimage Circuit)

Chapel of the Buddha of Infinite Light (22) This is the second of the chapels consecrated to Amitabha, the Buddha of Infinite Light. The entrance is protected by two fierce deities, a red Hayagriva (Tibetan: Tamdrin) and a blue Vajrapani. There are also statues of the eight bodhisattvas. Pilgrims generally pray here for the elimination of impediments to viewing the most sacred images of the Jokhang, Jowo Sakyamuni, which waits in the next chapel.

Outside the chapel are statues of King Songtsen Gampo with his two queens and also Guru Rinpoche (with a big nose).

Chapel of Jowo Sakyamuni (23) The most important shrine in Tibet, this chapel houses an image of Sakyamuni at the age of 12 years. You enter via an anteroom containing two protector statues: Achala (Tibetan: Miyowa) and Vajrapani and the Four Guardian Kings. The 1.5m statue of Sakyamuni is covered in silks and jewellery and flanked by silver pillars with dragon motifs. Pilgrims touch their forehead to Sakyamuni's left leg before being tapped on the back by a monk bouncer when it's time to move on.

THE JOKHANG

1	Prayer Poles	28	Chapel of Maitreya
2	Incense Burners	29	Chapel of the Hidden Jowo
3	Stele	30	Chapel of the Seven Buddhas
4	Guardian Kings	31	Chapel of the Nine Amitayus
5	Ticket Office	32	Chapel of the Kings
6	Main Assembly Hall	33	Chapel of Tara
7	Naga Chapel	34	Chapel of Lhobdak Namka
8	Nojin Chapel		Gyaltsen
9	Guru Rinpoche Statue	35	Chapel of Sakyamuni
10	Avalokiteshvara Statue	36	Chapel of Eight Medicine
11	Maitreya Statue		Buddhas
12	Maitreya Statue	37	Chapel of Sakyamuni
13	Maitreya Statue	38	Chapel of Five Protectors
14	Guru Rinpoche Statue	39	Anteroom
15	Chapel of Tsongkhapa	40	Chapel of Three Kings
	& His Disciples	41	Chapel of Songtsen Gompo
16	Chapel of the Buddha of	42	Chapel of Avalokiteshvara
	Infinite Light	43	Chapel of Sakyamuni
17	Chörten	44	Prayer Wheel
18	Chapel of the Eight Medicine	45	Closed
	Buddhas	46	Closed
19	Chapel of Avalokiteshvara	47	Closed
20	Chapel of Maitreya	48	Closed
21	Chapel of Tsongkhapa	49	Closed
22	Chapel of the Buddha of	50	Chapel of Songtsen
	Infinite Light		Gampo
23	Chapel of Jowo Sakyamuni	51	Zhelre Lakhang
24	Chapel of Maitreya	52	Chapel of Guru Rinpoche
25	Chapel of Avalokiteshvara	53	Chapel of Samvara
	(Riding a Lion)	54	Palden Lhamo Statues
26	Guru Rinpoche Shrine	55	Tantric Chapel (Pelchok
27	Chapel of Amitayus		Dukhang) (third floor)

To the rear of Sakyamuni are statues of the seventh and 13th Dalai Lamas, Tsongkhapa and 12 standing bodhisattvas.

Chapel of Maitreya (24) The Maitreya enshrined here is a replica of a statue that came to Tibet as part of the dowry of Princess Bhrikuti, King Songtsen Gampo's Nepalese wife. Surrounding the statue are eight images of Tara, a goddess who is seen as an embodiment of the enlightened mind of Buddhahood and who offers protection against the Eight Fears – hence the eight statues.

Chapel of Avalokiteshvara (Riding a Lion) (25) Look to the left of the chapel for this – not the largest of the statues within – statue of Avalokiteshvara on the back of a lion. The other statues of the chapel are all aspects of Avalokiteshvara.

Some pilgrims exit this chapel and then follow a flight of stairs to the next floor, while others complete the circuit on the ground floor. If you're chapelled out (you've seen the important ones already) continue on upstairs, but look out first for a small hole in the wall which pilgrims place their ear up against to hear the beating wings of a mythical bird that lives under the Jokhang.

Guru Rinpoche Shrine (26) Two statues of Guru Rinpoche and one of King Trisong Detsen can be found next to the stairs. Next to the shrine is a painting of the Medicine Buddha and some fine murals protected by an iron grill.

Chapel of Amitayus (27) Inside are nine statues of Amitayus (Tibetan: Tsepame), the red Buddha of Longevity, along with images of both Green and White Tara.

Chapel of Maitreya (28) This, another Maitreya chapel, houses the Maitreya statue that is borne around the Barkhor on the 25th day of the first lunar month for the Mönlam festival. The Maitreya's yearly excursion is designed to hasten the arrival of the Future Buddha.

Manjushri and Avalokiteshvara flank the Buddha. Look out also for the carving of the sacred goat mentioned in the Jokhang History section earlier in this chapter.

Chapel of the Hidden Jowo (29) This is the chapel where Princess Wencheng is said to have hidden Jowo Sakyamuni for safekeeping after the death of her husband. Inside is a statue of Amitabha and the Eight Medicine Buddhas.

From this point there are several chapels of limited interest to non-Tibetologists. The **Chapel of the Seven Buddhas** (30) is followed by the **Chapel of Nine Amitayus** (31). The last of the ground-floor chapels is the **Chapel of the Kings** (32) which contains some original statues of Tibet's earliest kings. The central figure is Songtsen Gampo, and he is flanked by images of King Trisong Detsen (left) and King Ralpachen (right). On the wall outside the chapel is an interesting mural depicting the construction of the Jokhang and the Potala.

Upper Floor

At this point (if you did not do so earlier) you should return to the rear of the ground floor and climb the flight of stairs to the upper floor of the Jokhang. The upper floor of the Jokhang's inner sanctum is also ringed with chapels, though some of them are closed. Notice the doorframes of the **Chapel of Samvara** (53) and the **Chapel of Guru Rinpoche** (52), which date back to the 7th century.

As you begin the circuit, you will pass two new rooms (35, 37) featuring **Sakyamuni** flanked by his two main disciples and one (36) featuring the **Eight Medicine Buddhas**. The chapel in the south-west corner is the **Chapel of Five Protectors** (38) and has some fearsome statues of Hayagriva, Shri Devi (Tibetan: Palden Lhamo) and other protector deities. Next is the **Chapel of the Three Kings** (40), dedicated to Songtsen Gampo, Trisong Detsen and Ralpachen. Also featured in the room are Songtsen Gampo's two wives, various ministers and symbols of royalty such as an elephant and horse.

Also worth a look is the **Chapel of Songtsen Gampo** (41), the principal Songtsen Gampo chapel in the Jokhang. It is positioned in the centre of the western wall (directly above the entrance to the ground-floor inner sanctum). The king is flanked by his two consorts, his Nepalese wife to the left and Chinese wife to the right. His *chang* (barley beer) container is placed in front of him.

Most of the other rooms are currently closed, the main exception being the meditation cell or **Chapel of Songtsen Gampo** (50) to the south of the floor's north-eastern corner, which has an incredible carved doorway smeared with decades of yak butter. Before you leave the second floor by the stairs in the south-east corner, ascend half a floor up to two statues of the protectress Shri Devi (54), one wrathful, the other benign. You can sometimes gain access to a **Tantric Chapel** (55) up on the third floor.

Other Things to See

After exploring the interior of the Jokhang, the best part is arguably spending some time on the **roof**. There are various levels with stunning views of the sweeping, gilded roofs of the Jokhang, sometimes with the Potala as a breathtaking backdrop. It is also possible to find monks debating up here in the afternoon. The orange coloured building on the north side holds the private quarters of the Dalai Lama.

Back on the ground floor, if you're not utterly exhausted you could have a brief look at the **Tara Chapel** (33), featuring statues of the 21 manifestations of this bodhisattva.

It's worth finishing off a visit with a walk around the **Nangkhor**, the circuit of prayer wheels that encircles the Jokhang's inner sanctum.

THE POTALA

The Potala is Lhasa's cardinal landmark and a structure that deserves a place as one of the wonders of eastern architecture. It looks best from a distance and it can be viewed and photographed from various places around town – notably from the top of Chagpo Ri.

The Potala is a structure of massive proportions, an awe-inspiring place to explore, but still many visitors come away slightly disappointed. Unlike the Jokhang, which hums with activity, the Potala lies dormant like a huge museum, and the lifelessness of the building constantly reminds visitors that the Dalai Lama has been forced to take his government elsewhere. That said, your first sight of the Potala will be a magical moment that you will remember for a long time. It's hard to take your eyes off the place.

Opening hours for the Potala are Monday to Friday from 9 am to 12.30 pm, though groups can sometimes get access in the afternoons at around 3.30 pm and at weekends. It's worth getting there early as there's a lot to see and the lower rooms in particular tend to close early.

There is a high mark-up on the entry charge for 'foreign friends' – Y40 as opposed to the Y1 paid by locals and pilgrims. More annoying are the extra charges you have to pay to get access to the roof and the exhibition room, both Y10.

Photographs of the interior of the Potala are only allowed after

paying a fee of Y50. This is generally enforced, though if you find yourself alone in a room with a monk you can occasionally get away with a polite request – though don't count on it.

History

Marpo Ri, the 130m high 'Red Hill' that commands a view of all Lhasa, was the site of King Songtsen Gampo's palace in the 7th century, long before the construction of the present-day Potala. There is little to indicate what this palace looked like, but it is clear that royal precedent was a major factor in the fifth Dalai Lama's choice of this site when he decided to move the seat of his Gelugpa government from Drepung Monastery to more spacious quarters.

Work began first on the Potrang Karpo, or White Palace, in 1645. The nine storey structure was completed three years later, and in 1649 the fifth Dalai Lama moved from Drepung Monastery to his new residence. However, the circumstances surrounding the construction of the larger Potrang Marpi, or Red Palace, are subject to some dispute. It is agreed that the fifth Dalai Lama died in 1682 and his death was concealed until the completion of the Red Palace 12 years later in 1694. In some accounts, the work was initiated by the regent who governed Tibet from 1679 to 1703 and foundations were laid in 1690 (after the fifth's death). In other accounts, the Red Palace was conceived by the fifth Dalai Lama as a funerary chörten and work was well under way at the time of his death. In any event,

Early 19th century etching of the Potala by Thomas Allom.

the death of the fifth Dalai Lama was not announced until he was put to rest in the newly completed Red Palace.

There is some scholarly debate concerning the Potala's name. The most probable explanation is that it derives from the Tibetan name for Avalokiteshvara's Pure Land, also known as Potala. Given that Songtsen Gampo and the Dalai Lamas are maintained to be reincarnations of Avalokiteshvara, this connection is compelling.

Since its construction, the Potala has been the home of each of the successive Dalai Lamas, although since construction of the Norbulingka summer palace in the late 18th century, it has served only as a winter residence. It was also the seat of the Tibetan government, and with chapels, cells, schools for religious training and even tombs for the Dalai Lamas it was virtually a self-contained world.

The 13th Dalai Lama undertook some renovation work in the early 20th century, demolishing sections of the White Palace to expand some chapels. The Potala was also shelled briefly during the 1959 popular uprising against the Chinese. Fortunately, and miraculously, the damage was not extensive. The Potala was also spared during the Cultural Revolution, reportedly at the insistence of Zhou Enlai (a Chinese leader), who is said to have deployed his own troops to protect it. The Potala was reopened to the public in 1980 and final touches to the US$4 million renovations were completed in 1995.

Inside the Potala

Entrance to the Potala is via Shöl village nestled at the southern foot of Marpo Ri. It was once Lhasa's red light district as well as housing a prison, printing press and some ancillary government buildings. Today it is an undistinguished cluster of Tibetan-style buildings and gift shops. Two steep access ramps snake up the southern side of the hill from Shöl and will almost certainly leave you puffing (there is also a northern ramp which may offer access to the Potala on days that it is officially closed). Visitors who arrive by car can drive to the top of the Potala (west side) and then walk down floor by floor.

The eastern entrance to the Potala takes you into **Deyang Shar**, the external courtyard of the White Palace, where there is a small gift shop and some pit toilets with some of the best views in Lhasa. From here a flight of steps leads up into the White Palace and the former living quarters of the Dalai Lamas. From there, you continue up to the roof of the Red Palace and then make a gradual journey downwards into the labyrinthine bowels of the Potala, before exiting out of the northern side.

Roof As you arrive on the roof turn right into the private quarters of the 13th and 14th Dalai Lamas. The first room you come to is the **Throne Room**, where the Dalai Lamas would receive official guests. The large picture on the left is of the 13th Dalai Lama – the matching photo of the present Dalai Lama has been removed. The trail continues clockwise to the **Reception Hall**, which has a fine collection

RED PALACE OF THE POTALA

2ND FLOOR

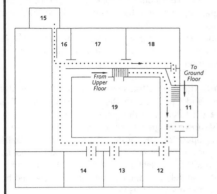

UPPER FLOOR

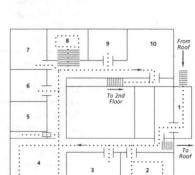

GROUND FLOOR

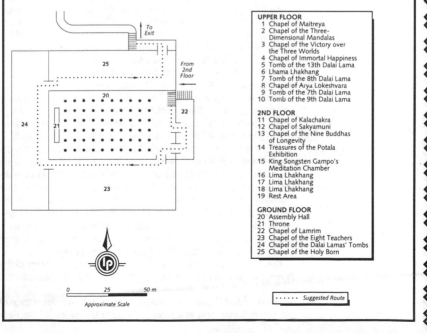

UPPER FLOOR
1 Chapel of Maitreya
2 Chapel of the Three-Dimensional Mandalas
3 Chapel of the Victory over the Three Worlds
4 Chapel of Immortal Happiness
5 Tomb of the 13th Dalai Lama
6 Lhama Lhakhang
7 Tomb of the 8th Dalai Lama
8 Chapel of Arya Lokeshvara
9 Tomb of the 7th Dalai Lama
10 Tomb of the 9th Dalai Lama

2ND FLOOR
11 Chapel of Kalachakra
12 Chapel of Sakyamuni
13 Chapel of the Nine Buddhas of Longevity
14 Treasures of the Potala Exhibition
15 King Songsten Gampo's Meditation Chamber
16 Lima Lhakhang
17 Lima Lhakhang
18 Lima Lhakhang
19 Rest Area

GROUND FLOOR
20 Assembly Hall
21 Throne
22 Chapel of Lamrim
23 Chapel of the Eight Teachers
24 Chapel of the Dalai Lamas' Tombs
25 Chapel of the Holy Born

0   25   50 m
Approximate Scale

· · · · · · Suggested Route

of bronze statues and fine views from the balcony. Next comes the **Meditation Room**, which still displays the ritual implements of the present Dalai Lama on a small table to the side of the room. The final room, the **Bedroom of the Dalai Lama** has some personal effects of the Dalai Lama on show, like his bedside clock. The mural above the bed is of Tsongkhapa, the founder of the Gelugpa order of which the Dalai Lama is the head.

From the roof you can catch some great views of Lhasa, before heading across the courtyard and up into the Red Palace. See the floor plans for orientation.

Upper (3rd) Floor The main attractions on the 3rd floor are the Chapel of Maitreya and the Tomb of the 13th Dalai Lama. The **Chapel of Maitreya** (Red Palace of the Potala map key No 1) contains an exquisite Maitreya image commissioned by the eighth Dalai Lama which stands opposite the throne of the successive Dalai Lamas. To the right of the throne is a wooden Kalachakra *mandala*. The walls are stacked with the collected works of the fifth Dalai Lama. The chapel was unfortunately damaged in a fire in 1984 (caused by an electrical fault) and many thangkas were lost.

From here you can ascend onto the roof of the Red Palace for an extra Y10 before continuing onto the other halls. The **Chapel of Three-Dimensional Mandalas** (2) houses jewel-encrusted mandalas of the three principal Tantric deities of the Gelugpa order. The **Chapel of the Victory Over the Three Worlds** (3) houses a library and displays examples of Manchu texts. The main statue is a golden Avalokiteshvara, while the picture by the exit is of the Manchu Chinese Emperor Qianlong. The **Chapel of Immortal Happiness** (4), once the residence of the sixth Dalai Lama whose throne remains, is now dedicated to Amitayus, the Buddha of Longevity.

From here a long corridor leads off the main circuit to a gallery which overlooks the **Tomb of the 13th Dalai Lama**. You can normally look down on the chörten from above and then descend to look at it at ground level but the room was closed at time of research.

The north-west corner houses the **Lhama Lhakhang** (6) and the **Tomb of the Eighth Dalai Lama** (7), constructed in 1805. From here steps lead up into the small but important **Chapel of Arya Lokeshvara** (8). Allegedly this is one of the few corners of the Potala that dates back to King Songtsen Gampo's 7th century palace. It is the most sacred of the Potala's chapels and the image of Arya Lokeshvara inside is the most revered image housed in the Potala. There are many other highly revered statues in the chapel, including those of Tara and Avalokiteshvara which flank the main statue.

The last two rooms on this floor are the jewel-encrusted **Tomb of the Seventh Dalai Lama** (9) and **Tomb of the Ninth Dalai Lama** (10).

Second Floor If you're exhausted already (still two floors to go!) you can rest your legs at a reception area in the middle of the floor

(19). Otherwise the first of the chapels you come to on the 2nd floor is the **Chapel of Kalachakra** (11). It is noted for its stunning three-dimensional mandala, which is over 6m in diameter and finely detailed with over 170 statues. A statue of the Tantric deity Kalachakra stands next to the mandala. The next two halls hold the **Chapel of Sakyamuni** (12) and the **Chapel of the Nine Buddhas of Longevity** (13).

The last room on the south side currently houses a **Treasures of the Potala Exhibition** (14). The collection is small but of a very high quality and includes such famous items as a three-dimensional mandala made of over 20,000 pearls, a crystal Sakyamuni Buddha and a bronze statue of a lotus whose leaves open out to reveal miniature statues inside. Other items include antique armour, festival costumes and thangkas. Entry to this room costs an additional Y10.

Continue clockwise to the north-western corner where you'll find a small corridor which leads to **King Songtsen Gampo's Meditation Chamber** (15), which, along with the Chapel of Arya Lokeshvara on the upper floor, is one of the oldest rooms in the Potala. Today it is crowded with statues, the most important being that of King Songtsen Gampo himself.

The next three rooms are all linked and are chock-a-block full of Chinese bronze statuary.

First Floor Currently closed.

Ground Floor The lower floor is reached via a number of steep, dark staircases and holds the beautiful **assembly hall** (20), which is the largest hall in the Potala and is its physical centre. The large throne that dominates one end of the hall was the throne of the sixth Dalai Lama (21). Four important chapels adjoin the hall.

The first chapel you come to is the **Chapel of Lamrim** (22). Lamrim means literally the 'gradual path', and is used to refer to the graduated stages that mark the path to enlightenment. The central figure in the chapel is Tsongkhapa, the founder of the Gelugpa order, with whom lamrim texts are usually associated.

The next chapel, the long **Chapel of the Eight Teachers** (23), is consecrated to eight Indian teachers who brought various Tantric practices and rituals to Tibet. The central figure is a silver statue of Guru Rinpoche (one of the eight), who is flanked by his consorts, as well as statues of the Eight Teachers on his left and a further eight statues of himself on the right.

In the west wing of the assembly hall is one of the highlights of the Potala, the awe-inspiring **Chapel of the Dalai Lamas' Tombs** (24). The hall is dominated by the huge 14m-high chörten of the 10th Dalai Lama, gilded with some 3700kg of gold. Flanking it are two smaller chörtens containing the 10th (right) and 12th (left) Dalai Lamas. Eight other chörtens represent the eight major events in the life of Buddha.

The final chapel visited is the **Chapel of the Holy Born** (25), which contains statues of the first four Dalai Lamas as well as larger statues of the fifth Dalai Lama and Sakyamuni. Also within the chapel is the tomb of the 11th Dalai Lama, who died at the age of 17 years.

At this point, you exit the Potala by a path that winds down to the prayer wheels of the Potala kora and Dekyi Nub Lam.

SITES AROUND THE POTALA

A morning visit to the Potala can easily be combined with an afternoon excursion to some of the sights nearby or a circuit of the Potala kora.

Drubthub Nunnery & Palha Lu-Puk

After you exit the Potala, a path takes you back down on to Dekyi Nub Lam at the site of Lhasa's old West Gate (former City Gate). Several chörtens have been rebuilt and you can get some good shots of the Potala from here.

On the other side of Dekyi Nub Lam, a road leads around the eastern side of Chagpo Ri, the hill that faces Marpo Ri, site of the Potala. Take this road past piles of mani stones and prayer flags to the **Drubthub Nunnery** on the right. The nunnery is dedicated to Tangtong Gyelpo, the 15th century bridge maker, medic, and inventor of Tibetan opera, whose white-haired statue graces its main hall.

After the nunnery, look for a flight of stairs 100m on the right. The stairs lead up to **Palha Lu-puk**, a cave temple that is said to have been the 7th century meditational retreat of King Songtsen Gampo. Entry costs Y15.

The main attraction of the cave is its relief rock carvings. Some of them are thought to be over 1000 years old. Altogether there are over 70 carvings of bodhisattvas in the cave and on the cave's central column. Work on the carvings was probably undertaken at three different historical periods, but the oldest are generally the ones lowest on the cave walls. Many of the carvings were damaged in the Cultural Revolution and have since been repaired.

The yellow building above Palha Lu-puk is a chapel that gives access to the smaller meditation cave of King Songtsen Gampo's Chinese wife, Princess Wencheng. It is of less interest than Palha Lu-puk, but worth a quick look if you are in the area.

Chagpo Ri

Apart from Palha Lupuk, there are a couple of other points of interest on Chagpo Ri (Iron Mountain), though the steel telecom mast that graces its summit is probably not one of them. The hill was once the site of Lhasa's principal Tibetan medical college. Founded in 1413 by the fifth Dalai Lama, it was destroyed in the 1959 popular uprising.

Today, the hill's main point of interest is a series of **rock carvings** on cliff walls at three different places. Altogether there are over 5000 carvings, some of them dating back to the 7th century. The first carvings are thought to have been commissioned by King Songtsen Gampo and executed by Nepalese artists. The tradition of carving images on the cliffs of Chagpo Ri continued for another 1000 years.

The best place to see the carvings is on the south-west end of the hill. Get there by following the Lingkhor kora (see the boxed text 'Lhasa's Pilgrimage Circuits' earlier in this chapter) or by taking a track that leads southwards from Dekyi Nub Lam. There are more carvings on the north-east end of the hill.

Finally, for stunning views of the Potala, take the trail that begins opposite the exit from the Potala and walk 20 minutes to the summit of Chagpo Ri.

Bompo Ri

Several hundred metres to the west of Chagpo Ri, Bompo Ri is another hill with a couple of interesting sights. At the foot of the hill, close to Dekyi Nub Lam, is one of Lhasa's four former royal temples, **Kunde Ling**. The *ling* (royal) temples were appointed by the fifth Dalai Lama, and it was from one of them that regents of Tibet were generally appointed. There are only a couple of restored chapels open, but it is worth a quick look all the same.

At the top of the hill is the **Gesar Ling**, a Chinese construction that dates back to the 18th century. It is the only Chinese-style temple in Lhasa and a quiet place for an afternoon walk. The main temple has a central statue of Gesar, flanked by Guru Rinpoche on the left and Ekajati, the Dzogchen deity on the right. A separate yellow chapel on the kora behind has statues of an orange-coloured Manjushri flanked by Sakyamuni, Vajrapani and Avalokiteshvara.

Lukhang Temple

Lukhang is a little-visited temple on a small lake island behind the Potala. The lake is in the Chingdröl Chiling (Liberation) Park, which is entered from north of the CAAC building or from directly behind the Potala. It is open daily and entry is Y5 (Y2 for locals).

The Lake of the Naga King in the park was created during the construction of the Potala. Earth used for mortar was excavated from here, leaving a depression that was later filled with water. Naga (also known as *lu*) are a subterranean dragon-like species which were thought to inhabit the area, and the Lukhang, or Chapel of the Dragon King, was built by the sixth Dalai Lama to propitiate them. You can see Luyi Gyalpo, the Naga King, at the rear of the ground floor of the Lukhang. He is riding an elephant and protective snakes rise from behind his head.

The Lukhang is celebrated for its 2nd and 3rd-floor murals which date from the 18th century. Bring a torch. The 2nd-floor murals tell a story made famous by a Tibetan opera, while the murals on the 3rd floor depict different themes on each of the walls – yogis demonstrating yogic positions (west), masters of Buddhism (east) and the life cycle as perceived by Tibetan Buddhists (north). The 3rd floor also contains a statue of 11 headed Avalokiteshvara as well as a meditation room used by the Dalai Lamas. It is reached by a flight of stairs around the back.

OTHER TEMPLES & MONASTERIES IN THE TIBETAN QUARTER

The old Tibetan quarter of Lhasa, around the Barkhor Square, has a number of smaller active temples and shrines little visited by foreigners. It is worth spending a morning or an afternoon checking them out. Generally you will receive a friendly reception. Try and keep it that way by respecting local customs (see the boxed text 'Visiting Monasteries' in the Facts about Tibet chapter) and asking politely for photographs.

Ramoche Temple

Ramoche is the sister temple to the Jokhang. It was originally built to house the Jowo Sakyamuni image that is now in the Jokhang. The principal image in Ramoche is Akshobhya, brought to Tibet in the 7th century as part of the dowry of King Songtsen Gampo's Nepalese wife. The image represents Sakyamuni at the age of eight years. It is said to have been badly damaged by Red Guards during the Cultural Revolution.

Built at the same time as the Jokhang, it is thought that, unlike the Jokhang, Ramoche was originally built in Chinese style. It was later rebuilt in Tibetan style and by the mid-15th century had become Lhasa's Upper Tantric College, Gyutö (see Gyume, following for information about Lhasa's Lower Tantric College). Today Ramoche is a little tired, and down at heel. It suffered extensive damage during the Cultural Revolution and, unlike other Lhasa sights, renovations seem to have been carried out with little zeal.

The Akshobhya image can be seen in the Tsangkhang, a small chapel at the far rear of the temple. There is a circumambulation circuit lined with prayer wheels around the perimeter of the temple. A steep Y20 entry fee is exacted on foreign visitors, and the zealous monk who collects the fee is not particularly interested in student cards.

Tsepak Lhakhang

As you exit Ramoche look for an entrance just to the right. Pass a row of prayer wheels to a delightful chapel with three large statues. The central image is Amitayus, the Buddha associated with longevity. He is flanked by Maitreya and Sakyamuni (the Buddha of the Past). The young monks tending this place are very friendly, which comes as a relief after the sullenness of the residents next door at Ramoche.

Gyume

Gyume, or the Lower Tantric College, is just down the road from the Yak Hotel, across from the Kirey Hotel. It is easy to miss – look for an imposing entrance set back from the road. This place gets very few foreign visitors.

Gyume was founded in the mid-15th century and in its time was one of Tibet's foremost Tantric training colleges. In Lhasa, its importance was second only to the monasteries of Sera and Drepung. Over 500 monks were once in residence, and students of the college underwent a physically and intellectually gruelling course of study. The college was thoroughly desecrated during the Cultural Revolution, and now only a handful of monks and novices are in residence here.

There is not a great deal to see nowadays at Gyume but the main dukhang (assembly hall) is worth a visit. The main statues are of Tsongkhapa, the 13th Dalai Lama and Sakyamuni. There are a few chapels on the 2nd and 3rd floors but these are often shut.

Gyume does not have regular opening hours and you may have to try several times before you find it open.

Meru Sarpa Monastery

This small but active monastery is opposite the Kirey Hotel. There is also a printing press on the grounds and workers are normally happy to show visitors if you can track one of them down. Look in the room above the main entrance to Dekyi Shar Lam.

Karmashar Temple

Situated about 150m south-east of Barkhor Square, this quiet but interesting temple was once the home of Lhasa's main oracle. Statues inside are of Guru Rinpoche, Avalokiteshvara, Tsongkhapa and the Karmashar oracle (far right). There are also some nice original murals of Atisha, Tsongkhapa and Amitayus on the upper walls.

Ani Sangkhung Nunnery

This small active nunnery (*ani* is Tibetan for nun) is the only one within the precincts of the old Tibetan quarter. Again, there is not a great deal to see, but the nuns are friendly and seem genuinely pleased to have a foreign guest. Many visitors end up paying for their visit with a free English lesson. There is an official Y10 entry charge, but the nuns rarely seem to demand it.

The site of the nunnery probably dates back to the 7th century but it was a monastery at least until the 15th century. The main hall is up a flight of stairs on the 2nd floor. The principal image is a 1000 armed Avalokiteshvara. A small alley to the side of the main chapel leads down to the old meditation chamber of King Songtsen Gampo.

The nunnery is a little difficult to find. It is on a narrow street south-east of the Barkhor Square. Look for the only yellow building on the street or ask for the *ani gompa*.

Muslim Quarter

There are a couple of mosques in the area south-east of the Barkhor circuit, serving Lhasa's 2000-strong Muslim population. It is dubious whether it is worth the effort of seeking them out (non-Muslims are denied entry) but the Muslim quarter is worth a stroll, especially at lunchtime on Friday when weekly prayers are held and the quarter is full of wispy beards and skull-caps. The main mosque is in a small market square south-east of the Barkhor and a newer mosque is west of the Ani Sangkhung Nunnery.

Both the Muslim quarter and the Ani Sangkhung Nunnery can be visited as part of the Lingkhor circuit (see boxed text 'Lhasa's Pilgrim Circuits' earlier in this chapter).

THE NORBULINGKA

The Norbulingka, the Summer Palace of the Dalai Lamas, about 10 minutes walk south of the Lhasa Hotel in the western part of town, rates behind the other points of interest in and around Lhasa, such as the Jokhang, the Potala, and also the Sera and Drepung monasteries. The gardens are poorly tended and the palaces themselves are something of an anticlimax, especially as most rooms are currently closed to the public. Avoid the zoo at all costs – it is thoroughly depressing.

Having said this, the Norbulingka is well worth a visit and the park is a great place to be at festival times and public holidays. During the seventh lunar month of every year the Norbulingka is crowded with picnickers for the Shötun (Yoghurt) festival. Traditional Tibetan opera performances are also held at this time.

The Norbulingka is open daily from 9 am to midday and 3.30 to 5.30 pm. There is a Y25 entry charge. Entry on Sundays costs Y1 but only the gardens are open.

History

The first summer palace to be constructed in the Norbulingka, or Jewel Park, was founded by the seventh Dalai Lama in 1755. Rather than using the palace as a simple retreat, he decided to use the wooded environs as a summer base from which to administer the country, a practice that was to be followed by each of the succeeding Dalai Lamas. The grand procession of the Dalai Lama's rich entourage relocating from the Potala to the Norbulingka grew to become one of the highlights of the Lhasa year.

The eighth Dalai Lama (1758-1804) initiated further work on the Norbulingka, expanding the gardens and digging a lake which can be found south of the New Summer Palace. The 13th Dalai Lama (1876-1933) was responsible for the three palaces in the north-west corner of the park and the 14th Dalai Lama built the New Summer Palace in 1956.

In 1959 the 14th Dalai Lama made his escape disguised as a Tibetan soldier from the Norbulingka. Unfortunately all the palaces of the Norbulingka were damaged by Chinese artillery fire in the popular uprising that followed the Dalai Lama's flight.

At the time the compound was surrounded by some 30,000 Tibetans determined to defend the life of their spiritual leader. Repairs have been undertaken but have failed to restore the palaces to their full former glory.

Palace of the Eighth Dalai Lama

This is the first of the palaces you come to from the entrance to the Norbulingka. Also known as the Kelsang Potrang, it was first used as a summer palace by the eighth Dalai Lama and was used by every Dalai Lama to the 13th. It is of limited interest to visitors today. Only the main audience hall is open, which features 65 hanging thangkas and a throne backed by statues of the Eight Medicine Buddhas.

New Summer Palace

The New Summer Palace, or Takten Migyü Potrang, in the centre of the park was built

by the present (14th) Dalai Lama between 1954 and 1956 and is without a doubt the most interesting of the Norbulingka palaces.

The first of the rooms you visit is the **Dalai Lama's Audience Chamber**. Note the murals on the chamber's walls. They depict the history of Tibet in 301 scenes (but don't bother looking for the Cultural Revolution). As you stand with your back to the window the murals start on the left hand wall with Sakyamuni Buddha and show the mythical beginnings of the Tibetan race and the first agricultural field in Tibet. The wall in front depicts the building of the circular monastery of Samye, as well as Ganden, Drepung and others. The right wall contains the histories of the Dalai Lamas, concluding with he reincarnation of the current Dalai Lama.

Next come the **Dalai Lama's Private Quarters**, which consists of a meditation chamber and a bedroom. The rooms have

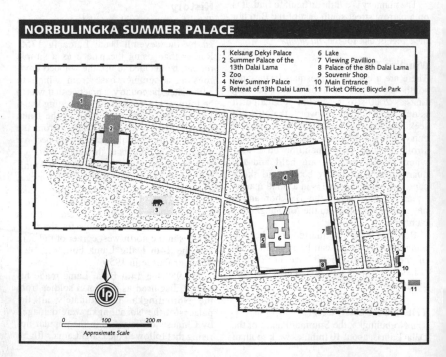

NORBULINGKA SUMMER PALACE

1 Kelsang Dekyi Palace
2 Summer Palace of the 13th Dalai Lama
3 Zoo
4 New Summer Palace
5 Retreat of 13th Dalai Lama
6 Lake
7 Viewing Pavillion
8 Palace of the 8th Dalai Lama
9 Souvenir Shop
10 Main Entrance
11 Ticket Office; Bicycle Park

0   100   200 m
Approximate Scale

Sera Monastery
One of Lhasa's great Gelugpa monasteries, which survived the Cultural Revolution better than most.

Lhasa
The treasures of the once forbidden city can still be experienced despite Chinese encroachment.
Top left: New Summer Palace, the Norbulingka. **Top right:** Woodcarvings, Barkhor Square.
Middle left: Cardsharps? **Bottom left:** Setting prayers in motion, Barkhor circuit.
Bottom right: Monastery door, Drepung.

been maintained (almost!) exactly as the Dalai Lama left them, and apart from the usual Buddhist images they contain the occasional surprise: a Phillips radiogram and a stylish European bed among other things.

The **assembly hall**, where the Dalai Lama would address heads of state, is home to a gold throne backed by cartoon-style murals of the Dalai Lama's court (left) and all 14 Dalai Lamas (right). Look out for the British representative Hugh Richardson in a top hat and several Mongolian ambassadors. The first five of the Dalai Lamas on the right hand wall lack the Wheel of Dharma, symbolising their lack of governmental authority. The final room to be visited is the meeting room of the Dalai Lama's mother.

South of the New Summer Palace is the artificial lake commissioned by the eighth Dalai Lama. The only pavilion open here during the time of research was the personal retreat of the 13th Dalai Lama in the south-western corner, featuring a stuffed tiger in the corner.

Summer Palace of the 13th Dalai Lama

The Summer Palace of the 13th Dalai Lama (Chensek Potrang) is in the western section of the Norbulingka, just north-west of the zoo (the shrieks of deranged monkeys should be warning enough to give the zoo a wide berth).

There is not a lot to see in the two storey palace, but it is worth a visit all the same.

The First Wheels in Lhasa

There used to be three dilapidated vehicles slowly rusting away in the gardens of the Norbulingka. The 1931 Dodge and two 1927 Austins were brought to Tibet in pieces on the backs of yaks and delivered to the 13th Dalai Lama as gifts. It was not until the 1950s that the present Dalai Lama got the vehicles going – they were then the only cars in Lhasa. They soon ran out of petrol.

The ground floor assembly hall holds the 13th Dalai Lama's throne and is stuffed full of various buggies, palanquins and bicycles. The 2nd floor living quarters are currently closed.

Close to the Chensek Potrang is another, smaller building, the Kelsang Dekyi Palace, also built by the 13th Dalai Lama.

OTHER LHASA SIGHTS
Tibetan Traditional Hospital

The original Tibetan Traditional Hospital (Mentsikhang) of Lhasa sat atop Chagpo Ri opposite the Potala. It was destroyed by artillery fire in the 1959 uprising. This one, on the north side of Yuthok Lam, was set up by the 13th Dalai Lama in 1916.

Tibetan medical science is an arcane field whose theories are backed up by Tantric texts. Diagnosis is largely carried out by taking various pulses, and illnesses are thought to result from imbalances between 'humours'. It obviously owes something both to Indian medicine and to Chinese medicine. The influence of the latter can be seen in the use of *moxibustion*, a treatment that involves burning a downy plant material on the skin. Surgery is never used in Tibetan medicine, and patients requiring treatment of this kind have to visit one of Lhasa's Chinese hospitals.

Tibetan doctors still train at the Tibetan Medical Hospital, and on the top floor the traditional medical and teaching thangkas are kept. If you are interested to see the clinic, you should make a polite request for one of the staff to show you around. Don't just go barging in. A short educational video is normally shown and a Y10 donation is expected.

Carpet Factory

You do not necessarily have to be in the market for a carpet to call into the carpet factory. The weaving process is still carried out by hand on vertical looms, and the factory makes for an unexciting but most interesting visit. It is in the south-east of town on Chingdröl Shar Lam near the Tibet University.

Tibetan Medicine

The basic teachings of Tibetan medicine share much with other Asian medical traditions, which according to some scholars made their way to the east via India from ancient Greece. While the western medical tradition treats symptoms that indicate a known medical condition (measles or mumps, say), the eastern medical tradition looks at symptoms as indications of an imbalance in the body and seeks to restore that balance.

It is wrong to assume, however, that Tibetan medicine was practiced by trained doctors in clinics scattered across the land. The Tibetan medical tradition is largely textual, derives from Indian sources and was studied in some monasteries in much the same way that Buddhist scriptures were studied. When Tibetans needed medical help they usually went to a local 'apothecary' who sold concoctions of herbs; equally, help was sought in prayers and good luck charms.

The theory of Tibetan medicine is based on an extremely complex system of checks and balances between what can be broadly described as three 'humours' (related to state of mind), seven 'bodily sustainers' (related to the digestive track) and three 'eliminators' (related to the elimination of bodily wastes). And if the relationship of the three humours of desire, egoism and ignorance with bodily functions were not complex enough, there is the influence of harmful spirits to consider. There are 360 harmful female influences, 360 harmful male influences, 360 malevolent Naga (water spirits) influences and finally 360 influences stemming from past karma. All these combine to produce 404 basic disorders and 84,000 illnesses!

How does a Tibetan doctor go about assessing the condition of a patient? The most important skill is pulse diagnosis. A Tibetan doctor is attuned to 360 'subtle channels' of energy that run through the body's skin and muscle, internal organs, and bone and marrow. The condition of these channels can be ascertained through six of the doctor's fingers (the first three fingers of each hand). Tibetan medicine also relies on urine analysis as an important diagnostic tool.

If Tibetan diagnostic theory is mainly Indian in influence, treatment owes as much to Chinese medicine as to Indian. Herbal concoctions, moxibustion and acupuncture are all used to restore balance to the body. Surgery was practiced in the early days of Tibetan medicine, but was outlawed in the 9th century when a king's mother died during an operation.

Lhasa Museum

There's a grand-looking new museum out in the west of town just opposite the Norbulingka Park. At time of research the building was closed and looked like staying that way but it might be worth asking about.

FESTIVALS

If it is at all possible, try and time your visit to Lhasa with one of the city's festivals. Pilgrims often flock to Lhasa at these times and the city's pilgrim circuits take on a colourful, party atmosphere. The New Year and Saga Dawa festivals are particularly exciting as thousands of pilgrims flood into town.

For a list of festivals in Lhasa see Cultural Events in the Facts for the Visitor chapter.

PLACES TO STAY

As a general rule of thumb, accommodation in Lhasa divides into inexpensive Tibetan-style accommodation in the central Barkhor area and less conveniently located upmarket digs on the outskirts of town. Almost all independent travellers head straight into the Barkhor area, where five Tibetan-style hotels dominate the backpacker market.

The simple reason for this is that this is the most interesting area of town, the service (while basic) is friendly in these hotels, and they are the best places to meet other travellers and get the current low-down on travel in Tibet.

PLACES TO STAY – BUDGET

Possibly the most popular place with individual travellers is the *Yak Hotel* (☎ 6323496). The hotel has two courtyards: one at the front and one to the rear. The rooms that front onto the rear courtyard are quietest, but at busy times of the year it will be difficult to find a vacant room. A shop next to reception sells soft drinks, beer and other essentials and there is a bicycle hire and Shigatse Travels office upstairs.

The Yak has a wide range of rooms available, including some excellent mid-range options (see Places to Stay – Mid-Range). Gloomy five or six-bed dorms cost Y25 per person and there are also some nice but dark doubles for Y90 in the back courtyard (rooms are quieter here and there's a nice sitting area). A few triples are also available at Y40 per bed. The availability of hot water has improved at the Yak over the last couple of years. Hot showers, in the far corner of the rear courtyard, are available most of the year from around 8 to 9 am and 5 to 7 pm.

The *Banak Shol* (☎ 6323829), once *the* place to stay back in the early days of independent travel, is the second most popular hotel among individual travellers. It is not as clean or as efficiently run as the Yak, but it does have a charm that the larger Yak doesn't. Guests can titillate themselves with the thought they have checked into a medieval monastic retreat (well, almost) as they enjoy the cosy Tibetan-style rooms fronted by verandas that face into the inner courtyard. In the evenings, guests sometimes retire to the roof for an impromptu party. The Kailash Restaurant on the 2nd floor has also taken off as one of Lhasa's most popular places to eat.

Four-bed dormitories are Y25. Pokey single rooms cost Y35 and all face onto the noisy main road. Doubles are better at Y60.

Prices vary according to the number of travellers in town. Laundry is free, though they won't wash your crusty socks after a week's trekking.

Snowlands (☎ 6323687), like the Banak Shol, is another of Lhasa's long-stayers. It was a favourite back in the mid-1980s and has changed very little since then (they certainly haven't cleaned the toilets). Many of Lhasa's repeat visitors, particularly those involved in carpet buying and aid work, seem to make this place their base, though they generally tend to look down their noses at the mere mortals who are passing through. Rooms, mainly doubles and five-bed dorms, are in a quadrangle that faces onto an inner courtyard.

Nowadays, Snowlands is quieter than the Yak or the Banak Shol, though you pay for your solitude with lower service standards. Dormitory beds with a locker are Y25. Double rooms cost Y60. The shower block in the corner of the courtyard has pretty reliable water round the clock though there's a frustrating lack of wash basins elsewhere.

The fourth and least popular of the Barkhor area's Tibetan-run hotels is the *Kirey Hotel* (☎ 6323462). This place deserves more custom than it gets. It is super friendly, clean and has reliable hot water from 9 am to 9 pm in the shower block around the back. Tashi II Restaurant is on the premises and there's a sitting area on the roof above reception. Laundry is free – put it in the bags provided and hand it in to reception before 9 am. The only grumble is the dodgy plumbing in the toilets. Beds in a three-bed dorm cost Y25, while beds in a comfortable double cost Y35.

The newest of the budget hotels is the *Pentoc Guesthouse* (☎ 6326686, fax 633 0700, email pentoc@public.east.cn.net), in a great location near the Snowlands, 50m north of Barkhor Square. It's a stylish place with some nice touches like free videos every night at 8 pm, print-outs of news reports and individual bed lights in the dormitories. Beds in clean but very small six-bed dorms cost Y30. Singles cost Y80 and doubles cost Y120. Prices vary throughout the season. Rooms overlooking the street can be noisy during the day.

In the unlikely event that all these are booked solid you might try the **Tashi Targyel Hotel** further up from the Pentoc and Snowlands. Beds in a clean, bright but characterless double are Y25, and some rooms even have a view of the Potala. Round-the-clock hot water is available in a washroom on the floor below.

PLACES TO STAY – MID-RANGE

The last couple of years have seen a rise in the number of mid-range options. Most of these are in shiny faceless Chinese hotels but the old backpacker hotels now offer excellent mid-range options and remain the best places to stay.

All of the budget hotels mentioned earlier offer mid-range doubles with private attached bathroom, carpet, TV etc. The **Yak Hotel** has excellent doubles with Tibetan-style décor for Y250 but these are often booked out by tour groups. The **Banak Shol** and **Snowlands** both have doubles for around Y250 and some nicely decorated Tibetan-style three-bed suites for Y350. The **Kirey** has the best value doubles for Y120.

Most of the other mid-range options are Chinese-style hotels that are either bursting with tour groups or deserted and languishing in lifeless apathy. The one exception is the **Hotel Kyi Chu** (☎ 6338824, fax 6320234), a friendly and well-run choice west of Tashi I Restaurant. Room rates are Y180/280 for a carpeted single/double and Y350 for a well-furnished four-bed room. A 20% discount is given in winter (November to April inclusive). All rooms have private bathroom.

Other hotels include the **Sunlight Hotel** (☎ 6322227), about 1km east of the Barkhor circuit. This a lifeless kind of place with smoky standard doubles at Y280. It is quite a long trudge from here to the more interesting parts of town, and no bicycle hire is available.

The **Himalaya Hotel** (☎ 6322293) is on Lingkhor Shar Lam. Like the more upmarket Tibet Hotel, an attempt has been made to give this place something of a Tibetan character. The result is a slightly depressing fusion of Tibetan design and Chinese hotel management. Glum doubles are available from Y275. A new block of three-star rooms is being built.

A couple of other places with rates of between US$30 and US$40 for standard doubles include the **Gold Grain Hotel** (☎ 6330359, 14 Yuthok Lam), **Gang Gyen Hotel** (☎ 6337666) on Dekyi Shar Lam, the **Yinqiao Hotel** (☎ 6330663) near the telecom building on the corner of Lingkhor Chang Lam and Lingkhor Shar Lam, the **Airway Hotel** (☎ 6333442) just east of the Potala and the **Tibet Royal Hotel** (☎ 6333988, 51 Chingdröl Shar Lam). There's little difference between these Chinese-run hotels, though the Airway Hotel boasts views of the Potala from its west-facing rooms.

PLACES TO STAY – TOP END

Up until recently there was only one place in town that even approached international standards. However in 1997, the Holiday Inn group pulled out of Tibet under increasing pressure from pro-Tibetan groups. The hotel was returned to the government and it reverted to its original name, the **Lhasa Hotel** (☎ 6832221, fax 6835796). It is thought that eventually another large hotel chain will buy the lease for the hotel and take over where Holiday Inn left off.

Standards at the Lhasa Hotel have begun to slide but there is still a decent selection of restaurants and bars, international direct-dial phones, satellite TV, in-house movies, a clinic with both western and Tibetan doctors and over 480 air-con rooms. The hotel no longer has a travel department, but vehicles are available for hire at the front desk at rates that are quite competitive. There are also a couple of independent travel agencies based on the ground floor of the hotel.

Rates for economy doubles are around Y700, while standard doubles weigh in at around Y1147. Budget travellers who are looking for some comfort and a hot shower in the winter months (when hot water is generally not available at the other hotels around town) might want to ask about the economy triples. If you can get three people together and organise a discount, the result should be quite affordable.

A couple of hundred metres up the road from the Lhasa Hotel is the *Tibet Hotel* (☎ 6334966, fax 6836787). In keeping with its name, it strives to create a Tibetan ambience, but the results are somewhat surreal. Look for the wall frescoes of Tibetan landscapes set off by chandeliers and fairy lights. Service tends to dodder somewhere between apathy and incompetence, and there are sometimes water cuts. This said, the plush rooms come with nice touches such as a hair dryer, and are considerably cheaper than those at the Lhasa Hotel. Standard doubles are Y580.

Like the Lhasa Hotel, the Tibet Hotel has a host of guest services. International direct-dial phones, satellite TV and foreign exchange are all available.

The *Grand Hotel* (☎ 6826096) on Dekyi Nub Lam used to serve as the government guesthouse but now operates as a plush and comfortable three-star option with standard rooms for Y420.

All the above hotels offer a minimum 20% discount in the winter months (November to March inclusive). Prices quoted are high season.

PLACES TO EAT

The restaurant scene in Lhasa has improved immensely over the last few years, though sadly this is for the most part due to Han Chinese immigration. Most individual travellers stick to the Tibetan quarter around the Barkhor Square area when it comes to meals. Tibetan cooking may not be one of the world's most exciting cuisines, but there are a few Tibetan restaurants in this area that serve up some very tasty dishes.

Tibetan Quarter

Tashi's Restaurant (Tashi I) deserves a special mention. This place has been running for a while now, and despite increased competition continues to be a favourite. The service is very friendly, the prices are cheap and everything on the menu is good. Special praise is reserved for the *bobis* (chapatti-like unleavened bread), which most people order with seasoned cream cheese and fried vegetables or meat. Tashi's cheesecakes are to die for.

Tashi II in the Kirey Hotel offers the same dishes as the first Tashi restaurant and is a little quieter, though the décor is not quite as pleasant.

The *Kailash Restaurant* on the 2nd floor of the Banak Shol hotel is one of the best hotel restaurants. Prices are definitely higher than at the Tashi restaurants but dishes on offer include vegetarian lasagne and yak burgers (as good as those at the Lhasa Hotel and much cheaper). The roof is a great place for a beer in summer. The restaurant's breakfasts (muesli brought in from Kathmandu, among other things) have also achieved a devoted following.

The *Third Eye Restaurant*, not far from the Yak Hotel, offers good breakfasts and Nepalese food. Sizzlers are recommended for around Y18.

The *Alougang Restaurant*, also known as the Pink Curtain due to the curtain that hangs at the entrance, is popular with locals and travellers alike. There are some good stir-fried vegetable dishes available, but the most popular dishes are the curry potatoes, the 'lambs French fries' and the sweet and sour lamb (the latter is excellent). The 'Pink Curtain' is close to the No 2 minibus stand and a block west of Barkhor Square.

Snowlands Restaurant, attached to the Snowlands Hotel, is a slightly more upmarket place that serves a mix of Tibetan and Nepalese food in civilised surroundings. Most dishes are around Y25 to Y35.

Next door to the Yak Hotel is the *Crazy Yak Saloon*. It isn't as popular as it perhaps deserves to be. The food might be a little expensive and the menu a bit short, but what they have is very good. The Tibetan-style interior is also probably the best in this part of town and there's live music whenever a group is in town. The food is mainly Chinese with a couple of Tibetan items thrown in.

Down in the Barkhor Square area there are also a couple of restaurants. Both the

Welcome Restaurant and the *Barkhor Café* have roof-top dining areas which provide great views of the Jokhang and Barkhor Square. The food at the Barkhor Café is probably the better of the two (especially the breakfasts), though the Welcome Restaurant maintains a more Tibetan flavour. Prices are a little higher than elsewhere but a late afternoon beer enjoyed gazing over Barkhor Square is worth indulging in.

The prize for the best location in town must go to the *Makye Amye Restaurant* on the first floor of a building overlooking the south-east corner of the Barkhor circuit. This foreign-run restaurant serves decent western and Nepalese cuisine plus treats like great brownies and Kahlúa coffee. It has a pretty good vibe and, voyeurism aside, it's a great place to kick back with a beer or pot of tea and watch the Barkhor below. The future of the restaurant looks a little uncertain so don't be surprised if things change during the life of this book.

There are also many other local restaurants in the Tibetan quarter. Along Dekyi Shar Lam between the Kirey and Banak Shol hotels are a number of *Muslim restaurants*. One such restaurant can be found on Dekyi Shar Lam just east of the Bank of China. There are some excellent and cheap noodle dishes on offer such as *ganban mian*, a kind of stir-fried spaghetti bolognaise.

The *Friend's Corner Restaurant* on Dekyi Shar Lam not far from Tashi I currently has the best Chinese food in this part of town, though it is owned and run by a Tibetan couple. They serve most of the dishes listed in the Language chapter. The Han Chinese chef keeps threatening to leave so standards might change in the future.

West Lhasa

The best Chinese food in town is found in the west of town, which is predominantly Han Chinese. This area is such a long hike from the Tibetan quarter that few travellers make the effort.

In the vicinity of the Lhasa Hotel are some upmarket dining options, both Tibetan and Chinese. But the best upmarket restaurants in town are actually in the hotel itself. Travellers who can't afford the prices (and they are fairly expensive) should call in to the snack bar just off the foyer: *One Minzu Lane* (the hotel's address). This place has affordable coffee, sandwiches and sundaes. Afternoons often see this place crowded with refugees from the Tibetan quarter sipping on a coffee and wolfing down a banana split for Y28.

Still inside the Lhasa Hotel and next door to One Minzu Lane is the *Hard Yak Café*. Good meals – including the famous yak burger with French fries (Y65) – are available here for between Y60 and Y90. Other restaurants include the *Gya Se Kang* (Chinese food), the *Everest* (international buffet) and the *Himalaya* (Indian and Tibetan). The Y170 buffet price tag will put these out of reach for most travellers, but for those with some extra cash to spend on a splash-out meal this is some of the best food available in Lhasa.

A more modest restaurant opposite the Lhasa Hotel is the *Yeti Café* where you can get some unusual Tibetan dishes in very pleasant surroundings for around Y40 a dish.

Self-Catering & Trekking Supplies

Lhasa is the best place to stock up on food supplies for trips to Kailash and the Nepalese border. Instant noodles are readily available in a thousand flavours. Other popular buys include biscuits, peanuts, salted peas and various fruits in a jar.

In the Tibetan quarter the wholesale shops near the Kirey Hotel offer the best prices for basic food supplies and are the places to stock up for a long trip. The Lhasa Foreign Trade Building is also very well stocked.

The Tromsikhang Market area just south of here has a small selection of fresh vegetables, puffed rice and yoghurt. Ramoche Lam, the street leading to the Ramoche Temple, also has a small vegetable market, though the best local produce market lies in a covered lane just east of the Potala.

For imported luxury items like chocolate, biscuits and cornflakes check out the Pentoc

Guesthouse and shop. There is also a little bakery across from the CAAC office which sells cans of Pringles and Bordeaux wine among the cakes and pastries.

ENTERTAINMENT

There is not a great deal in the way of entertainment options in Lhasa. Evenings see most travellers heading off to one of the restaurants in the Tibetan quarter and then retiring to the Yak or Banak Shol hotels, which are sometimes the scene of an impromptu party. The *Kailash Restaurant* in the Banak Shol hotel often stays open late if there are enough customers guzzling beer and swapping stories of Tibetan adventures. *Makye Amye* is a good place for a beer or hard to find drinks such as Kahlúa, and sometimes stays open until the early hours if there are enough people around.

In the west of town near the Grand Hotel, *Gleckes Fresh Beer* (☎ 6826552) on Dekyi Nub Lam brews its own dark and lager-style beer. Prices are Y30 for a pitcher of light beer, Y38 for a dark beer and there's the standard Budweiser and San Miguel as well. Food is served but it's nothing special. Gleckes is open all day and closes at midnight.

Karaoke bars and discos are a recent addition to the nightlife scene. Generally not many travellers venture into these places and some of those who have claim to have been harassed by plain-clothed PSB. Several of the discos around town, however, have uniformed PSB as door staff. If you venture into any of these places you can expect to be monitored. Foreigners will be dissuaded from dancing with locals in no uncertain terms. It is best to avoid these places. There is no need to be overly paranoid, providing you keep a relatively low profile. Most are in the Chinese west of town though there is one across from Snowlands Hotel on the first floor.

Lhasa's cinemas are very unlikely to be showing anything you would actually want to watch, though the *Pentoc Guesthouse* shows free videos every night at 8 pm in its lobby.

Unfortunately there is almost nothing in the way of cultural entertainment in Lhasa. For performances of Tibetan opera and dancing you will probably have to wait for one of Lhasa's festivals (see Festivals earlier in this section). The *Tibetan Dance & Drama Theatre* opposite the Lhasa Hotel is mostly a lost cause, though it might be worth enquiring at the Lhasa Hotel whether there will be any performances that coincide with your visit – it is unlikely.

SHOPPING

Lhasa is no longer the backwater it once was, and it is now a reasonably good place to stock up on basic supplies. Bring your own medical supplies. Items such as water-purifying tablets are not easy to find.

Photography

It is still a good idea to come with your own film supplies, but slide film is now relatively easy to find in Lhasa (though slide processing is still impossible). A profusion of photographic shops are clustered around the entrance to the Workers' Cultural Palace, just east of the Potala square. Prices for 100ASA Sensia or Ektrachrome can normally be haggled down to around Y50 for 36 exposures. Print film is available everywhere.

Chinese black and white film is cheap and available everywhere but is amazingly expensive to process in Lhasa so you won't save much over colour film.

Clothes

For good-quality warm clothes it would be a good idea to think ahead and bring whatever you need. There are a couple of places around town selling down jackets and so on, but the quality is not very good and you will have a poor selection to choose from.

West of the Kirey Hotel on Dekyi Shar Lam are a couple of small operations selling army surplus jackets and so on. There is a better selection up on the 2nd floor of the Lhasa Foreign Trade Building in the west of town just before the Lhasa Hotel, including some down jackets and sleeping bags. The best quality down jackets cost around Y200.

Mount Green Trekking and Yeti Mountaineering have down jackets, fleeces and gloves; Mount Green's stock are made in Nepal while Yeti's are China made.

Long-Distance Travel & Trekking Equipment

For food supplies see Self-Catering & Trekking Supplies in the Places to Eat section earlier. For basic items such as thermoses and water canisters, the best place to shop is the Barkhor area. The lanes that run from the Tromsikhang Market down to the Barkhor circuit have numerous stalls selling everything from ropes and twine to enamel mugs.

Quality sleeping bags are almost impossible to find in Lhasa. Look out for notices at the Yak and Banak Shol hotels advertising used sleeping bags for sale. They usually get snapped up very quickly. Surprisingly, there are sometimes decent sleeping bags for sale on the 2nd floor of the Lhasa Foreign Trade Building, as well as useful things like penknives, enamel mugs etc.

Trekking gear is available for rent at Mount Green Trekking. For more information on trekking supplies see the Trekking chapter.

Canned oxygen is available from the Pentoc Guesthouse reception.

Souvenirs

Most travellers do their souvenir shopping on the Barkhor circuit. Expect to be offered some outrageous prices for anything you are interested in and then settle down for some serious haggling. There is an awful lot of junk for sale in this part of town, but even some of the junky items have a certain charm.

Popular purchases include prayer wheels, rings, daggers and prayer flags, all of which are fairly portable. There are carpet stalls at a couple of points on the Barkhor circuit. Some travellers buy a carpet or two and send them home. Those with a particular interest in carpets might want to check out the

carpet factory on Chingdröl Shar Lam, though it doesn't sport a particularly exciting selection.

There are a couple of thangka workshops on the south side of the Barkhor circuit and also one in a lane to the north of the Barkhor. There is also a tent workshop in the backstreets north of the Yak Hotel which sells ready-made tents and door hangings (around Y80) and which will make anything you ask of them in a day or so.

For better quality souvenir items at marked-up prices, look out for the antique shops tucked away behind the stalls on the Barkhor circuit. The Buy & Sell Antiques Shop opposite the Yak Hotel is another place worth checking out. The Pentoc Guesthouse shop has some interesting items such as yak tails, hand-made Tibetan paper, and fabulous kitsch such as *om mani padme hum* fridge magnets! They also have the best postcards in town as well as Tibetan calendars.

Most tourist sites have some souvenir shops. The shops around the Potala offer a selection of oil paintings by local artists, thangkas, antiques, souvenir books, postcards and the best selection of T-shirts in town, though prices have been pushed up by the tour groups. Another souvenir shop just inside the entrance to the Norbulingka has probably the best selection of paintings and colour coffee-table books about Tibet. They are hefty items but you could always send them home. There are more shops outside the Norbulingka.

Most of these kind of shops are run by Han Chinese from other provinces. Tibetans sell trinkets from blankets outside the Potala and the Lhasa Hotel.

Finally, both the Tibet Hotel and the Lhasa Hotel have souvenir shops. Most of the items for sale in both these shops are fairly expensive, but at least the quality is good.

GETTING THERE & AWAY

While there are theoretically a number of ways to get to Lhasa, the main approach routes are by air from Chengdu (in Sichuan), by bus from Golmud (in Qinghai), and overland or by air from Kathmandu. For information on these services into Tibet see the Getting There & Away chapter.

Air

At the time of writing Lhasa had air connections to Kathmandu (Tuesday, Thursday and Saturday, Y1850), Chengdu (twice daily, Y1200), Chongqing (Tuesday, Y1300) and Xi'an (Wednesday, Y1320) – a twice weekly flight to Beijing required a change of aircraft in Xi'an or Chengdu. There have been rumours of a Hong Kong or a Canton flight for years though nothing has yet materialised.

For information on flights from Chengdu or Kathmandu into Lhasa see the Getting There & Away chapter. Flying *out* of Lhasa is considerably easier and cheaper than flying in. No permits are necessary – just turn up to the CAAC (☎ 6333446) booking office on Nyangdren Chang Lam and buy a ticket, preferably several days in advance of your intended departure date. The bank at the CAAC office doesn't change travellers cheques so bring the cash with you. Discounted fares of up to 25% are sometimes available on the Kathmandu flight.

Lhasa's Gongkar airport is 95km from town (see the Getting Around section later in this chapter). There is no Tibet Tourism Bureau (TTB) permit check on arrival from Chengdu, though you should hold on to your luggage stub as officials check these zealously. If you are departing for or arriving from Kathmandu you may be faced with a Y100 fine if you are travelling on an individual visa with no TTB permit. Departure tax is Y50 for domestic flights, Y90 to Kathmandu.

Bus

The only bus service between Lhasa and the outside world is to Golmud in Qinghai Province. The journey takes anywhere between 30 and 50 hours. Mishaps of one sort or another are almost inevitable, and it is not unusual to arrive in Lhasa at an hour when the city is the domain of rabid dogs and all the hotels are closed – you will just have to hammer on the doors and get the staff out of bed.

Tickets for buses from Lhasa to Golmud can be bought at the main bus station south of the Lhasa Hotel. Prices are Y424 for a Japanese sleeper bus or Y244 for a clapped-out Chinese bus. There are also sleeper buses which continue on all the way to Xining, the capital of Qinghai Province, for Y664 (foreigners' price). Hard-core masochists might be attracted by the epic nonstop 3287km sleeper bus to Chengdu (3 days and four nights, Y1004), though most sane people will take the plane for an extra Y200. The bus travels via Golmud and Xining rather than the more direct and pulse-quickening Sichuan Tibet Highway. For more information on the Lhasa-Golmud route see the Qinghai-Tibet Highway section of the Getting There & Away chapter.

Other services operating from the main bus station include those to Tsetang (three daily, Y60), Shigatse (daily, Y80), Chamdo (daily, Y302) and Bayi (Y310), though foreigners might have problems getting on the last two buses. All prices quoted are foreigners' prices, which are double local price.

Few foreigners use the bus station's Shigatse service as there are minibuses departing from in front of the Kirey Hotel from 7 am. They do the trip quicker than the public buses and cost only Y38. Since the completion of the Lhasa-Shigatse Highway, there is no public transport direct to Gyantse. It is necessary to travel to Shigatse first and then change to a private minibus or a public bus.

Lhasa's city bus station is located southwest of the Barkhor Square and has several departures daily to both Medro Gungkar (Chinese: *mòzhú gongka*) to visit Drigung Til Monastery, and Lhundrub (*línzhou*) to visit Talung Monastery, and for the road to Reting Monastery.

Buses to Ganden (2½ hours, Y8), the Samye ferry crossing (Y23) and Tsetang (advertised as Shannan, the name of the county, Y30) leave every morning from the west side of Barkhor Square.

Minibus

Minibus connections between Lhasa and Shigatse have already been mentioned in the bus section above. Besides this service, a host of other minibus routes have sprung up in recent years. One area to look for these is directly west of the Barkhor Square, from where there are daily minibuses to Tsurphu Monastery in Ü Province (Y18, leaves when full from around 7 am onwards) and frequent services to Drepung Monastery.

There are also daily minibus services to Naqu (via Damxung, Y48), Samye in Ü (Y25) and Shigatse in Tsang (Y38) from in front of the Kirey Hotel. Minibuses congregate around 7 am and depart when full. They may use aggressive tactics to get you onto their vehicle. Minibuses are normally quicker than the buses, though there can be interminable stops.

There are no longer buses to the Nepalese border (Zhangmu), though the private agencies in the Tibetan quarter advertise weekly minibuses to Zhangmu, departing Thursday. These are minibuses which are travelling to pick up groups so beware that if a tour is cancelled so is the minibus (and your booking). Seats cost between Y250 and Y350 for the two day trip, normally with an overnight stop at Shigatse's Tenzin Hotel.

Other services scatted around town include minibuses to Chushul and Yangpachen from opposite the CAAC office on Nyangdren Chang Lam.

Rented Vehicles

Rented vehicles have emerged as the most popular way to get away from Lhasa in recent years, even though you can still travel along most of the main routes by public transport. The most popular route is a leisurely and slightly circuitous journey down to Zhangmu on the Tibetan-Nepalese border, taking in Yamdrok-tso, Gyantse, Shigatse, Sakya, Everest Base Camp and Tingri on the way (see the Tsang chapter for more information). Other popular trips include both Mt Kailash and Nam-tso. See the boxed text for a list of rough prices for various trip options.

Check the Information section at the start of this chapter for a listing of some of the travel agencies around town. It is often

worth spending a few hundred yuan extra (it is not much spread over five or six people) to hire a vehicle from a bigger and more reliable agency. If you are organising a long trip to a destination like Kailash then read the advice given in the boxed text 'Contracts' in the Getting Around chapter.

It is also important to talk to other travellers and get the latest on which agencies (and there are always a few) are ripping people off.

Hitching

There are relatively few people hitching out of Lhasa these days. One of the problems is that the city is so spread out that getting to the edge of town is a trip in itself. You are better off getting a local service out of town and then hitch along the road.

GETTING AROUND

For those travellers based in the Tibetan quarter of Lhasa, most of the major inner-Lhasa sights are within fairly easy walking distance. Sights such as the Norbulingka over in the west of town however, are a long trudge and it's better to take a minibus or hire a bicycle.

To/From Gongkar Airport

Gongkar airport is an inconvenient 95km away from Lhasa. Airport buses leave at 6 am for the morning flights to Kathmandu and Chengdu from the courtyard behind the CAAC building. Private buses leave at other times when full. The price is Y30 from Lhasa to Gongkar and Y25 from Gongkar to Lhasa. It is possible to stay the night at Gongkar if you can't face the early start.

Signs on the notice boards at the Yak, Snowlands and Banak Shol hotels and at the Pentoc Guesthouse regularly advertise seats on a hired Land Cruiser to the airport. Hiring a vehicle for this trip should cost around Y400, which is fairly reasonable if you can get six or seven people together. Taxis are cheaper at around Y200 but can only fit three comfortably. The road has been asphalted for its entire length and it is a relatively smooth drive.

Shared taxis sometimes run to and from Gongkar airport for Y25 per person. This price assumes that there are four paying passengers in the car. A further problem is that these airport taxis can be tricky to track down in Lhasa.

Minibus

Privately run minibuses are frequent on Dekyi Shar Lam and if you need to get up to the area around the Lhasa Hotel or the bus station this is the quickest and cheapest way to do it. There is a flat Y2 charge.

Land Cruiser Rates in Lhasa

Prices for Land Cruiser hire (with driver) fluctuate throughout the year depending upon the season, the number of available vehicles and the number of tourists. August and September are probably the most expensive times to hire a vehicle. Prices can also vary considerably between agencies so it's worthwhile shopping around, though remember cheapest isn't always best. Prices depend largely on the kilometres driven (roughly Y3.50 per kilometre) not the time taken, meaning that you can often add an extra day to your itinerary for the same cost. If you are not returning with your vehicle you can expect to pay an extra 50% of the one way hire rate for the vehicle to return empty. Prices are higher on trips where a permit and both guide and driver are needed. Guide fees are normally calculated at Y150 per day.

Some approximate prices are given below:

trip	duration	cost
Lhasa-Ganden or Tsurphu	day trip	Y400
Lhasa-Nepal Border direct	3 days	Y2400
Lhasa-Nepal border via Yamdrok-tso, Gyantse, Shigatse, Sakya & Everest Base Camp	7 days	Y4500-Y6000. Price includes permits and guide and should also include the Y400 Land Cruiser fee to enter the Qomolangma Nature Preserve (though it generally does not cover the Y65 individual entry fee).
Lhasa-Nam-tso-Lhasa	3 days	Y1500-Y1700. You can sometimes add on a visit to Tsurphu Monastery for no extra charge, though some agencies charge up to Y150 extra.
Lhasa-Nam-tso-Reting-Drigung Til-Lhasa	5 days	Y2800
Lhasa-Gyantse-Shigatse-Lhasa	2 days	Y2000
Lhasa-Samye-Mindroling Monastery-Tsetang-Lhasa	3 days	Y2800. Price includes guide and permits.
Lhasa-Drigung Til-Tidrum-Lhasa	2 or 3 days	Y1100
Lhasa-Talung-Reting-Drigung Til-Lhasa	4 days	Y1500
Lhasa-Yamdrok-tso	day trip	Y1000
Mt Kailash	15-24 days	Y24,000. Or priced from US$500 per person with guide, permits and support truck. There's little price difference between returning to Lhasa and getting off in Zhangmu. See Mt Kailash section in Western Tibet chapter for more details.

The main minibus routes are:

No 2 From a block west of Barkhor Square, eastwards past the Potala to the Norbulingka and main bus station and back.

No 3 From a block west of Tashi I Restaurant along Dekyi Shar Lam past the Potala, Lhasa Hotel and out to Drepung Monastery. Returns east along the same route except it detours behind the Potala and the Lukhang.

No 5 From Nyangdren Chang Lam (and sometimes Dekyi Shar Lam) north to the Sera Monastery.

Taxi

Taxis are plentiful and charge a standard fare of Y10 to anywhere within the city. However, few Chinese drivers will know the Tibetan names for even the major sites, so you may have to ask for, say, the *dajiaosi* instead of the Jokhang.

Pedicab

There is no shortage of pedicabs plying the streets of Lhasa, but as they are slow and relatively expensive there is little incentive to use them. A trip between the Yak Hotel and the Lhasa Hotel for example costs at least Y10 (after much haggling) and takes around 25 minutes. If you are headed to the Potala, bear in mind that pedicabs are not allowed to proceed further west than Nyangdren Chang Lam so you'll have to walk half the distance anyway. You'd be better off hiring a bicycle and peddling yourself around.

Bicycle

Bicycle is without a doubt the best way to get around once you have acclimatised to the altitude. You can hire bicycles at the Yak, Banak Shol and Snowlands hotels. Mountain bikes can be hired from the Pentoc Guesthouse for around Y60.

Most bicycle hire places charge a standard Y2 an hour or Y20 per day. No deposit is required if you are a guest of the hotel, if not you'll have to hand over a deposit of around Y200 to Y400.

Bicycle theft has been a bit of a problem in Lhasa for some time now. Make it a rule to park your bike in the designated areas

patrolled by matronly bicycle attendants (there is a flat charge of Y0.30) and your bike will go unmolested. A bike chain is a good idea.

Leaving it unattended (particularly at night) and wandering off for an hour is almost an invitation to theft. Naturally it goes without saying that expensive mountain bikes require more care than a rusty old Flying Pigeon.

Nowadays it is even possible to buy mountain bikes in Lhasa. Check the area in the vicinity of the Potala on Dekyi Nub Lam for bike shops. Prices fluctuate around Y500. Don't expect the quality to be up to international standards, but plenty of travellers still manage to do long trips without having the bikes fall apart. The most important thing to check is the gears.

Those who have ridden their bikes through to Kathmandu report that the bikes have a high resale value there – possibly more than the original price in Lhasa, though this will depend on the condition of the bike when you arrive.

AROUND LHASA

Within easy cycling distance of central Lhasa are the major Gelugpa monasteries of Sera and Drepung. Both are worth visiting, even if you have only a brief stay in Lhasa.

Drepung Monastery

About 8km to the west of central Lhasa, Drepung was once the world's largest monastery, with a population of around 10,000 monks. The word Drepung literally translates as 'rice heap', a reference to the huge numbers of white monastic buildings that once piled up on the hillside. It has suffered through the ages with assaults by the kings of Tsang and the Mongols, but it was left relatively unscathed during the Cultural Revolution and there is still much of interest left intact.

Drepung is open from approximately 9 am to 4 pm. There may be breaks for lunch (any time from noon to 2 pm) and some or all chapels and colleges may be closed on Sunday. There is a Y30 entry charge, though no one seems bothered to collect it. If they do, a student card should give you a reduction of Y15.

A restaurant near the bus stop serves life-reviving tea for Y1 a mug and momos for two mao each.

History Drepung was founded in 1416 by a charismatic monk and disciple of Tsong-khapa called Jamyang Chöje. He was able to raise funds for the project quickly and within a year of completion the monastery already hosted a population of some 2000 monks.

In 1530 the second Dalai Lama established the Ganden Palace, the palace that was home to the Dalai Lamas until the fifth built the Potala. It was from here that the early Dalai Lamas exercised their control over central Tibet, and the second, third and fourth Dalai Lamas are all entombed here. Meanwhile the monastic population of Drepung continued to grow. By the time of the fifth Dalai Lama in the early 17th century, the number of resident monks was somewhere between 7000 and 10,000. Today there are around 600 monks in residence.

Ganden Palace From the car park follow the kora circuit clockwise around the outside of the monastery until you reach steps up to the Ganden Palace. Prior to the construction of the Potala, this was the residence of the Dalai Lamas and headquarters of the Tibetan government. You can see the former residence of the Dalai Lamas at the top right of the main building.

The first hall on the left is the Sanga Tratsang, a recently renovated chapel housing statues of the protectors Palden Lhamo, Yamantaka (Tibetan: Dorje Jigje), Mahakala (Nagpo Chenpo) and Damaraja (Chögyel), arranged around a central statue of the fifth Dalai Lama.

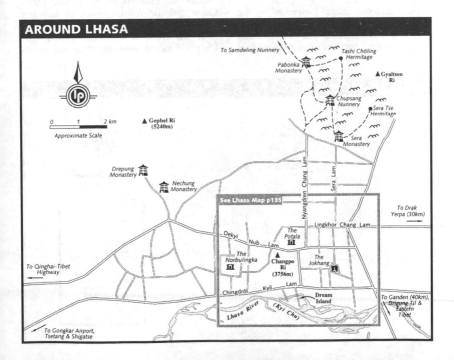

AROUND LHASA

Head up across the main courtyard, where Cham dances are still held during the Shötun festival, up to a single chapel on the first floor of the main building. Exit out the back.

Main Assembly Hall The main assembly hall, or tsogchen, is the principal structure in the Drepung complex. The huge hall itself is now only used on special occasions, but it is possible to imagine it crowded with monks in the monastery's heyday. It is reached through an entrance on the west side.

The interior of the hall is very atmospheric, draped with thangkas and marked by over 180 supporting columns, some of which are adorned with ancient armour used for festival dances. Sculptures of interest include those of Tsongkhapa, Jamyang Chöje (Drepung's founder) and a series of Dalai Lamas – the seventh, third, fourth, fifth (raised above the others), ninth and eighth. At either end of the altar is a group of eight *arhats*.

The backroom chapel is flanked by the protector deities Vajrapani (blue) and Hayagriva (red) and features statues of Sakyamuni Buddha with his two disciples, the Buddhas of the Three Ages and nine chörtens. To the east is Tsongkhapa. Look out for several small images of Songtsen Gampo perched on the columns.

Back by the main entrance, steps lead up to the 1st floor, past a small kitchen and up to the 2nd floor. At the top of the stairs to the right is the Hall of the Kings of Tibet and to the left is a chapel containing the head of a two storey Maitreya. Pilgrims prostrate themselves here and drink from a sacred white conch shell.

Continue clockwise through the Sakyamuni Chapel, stuffed with chörtens and then descend to the **Chapel of Maitreya**. This chapel contains the assembly hall's most revered image, a massive statue of Maitreya, the Future Buddha, at the age of 12. The statue rises through three floors of the building from a ground-floor chapel, that is usually closed, and is flanked by Tsongkhapa and Jamyang Chöje. The chörtens behind contain the remains of the second Dalai Lama and the former abbot of Labrang Monastery in Gansu.

To the right of this chapel is a Tara Chapel. Tara is a protective deity, and in this

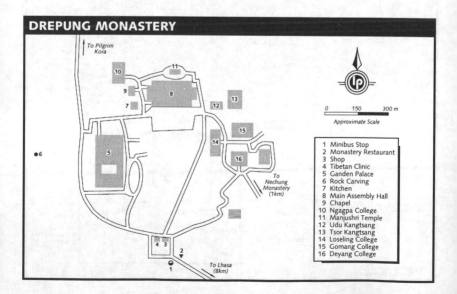

DREPUNG MONASTERY

To Pilgrim Kora

To Nechung Monastery (1km)

To Lhasa (8km)

0   150   300 m
Approximate Scale

1 Minibus Stop
2 Monastery Restaurant
3 Shop
4 Tibetan Clinic
5 Ganden Palace
6 Rock Carving
7 Kitchen
8 Main Assembly Hall
9 Chapel
10 Ngagpa College
11 Manjushri Temple
12 Udu Kangtsang
13 Tsor Kangtsang
14 Loseling College
15 Gomang College
16 Deyang College

case the three Tara images in the chapel are responsible for protecting Drepung's drinking water, wealth and authority respectively. There are also some lovely examples of Tibetan Kangyur scriptures here.

Ngagpa College Ngagpa is one of Drepung's four colleges, and was devoted to Tantric study. The chapel is dedicated to Yamantaka, a Tantric meditational deity who serves as an opponent to the forces of impermanence. The Yamantaka image is said to have been fashioned by Tsongkhapa himself and still stands in the chapel. Working clockwise other statues include Palden Lhamo (second clockwise), Mahakala (fourth), White Tara (fifth), Tsongkhapa (sixth), the fifth Dalai Lama (eighth), the Nechung oracle in the corner and a small Dorje

Drakden (see Nechung Monastery later in this chapter) by the door.

As you follow the pilgrim path (clockwise) around the back of the assembly hall you will pass the small Manjushri Temple where pilgrims peer in to see a holy rock painting and get hit on the back with a holy iron rod!

Loseling College Loseling is the largest of Drepung's colleges, and studies here were devoted to logic. The main hall houses a throne used by the Dalai Lamas, an extensive library and a long altar decorated with statues of various Dalai Lamas, Tsongkhapa and former Drepung abbots. There are three chapels to the rear of the hall. The one to the left houses 16 arhats which pilgrims walk under in a circuit, the

Monasteries in Tibet

The great Gelugpa monasteries of Drepung, Sera and Ganden were like self-contained worlds. Drepung, the largest of these monasteries, was home to around 10,000 monks at the time of the Chinese takeover in 1951. Like the other major Gelugpa institutions, Drepung operated less as a single unit than as an assembly of colleges, each with its own interests, resources and administration.

The colleges, known as *tratsang*, were in turn made up of residences, or *kangtsang*. A monk joining a monastic college was assigned to a kangtsang according to the region he was born in. For example, Drepung's Loseling college is thought to have been made up 60% of monks from Kham, while Gomang college was dominated by monks from Amdo and Mongolia. In total Loseling had 23 kangtsang, but the three most powerful kangtsang were all Kham controlled. This gave the monastic colleges a distinctive regional flavour, and meant that loyalties were generally grounded much deeper in the colleges than in the monastery itself.

At the head of a college was the abbot or *khenpo*, a position that was filled by contenders who had completed the highest degrees of monastic studies. The successful applicant was chosen by the Dalai Lama. Beneath the abbot, was a group of religious heads who supervised prayer meetings and festivals and a group of economic managers who controlled the various kangtsang estates and funds. There was also a squad of huge monk police known as *dob-dobs*, who were in charge of discipline and administering punishments.

In the case of the larger colleges, estates and funds were often extensive. Loseling College had over 180 estates and 20,000 serfs who worked the land and paid taxes to the monastery. Monasteries had their fingers in most forms of trade. For the most part, these holdings were not used to support monks – who were often forced to do private business to sustain themselves – but to maintain an endless cycle of prayer meetings and festivals that were deemed necessary for the spiritual good of the nation.

central chapel has a large Maitreya image, and the chapel to the right has a small Sakyamuni statue.

On the 2nd floor you'll come to a small chapel full of angry deities and then you pass under the body of a stuffed goat draped with one mao notes before entering the *gönkhang* (protector chapel). There are more protective deities here including Mahakala, Dorje Drakden (see Nechung Monastery later in this chapter) and Yamantaka (see the previous entry for Ngagpa College).

Gomang College Gomang is the second largest of Drepung's colleges and follows the same layout as Loseling. The main hall has a whole row of images including Maitreya, red Amitayus, and the seventh Dalai Lama. Again there are three chapels to the rear: the one to the left houses three deities of longevity, but more important is the central chapel, chock-a-block with images. Like Loseling, there is a single protector chapel on the 2nd floor. Women are sometimes not allowed into this chapel.

Deyang College The smallest of Drepung's colleges, this one can safely be missed if you have had enough. The principal image in the main hall is Maitreya, flanked by Manjushri, Tara, the fifth Dalai Lama and others.

Drepung Kora The Drepung kora climbs up to around 3900m and probably should not be attempted until you have had four or five days acclimatising in Lhasa. It takes about 1½ hours at a leisurely pace (it is possible to do it quicker at hiking speed). Look for the path that leads from the north-west corner of the parking area in front of the monastery. The path passes carvings of Tara to the east, climbs up to a patch of prayer flags and then heads down the east side past a high wall used to hang a giant thangka during the Shötun (Yoghurt) festival. There are good views along the way.

Hard-core acclimatised trekkers might want to consider the three-hour climb up to

a white retreat perched high on the steep rock face, for spectacular views.

Getting There & Away It takes around 45 minutes to cycle from the Barkhor area of Lhasa to the base of the hill on which Drepung is situated (look for Drepung above you and to the right). A dirt road leaves the main road up to Drepung and, unless you have a mountain bike, you will be best off leaving your bike at the base of the hill. There should be someone to look after your bike just after the turn-off. The walk up to Drepung takes around 30 minutes.

The easy way to get out to Drepung is to take a minibus. Buses run from the minibus area in front of Barkhor Square and cost Y3 to the base of the hill or, if you're lucky, up to the parking area in front of Drepung. The No 3 minibus also goes there from a block west of Tashi ! Restaurant, Lhasa.

Nechung Monastery

Nechung is only 10 minutes walk downhill from Drepung. Until 1959, it was the seat of the State Oracle. Oracles serve as mediums or mouthpieces of protective deities in Tibetan Buddhism and are thought to be possessed by the deity in question. The oracle at Nechung was the medium of Dorje Drakden, an aspect of Pehar, protector of the Buddhist state, and no important decision would be made by the Dalai Lamas without first consulting him. In 1959 the State Oracle fled with the Dalai Lama to India and Nechung is now cared for by a small number of resident monks.

Nechung Monastery is an eerie place associated with possession, exorcism and other pre-Buddhist rites. Note the blood-red doors at the entrance painted with flayed human skins and the scenes of torture along the top of the outer courtyard. For images of Dorje Drakden, the protective spirit manifested in the State Oracle, see the backroom chapel to the left of the main hall. The statue on the left shows Dorje Drakden in his wrathful aspect, the one on the right has him in a more conciliatory frame of mind. In between the two is a sacred tree.

The Nechung Oracle

Every New Year the Dalai Lama would consult the Nechung oracle on important matters of state. As the oracle prepared himself for the ordeal he would strap on bracelets in the shape of a human eye and an elaborate headdress of feathers, so heavy that it had to be lifted onto his head by two men.

As the oracle whipped himself into a trance to dislodge the spirit from his body, eyewitness accounts describe how his eyeballs would swell and roll up into his sockets, and how his mouth would open wide, his tongue curl upward and his face swell and redden. As he started to make out the future in a steel mirror he would answer questions in an anguished and tortured, hissing voice, which would then be translated for the court by a clerk. After the trance the oracle would faint and would have to be carried away.

On the 1st floor is an audience chamber with a throne used by the Dalai Lamas when they consulted with the State Oracle. The 2nd floor features a huge new statue of a wrathful Guru Rinpoche surrounded by new paintings that are halfway through completion.

Nechung has the same basic opening hours as Drepung, and at the time of writing entry was free.

Sera Monastery

Sera Monastery, around 5km north of central Lhasa, was along with Drepung one of Lhasa's two great Gelugpa monasteries. Its once huge monastic population of around 5000 monks has now been reduced to several hundred, and building repairs are still continuing. Nevertheless the monastery is worth a visit, particularly from around 3.30 pm onwards when debating is usually held in the monastery's debating courtyard.

Sera is frequently invaded by video-camera toting tour groups who toss money to the child beggars who infest the place. Try not to encourage the children, and if the tour groups annoy you sit down and wait them out – they very rarely linger long.

Like Drepung, Sera has opening hours from around 9 am to 4.30 pm daily (a long lunch break is to be expected) and there is an entry charge of Y30, though this is not strictly enforced. Photography fees are out-

rageously high (Y850 – over US$100 – to use a video).

There is a restaurant by the monastery entrance which serves basic thugpa and sweet tea for a couple of yuan.

History Sera was founded in 1419 by Sakya Yeshe, a disciple of Tsongkhapa also known by the honorific title Jamchen Chöje. In its heyday, Sera hosted a huge monastic population and five colleges of instruction, but at the time of the Chinese invasion in 1959 the colleges numbered three. Like Drepung, the colleges of Sera specialised: Sera Me in the fundamental precepts of Buddhism; Sera Je in the instruction of itinerant monks from outside central Tibet; and Sera Ngagpa in Tantric studies.

Sera survived the ravages of the Cultural Revolution with little damage, although many of the colleges were destroyed.

Sera Me College Follow the pilgrims clockwise, past the Shampa Kangtsang residential hall and several minor buildings, to the Sera Me College. This college dates back to the original founding of the monastery. The central image of the **main hall** is a copper Sakyamuni, flanked by Maitreya and Manjushri. To the rear of the hall are five chapels. To the far left is a dark chapel dedicated to Ta-og, Dharma Protector of the East. Look out for the dorje (thunderbolt) symbols, masks, knives and horns tied to the pillars. The next chapel is undistinguished, with a central statue of Tsongkhapa and a chörten. The central chapel contains statues of the Present, Future and Past Buddhas: Sakyamuni, Maitreya and Dipamkara, as well as 16 arhats depicted in their mountain grottos.

The next chapel is home to Miwang Jowo, a Sakyamuni statue that dates from the 15th century and is the most sacred of the college's statues. The entrance to the chapel is flanked by the protectors Hayagriva (red) and Achala (blue). The last chapel is dedicated to Tsongkhapa and there are also images of several Dalai Lamas as well as Sera's founder and first abbot.

There are also two chapels on the upper floor. The first, after you mount the stairs is dedicated to Sakyamuni. The second is a Tara chapel and has 1000 statues of this protective deity.

Sera Ngagpa College A Tantric college, Ngagpa is also the oldest structure at Sera. The **main hall** is dominated by a statue of Sakya Yeshe, founder of Sera, and he is surrounded by other famous Sera lamas. There

are two chapels to the rear of the hall, one with 16 arhats and a large Sakyamuni statue and one with a statue of the protective deity Yamantaka, as well as Vaishravana (Tibetan: Namtöse), the Guardian of the North who rides a snow lion and holds a mongoose that vomits jewels. There are also a couple of rooms upstairs.

Jarung Kangtsang Most pilgrims pay a quick visit to this residential college.

Sera Je College This is the largest of Sera's colleges. It has a breathtaking **main hall**, hung with thangkas and lit by shafts of light from high windows. There are also two thrones, one for the Dalai Lama and the smaller for the Panchen Lama, as well as several chörtens holding the remains of Sera's most famous lamas.

To the left of the hall is a passage which leads, via a chapel dedicated to the Buddhas of the Three Ages (present, future and past), to the most sacred of Sera Monastery's chapels, the **Chapel of Hayagriva**. Hayagriva is a wrathful meditational deity whose name means 'horse-headed'. He is the chief

SERA MONASTERY

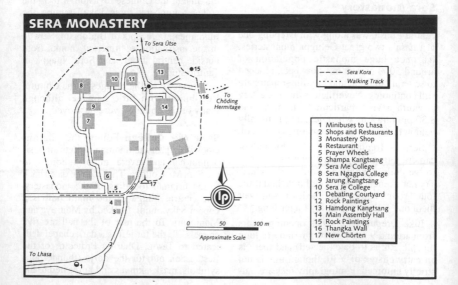

Legend:
- – – – – Sera Kora
- · · · · · Walking Track

1 Minibuses to Lhasa
2 Shops and Restaurants
3 Monastery Shop
4 Restaurant
5 Prayer Wheels
6 Shampa Kangtsang
7 Sera Me College
8 Sera Ngagpa College
9 Jarung Kangtsang
10 Sera Je College
11 Debating Courtyard
12 Rock Paintings
13 Hamdong Kangtsang
14 Main Assembly Hall
15 Rock Paintings
16 Thangka Wall
17 New Chörten

To Sera Ütse
To Chöding Hermitage
To Lhasa

0   50   100 m
Approximate Scale

protective deity of Sera, and there is often a line of pilgrims waiting to touch their foreheads to his feet in respect. There is a second chapel for him on the upper floor, but here he is in another aspect with nine heads. The chapels to the rear of the hall are of less interest. There are three altogether and these are devoted to Maitreya, Tsongkhapa and Manjushri, who is depicted turning the Wheel of Dharma.

To the right of Sera Je is Sera's **debating courtyard**. There is usually debating practice here in the afternoons from around 3.30 to 4 pm. You will hear it (much clapping of hands to emphasise points) as you approach Sera Je. It is well worth your time and provides a welcome relief from peering at Buddhist iconography.

Hamdong Kangtsang Hamdong served as a residence for monks studying at Sera Je College. The back left chapel contains an image of a Sera lama who died in 1962, plus an image of Tara who is said to protect Sera's water supply. It is of fairly limited interest.

Main Assembly Hall The main assembly hall is the largest of Sera's buildings and dates back to 1710. The main hall is particularly impressive and is noted for its wall-length thangkas. A statue of Maitreya is the centrepiece and he is flanked by other figures including Dalai Lamas on your right, while to the left is the large throne of the 13th Dalai Lama. Behind the throne is a figure of Sakyamuni flanked by the 13th Dalai Lama and Sakya Yeshe, the founder of Sera.

Of the three chapels to the rear of the hall, the central is the most important, with its 6m Maitreya statue. The statue rises up to the upper floor, where it can also be viewed from the central chapel. Also on the upper floor (to the far left of the central chapel) is a highly revered statue of a 1000 armed Avalokiteshvara. You exit out the back.

Sera Kora The Sera kora (pilgrimage circuit) takes less than an hour and is well worth the time. It starts inside the entrance and heads west, following an arc around the

outskirts of the monastery. On the descent, look out for several brightly coloured rock paintings. The largest ones on the eastern side of the monastery are of Yamantaka, Tsongkhapa and Guru Rinpoche. You can cut through to here by heading east from the Hamdong Kangtsang. Next to the rock paintings is a support wall used to hang a giant thangka during festivals.

A path leads up the side steps of this wall to the **Chöding Hermitage**, a short five minute climb. The hermitage was a retreat of Tsongkhapa, and predates Sera. There is not a great deal to see, but it is a short walk and the views from the hermitage are worthwhile. A path continues east around the hillside, past a holy spring to a viewpoint which has fine views of Sera and Lhasa beyond.

Sera Ütse Sera Ütse was another retreat used by Tsongkhapa. It is of more interest than Chöding, but it is also more of a climb. From Sera the walk takes around 1½ hours. To get there, take the tree-lined road that bisects Sera Monastery and continue climbing the ridge via a switch-back path. This walk should not really be attempted until you have had at least a few days in Lhasa acclimatising to the altitude. Another thing worth bearing in mind is that the white granite rock faces of the hills around Sera give off a lot of glare and can make for hot walking, particularly in the summer months. It is a good idea to get an early start.

Getting There & Away Sera is only a half-hour bicycle ride from the Barkhor area of Lhasa. Leave your bicycle next to the monastery restaurant.

Alternatively head down to the intersection of Nyangdren Chang Lam and Dekyi Shar Lam (the last turn before the main post office as you head west) and look for the No 5 minibuses and jeeps that wait on the corner. They head up to Sera every 10 minutes or so whenever they are full and cost Y3.

Pabonka Monastery

Pabonka is one of the most ancient Buddhist sites in the Lhasa region. It is little visited, but is only a one hour walk from the Sera Monastery turn-off and is well worth the effort.

Built on a flat-topped granite boulder, Pabonka may even predate the Jokhang and Ramoche. It was built in the 7th century by King Songtsen Gampo. The Tibetan king Trisong Detsen, Guru Rinpoche and Tibet's first seven monks all meditated here. A monk named Thonmi Sambhota reputedly invented the Tibetan alphabet here. In 841 it was destroyed by the anti-Buddhist King Langdharma and rebuilt in the 11th century. It was restored again by the fifth Dalai Lama, who added an extra floor to the two storey building. It suffered more damage in the Cultural Revolution and has undergone repairs in recent years.

The first building you come across is the **Rigsum Gonpo Temple**, whose most famous relic is the carved mantra *om mani padme hum* on display by the entrance. Continue uphill, walking clockwise around the Pabonka rock (said to represent a female tortoise) to the **Palden Lhamo Cave**, where King Songtsen Gampo once meditated. Images inside are of Songtsen Gampo, Guru Rinpoche, Trisong Detsen and the protectoress Palden Lhamo.

The main **Pabonka Podrang** is placed on top of the ancient rock. There is nothing to see on the ground floor of the Pabonka, but the upper floor has an assembly hall with a fine Sakyamuni statue. Other items of interest include some old thangkas and statues of the fifth and 13th Dalai Lamas, Songtsen Gampo, Guru Rinpoche and Trisong Detsen. The throne is for the Panchen Lama.

Further above the Pabonka Podrang are the remains of 108 chörtens, the yellow temple of Princess Wencheng and a sky burial site.

Walks Around Pabonka A few intrepid (and fit) travellers use Pabonka as a base for walks farther afield. These are serious day walks and should not be attempted until you are well adjusted to the altitude. Midday can be hot here so bring enough water.

For those who aren't so fit, an easy, short walk from Pabonka leads up to **Tashi Chöling Hermitage**. There is not a lot left to see at the hermitage, but again it affords good views. From Pabonka look for another granite boulder to the north-east (it is very close), and just before the boulder look for a path that leads up to a wider trail. The whole walk takes only around 20 minutes.

From Tashi Chöling, it is possible to take a slightly more arduous hike to **Chupsang Nunnery**. The trail drops down to the right from Tashi Chöling and follows a ravine. Ask for the *ani gompa* (nunnery) at the first village you reach. There are some 80 nuns resident at Chupsang and it's a very friendly place. The entire walk takes from 30 to 40 minutes. You could also get to the nunnery from the road between Sera and Pabonka and then follow paths west around the base of the hill to Pabonka itself.

Samdeling Nunnery is a tough four hour hike from Tashi Chöling (allow around two hours for the descent). Take some water with you, though you will probably receive some butter tea from the nuns if you make it to the top. The trail heads to the left from Tashi Chöling and follows a steep ridge. The nunnery, home to more than 80 nuns, is at an altitude of over 4200m.

Getting There & Away To get to Pabonka, take a minibus or jeep to the Sera Monastery turn-off (see the Sera Monastery section earlier). Rather than take the turn to Sera, look for a left turn a little up the road. The walk from here is fairly straightforward. You need to make a right turn at a T-junction, but you will see Pabonka up ahead to the left perched on its granite boulder. The monastery to the right is actually the Chupsang Nunnery.

Ü

HIGHLIGHTS

- **Ganden Monastery** – the main seat of the Gelugpa order is an excellent day trip from Lhasa

- **Tsurphu Monastery** – visit the Karmapa; also a day trip from Lhasa

- **Nam-tso** – a stunningly turquoise high-altitude lake ringed with 7000m snowy peaks

- **Samye Monastery** – take a relaxing ferry across the Yarlung Tsangpo to Tibet's first monastery

- **Yumbulagang** – the first building in Tibet, set in a stunning location in the Yarlung valley

The traditional province known in Tibetan as Ü is the more easterly of the two central provinces that have long been at the centre stage of Tibetan politics and history. The other central province is Tsang, and its capital is Shigatse. In modern Chinese terms Ü consists mainly of Lhasa and Shannan prefectures. Travel in Lhasa Prefecture does not require a permit but, officially, once you leave the prefecture you need a permit from the PSB to visit most sites.

The province of Ü is effectively the heartland of all greater Tibet. It was from here, in the Yarlung valley, that the earliest Tibetan kings launched their 6th century conquest and unification of the Tibetan plateau and ruled from Lhasa for three centuries. Political power later shifted to Sakya and Shigatse in Tsang, but returned to Ü when the fifth Dalai Lama reunited the country with Mongol support in 1642, and again made Lhasa the capital.

For most individual travellers the principal attractions of Ü are Ganden, Tsurphu and Samye monasteries and the impressive turquoise lake, Nam-tso. The first two can be visited as day trips from the capital, whereas it's best to take around three days for a visit to either Samye Monastery or Nam-tso.

The ancient province is also host to a large number of other sights that are little visited by foreign travellers. Lhamo La-tso, the oracle lake of the Dalai Lamas and a place of great spiritual importance for the Tibetan people, is growing in popularity though it's not easy to get to. The Yarlung valley, site of Yumbulagang and the nearby tombs of the Tibetan kings at Chongye, is well worth a visit, as are the smaller monastery complexes in the area, such as Mindroling. Around 100km north-east of Lhasa, Drigung Til Monastery and nearby Tidrum Nunnery offer an excellent three day trip deep into the Tibetan countryside.

The entries in this chapter start off with day trips from Lhasa and then head off in spokes to the north-west, north-east and then south of the capital.

Getting Around

With the exception of a few of Ü's major attractions, public transport is a rarity. Ganden, Tsurphu and Samye monasteries are linked with Lhasa by public buses and minibuses, as is Tsetang – the nearest major town to the south-east of Lhasa and a good base for visits to the Yarlung valley – but otherwise rented vehicles, hiking and hitching are the only ways to get around.

Travellers planning on renting vehicles should turn to the Information section of the Lhasa chapter for a listing of travel agencies. For a list of rough prices and sample itineraries, see the boxed text 'Land Cruiser Rates in Lhasa' in the same chapter.

Some Ü sights, such as Nam-tso, are already popular destinations, and prices should be fairly competitive. In the case of less frequently travelled routes, travel agents tend to quote a little wildly. Calculate the distances involved and remember that there

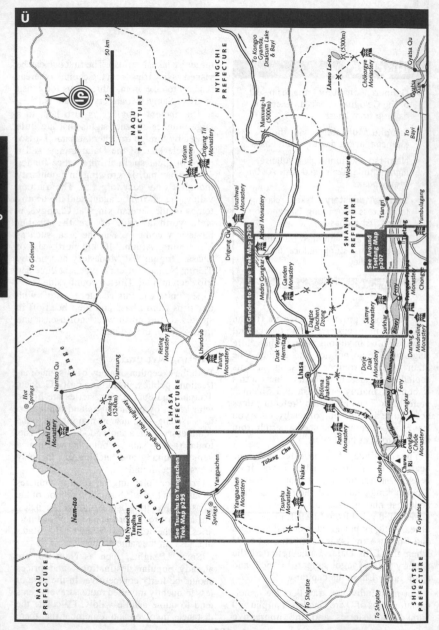

Ü

See Ganden to Samye Trek Map p290

See Around Tsetang Map p207

See Tsurphu to Yangpachen Trek Map p295

is a general charge of between Y3 and Y4 per kilometre.

There are a lot of hiking possibilities in Ü. Day hikes around Tidrum Nunnery, Samye Monastery and the Yarlung valley are covered in this chapter and the treks from Tsurphu to Yangpachen and also Ganden to Samye are covered in detail in the Trekking chapter. Those with a keen interest in extended hikes, however, should get hold of Victor Chan's *Tibet Handbook – a pilgrimage guide*, which has exhaustive details on innumerable treks and hikes in the Ü region.

GANDEN MONASTERY

Ganden (4500m) was the first Gelugpa monastery and has remained the main seat of this major Buddhist order ever since. It was founded in 1417 by Tsongkhapa, the revered reformer of the Gelugpa order, and images of him and his first two disciples are found throughout the monastery. When he died two years later, the abbotship of the monastery passed on to these disciples, Gyatsab Je and Kedrub Je. The post came to be known as the Ganden Tripa and was earned through schol-

arly merit. It is the Ganden Tripa, not, as one might expect, the Dalai Lama who is the head of the Gelugpa order.

Ganden means 'joyous' in Tibetan and is the name of the western paradise (also known as Tushita) that is home to Maitreya (Tibetan: Jampa), the Future Buddha. There is a certain irony in this, as of all the great monasteries of Tibet, it was Ganden that suffered most at the hands of the Red Guards, possibly because of its political influence.

Today it is the scene of frenetic rebuilding, but this does not disguise the ruin that surrounds the new. The destruction was caused by artillery fire and bombing in 1966. The debris sprawls around a natural protected bowl high above the Kyi Chu valley. Ganden might be a depressing experience were it not for the obvious zeal with which work teams are carrying out the large-scale reconstruction of the monastic buildings.

If you only have time for one monastery excursion outside Lhasa, Ganden would probably be the best choice. Samye Monastery is a strong contender, but it is more time consuming to reach. Ganden, just 40km north-east of Lhasa, with its stupendous

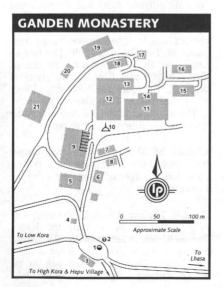

GANDEN MONASTERY

1	Buses to/from Lhasa
2	Toilets
3	Monastery Guesthouse & Restaurant
4	Monastery Shop
5	Jangtse College
6	Ngam Chö Khang
7	Gomde Khang
8	Debating Courtyard
9	Shartse College
10	White Chörten
11	Assembly Hall
12	Golden Tomb of Tsongkhapa
13	Maitreya Chapel
14	Golden Throne Room
15	Residence of Ganden Tripa
16	Chapel
17	Shoba Kangtsang
18	Zungjung Kangtsang
19	Amdo Kangtsang
20	Tsar Kangtsang
21	Dreu Kangtsang

views of the surrounding Kyi Chu valley and fascinating pilgrim *kora* (ritual circumambulation circuit), is an experience unlike the other major Gelugpa monasteries in the Lhasa area.

Ganden was temporarily closed to tourists in 1996 after violent demonstrations against the government's banning of Dalai Lama photos. There are currently no restrictions on visiting the monastery.

There is a Y15 admission charge for Ganden, but it is not collected very scrupulously and there is no one checking tickets.

The Monastery

Ganden is an interesting place in which to wander aimlessly. The sheer ochre walls of many of the buildings make great backdrops for photographs, there are always streams of friendly pilgrims making the rounds and there is usually a yak or two lurking in the shadows. New chapels and residences are being opened all the time.

Buses and rented vehicles stop in a car park to the south of the monastery. There is a restaurant here, which also offers basic accommodation on the upper floor and has good views of the monastery. (See Places to Stay & Eat later.)

Ngam Chö Khang The first chapel you reach from the car park is Ngam Chö Khang. It is built on the site of Tsongkhapa's original assembly hall, or *dukhang,* and has a small shrine with images of Tsongkhapa and his two principal disciples. These disciples were responsible for elucidating on and distilling his thought into the body of beliefs that would become the basis of the Gelugpa order. On the left is a protector chapel, or *gönkhang,* that houses four protective deities. The largest image is of Yamantaka (Tibetan: Dorje Jigje).

Debating Courtyard Further to the northeast the Gomde Khang (a building that serves as living quarters for monks), is the debating courtyard. There is often debating here in the afternoons; you should be able

to hear the clapping of hands as you pass if there is a debate in progress.

Assembly Hall This recently renovated assembly hall is still under repair but should be completed before long. You can normally pop in to see the craftsmen at work.

Golden Tomb of Tsongkhapa The red fortress-like structure of Tsongkhapa's mausoleum, or Serkhang, is probably the most impressive of the reconstructed buildings at Ganden. Look for its inclining walls and the four high windows above the prominent white *chörten* (stupa).

The entrance leads into an open courtyard. The chapel straight ahead is the domain of the protective deity Dhamaraja (Tibetan: Chöyel). Women are not allowed in to this chapel for fear that the god's wrathful appearance might disturb their tender sensitivities.

Climb the rickety stairs up to the 1st floor hall which houses a throne for the Dalai Lama.

Next to the hall is the Yangchen Khang chapel which houses Tsongkhapa's tomb. Both the original tomb and the preserved body of Tsongkhapa inside it were destroyed by Red Guards. The new silver and gold chörten was built to house salvaged fragments of Tsongkhapa's skull. The images seated in front of the chörten are of Tsongkhapa flanked by his two principal disciples. The room also holds several holy relics attributed to Tsongkhapa.

The top floor of the building houses an interesting traditional printing press.

Chapel of Maitreya This small chapel just across from the exit of the Serkhang holds large images of Tsongkhapa and the Future Buddha.

Golden Throne Room On the other side of the path from the Serkhang, the Golden Throne Room, or Ser Trikhang, is a narrow, red building that houses the throne used by the Ganden Tripa. The cloth bag on the throne contains the yellow hat of the Dalai

Lama. Evidently he forgot it when he fled to India; if you are heading to Dharamsala, you might offer to drop it off to him ... then again, maybe not. The throne room is actually part of the main assembly hall below it.

Residence of the Ganden Tripa South of the Ser Trikhang, the Residence of the Ganden Tripa or Zimchung Tridok Khang contains another, lesser throne used by the Ganden Tripa on its 1st floor. The ground floor houses four chapels, all of which are worth visiting. The room with just a bed and a seat marks the place where Tsongkhapa is thought to have died. The middle room is reserved for visits by the Dalai Lama, while the other main room is a protector chapel. All have excellent murals.

Amdo Kangtsang The 'Amdo' of Amdo Kangtsang's name refers to the Tibetan province that is now Qinghai. Tsongkhapa himself was from Amdo, and many monks came from the province to study here. There are some interesting chapels to the rear of the building and many *thangkas* (religious paintings) and other paintings on the walls. To the left of the main chapel are paintings of the 35 Buddhas of Confession.

Others There are several other residential houses which have recently been restored, among them the Shoba, Zungjung and Dreu kangtsangs. Two other colleges, the grand-looking Shartse College and the smaller Jangtse College, are still being restored. All welcome visitors if you have the energy to work your way around them.

Ganden Kora

The Ganden kora is a simply stunning walk and should not be missed. There are superb views of the Kyi Chu valley along the way and there are usually large numbers of pilgrims and monks offering prayers, rubbing holy rocks and prostrating themselves along the path.

There are actually two parts to the walk: the high and low kora. The high kora climbs

Wanbo Ri south of Ganden and then drops down the ridge to join up with the lower kora.

To walk the **high kora** follow the path south-east of the car park, away from the monastery. After a while the track splits – the left path leads to Hepu village on the Ganden-Samye trek, the right path heads pretty much straight up the ridge to a collection of prayer flags. Try to follow other pilgrims up. It's a tough 40 minute climb up to the top of the ridge – don't try this one unless you're well acclimatised. Here pilgrims burn juniper incense and give offerings of *tsampa* (roast barley flour) before heading west down the ridge in the direction of the monastery, stopping at several other shrines en route.

The **low kora** is an easier walk of around 45 minutes. From the car park bear left for the trail that heads west up and then around the back of the ridge behind the monastery. The trail winds past several isolated shrines and rocks which are rubbed for their healing properties or squeezed through to test the amount of sin a pilgrim carries. There is also a **sky burial site** and several rock carvings along the route. The sky burial site is reached shortly after the path begins to descend. Some pilgrims undertake a ritual simulated death and rebirth at this point, rolling around on the ground.

Towards the end of the kora, on the eastern side of the ridge, is **Tsongkhapa's Hermitage**, a small building with a relief image of Tsongkhapa and two Buddha images carved in rock. These images are believed to have the power of speech. Above the hermitage is a brilliantly coloured rock-painting that is reached by a narrow, precipitous path. It is definitely worth the climb uphill. From the hermitage the kora drops down to join the main buildings of the monastery.

Places to Stay & Eat

The *Monastery Guesthouse* to the south of the car park has very basic accommodation for Y12. It is used mainly by travellers who are planning to do the Ganden to Samye trek (see the Trekking chapter). The *restaurant* underneath the guesthouse has low-grade *thugpa* (Tibetan noodle dish, almost inedible unless you are *very* hungry) and little else. Just up the road from the car park is a well-stocked **shop** with everything from sweets and candles to instant noodles and beer, but you're better off bringing your own food.

Getting There & Away

Ganden is one of the few sights in Ü that is connected to Lhasa by public transport. There is a small tin shack on the south-western corner of the Barkhor circuit selling tickets (Y8) for a bus service that leaves from in front of Barkhor Square at 6.30 am. The bus takes around 2½ hours to get out to Ganden and leaves the monastery for the return journey at around 2 pm. Tickets cost Y16 return and should be bought on the afternoon of the day before you visit. An additional 7.30 am service sometimes operates – ask at the aforementioned tin shack the day before you intend to go.

If you can get a group of people together, Ganden is worth visiting in a rented vehicle. You can stop for photos on the long, panoramic haul up to the monastery itself and you have control over when you leave. A Land Cruiser for the day trip should cost around Y400.

DRÖLMA LHAKHANG

This small but significant monastery is only 30 minutes by bus south-west of Lhasa, but very few travellers make it here. It's worth a stop for those interested in Tibetan Buddhism and is an easy break on any Land Cruiser trip south.

As you take the Lhasa-Tsetang road out of Lhasa, you will pass a blue Buddha rock carving at the base of a cliff about 11km south-west of town. Five kilometres further is Netang and the monastery.

Drölma Lhakhang is associated with the Bengali master Atisha. Atisha came to Tibet at the invitation of the king of the Guge Kingdom in Western Tibet and subsequently travelled extensively in Tibet. His teachings were instrumental in the so-called second diffusion of Buddhism in the 11th century.

Drölma Lhakhang was established at this time by one of Atisha's foremost disciples, Drömtonpa. Drömtonpa was the founder of the Kadampa order, to which the monastery belongs. Atisha died at Netang.

The monastery was spared desecration by the Red Guards during the Cultural Revolution after a direct request from Bangladesh (which now encompasses Atisha's homeland) that the monastery be left untouched. Apparently, Zhou Enlai intervened on its behalf.

The entrance and exit of the monastery are both protected by two guardian deities. They are very ancient, and may even date back to the 11th century founding of the monastery.

From the entrance, you pass into the first chapel, which contains a number of chörtens. The chörtens hold the relics of former Kadampa teachers. Statuary includes an image of Atisha and the Eight Medicine Buddhas.

The middle chapel houses a number of relics that are purported to be associated with Atisha. The central image is an 11th century statue of Sakyamuni (Tibetan: Sakya Thukpa) from India. There are many statues in this room of Tara (Tibetan: Drölma), after whom the monastery is named. The rear chapel is said to be where Atisha himself once taught. It is dominated by the Buddhas of the Three Ages and the Eight Great Bodhisattvas.

Really keen gompa stompers can plod out a further hour west from Drölma Lhakhang to **Ratö Monastery**. This Gelugpa institution is renowned for its fine wall murals. It is reached via a track that heads south from the main road just after Drölma Lhakhang.

Getting There & Away

Any bus headed south from Lhasa (ie to Shigatse, Samye Monastery or Tsetang) will take you past the entrance to the monastery. You could also take a minibus to Chushul or Gongkar. These both leave from outside the Civil Aviation Administration of China (CAAC) office but only depart when full. To get back, flag down anything that comes by.

TSURPHU MONASTERY

Tsurphu Monastery (4480m), around 70km north-west of Lhasa, is the seat of the Karmapa branch of the Kagyupa order of Tibetan Buddhism. The Karmapa are also known as the Black Hats, a title that dates back to 1256, when the second Karmapa was invited to China by the emperor of the Yuan Dynasty, Kublai Khan, and presented with a black hat embellished with gold. The hat, said to be made from the hair of holy women, is now kept at Rumtek Monastery in Sikkim.

It was the first Karmapa, Dusum Khyenpa, who instigated the Tibetan Buddhist tradition of *trulku*, or the practice whereby a lama could choose his next reincarnation. The Karmapa lineage has been maintained until this day. Before his death, the first Karmapa indicated to followers certain signs that would enable them to find his reincarnation. It was a practice that was widely adopted by other orders, notably the Gelugpa in the form of the Dalai Lama and Panchen Lama lineages.

Tsurphu Monastery fared badly in the Cultural Revolution and much of it is ruined today. Visiting it has become a popular day trip in recent years, however, mainly due to the presence of a recently installed Karmapa.

The Karmapa order is one of the most popular Buddhist movements outside Tibet, particularly in the USA. There is some dispute as to the young Karmapa's incarnate authenticity, with a rival group in Delhi calling foul play and staging protests (see the boxed text 'The Karmapa Connection' over the page), but this has not stopped local Tibetans and visiting foreigners cruising up to the monastery in droves to receive a blessing. Many people are impressed with the Karmapa, others come away with the feeling that he is terribly bored by the whole proceedings. The Karmapa makes a daily appearance at 1 pm.

Tsurphu has an annual festival around the time of Saga Dawa festival in the fourth lunar month of the Tibetan calender. There is plenty of free-flowing *chang* (Tibetan barley beer) and also *cham* dancing, the highlight of which is the dance of the Karmapa.

Because of the attention given to it by foreign disciples, Tsurphu seems to attract the watchful eye of the Chinese authorities and you should be careful what you say and to whom.

For details on the three or four day trek from Tsurphu to Yangpachen monasteries see the Trekking chapter.

History

Tsurphu was founded in the 1180s by Dusum Khyenpa, the first Karmapa, some 40 years after he founded the Karmapa order in Kham, his birthplace. It was the third Karmapa monastery to be built, and after the first Karmapa's death it became the head monastery for the order. The second Karmapa was discovered nine years later. He visited China at the invitation of Kublai Khan and spent the latter part of his life supervising extensions to Tsurphu.

The Karmapa order traditionally enjoyed strong ties with the kings and monasteries of Tsang, a legacy that proved a liability when conflict broke out between the kings of Tsang and the Gelugpa order. When the fifth Dalai Lama invited the Mongolian army of Gushri Khan to do away with his opponents in Tsang, the Karmapa's political clout effectively came to an end and Tsurphu Monastery was sacked. Shorn of its political influence, Tsurphu nevertheless bounced back as an important spiritual centre and is one of the few Kagyupa institutions still functioning in the Ü region. When the Chinese forces invaded in 1950, there were around 1000 monks in residence.

The 16th Karmapa fled to Sikkim in 1959 after the popular uprising in Lhasa and founded a new Karmapa monastery in Rumtek. He died in 1981 and his reincarnation was announced, amid great controversy, by the Dalai Lama and other religious leaders in June 1992 as an eight-year-old Tibetan boy from Kham, Ugen Thinley Dorje.

The Monastery

Extensive renovations have been undertaken at Tsurphu, and are continuing apace now that the Karmapa is installed there. New chapels are opening all the time.

Assembly Hall The large central building is in the main courtyard. It houses a chörten containing the relics of the last (16th) Karmapa who died in 1981, as well as statues of Amitabha (Tibetan: Öpagme) and Sakyamuni. The audience chamber of the present Karmapa is on the upper floor and it is here that guests are received each day at 1 pm. It is not possible to carry bags into the audience chamber.

Protector Chapel Walking west (clockwise) around the monastery complex you come to the protector chapel, or gönkhang, of the main hall. There are five main rooms here all stuffed to the brim with wrathful deities. The corridor between them is lined with moth-eaten stuffed goats, wolves and even a yak or two.

The first room you come to is dedicated to Tsurphu's protector deity, an aspect of blue Mahakala (Tibetan: Nagpo Chenpo) called Bernakchen. There is also a photo of statues of Palden Lhamo and Hayagriva (Tamdrin).

The Karmapa Connection

Anyone who thinks of the Tibetans as a lofty, spiritually absorbed people should think again. Tibetan history has been dogged by factional intrigue, and the intrigues continue into the late 20th century.

In 1981 the 16th Karmapa died in Chicago. Administration of the Karmapa sect in Sikkim was subsequently passed down to four regents. Two of them, Situ Rinpoche and Shamar Rinpoche, were to become embroiled in a dispute that has caused a painful rift in the exiled Tibetan community.

At the centre of the dispute is the young man with an angelic smile who dispenses blessings at Tsurphu Monastery – the 17th Karmapa. In early 1992 the four regents announced the discovery of a letter written by the 16th Karmapa that provided critical clues as to the whereabouts of his reincarnation. Curiously, just a month later, one of the regents was killed in a car crash in Sikkim. The local press declared 'suspicious circumstances', but if there were, they were never investigated – apparently at the request of figures close to the regent.

Two weeks after the accident, Shamar Rinpoche announced that the mystery letter was a fraud. The announcement was tardy. A search team was already in eastern Tibet, with Chinese permission, on the trail of the Karmapa's 17th reincarnation. By early June clues from the letter had been deciphered, the boy had been found and the Dalai Lama had made a formal announcement supporting the boy's candidature. This was against a background of a brief occupation of Sikkim's Rumtek Monastery (now the head Karmapa monastery) by Indian troops and brawling by monks divided over the issue.

Shamar Rinpoche initially opposed the Dalai Lama's support, but after talks with the Dalai Lama he changed his mind. Several days later, he changed his mind again. Aided by western supporters he began a letter-writing campaign. Meanwhile, the Chinese authorities formally enthroned the 17th Karmapa at Tsurphu, using the occasion to announce that they had a 'historical and legal right to appoint religious leaders in Tibet'.

The issue still refuses to go away. Death threats have been made to various lamas who support the young 17th Karmapa (otherwise known as Ugen Thinley Dorje). And in March 1994, Shamar Rinpoche announced that he had discovered the rightful reincarnation, a boy named Tenzin Chentse who had been spirited out of China via Chengdu, Hong Kong and

The third room features a wrathful form of Guru Rinpoche and the fourth room features the Kagyupa protector Dorje Phurba holding a ritual dagger. The fifth room has a statue of Tseringma, a protectress associated with Mt Everest, on a snow lion.

Residence of the Karmapa The large building behind the gönkhang is the Serdung Chanpo, which serves as the residence of the Karmapa. It is usually possible to visit the cavernous ground floor assembly hall, which features a large statue of Sakyamuni flanked by Guru Rinpoche and the 16th Karmapa, who wears the characteristic black hat. It is sometimes possible to go into the upper chapels featuring new statues of all 16 previous Karmapas.

Lhakhang Chenmo This building to the right of the Serdung Chanpo houses a new and remarkably ugly 20m high statue of Sakyamuni, which replaces the celebrated 13th century image that was destroyed during the Cultural Revolution. You can view the statue from a 2nd floor balcony but even with the new perspective it just doesn't get any better-looking.

The Karmapa Connection

into India. The fact that the boy was able to obtain travel papers points to high-up official involvement. There is much conjecture that the Chinese authorities are revelling in a dispute that is dividing the exiled Tibetan community and may even have fanned the flames a little here and there. Tenzin continues to live in New Delhi under 24 hour protection and both Karmapas have received death threats.

The stakes are high. The Karmapa sect has estimated assets of around US$1.2 billion and up to one million followers, including many in the USA. More important to the Chinese is the fact that the Karmapa ranks as the third most important lama in Tibet after the Panchen Lama, whose reincarnation remains under house arrest in Beijing, and the Dalai Lama (see the boxed text 'The Panchen Lama' in the Tsang chapter).

The official Chinese position is that the 17th Karmapa installed at Tsurphu is the only rightful claimant. And here lies the rub – with the Tibetan community divided now between Chinese-administered Tibet and an exiled government in Dharamsala, the question of where incarnate lamas are to be found is likely to be an increasingly prickly issue. For the Chinese authorities, the more incarnate lamas found in Tibet the better, as this weakens the spiritual authority of the Government in Exile and lends credence to their own claims that there is only one Tibet – a Chinese-controlled Tibet.

Ugen Thinley Dorje, the 17th Karmapa, makes a daily public appearance at Tsurphu Monastery.

Chökang Gang Monastery Behind the Serdung Chanpo and Lhakhang Chenmo is the sprawling residence of the Regent of Tsurphu, where a couple of rooms have been restored: one on the 2nd floor and another downstairs. There is also an assembly hall accessed from a side entrance just by the main western entrance, which has statues of Sakyamuni, flanked by Maitreya and Guru Rinpoche and protected by blue Mahakala and red Hayagriva.

Returning back to the main courtyard the building to the right of the assembly hall has a small printing press but is often closed.

Tsurphu Kora

The Tsurphu kora, a walk of two or three hours, is quite taxing if you are not accli-matised to the altitude. It winds its way up some 150m above the monastery, providing splendid views of Tsurphu below. Above the monastery are some meditation retreats and faint traces of rock paintings. You may not have time for the kora if you have to return on the public minibus.

To follow this kora take the road west of Tsurphu and bear left. Up ahead is a turn-off that snakes uphill eventually to the top of the ridge overlooking the monastery. From here the trail is fairly obvious, descending eastward down the ridge into a gully before returning to the entrance of Tsurphu.

Places to Stay & Eat

There is no longer a monastery guesthouse at Tsurphu, though it is possible to *camp*

Nomads

The nomads of Tibet *(drokpas)* travel in groups of several up to 20 or more families. They live in four-sided yak-hair tents, which are usually shared by one family, though a smaller subsidiary tent may be used when a son marries and has children of his own. The various families of a group pitch their tents at quite a distance from each other, however, usually because the poor quality of grazing land means that yaks have to cover a large area of land to feed. The decision to move from one area to another is made together by all the families in a particular group.

The interior of a nomad tent holds all the family's possessions. There will be a stove for cooking and boiling water. The principal diet of nomad people is tsampa and yak butter (mixed together with tea), dried yak cheese and sometimes yak meat. The tent will also house a family altar with Buddha images and yak-butter candles that are left burning night and day. Next to the altar is a box that contains the family's jewellery and other valuables. In the warm summer months it is not unusual for nomad people to sleep outside their tent on a sheep-skin, covering themselves with rough yak-hair blankets.

Tending the herds of yaks and sheep is carried out by the men during the day. Women and children stay together in the camp where they are guarded by one of the men and the fero-cious Tibetan mastiffs that are the constant companions of Tibet's nomads. The women and children usually work during the day doing daily chores around the camp, weaving blankets and tanning sheep skins. Women are normally in charge of making dairy products such as butter and cheese.

Nomads graze their herds through the summer months and into late autumn. By this time the herds should be strong and healthy, and with the onset of winter it is time to go to the markets of some urban centre. The farmers of Tibet do the same, and trade between nomads and farmers provides the former with tsampa and the latter with meat and butter.

The nomads of Tibet have also traditionally traded in salt, which is collected from the Chang-tang plateau and transported south in bricks, often to the border with Nepal, where it is traded

nearby. There are a couple of basic *restaurants* here and a small shop.

Getting There & Away

Minibuses head out to Tsurphu from Barkhor Square in Lhasa from around 7 to 7.30 am, leaving whenever they're full. The timings aren't ideal as the minibuses take around 2½ hours to get to Tsurphu and return shortly after the Karmapa's blessing at 1 pm, thus only allowing a couple of hours to look around the place. Tickets cost Y18.

You could hire a Land Cruiser for around Y400 or even tag a visit here on to a trip to Nam-tso. You should agree to this in advance with your travel agency. Some will let you detour here for free, others will add on up to Y150 to the price of the tour.

NAM-TSO

Nam-tso (4718m), approximately 190km north-west of Lhasa, is the second largest salt-water lake in China, the first being Kokonor (Qinghai Lake) in Amdo (Qinghai Province). It is over 70km long and reaches a width of 30km. The Nyenchen Tanglha mountain range, with peaks of over 7000m, towers over the lake to the south – it was these mountains that Heinrich Harrer and Peter Aufschnaiter crossed on their incredible journey to Lhasa. Getting to the lake requires crossing the range via the road over the Largen-la (5150m) or on foot over the Kong-la (5240m).

Nomads

for grain. These annual caravans are fast dying out. Traditional life suffered its greatest setback in 1968 when nomads were collectivised and forcibly settled by the government. In 1981 the communes were dissolved and the collectivised livestock was divided equally with everyone getting five yaks, 25 sheep and seven goats. Nomads today generally rank among the poorest people in Tibet.

The nomads, like the farmers of Tibet, take their dead to high places and leave them for the birds. However, a ceremony, where the dead body is placed in a sitting position for a day and prayers are recited over it, is usually conducted first.

Nomad marriage customs, however, differ from those of farming communities in many ways. To a certain extent they are arranged by the families involved. When a child comes of a marriageable age, enquiries are made and when a suitable match is found the two people meet and exchange gifts. If they like each other, these informal meetings and ritual exchanges of gifts may go on for some time. The date for a marriage is decided by an astrologer, and when the date arrives the family of the son rides to the camp of their prospective daughter-in-law to collect her. When they arrive there is a custom of feigned mutual abuse that appears to verge on giving way to violence at any moment. This may continue for several days before the son's family finally carry off the daughter to their camp and she enters a new life.

Nomad herders or *drokpas* wearing the traditional heavy sheepskin coat known as a *chuba*.

Visits to Nam-tso, also known as Tengri Nor (Sky Lake), have become increasingly popular with individual travellers over the last few years. The water is a miraculous shade of turquoise blue and there are magnificent views of the nearby mountains. The wide open spaces are intoxicating and are dotted with the tents of local *drokpas* (nomad herders).

Whatever you do, however, do not sign up for a lift out here until you have been in Lhasa for at least a week. It is not unusual for visitors to get AMS on an overnight stay out at the lake. The sudden altitude gain of 1100m is not to be treated lightly.

Tashi Dor Monastery

Most travellers head for Tashi Dor Monastery, situated on a hammerhead of land that juts into the south-eastern corner of the lake. The monastery has a superb location at the foot of two wedge-shaped hills, with views across the turquoise waters to the huge snowy Nyenchen Tanglha massif.

The small chapel occupies just one of the numerous deserted caves honeycombed into the rock face. As you drive around the lake you will spot the two splinters of rock that mark the entrance to the cave. There is a highly dubious Y15 'entrance fee' to the monastery area.

The main attraction is just to take in the scenery, but there are some fine walks as well. The short kora takes less than an hour and passes a hermitage cave decorated with prayer flags and then a rocky promontory full of cairns, ending up on the eastern side at a huge *mani* (prayer wall). From here you can walk up to the top of the hill for good views.

If you have enough time it's well worth walking around the larger of the two hills. There are superb views to the north-east of the Tangula Shan mountains, marking the modern border between Tibet and Qinghai.

Another main attraction of a trip to Nam-tso is to get a peek at the otherwise inaccessible nomadic life of the Changtang, Tibet's vast northern plateau. You may get the opportunity to stop at the brown or black spider-like nomad tents. Make sure you are not forcing any hospitality and watch out for vicious dogs.

Places to Stay & Eat

There is basic *accommodation* at Tashi Dor Monastery for Y15 per person. It's really advisable to have a sleeping bag, though some bedding is provided. The *guesthouse* was being rebuilt at the time of research but should be completed by the time this guide is published. It won't fit more than around 10 people, so if there happens to be two groups up there at once there will be problems.

There is good *camping* 100m west of the monastery at the foot of the cliffs. Remember to carry out yours and as much of other people's rubbish with you before the site turns into a huge rubbish dump. Wilderness camping rules apply when going to the toilet – bury the waste and burn your toilet paper.

There is no food available at Nam-tso but you can get boiled lake water for Y2 a flask. There's no taste of salt. The only shops are at Namtso Qu, the local government centre 25km east, where there is also a basic *guesthouse* with cheap and basic rooms.

Getting There & Away

There is no public transport to Nam-tso. Most travellers band together in a group and hire a minibus or a Land Cruiser for the six or seven hour drive. The average price for a three day return trip is around Y1500 to Y2000 (Y300 to Y400 per person). Look out for notices at the Yak and Banak Shol hotels in Lhasa if you are interested in joining such a group. Many groups also stop off at the hot springs at Yangpachen (entry Y20).

The nearest town to Nam-tso that is linked to Lhasa by public transport is Damxung (Chinese: Dangxiong) on the Qinghai-Tibet Highway. One option is to take a Naqu-bound bus as far as Damxung, the other is to take a minibus from in front of the Kirey Hotel in Lhasa. The latter is cheaper and probably more convenient. Minibuses to Damxung cost around Y20 and theoretically leave daily at around 7 am,

THE WORLD OF A MONK

The western term 'monk' is slightly misleading when it is used in Tibetan Buddhism. The Tibetan equivalent would probably be *trapa*, which means literally 'scholar' or 'student', and is an inclusive term that covers the three main categories of monastic inmates. These should be distinguished again from lamas, who as spiritual luminaries have a privileged position in the monastic hierarchy, may have considerable wealth and, outside the Gelugpa order, are not necessarily celibate.

The first step for a monk, usually after having completed some prior study, is one of two lesser vows: the *genyen* or *getsul* ordinations – renunciations of secular life that include a vow of celibacy. This marks the beginning of a long course of study which is expected to lead to

the full *gelong* vows of ordination. While most major monasteries will have a number of gelong monks, it is by no means certain that all monks achieve gelong status.

These three divisions do not exhaust the categories of monks in a monastery. There are usually specific monastic posts associated with administrative duties, with ritual and with teaching. Gelong vows are also supplemented by higher courses of study, which are rewarded in the Gelugpa order by the title *geshe*. In pre-modern Tibet, the larger monasteries also had divisions of so-called 'fighting monks', or monastic militias. To a large extent they served as a kind of police force within a particular monastery, but there were also times when their services were used to hammer home a doctrinal dispute with a rival monastery.

Above: Printing blocks of Buddhist scripture and caretaker monk at Ganden Monastery, Ü, the main seat of the Gelugpa order.

Right: Novice monk, Drepung Monastery, Lhasa.

Over page: Time to reflect, Drepung Monastery.

CALUM MACLEOD

but it would be best to check at Kirey's reception desk for the latest details.

There are several *restaurants* in Damxung and there's a pretty good *County Government Guesthouse* here. It's in a government compound, over the river from the main Qinghai-Tibet Highway and has an English sign that says 'DX Hostelre'. Beds range from Y20 to Y40 and there are no washing facilities.

From Damxung, you have the option of hitching or hiking out to the village of Namtso Qu or to Tashi Dor Monastery. Both are around 40km away. Some travellers have been lucky and got lifts with trucks or even jeeps, but it seems that most end up walking. If you are trekking in to Nam-tso the best pass to use is the 5150m Largen-la (around 15km out of Damxung) and the best way out is via the Kong-la. For more information on this demanding walk see the Trekking chapter.

Some intrepid travellers have made it out to Nam-tso on a mountain bike, though the shiny wheels seem to drive most nomads' dogs even more berserk than normal. Wolves have been spotted around the Largen-la and the Kong-la.

DRAK YERPA

Drak Yerpa, around 30km to the north-east of Lhasa, is probably not of great interest for the average traveller but, for those with a particular interest in Tibetan Buddhism, Yerpa is one of the holiest cave retreats in Ü. Among the many ascetics who have sojourned here and contributed to the area's great sanctity are Guru Rinpoche and Atisha, the Bengali Buddhist who spent 12 years proselytising in Tibet. King Songtsen Gampo also meditated in a cave here, after his Tibetan wife established the first of Yerpa's chapels.

At one time the hill at the base of the cave-dotted cliffs was home to Yerpa Monastery. The monastery, however, was effectively laid to waste in the Cultural Revolution and there is very little to see nowadays.

From the ruins of the monastery it is possible to see some of the **cave retreats** a couple of hundred metres away at the foot of the cliffs. There are others higher up. Many were desecrated by Red Guards, but some have survived. Monks have begun to return to Yerpa, so expect some of the caves to be occupied.

Getting There & Away

It is possible to hike from Lhasa to Yerpa in a single day. You should come prepared with a tent and sleeping bag, however, as there is no formal accommodation in the area.

To walk to Yerpa, head up to the intersection of Lingkhor Chang Lam and Lingkhor Shar Lam and turn east on the road opposite the telecom building. This road follows the northern bank of Kyi Chu east out of Lhasa. About 2½ to three hours out of Lhasa, you will reach a hydroelectric power station. Shortly after this the road bears left up a mountainside to a pass. Yerpa village is visible from here, as is the side valley that leads from the village to Yerpa itself. Reckon on the entire walk taking between seven and eight hours.

TALUNG MONASTERY

Talung Monastery, around 65km north of Lhasa, is one of a number of monasteries (see Drak Yerpa earlier and Reting and Drigung Til monasteries following) that can be visited in a circuit north and east of Lhasa with a rented vehicle. Public transport in this part of Ü is almost nonexistent. It is even possible to tack on a visit to Reting and Talung or Drigung Til with a visit to Nam-tso, ending up with an intrepid clockwise circuit of around five days.

The sprawling monastic complex of Talung – it may at one time have had a population of some 7000 monks – was dynamited by Red Guards and now lies in ruins in the green fields of the Pak valley. Rebuilding is being undertaken, but not on the scale of other more important monasteries in the area such as Ganden. Talung was the seat of the Talung school of the Kagyupa order.

The site's most important structure was its **Tsuglhakhang**, or grand temple, the Red

Jokhang of Talung. The building is reduced to rubble but its walls remain. It once housed a two-storey statue of Sakyamuni.

RETING MONASTERY

Pre-1950 photographs show Reting Monastery sprawling gracefully across the flank of a juniper-clad hill in the Rong Chu valley. Like Ganden Monastery, it was devastated by Red Guards and its present remains hammer home the tragic waste caused by the ideological zeal of the Cultural Revolution.

The monastery dates back to 1056. It was initially associated with Atisha, the Bengali scholar who first came to Tibet via the Guge Kingdom of Western Tibet and then travelled to Ü, where he emerged as a principal catalyst in the revival of the near moribund Buddhist faith. In its later years, the monastery had an important connection with the Gelugpa order and the Dalai Lamas. Two regents – the de facto rulers of Tibet for the interregnum between the death of a Dalai Lama and the majority of his next reincarnation – were chosen from Reting abbots.

As is happening with other destroyed monasteries in Tibet, monks here have begun the slow and arduous process of rebuilding the work of centuries which was reduced to a pile of rocks with a few well-placed sticks of dynamite. The **main assembly hall** has been reconstructed and contains murals of Tsongkhapa, other prominent lamas and Tantric deities associated with the Gelugpa order. The **chapel** to the rear of the hall contains Reting's most important image, a gold statue of Guhyasumaja (Tibetan: Sangdu) – said to be the personal Tantric deity of Atisha.

Getting There & Away

Yerpa, Talung and Reting monasteries are probably best visited together in a rented vehicle. You might find it difficult to find companions to share the costs with, but this is not necessarily the case. There is usually a reasonable number of travellers in Lhasa with an interest in Tibetan Buddhism and a will to escape the madding crowds.

A trip of this sort is not so common so it would probably be worth shopping around for quotes on vehicles. The costs for a two day trip should probably be between Y1000 and Y1300 for a Land Cruiser. It may be possible to do it cheaper.

You could tack on Drigung Til Monastery and make a nice loop for a few hundred yuan more. A longer trip incorporating Nam-tso would cost around Y2800. It is not necessary to have a guide or permits for this trip.

On public transport you could get as far as Lhundrub, if not a little further, on a daily bus from Lhasa's city bus station, south of the Barkhor. After this you'd have to rely on hitching, though if you have food and enough time you shouldn't have any major problems.

DRIGUNG TIL MONASTERY & TIDRUM NUNNERY

Neither Drigung Til nor Tidrum, around 120km north-east of Lhasa, have become popular destinations for individual travellers. They can only be reached by rented transport or by hitching. There are few intrinsic sights but the valleys have an untouched and timeless quality that make them seem much further from Lhasa than they actually are. Most people who make it out here agree that it is well worth the effort.

If you have the time on the way to Drigung it's worth stopping at **Katsel Monastery**, just across the Kyi Chu from Medro Gungkar. There's not much to see but the temple has significance as one of the original Demoness Subduing Temples (see the boxed text 'Demoness Subduing Temples' in the Lhasa chapter). As you continue up the valley you pass countless chörtens.

Half way up the valley you come to Drigung Qu village, where there is a basic *guesthouse* offering beds for Y8 and several shops selling supplies. Drigung Qu could serve as a useful base to explore the local fort on a hillside to the north of the village, or nearby Uruzhwai Monastery, 2km south of the village and dedicated to the Dzogchen deity Ekajati (Tibetan:

Tsechigma). From Drigung Qu it is about 35km to Drigung Til.

Drigung Til Monastery

This is the head monastery of the Drigung school of the Kagyupa order. Although it suffered some damage in the Cultural Revolution, the monastery is in better shape than most of the other monastic centres in this part of Ü. It was first established in the mid-12th century. By 1250 it was already vying with Sakya for political power – as it happened, not a particularly good move. The Sakya forces joined with the Mongol army to sack Drigung Til in 1290. The monastery is thought to have been completely destroyed. Thus chastened, the monastery subsequently devoted itself to the instruction of contemplative meditation. There are currently 210 monks at the monastery.

Drigung Til sprouts from a high, steep ridge overlooking the Drigung valley. A steep thread of a path makes its way up into the monastic complex, although there is also vehicle access from the eastern end of the valley. The 180° views from the main courtyard are impressive and a serene stillness pervades the site.

The **main assembly hall** is probably the most impressive of the buildings at the monastery. The central figure inside is Jigten Sumgon, the founder of the monastery. Guru Rinpoche and Sakyamuni are to the left. Upstairs on the 1st floor you can see statues of Jigten Sumgon and his two successors, all wearing red hats. Jigten's footprint is set in a slab of rock at the foot of the statue. From the 1st floor you can go upstairs again to a balcony and a circuit of prayer wheels. Steps from here lead up to the funeral chörtens of two previous abbots.

The monastery **kora** then heads up the hill up to the main *dürtro* (sky burial site). This is the holiest sky burial site in the Lhasa region – people will travel hundreds of kilometres to bring their deceased relatives here. It is sometimes possible to observe the sky burial but it is absolutely essential that you gain permission from the family of the deceased and the senior lama who conducts the

ceremony. The lama requests that you do not take photos. Please do not abuse his and the deceased family's hospitality by sneaking any shots. If they do not want you to attend then just let it go. It's not worth coming all the way to Drigung just on the off-chance that there will be a burial.

As you follow the kora along the ridge and down to the monastery ask the monks for the path to the gönkhang. This **protector chapel** is dedicated to Abchi, the protectress of Drigung, who can be seen to the left of the main statue of the Jigten Sumgon. To the right of the chapel there is another statue of Abchi riding a horse which is next to Tseringma, the goddess of Mt Everest, who is riding a snow lion. Also look out for the pair of yak horns on the left wall of the chapel, after which Drigung is said to be names (a *dri* is a female yak), and the stuffed snow leopard on the right.

It is possible to stay in the *Monastery Guesthouse* in the main courtyard for Y15 per night. There's a small monastery shop here but no food, only boiled water, so bring supplies with you.

Tidrum Nunnery

About three hours walk to the north of Drigung Til up a side valley is Tidrum Nunnery (4325m), with its **medicinal hot springs**. The small nunnery has a great location in a narrow gorge at the confluence of two streams. The hot springs are delightful and are in a mercifully concrete-free zone. There are separate men's and women's baths. Bathing should be free, though 'big noses' sometimes get asked for a Y5 fee. A towel and flip flops are very useful.

There are two guesthouses next to the springs. Both offer beds for Y15 but the *Nunnery Guesthouse* is much nicer than the *government blocks*. There is a shop selling biscuits and beer but you should bring all your food with you.

Walks Around Tidrum If you have a day to spare you could do a tough day hike circumambulating the caves of Yeshe Tsogyel, Guru Rinpoche's consort and the one-time wife of King Songtsen Gampo. Pilgrims should do the hike clockwise but it's easier to find the route anticlockwise so that is how we describe it here.

First head north up the gorge behind the nunnery for about 1½ hours until you get to Dranang Monastery, where the valley divides. The caves are straight up the high ridge in front of the *gompa* but it's really too steep to climb up. If you're only on for a short walk you could turn back from here after visiting the monastery.

From Dranang take the left (west) valley and after five minutes or so start to climb to the left and then follow the path heading south-west up the side valley. The path turns to the right and continues up to the head of the valley in one to 1½ hours. From here you have to make your way up the steep scree to the pass, from where you get fabulous views of a wide cirque in the next valley.

Follow the rim of the cirque. At the far end of the rim the path drops a little and continues in a southerly direction. Don't descend to the valley on the right, you need to get to the pass which divides the Tidrum valley from this valley to the right. From the prayer flags of the pass, paths descend steeply to a sky burial site. From here continue right as the left-hand valley becomes very steep lower down. The right valley descends for almost 800m down to Tidrum.

Getting There & Away

The best way to get to Drigung Til and Tidrum is again by rented vehicle. The trip should take around four hours. It's worth spending at least one night in Tidrum or Drigung, more if you want to do any hikes. A two or three day trip should cost around Y1200, but as usual it pays to shop around. It is also possible to visit Drigung as part of a loop from Lhasa taking in Reting (around Y1500), or as a longer five day trip taking in Nam-tso and Reting (around Y2800).

If you are hitching you can take a bus to Medro Gungkar and hitch from there. Buses leave from the city bus station at around 10 am, so if you want an early start it's better to take the 6.30 am Ganden bus, get off on

the main road before the long climb up to the monastery and hitch from there. It's relatively easy to get a lift to Drigung Qu village, 35km before Drigung Til, but it's harder to get a lift up to the monastery itself.

DRAKSUM LAKE

The Swiss-style alpine Draksum (Basum) Lake, surrounded by 6000m peaks, is situated around 270km east of Lhasa along the road to Sichuan. It's a two day drive, with a stop in Kongpo Gyamda, the district capital. The lake is around 40km along a branch road.

There is local tourism authority **accommodation** at the lake and it should also be possible to stay with villagers. It would be a great place to have a tent. There is a temple on an island in the middle of the lake and a two day pilgrim circuit around the lake.

Very few travellers visit the lake. It is difficult, though not impossible, to visit without your own transport (plus a guide, permits etc), but you leave yourself open to fines if you travel without a permit. The nearest major checkpoint is a particularly nasty one at Bayi which shouldn't affect you, but you would also have to keep a low profile in Kongpo Gyamda.

GONGKAR

Gongkar's main claim to fame is its airport. There was once a fort here – Gongkar Dzong – but it now lies in ruins. Around 10km back on the road to Lhasa is the fort and **Gongkar Chöde Monastery**. This small Sakyapa monastery is by no means an important sight, but is worth heading out to if you are stuck with a whole afternoon or morning in Gongkar.

Places to Stay & Eat

There are a couple of decent places to stay near the airport if you can't face an early bus trip or you are headed to Gongkar from places other than Lhasa. The officially sanctioned abode for foreigners is the *Airport Hotel* (☎ 6182243), where surly staff will give you a bed in a comfortable carpeted double for Y70 per bed. There was no hot

Kilometre Markers along the Yarlung Tsangpo

Chushul to Tsetang

72	Chuwo Ri, one of Ü's four holy mountains
73	Monastery on side of Chuwo Ri
80	Ruins of Gongkar Dzong
82	Gongkar Chöde Monastery
93	Gongkar Airport
103	Gongkar Xian Town
112	Ferry to Dorje Drak
142	Turn-off Dranang Monastery (signposted as 'Zhatong')
147	Road to Mindroling Monastery
148/9	Tsongdu Tsokpa Monastery
155	Samye Ferry
190	Tsetang Town

water at the time of research. Foreigners are not allowed to stay in the cheaper rooms. Evening meals are served at the hotel between 7 and 8 pm – if you are late you miss out.

The *Wujin Zhaodaisuo*, next to the Airport Hotel, has pretty good rooms with bathroom for Y50 per person, as well as cheaper rooms with no bathroom for Y30/ Y25 a triple/double. Showers cost an extra Y10 for all rooms.

On the corner of the main road is a *hotel* with no English sign. Rooms in a hospital-ward style dormitory are Y30. Beds in a triple with communal bathroom are Y40. Doubles with private bathroom cost Y50 per person.

There is also a very basic *Tibetan guesthouse* with beds for Y10. The main Lhasa-Tsetang road running through Gongkar is the best place for *restaurants*. The food is fairly average Sichuanese fare.

Getting There & Away

Airport buses run from the Lhasa CAAC booking office to Gongkar every morning at 6 am and cost Y30. Private buses run when full from opposite the CAAC office. Return

buses to Lhasa are timed to coincide with the arrival of flights from Chengdu and Kathmandu. There are plenty of minibuses from Tsetang to Gongkar, particularly in the afternoon.

Outside of these times you may find a stray taxi who will take you back to Lhasa for as little as Y25. Otherwise you should not have to wait too long to find a bus returning from Samye Monastery or Tsetang to Lhasa.

DORJE DRAK MONASTERY

Dorje Drak, along with Mindroling, is one of the two most important Nyingmapa monasteries in Ü. It is less accessible and not as well restored as Mindroling, and consequently gets few western visitors. The monastery, on the north bank of the Yarlung Tsangpo, can be reached via a ferry from kilometre marker 112 on the Lhasa-Tsetang road. Some trekkers approach Dorje Drak from Lhasa, which is a hike of around four days.

MINDROLING MONASTERY

Mindroling Monastery is a very worthwhile detour from the Lhasa-Tsetang road between the Samye ferry crossing and Gongkar. It is the largest and, along with Dorje Drak, the most important Nyingmapa monastery in Ü. Parts of it were dynamited during the Cultural Revolution, but most of it has been beautifully restored.

Although a small monastery was founded at the present site of Mindroling as early as the 10th century, the usual date for the founding of Mindroling is given as the mid-1670s. The founding lama, Terdak Lingpa, was held in high esteem as a scholar and counted among his students the fifth Dalai Lama. The monastery was razed during the Mongol invasion of 1718 and later restored.

There are two entrances. If you come by foot you will probably enter from the east – cars enter from the south. The central building of Mindroling is an elegant brown stone structure on the west side of the courtyard. Note in particular the impressive masonry –

the fit between the many different sized stones used in the building is nearly perfect.

The most important **chapel** of the main hall is the one to the rear, where you can see a large Sakyamuni image. In the hall itself is a statue of Terdak Lingpa in a glass case. There are more chapels on the 2nd floor, though you'll need to find a monk willing to open them up. The main **assembly hall** of Mindroling lies to the north of the central courtyard.

On the main road 1½km towards Tsetang is the small **Tsongdu Tsokpa Monastery**. The original monastery across the road has been converted into a housing block.

Getting There & Away

There is no direct public transport to Mindroling. One possibility is to take the Lhasa-Tsetang bus and get off at kilometre marker 147 by the English sign to the monastery. The monastery is around 8km south of the road, and the last section involves an uphill climb – it is not too punishing, however. You cannot see the monastery until you round a ridge and are below it – it appears on the right. You should be able to hitch a lift pretty easily.

Mindroling is easily slotted into a Yarlung valley excursion if you have a rented vehicle. It should add very little to the cost of your trip, as it is only a 16km detour all up.

SAMYE MONASTERY

Samye is deservedly the most popular destination for travellers in the Ü region. Samye, in the middle of the sandy Samye valley and approached via a beautiful river crossing, has a magic about it that makes many travellers stay longer than they had intended. No journey in Ü is complete without visiting Samye.

History

Samye was Tibet's very first monastery and has a history that spans over 1200 years. It was founded in the reign of King Trisong Detsen (who was born nearby), though the exact date is unknown and subject to some debate – probably between 765 and 780. Whatever the case, Samye represents the Tibetan state's first efforts to allow the Buddhist faith to set down roots in the country. Of course the Bön majority at court, whose religion prevailed in Tibet prior to Buddhism, were not at all pleased with this development.

Buddhism's victory over the Bön dominated establishment is symbolised by Guru Rinpoche's victory over the massed demons of Tibet at Hepo Ri, just to the east of Samye. It was this act which paved the way for the introduction of Buddhism in Tibet.

Shortly after the founding of the monastery, Tibet's first seven monks were ordained here by the monastery's Indian abbot, Shantarakshita, and Indian and Chinese scholars were invited to the monastery to assist in the translation of Buddhist texts into Tibetan.

Before long, disputes broke out between followers of Indian scholarship and Chinese. The disputes culminated in the Great Debate of Samye, an event that is heralded by Tibetan historians as a crucial juncture in which the future course of Tibetan Buddhism was decided. The debate, which probably took place in the early 790s, was essentially an argument between the quietist Indian approach to bodhisattvahood via textual study and scholarship and the more immediate Chan (Zen) influenced approach of Chinese masters, who decried scholarly study in favour of contemplation on the absolute nature of Buddhahood. The debates came out on the side of the Indian scholars.

Samye has never been truly the preserve of any one of Tibetan Buddhism's different orders. The influence of Guru Rinpoche, however, in establishing the monastery has meant that the Nyingmapa order has been most closely associated with the monastery. Images of the Guru dominate the monastery. When the Sakyapa order came to power in the 15th century it took control of Samye, and Nyingmapa influence declined, though not completely.

Samye has been damaged and restored many times throughout its long history. Inevitably, the most recent assault on its antiquity was by the Chinese during the Cultural Revolution. Many of the monastery's structures, including the all-important, gold-topped Ütse, were badly damaged and vast numbers of relics and images were stolen or destroyed. Nevertheless, Samye did not fare as badly as some of the other temples in Ü. Extensive renovation work has been going on since the mid-80s and there are now 130 monks at Samye.

Permits

A travel permit is needed to visit Samye and it's not all that easy to get one. Shigatse PSB occasionally issues them to individual travellers; Lhasa never does. If you come with a Land Cruiser group your agency will get you one.

At the time of research many travellers were turning up at the ferry point on the

Tsetang side without a permit, paying Y50 to the PSB officers and crossing without any problems. Whether this will continue to happen is open to question. You'll just have to go and see. Don't trust the travel agencies in Lhasa to tell you the truth. Trekkers coming from Ganden Monastery were being fined several hundred yuan after crossing from the Samye side. There are no PSB checks in Samye – just at the ferry crossing on the south bank.

The Monastery

Samye Monastery is designed to represent the Buddhist universe and many of the buildings in the courtyard are cosmological symbols. The square in front of the monastery guesthouse has some interesting bits and pieces. The stubby isolated building to the north is the remains of a nine storey tower used to display festival thangkas.

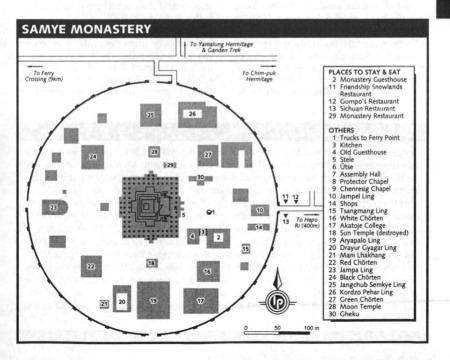

SAMYE MONASTERY

To Yamalung Hermitage & Ganden Trek

To Ferry Crossing (9km)

To Chim-puk Hermitage

To Hepo Ri (400m)

0   50   100 m

PLACES TO STAY & EAT
2 Monastery Guesthouse
11 Friendship Snowlands Restaurant
12 Gompo's Restaurant
13 Sichuan Restaurant
29 Monastery Restaurant

OTHERS
1 Trucks to Ferry Point
3 Kitchen
4 Old Guesthouse
5 Stele
6 Ütse
7 Assembly Hall
8 Protector Chapel
9 Chenresig Chapel
10 Jampel Ling
14 Shops
15 Tsangmang Ling
16 White Chörten
17 Akatoje College
18 Sun Temple (destroyed)
19 Aryapalo Ling
20 Drayur Gyagar Ling
21 Mani Lhakhang
22 Red Chörten
23 Jampa Ling
24 Black Chörten
25 Jangchub Semkye Ling
26 Kordzo Pehar Ling
27 Green Chörten
28 Moon Temple
30 Gheku

The Ütse The central building of Samye, the Ütse, comprises a synthesis of architectural styles. The ground and 1st floors were originally Tibetan in style, the 2nd floor was Chinese and the 3rd floor Indian. There is much scholarly debate on this issue and without a trained eye there is little way of telling anyway.

Just to the left of the entrance is a **stele** dating from 779. The elegant Tibetan script carved on its surface proclaims Buddhism as the state religion of Tibet by order of King Trisong Detsen.

From here the entrance leads into the first of the ground floor chambers: the **assembly hall**. As you enter the hall a row of figures greet you on the left; Vairocana, a translator; Shantarakshita, Samye's first abbot; Guru Rinpoche; Trisong Detsen and Songtsen Gampo. On the right are two groups of three statues: the first group are associated with the Kadampa order; the second group is multidenominational, including lamas from the Nyingmapa, Sakyapa and Gelugpa orders.

To the rear of the assembly hall are steps leading into Samye's most revered chapel, the **Jowo Khang**. You enter the inner chapel via three doors – an unusual feature. They symbolise the Three Doors of Liberation:

those of emptiness, signlessness and wishlessness. An inner circumambulation route around the inner chapel follows at this point.

The centrepiece of the inner chapel is a 4m statue of Sakyamuni. Bodhisattvas and protective deities line the side walls of the chapel, and the walls themselves are decorated with ancient murals. Look also for the panelled ceiling – each of the panels is adorned with a Tantric mandala.

To the right of the hall is a gönkhang (protector chapel) with statues of deities so terrible that they must be masked. Watch out for the stuffed snake over the exit.

Before ascending to the 1st floor, take a look at the **Chapel of Chenresig**, outside and to the left of the main assembly hall, which features a 1000 armed statue of Avalokiteshvara (Tibetan: Chenresig).

The main feature of the **1st floor** is an upper extension of the inner chapel. This houses an image of Guru Rinpoche in a semi-wrathful aspect. There is an inner kora path around the hall.

Some of the 2nd-floor murals outside this hall are very impressive; the ones on the south wall depict Guru Rinpoche, the ones to the left of the main door show the fifth Dalai Lama with the Mongol Khan Gushri with various ambassadors showing obeisance.

The Samye Mandala

Samye's overall design was based on the Odantapuri Temple of Bihar, India, and is a mandalic representation of the universe. The central temple represents Mt Meru (or Sumeru), and the temples around it in two concentric circles represent the oceans, continents and subcontinents that ring the mountain in Buddhist cosmology.

At the centre of the monastery grounds is the Ütse, the most impressive of the monastery buildings, and at the centre of this is a central pole which represents the core of the universe. Directly to the north is a Moon Temple and to the south a Sun Temple (now destroyed). Ringing the Ütse are four large chörtens, which are named after their colours: red, black, green and white. These were destroyed in the Cultural Revolution but have been rebuilt recently – they look decidedly concrete and slightly out of place. Surrounding the chörtens are 12 ling chapels, four major ones and eight minor ones. The four major ling chapels represent the four continents, the minor ling chapels are subcontinents. The complex originally had 108 buildings (an auspicious number to Tibetans) and there were 1008 chörtens on the circular wall which rings the monastery.

Also on the 2nd floor are the three rooms of the Dalai Lama's quarters (left) and another protector chapel and Amitayus (Tibetan: Tsepame) chapel (right).

The **3rd floor** is a recent addition to the Ütse. It holds a mandala base but is normally closed. Walk around the back to a ladder leading up to the **4th floor**. This is a sacred chapel of great significance. The main image is of Kalachakra (Tibetan: Dukor), a Tantric deity. The pillars around the central core are meant to symbolise the Four Kings, the 16 arhats and the 21 manifestations of Tara.

Back on the ground floor you can follow the prayer wheel circuit around the Ütse, and look at the interesting murals showing the founding of the monastery. It is also possible to climb up to the monks' quarters on the outer first floor and then up onto the roof.

The Ling Chapels & Chörtens As renovation work continues at Samye, the original ling chapels and the coloured chörtens are gradually being restored. Take a wander around and see which ones are open. Following is a clockwise tour of the chapels open at the time of research.

The **Tsangmang Ling**, once the monastery printing press, is now open. **Akatoje College**, opened in 1997, is now a college for monks. The restored **Aryapalo Ling** was Samye's first building and is now looked after by a charming couple of monks. **The Drayur Gyagar Ling** was the original centre for translation of texts, as depicted on the wall murals. The main statue on the upper floor is of Sakyamuni, flanked by his Indian and Chinese translators.

The **Jampa Ling** on the west was where Samye's Great Debate was held. On the right as you go in, look out for the mural depicting the original design of Samye with zigzagging walls. There is an unusual semicircular inner pilgrimage path here that is decorated with images of Maitreya.

To the north is the **Kordzo Pehar Ling**, the home of the oracle Pehar, until he moved to Nechung Monastery outside Lhasa. Several chapels have been renovated inside.

It is also possible to enter the Green and White chörtens, though there is little of interest inside.

Hepo Ri

Hepo Ri is the hill to the east of Samye where Guru Rinpoche vanquished the demons of Tibet. King Trisong Detsen later established a palace here. Paths lead up the side of the hill from the road leading from Samye's east gate. A 30 minute climb takes you to the top, festooned with prayer flags and offering great views of Samye below. Early morning is the best time for photography.

Chim-puk Hermitage

Chim-puk Hermitage is a warren of caves that was once a retreat for Guru Rinpoche. It is a popular day hike for travellers spending a few days at Samye. The walk takes around four or five hours up and around three hours down. Take some water with you. If you are lucky you might find a pilgrim truck headed up there, otherwise you could hire a tractor in Samye. Ask at the reception of the Monastery Guesthouse.

Chim-puk is to the north-east of Samye. If you head out of the monastery in this direction you should be able to find a path leading east through some fields. Keep following this track, bearing left. The path crosses through desert-like territory for a couple of hours before ascending into the surprisingly lush area in which the caves are found.

Many of the caves are occupied by hermits so don't just go barging into them. There is a small monastery built around Guru Rinpoche's original **meditation cave** halfway up the hill. It might be possible to stay the night here if you have a sleeping bag and food. There are splendid views of the Samye valley from up here.

If you are feeling fit and acclimatised it is possible to climb up to the top of the peak above Chim-puk. You'll probably only have enough time to do this if you get a lift to Chim-puk or stay the night there. To make this climb from the Guru Rinpoche cave follow the left-hand valley behind the caves and slog it uphill for 1½ hours to the top of the ridge, where there are several clumps of prayer flags. From here you can drag yourself up along a path for another 90 minutes to the top of the conical peak, where there are a couple of meditation retreats and fine views of the Yarlung Tsangpo (Brahmaputra) valley. On clear days you can see several massive Himalayan peaks to the south-east.

If you managed to get a lift up to Chimpuk it is possible to take another route back to Samye in around three to four hours. From the peak descend back down to the ridge-line above Chim-puk but instead of heading straight down the way you came up, cut down the other (west) side of the ridge that divides Chim-puk from the Samye valley. Follow paths along the western side of this ridge, slowly descending in the direction of Samye. After two hours you get to the valley floor, from where it is an easy hour's walk to Samye.

Other Things to See

It is possible to head up the valley directly behind Samye to **Yamalung Hermitage**, around 20km from Samye (see the Ganden to Samye Trek map in the Trekking chapter). It's really too far to hike there and back in a day but you could probably hire a tractor to take you there for around Y50 return. For details of this valley see the final stages of the Ganden to Samye trek and its map in the Trekking chapter.

Places to Stay & Eat

There is really only one place to stay, the new *Monastery Guesthouse* just in front of the Ütse compound. It lacks the intimacy of the old guesthouse next door (now used by monks) but it's still pretty good. Basic ground floor rooms are available for Y10 a bed; middle floor rooms have better beds and windows for Y15 to Y20. Carpeted rooms on the top floor cost Y25, including the much sought after corner room with its great views of the Ütse.

The best places to eat are just outside the eastern gate of the monastery. *Gompo's Restaurant* is the most popular and the food is cheap and tasty. The Amdo *momos* (dumplings) are worth trying. Gompo is an excellent source of information on the region and is mellow as can be. Next door, the *Friendship Snowlands Restaurant* is also pretty good, but only if the owner is in the kitchen.

The *Sichuan Restaurant* offers Chinese food but you'll have to refer to the Chinese Food section in the Language chapter as no English is spoken here. Travellers have complained of overcharging and there's little you can do about it since the owner is also the local PSB officer! There's a basic *hotel* on the upper floors but you should make sure your papers are in order if you decide to stay here. All in all, you're better off at the Monastery Guesthouse.

Finally, the *Monastery Restaurant*, just to the north of the Ütse, offers basic food like thugpa and fried noodles. Prices are cheap, food is average and there's an English menu.

In front of the Monastery Guesthouse is a shop that is reasonably well stocked with instant noodles, sweets, biscuits, candles, cigarettes, soft drinks, beer (essential for any monastic sojourn) and so on.

Getting There & Away

All buses from Lhasa to Tsetang pass by the Samye ferry departure point, which makes getting to Samye from either Lhasa or Tsetang fairly easy. Permits are officially required for Samye Monastery and have posed problems for some travellers, see Samye Monastery Permits earlier in this section.

A bus service also runs from just west of Barkhor Square in Lhasa to the Samye ferry. It leaves at around 7.30 am and costs Y23. There is also a bus to Tsetang (referred to as Shannan, the name of the prefecture) that leaves an hour or so later. You might try getting tickets the day before, but the best course of action is to get there before 7 am on the day you want to leave and ask around for the Samye bus. There is also a minibus to Samye that leaves from opposite the Kirey Hotel in Lhasa at roughly the same time.

Buses to Tsetang also leave from Lhasa's main bus station at around 7.30 am but until the pricing system changes you'll be paying twice the local price. Foreigners' price is Y70.

All buses drop off Samye passengers at the ferry crossing. River crossings are irregular (operating whenever there are enough people – about 30 seems the average) in flat-bottomed boats powered with a small motor. Locals pay Y3 for the crossing but the PSB have ordered that foreigners should pay Y10. Anyone who turns up with a guide can expect to be charged a lot more.

The river crossing, one of the few in Tibet, is a fantastic ride. It takes a little over an hour, and much careful navigation around the sandbanks. On the other side, you hop across other boats moored against the banks of the Yarlung Tsangpo to avoid getting your feet wet.

It is a 9km walk from the ferry to Samye and almost everyone – Tibetans included – jumps on a truck for the ride. The cost is Y3, though some truck drivers will again try to charge Y10, and you can expect a crowded, bumpy 30 minute ride – lots of fun if you are in the mood for it. There is sometimes a Land Cruiser waiting at the ferry point, which takes passengers to the monastery for Y10.

Trucks leave Samye for the ferry terminal at around 8 am and 2 pm, though it's worth checking these times with the guesthouse manager. Buses to Tsetang and Lhasa wait for passengers on the other side of the river.

See the Ganden to Samye trek in the Trekking chapter for information on the popular trek between the two monasteries.

TSETANG

Tsetang (3550m), 183km south-east of Lhasa, is the second largest town in the Ü region and the third largest in Tibet. It is the capital of Shannan Prefecture and an important administrative centre and army base for the Chinese government. For travellers Tsetang is of interest mainly as a jumping board for exploration of the Yarlung valley area. The major obstacles in your way are a lack of budget accommodation, permit hassles (see the Yarlung valley section later in this chapter) and a concerted effort on the part of the Chinese authorities to charge foreigners double for everything.

Like Lhasa and Shigatse, Tsetang is divided into a new Chinese town and an old Tibetan quarter. The main street that leads south of the traffic circle consists entirely of soulless department stores, government offices and karaoke bars; the result of rapid Chinese immigration and its associated economic boom. The Tibetan quarter is in the east of town, clustered around Gangpo Ri, one of Ü's four sacred mountains. It's a shabby, dispirited affair compared to its equivalent in Lhasa but there are still a few interesting monasteries to see.

Information

The new telecom office is the place to make international calls. It's also worth trying at the Tsetang Hotel, especially as they'll normally let you arrange to be called back if things aren't that busy. The hotel is also the only place in town to change money, though strictly speaking you should be a guest to do this.

The PSB office is the big green building near the Regional Guesthouse. They play things strictly by the book and won't help with permits so avoid the place.

China International Travel Service This branch office of CITS, also known as Hongshan (Red Mountain – the Chinese name for Gangpo Ri) Travel Service is at the back of the Tsetang Hotel and is the place to hire a vehicle to get out to Yumbulagang and Chongye. If there happens to be a small group of you in town, hiring a vehicle (which holds five or six people) for an excursion out to the Yarlung valley should be fairly economical. A half day trip (without guide) to Trandruk Monastery and Yumbulagang costs Y150 and a full day tour (with guide) to Trandruk, Yumbulagang and Chongye costs Y450.

Monastery Kora

There are a couple of small monasteries in the Tibetan quarter which are worth a brief visit. Most pilgrims visit them in a clockwise circuit.

From the market head east to a small square and continue down the street to the right of the bank. After 200m you'll come to **Tsetang Monastery**. This 14th century monastery was originally a Kagyupa institution but by the 18th century the Gelugpas had taken it over. The Chinese smashed the place to pieces but it's been well restored. You may have to track down the friendly caretaker to show you around; there are good views from the roof.

From here head north and then east to the **Ngachö Monastery**, a somewhat livelier place. Monks are more than happy to show you around in return for a look at the photos in your Lonely Planet guide. On the top floor is the bed and throne of the Dalai Lama. A side chapel is devoted to medicine with images of Tangtong Gyelpo and the Eight Medicine Buddhas.

A pilgrim path leads down from the mon-astery, follows the base of Gangpo Ri to a small shrine and then heads up to a bundle of prayer flags. From here one path ascends the hill to some hermitage caves, the other descends to **Sang-ngag Zimche Nunnery**.

This nunnery was largely spared the outright destruction suffered by Tsetang Monastery and has some important images in its main chapel. The principal image is of Avalokiteshvara, and dates back to the time of King Songtsen Gampo – according to some accounts the statue was fashioned by the king himself. The walls are draped with some fine old thangkas and there are a couple of small chapels with more images to the rear of the building. There is a Y5 entrance fee. You can grab a nice cup of tea at a stall below the nunnery before following the path down to Tsetang Monastery and back to town.

Market

If you are really stuck for something to do in Tsetang, you might wander down to the market just south of the Tsetang traffic circle. There are a few thangkas for sale but

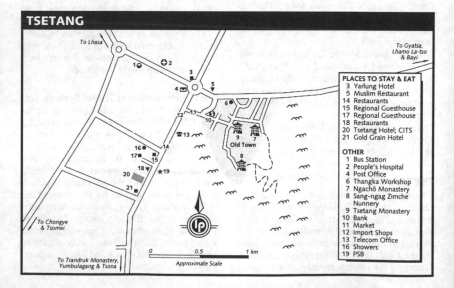

TSETANG

To Lhasa

To Gyatsa,
Lhamo La-tso
& Bayi

Old Town

To Chongye
& Tsomei

To Trandruk Monastery,
Yumbulagang & Tsona

0   0.5   1 km
Approximate Scale

PLACES TO STAY & EAT
3   Yarlung Hotel
5   Muslim Restaurant
14 Restaurants
15 Regional Guesthouse
17 Regional Guesthouse
18 Restaurants
20 Tsetang Hotel; CITS
21 Gold Grain Hotel

OTHER
1   Bus Station
2   People's Hospital
4   Post Office
6   Thangka Workshop
7   Ngachö Monastery
8   Sang-ngag Zimche
    Nunnery
9   Tsetang Monastery
10 Bank
11 Market
12 Import Shops
13 Telecom Office
16 Showers
19 PSB

not much else. It closes reasonably early at around 6.30 pm.

Places to Stay

Finding good budget accommodation is a problem in Tsetang. There are cheap hotels, like the *Yarlung Hotel* on the main roundabout (Y15 a bed), but they are prevented from accepting foreigners by Tsetang's strong PSB presence.

The cheapest official place we found was the *Regional Guesthouse (diqu zhaodaisu)* on the main street. Here you can get a bed in a comfortable and carpeted double for Y100. Unofficially they have a whole range of cheaper rooms in a separate block, where you might be able to get a bed for Y50 (which is still double local price). For a shower, head out to a washhouse just off the main road which offers hot showers in pretty clean surroundings for Y5 (though they often try to charge foreigners Y10).

Tsetang's premier lodging is the *Tsetang Hotel* (☎ 7821899, fax 7821688), just down the road from the guesthouse. It is a tacky attempt to create a tourist-class hotel, but you have to give them credit for trying. Rooms are comfortably furnished. Economy doubles are Y500, triples Y690, and quads are Y800, though you might be able to get a discount if there are no groups in sight. The Cantonese restaurant is pretty good but somehow the food isn't as tasty when you know the English menu is double the price of the Chinese.

Further south is the new *Gold Grain Hotel*, which is better value, with comfortable singles/doubles for Y180/200.

Places to Eat

The main north-south drag is the best place to seek out restaurants; north of the Tsetang Hotel all the way to the traffic circle the road is lined with *Chinese restaurants*. The flashy places serve hot-pot and are generally expensive – it is notoriously difficult to keep track of the price when eating hot-pot and it is easy to get ripped off. There are a number of humble-looking places that serve up typical Chinese fare for prices of around

Y15 to Y20 per dish. None of them have English menus – check out the Chinese Food section in the Language chapter. There are also a few *Tibetan restaurants*.

If you are self-catering or looking for hiking supplies then the *import shops* near the market can seem like the promised land. Feast on such goodies as chocolate, honey, crackers, US cookies, beef jerky, canned ham, wine and Budweiser.

Getting There & Away

There are direct buses from Lhasa's Barkhor Square and main bus station to Tsetang, though most travellers make their way first to Samye, spend a day or so at the monastery, and then travel on to Tsetang.

Transport out of Tsetang is fairly minimal. Buses and minibuses to Lhasa (and the Samye ferry) leave hourly between 9 am and 2 pm and cost between Y30 and Y35. Afternoon minibuses to Gongkar run until about 6 pm. There are also buses headed south to Tsomei (via Chongye) and Tsona (via Yumbulagang) at 8.30 am but you have more chance of getting on these buses if you flag them down outside of town since both these destinations are off-limits to foreigners.

Some travellers band together in Lhasa for a three or four day trip out to the Yarlung valley by way of Tsetang. This way it is possible to visit Samye Monastery, drive on to Tsetang, spend the night there, visit the Yarlung valley sights and then head back to Lhasa via Mindroling Monastery and possibly Gongkar. The total cost (including permits and guide) for a Land Cruiser on a trip of this sort is around Y2800, though you might find it cheaper. It's more cost-effective to add a Yarlung extension onto a trip to the Nepalese border if you are headed that way.

AROUND TSETANG
Gangpo Ri

Gangpo Ri (4130m) is a mountain of special significance for Tibetans as it is the legendary birthplace of the Tibetan people (see the boxed text 'Mythology of the Yarlung Valley'). The **Gangpo Ri Monkey**

Cave where the monkey meditated can be visited near the summit of the mountain. The walk there and back will take close to a full day. Do it in the spirit of a day walk in the hills, rather than as a trip specifically to see the Monkey Cave, as the cave itself is rather disappointing.

Around 2km south of the Tsetang Hotel is a trail that leads up the slopes of Gangpo Ri for around 3km (an altitude gain of about 550m) to the cave.

There is a pilgrimage circuit around Gangpo Ri but the walk would probably require two days. Very fit walkers (and Tibetans) can do it in one day, taking around 11 hours. The walk starts a couple of kilometres east of town, along the road to Bayi and heads south up a dry valley to the Gangpo-la and Monkey Cave. You could probably sleep here if you had a sleeping bag, some food and a sense of adventure,

before descending the next day to the main road south of Tsetang.

Yarlung Valley

Yarlung is considered the cradle of Tibetan civilisation (see the boxed text), and it was from Yarlung that the early Tibetan kings unified Tibet in the 7th century. The massive burial mounds of these kings can be seen in Chongye. Yumbulagang, another major attraction of the area, is perched on a crag like a medieval European castle and is considered the oldest building in Tibet.

The major attractions of the Yarlung valley can be seen in a day or two, but it is worth giving yourself some extra time here. The main problem is the permit situation (see the following Permits section). Transportation in the area is also somewhat hit and miss, but it is a beautiful part of Tibet for extended hiking and day walks. Yarlung

---

Mythology of the Yarlung Valley

The Yarlung valley is considered the cradle of the Tibetan people. The story goes that Avalokiteshvara (Chenresig), the Bodhisattva of Compassion, descended from the heavens to the Land of Snows long ago in the form of a monkey. He meditated in a cave on the slopes of Gangpo Ri, before being drawn from his solitude by Sinmo, a white demoness. It seems she got his attention by sitting outside his cave and weeping – oldest trick in the book, but one that is especially effective with a Bodhisattva of Compassion. One thing led to another and before too long they had six children – the beginnings of the Tibetan race. A strip of land nearby (now less than romantically known as 'Commune No 9') is the site of the legendary 'first field in Tibet'.

The contours of the valley shelter a wealth of other such legends. The mountain of Lhabab Ri is said to be the site where the first of the Tibetan kings, Nyentri Tsenpo, descended from heaven on a sky cord, whereupon he was recognised by 12 local chieftains. Subsequent Tibetan kings all ascended back to heaven using the handy sky cord until Drigum Tsenpo, whose name means 'slain by pollution', accidentally cut the cord in a show of marksmanship. From this time the remains of Tibetan kings were earth-bound and buried in the funerary mounds of Chongye.

Then in 1943 three Americans fell from the sky. They had lost their bearings and run out of fuel while on a mission flying supplies from India to Kunming over 'The Hump', China's only supply line during WWII. They managed to bail out of their B-24 bomber and landed on mountain slopes above Tsetang. They finally made it to Lhasa and then safely back home to Idaho but only after they narrowly escaped a mob of Tibetans furious that foreigners had been high enough to look down on the Dalai Lama.

sees a lot fewer foreign travellers than the other major destinations of Ü and Tsang.

Some travellers have spent a week or more hiking in the Yarlung valley region, and have successfully stayed with Tibetan families in the villages. This doesn't happen so much now that the PSB has tightened up travel regulations, but you still might be offered a place to stay, either at a home or a monastery. If you opt to do this, always offer a gift or some money in return for the favours given by the locals and try to make sure that the reception for future travellers remains a welcome one.

Permits At the time of research permits were needed to visit anywhere outside Tsetang township, though there weren't actually any checks in the valley. If you head off on foot before dawn to Yumbulagang or Rechung-puk there is little chance of being caught, though the likelihood rises rapidly in Chongye, especially if you stay the night. We spent a couple of days in the Yarlung valley with no permits and saw no checks, though we might just have been lucky.

If you are on a Land Cruiser tour your driver or guide will arrange a permit from Tsetang PSB. The only way to get one otherwise is to hire a Land Cruiser for a half or full day from CITS at the Tsetang Hotel and they will get you one.

Sheldrak Cave Sheldrak Cave is the preserve of hardy hikers and Tibetan pilgrims. It is a tough six hour climb to the west of Tsetang with an altitude gain of around 1000m.

For Tibetans, Sheldrak is one of Tibet's holiest pilgrimage destinations. It is the site of Guru Rinpoche's first meditation cave. At the invitation of King Trisong Detsen, Guru Rinpoche came to Tibet to exorcise the land of demons and the influence of Tibet's indigenous Bön faith. According to legend, it was here in the Crystal Cave that he got the job done. Unless you have a keen interest in Tibetan pilgrimage sites, this is another attraction that it would be best to treat as a strenuous hike.

The cave is reached from the road that heads out to Chongye from Tsetang. About 4km from the centre of Tsetang there is a large chörten known as the Tsechu Bumpa. It's worth trying to hitch a ride on a tractor along this section. From the chörten a trail heads west from the Chongye road up the Sheldrak valley to Sekhang Zhirka village, a sky burial site and then a small monastery. From here it is a tough climb of less than an hour to Sheldrak. The cave itself has a small chapel and provides great views of the surrounding countryside.

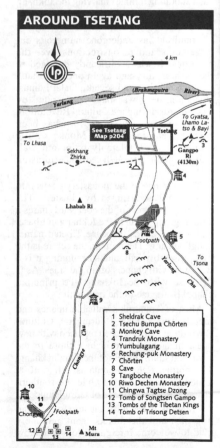

AROUND TSETANG

1 Sheldrak Cave
2 Tsechu Bumpa Chörten
3 Monkey Cave
4 Trandruk Monastery
5 Yumbulagang
6 Rechung-puk Monastery
7 Chörten
8 Cave
9 Tangboche Monastery
10 Riwo Dechen Monastery
11 Chingwa Tagtse Dzong
12 Tomb of Songtsen Gampo
13 Tombs of the Tibetan Kings
14 Tomb of Trisong Detsen

Trandruk Monastery Around 7km south of the Tsetang Hotel, Trandruk is one of the earliest Buddhist monasteries in Tibet, having been founded at the same time as the Jokhang and Ramoche in Lhasa. Dating back to the 7th century reign of Songtsen Gampo, it is one of the 'Demoness Subduing' temples of Tibet. King Songtsen Gampo's Chinese wife, Princess Wencheng, divined the presence of a subterranean demoness in Tibet. Only by pinning this demoness down, it was felt, could the Buddhist faith take root in the high plateau. The location of Trandruk – which is one of 12 such subduing temples that ring the Jokhang in concentric circles like a mandala – corresponds to the demoness's left shoulder.

Trandruk has undergone numerous enlargements and reconstructions over the centuries. It was significantly enlarged in the 14th century and again under the auspices of the fifth and seventh Dalai Lamas. The monastery was badly desecrated by Red Guards during the Cultural Revolution, and extensive restoration work has been carried out since 1988. Monks at the monastery will solemnly point out wall paintings that were defaced and still await restoration.

The entrance of the monastery opens into a courtyard area ringed by cloisters. The building to the rear of the courtyard shares a similar ground plan to the Jokhang in Lhasa, and indeed shares the same Tibetan name: Tsuglhakhang. The room in the centre is the main assembly hall, and surrounding it is a walkway with chapels off to the sides. As is the case with the Jokhang, the principal chapel is the one to the rear centre.

Most of Trandruk's valuable images and murals were damaged during the Cultural Revolution and have been replaced with new ones. Images of note include those in the north and south chapels of the Tsuglhakhang. The northern chapel contains a fine 1000 armed Avalokiteshvara, while the southern chapel has a huge image of Guru Rinpoche.

Trandruk is a significant stop for Tibetan pilgrims, and the monks seem genuinely glad to welcome foreign visitors and show them around. It is a lively place and well worth a brief visit en route to Yumbulagang. Theoretically, there is an entry charge of Y15, but the monks do not seem particularly concerned about collecting it.

Getting There & Away Trandruk is in a small Tibetan village around 6km or 7km south of the Tsetang Hotel. It is possible to walk there in 1½ hours, but there is also a steady stream of tractors plying the road between Trandruk and Tsetang. Getting a lift should only cost Y1 or Y2. One possibility is to hitch as far as Trandruk and then walk out to Yumbulagang, which is another 5km down the road. Try to head out around dawn if you don't have a travel permit (see Permits section earlier).

Yumbulagang This fine, tapering finger of a structure that sprouts from a craggy ridge overlooking the patchwork fields of the Yarlung valley is reputed to be the oldest building in Tibet. At least that is the claim for the original structure. Most of what can be seen today dates from 1982. It is still a remarkably impressive sight, and should not be missed.

The founding of Yumbulagang stretches back to a time of legend; myths converge on the structure in bewildering profusion. The standard line is that it was built to accommodate King Nyentri Tsenpo, a likely historical figure who has since been swallowed up by the mythology of Tibet. Legend has him descending from the heavens and being received by the people of the Yarlung valley as a king. Buddhist holy texts are also thought to have fallen from the heavens at Yumbulagang at a later date.

There has been no conclusive dating for the original Yumbulagang, though some accounts indicate that the foundations may have been laid more than 2000 years ago. They are probably inaccurate. It is more likely that it dates back to the 7th century, when the country first came under the rule of Songtsen Gampo.

The design of Yumbulagang indicates that it was originally a fortress and probably much larger than the present structure. Today it serves as a chapel and is inhabited by a few monks. Its most impressive feature is its **tower**, and the prominence of Yumbulagang on the Yarlung skyline belies the fact that this tower is only some 11m tall. It is possible to climb up to the top storey of the tower via a couple of rickety stepladders but there's little to see.

The ground floor **chapel** is consecrated to the ancient kings of Tibet. A central Buddha image is flanked by Nyentri Tsenpo on the left and Songtsen Gampo on the right. Other kings and ministers line the side walls. There is another chapel on the upper floor with a Avalokiteshvara image. There are some excellent murals by the door which depict, amongst other things, Nyentri Tsenpo descending from heaven on a sky cord and Guru Rinpoche arriving at Sheldrak.

It does not take all that long to explore Yumbulagang. Perhaps the best part of a visit is the walk up along the ridge above the building. There are fabulous views of Yumbulagang and the Yarlung valley from a promontory topped with prayer flags. It is an easy 10 minute climb.

Getting There & Away Unless you have hired transport, you will probably have to walk from Trandruk Monastery to Yumbulagang. There are plenty of tractors on the road between Trandruk and Tsetang, but fewer between Trandruk and Yumbulagang. It is a walk of around 6km, and for the most part it follows a shady, tree-lined stretch of road. From Tsetang it takes around 2½ to three hours.

Rechung-puk Monastery The remains of Rechung-puk Monastery are really only an attraction for serious pilgrim types or those with time to hike around the Yarlung valley region. It is easily accessible on foot from Trandruk Monastery or from Tsetang, but little remains of its former grandeur. As ever, it's most interesting to visit with a bunch of pilgrims.

Rechung-puk is associated with the illustrious Milarepa (1040-1123), founder of the Kagyupa order and revered by many as Tibet's greatest song writer and poet. It was his foremost disciple, Rechungpa (1083-1161), who founded Rechung-puk as a cave retreat. Later a monastery was founded at the site, which eventually housed up to 1000 monks. The draw of the monastery to pilgrims is the cave itself where they are hit on the back with holy relics.

To get to Rechung-puk, follow the road between Yumbulagang and Trandruk and take the road to the west (left) at kilometre marker 132, about half way between the two. You can see the ruins of the monastery up on the ridge that divides the two channels of the Yarlung valley. The road enters a small village and then bends to the south (left), finally crossing a river next to a small school. A couple of kilometres from the main road is a second village, from where it is a steep 20 minute walk up to the monastery, passing a white chörten.

A path leads over the ridge from the cave, past some ruined chapels and down to the minor road. From here you can head west along a dirt track towards a large chörten and then join the main road from Tsetang to Chongye.

Alternatively you can walk down the eastern side of the Chongye valley to a holy cave and, a couple of hours after that, Tangboche Monastery.

Tangboche Monastery Around 15km south-west of Tsetang on the road to Chongye, Tangboche is not an important site and should not be too high on most travellers' itineraries. Nevertheless, the monastery was less badly damaged during the Cultural Revolution than many of the other monastic sites of Ü and some highly rated murals have survived intact.

The monastery is thought to date back to 1017 and was instrumental in the revival of Buddhism in central Tibet. Atisha, the renowned Bengali scholar, stayed here in a meditation retreat. The murals, which for most visitors with an interest in things Tibetan are the main attraction of the monastery, were commissioned by the 13th

Dalai Lama in 1913. They can be seen in the monastery's main hall – one of the few monastic structures in this region that was not destroyed by Red Guards.

Tangboche is easily visited if you are travelling by rented transport between Tsetang and Chongye. You should be able to see the building on the left once you're about 15km out of Tsetang. You have to look carefully, as it is partially obscured by a village. There is a short trail from the road to the village and monastery. It is a dusty 12km walk from Trandruk Monastery to Tangboche.

Chongye Valley

Most visitors to Chongye go there as a day trip from Tsetang, and combine the visit with seeing the attractions in the Yarlung valley. It is possible to stay in the town of Chongye but you leave yourself open to permit hassles this way. If you want to visit the surrounding sites and don't have a permit it's worth detouring around the central PSB office and generally keeping a low profile. A road on the eastern side of the valley by-passes the centre of town and leads to the Chongye tombs.

There probably is not enough of interest to the average traveller to warrant a stay of more than a day or so in the area. The huge burial mounds of the ancient kings of Ü are, pretty much as their name suggests – mounds – and not particularly exciting for anyone without a degree in archaeology.

Like the Yarlung valley, Chongye is a beautiful valley enclosed by rugged peaks. The views from some of the burial mounds are superb. It is also well worth climbing up to Riwo Dechen Monastery and the ruins of the old *dzong* (fort) behind it for more views of the mounds.

Chongye Town Chongye town is a dusty street, lined with the occasional shop and restaurant, that culminates in a T-junction. To the far right of the junction as you come from Tsetang there is a basic *Government Guesthouse* (next to the PSB compound) with beds for around Y20. It is not a town in which you'll want to linger for long, but it

makes a good base for hikes in the Chongye valley area. Chongye is around 27km south of Tsetang and is not that easy, though by no means impossible, to hitch there. If you can get hold of a bicycle it is possible to ride out to the town in a few hours.

From Chongye town, most of the important sights are easily accessible on foot.

Chongye Burial Mounds The Tombs of the Kings at Chongye represent one of the few historical sites in the country that give evidence of a pre-Buddhist culture in Tibet. Most of the kings interred here are now firmly associated with the rise of Buddhism on the high plateau, but the methods of their interment point to the Bön faith. It is thought that the burials were probably officiated at by Bön priests and accompanied by sacrificial offerings.

Sky burial is the most popular means of disposing of the dead these days but recent archaeological evidence seems to suggest that burial might have been quite widespread in the time of the Yarlung kings, and may not have been limited to royalty.

Accounts of the location and number of the mounds differ. Erosion of the mounds has also made some of them difficult to identify positively. It is agreed, however, that there is a group of 10 burial mounds just south of the Chongye Chu.

The most revered of the mounds, and the closest to the main road, is the **Tomb of Songtsen Gampo**. It is the largest of the mounds and has a small Nyingmapa temple atop its 13m-high summit.

The southernmost of the group of mounds, high up on the slopes of Mt Mura is the **Tomb of King Trisong Detsen**. It is about a one hour climb, but there are superb views of the Chongye valley from up here.

Chingwa Tagtse Dzong The dzong, or fort, can be seen clearly from Chongye town and the Chongye burial mounds, its crumbling ramparts straddling a ridge of Mt Chingwa. It was once one of the most powerful forts in central Tibet and dates back to the time of the early Yarlung kings. The dzong is also celebrated as the birthplace of the fifth Dalai Lama. There is nothing to see in the fort itself, but again you are rewarded with some great views if you take the hour or so walk up from Chongye town. Paths lead up from the centre of town, from the nearby ruins of the red chapel and from the gully behind Riwo Dechen Monastery.

Riwo Dechen Monastery Riwo Dechen Monastery sprawls across the lower slopes of Mt Chingwa below the fort. It is well worth visiting this active Gelugpa monastery. The monks are friendly and there are surprisingly large numbers of them (around 70 at the moment) Extensive restoration work has been carried out here, making this one of the largest monasteries in this part of Tibet. There are some nice walks up to the ridge to the north of the monastery and then down to the fort.

Riwo Dechen Monastery can be reached by a half hour walk from Chongye's excellent old Tibetan quarter. Turn west at the town's T-junction and ask for the 'gompa'. Half-way up is a grand, new chörten. It is sometimes possible to stay the night at the monastery – a magical experience.

LHAMO LA-TSO

Around 115km to the north-east of Tsetang, Lhamo La-tso is one of Ü's most important pilgrimage destinations. The *la* of La-tso is a Tibetan word that means 'soul' or 'life spirit'. La resides in both animate and inanimate forms such as lakes, mountains and trees. The two may sometimes be connected, as in the Tibetan custom of planting a tree at the birth of a child – such a tree is known as a *la-shing*. In the case of Lhamo La-tso, the la here is identified with the spirit of Tibet itself.

The Dalai Lamas have traditionally made pilgrimages to Lhamo La-tso to seek visions which appear on the surface of the oracle lake. The Tibetan regent journeyed to the lake after the death of the 13th Dalai Lama and had a vision of a monastery in Amdo that led to the discovery of the present Dalai Lama. The lake is also considered to be the home of Palden Lhamo, Tibet's protectress deity.

Lhamo La-tso is difficult to reach and receives very few foreign visitors. You should come prepared with a tent and enough food supplies for around a week. Be prepared for cold weather – the lake is at an altitude of over 5000m.

The nearest accommodation to Lhamo La-tso is at *Chökorgye Monastery*, which is around four hours hard walking from the lake over a high pass of around 5300m. You have to be fit, acclimatised and well equipped to attempt this. Nothing is charged for staying at the monastery, but it is appropriate to make a donation when you leave. Do your best to keep the monks well disposed toward the occasional foreign visitor.

Getting There & Away

It is possible to hike all the way from Samye Monastery or from Tsetang to Lhamo La-tso. From Samye it is a taxing seven to eight day walk; those considering this trek should refer to Victor Chan's *Tibet Handbook – a pilgrimage guide*, which has full details of the hike. From Tsetang, it may be possible to hitch a lift to Gyatsa Qu, from where it is a two day walk up to Chökorgye Monastery.

Most travellers approach Lhamo La-tso by rented vehicle from Lhasa or Tsetang. Land Cruisers should complete the road between Tsetang and Gyatsa in around five hours – reckon on around seven hours in a Chinese truck. You can cross the river by vehicle at Gyatsa Qu. On the other side a truck is sometimes available to ferry pilgrims and travellers up to Chökorgye Monastery. You will have to keep a low profile at Gyatsa if you don't have a permit. It would be wise to check on the current situation before heading out there.

Tsang

HIGHLIGHTS

- **Yamdrok-tso** – the turquoise waters of this coiling 'scorpion' lake
- **Tashilhunpo Monastery** – spectacular chapels and tombs of the Panchen Lamas
- **Gyantse's Kumbum** – the most stunning architectural wonder in Tibet
- **Mt Everest** – magnificent views from Rongphu Monastery
- **Sakya Monastery** – the breathtaking assembly hall, one of Tibet's greatest treasures

The traditional Tibetan province of Tsang lies to the west of Ü, the province with which Tsang has long shared political dominance over the Tibetan plateau. With the decline of the Lhasa kings in the 10th century, the epicentre of power moved to Sakya, under Mongol patronage from around the mid-13th to the mid-14th centuries.

After the fall of the Sakya government, power shifted back to Ü and then back to Tsang again. But until the rise of the Gelugpa order and the Dalai Lamas in the 17th century, neither Tsang nor Ü effectively governed the whole of central Tibet, and the two provinces were usually rivals for power. Some commentators see the rivalry between the Panchen Lama and Dalai Lama as a latter-day extension of this provincial wrestling for political dominance.

The two major urban centres of Tsang are Shigatse and Gyantse. Both contain important historical sights and have emerged as popular destinations for travellers.

A large number of travellers make their way through Tsang from Lhasa to Kathmandu – usually in rented vehicles – via Yamdrok-tso, Gyantse, Shigatse, Sakya,

Everest Base Camp, Tingri and Zhangmu. It is a convenient route along the 725km Friendship Highway that takes in Tsang's most important attractions. By public transport it is possible to get as far as Lhatse but after that you must rely on your thumb.

Most of Tsang's sights involve detours from the highway. Sakya is a 21km detour from the highway, close to Lhatse, while Everest Base Camp is a 71km detour from Shegar by vehicle or a three day trek from Tingri.

The entries in this chapter follow a southwesterly route through Tsang from Lhasa to the Nepalese border, taking in the main attractions of the area on the way.

YAMDROK-TSO

On the old road between Gyantse and Lhasa, the dazzling Yamdrok-tso (4488m) can be seen from the summit of the Kamba-la pass (4794m). The lake lies several hundred metres below the road, and in clear weather is a fabulous shade of deep turquoise. Far in the distance is the huge massif of Mt Nojin Kangtsang (7191m).

Yamdrok-tso is a coiling, many-armed body of water that doubles back on itself like a scorpion at its south-west extent, effectively creating a large island within its reaches. For Tibetans, it is one of the four holy lakes of Tibet (the others are Lhamo La-tso, Namtso and Manasarovar), and the home of wrathful deities. The Chinese, on the other hand, have a more pragmatic interest in the lake as the site of a hydroelectricity generating station (see the boxed text 'Down the Drain').

Devout Tibetan pilgrims and the occasional western trekker circumambulate the lake, a walk of around seven days. Most western travellers, however, are content with a glimpse of the lake from Kamba-la and views from the town of Nangartse, where you can stay the night. For those interested in a day walk on the shores of the lake, see the following entry on Samding Monastery.

Leaving Yamdrok-tso is as spectacular as arriving, since you have to cross the 5045m Karo-la, with its awesome roadside views of the Nojin Kangtsang Glacier. It was here that Colonel Younghusband's British troops clashed with Tibetan forces en route to Lhasa in what is thought to be geographically the highest battle in British history. See the boxed text 'Bayonets to Gyantse' later in this chapter.

Getting There & Away

There is no public transport to Yamdrok-tso. Most travellers visit the lake with a rented vehicle en route from Lhasa to Gyantse and on into Tsang. It's also possible to hire a vehicle for a four day loop from Lhasa, visiting the lake, Gyantse and Shigatse.

If you are hitching you can get a bus to Chushul and then hitch from just over the Yarlung Bridge. Alternatively you can get a minibus to Shigatse and then Gyantse and then hitch from there. The advantage of this route is that you can get a travel permit for the lake from the Shigatse PSB. At the time of research it was relatively easy to hitch as large convoys of trucks were shuttling between Chushul and a hydroelectric plant near Longma, about 40km east of Gyantse. Nangartse to Chushul should cost around Y25.

Trekkers who want to hike here should see Victor Chan's *Tibet Handbook – a pilgrimage guide*, which has highly detailed information on the various approaches to the lake and hiking around it.

Nangartse

Nangartse (4500m) is the largest town on the lake side and a popular place to stop for the night. It's not a particularly attractive place but there is a small monastery in the south of town, an old Tibetan quarter and small fortress to the north, and there are plenty of opportunities for walks nearby (see Samding Monastery). You can't actually walk to the lake shore (you'll soon find yourself up to your knees in bog) but the

---

Down the Drain

Yamdrok-tso is one of Tibet's holiest lakes and an important centre for pilgrimage. Yet what one devout Tibetan Buddhist perceives as a sacred body of water, another pragmatic Chinese engineer views as a natural resource just waiting to be utilised for the development of the country.

Yamdrok-tso has an unusual location locked in a high bowl above the Yarlung Tsangpo (Brahmaputra River) and the Chinese government has long harboured a plan to utilise gravity to create a hydroelectric supply. By the mid 1980s the Chinese leadership had sanctioned a plan to build a 6km tunnel 10m below the surface of the lake that would send the waters of the lake dropping some 846m into the Yarlung Tsangpo. Work was temporarily halted after opposition by the Panchen Lama, but by 1997 the turbines had started to produce electricity for the Lhasa region. You can see the pumps from the Lhasa-Shigatse road near Chushul.

The project is highly controversial, and not only because of the reverence Tibetans have for the lake. Yamdrok-tso is a dead lake with no outlet and no perennial source of water. Water drained from it can never be replenished naturally. Chinese scientists claim that excess power will pump river water back up into the lake. Environmentalists fear that the lake, an important breeding ground for the endangered black-necked crane, could be dry within 20 years.

Water levels do indeed seem to be dropping and the section of water around Nangartse is now cut off from the main body of the lake. Many Tibetans further claim that the energy produced by the lake's hydroelectric supply will be directed mainly at fuelling Chinese migration into Lhasa. The Chinese reaction is predictable: other hydroelectric sites are in the pipeline.

views are still good and birdwatchers in particular will have a field day here during the summer months.

Places to Stay & Eat The best place to stay is the Tibetan-style *Grain Guesthouse*, above the Sichuan Restaurant on the south side of the street. Look for a purple sign that says 'Guesthouse'. Dorm beds are Y20 or Y30, depending on the quality of the bed and the carpet around it. Washing facilities consist of a flask of hot water and a basin

(the pit toilets will make your eyes water) but it's a friendly and comfortable place.

The other place to stay is the *Hotel for Foreigners* (both hotels can take foreigners), where beds vary from Y15 to Y30. Rooms are comfortable but the place lacks the charm of its competition across the street.

There are several relatively expensive Chinese restaurants in town, including the *Sichuan Restaurant* on the ground floor of the Grain Guesthouse. A cheaper option is the *shop* 50m east of the guesthouse which sells *shuijiao* (Shandong-style dumplings)

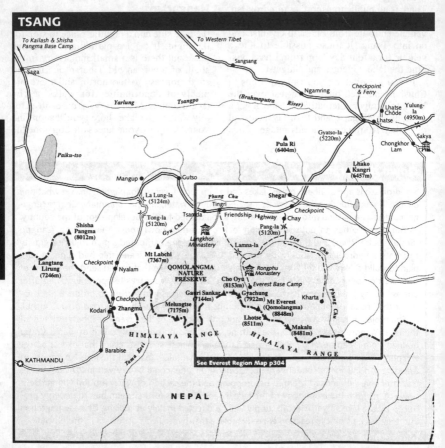

by the bowl or the weight. The *Nanjiang Restaurant* next door is also good.

Samding Monastery

Samding is a monastery on the shores of Yamdrok-tso, around 10km to the east of Nangartse. Sited on a ridge that separates the south-bearing northern arm of the lake from Dumo-tso (a smaller lake between the northern and southern arms of Yamdrok-tso) the monastery provides excellent views of the Dumo plain and the mountains to the

south. You can walk there from Nangartse in about two hours.

The founding of Samding probably took place in the mid-14th century. It is associated with Bodong Chokle Nangyel (1306-86), a monk who founded an obscure sub-order derived from Nyingmapa and Sakyapa teachings. The order never prospered and was for the most part restricted to Samding and other smaller monasteries in the Yamdrok-tso area. The monastery is noted for the unusual fact that it is traditionally headed by a female incarnate lama named

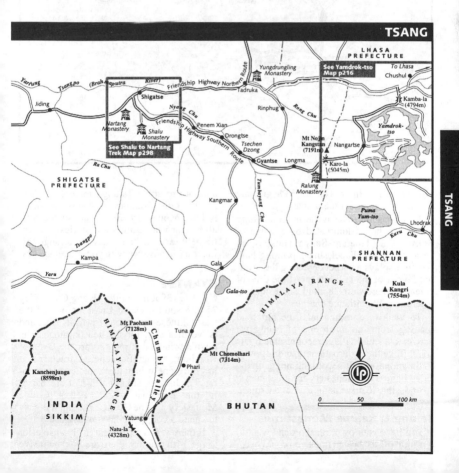

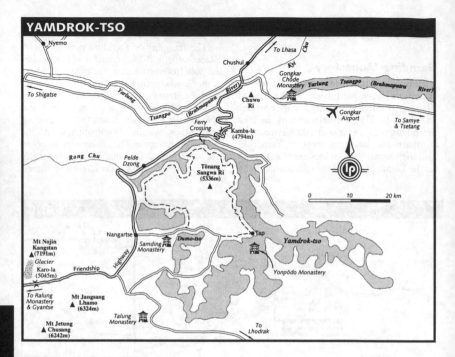

Dorje Phagmo. Images of Dorje Phagmo are common throughout the monastery.

It is possible to visit the main *dukhang* (assembly hall), dominated by a statue of Sakyamuni (Tibetan: Sakya Thukpa), an eerie protector chapel, and a printing hall, which displays a carpet depicting the original layout of the monastery. At the time of research, there were 38 monks in residence. There is a Y8 entrance charge.

To walk to Samding take the dirt road leading from the north end of Nangartse across to a small village recognisable by its trees. Take the right path here and follow it to the monastery. It's worth climbing up the ridge behind the monastery for great views. It's possible to drive here in a Land Cruiser.

Talung & Ralung Monasteries

If you have your own transport and want to get right off the beaten track you could make a detour to either Talung Monastery, 13km south of the Nangartse-Gyantse road, or Ralung Monastery, 5km south of the road after Karo-la. Both monasteries are extremely remote. You'll have to arrange this itinerary in advance with your travel agency.

GYANTSE

Gyantse (3950m), in the Nyang Chu valley 254km south-west of Lhasa, is one of the least Chinese-influenced towns in Tibet and is worth a visit for this reason alone. The town's principal attractions are the Gyantse Kumbum, a magnificent tiered structure that has only one ruined and remote contemporary (at Jonang, 60km north-east of Lhatse) in the Buddhist world, Pelkor Chöde Monastery and the Gyantse Dzong. It is easy to spend a couple of days in Gyantse.

If there was a settlement in Gyantse prior to the 14th century, there are no conclusive records of its existence. But between the 14th and 15th centuries the town emerged as the centre of a fiefdom with powerful connections with the Sakyapa order. By 1440 Gyantse's most impressive architectural achievements – the Kumbum and the dzong – had been completed. Pelkor Chöde Monastery also dates from this period.

The monastery compound in the far north of town, which houses both Pelkor Chöde Monastery and the Gyantse Kumbum, once contained 15 monasteries. Little remains of them today. They were a particularly interesting collection, however, in that they brought together three different orders of Tibetan Buddhism in the one compound – a rare instance of multidenominational tolerance. Nine of the monasteries were Gelugpa, three Sakyapa and three belonged to the Bupa, an obscure order whose head monastery was Zhalu near Shigatse.

Gyantse's historical importance declined from the end of the 15th century, though it continued to be a major centre for the trade of wood and wool between India and Tibet. Its position at the crossroads of trade routes leading south to Bhutan, west to Shigatse and north-east to Lhasa turned Gyantse into the third largest town in Tibet by the time of the Chinese takeover. In 1904 it became the site of a major battle during Colonel Younghusband's advance on Lhasa, and the British troops spent a month here in the Gyantse Dzong before continuing to Lhasa (see the boxed text 'Bayonets to Gyantse' later in this section).

Gyantse has a horse racing and archery festival in the summer. It is traditionally held in the middle of the fourth lunar month, though tourist authorities are trying to fix it for sometime in June or July.

Orientation

Orientation in Gyantse is a fairly straightforward affair. Buses stop at the town's only major intersection. To the north is the Tibetan part of town. It is concentrated around the main road leading to Pelkor Chöde Monastery past the dzong, which looms over the town on a high ridge. To the

south is an incipient Chinese quarter, with some government buildings, shops, restaurants and a couple of hotels.

Pelkor Chöde Monastery

Founded in 1418, Pelkor Chöde was once a multidenominational complex of monasteries. Today much of the sprawling courtyard, enclosed by walls that cling to the hills backing on to the monastery, is bare and the remaining structures are attended by Gelugpa monks. The best way to get an idea of the

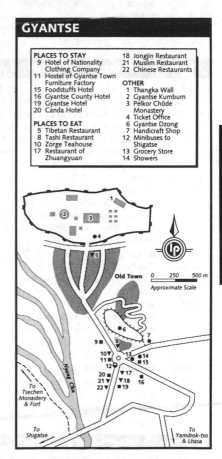

GYANTSE

PLACES TO STAY
9 Hotel of Nationality Clothing Company
11 Hostel of Gyantse Town Furniture Factory
15 Foodstuffs Hotel
16 Gyantse County Hotel
19 Gyantse Hotel
20 Canda Hotel

PLACES TO EAT
5 Tibetan Restaurant
8 Tashi Restaurant
10 Zorge Teahouse
17 Restaurant of Zhuangyuan

18 Jongjin Restaurant
21 Muslim Restaurant
22 Chinese Restaurants

OTHER
1 Thangka Wall
2 Gyantse Kumbum
3 Pelkor Chöde Monastery
4 Ticket Office
6 Gyantse Dzong
7 Handicraft Shop
12 Minibuses to Shigatse
13 Grocery Store
14 Showers

Old Town

0   250   500 m

Approximate Scale

To Tsechen Monastery & Fort

To Shigatse

Nyang Chu

To Yamdrok-tso & Lhasa

TSANG

original extent of Pelkor Chöde is to view it from the Gyantse Dzong.

Pelkor Chöde Monastery is a dark, gloomy place and if you want a good look at the various murals and *thangkas* it is a good idea to bring a torch. The entrance is flanked by statues of the Four Guardian Kings instead of the usual paintings. Keep and eye out for the jewel-vomiting mongoose. Just by the entrance on the left is a particularly spooky protector chapel.

The main chapel is to the rear of the assembly hall. There is an inner route around the chapel which is lined with murals. Inside, the central image is of Sakyamuni, who is flanked by the Buddhas of the past and future. Other bodhisattvas line the walls.

To the left of the main chapel is another chapel that is worth taking a look inside. It is crowded with images, some of them particularly noteworthy for their fine artistic accomplishment.

There are also a number of interesting chapels on the upper floor. Some of the statuary may be of Indian origin, but whatever the case there are many beautiful images here with startlingly vivid and lifelike facial expressions. The first chapel to the left after you mount the stairs is noted in particular for a three-dimensional mandala that dominates the room, the paintings of the 84

Kilometre Markers along the Friendship Highway

The following points of interest, towns and geographical features along with their appropriate km markers (distance from Beijing) may be of help to travellers, hitchhikers and, in particular, mountain bikers. One point worth bearing in mind is that the km marker system changes at some points and in certain regions the markers have disappeared – sometimes turning up as doorsteps in new buildings. There are enough of them left, however, for you to be able to keep a fairly accurate track of your progress and identify turn-offs to places of interest.

Lhasa to Shigatse

4647	Lhasa's eastern crossroads to Golmud or Shigatse
4656	Sakyamuni Buddha rock painting
4662/3	Netang village and Drölma Lhakhang
4673/4	Bridge
4696/7	Chushul
4703	Bridge over the Yarlung Tsangpo
4707	Monastery
4712	Views of Yamdrok-tso hydroelectric project on the far side of the river. The golf ball on the top of the hill is a radar and meteorological centre.
4718/9	Ruined fortress on left
4724	Monastery, village and ruined dzong
4732	Jagged peaks ahead and valley begins to narrow

4758	Road to Nyemo to north
4760	Restaurants
4781	Bridge over to south side
4801	Turn-off to Rin-puk
4821	Ferry to North Friendship Highway and Yungdrungling Monastery, restaurants
4835	Drakchik Ferry
4876	Ferry
4905	Shigatse

Shigatse to Tingri

4917	Nartang Monastery
4928	Gyeli village
4933	The very gentle mountain pass of Tso-la (4500m)
4936	Kangchen Monastery to right
4960/61	Jiding village and fort, restaurants and shops
4973	Dilong village

mahasiddhas that adorn the walls, and clay images of key figures in the Sakyapa lineage. Take a look at the 84 mahasiddhas, each of which is unique and shown contorted in a yogic posture. Other chapels are dedicated to Maitreya (Tibetan: Jampa), Tsongkhapa and the 16 arhats.

There is a Y30 entry fee for the Pelkor Chöde Monastery complex and this includes entry to the Gyantse Kumbum. There is a ticket office just inside the main gates but it's all a bit disorganised and you might be able to haggle the price down to Y15, the local price. Opening hours are, very roughly, 10 am to 1 pm and 3 pm to 6.30 pm.

Gyantse Kumbum

Commissioned by one of the early Gyantse princes in 1440, the Gyantse Kumbum is rated by many as Gyantse's foremost attraction. The chörten rises over four symmetrical floors and is surmounted by a gold dome. The dome rises like a crown over four sets of eyes that gaze serenely out in the cardinal directions of the compass. There are excellent views of the Kumbum from the hills behind the monastery.

A clockwise route spirals up through all six floors of the Kumbum taking in the chapels that line the walls of the chörten. There are two sets of four central chapels which extend to the floor above from the 1st

Kilometre Markers along the Friendship Highway			
5000	Marker showing 5000km from Beijing, small monastery and dzong	**Tingri to Nyalam**	
		5193/4	Tingri
5009	Village and start of climb to pass	5205	Tsamda hot springs and Snowland Lodge
5014/15	Yulung-la (4950m)		
5016	Road Works No 1 Camp	5209	Tashi Hotel on the left
5028	Sakya Bridge, turn-off to Sakya and Lhatse Co Guesthouse	5216	Two small Tibetan guesthouses
5036	Ruined dzong	5232	Gutso village
5052/3	Lhatse	5236	Mangup Monastery and ruined fort on west side of the river
5058	Checkpoint and road to Western Tibet		
5063	Start of climb to pass, with a height gain of around 1000m	5253	Three small guesthouses
		5255/6	Small guesthouse
5083	Gyatso-la (5220m)	5274	La Lung-la (5124m)
5100	Terrible roads 5km either way	5281	Bridge
5115	Views of Everest and the Himalaya Range	5284	Tong-la pass (5120m)
		5290	Short cut down the hillside, used by Land Cruiser drivers
5123/4	Monastery and fortress		
5133/4	Shegar turn-off, Kangjong Hotel	5303	Roadworkers hostel
5139/40	Shegar Checkpoint (passports only)	5311	Village
		5333	White chörten and track to Milarepa's Cave
5145	Turn-off to Everest Base Camp		
5155	Ruined dzong to left	5345	Nyalam
5162	Village	5357	Choksam Hotel
5170	Village	5376	(Approx) Checkpoint
5193/4	Tingri	5378	Zhangmu
		5386	Nepalese Border

and 3rd floors, and each of these is surrounded by smaller chapels in diminishing numbers and size as the floors ascend.

Much of the statuary in the chapels was damaged in the Cultural Revolution (see the Facts about Tibet chapter) and has only recently been restored. The murals, however, have weathered the years very well. They are of 14th century provenance and if they were not created by Newari (Nepalese) artisans they are obviously influenced by Newari forms. Experts also see evidence of Chinese influence and, in the fusion of these Newari and Chinese forms with Tibetan sensibilities, the emergence of a syncretic but distinctly Tibetan style of painting.

Whatever the case, there are an awful lot of murals to look at ('kumbum' means 10,000 images!) and unless you have a particular interest in the evolution of Tibetan Buddhist art it is difficult not to hurry through the last two floors. Lingering in a few of the chapels and having a close look at the wall frescoes is enough to give you an idea of what is on offer in other chapels.

Depending on the position of the sun, certain chapels are sometimes illuminated with a warm, soft light that allows flashless photographs. There is a photography charge of Y10 and the monks are insistent that you leave your camera with them if you don't pay.

First Floor The 1st floor has four main chapels in the cardinal directions. These are dedicated to Sakyamuni (along with two disciples, Medicine Buddhas and Guru Rinpoche) in the south; Sukhavati, the Pure Land of the West, home of red Amitabha (Tibetan: Öpagme) in the west; Dipamkara (Marmedze – Buddha of the Past) in the north and Tushita (another Pure Land and the home of Maitreya) in the east. In between are some excellent murals depicting minor Tantric and protector deities. Murals of the Four Guardian Kings in the east lead the way to the upper floors.

Second Floor The first four chapels clockwise from the stairs are dedicated to Manjughosa (a form of Manjushri), Avalokiteshvara (Tibetan: Chenresig), Amitayus (Tsepame), and Green Tara (Drölma). Most of the other chapels are devoted to wrathful protector deities, while others include White Tara (12th chapel from the stairs), Vajrapani (Chana Dorje; 14th) and Akshobhya (Mikyöba; 15th), a blue Buddha who holds a *dorje* (thunderbolt).

Third Floor This floor is dominated by a second series of two storey chapels at the cardinal points portraying the four Dhyani Buddhas (red Amitayus in the south, yellow Ratnasambhava in the west, green Amoghasiddhi in the north and blue Akshobhya in the east). There are several other chapels devoted to the fifth Dhyani Buddha, white Vairocana (Tibetan: Nampa Nangdze). Again most of the other chapels are filled with wrathful deities.

Fourth Floor The 11 chapels on this floor consist largely of teachers, interpreters and translators of obscure orders of Tibetan Buddhism. Exceptions include the Three Kings of Tibet (8th chapel clockwise from the steps), and Guru Rinpoche (10th chapel). You circumambulate this floor in a clockwise direction and find the passageway to the upper floors hidden behind the fourth statue in the eastern chapel – it's easy to miss in the gloom.

Upper Floors The 5th floor, also known as the Bumpa, has four chapels and gives access to the roof. A pathway at the back of the floor leads up to the 6th floor which takes you out at the level of the eyes and there are great views of the town and monastery. There is also a series of murals painted around a central cube. The top floor portrays a Tantric manifestation of Sakyamuni but may well be locked.

Gyantse Dzong

The 14th century Gyantse Dzong, or fort, is worth the stiff 20 minute climb to its upper limits, though more for the amazing views of Gyantse, the monastery compound at the end of town and the surrounding Nyang Chu valley, than for what is left of the dzong itself – not much, though renovations proceed apace.

Some of the dzong's buildings can be entered and explored, sometimes to upper floors by means of rickety wooden ladders. However, there is generally very little to see. About midway up through the fort complex is an **Anti-British Imperialists Museum** featuring a fabulously warped version of the 1904 British invasion. The displays start off with the predictable 'Tibet is an inalienable part of the motherland ...' Some of the more spurious facts quoted include the '10,000 British troops' (the British claim a thousand), the death of reporter Edmund Chandler (he actually returned home to write a best seller) and the claim that Tibetan troops were 'fighting to safeguard the (Chinese) motherland'.

Entry to the dzong is via an alley that runs from the left of the eastbound road from the roundabout. A couple of locals lounge by the entrance all day to nab the occasional foreign visitor for a Y20 entry charge. They do at least issue a ticket, and hopefully some of the money goes towards the ongoing renovations. They are not interested in student cards.

Places to Stay

The accommodation situation in Gyantse has been in flux for the last couple of years. In 1997 the PSB decided that foreigners could only stay in the Y400 a night Gyantse Hotel, effectively putting the town off limits to most budget tourists. Fortunately, by 1998 everyone was healthily ignoring this regulation and individual travellers were facing no problems. However, the regulation could rear its ugly head again.

Places to Stay – Budget

One good place is the *Hostel of Gyantse Town Furniture Factory* on the main junction. Decent, clean rooms with a table and chairs run at around Y30 per person. There are toilets and a nice sitting area with great views of the fort, but no washing facilities.

There's also a Tibetan teahouse next door, visible from the sitting area.

Five minutes walk north-west is the *Hotel of Nationality Clothing Company* (don't you love these snappy names?). This truck stop has been the mainstay of budget travellers for years but it's now very run down and you have to check the bedding for bed bugs. Beds in a three or five-bed room cost around Y15. Again there are no washing facilities.

The *Foodstuffs Hotel* just opposite the Furniture Hostel is a Chinese style hotel but it's better than it looks from the outside. Again there are no showers but rooms have a basin and TV – not bad for the money. Beds in a single/double are Y40/30.

All of these are better than the disintegrating *Gyantse County Hotel*, east of the main junction. Avoid this one.

If you stay in a cheapo hotel you can get a shower for Y5 at a washhouse on the eastern corner of the main junction. Opening hours are 10 am to 7 pm daily. Take flip-flops and a towel.

Places to Stay – Mid-Range

The *Canda Hotel* (Chan Da) is a new mid-range hotel that opened in 1998. At time of research it was great value with spotless doubles with private bathroom going for Y150.

The main group-tourist pad is the Chinese-style *Gyantse Hotel* (☎ 8172222, fax 8172366). It has all you would expect – obsequious staff, shiny lobby, awful coffee and clocks showing the wrong time in all the major capitals. They even provide a list of the replacement cost for anything in the room. Break the bathroom mirror and, as well as seven years bad luck, you'll get a bill for Y20!

Comfortable doubles/triples at the Gyantse Hotel, with attached bathrooms cost Y406/496. You can get laundry done for around Y3 or Y4 per piece.

Places to Eat

Dining out options in Gyantse have improved immensely in recent years, largely

Bayonets to Gyantse

The Younghusband Expedition, as it came to be known, is one of those controversial moments in the history of the British Empire when superior technology and military tactics were used to force business and political interests on the furthermost edges of the Empire. In this case the main contender for the much coveted jewel of Lhasa was the rapidly expanding Russian Empire.

Wild speculation about Russian designs on Tibet had reached epidemic proportions by the turn of the 19th century. And with Tibetans thumbing their noses at the British drafted Sikkim-Tibet convention of 1890, which allowed the free exchange of goods between India and Tibet, the British decided it was time for more persuasive tactics. Francis Younghusband, an army officer with rich experience of Central Asia, was the man chosen for the job. In 1903 Younghusband was instructed to advance on Gyantse from Yatung with an expeditionary force of some 1000 troops (plus 10,000 servants and 4000 yaks) to gain 'satisfaction' from the Tibetans.

Despite previous brushes with British firepower, the Tibetans seemed to have had little idea about what they were up against. Not far from the village of Tuna (about halfway between Yatung and Gyantse) a Tibetan army of some 1500 troops armed with swords, matchlock rifles and a motley assortment of foreign firearms confronted a British force armed with light artillery, Maxim machine guns and modern rifles. The Tibetan trump card was a charm marked with the seal of the Dalai Lama himself which each of the troops had been given with the assurance by monks that it would protect them from British bullets. Despite British attempts to achieve a peaceful solution and disarm the Tibetans, a false alarm killed 700 Tibetans in four minutes. The remaining Tibetans are said to have walked slowly away from the field, despondent that their protector deities had abandoned them.

The British buried the Tibetan dead (the Tibetans dug them up at night and carried them off for sky burial) and set up a field hospital, apparently dumbfounding the wounded Tibetans who couldn't understand why the British would try to kill them one day and save them the next.

The British continued their advance on Gyantse. On arrival they found that the Gyantse Dzong had been deserted by its troops. Curiously, rather than occupy the dzong, the British camped on the outskirts of Gyantse, content to watch the Union Jack flutter on top of the fort. After a month in Gyantse waiting for officials from Lhasa to arrive (they never came), a force of 800 Tibetan troops reoccupied the dzong under the cover of darkness. Meanwhile Younghusband sped off up to the Karo-la to overcome 3000 Tibetans who had dug themselves in at over 5000m – the highest battle in British military history and a valiant display of frozen stiff upper lip.

In early July, over six months after setting out from Yatung, and after nearly two months in Gyantse waiting for Lhasa officials, the British troops received permission from Britain to

due to Sichuanese and Muslim Chinese immigration. Most restaurants are concentrated in the stretch of road opposite the Gyantse Hotel. The best of the bunch is probably the *Restaurant of Zhuangyuan*. Prices are a little expensive (as most are in Gyantse) at around Y20 a dish, but you'll save yourself some money by ordering off the Chinese menu – it's 20% cheaper than the English

version! The *Jongjin Restaurant*, close by, is also OK, though marginally more expensive.

The *Tashi Restaurant* on the main junction has no connection to the one in Lhasa and serves average Chinese and Tibetan food, but at least it's got an English menu.

For something a bit cheaper try the *Muslim Restaurant* on the other side of the

Bayonets to Gyantse

re-take the Gyantse Dzong and march on Lhasa. The assault on the Gyantse Dzong involved a diversionary attack on the north-east front while the real attack took place on the south-west. Shelling was used to make breaches in the walls, and when one of the shells destroyed the Tibetan gunpowder supply (and much of the dzong with it) the Tibetans were reduced to throwing rocks at their attackers. The dzong fell in one day, with over 300 Tibetan dead and just four British casualties.

The fall of the Gyantse Dzong was the last straw in Tibetan attempts to repel the British incursion. The British proceeded to the Yarlung Tsangpo, which they finally crossed after five days of continual ferrying, and reached Lhasa without further incident.

Once in Lhasa there were some fine moments of imperial culture clash while Younghusband tried to ascertain where the bloody hell the Dalai Lama was (he had fled to Mongolia). British soldiers roamed the bazaars, quite miffed that the Tibetans largely ignored them, and one wrote proudly how he managed to find a sausage machine made in Birmingham and two bottles of Bulldog stout on a shopping trip to the Barkhor. Others tried to persuade monks to sell them the statues from the inside of the Jokhang. Earlier that year in Tuna, the stalwart British officers had even managed to rustle up a Christmas dinner of turkey, Christmas pudding and (frozen) champagne.

After a month Younghusband managed to get the Tibetan regent to sign an agreement in the throne room of the Potala, allowing the British to set up trade missions at Gyantse and Gartok (near Kailash) and the troops withdrew from their camp behind the Potala. A more profound agreement was signed in 1906 between the British and Chinese authorities, which assigned Tibet to China's sphere of influence, effectively ending both British and Russian influence in the region.

But for Younghusband himself the most significant event of the campaign was yet to come. As he looked out over Lhasa on the evening before his departure he felt a great wave of emotion, insight and spiritual peace rush over him: an almost religious awakening that changed his life. He went on to found the World Congress of Faiths in 1936, citing that 'that single hour on leaving Lhasa was worth all the rest of a lifetime'.

Francis Younghusband

---

road. You can get a good plate of *ganbian* (home-made noodles fried with yak meat) for Y6. The *chao mianpian* (fried noodle squares) are also recommended.

The **Zorge Teahouse** on the first floor above the main junction is a decent (if scruffy) place to read or write as you sip from a thermos of sweet milky tea. If you get hungry trekking around the Kumbum there's a basic tea and thugpa **restaurant** in the north of town by the entrance to the Pelkor Chöde Monastery.

Breakfasts are limited to *baozi* (Chinese dumplings) and *doujiang* (soya bean milk), and are found everywhere in restaurants opposite the Gyantse Hotel. For those who want to self-cater, there's a grocery store by the junction.

TSANG

Getting There & Away

All public transport to Gyantse nowadays is by way of Shigatse. It probably makes sense to at least overnight in Shigatse seeing you have to go there first, but if Gyantse is your destination and you do not want to bother with Shigatse, it is usually possible to get from Lhasa to Gyantse in a single day. Minibuses from Lhasa arrive in Shigatse around 3 pm and there are usually minibuses on to Gyantse from the minibus stand in front of the Shigatse bus station until around 5 pm. The trip takes two hours and costs Y25. Minibuses from Gyantse back to Shigatse leave on an irregular basis through the day from the main intersection.

If you're hitching to Yamdrok-tso you are best off walking a way along the road and trying from there. You'll probably get a lift as far as the hydroelectric engineering works 30km east of Gyantse, where there is a minor checkpoint. Show them your travel permit if you have one. From here you'll have to walk about 1km to find a truck leaving for Nangartse.

Most travellers heading to the Nepal border with hired vehicles pass through Gyantse. Many only give the place a few hours (including lunch) before travelling through to Shigatse for an overnight stop. It is worth considering overnighting in both Gyantse and Shigatse, however, as both have more than enough in the way of sights to keep you busy for a day.

Getting Around

All of Gyantse's sights can be reached comfortably on foot, which is just as well because apart from a few stray pedicabs there is not much else. It's possible to hire bikes from the Gyantse Hotel for a pricey Y5 per hour.

AROUND GYANTSE
Tsechen Monastery & Fort

The traditional village of Tsechen is around 5km north-west of Gyantse and offers a nice half-day trip out of Gyantse. There is a small monastery above the village but the main reason to hike out here is to climb up the ruined fortress, wander along the defensive walls and enjoy great views of the (often flooded) river valley below. It's a good idea to bring a picnic.

The fortress was believed to have been built as early as the 14th century and was used by the British during their 1904 invasion, though it was already partly ruined by then. It's possible to hike up to the right side of the fortress and then cross over to the highest ramparts on the left. You can expect to have your every move shadowed by several adolescents whose job is supposedly to stop foreigners taking pictures of the fort.

To get to Tsechen you can either walk or hitch along the main highway to Shigatse. The village is just past the turn-off south to Yatung. On the way back it is possible to cut through fields to the river (you'll be offered to share countless jerry cans of *chang* en route) and follow this back to the Gyantse Bridge. It's often possible to get a lift back on a tractor for a couple of yuan, otherwise it's about an hour-long walk.

YATUNG & THE CHUMBI VALLEY

The Chumbi valley is where Tibet dips a cautious toe into the Indian subcontinent between Sikkim and Bhutan. The lower-altitude subtropical scenery here differs immensely to that on the higher Tibetan plateau. Unfortunately, the Chumbi valley and Yatung, the county seat, have been decidedly off limits to foreigners for the last few years. There are large numbers of Chinese troops in the area, and the last thing the authorities want is foreign backpackers snooping about.

If the place ever opens up again then the main attractions of the area are said to be views of Mt Chomolhari from Gala-tso, as well as the tropical scenery around Yatung. There are public buses from Gyantse to Yatung but it's highly unlikely you'd be allowed on board. The main checkpoint en route is at Gala.

SHIGATSE

Shigatse (3900m) is the second largest town in Tibet and the traditional capital of Tsang.

Tsang
Top: Pelkor Chode Monastery and Gyantse kumbum. **Middle left:** One of the four holy lakes of Tibet, the fabulously turquoise Yamdrok-tso. **Middle right:** The monastery township of Sakya. **Bottom left:** Rugged border town of Zhangmu. **Bottom right:** Prayer flags and mani walls near Nyalam.

Tsang
Top: The seat of the Panchen Lama, Tashilhunpo Monastery, Shigatse.
Middle right: Gyantse kumbum eyes. **Bottom left:** Young pilgrim at Pelgye Ling, Nyalam.
Bottom right: Pilgrims circumambulating Rongphu Monastery.

RICHARD I'ANSON

TONY WHEELER

RICHARD I'ANSON

BRADLEY MAYHEW

Around 250km to the south-west of Lhasa (via the new road), Shigatse is one of the few places in Tsang with reliable and frequent transport connections with the capital.

Shigatse has long been an important trading town and administrative centre. The Tsang kings exercised their power from the once imposing heights of the Shigatse Dzong – the present ruins only hint at its former glory – and the fort later became the residence of the governor of Tsang. Since the Mongol sponsorship of the Gelugpa order, Shigatse has been the seat of the Panchen Lama, who is traditionally based in Tashilhunpo Monastery. The monastery is Shigatse's foremost attraction.

Like most modern Tibetan towns, Shigatse divides into a distinct Tibetan quarter and a newer Chinatown. The Chinese part of town comprises wide, dusty boulevards lined with building-block concrete cubes of the style beloved by Marxist town planners. The Tibetan part of town, which is for the most part clustered higgledy-piggledy between Tashilhunpo Monastery and the high ramparts of the Shigatse Dzong, is on

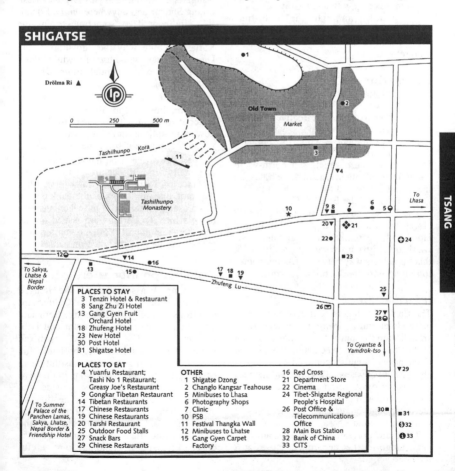

SHIGATSE

Drölma Ri ▲

Old Town

Market

Tashilhunpo Kora

0   250   500 m

Tashilhunpo Monastery

To Lhasa

To Sakya, Lhatse & Nepal Border

Zhufeng Lu

To Summer Palace of the Panchen Lamas, Sakya, Lhatse, Nepal Border & Friendship Hotel

To Gyantse & Yamdrok-tso

PLACES TO STAY
3   Tenzin Hotel & Restaurant
8   Sang Zhu Zi Hotel
13 Gang Gyen Fruit Orchard Hotel
18 Zhufeng Hotel
23 New Hotel
30 Post Hotel
31 Shigatse Hotel

PLACES TO EAT
4   Yuanfu Restaurant; Tashi No 1 Restaurant; Greasy Joe's Restaurant
9   Gongkar Tibetan Restaurant
14 Tibetan Restaurants
17 Chinese Restaurants
19 Chinese Restaurants
20 Tarshi Restaurant
25 Outdoor Food Stalls
27 Snack Bars
29 Chinese Restaurants

OTHER
1   Shigatse Dzong
2   Changlo Kangsar Teahouse
5   Minibuses to Lhasa
6   Photography Shops
7   Clinic
10 PSB
11 Festival Thangka Wall
12 Minibuses to Lhatse
15 Gang Gyen Carpet Factory
16 Red Cross
21 Department Store
22 Cinema
24 Tibet-Shigatse Regional People's Hospital
26 Post Office & Telecommunications Office
28 Main Bus Station
32 Bank of China
33 CITS

TSANG

the other hand a delightful place to be based for a few days.

Far too many travellers speed through Shigatse on their way to the Nepal border, giving the place just one afternoon to poke around Tashilhunpo and a night to rest up. This is a pity as, while it may not be exactly brimming in sights, Shigatse is a good place to hang out, kick back and enjoy a few beers on the roof of the Tenzin Hotel, gazing across at the ruins of the fort.

Finally, don't expect to get much sleep in Shigatse. By around 10 pm packs of dogs begin to wake up with a few stray yelps and howls and by midnight the night-time silence is torn to shreds by a cacophony of blood-curdling canine cries of attack and wild retreat.

Orientation

Shigatse is not a particularly big town, but orientation can initially be a bit confusing. Tashilhunpo Monastery effectively marks the western extent of town – beyond it is a nomad encampment – while the Shigatse Dzong does the same thing to the north. The two main Chinese streets run north-south parallel to each other. One of these holds the main post office and the other has the Shigatse Hotel and the Bank of China.

The Tibetan quarter is around the Tenzin Hotel and the market. From the Tenzin Hotel and the market the road runs westward, quickly narrowing into a dirt track that threads its way between Tibetan homes to join up with the Tashilhunpo *kora*.

Information

The Bank of China is next door to the Shigatse Hotel and is open on weekdays from around 9 am to 1 pm and 4 to 7 pm, and from 10 am to 4 pm on weekends, though you might have difficulties getting the correct exchange rates at weekends. Travellers cheques and cash in most currencies can be changed with a minimum of fuss, but it is not possible to arrange credit card advances – you will have to go to Lhasa for this service.

The main post office is open 9 am to 8 pm, though the fax department closes at 6 pm. It is possible to send international letters and postcards from here, but *not* international parcels. You can make international phone calls and send faxes, though it may take some time.

Public Security Bureau Shigatse PSB is the saviour of independent travel in Tibet. Not only are the staff remarkably friendly, but they will grant independent travellers a travel permit for almost anywhere in Shigatse Prefecture, including Gyantse, Nangartse, Shalu, Sakya, Everest Base Camp, Shegar and anywhere on the Friendship Highway. They sometimes even give permits to Samye and Saga (on the road to Kailash). Quite why they do this no one knows but make good use of it while it lasts because life will be much more difficult without them.

It might be possible to get a visa extension here, though probably only if your visa is about to expire. The office also has the powers to split an individual from a group visa, for example if someone becomes ill.

The PSB office is on the road that leads diagonally from the centre of town to the entrance of Tashilhunpo Monastery. It has the same opening hours as the bank except it is closed at weekends (and whenever else it feels like it). Permits are issued on the spot for a standard Y50, no matter how many destinations are listed on it.

Tashilhunpo Monastery

Tashilhunpo is associated with the Gelugpa order and is one of the six great Gelugpa institutions along with Drepung, Sera and Ganden in Lhasa and Kumbum and Labrang in Amdo. The monastery gets mixed reports from visitors. It is probably the largest functioning monastic institution in contemporary Tibet and is an impressive place to explore. On the downside, the monks here are sometimes unfriendly and there is conjecture that many of the English-speaking monks are in cohorts with the Chinese authorities. There is no direct evidence of this, but it would pay to be careful about voicing controversial opinions and handing out Dalai Lama pictures.

Opening and closing hours at Tashilhunpo are fairly arbitrary. It is theoretically open from 9 am to noon and 2 to 5 pm. In practice, you may be told by monks at, say, 4 pm, after you have already bought your ticket, that the monastery is already closed. If this happens, try smiling and showing them your ticket – getting annoyed only serves to deepen their conviction that the monastery is closed. There is a Y40 entry fee. (Some travellers have reported that the entry fee has decreased to Y30.)

There are severe restrictions on photographs inside the monastic buildings. The going cost for a photograph varies, but be prepared for a pricey Y80. This may be negotiable and once paid should cover more than one photograph, but do not count on it.

History Tashilhunpo Monastery was founded in 1447 by a disciple of Tsongkhapa, Genden Drup. Genden Drup was retroactively named the first Dalai Lama and he is enshrined in Tashilhunpo. Despite its association with the first Dalai Lama, Tashilhunpo was initially isolated from the mainstream of Gelugpa affairs, which were centred in the Lhasa region. The monastery's standing rocketed, however, when the fifth Dalai Lama declared his teacher – then abbot of Tashilhunpo – to be a manifestation of Amitabha (a deification of Buddha's faculty of perfected cognition and perception). Thus Tashilhunpo became the seat of an important lineage line: the Panchen Lamas.

The title Panchen means 'great scholar' and was the title traditionally bestowed on abbots of Tashilhunpo. But with the establishment of the Panchen Lama lineage of spiritual and temporal leaders – second only to the Dalai Lamas themselves – the spectre of possible rivalry was introduced into the Gelugpa order. Naturally it did not take long to emerge. The next Panchen Lama was declared ruler of Tsang and Western Tibet by the Qing Dynasty in China, a move that has been seen by many as part of a continuing effort by the Chinese to manipulate a schism between the Panchen Lama and Dalai Lama.

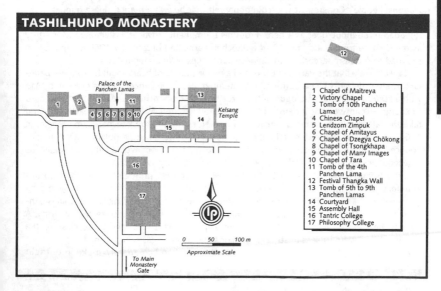

TASHILHUNPO MONASTERY

Palace of the Panchen Lamas

Kelsang Temple

1 Chapel of Maitreya
2 Victory Chapel
3 Tomb of 10th Panchen Lama
4 Chinese Chapel
5 Lendzom Zimpuk
6 Chapel of Amitayus
7 Chapel of Dzegya Chökong
8 Chapel of Tsongkhapa
9 Chapel of Many Images
10 Chapel of Tara
11 Tomb of the 4th Panchen Lama
12 Festival Thangka Wall
13 Tomb of 5th to 9th Panchen Lamas
14 Courtyard
15 Assembly Hall
16 Tantric College
17 Philosophy College

0   50   100 m
Approximate Scale

To Main Monastery Gate

TSANG

Of course it is arguable that such a schism did not require much prompting on the part of the Chinese. There have long been disputes between Lhasa and Shigatse over the autonomy of Tashilhunpo. In the early 1920s a dispute between the ninth Panchen Lama and the 13th Dalai Lama over taxes – and ultimately Tashilhunpo's right to self rule – led to the flight of the Panchen Lama to China. He never returned to Tibet. His successor, the 10th Panchen Lama, never escaped Chinese clutches and was largely kept in Beijing, only occasionally visiting Tashilhunpo. He died in 1989.

The Monastery Tashilhunpo is one of the few monasteries in Tibet that weathered the

The Panchen Lamas

Traditional abbots of Tashilhunpo Monastery, frequent rivals to the central authority of Lhasa and often pawns in Chinese designs on the high plateau, the Panchen Lamas, have often been the focus of decidedly unspiritual squabbles. The ninth Panchen Lama (1883-1937) ended up spending the last of his days in the clutches of a Chinese Nationalist warlord after attempting to use the Chinese as leverage to gain greater influence in Tibet during a disagreement with the 13th Dalai Lama. His reincarnation grew up in the control of the Chinese.

This Chinese connection hung over the 10th Panchen Lama like a grim cloud, and he was regarded with suspicion by his own people for much of his life. Even his authenticity was subject to doubt. There had been at least two other candidates for the position in Tibet itself, but the Chinese had forced Tibetan delegates in Beijing in 1951 to endorse the Chinese choice. It is said that in 1949 the 11-year-old Panchen Lama had written to Mao asking him to 'liberate' Tibet, although, to give him credit, it is unlikely he did it of his own volition. When the Panchen Lama became joint chairperson (with the Dalai Lama) of the Preparatory Committee for the Autonomous Region of Tibet (PCART) and later Vice-Chairman of China's National People's Congress, it was commonly felt that he was a mere Chinese puppet.

By the time he died of a heart attack at Shigatse in 1989, however, the Panchen Lama was regarded throughout Tibet as a hero. From his triumphant arrival at Tashilhunpo Monastery as the Chinese trump card in 1951, the Panchen Lama had become by 1965 a 'big rock on the road to socialism' according to Chinese authorities. What happened?

It seems likely that the Panchen Lama had a major change of heart about his Chinese benefactors after the 1959 Lhasa uprising. In September 1961, the Panchen Lama presented Mao with a 70,000-character catalogue of the atrocities acted upon Tibet and a plea for increased freedoms. His answer was a demand that he denounce the Dalai Lama as a reactionary and take the latter's place as spiritual head of Tibet. Not only did the Panchen Lama refuse, in 1964, with tens of thousands of Tibetans gathered in Lhasa for the Mönlam festival, he announced to the assembled crowds that he believed that Tibet would one day regain its independence and that the Dalai Lama would return in glory as its leader.

It must have come as a shock to the Chinese to see their protégé turn on them so ungratefully. They responded in time-honoured fashion by throwing him into jail, where he remained for 14 years, suffering abuse and torture. His crimes, according to the Chinese, included participating in orgies, 'criticising China' and raising a private insurrectionary army. A 'Smash the Panchen Reactionary Clique' campaign was mounted, and those close to the Panchen Lama were subject to struggle sessions and in some cases imprisoned.

After emerging from prison in early 1978, the Panchen Lama rarely spoke in outright

stormy seas of the Cultural Revolution relatively unscathed. It is a real pleasure to explore. Go to the monastery several times if you can – there is really too much to see in a single visit.

From the entrance to the monastery visitors get a grand view of the complex. Above the white monastic quarters is a crowd of ochre buildings topped with gold – the

tombs of the past Panchen Lamas. To the right and higher still is the great white wall that is hung with massive, colourful thangkas during festivals. The entire complex is surrounded by a high wall.

Chapel of Maitreya Walk up through the monastery and bear left for the first and

The Panchen Lamas

defiance of the Chinese authorities, but continued to use what influence he had to press for the preservation of Tibetan cultural traditions. Shortly before his death it is believed that he again fell out with the Chinese, arguing at a high-level meeting in Beijing that the Chinese occupation had brought nothing but misery and hardship to his people. Accordingly, many Tibetans believe that he died not of a heart attack but by poisoning. Others maintain that, exhausted and perhaps despairing, the Panchen Lama came home in 1986 to die as he always said he would on Tibetan soil.

Of course in Tibet the story doesn't just end here. In May 1995 the Dalai Lama identified Gedhun Choekyi Nyima, a six-year-old boy from Amdo, as the reincarnation of the Panchen Lama. Within a month the boy had been forcibly relocated to a government compound in Beijing and an irate Chinese government had ordered the senior lamas of Tashilhunpo to come up with a second, Chinese-approved choice. The abbot of Tashilhunpo was later arrested for 'revealing state secrets' (ie consulting the Dalai Lama over the selection) and the monastery was closed to tourists for a few months. Tashilhunpo's lamas eventually settled on Gyancain Norbu, the son of Communist Party members, who was formally approved in a carefully orchestrated ceremony. Beijing's interest is not only to control the education of Tibet's number two spiritual leader but also to influence the boy who will later himself be influential in identifying the reincarnation of the Dalai Lama.

Meanwhile the young 11th Panchen Lama remains under house arrest, causing him to be dubbed the 'world's youngest political prisoner'. For his ninth birthday the Canadian Embassy presented Gedhun with 1000 birthday cards from well-wishers. His future is still uncertain, though. It seems the Chinese are not only intent on influencing Tibet's spiritual leaders during their lifetime but also in their future lifetimes as well.

The late 10th Panchen Lama.

TSANG

probably most impressive of Tashilhunpo's sights, the Chapel of Maitreya. An entire building is hollowed out to house a 26m image of Maitreya, the Future Buddha. It was made in 1914 under the auspices of the ninth Panchen Lama and took some 900 artisans and labourers four years to complete.

The impressive, finely crafted serene-looking Maitreya looms over the viewer. More than 300kg of gold went into coating the Maitreya, much of which is also studded with precious stones. On the walls surrounding the image are a thousand more gold paintings of Maitreya against a red background.

Victory Chapel This newly opened chapel is centre for philosophy and houses a large statue of Tsongkhapa flanked by Maitreya and Manjushri.

Tomb of 10th Panchen Lama This impressive funeral chörten holds the remains of the 10th Panchen Lama who died in 1989 (see the boxed text, 'The Panchen Lamas'). His image is displayed in front of the tomb, surrounded by kaleidoscopic rainbow swirls. The ceiling of the chapel is painted with a Kalachakra mandala and the walls are painted with real gold Buddhas.

Palace of the Panchen Lamas The palace itself is the white building that rises over the red buildings in front of it. The palace has been the residence of the Panchen Lamas since the first Panchen Lama, although the present structure was built during the time of the sixth Panchen Lama (1738-80). It is not open to the public. It is possible, however, to enter a series of chapels in the anterior buildings, which are accessed from the courtyard of the tomb of the 10th Panchen Lama.

The **Chinese Chapel** is notable for its Chinese shrine built in respect for the Chinese emperor Qianlong. The **Lendzom Zimpuk** was a reception area for visiting dignitaries and includes two thrones, of which the left one was used by the Panchen Lama. Next is the **Chapel of Amitayus**,

which is dominated by an image of Amitayus, the Buddha of Long Life on the left, Sakyamuni in the centre and Manjushri to the right. The **Chapel of Dzegya Chökong**, up a small flight of stairs, is a protector chapel that houses the wrathful female deity who guards over Tashilhunpo. Next door is a **Chapel of Tsongkhapa**, in which Tsongkhapa and two of his principal disciples preside. The last two rooms are the **Chapel of Many Images**, which as its name suggests has many images, and the **Chapel of Tara**, a chapel with the 21 manifestations of Tara, a meditational deity associated with the enlightened activity of the mind.

Tomb of the Fourth Panchen Lama From the Tara Chapel you come to the 11m silver and gold funerary chörten of the fourth Panchen Lama (1570-1662). From here you pass through a dark walkway that leads out to the Kelsang Temple complex.

Kelsang Temple The centrepiece of this remarkable and complex collection of buildings is a large courtyard, which is the focus of festival and monastic activities. This is a fascinating place to sit and watch the pilgrims and monks go about their business. Monks congregate here before their lunchtime service in the main assembly hall. A huge prayer pole rears up from the centre of the flagged courtyard, while the surrounding walls are painted with Buddhas. There are splendid photo opportunities of the surrounding buildings.

There are so many chapels and points of interest in the Kelsang Temple that keeping track of them can be confusing. It is probably best to return to the Kelsang Temple several times. Attempting to see everything in one hit is to risk sensory overload and tedium. Tibetan pilgrims generally follow the path set out below. If you have limited time or interest then just check out the assembly hall and possibly some of the chapels above it.

From the main steps of the courtyard walk along the balcony of the middle floor to the Chapel of Sakyamuni, the silver chörtens of the Silver Tomb Chapel and the printing press of the Barkang.

The south side of the courtyard has rooms dedicated to Sakyamuni, Tara and Tsongkhapa. From here head past the kitchen into the **assembly hall**. This hall is one of the oldest buildings in Tashilhunpo, dating back to the original 15th century founding of the monastery. The huge throne dominating the centre of the hall is the throne of the Panchen Lamas. The hall is an atmospheric place, with rows of mounted cushions for monks and impressive thangkas depicting the various incarnations of the Panchen Lama suspended from the ceiling. The central inner chapel holds a wonderful statue of Jowo Sakyamuni, while the chapel to the right holds several images of Tara.

At this point, if you are not being shepherded around by a monk, ascend the stairs by the kitchen to see three packed chapels, featuring a kadam chörten, Sakyamuni with 10 arhats and then a well-dressed Maitreya. You then ascend to see four chapels positioned directly above the last three. These are dedicated to Tara, the fourth Panchen Lama, Maitreya and Tsongkhapa.

From here you descend a few steps and ahead on the left is a statueless protector chapel. Upstairs to the left is a room with fine views of a huge **Maitreya** statue sitting in the assembly hall below. Right of this is a spooky **Chapel of Sakyamuni** stuffed with Tantric symbols including old armour, stuffed snakes and, on the right, a statue of Palden Lhamo.

Descend a little way and pass through a long chapel with views of Jowo Sakyamuni below. Then climb up a small flight of stairs to the **chörten** of the first Dalai Lama, the second and third Panchen Lamas and several of Tashilhunpo's early abbots.

Finally on the homeward stretch you can visit the huge new **Tomb of the Fifth to the**

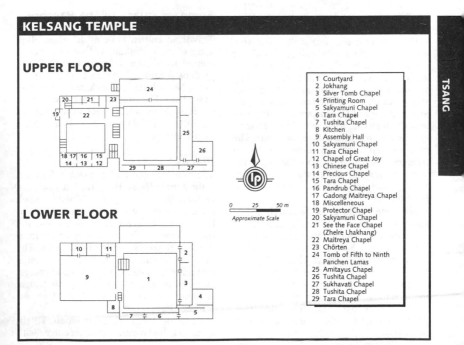

KELSANG TEMPLE

UPPER FLOOR

LOWER FLOOR

0   25   50 m
Approximate Scale

1 Courtyard
2 Jokhang
3 Silver Tomb Chapel
4 Printing Room
5 Sakyamuni Chapel
6 Tara Chapel
7 Tushita Chapel
8 Kitchen
9 Assembly Hall
10 Sakyamuni Chapel
11 Tara Chapel
12 Chapel of Great Joy
13 Chinese Chapel
14 Precious Chapel
15 Tara Chapel
16 Pandrub Chapel
17 Gadong Maitreya Chapel
18 Miscellaneous
19 Protector Chapel
20 Sakyamuni Chapel
21 See the Face Chapel
   (Zhelre Lhakhang)
22 Maitreya Chapel
23 Chörten
24 Tomb of Fifth to Ninth
   Panchen Lamas
25 Amitayus Chapel
26 Tushita Chapel
27 Sukhavati Chapel
28 Tushita Chapel
29 Tara Chapel

TSANG

Ninth **Panchen Lamas**. From here head around the top floor of the courtyard passing through the **Chapel of Amitayus**, a heady sutra chapel filled with chanting monks and incense and finally through three chapels dedicated to Amitabha, Tsongkhapa and Tara.

Other Buildings As you leave Tashilhunpo, it is also possible to visit the monastery's two remaining colleges. They are on the left hand side as you walk down towards the entrance/exit. The first is the **Tantric College** and the second is the brown **Philosophy College**. Neither is particularly interesting, but you may be lucky and be in time for debating, which is held in the courtyard of the Philosophy College.

Tashilhunpo Kora The kora around Tashilhunpo takes just an hour and provides photogenic views of the monastery. As with most walks in Shigatse, you should keep a watchful eye out for dogs – keep some stones at the ready.

From the entrance, follow the monastery walls in a clockwise direction and look out for an alley on the right. The alley follows the western wall for a while before opening out into a wider trail that leads into the hills above Tashilhunpo. The trail leads up past rock paintings of Guru Rinpoche and Avalokiteshvara to the 13 storey white wall used to hang a giant thangka at festival time. The path then splits in two: down the hill to complete the circuit of the monastery and (more interesting) along a ridge to the ruins of Shigatse Dzong, a walk of around 15 to 20 minutes.

For those staying at the Tenzin Hotel, the kora can also be approached by turning left out of the hotel and following the road past Tibetan homes before bearing left at the walls of the monastery. This path leads down onto the main road and on to the entrance of the monastery, where you can continue the kora, finishing back on the trail that leads back to the hotel. To avoid giving offence, try not to follow the route counterclockwise.

If you are fit and acclimatised you could hike up the side of the ridge behind the monastery to the Drölma Ri peak. A trail branches off from the Tashilhunpo kora.

Shigatse Dzong

Once the residence of the kings of Tsang and later the governor of Tsang, very little remains of the dzong. It was destroyed in the popular uprising of 1959. Pictures taken before the Chinese occupation, however, show an impressive structure that bears a remarkable resemblance to the Potala, though a smaller version.

The main attraction of the Shigatse Dzong today are the views it commands over Shigatse and the surrounding valleys. One approach is via the Tashilhunpo kora. The other is to turn left out of the Tenzin Hotel and after about 100m look for an paved alley heading north (right). Watch out for dogs. The walk takes around 20 to 30 minutes.

Summer Palace of the Panchen Lamas

This little known building is around 1km south of the Tashilhunpo Monastery, hidden behind trees in a walled compound. The gardens form the Panchen Lamas' version of the Norbulingka, though there's a lot less to see here. The complex is not always open but it might be worth a look to find out, especially on holidays when it is a popular picnic ground.

Places to Stay

The most popular budget place in Shigatse is the *Tenzin Hotel*. Be warned, it's far from perfect: the hot shower only works when there's a group around, the staff are not to be trusted with hiring vehicles and the rooms have seen better days. But apart from this, the Tenzin is a delightful little inn. The upstairs veranda is a great place to lounge around in the late afternoons and evenings, and they even keep cold beer in the fridge. A laundry service is available for around Y1 per piece.

Beds cost Y25 in the dorm rooms, Y30 in nicer four-bed rooms. Modern doubles with a view of the fort are anywhere between Y60 and Y100 and there are also overpriced doubles with private bathroom. There's only one toilet for everyone. A solar shower is available on the top floor, though 'solar' in Shigatse seems to be a local Tibetan euphemism for 'cold'. More reliable showers are found downstairs.

The other hotel that sees a fair number of foreign guests is the **Gang Gyen Fruit Orchard Hotel**, opposite the entrance to Tashilhunpo Monastery. It comes firmly from the concrete box school of Chinese hotel design but at least it's pretty clean and it has a perfect location for visiting the Tashilhunpo or catching a morning minibus to Lhatse. Dorm beds are Y15, beds in a nicer triple/double cost Y30/40. The manager will normally open up one of the suites and let you use the hot shower there.

Just down the road and around the corner from the Tenzin is the Chinese-style **Sang Zhu Zi Hotel** (☎ 8821135), an uninspiring but comfortable enough place to stay. Double rooms with private bathroom cost Y160. They might give a room for Y80 to a solo traveller if they're not too busy. Hot showers are available in the evening and for an hour or two in the morning.

A newer hotel is the **Zhufeng Hotel** (☎ 8823383), a five minute walk south-east of the Orchard Hotel. Doubles come with private bathroom and hot water and are excellent value at Y50 per person. 'Zhufeng' means 'Everest' in Chinese.

The government has been planning to build a new three star hotel a couple of hundred metres north of the post office and it may now have opened. The **Post Hotel** opposite the Shigatse Hotel is overpriced and has little to recommend it.

Finally, the lap of luxury in Shigatse is the **Shigatse Hotel** (☎ 8822550), inconveniently located in the far south of town next to the Bank of China. Prices here are reasonably negotiable, as occupancy rates are likely to be always lowish. Chinese or Tibetan-style standard doubles with attached bathrooms (24 hour hot water!) cost Y450, economy triples cost Y480 and singles are available for Y430. Rooms should be comfortable enough as they were recently renovated. High-fliers might like to enquire about the Tibetan suites at Y1540. There's a 20% discount on all rooms from November to April.

Places to Eat

Shigatse is swarming with good restaurants, most of them Chinese. Many travellers find the food better here than in Lhasa, though prices are slightly higher.

Unfortunately in 1998 most of the backpacker restaurants in the vicinity of the Tenzin Hotel were demolished. If they are eventually rebuilt look out for **Greasy Joe's** (aka the Yingbin Restaurant), the **Yuanfu Restaurant** with its famous speciality fish-tasting eggplant and **Tashi 1**. The only restaurant left standing at time of research was the **Tenzin Restaurant** on the ground

---

Brain Cord for Two?

The English menus of Shigatse's backpacker restaurants offer the town's only real entertainment. If you do actually want to order anything, however, you'll need some help. Vegetarians might not immediately be attracted to a steaming dish of 'Brain Cord' but will probably be immensely relieved to get a plate of inoffensive bean curd. When it slowly dawns on you that the 'Fry Bean (Not Not)' is actually *stir-fried* bean curd, you might start to think it's all a bit of a conspiracy, but once you get the swing of things you'll soon recognise more. How about 'Coipew Thread Soup'? No? Well, we'll help you with this one (cucumber and pork soup) but from now on you're on your own ...

floor of the Tenzin Hotel, run by a Chinese couple who serve up tasty Sichuanese food.

Worth a try is the *Gongkar Tibetan Restaurant* to the west of the Sang Zhu Zi Hotel. It is Chinese run but has an English menu.

For Tibetan food you could try the *Tarshi Restaurant*, five minutes walk south of the Tenzin Hotel, though it's nothing special. There's a Tibetan-style teahouse called the *Changlo Kangsar* a couple of hundred metres north of the Tenzin Hotel where you can get a flask of sweet tea for Y4.

There are some decent *Tibetan restaurants* east of the Orchard Hotel. A bowl of *hipduk* (square noodles in thick soup) or *shemdre* (rice, potatoes and yak meat on rice) makes for a good lunch after a visit to the Tashilhunpo. The best Chinese restaurants in town are down the east end of this street towards the post office, though there's not an English menu in sight.

Out near the Shigatse Hotel are a number of other restaurants, some with English menus. There are also some dumpling shops next to the bus station – a good place to grab a snack while waiting for a bus.

Shopping

The market in front of the Tenzin Hotel is probably the best place outside Lhasa to pick up souvenirs like prayer wheels, rosaries and wooden masks. Bargain hard.

Getting There & Away

Between Lhasa and Shigatse most travellers use the minibus service that costs Y38. This is a big saving on the slower and less comfortable public bus service which runs from the main Lhasa bus station for Y74. It remains to be seen, however, whether the authorities will continue to turn a blind eye to this situation. Some of the minibuses have been stopped and fined and the drivers told that they are not to take foreign passengers.

Minibuses for Lhasa leave between 7.30 and 8 am from a crossroads at the eastern edge of town. There are also buses from in front of the main bus station around the same time but the bus station charges foreigners double unless you can come up with a Chinese student card. The trip takes around seven hours.

Buses to Gyantse depart from the main bus station whenever full from around 10 am until 5 pm. The journey takes two hours and costs Y25 (Y50 on a government bus). There is also an 8 am departure to Yatung which passes within 5km of Gyantse, though you'll have to persuade the bus driver to let you on the bus as Yatung itself is off-limits to foreigners.

From the main bus station there are also buses every other day at 8.30 am for Sakya (Y54). These return to Shigatse the next day so you get either an afternoon or 2½ days at Sakya – neither one ideal. An alternative is to take the daily bus to Lhatse, get off at the Sakya turn-off and hitch the remaining 25km. You'll most likely have to pay the full fare to Lhatse though. Private minibuses depart daily at around 8 am to Lhatse (Y30).

Those heading out to the Nepal border or Tingri really have very few options. One possibility is to enquire at the Shigatse or Tenzin hotels for minibuses or Land Cruisers heading out to the border to pick up tour groups. The cost for hooking up with one of these is around Y250. You will probably need to go out to the hotel three or four days in a row before you get lucky, and there is always the chance that you will not. Thursday night is a good time to ask at the Tenzin as minibuses from Lhasa normally stop the night here. Otherwise start hitching from Lhatse.

Rented Vehicles Renting vehicles in Shigatse is more difficult than in Lhasa and prices are not as competitive. The few agencies operating in town have a reputation for ripping travellers off and should be treated with caution.

China International Travel Service (CITS) has a branch near the Shigatse Hotel. Prices are not cheap but surprisingly, this is probably the most reliable outfit around. Sample prices are Y3400 for a three day trip to

Rongphu or Y3800 to Rongphu and the Nepalese border (Y4400 return). Take care and ask around before you commit yourself to anything.

Getting Around

Shigatse is not that big and can be comfortably explored on foot. For trips out to the Shigatse Hotel, however, you might want to use the pedicabs or the tractors, which are abundant – there is usually a small crowd of them on every corner. Prices are negotiable, but should work out around Y3 per head after a little haggling. A ride in a tractor from the centre of town to the Tashilhunpo should cost Y1.

A ride anywhere in town in one of the many taxis will cost Y10.

AROUND SHIGATSE

There are a number of sights around Shigatse, though few of them are visited by western travellers, mainly because of difficulty of access. For information on the trek from Shalu to Nartang see the Trekking chapter. It is even possible to visit Gyantse as a day trip from Shigatse.

Shalu Monastery

Shalu Monastery is around 19km south-east of Shigatse, a few kilometres off the Shigatse-Gyantse road and is easily spotted because of its Chinese-style green tiled roof. The monastery, which dates back to the 11th century, rose to prominence in the 14th century, when its abbot, Büton Rinchen Drup, emerged as the foremost interpreter of Sanskrit Buddhist texts of his day. A sub-order, the Büton, formed around him. Shalu was also a centre for training in skills such as trance walking, made famous by the flying monks of Alexandra David-Neel's *Magic & Mystery in Tibet*.

Shalu divides into a Tibetan-style monastery founded in the 10th century and the Chinese-influenced inner Serkhang, which was founded in the 15th century. The former was destroyed in the Cultural Revolution, but the Serkhang has survived reasonably well. Major renovations were being carried out at the time of writing.

Shalu is noted for its 14th century murals which fuse Chinese, Mongol and Nepalese Newari styles, but it's hard for most non-specialists to discern much. The best murals line the walls of a corridor that rings the central assembly hall – bring a torch to really appreciate these.

The only chapel open at time of research was the south chapel of the inner Serkhang. On the left is a statue of Büton in front of three 14th century mandalas. There are also statues of the monastery's founder and the Tantric deity Kalachakra (Tibetan: Dukor). When it reopens, the west chapel should contain a black stone statue of Avalokiteshvara, the monastery's holiest relic.

Walks Around Shalu From Shalu you can take an hour's walk up to remote Ripuk Monastery, where there are nice views of the Shalu valley. Follow the path in front of Shalu Monastery around the left of the monastery walls and continue out of the village. Head south-west over a stream following a dirt track up to a large *om mani padme hum* made up of lots of little stones on a rise ahead. You can see the monastery from here. There's not much to see, just one main chapel and a large chörten surrounded by some wind-operated prayer wheels, but the monks and nuns are friendly.

If you are feeling fit you could head back down to the main Shalu valley and cut out to the remains of a small dzong 1½ hours walk south of Shalu. For a map of the valley and details of the trek from Shalu to Nartang see the Trekking chapter.

Getting There & Away Shalu is one of the more accessible sights around Shigatse, as it is only 4km south off the main Shigatse-Gyantse road. If you take a Gyantse-bound minibus from Shigatse, get off at the village of Tsündu and look out for the turn-off a couple of hundred metres past a hill covered with prayer flags. From here it's an hour's walk up to Shalu village, passing the small Gyanggong Monastery en route. A shop in

Shalu village sells soft drinks and thugpa only. Bring a hat, sunscreen and water.

SAKYA

The monastic town of Sakya (4280m) is one of Tsang's most important historical sights and, even more than Gyantse, is very Tibetan in character, making it an interesting place to spend a day or so. Sakya's principal attractions are its northern and southern monasteries on either side of the Trum Chu. The fortress-like southern monastery is of most interest. The original, northern monastery has been mostly reduced to picturesque ruins, though restoration work is ongoing.

Sakya is a small town, making orientation a simple affair. The modern section is clustered to the east of the southern monastery, and this is where you will find Sakya's few hotels, restaurants and shops.

Do not expect too much of Sakya in terms of basic comforts – food is good but limited and accommodation is very basic. But if you are doing the Tibet grand tour – Lhasa and environs, Gyantse, Shigatse, Everest and the border – Sakya offers the opportunity for an overnight stay or longer in a town that has suffered little from the encroachments of the modern Chinese world. Local villagers and monks are friendly but show a rougher, coarser edge than Tibetans elsewhere.

One characteristic feature of the Sakya region is the colouring of the buildings. Unlike the standard whitewashed effect that you see elsewhere in Tibet, in Sakya the buildings are ash grey with white and red vertical stripes. The colouring is thought to either symbolise the Rigsum Gonpo, the three most important bodhisattvas, or stand as a mark of Sakya authority – at the end of the day it's probably a mixture of both. Sakya itself literally means 'pale earth'.

Permits

There is much debate as to whether or not a permit is required for Sakya. If you are worried about this, you can pick one up with no hassles for Y50 in Shigatse. On the other hand, if you simply turn up without one, no one seems to care in the least. Those coming by rented vehicle from Lhasa will have one arranged by their travel agency.

History

Sakya Monastery was founded in 1073 by Kön Könchog Gyelpo, a member of the influential Kön family. The 11th century was a dynamic period in the history of Tibetan Buddhism, largely due to renewed contacts with Indian Buddhists. The Kagyupa order was founded by Marpa and his disciple Milarepa at this time, and in Sakya the Kön family established a school that came to be called the Sakyapa.

Unlike most other schools and monasteries, which were headed by a succession of incarnate lamas, the abbotship of Sakya was hereditary and restricted to sons of the Kön family. It is thought that in the early days of Sakya at least one Kön son would marry in order to perpetuate the Kön line, but later abbots of Sakya themselves married.

By the early 13th century Sakya had emerged as an important centre of scholastic study. This was initially aided by the assistance of Indian translators such as Shakyashribhada, who came to Sakya in 1204. But before long Tibetan scholars began to make their own unique contributions to Buddhist scholarship. The most famous of these was a Sakya abbot, Kunga Gyaltsen (1182-1251), who came to be known as the Sakya Pandita, or the Scholar from Sakya.

Sakya Pandita wrote influential texts on perception and logic, and his learning gave rise to his being identified as a manifestation of Manjushri, the bodhisattva of insight.

It was no doubt Sakya Pandita's scholastic and spiritual eminence that led to his representing the people of Tibet to the Mongol prince Godan (the son of Ghengis Khan) when the Mongols threatened to invade Tibet in the mid-13th century. Sakya Pandita made a three year journey to Mongolia, arriving in 1247, and after meeting with Godan offered him overlordship of Tibet. Sakya Pandita defended his actions by noting that resistance to the Mongols was pointless.

After Sakya Pandita's death in 1251, one of his nephews became the abbot of Sakya and, with the Mongol support of Kublai Khan, the ruler of all Tibet. It was the first religious government with a lama as head of state, thus setting an important precedent for Tibetan government.

The relationship between Tibetan lamas and their Mongol masters, which the Tibetans characterised as like that between religious teacher and patron, set yet another important precedent; one that was open to various interpretations, would trouble the Tibetan state for centuries to come and justify Chinese claims over the high Plateau.

As it was, Mongol overlordship and Sakya supremacy were relatively short-lived. Mongol corruption and rivalry between the Sakyapa and Kagyupa orders led to the fall of Sakya in 1354, when power fell into the hands of the Kagyupa and the government moved to Nedong in Ü.

Sakya was to remain a powerful municipality, however, and like Shigatse enjoyed a high degree of autonomy from successive central governments.

Sakya Monastery

The immense, thick-walled southern monastery is Sakya's main attraction. It crouches grim and forbidding among the cluster of Tibetan houses that make up Sakya township. For good views of the monastery, climb up into the northern hills on the other side of the river.

The southern monastery was established in 1268 and is designed defensively, with watchtowers on each of the corners of its high walls. There may once have been further walls intervened by a moat, but no trace of them remains today. It is possible to walk around the top of these outer walls.

Entry to Sakya Monastery is via the east

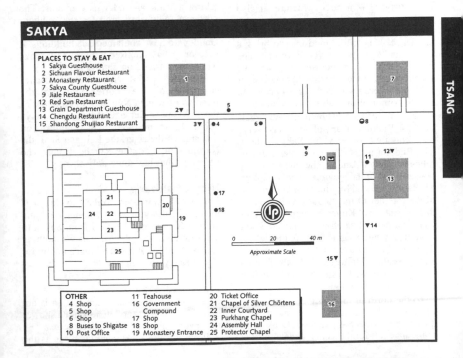

SAKYA

PLACES TO STAY & EAT
1 Sakya Guesthouse
2 Sichuan Flavour Restaurant
3 Monastery Restaurant
7 Sakya County Guesthouse
9 Jiale Restaurant
12 Red Sun Restaurant
13 Grain Department Guesthouse
14 Chengdu Restaurant
15 Shandong Shuijiao Restaurant

21
24 22
23
20
19
25
17
18

0   20   40 m
Approximate Scale

TSANG

OTHER
4 Shop
5 Shop
6 Shop
8 Buses to Shigatse
10 Post Office
11 Teahouse
16 Government
    Compound
17 Shop
18 Shop
19 Monastery Entrance
20 Ticket Office
21 Chapel of Silver Chörtens
22 Inner Courtyard
23 Purkhang Chapel
24 Assembly Hall
25 Protector Chapel

wall, though it is sometimes also possible to enter via the south wall – no one seems to mind.

Directly ahead of the east-wall entrance is the entrance to the central courtyard of the monastery, an impressive area with a towering prayer pole that is surrounded by chapels. This central section is open from 9 am to noon and may also be open in the afternoon from around 3 to 4 pm. Try to tag along with a group if possible as the monks will open up more rooms.

The chapel to the left (south) is the **Purkhang Chapel**. Central images are of Sakyamuni and Manjushri, while wall paintings behind depict Amitayus, Tara, Vijaya (Tibetan: Namgyelma – trinity of Long Life), as well as the Medicine Buddha, two Sakyamunis and Maitreya. Murals on the left wall depict Tantric deities central to the Sakya school.

The **main assembly hall** to the west of the courtyard is a huge structure. It also tends to be very dark, though morning sunshine lights the place up with a diffuse ambience. It is still a good idea to bring a good torch with you if you have one. The hall's ceiling is supported by massive sacred pillars, which are draped in fake tiger skin or plastered with coins and amulets. In the far corner of the hall is a huge drum.

The walls of the hall are lined with larger-than-life Buddhas, many of which also serve as reliquaries for previous Sakya abbots. The Buddha in the far left corner contains relics of Sakya Pandita; the one next to it houses those of the previous abbot of Sakya. The largest central Buddha contains remains of the founder of the monastery. In front of this are statues of Kunga Nyingpo, the abbot who first put Sakya on the map, and Sakya Pandita, Nyingpo's grandson. To the right of the central Buddha are statues of Manjushri and a seated Maitreya. Sakya's famous library is accessed from this hall but it is rarely opened up to tourists.

To the north of the courtyard is a chapel containing 11 silver chörtens, again reliquaries for former Sakya abbots. Look to the immediate left for the sand mandala. A door leads to another chapel with more amazing chörtens.

On either side of the east-wall entrance are stairs leading up to two 2nd-floor chapels. Neither of them is of immense interest and they may not be open.

There are a couple of chapels open outside this central complex, though the most interesting is the very spooky **protector chapel** of the Pakspa Lhakhang, where scary monsters, masks and stuffed wolves await you in the dark recesses.

Finally, climb up onto the walls of the monastery for superb views of the surrounding valley and the interior buildings of Sakya Monastery.

Northern Monastery

Very little remains of the monastery complex that once sprawled across the hills north of the Trum Chu. It is still worth climbing up through the Tibetan town and taking a walk around what remains. The northern monastery predates the southern monastery, and in its time is alleged, like Ganden, to have contained 108 buildings. It may once have housed some 3000 monks who concentrated on Tantric studies.

Aim for the white chörten, which is a reconstruction of a chörten that held the remains of Kunga Nyingpo, the founder of the Sakyapa order and the second Sakya abbot. There are three main complexes on this side of the river, the Labrang Shar, the Namja Chu and the Rinche Gang. The Labrang Shar has some holy caves.

Ujay Lhakhang

This small monastery linked to Sakya is located in the village of Chongkhor Lam, around 5km along the road from Sakya to the Friendship Highway. There's nothing special here but it's a good place to aim for if you fancy an hour's walk.

Places to Stay

Hedonists beware – accommodation is not luxurious in Sakya and there's not a shower for several hundred square kilometres.

Probably the most popular place is the

Sakya Guesthouse (there's no English sign). Rooms are basic with dirt floors and no electricity but it's bearable if you have a sleeping bag. There's a certain timeless feel about the place. Beds should cost Y8 per person but foreigners are asked to pay anything from Y10 to Y20 (one group was asked Y50!). The scenic pit toilets offer great views of the northern monastery.

Another place well worth checking out is the *Grain Department Guesthouse* (Chinese: *liangshiju zhaodaisuo*). There's a whole range of rooms here arranged around a large courtyard. Most are pretty grim, but there is one suite of three interconnected rooms (sleeping up to 12) that are by far the best rooms in town. Beds are around Y20, though the price depends upon how wealthy the manager thinks you look. Other rooms in the concrete block overlooking the main street are cheap but spirit-crushing at Y13 a bed.

Finally, one place to avoid is the *Sakya County Guesthouse* (no English sign). This decrepit fleapit is on its last legs and even the staff (if you can track them down) will recommend you go elsewhere.

Places to Eat

Sakya now has a few restaurants set up by Sichuanese immigrants and the food, although relatively pricey, is excellent.

One popular place is the *Sichuan Flavour Restaurant* just outside the Sakya Guesthouse. Recommended dishes are spicy chicken with peanuts (*gongbao jiding*) or fish-resembling eggplant (*yuxiang qiezi*). Dishes are around Y20.

Another good choice is the *Red Sun Restaurant* opposite the County Guesthouse. Both this and the Sichuan Flavour Restaurant have English menus. The *Jiale Restaurant* also has an English menu but it is 50% more than the Chinese one so avoid it out of principle. To be fair, all restaurants in Sakya do this but the Jiale is the worst offender.

Other restaurants include the *Chengdu Restaurant* (no English menu) and the *Shandong Shuijiao Restaurant*. *Shuijiao*

are Chinese-style ravioli and make a good cheap lunch. Buy them by the bowl or weight (half a jin is enough for one person and costs about Y5).

There are several shops about, where you can stock up on instant noodles, soft drinks and dry, crumbly biscuits.

Getting There & Away

There are buses every other day from Shigatse to Sakya, returning to Shigatse the following day. As these are government buses tickets cost Y54, twice the local price, though you might be able to get the local price on the way back. Buses in Sakya run from the Sakya County Guesthouse.

Another option is to take a bus to the Sakya turn-off and then hitch the remaining 25km. The distance between Shigatse and the turn-off is 127km (km marker 5028). There's a guesthouse at the turn-off, the *Lhatse Co Guesthouse*, so you won't be stuck if you can't get a lift. Beds cost Y15 and are as good as anything you'll find in Sakya, though the only food available is instant noodles.

You might find the occasional bus from Sakya to Lhatse but you'll probably have to change transport at the Sakya turn-off. If you are hitching this way it's worth heading out early to catch the morning minibuses that run from Shigatse to Lhasa.

LHATSE

Approximately 150km south-west of Shigatse and some 30km west of the Sakya turn-off, Lhatse (4050m) is essentially just a truck stop. It is a dusty little place that lines the Friendship Highway, but has some good restaurants, well-stocked shops and a few guesthouses. Most of the traffic here is en route to Zhangmu on the Nepal border, but some vehicles take the turn-off 6km down the road for Ali in Western Tibet – see the Western Tibet chapter for more details.

If you get stuck in Lhatse for a day or so (perhaps trying to hitch out of the place) there are a couple of attractions in the vicinity that can be hiked to in a day, but it should be emphasised that they are minor attractions and probably of most interest to the archaeologically minded.

At each end of town, there are ruined **dzongs**, though there's not much to see except the views of the plain below. At the west end of town is the small **Changmoche Monastery**.

About 1km short of Lhatse as you come in from Shigatse, at km marker 5052, is a northbound trail that heads out to the ruins of **Lhatse Chöde** and **Drampa Gyang Temple**. The latter is one of King Songtsen Gampo's Demoness Subduing Temples, in this case pinioning the troublesome demoness' left hip; there is little to see today. The ruins of the dzong mark the sight of the old chöde administrative centre of Lhatse.

It is around 20km to either the chöde or Drampa Gyang. The trail forks around 8km after the turn-off, with the left fork heading out to the chöde and the right fork heading out to Drampa Gyang. If you hang around the road junction you might just get a lift on a tractor.

Places to Stay

There are a few guesthouses along the Friendship Highway in Lhatse. The most popular is the *Lhatse Hotel* which has a wide variety of rooms set around a huge courtyard – the east side has the cheapest rooms, the west is more upmarket and the best rooms are above the reception on the south side.

Beds in a basic eight-bed or four-bed dormitory are Y15 or Y20 respectively. Y30 will get you a bed in a triple with carpet, Y40 gets you all this plus a TV and Y50 gets you a bed in a double in the main hotel overlooking the main road. Top of the range is a comfortable Tibetan-style double at Y80 per person. Hot showers are available from 2 to 8 pm and cost an additional Y5. The cleanest toilets are hard to find in the upper floor of the main hotel block in the south-east corner.

Other places to stay include the *Fuli Guesthouse*, a basic truck stop 50m west which has rooms for Y10, or the *Lhatse Guesthouse* 100m to the east which has a

similar range of rooms to the Lhatse Hotel and for similar prices. The *Lazi Highway Hotel* (Chinese: *gongluduan zhaodaisuo*) looks really grim from the outside but once inside it's only a little bit grim; beds cost Y10/15/20 in a triple/quad/quad with a TV.

Places to Eat

There are two restaurants in the Lhatse Hotel. Best is the Tibetan-style *Lhatse Friendship Restaurant* in the main courtyard, which has an English menu (kind of). The *Tashi No 2 Restaurant* next to reception has decent Chinese food but nothing else.

Lhatse has numerous other restaurants as it's a fairly busy truck stop. The eastern end of town is the best place to look for good Chinese food; wander in and take a look in the kitchen – no one seems to mind. Worth trying are the *Welcome* and *Great Wall* restaurants.

Getting There & Away

Daily minibuses run between Shigatse and Lhatse. In Lhatse they circle for customers every morning 150m east of the Lhatse Hotel and depart when full. The cost is Y25. There may also be a once weekly bus service to/from Sakya but no one was willing to confirm it absolutely in either Lhatse or Sakya.

Almost all truck traffic stops in Lhatse but getting a lift westwards out of Lhatse can prove tricky as there is a traffic checkpoint 6km west of Lhatse. This checkpoint doesn't affect foreigners directly but it will scare off any prospective lift that doesn't have permission to carry foreigners. It might be worthwhile walking 1½ hours to the checkpoint and then looking for a lift a kilometre or two on the other side.

For information on hitching from here out to Ali and Kailash, see the Western Tibet chapter.

A ride from Lhatse to Zhangmu should cost around Y150, though this will probably require some determined bargaining. Those looking at hitching to Tingri or Shegar will probably have to pay around Y40 to Y50, but again this depends on how hard you bargain.

It will probably also help if you have a travel permit for Tingri, Nyalam and Zhangmu, though this is by no means necessary.

SHEGAR (NEW TINGRI)

Not so many travellers stop over in Shegar (4050m). However it's a good place to spend the night before heading off to Everest Base Camp (whose access road is only 12km further on). Shegar is also a possible last stop before the Nepal border, though most travellers spend the night at Tingri, which provides views of Everest.

The town itself, a 7km diversion northwest of the Friendship Highway, is worth a visit for the ruins of **Shegar Dzong**, the Crystal Fortress, once the capital of the Tingri region. The remains of defensive walls snake incredibly over the abrupt pinnacle that looms over the town. A kora trail up to the peak leads up from the western side of town. Morning light is best for photography.

Also of interest here is **Shegar Chöde Monastery**, a small Gelugpa institution at the foot of the mountain. If you climb up to the wall behind the monastery you can get a peek at the top of Everest far in the distance. Paths continue up from here around to the dzong.

Places to Stay & Eat

The *Kangjong Hotel* is a friendly new Tibetan guesthouse right on the highway at the turn-off to Shegar. The rooms are basic but clean and cost Y20 per bed. The real attraction of the place is the restaurant and sitting area which offers wall-to-wall comfy sofas arranged around a warm stove. Good food is available at around Y15 a dish and you can sit back with a thermos of sweet tea for Y4. You can leave bags here if you are off to Everest for a few days.

Just across the road is the *Qomolangma Shegar Guesthouse*, a ridiculously expensive attempt to capture passing tour groups for the night. Economy doubles cost Y350 and are in varying states of disrepair.

There is a basic *guesthouse* with rates around Y10 and a couple of well-stocked shops in Shegar itself. Next to the Shegar checkpoint at km marker 5140 is a basic *truck stop* with beds for around Y15.

Getting There & Away

There is no public transport to or from Shegar. A ride from Shegar to Lhatse should cost between Y30 and Y50. It may be possible to hitch from the Friendship Highway to Shegar, but the chances are you'll end up walking the 7km stretch of road. It's 6km from the Shegar turn-off to the Shegar checkpoint and another 6km to the Everest turn-off.

THE EVEREST REGION

This section is aimed at the majority of travellers who visit Everest as part of a Land Cruiser trip. It is also aimed to give you an overview of the region to help you decide what kind of trip to take. For multi-day treks to and from Everest, see the Trekking chapter. The Tibetan approach to Mt Everest (8848m) provides far better vistas of the world's highest peak than those on the Nepal side.

Views of the mountain can even be had on the Friendship Highway in the vicinity of Tingri. But it is from Rongphu (sometimes spelt Rongbuk) Monastery and the Everest Base Camp that the true grandeur of Everest's sheer north face becomes apparent.

The Tibetan name for Everest is generally rendered as Qomolangma, and some 27,000 sq km of territory around Everest's Tibetan face have been designated as the Qomolangma Nature Preserve. Planning of the project was cooperative and included local Tibetan organisations, the Chinese Academy of Sciences and The Mountain Institute of the USA. For more information on the park see the aside in the Trekking chapter.

For foreign travellers, the Everest Base Camp has become the most popular trekking destination in Tibet and is an increasingly popular itinerary on a Land Cruiser trip to the border. This doesn't mean that the region is exactly swarming with hikers, but it is also not realistic to expect that you will be the only one up there. In the warm summer months there might be anywhere between 10 and 20 travellers camping around or staying in Rongphu Monastery, close to the Base Camp.

There are several ways to get to Rongphu Monastery: by Land Cruiser, on foot or by a mixture of walking and hitching. For those who want to reach the Base Camp the easy way, you can drive all the way from Shegar in a 4WD. It is a rough drive, but far less rough than doing it on foot. Buy your 'Wimps Anonymous' T-shirt in Lhasa before you go and hold your head high as you wave to the real travellers you leave behind in a cloud of dust. See the Getting There & Away section for more information on transport options.

Finally, whatever you do, do not attempt walking to Base Camp directly after arriving in Tingri from the low altitudes of the Kathmandu valley. Land Cruiser trips often reach Base Camp within two days of leaving Zhangmu and the altitude gain of over 2600m in less than 30 hours leaves most people reeling from the effects of AMS (Acute Mountain Sickness) also known as altitude sickness.

What's in a Name?

In 1849 the Great Trigonometrical Survey of India mapped the heights of peaks in the Himalaya Range. The calculations were carried out from the Indian foothills of the Himalaya Range, and three years later the computed results showed a peak known to the West as Peak XV to be the highest mountain in the world. This came as a surprise, as until this time a mountain called Kangchenjunga near Sikkim was thought to be the peak whose head rose closest to the heavens. Peak XV was rather an ignominious name for the highest mountain in the world, and immediately a search began for its real name.

Western linguists working in Nepal and India reported various local names for the mountain. In Nepal, it was claimed, XV was known as Devadhunga, 'Abode of the Gods'. German explorers, on the other hand, reported that the Tibetan name was Chingopamari. In 1862 the Royal Geographic Society opted for an alternative Nepalese name for the mountain: Gaurisanka.

In the meantime, Andrew Waugh, Surveyor General of India, embarked on a mission of his own – to have the mountain named after the head of the Great Trigonometrical Survey, Sir George Everest. He met with much opposition, largely because it was argued that a local name would be more appropriate. In 1865 the Royal Geographic Society decided to back the Everest contingent due to uncertainties surrounding Gaurisanka (in 1902 it was determined that Gaurisanka was another peak, some 50km from Everest).

The Everest name stuck amid much controversy, not least due to the fact that there were probably no shortage of experts who knew the true Tibetan name for the mountain to be Chomolangma (or Qomolangma, as the Chinese have transliterated it), which can be interpreted as the Goddess Mother of the Universe. After all, as early as 1733, the French produced a map in which Everest is indicated as Tschoumou Lancma. According to Tibetan scriptures safeguarded at Rongphu Monastery Chomolangma is the name of the mountain while the goddess who dwells there is called Miyo Langsangma. She is one of a group of five well-known long life sisters called the Tsering Che Nga, Tibetan deities that predate Buddhism.

The Tibetans and Chinese have no truck with the westernised name of the world's loftiest peak. Trekkers who make it up to Everest Base Camp have to make do with a posed photograph in front of a slab of rock inscribed with the words 'Mt Qomolangma Base Camp'.

Just as importantly, do not be tempted by the enthusiasm of others to climb any higher than you feel comfortable. As Base Camp becomes more popular, many travellers are starting to set their sights at advanced Base Camp and higher. It is probably only a matter of time before some idiot decides to scale the peak itself and dies up there. Chinese scientific teams at Base Camp will remind travellers that there is no rescue service up here in the shadow of Everest.

Permits

Permits for Everest Base Camp are readily available in Shigatse PSB for Y50. The big question is do you need one? Theoretically, yes. On the other hand, the only place it is likely to be checked is a nasty little checkpoint at the village of Chay, around two to three hours walk from the Pang-la turn-off.

However the guards here are more concerned with selling you a park permit: individuals must pay Y65, while vehicles face a whopping Y400. Your travel agency should pay the Y400 fee (but not the individual fee) but this is something you should check with them before you set out.

Those at the Chay checkpoint don't seem to be too worried about travellers leaving the Everest region, so you probably won't have to worry about any permits if you trek in from Tingri and leave via Chay.

What to Bring

If coming by Land Cruiser you don't need much more than some food and warm clothes. There are places to stay and eat en route, however you will be safest to bring some emergency food with you.

If you decide to hitch/walk in and out via Chay then you don't really need a stove. A sleeping bag is a nice luxury but not mandatory. Water purification is a good idea, as are sachets of hot drinks and packets of instant noodles.

Shegar to Everest by Road

The Everest access road turns off the Friendship Highway around 6km west of the Shegar checkpoint shortly after km marker 5145. The 63km drive takes around five hours and it's a bumpy ride – make sure you tie everything down securely.

About 3km from the Friendship Highway you get to the village of Chay (4300m), where you must pay an entrance fee to the Everest region. It is possible to find accommodation here for around Y15 but there's not much food available.

From Chay, it is a winding drive up to Pang-la (5120m). The views here are stupendous on a clear day, featuring a huge sweep of the Himalaya Range that includes Makalu, Lhotse, Everest, Gyachung Kang and Cho Oyu. A plaque on the pass shows you what's what. You can climb up a scree slope to the left for slightly wider views.

The road descends past a couple of photogenic villages and ruins into the fertile Dzakar valley and the village of Tashi Dzom (also known as Peruche), where you can get lunch and a bed for the night. The dirt road bumps up the wide valley passing the villages of Pasum and Chö Dzom, both of which offer accommodation. From Chö Dzom the road turns south towards Rongphu. The first views of Everest appear half an hour before you arrive at Rongphu.

For detailed information about the trek to Everest Base Camp, see the Trekking chapter.

Rongphu Monastery Although there were probably monastic settlements in the area for several hundred years, Rongphu Monastery is the main Buddhist centre in the valley and once coordinated the activities of around one dozen smaller religious institutions, all of which are now ruined. It was established in 1902 by a Nyingmapa lama.

While not of great antiquity, it can at least lay claim to being the highest monastery in Tibet, and thus the world, at 4980m. There were once 500 monks and nuns living here, but locals report that there are now only 20 nuns and 10 monks. The nuns and monks use the same prayer hall but have separate residences.

Renovation work has been ongoing at the monastery since 1983 and some of the interior murals are quite stunning. The monastery itself makes a fabulous photograph with Everest thrusting its head skyward in the background.

Basic accommodation is available at the monastery for Y25 per bed. Only one thermos of boiling water is supplied per day. There is also a shop and restaurant on the grounds and a surprisingly large variety of packaged goods available, including left over stock from expeditions. Egg, meat, noodle and potato dishes are served on order for around Y10 each; an omelette wrapped in a *chapatti* costs Y5. Camping on the greens of the monastery costs Y10 per tent and there is a water supply at the southern side of the monastery.

Rongphu to Everest Base Camp It is just over a two hour (8km) walk from Rongphu Monastery to the Base Camp. Vehicles do the trip in around 10 to 15 minutes. The walk is fairly straightforward, even if the altitude has you puffing within a few minutes of starting out.

Above Rongphu the valley expands into a large glacial outwash plain. There is a short cut from behind the big chörten at the monastery which cuts through a meadow

The Assault on Everest

There had been 13 assaults on Everest before Edmund Hillary and Sherpa Tenzing finally reached the summit in the major British expedition of 1953 led by John Hunt. Some of them verged on insanity.

In 1934 Edmund Wilson, an eccentric ex-British army captain, hatched a plan to fly himself from Hendon direct to the Himalaya Range, crash land his Gypsy Moth halfway up Everest and then climb solo to the summit, despite having no previous mountaineering experience (and marginal flying expertise). Needless to say he failed spectacularly. When his plane was impounded by the British in India he trekked to Rongphu in disguise and made a solo bid for the summit. He disappeared somewhere above Camp III, and his body was later discovered by the mountaineer Eric Shipton at 6400m, who read Wilson's diary until the entries abruptly finished on May 31st. A second solo effort was later attempted by a Canadian in disguise from the Tibet side. It was abandoned at 7150m.

From 1921 to 1938 all expeditions to Everest were British and were attempted from the north (Tibetan) side, along a route reconnoitred by John Noel – disguised as a Tibetan (with blue eyes) – in 1913. In all, the mountain claimed 14 lives. Perhaps the most famous early summit bid was by George Mallory and Andrew Irvine (then aged 22), who were last seen going strong above 7800m (26,000ft), before clouds obscured visibility. The two were never seen again. It is conceivable that the two reached the top and the possibility, however slight, has become one of mountaineering's most enduring mysteries. It was Mallory who, when asked why he wanted to climb Everest, famously quipped 'because it is there'.

With the conclusion of WWII and the collapse of the British Raj, the Himalaya Range became inaccessible. Tibet closed its doors to outsiders, and in 1951 the Chinese invasion wedged the doors shut even more tightly. In mountaineering terms, however, the Chinese takeover had the positive effect of shocking the hermit kingdom of Nepal into looking for powerful friends. The great peaks of the Himalaya suddenly became accessible from Nepal.

Much to their dismay, the British found that the mountain was no longer theirs alone. In 1951, Eric Shipton led a British reconnaissance expedition that explored the Nepal approaches to Everest and came to the conclusion that a Nepal assault might indeed meet with success. In 1952, however, the Nepalese issued only one permit to climb Everest – to the Swiss. The

and then past a superbly photogenic complex of ruins called **Rong Chung**. Until the Communist takeover this was a thriving meditation retreat. Permission to rebuild has not yet been granted. From Rong Chung the trail descends from the shelf to meet the road at a sacred spring.

The road climbs up through a jumble of boulders and glacial debris favouring the left side of the valley. Passing the recently rebuilt **Sherab Chöling Hermitage** (signposted as the Guru Rinpoche Monastery) the road runs into the terminal moraine of the Rongphu Glacier, mounds of stone and silt barricading the valley. You may see herds of deer and yak on the hillsides.

It is still 30 minutes from here to Base Camp. The road snakes through the moraine to reach a sandy plain. Everest Base Camp (5200m) is at the far edge of this plain. The site has a couple of permanent structures and there are usually tents belonging to various expeditions. Endowed with springs, Everest Base Camp was first used by the 1924 British Everest expedition.

There is little to see at the Everest Base Camp, but the views of Everest more than make up for this. Have a photo taken at the

The Assault on Everest

Swiss, who together with the British had virtually invented mountaineering as a sport, were extremely able climbers, and British climbers secretly feared that the Swiss might mount a successful ascent on their first attempt; something that eight major British expeditions had failed to achieve. As it happened, the Swiss climbed to 8595m on the south-east ridge – higher than any previous expedition – but failed to reach the summit.

The next British attempt was assigned for 1953. Preparations were particularly tense. It was generally felt that if this attempt was unsuccessful, any British hopes to be the first to reach the summit would be dashed. There was considerable backroom manoeuvring before the expedition set off. As a result, Eric Shipton, who had led three previous expeditions (including one in 1935), was dropped as team leader in favour of John Hunt, an army officer and keen Alpine mountaineer but relatively unknown among British climbers.

Shipton's 1951 expedition had at the last minute accepted two New Zealand climbers. One of them was Edmund Hillary, a professional bee-keeper and a man of enormous determination and seemingly unlimited reserves of strength. He was invited again to join Hunt's 1953 expedition. Also joining the 1953 expedition was Sherpa Tenzing, a Sherpa who had set out on his first Everest expedition at the age of 19 in 1935 and who had subsequently become infected with the dream of conquering the world's highest peak.

On 28 May 1953, Hillary and Tenzing made a precarious camp at 8370m on a tiny platform of the south-east ridge approach to the summit, while the other anxious members of the expedition waited below at various camps. The two men feasted that night on chicken noodle soup and dates. At 6.30 am the next morning they set out.

Almost immediately they were in trouble, confronted with a vast, steep sweep of snow. It was the kind of obstacle that had turned back previous expeditions, but Tenzing agreed with Hillary that it had to be risked. It was a gamble that paid off. The next major obstacle was a chimney-like fissure which the two men squirmed up painfully. Struggling onwards they suddenly found themselves just metres away from a snow-clad dome. At 11.30 am, 29 May, they photographed each other standing at the closest point to the heavens it is possible to reach on foot. Everest had finally been won, though to this day neither will reveal who got there first.

Base Camp marker, which disappointingly does not even mention the word 'Everest'. It reads: 'Mt Qomolangma Base Camp' and the Chinese below indicates 5200m above sea level. On a small hill to the side of the Base Camp marker are a couple of prayer poles. Clamber up for great views of the world's highest peak. You can also walk on to the edge of the Rongphu Glacier across the gravel plain just 15 minutes away. There is a creek to ford along the way – try to cross it as high up as possible and in the early morning before water levels rise.

Onwards from Base Camp Expeditions farther from Base Camp are only for very experienced trekkers or mountaineers. It is easy, once you have reached Base Camp, to succumb to the temptation to push just a little farther. Do not do it without adequate preparation. At the very least, spend a couple of days acclimatising in the Rongphu area and doing day hikes to higher altitudes. AMS can strike anyone at these altitudes, and the nearest real help is far away in Shigatse. See the Health section in the Facts for the Visitor chapter for more details.

If you have been in Tibet for a couple of weeks and are fully acclimatised it is possible to cross the creek and head up the path on the left side of the moraine. After 1¼ hours you get to a sandy camp, which offers excellent views of the main Rongphu Glacier, Guangming Peak (6533m) and Mt Pumori (7165m).

A trail continues up the side valley to Camp I and the East Rongphu Glacier but it's too far and too high to go safely in a single day. Don't attempt it unless you have a tent, stove and several days to acclimatise slowly. From the sandy camp it is a minimum three hour walk back to Rongphu Monastery.

Getting There & Away

Rented Vehicles It is perfectly feasible to hire a Land Cruiser in Shigatse or Lhasa to see the Everest region. Many travellers elect to include Everest as part of a 'package' of sights between Lhasa and the Nepal border.

Land Cruisers can lurch all the way up to Base Camp, but if you want to do some walking and turn up at Base Camp looking like you have trekked the whole way, leave the Land Cruiser at Rongphu.

Hiring a Land Cruiser in Lhasa purely to visit Everest will cost almost as much as a border trip incorporating Everest – around Y5000 or more. Shop around. In Shigatse, prices for Everest with a stop-over at Sakya en route were between Y4000 and Y4500. Shopping around and some determined haggling can bring the price down lower than this, but be wary of deals that seem too good to be true. You'll need a minimum of one night at Rongphu; two nights is much better.

Trekking The Trekking chapter has information about the logistics of hiking in and out of the Everest region from Shegar and Tingri.

Hitching Not everyone wants to trek the entire distance, however, and it is possible to use a combination of hiking and hitching to get to Rongphu. There are normally up to five Land Cruisers a day headed up to Rongphu and you might well be able to score a ride at least part of the way. There is accommodation along the road at Tashi Dzom, Pasum and Chö Dzom, all a day's walk from each other and some food is available. You'll need a few days and a flexible itinerary for the trip but you will have more opportunities to stop and explore sites en route. See the Trekking chapter for information on accommodation and sights en route.

TINGRI

Tingri (4390m), a huddle of Tibetan homes that overlook a sweeping plain bordered by the towering Himalaya Range, is where most travellers spend their last night in Tibet en route to Nepal, or their first night en route to Lhasa from Kathmandu. For newcomers from Kathmandu, the discomforts of the sudden altitude gain are likely to make it an unpleasant stay. There is little in the way of sights around Tingri, though views of

Everest and the muscular-looking massif of Cho Oyu more than compensate for this.

Ruins on the hill overlooking Tingri are all that remain of the **Tingri Dzong**. This is a fort that was not blown up by Red Guards but rather destroyed in a late 18th century Nepalese invasion. On the plains between Shegar and Tingri many more ruins that shared the same fate can be seen from the Friendship Highway.

Those planning on using Tingri as a base to trek into the Everest region should consult the Everest section of the Trekking chapter.

Langkhor Monastery

One minor sight you might want to head out to is Langkhor Monastery, about 20km south-west of Tingri. It is associated with Padampa Sangye, an Indian ascetic who was an important figure in the 11th to 12th century second diffusion of Buddhism on the Tibetan plateau. Restoration work has been undertaken at Langkhor and there are some fine old woodcarvings but in general it's not a spectacular site. The best thing about the trip is the ever changing view of the Tingri plain – a classic case of it being better to travel than to arrive.

You can hike out to the monastery and village in around five hours but a better option is to hire a pony and cart for the bumpy ride out there. Most villagers have a cart and though it's not a comfortable 4½ hour return ride (bring some padding!) you'll get to see much more this way. The cost for a pony, cart and driver is around Y50.

The track heads south-west from Tingri through the villages of Shegar, Sala and Injum and then turns west towards Langkhor. On the way back you could head north to the village of Dongba and then continue past ancient ruins to the main highway at km marker 5202. You could also visit the hot springs at Tsamda, 10km west of Tingri, as part of a trip to Langkhor. There is a small hotel, the *Snowland Lodge*, at the springs.

Places to Stay & Eat

All accommodation is on the Friendship Highway. Most budget travellers passing through in rented vehicles stay in the *Everest View Hotel* (or the 'Lao Dhengre Haho Everest Veo Hotel & Restaurant' as the sign cryptically advertises), a shabby little place arranged around a compound. Beds are Y20 and basic food is available.

Other basic truck stops nearby include the *Amdo Hotel* and *Himalaya Hotel*, both of which offer beds for Y20. There are several Chinese restaurants nearby which cater largely to the local army garrison. All the English menus are the same, with dishes starting around Y20.

The nicest place by far is the *Everest Snow Leopard Hotel*, about 400m east of the other hotels. The all-brick rooms are spotlessly clean, very cosy and there are some nice touches like unsolicited buckets of hot and cold water and views of Cho Oyu from most of the rooms. There's also a nice restaurant and sitting area, which doubles as reception. Rates are officially Y60 per bed but this normally crumbles to around Y30 if you don't arrive in a flashy Land Cruiser.

Getting There & Away

There is no public transport along this stretch of the Friendship Highway. Hitching a lift with trucks bound for the border from Shigatse or Lhatse would be the best bet. You will have to pay for the lift. The sum is entirely negotiable, but don't be surprised if it is as high as Y100 (around Y50 to Nyalam).

NYALAM

Nyalam (3750m) is a one-street town around 30km before the Nepal border. It has been steadily growing in size and facilities have been improving over the last few years. This no doubt due to burgeoning trade opportunities with nearby Nepal.

Some tour groups coming up from Kathmandu spend the night at Nyalam, but most groups coming from Lhasa stay in Tingri, 150km to the north-east. Even if you do not have time to spend the night, it is worth stopping for lunch in Nyalam and poking around. The Nepalese influence that is so prevalent in nearby Zhangmu can also be felt here; there are normally plenty of

Nepalese and Indian pilgrims shivering in down jackets and bobble hats.

From Nyalam the road drops like a stone off the Tibetan plateau into a mossy gorge of waterfalls and cascades. During the summer monsoons the road submerges into a sea of cloud, no doubt one of the reasons why Nyalam means 'The Gateway to Hell' in Tibetan.

For those who want to use Nyalam as a base for treks, Gary McCue has a section on treks around Nyalam in his book, *Trekking in Tibet – a traveler's guide*. One possible

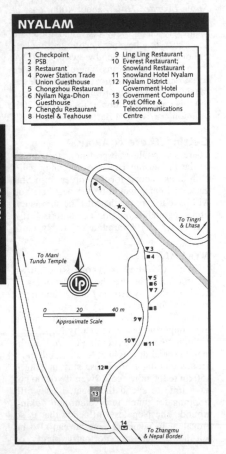

NYALAM

1 Checkpoint	9 Ling Ling Restaurant
2 PSB	10 Everest Restaurant;
3 Restaurant	Snowland Restaurant
4 Power Station Trade	11 Snowland Hotel Nyalam
Union Guesthouse	12 Nyalam District
5 Chongzhou Restaurant	Government Hotel
6 Nyilam Nga-Dhon	13 Government Compound
Guesthouse	14 Post Office &
7 Chengdu Restaurant	Telecommunications
8 Hostel & Teahouse	Centre

day hike takes you up the valley behind Nyalam for three hours to some *drokpa* (herders') camps.

The closest cultural sight to Nyalam is Nyalam Pelgye Ling, a small temple that is associated with the **Cave of Milarepa**, the famous Buddhist mystic and composer of songs who lived in the late 11th and early 12th centuries. The temple is around 10km north of Nyalam, and a path leads down to it from a white chörten near km marker 5333 on the Friendship Highway. It takes around three hours to hike here from Nyalam.

In the town itself is a small *mani lhakhang* housing a large prayer wheel and the nearby **Mani Tundu Temple**. There's not much to see but it's a nice five minute walk and there are often a few pilgrims around. To get there take the road that branches off from the southern end of town.

Amazingly enough there are even a couple of full-size pool tables underneath the Snowland Restaurant which could easily divert some of your time.

Information

The post office at the top (southern) end of town is the place to send mail and even make international phone calls. The office is open from 9.30 am to 12.30 pm and 3.30 to 6 pm and there's a night trunk call office next door open until 11 pm.

There's nowhere to change money in Nyalam.

Places to Stay

There are a couple of cheap places to stay on the main square. The *Power Station Trade Union Guesthouse* is a good value budget place, despite its unlikely name. Dorm beds are Y15 and they back onto the river below. The toilet is pretty grim.

The *Nyilam Nga-Dhon Guesthouse* (☎ 2113) is nearby. There are a range of clean rooms, starting at Y20 for a bed in a quad and moving up to Y35 for a bed in a triple or quad with carpet. The best room in the house (and probably Nyalam) is a pleasant double for Y60 which has a sitting area and a river view. The hotel is a bit cramped but the owners are friendly and there's a clean toilet and washing block.

The other choice is the **Snowland Hotel Nyalam** (☎ *2111*) further up the road. It's a small and intimate place and is where most groups stay. Beds are Y30 in Tibetan-style doubles or more comfortable five-bed rooms. The upper floor has modern style doubles for Y60 and Y120 and a toilet block and solar shower on the roof.

The **Nyalam District Government Hotel** down the road is shabby and depressing and foreigners have to pay 50% more for the privilege to stay here. There's no reason to stay here.

There's also a small teahouse and **hostel** near the central square where you can get basic food and very basic accommodation for Y15 a bed.

Places to Eat

There are several Chinese restaurants near the main square including the **Chengdu Restaurant**, **Chongzhou Restaurant** and **Ling Ling Restaurant**. The latter has an English menu and slightly inflated prices. Dishes are around Y15 to Y20.

The classiest place for a final Chinese dinner before the hedonistic delights of Kathmandu is the third-floor **Snowland Restaurant**. Vegetarian dishes are around Y12 to Y20, and meat dishes cost Y20 to Y30.

There are several other cheap restaurants offering a mixture of western and Nepalese food. Try the **Everest Restaurant** underneath the Snowland Restaurant.

Getting There & Away

There are usually a few Land Cruisers headed down to Zhangmu to pick up groups; most leave sometime before 10 am and you can normally get a lift. It's a stunning 30km down to Zhangmu and you could even walk it if you are keen. There's a good chance you'll get a lift somewhere along the route if you start flagging. You might even have to walk some of the way if the road is washed out.

Most travellers heading into Tibet will already have arranged their own transport in Kathmandu or Zhangmu in order to get past the Zhangmu checkpoint (see the following section). If you are hitching eastwards it's worth walking past the Nyalam checkpoint by the river.

From Tingri you'll have to hitch a ride to Nyalam (expect to pay about Y50).

ZHANGMU

Zhangmu (2300m), also known as Khasa in Nepali and Dram in Tibetan, is a remarkable town that hugs the rim of a seemingly never-ending succession of hairpin bends down to the customs area at the border of China and Nepal. After Tibet, it all seems incredibly green and luxuriant, the smells of curry and incense in the air are smells from the subcontinent and the babbling sound of fast-flowing streams that cut through the town is music to the ears.

Zhangmu is a typical border town, much larger than Nyalam, and has a restless, reckless feel to it. The population is a fascinating mix of Han, Tibetan and Nepalese, the shops brim with goodies from India, Nepal and China, and in curry shops Tibetans watch videos of Indian soap operas. Chinese officials strut around town with coiffured hairstyles, micro-thin socks and jackets hanging off their shoulders like parading generals. Meanwhile Indian traders squeeze their Tata trucks through the congested twisting streets, sending western tour groups running for their lives. It is well worth spending a little time exploring the place.

There are nice views of the town from the back of the mani lhakhang, halfway up the town.

Information

CITS has an office just next to the Zhangmu Hotel. It arranges transport and Tibet Tourism Bureau (TTB) permits for travellers who turn up from Nepal without pre-arranged transport or a guide.

Moneychangers deal openly in front of the Zhangmu Hotel and will change any combination of Chinese yuan, US dollars or Nepali rupees. There are two branches of

TSANG

the Bank of China in town, one right next to the Zhangmu Hotel but they'll tell you to go to the moneychangers.

The post office is at the top of town, a *long* hike from the Zhangmu Hotel.

Places to Stay

The main hotel in Zhangmu is the *Zhangmu Hotel* (☎ 2221), right down in the south of town next to customs. As you might expect of the last official foreigner's abode in Tibet, it is expensive and apathetically run. It's also the only hotel in Tibet whose reception is on the top floor!

Standard doubles cost Y400 per bed, and while the rooms are really very luxurious, hot water can be a bit dicey. Bottom floor triples are available for Y50 per bed.

Most budget travellers sensibly give the Zhangmu Hotel a miss in favour of the *Gang Gyen Hotel* (☎ 2188) across the road. Rooms are officially Y70 for a double or Y50 per bed in a five bed dorm but the latter normally slides down to around Y30. The dorms are nice and spotlessly clean, though the communal bathrooms are a little grim.

Hot showers are available on the roof and are free for guests (Y5 for non-guest).

Another possibility is the *Weijian Hostel*, a funky collection of wooden shacks that go for around Y20 per person. This is also the site of the Kangle Bathhouse, where you can get a hot shower for Y5.

There are several other accommodation options in Zhangmu, though none of them are up to much. The *Zangbao Guesthouse* is a big block halfway up the town which has beds for around Y30. There are several others further up in town but they are all pretty inconvenient for crossing the border.

Places to Eat

There is no shortage of restaurants in Zhangmu. The *Gang Gyen Hotel* has a popular ground floor restaurant that serves Nepalese food and western breakfasts. Buffet dinners at the Zhangmu Hotel's *restaurant* cost Y90 and you can also order à la carte at around Y20 to Y40 a dish.

Wander further up the hill for a good selection of Chinese, Tibetan and Nepalese cuisine – for anyone who has come in from other parts of Tibet, it is paradise. The *Xianrong Restaurant* at the first major switchback serves good Chinese food. There's no English menu but they serve most of the dishes listed in the Language

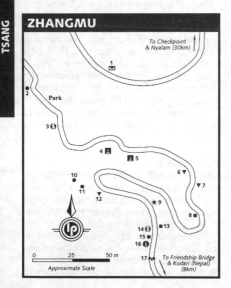

ZHANGMU

To Checkpoint & Nyalam (30km)

Park

To Friendship Bridge & Kodari (Nepal) (8km)

0   25   50 m
Approximate Scale

chapter at the back of the book. For Muslim food try the *West Restaurant of Muslims*. For Tibetan food try the *Lhasa Restaurant*.

Getting There & Away

To Kathmandu Access to Nepal is via the Friendship Bridge and Kodari, around 8km below Zhangmu. Traffic on the stretch of no-man's land between the two countries has increased over the last couple of years and it has now become quite easy to hitch a lift, though you will probably have to pay. Around Y15 should do the trick, but the amount depends entirely on who is giving the lift.

If you decide to walk, it takes a couple of hours down to the bridge. There are porters at both customs points who will carry your pack for a few rupees or Renminbi (RMB). Look out for short cuts down between the hairpin bends of the road. They save quite a bit of time if you find them, though they put a real strain on the knees.

It is possible to get a Nepali visa at the border for the same price as in Lhasa, though it would be sensible to get one in Lhasa just in case. There are a couple of hotels on the Nepalese side, which offer rooms for around Rs 80. For those looking at continuing straight on to Kathmandu, there are a couple of buses a day from Kodari that leave whenever they are full. If you can't find a direct bus you'll have to change halfway at Barabise. The other option is to hire a vehicle. There are usually touts for vehicles to Kathmandu in front of the hotels on the Nepalese side. The cost is around Rs 1500 to Rs 2000. Most of the ve-hicles are private cars, and small ones at that; you will be hard pressed to fit more than three people into one, especially if you have big packs. Depending on the condition of the road, it should take around four to five hours from Kodari to Kathmandu.

Nepal is 2¼ hours behind Chinese time.

Into Tibet For information on getting to Zhangmu from Kathmandu see the Land section in the Getting There & Away chapter. It is very difficult nowadays to hitch from Zhangmu into the rest of Tibet. The check-point a couple of kilometres above town will not let you cross without TTB permit. This can only be obtained from the CITS office next to the Zhangmu Hotel and they will only give you one once you have booked a Land Cruiser with them or can prove that you have your own Land Cruiser and guide. Some travellers have tried sneaking across the checkpoint before dawn but it's a long hike up there so you'd have to leave ex-tremely early. Plus you'll still have to bluff your way across the Nyalam checkpoint.

There are usually a number of empty Land Cruisers that have brought groups from Lhasa to the border and who would like to make some extra cash by transport-ing new arrivals back, but CITS will normally make sure that you end up paying around US$130 for the ride. If you are trav-elling alone or in a couple you'll probably have to hang around waiting for other trav-ellers to share the cost. Land Cruiser drivers normally wait at Chinese customs for new arrivals, but alternatively you can ask around at the hotels in Zhangmu.

TSANG

Western Tibet

HIGHLIGHTS

- **Wild Adventure** – Western Tibet is one of the most beautiful and remote parts of Asia

- **Mt Kailash** – the three or four day pilgrim circuit around the auspicious holy mountain

- **Lake Manasarovar** – the sacred lake is an ocean of turquoise bordered by snowy peaks

- **Tsaparang & Thöling** – ruins of the ancient Guge Kingdom

- **Rutok** – hilltop ruins of a series of Monasteries and a dzong, overlooking a traditional Tibetan village and close to some prehistoric rock carvings

Western Tibet, or Ngari as it is known to Tibetans, is the most inaccessible part of the Tibetan Autonomous Region. The Chinese authorities do their best to make it even more inaccessible by putting as many hurdles as possible between individual travellers and the main attractions of the region: sacred Mt Kailash, Lake Manasarovar (Tibetan: Mapham yum-tso) and the ruined capital of Tsaparang.

Until recently, Western Tibet has largely been the preserve of western tour groups and the occasional intrepid traveller with a taste for adventure and plenty of time to spare. This situation, for good or for bad, is starting to change. Over the last few years, it has become slightly easier to obtain permits for the region, and local authorities have become more relaxed about the arrival of individual travellers.

The journey from Lhasa is marked by stunning, if desolate, scenery and Kailash and Manasarovar are two of the most remote travel destinations in the world. At the end of the day, the main attractions of what is likely to be a three week trip are a mountain and a lake, but what a mountain, what a lake, and for the truly intrepid there are the other-worldly ruins of Tsaparang, the little visited monastery at Rutok and Western Tibet's almost unknown prehistoric rock carvings.

Visitors not overly fussed by the spiritual significance of Kailash are likely to come away with the feeling that it was one of those 'been-there-done-that' adventures, with the difficulty of access and the cachet of having been to one of the most remote corners of the globe as much an attraction as the destination itself.

History

Most histories of Tibet begin with the kings of the Yarlung valley region and their unification of central Tibet in the 7th century. But it is thought that the Shangshung Kingdom of Western Tibet probably ruled the Tibetan plateau for several centuries prior to this. According to some scholars, the Bön religion made its way into the rest of Tibet from here. The Shangshung Kingdom may also have served as a conduit for Tibet's earliest contacts with Buddhism.

There is little material evidence of the Shangshung Kingdom in modern Tibet. Khyunglung Monastery, around 95km north-west of Lake Manasarovar, and ruins in its near vicinity are thought to mark the site of the old kingdom. Those with a particular interest in this archaeological site and other remote monasteries in the area should go prepared with a copy of Victor Chan's *Tibet Handbook*.

The next regional power to emerge in Western Tibet was the Guge Kingdom in the 9th century. After the assassination of the anti-Buddhist Lhasa king, Langdharma, one of the king's sons, Wosung, established the kingdom west of Manasarovar and Kailash at Tsaparang. The Guge Kingdom, via contacts

WESTERN TIBET

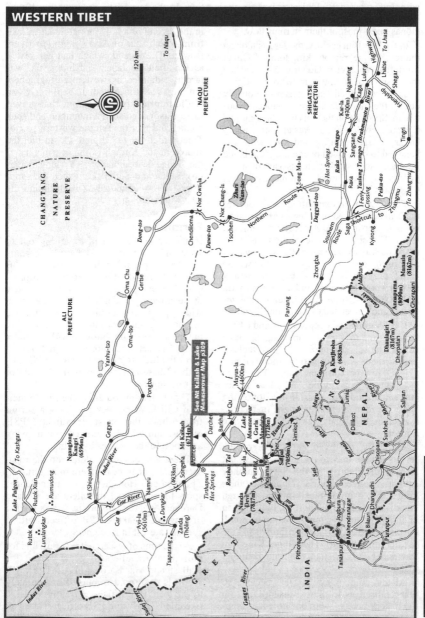

with India, led a Buddhist revival on the Tibetan plateau and was home to over 100 monasteries, most of them in ruins now.

In the late 16th century, the Jesuits took an interest in the remote kingdom of Guge. From their enclave in Goa, rumours reached the Jesuits of a kingdom whose religion strongly resembled Catholicism – probably due to the monastic nature of Tibetan Buddhism. Speculation that this was the long-lost Christian civilisation of Prester John – a legendary Christian priest and king who was believed to have ruled over a kingdom in the Far East – soon sparked enthusiasm for an expedition to this faraway community of lost Christians.

The first Jesuit expedition to set out for the kingdom ended in failure with the death of its leader in 1603. A second expedition, led by Father Antonio de Andrede in 1624, made its way to the head of the Mana valley disguised as pilgrims and looked down on Tibet only to be turned back by heavy snows, snow blindness and acute mountain sickness (AMS). A month later they returned and descended to the Guge Kingdom.

If de Andrede had expected to find Christians waiting for him at Tsaparang, the Guge capital, he was disappointed. Nevertheless, he did meet with surprising tolerance and respect for the Christian faith. The Guge king agreed to allow de Andrede to return and set up a Jesuit mission the following year. The foundation stone of the first Christian church in Tibet was laid by the king himself.

Ironically, the evangelical zeal of the Jesuits led not only to their own demise but also to the demise of the kingdom they sought to convert. Lamas, outraged by their king's increasing enthusiasm for an alien creed, enlisted the support of Ladakhis in laying siege to Tsaparang. Within a month the city fell, the king was overthrown and the Jesuits imprisoned. The Guge Kingdom foundered on Christian zeal and factional manoeuvring.

At this point, Western Tibet became so marginalised as to almost disappear from the history books – with one notable exception. In the late Victorian era, a handful of western explorers began to take an interest in the legend of a holy mountain and a lake from which four of Asia's mightiest rivers flowed. The legend, which had percolated as far afield as Japan and Indonesia, was largely ridiculed by western cartographers but in 1908 the Swedish explorer Sven Hedin returned from a journey that proved there was indeed such a mountain and such a lake, and that the remote western part of Tibet which they occupied was in fact the source of the Karnali (a major tributary of the Ganges), Brahmaputra (Yarlung Tsangpo), Indus and Sutlej (Langchen Tsangpo) rivers. The mountain was Kailash and the lake Manasarovar.

Permits

In theory all foreigners travelling out to Western Tibet must have a fistful of permits – a travel permit, military permit, TTB permit, Cultural Affairs Permit ... In practice, however, many travellers – mainly those hitching – don't bother. The catch with applying for permits and doing the trip officially is that the authorities only give out permits to tour groups with a guide, Land Cruiser and (normally) a truck to carry the fuel. If you arrange a trip like this with a Lhasa agency they will take care of all relevant permits.

Those planning on doing the trip on their own will have no luck obtaining a permit from either the Lhasa or Shigatse PSB offices, and will be better off not drawing attention to themselves by trying.

There are local checkpoints on the road, specifically near the northern route turn-off, Zhongba and Hor Qu but the main danger spots for individual travellers are Ali and Darchen, where there are usually a couple of English-speaking PSB officers with a special interest in foreigners.

At the time of research it was possible for individual travellers to get a permit for Kailash and Manasarovar in Ali. The key it seems is to surrender yourself immediately to the local PSB officer, currently Mr Li, a likeable Hui Muslim PSB officer. Here you

Sven Hedin

Sven Hedin was born in Stockholm in 1865. From a young age he was inspired by tales of journeys to the empty spaces of maps. By the age of 15 he had already decided that he too would become an explorer, and undertook a fanatical regime of training that included learning languages (Russian, Tatar, Persian, Tibetan, Turkish and Arabic), naked romps in the snow (to improve his physical endurance), cartography and drawing. He was nothing short of a man obsessed, and at 21 he made his first long journey – 1500km by steamer across the Caspian Sea, on horseback across Persia, to the Gulf, Baghdad and back through Persia. It established his reputation in Europe as a hardy traveller.

Hedin continued his travels, winning the approbation of other renowned explorers and, importantly, the Royal Geographic Society, which heaped him with honours. A close encounter with death in the Taklamakan desert of Chinese Turkestan made him more cautious, but it did nothing to dampen his enthusiasm. And having explored much of Central Asia, he turned his attention to Tibet and the forbidden city of Lhasa. Thwarted in his goal by zealous Tibetan border patrols and then beaten to the post by the British Younghusband expedition of 1904, Hedin suddenly lost interest in Lhasa and turned his gaze westward to the vast unmapped regions of Western Tibet.

The British Indian administration was none too keen on this idea. When Hedin arrived at Shimla in northern India in early 1906, he received a frosty reception and was prohibited from continuing on to Tibet. For the next few months, with characteristic resolve, he played a cat-and-mouse game with the British authorities, finally breaking into Tibet in August 1906 from Leh in Ladakh.

Over the next two years, Hedin cut two great swathes across Tibet, filling in 100,000km of blank spaces on maps of Tibet, discovering the sources of the Brahmaputra (Yarlung Tsangpo), Sutlej and Indus rivers, circumambulating Mt Kailash and returning with reports of a trans-Himalayan mountain range that intervened between the Himalaya to the south and the Kunlun range to the north. On one of his trips to the Changtang plateau Hedin's party travelled for 55 days without meeting another soul.

If Hedin expected to return to Europe a conquering hero, he was disappointed. Although his speeches at the Royal Geographic Society were received to fabulous applause, there were elements in the British geographical establishment who doubted some of his claims and acrimonious debate broke out. Not long after he published accounts of his journey (running to a massive 13 volumes in two works: *Transhimalaya* and *Southern Tibet*), he found a more welcome reception in Germany. His support of Germany in WWI led to his being struck off the membership of the Royal Geographic Society, and his similar support in WWII led to his being spurned by his own countrymen. His death went almost unnoticed in 1952.

Sven Hedin, intrepid explorer of Western Tibet.

may have to eat a slice of humble pie and pay a fine of a couple of hundred yuan but you should receive in return a little goody-goody badge and, more importantly, a Y50 permit for Kailash and Darchen, making the rest of your trip delightfully legal. Even with the fine, you have got away with doing the trip a lot more cheaply than if you had done it officially. Be warned however, this could change at any time so it's worth checking with other travellers before you head off.

Shigatse PSB will sometimes give a permit to Saga, the first town on the southern route after the northern turn-off, for Y50. This can be very useful in getting you started along the road, though don't tell them you are going to Kailash.

When to Go

May, June, and from mid-September to early October are probably the best times to head out to Western Tibet. Rates for Land Cruiser hire are cheapest in May. In April the Mayun River, around 100km north-west of Paryang, is often still frozen creating a difficult crossing. Roads along the southern route in particular are sometimes made impassable by July and August's mini-monsoon although work is under way to complete bridges across the most difficult rivers. The Drölma-la pass on the Kailash kora is normally blocked with snow from mid-October to early April.

What to Bring

A sleeping bag is essential as are warm clothes. A tent is highly recommended, especially if you are trekking around Kailash, though you could conceivably get by without one. Several large water bottles or jerry cans are useful for carrying water.

Most people end up dining on Chinese instant noodles for their entire Western Tibet trip. This is not an ideal option (the combined MSG of 20 or 30 bags of noodles is probably enough to kill a small rodent!) but you have little choice, especially if you are hitching. It's worth bringing along as much food as you can carry or you can stuff in

your truck. Possibilities include dried fruit, bottled fruit, potatoes, peanuts, potatoes, boiled eggs, Snickers bars and dehydrated food from home. For more culinary ideas see the Food sections in the Facts for the Visitor and Trekking chapters. A small stove could well save your taste buds.

Getting There & Away

Most travellers approach Western Tibet from Lhasa, it's the easiest place to organise permits and find travelling companions. In 1998 an increasing number of individual travellers were successfully taking the difficult road from Kashgar in Xinjiang to Ali (some after arriving there via the Karakoram Highway from Pakistan). Some of them were even travelling by bicycle. Whether this route will remain relatively open is anyone's guess. Some trekking groups arrive in the region by walking for five or six days from Simikot in western Nepal.

There is no public transport for any of these routes. The only motorised options are to hire a vehicle or to hitch.

Land Cruiser Trips This is the most popular way to get out to Kailash. In July and August you'll probably find three or four trips being advertised on Lhasa's notice boards at any one time. Costs depend on a multiplicity of factors but average around US$600 per person for six people on an 18 day trip with a Land Cruiser, truck, two drivers, a guide, permits and fuel. Additional days or changes in the routing (for example getting dropped off in Zhangmu) seem to add little to the cost of the trip.

You really need a minimum of a week to arrange a trip of this sort. See the Getting Around chapter and the boxed text 'Planning a Land Cruiser Trip to Mt Kailash' for some basic rules. There's a list of agencies in the Travel Agencies section of the Lhasa chapter.

Hitching For those hitching, it is the northern route that has the most traffic (see the following section).

PILGRIMAGE

BRADLEY MAYHEW

Pilgrimage is practised throughout the world, though as a devotional exercise it has been raised to a level of particular importance in Tibet. This may be because of the nomadic element in Tibetan society; it may also be that in a mountainous country with no roads and no wheeled vehicles, walking long distances became a fact of life, and by visiting sacred places en route this could be combined with accumulating merit. To most Tibetans their natural landscape is imbued with a series of sacred visions and holy 'power places'; mountains can be perceived as a mandala image, rocks assume spiritual dimensions, and the earth is imbued with healing powers.

The immediate motivations of pilgrimage are many, but for the ordinary Tibetan it amounts to a means of accumulating merit *(sonam)* or good luck *(tashi)*. The lay practitioner might go on pilgrimage in the hope of winning a better rebirth, cure an illness, end a spate of bad luck or simply because of a vow to take a pilgrimage if a bodhisattva granted a wish.

In Tibet there are countless sacred destinations, ranging from lakes and mountains to monasteries and caves that once served as meditational retreats for important yogin. Specific pilgrimages are often proscribed for specific ills; certain mountains for example expiate certain sins. A circumambulation of Mt Kailash offers the possibility of liberation within three lifetimes, while a circuit of Lake Manasarovar can result in spontaneous Buddhahood. A circuit of Mt Tsari in south-eastern Tibet can improve a pilgrim's chances of being reborn with special powers such as the ability to fly.

Pilgrims and prayer flags at the high point of the auspicious Mt Kailash kora – the 5630m Drölma-la.

TONY WHEELER

Pilgrimage is even more powerful in certain auspicious months; at certain times a circumambulation of Mt Bonri is reckoned to be 700 million times more auspicious than those of other mountains.

The three foremost pilgrimage destinations of Tibet are all mountains: Mt Kailash, in Western Tibet; Mt Tapka Shelri and the Tsari valley, in south-east Tibet; and Mt Lapchi, east of Nyalam. Lakes such as Manasarovar, Yamdrok-tso, Nam-tso and Lhamo La-tso attract pilgrims partly because their sacred water is thought to hold great healing qualities. The cave hermitages of Drak Yerpa, Chimphug and Sheldrak are particularly venerated by pilgrims for their associations with Guru Rinpoche.

On a Pilgrimage

BRADLEY MAYHEW

Pilgrims often organise themselves into large groups, hire a truck and travel around the country visiting all the major sacred places in one go. Pilgrim guidebooks have existed for centuries to help travellers interpret the 24 'power places' of Tibet. Such guides even specify locations where you can urinate or fart without offending local spirits (and probably your fellow pilgrims).

Pilgrimage is naturally not just a matter of walking to a sacred place and then going home. There are a number of activities that focus the concentration of the pilgrim. The act of kora, of circumambulating the object of devotion is chief among these. Circuits of three, 13 or 108 koras are especially auspicious, with sunrise and sunset the most auspicious hours. Prostration *(chaktsal)* is a powerful way of showing devotion. Prostration follows a sequence – placing your hands in a namaste position, touching one's forehead, throat and heart, getting down into a half-prostration (like Muslim prayer) and then lying full on the ground with one's hands stretched out. The

GREG CAIRE

Above: Prostrating pilgrim taking a rest on the Barkhor, Lhasa. The thick apron protects his clothes and the wooden blocks (slung over his left shoulder) protect his hands.

Left: Thousands of pilgrims make a pilgrimage on the first day of the sixth lunar month on the outskirts of Lhasa.

Below: Keen pilgrims show their devotion by prostrating themselves along Lhasa's 8km Lingkhor.

Bottom: Raising the Tarboche flagpole during Saga Dawa, Lha Chu valley, Mt Kailash kora.

particularly devout carry out whole pilgrimages like this, stepping forward the length of their body after each prostration and starting all over again.

Most pilgrims make offerings during the course of a pilgrimage. *Kathaks*, white ceremonial scarves, are given to lamas or holy statues as a term of respect. Offerings of yak butter or oil, fruit, tsampa, seeds and money are all left at altars, and bowls of water and chang are replenished. Monks often act as moneychangers, converting Y10 notes into a wad of one mao notes, that makes limited funds go further.

Outside chapels, at holy mountain peaks, passes and bridges you will see pilgrims throwing offerings of tsampa or printed prayers into the air (often with the cry 'ou, ou, ou!'). Pilgrims will also collect sacred rocks, herbs, earth and water from a holy site to take back home to those who couldn't make the pilgrimage. Other activities include adding stones to a cairn, rubbing special healing rocks and squeezing through narrow gaps in a rock as a method of sin detection. While circumambulating a pilgrimage site, there are usually stops of particular spiritual significance such as rock-carved syllables or painted Buddha images. Many of these carvings are said to be 'self-arising', ie not having been carved by a human hand. The Kailash kora, for example is a treasure trove of these, encompassing sky burial sites, stones that have 'flown' from India, monasteries, bodhisattva footprints, and even at one point a lingam, or penis-print.

Other pilgrimages are carried out purely to visit a renowned holy man or teacher. Blessings from lamas, trulkus (reincarnated lamas) or Rinpoches are particularly valued, as are the personal possessions of famous holy men. According to Keith Dowman in his book Sacred Tibet, the underpants of one revered lama were cut up and then distributed amongst his eager followers!

BRADLEY MAYHEW

CARRY WEARE

Western Tibet
Top: Lake Manasarovar from Chiu Monastery. **Middle left:** Drölma-la, Mt Kailash kora.
Middle right: Pilgrims rest near Lhatse. **Bottom:** Little Drölma-la, Tirthapuri kora.

Travellers planning on hitching out to Western Tibet should travel to Lhatse first (see the Lhatse section of the Tsang chapter). It is a small place and all the westbound traffic is either heading for the Nepalese border or out to Ali. Most travellers walk the 6km from Lhatse to the checkpoint and turn off for Western Tibet. It is very rare to have any problems at this checkpoint – most people just walk straight through it – but it's probably the best place to begin hitching, since the ferry crossing just west of the turn-off has recently been replaced with a bridge. Some travellers have managed to get lifts all the way to Ali from this point, some in Land Cruisers.

Truck drivers are increasingly reluctant to give foreigners lifts and more hitchhikers turn back than actually make it. One traveller wrote how he placed a stone on the roadside for every truck that passed him in the three days he waited for a lift. After three days he gave up and headed back to Lhasa to rent a Land Cruiser, leaving behind a sizeable roadside chörten. You need to be very flexible with your itinerary, carry plenty of supplies and more importantly you need to have sufficient time (minimum three weeks) remaining on your visa.

ROUTES TO WESTERN TIBET

There are two routes from Lhasa to Western Tibet: a northern route and a southern route. The northern route is considerably longer than the southern route: about 1700km versus 1200km to Ali.

If your objective is Mt Kailash and Lake Manasarovar and you've hired a Land Cruiser, the southern route is the way to travel. The road is generally better and on a good run it can be covered in four days

---

Planning a Land Cruiser Trip to Mt Kailash

Any pilgrimage worth its salt involves its fair share of trials and tribulations but with careful planning it's possible to avoid many of the common pitfalls of arranging a trip to Kailash.

Obviously the first step is to draw up a proposed itinerary for the trip. This will allow the various agencies to give you a firm quote based on distance covered and number of days on the road (see the boxed text 'Dealing with an Agency' in the Getting Around chapter). The agencies may even suggest changes to your proposal based on the current road conditions, travel times, accommodation en route etc. One point to consider carefully when drawing up an itinerary is the rate of altitude gain. Build in an extra day early on to acclimatise – after Lhatse nowhere is lower than 4500m.

Most basic itineraries take around 17 to 21 days which allows for six days to get to Kailash, stopping en route at places like Sakya Monastery, a couple of days around Manasarovar to rest up and enjoy the lake, four days on the Kailash kora and four to five days to get back. A visit to Thöling or Tsaparang will add on at least three days, probably four. An itinerary which takes in both the northern and southern routes will eat up a minimum of three weeks, probably 24 days. A final consideration if you are headed to Nepal is whether to take the shortcut from Saga to Zhangmu.

With an itinerary you can start to recruit travellers to share the costs of the trip. The notice boards at Lhasa's budget hotels are the best places to post an advert. The final number of people in your group determines the type of vehicle you rent. Most groups of five or six take one Land Cruiser and one truck to carry supplies, petrol and normally one passenger. Remember you have a guide as well. Groups of four may be able to hire just a Land Cruiser, though agencies are normally loathe to do this.

Andre Ticheler

from Lhasa, as opposed to six or seven (or more) on the northern route. The scenery, with its vast sweeping plains, sand dunes and the Himalaya range in the distance, is also more majestic on the southern route. The drawback is that apart from the fact that it is notoriously difficult to hitch this way (you are at the mercy of paying tourists who are generally not interested in free-loaders), the southern route is also subject to seasonal closure (see the When to Go section earlier in this chapter). This could soon change though, as work to improve the southern route has recently been completed.

Meanwhile most hitchhikers take the northern route, the destination of which is the Chinese town of Ali, or Shiquanhe, over 300km north-west of Kailash. It's easier to get a lift to Ali on this route and you can arrange a permit there for Kailash.

Lhatse to the Northern Turn-Off

Both the northern and southern routes follow the same road beyond Lhatse and on to the northern turn-off past Sangsang. For information on the places on the road to Lhatse see the Tsang chapter.

From Lhatse onwards there is little in the way of food or accommodation. There are truck stops strategically situated a day's travel from each other along the early section of the northern road, but all it takes is a breakdown (a frequent occurrence) and a delay of a few hours to fall completely out of sync with this arrangement.

Just 4km beyond Lhatse the paved road ends, from there its dust and corrugations all the way to Ali. Around 6km after Lhatse, the road leaves the Friendship Highway at km marker 2140 and bears west. It is approximately 240km from here to the northern road turn-off. The condition of the road shared by both routes is relatively good, and trucks generally average around 40km/h or more.

From the bridge across the Yarlung Tsangpo (Brahmaputra), 2km after leaving the Friendship Highway, the road soon enters a surprisingly lush (well, during the summer at least) river valley, scattered with

Tibetan villages. This is a beautiful area for photographs if your driver is amenable to the idea of stopping occasionally. **Lulung village**, 31km from Lhatse, has many buildings decorated with what looks like the red, white and blue of the French tricolour. These are actually the colours of the three bodhisattvas connected with the Sakya Monastery, not some curious linkage with French culture!

The road edges around the north side of a lake and climbs up to a pass. At km marker 2085, 61km from Lhatse the road passes through the very small town of **Kaga** (Kajia), the Tibetan town is to the right of the road while there is a *truck stop* on the left, a little further on, with basic food, beer and accommodation for around Y15. The town is next to the very picturesque **Ngam-ring-tso** and a turn-off runs round the east side of the lake to the larger settlement of Ngamring, on the north-east side of the lake and about 6km off the main route.

Within 10km of Kaga, 70km west of Lhatse, you'll pass the last trees for many days and soon after you'll also leave the last agricultural fields for days to come. Just beyond km marker 2060, mani stones and prayer flags mark the start of a path to a hilltop monastery overlooking the road from the north. The road then makes a zigzag ascent to the 4700m Kar-la before dropping down to Sangsang.

Sangsang, 122km west of Lhatse, is a larger town than Kaga with a couple of *guesthouses*, one near the road and another in the village to the north of the road. Expect to pay around Y20 for very basic accommodation. On the eastern edge of the town there's also a shop and a *Chinese restaurant* as well as a cosy little Tibetan *pub*, marked by the huge stack of empty beer bottles which will become a familiar sign of Chinese influence as you continue further west.

From Sangsang the route passes through a succession of valleys and follows a gorge into the spectacular wide ravine of the Raka Tsangpo. Emerging from this ravine it skirts around a lake and then crosses a flood plain, prone to flood damage during the monsoon.

The route then climbs a series of passes before dropping down again past the tiny settlement of **Raka**, near km marker 1912 and about 6km before the junction where the northern and southern routes split, 120km from Sangsang. The *Lhato Tea House* (there's actually a sign in English) is the last such stop for many kilometres and there may be a checkpoint here. Confusingly, many maps show Raka (or Raga) right at the crossroads, in fact the turn-off is marked only by a weather-worn sign in Tibetan and Chinese pointing to Ali.

Zhangmu to Saga

This short cut from Zhangmu on the Nepal border to Saga on the southern route to Western Tibet saves 250km (at least a day of travel) and is used by tour groups travelling from Kathmandu to Kailash (or the reverse) and by individual travellers who have hired vehicles and want to leave for Nepal after visiting Western Tibet.

See the Nyalam and Zhangmu sections in the Tsang chapter for more details of the first part of this route, which follows the Friendship Highway. From Kathmandu the road climbs steadily uphill out of the Kathmandu valley, past breathtaking views through a luxuriant, deep gorge shifting to a windy barren pass. Past Nyalam the road climbs to the 5120m Tong-la then drops down before climbing to the second high point of the double pass, the Lalung-la (5124m). Soon after the pass the shortcut turns west off the Friendship Highway, rounding some hills at the start of a vast plain. To the south there are views of **Shisha Pangma** (8012m), known to the Nepalese as Gosainthan it's the only 8000m plus mountain planted completely inside Tibet. The road passes just a few kilometres south of the huge lake, **Peiku-tso**, and provides access to the north base camp of the mountain.

The road, most of it very bad, continues across the plain although stunning Himalayan views compensate for the discomfort. The route then follows a narrow gorge before climbing to a pass and dropping steeply down to a ferry crossing over the Yarlung Tsangpo.

Supposedly it doesn't operate until 9.30 am although it often seems to be under way by 8 am. Ferry costs are for the vehicle only and not for passengers. It's not far from the crossing to Saga where you pick up the southern route.

The Southern Route

From the northern turn-off it is 60km to Saga which is also the junction for the short cut from Zhangmu on the Nepalese border, see the previous entry.

Saga Saga (Sajia, 4600m) is the last town of any size on the southern route. Turn left off the main road towards a vast Soviet-style people's hall and look out for the town's two *hotels*, one Tibetan (Y25 for dirty dorm beds) the other Chinese (Y45 for a bed in a basic room with a stove). Just down from the hotels there are a couple of excellent *Chinese restaurants* and the last well-stocked shops en route. There is also an unmarked *PLA Hotel*, which offers similar standards for Y45 per bed. To find it, turn right at the hall and continue through the arches to an unmarked block.

Zhongba From Saga it is 145km to Zhongba. The road is good, and most trucks can complete the trip in around four hours. 'New' Zhongba, a small dusty town with a couple of shops, hotels and a restaurant has little to recommend it. 'Old' Zhongba is a couple of kilometres away and is largely a ghost town. Given a choice, try to stay at Saga.

The *Tashi Hotel* on the eastern entrance to town has beds in a grimy room for Y15 and awful *thugpa* for Y10. Better is the *Hotel Kailash* in the middle of town, with dorm beds for Y20 and good thugpa for Y6. There is a small monastery at the western end of town on a hill, however it's not worth a special stop. Fourteen kilometres past Zhongba, on the far side of a bridge, is another checkpoint, this time for the driver's license.

Paryang Paryang (Paiyang, 4750m) is 110km on from Zhongba and 10 hours drive from Saga and is the next town of any significance. It is a squalid place, littered with bones and broken beer bottles and infested with dogs. The friendly *Tashi Hotel* has rudimentary but clean dorm beds for Y25 and the *Yak Hotel* has basic dorm rooms for Y20. Both hotels have simple meals available, but there are no restaurants as such.

From Zhongba onwards the southern road deteriorates. The section between Zhongba and Paryang is particularly prone to sand being swept down from the sand dunes on either side of the road. Many trucks get stuck briefly here – experienced drivers carry long poles which they wedge between both the twin rear wheels of their trucks for traction. You should not have any real problems with this section of road if you are in a 4WD, however.

Paryang to Darchen After Paryang, on the long haul to Darchen (around 300km or 12 hours of driving), the problem is not so much sand as river crossings. The first of these comes around 20km out of Paryang. The crossing here is fairly obvious, but it still pays to get out and have a good look before attempting it. A couple of hours on from this crossing there are three tributaries of the same river to cross. It is not uncommon for trucks to get stuck in one of these for days at a time. The best crossing point is not obvious as there are tracks approaching the rivers in a multitude of directions. The best advice is to walk along the banks

and look for the least sandy stretches of river.

There is yet another, very similar river crossing near the top of the Mayun-la, though this one is an ice river. Again, you should follow the same procedure and cross with extreme caution. From here it's around 30km to the top of the pass. The section of the southern route from Zhongba to Darchen has some of the most panoramic scenery of either route. If you get an early start and do not get bogged in sand or a river, it should be possible to complete the Paryang-Darchen run in a long day.

If you are running late you can spend your last night on the road at Hor Qu, about 40km before Darchen. Beds in the local *PLA camp* cost Y30 and there is also an unmarked *guesthouse* on the southern fringe of town, which offers beds for Y20. There is normally hot water available here.

There's another checkpoint between Hor Qu and Barkha and a final military checkpoint just beyond Barkha and only a short distance before the turn-off to Darchen, the closest town to the Kailash kora (see the Darchen entry later in this chapter).

The Northern Route

The northern route is the more difficult and longer of the two routes from Lhasa to Western Tibet but is the more popular of the two with hitchhikers because more traffic uses this route. In part this is because the

---

WESTERN TIBET

Four Rules of Travel in Western Tibet

- If all you can see of the last Land Cruiser to cross the river is its roof – the crossing is too deep.
- If you've been hitching through Western Tibet on Tibetan pilgrim buses and after two weeks you still do not have body lice – your karma is very good.
- If you're travelling through Western Tibet with a Nepalese trekking crew and their first action on arriving at a hotel is to start digging a pit toilet in the car park – the hotel toilets are not good.
- If the hotel manager kicks aside a goat head before opening your room door – do not expect high standards at this establishment.

route is less likely to be affected by rain making rivers too high to cross.

From Sangsang, there is basically nothing in the way of accommodation before Tsochen (Cuojin), 355km away. The road can be even worse once you get beyond the northern turn off but that's only likely to be the difference between bad and very bad. The stretch of 410km between the turn-off and the northern road proper, which links Ali to Naqu, is often very hard going. Road conditions along this stretch can easily slow your progress down to between 15 and 25km/h. The one compensation for the shocking state of the road after the northern turn-off is the frequently breathtaking scenery the road winds through. If you're travelling by Land Cruiser and camping the possibilities for putting up a tent along the road are often excellent, there's no shortage of grassy riverside spots with beautiful mountain views as a bonus. Nomads' herds of goats and sheep are a common sight along this route.

King Tiger Hot Springs & Daggyai-tso
Only 21km north of the junction are the Tag Gyal Chutse, the 'King Tiger Hot Springs', a collection of gushing geysers, bubbling hot springs, puffing steam outlets and miscellaneous smoking holes in the ground. They stretch from beside the road down to and across both sides of the fast flowing river which issues out of the lake. In places the hot water pours straight into the river so if you've already accumulated an excess of Tibetan road dust this would be a good place to pause and wash it off.

From the hot springs the road runs around the western side of a lake then through a wide valley, one of the stretches of flat terrain in Western Tibet where every driver seems to have been intent on finding his own new route. As a result, myriad different tracks fan out across the plain. From a low pass the route descends to a much larger lake, Daggyai-tso, the waters of the lake a miraculous shade of the deepest blue imaginable.

North to Tsochen For 25km the road runs along the eastern side of this lake, mountain

ranges closing it in on both sides, before climbing to the 5500m Song Ma-la and then following a long valley cut by a fast flowing mountain stream and eventually descending to a bridge and checkpoint. Checking the paperwork of passing vehicles doesn't seem to be a priority at this checkpoint. From here the valley widens out before the route reaches Tsochen, the major outpost between the turn-off and the northern road proper.

Tsochen Tsochen, 235km from the northern turn-off and 173km south of the northern road proper, is one of those miserable Western Tibetan hybrids, a depressing combination of the ugliest of Chinese and the slummiest of Tibetan urban conglomerations. Getting there late and leaving early is definitely a good idea, although it does seem to have improved in recent years. There are even a handful of reasonable looking restaurants (formerly there were none) including the *Friendship Restaurant* with a sign in English. There are several stores with basic food supplies.

The *Gaoyuan Lüshe* (Plateau Hotel in English, not that there is an English sign) has basic accommodation at around Y25, it's on the south side of Tsochen's single wide street and easily identified by the satellite dish and telecommunications tower in its compound. Adjacent is the *Bank Guest House*, nothing there in English either.

Tsochen to Gertse From Tsochen the route climbs through green rolling hills, look back over Tsochen for views of the intense blue of Zhari Nam-tso, backed by snow capped peaks in the distance. The route crosses the relatively insignificant Tsochen-la and then, 43km north of Tsochen, the more impressive 4900m **Nor Chung-la** (Small Wild Yak Pass) before descending to the turquoise waters of **Dawa-tso**. The road circles around the lake before climbing up a narrow ravine beside a swift flowing river. For the next 50km the route crosses from one attractive valley to another, sometimes connected by the river and gorge, other times by passes.

The road crosses the **Nor Gaw-la** (Wild Yak Head Pass), another nearly 5000m pass, 94km north of Tsochen, and there may indeed be yak skulls entangled in the prayer flags among the mani stones. From the pass the route descends to a bridge, 109km from Tsochen, at **Chendiloma**, with a small *guesthouse*, *restaurant* and *teahouse*, and then drops down into another valley that continues most of the way to the northern road proper.

From around 10km before Chendiloma for the next 50km the road runs right alongside a beautiful, small, snow-capped mountain range, running north-south and with glaciers from the higher peaks often coming down to what looks like a stone's throw west of the road. The valley narrows towards its northern end and the road suddenly pops out onto a wide plain before meeting the northern road proper, just south of Dong-tso. So many different routes fan out across the plain at this point that it's difficult to pinpoint exactly where the routes meet, 173km north of Tsochen. Some trucks travelling the northern road come this far to collect salt that is mined from a salt lake near the junction and take it back to Lhasa or Shigatse.

From the junction it's 84km west to Gertse, the road often forming a single lane, banked up on the edges, across the plain. In between it's the multiple trails typical of routes across the wide, empty plains of Western Tibet.

Gertse Gertse (Gaize) has several roads running off the bleak east-west main street. There's a long line of chörtens and mani walls studded with yak and goat horns and draped with prayer flags stretching off to the north of the town. Accommodation is available for Y25 at the *Government Guesthouse*, opposite the hospital at the eastern end of town, or there's a second unmarked *guesthouse* costing Y15. The town has a number of *Sichuan restaurants* with surprisingly good food (even some fresh vegetables). Just wander into the kitchen and point out what you want. *Chong Wei*, across the road from the guesthouse and a few steps to the right, is

one place which can turn out some pleasant culinary surprises. There are a number of shops, the usual collection of rickety pool tables in the street and, if your Land Cruiser or truck is on its last legs, some rudimentary repair places.

Gertse to Gegye It's 373km, most of them not very inspiring, from Gertse to Gegye, the next town of any size. **Oma Chu**, a small village, is 54km west, the road runs through a wide valley and is often raised above the surrounding plain with drainage channels on each side. For about 150km from Oma Chu to between Yanhu-tso and Pongba the route is regularly identified by small marker posts. In winter, when this route is often snow-covered, they identify the route across the otherwise trackless plain.

Another 45km takes the road past the small **Oma-tso** from where it's another 73km to **Yanhu- tso** with a small salt-mining community at its western end. Stopping here is probably not a good idea. It is a depressing little place populated by alcoholic Tibetans, mad dogs and broken beer bottles. From Yanhu-tso the road turns south to Pongba. Another route continues west from the turn-off to meet the Ali-Kashgar road just north of Lake Palgon. The Pongba road climbs up a ravine and crosses a pass before descending to the town, 96km from the turn-off.

Pongba (Xiongba) is another dismal little place populated by mad Tibetans, alcoholic dogs and broken beer bottles. If you ever drag yourself away from Pongba, the last stretch of road between here and Ali is fairly good. An hour or so out of Pongba, the road enters a gorge and follows the Indus River to Gegye, 105km from Pongba.

Gegye The town of Gegye (Geji) is a good place to stop for lunch or for the night. As you enter town, there is a road running off to the north that leads past lots of shops and the odd *restaurant* serving standard Chinese fare – which tastes very good after a couple of days of pot noodles. There is also a *hotel* with beds for Y20.

Gegye to Ali Ali is just 112km from Geg-ye; 30km before Gegye the road reaches the brand new Indus River, not far from its Kailash birthplace, and follows it all the way to Ali. At first it's a gently looping river, spreading out in multiple channels across the valley floor, but later it straight-ens out and the valley narrows.

Ali emerges like a bizarre mirage, from a distance it looks very large and modern and the shock is reinforced when you actually reach the town. It has clusters of modern looking buildings, shops, neon signs, paved roads and hordes of taxis, just like Beijing. Here you will drive onto your first bitumen road since Lhatse and it's an amazing expe-rience to glide smoothly into town after five or six days of bone-jarring bouncing around. See the separate Ali section for more details on the town.

Ali to Kailash From Ali to Darchen, the only town in the near vicinity of the Kailash pilgrimage circuit, is around 330km. It is perhaps 50km further if you have to take the longer route on the west bank of the Gar River from Ali to Namru. The shorter route depends on being able to cross the Gar River further to the east, which may not be possible if it's particularly high.

After the road from Ali meets the river, for 100km or so there are many streams to ford along this broad river valley. Most ve-hicles seem to get stuck in at least one of them. If your driver is not familiar with the road, have him drive carefully and stop at the streams to look for the best crossings. Deep ruts in the sand and gravel normally indicate where other vehicles have been bogged down. At Namru a road turns off south to climb over the 5610m Ayi-la to Thöling and Tsaparang.

The road from Ali to Darchen is quite a spectacular ride, but by no means outstand-ing in comparison with the rest of the northern or southern routes. Mt Kailash comes into view on the left around 30 or 40 minutes before reaching Darchen.

Providing there are no serious breakdowns and you do not spend too long languishing in a stream, there is no reason you can't com-plete the trip in a single day. One last thing to be careful of, just before reaching Darchen is a fairly deep river crossing. It comes up at the last minute before the town, around 6 or 7km after leaving the main road.

Humla (Nepal) to Kailash

In mid-1994 the authorities opened up another border crossing between Nepal and Tibet. This route is open only to tour groups who trek in from Humla, a restricted region in the far west of Nepal. You will need a specially endorsed Chinese visa, see Lonely Planet's *Trekking in the Nepal Himalaya* for more information.

Trekkers start by travelling by road or flying from Kathmandu to Nepalganj, then flying from there to Simikot in the far west of Nepal. From Simikot it's a five or six day walk to the Tibetan border, crossing the Humla Karnali to the small border post at Sher (Shera). From there it's a 28km drive to Purang (Taklakot in Nepali), through Khojarnath, and 107km on to Kailash via Manasarovar. See the Purang section for more details on that town.

Although the trekking season in Nepal customarily starts after the monsoon finish-es, at the end of September or in early October, and ends when the monsoon arrives in April, it's necessary to make this trek during the monsoon in order to get to Tibet before the winter weather arrives.

Khojarnath From the Nepalese border the road makes a long descent to a stream and then follows the Humla Karnali to the village of Khojarnath (3790m), 10km north of Sher.

Khojarnath is the first large village in Tibet and boasts the **Korja Monastery**, an important monastery of the Sakya order. This monastery escaped most of the ex-cesses of the Cultural Revolution, though the silver statues and some other items described by earlier travellers have disap-peared. The new statues are of Guru Rinpoche, Avalokiteshvara (Tibetan: Chen-resig), Manjushri (Jampelyang), Vajrapani

(Chana Dorje), Green Tara (Drölma) and Sakyamuni (Sakya Thukpa). The entrance to the hall is flanked by the Four Guardian Kings.

The **main hall** – large, empty and under restoration – is presided over by a figure of Maitreya (Jampa). Hanging from the ceiling are the stuffed carcasses of a yak, an Indian tiger, a snow leopard (Tibetan: *chen*) and a wolf (*changu*). Like the statues these are replacements, dating from 1985.

From Khojarnath the road passes Kangtse, presided over by a hilltop monastery to the west, fords two rivers, passes through two villages and eventually enters Purang, 18km north, along a walled road lined with willow trees. Make the most of them, there will be no more trees for a long time.

Kashgar to Ali

For information on this remote route from China's Muslim Xinjiang province see the Xinjiang-Tibet Highway section in the Getting There & Away chapter. Although the route is officially off limits, in fact many travellers are making the arduous trip by bicycle and by hitching rides on trucks. Halfway between the two towns the road passes through the remote Aksai Chin region. The construction of this road, through a triangle of territory which India claimed as part of Ladakh, was a principal cause of the border war between India and China in 1962. The fact that the Chinese managed to build this road without India even realising it was under construction is an indication of the utter isolation of the region.

Further south the road skirts around the eastern end of Lake Palgon and soon after arrives at new Rutok Xian, where a permit checkpoint awaits the unwary. The old town of Rutok, overlooked by a ruined hilltop *dzong* (fort) and a recently restored monastery, is about 10km west of the road and a few kilometres to the south of the new town. There are interesting prehistoric petroglyphs just south of old Rutok and a larger batch right beside the Rutok-Ali road, 30km further south. For more on these ancient rock carvings see the boxed text 'Prehistoric Petrogylphs' in the Rutok section later in this chapter.

ALI

Also known as Shiquanhe in Chinese and Senge Khabab (Town of the Lion) in

---

China's Gifts to Western Tibet

Chinese settlement has certainly brought a number of things to Western Tibet, like beer bottles. Western Tibet is simply too remote and the roads too terrible to contemplate returning empty beer bottles. As a result the whole region is submerging under mountains of beer bottles, most of them broken. When a truck or Land Cruiser driver needs to add oil, transmission fluid, brake fluid or some other vital liquid to his vehicle he doesn't think, 'where did I put the funnel?' No, he just reaches down and picks up the nearest beer bottle, expertly smashes the bottom off and there's your instantly disposable funnel.

Then there's Chinese architecture, rapidly sweeping right across Tibet, elbowing traditional Tibetan design to one side and replacing it with more bizarrely designed buildings heavily dependant on white lavatory tiles and bright blue tinted glass to get the message across.

Finally we cannot forget Chinese entertainment, karaoke bars and nightclubs are everywhere, even remote Ali has a casino and no Tibetan Chinatown is complete without a string of brothels. Even Darchen, starting point for the circuit of holy Mt Kailash, has one. In most towns they're cheerless affairs with a row of closet-sized plywood partitions fronted by the young workers who while away the waiting time watching TV, playing mah jong or, most often, knitting.

Tibetan, Ali is the capital of Ali Prefecture. There is nothing much to see, but it is a good place to clean up, have some decent food, do some shopping and rest for a while before heading off to the real attractions of Western Tibet.

The town itself is situated at the confluence of the Indus and Gar rivers, and is thoroughly Chinese. There are plenty of Tibetans wandering the streets but, like you, they are probably visitors from farther afield. The town has a population of about 5000 and there's a big army presence.

Ali is basically just two cross streets, lined with shops, restaurants, nightclubs and karaoke bars, the occasional department store and lots of government buildings. More of them are popping up at a breakneck pace.

Ali is another centre for the white-tile-and-blue-glass school of architecture which is sweeping across Tibet. After the barren emptiness of the surrounding country Ali, with its bright lights, bustling crowds and modern looking buildings, comes as a real shock.

Information
There's a PSB office in the Ali Guesthouse but the main office is just the other side of the roundabout. Ali has two banks and two post and telephone offices. Only the bank near the army post south-west of the roundabout will change foreign currency and only if you can track down the appropriate person. You cannot change travellers cheques. Only the post and telephone office by the roundabout has a line for international calls and although you may have to wait for what appears to be a single international line it's generally quite easy to make overseas connections. The office is supposedly open 9.30 am to 1.30 pm and 4.30 to 6.30 pm.

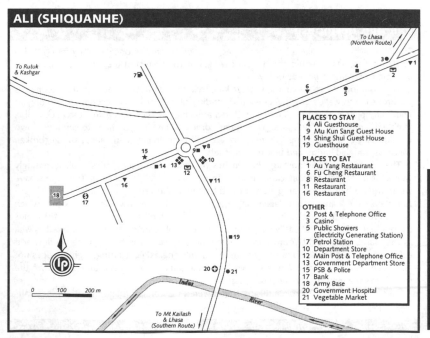

ALI (SHIQUANHE)

To Lhasa
(Northen Route)

To Rutuk
& Kashgar

PLACES TO STAY
4 Ali Guesthouse
9 Mu Kun Sang Guest House
14 Shing Shui Guest House
19 Guesthouse

PLACES TO EAT
1 Au Yang Restaurant
6 Fu Cheng Restaurant
8 Restaurant
11 Restaurant
16 Restaurant

OTHER
2 Post & Telephone Office
3 Casino
5 Public Showers
(Electricity Generating Station)
7 Petrol Station
10 Department Store
12 Main Post & Telephone Office
13 Government Department Store
15 PSB & Police
17 Bank
18 Army Base
20 Government Hospital
21 Vegetable Market

To Mt Kailash
& Lhasa
(Southern Route)

Indus
River

0   100   200 m

WESTERN TIBET

Places to Stay

The rambling and decrepit *Ali Guesthouse* is on the right shortly after you pull into town on the northern route from Lhatse. It's the official foreigner's abode in Ali, all visitors in groups stay there and will have to pay Y120 per person, an extortionate figure when local guests pay from Y16 to Y35 for the same run down facilities. The rooms are reasonably comfortable and have attached bathrooms although there is no running water and you have to flush the toilets by hurling in a bucket of water, scooped out of the bathtub. Hot showers are available for Y10 at the somewhat slimy public showers at the back of the electricity generating station across the road from the guesthouse. Look for the suggestion box next to reception, perched so high on the wall that most Chinese and Tibetans would have trouble reaching it.

Ali has a surprising number of guesthouses which will take foreigners, officially or not. Typically they will initially ask Y80 to Y100 per bed for foreigners but will soon come down to Y30 to Y40. The *Mu Kun Sang Guest House* is right on the roundabout and can be noisy because of the adjacent dance hall. Climb the spiral stairs to the guesthouse office. The *Shing Shui Guest House* is quieter, although still conveniently close to the centre. Towards the market and river there's another, cheaper, *guesthouse*.

Places to Eat

Ali has numerous restaurants although, given the town's remote location, it's hardly surprising that food can be rather expensive. The best hunting ground for restaurants is beside the roundabout marking the centre of town and from there south towards the market and river. Sichuan fare is the standard cuisine and most places will let you pick and choose in the kitchen. More expensive restaurants include the *Fu Cheng*

The Ali Guesthouse

The Ali Guesthouse is like a half abandoned mansion where the once wealthy family, fallen on hard times, has retreated into the back wing, leaving the rest of the formerly magnificent building to fall into apathetic decay.

The front lobby sets the mood, you walk in, trying not to notice that half the glass panels are broken, and walk across hectares of filthy-dirty tiled floor to the reception desk, only to find it completely deserted. A row of tattered arm chairs is lined up against the back wall, a jumble of empty beer bottles are piled in one corner. To find life you have to continue down the side alley to the last wing, where rooms are still in use. In between is just garbage, broken windows, tangled wiring and blocked up toilets.

The rooms, with their nostalgic hint at the guesthouse's former glories, look surprisingly well kept at first glance but closer inspection reveals that all is not well. The rooms have western-style bathrooms complete with bathtubs with showers, flush toilets and sinks. Unfortunately the water system failed long ago so the baths are now filled with water which you scoop out with a bucket in order to flush the toilet. Don't try to use the sink, the drains are blocked. All this is not easily visible because the hotel's electrical wiring has failed as well as the plumbing. To light your room an extension cord snakes in through the window and extends to a bare light bulb hanging from the room's original light fitting. Lighting does not extend to the bathrooms. Want a shower? Well the public showers can be found down the road in the town electricity generating station.

All of this would be merely amusing if you weren't a 'foreign friend' and therefore entitled to pay way over the odds for Western Tibet's number one hotel.

Restaurant (with a sign in English) and the *Au Yang Restaurant*. The lethargic *Ali Guesthouse* sometimes raises the energy to feed its guests.

Ali also has nightclubs, dance halls, karaoke bars and even a casino.

Shopping
It is not as if you are likely to leave Ali loaded down with souvenirs, but it is a good place, indeed the only place for hundreds of kilometres, to stock up on some supplies. There is a small shop in Darchen, but its prices are higher. There are several department stores in Ali and a host of small shops selling basic supplies including cup noodles, biscuits, sweets and drinks.

Getting There & Away
See the Southern Route and Northern Route entries earlier in this chapter for information on getting to Ali from Lhatse and Lhasa and onward travel from Ali to Darchen and Mt Kailash. See also the section on travelling from Kashgar in Xinjiang.

Getting Around
Taxis are part of the 'mirage in the desert' shock of arriving in Ali, the town seems to be thronged with little Daihatsu Charades, just like Beijing. In fact there are probably only a dozen taxis in the town, ricocheting around like birds in a cage. None of them would survive 5km beyond the city limits without falling apart on the potholes and corrugations or getting stuck in a sand drift. Within the city limits there's a standard taxi fare of Y10. Ali also has buses and motorcycle rickshaw devices but it's actually compact enough to walk anywhere in town.

MT KAILASH
Throughout Asia there is a myth of a great mountain, the navel of the world, from which flow four great rivers that give life to the areas they pass through. The myth originates in the Hindu epics, which speak of Mt Meru – home of the gods – as a vast column 84,000 leagues high; its summit kissing the heavens; its flanks composed of gold, crystal, ruby and lapis lazuli. These Hindu accounts placed Mt Meru somewhere in the towering Himalaya but, with time, Meru increasingly came to be associated specifically with Mt Kailash. The confluence of the myth and the mountain is no coincidence. There are probably no gods at its summit, but Kailash does indeed lie at the centre of an area that is the key to the drainage system of the Tibetan plateau, and from which issues four of the great rivers of the Indian subcontinent: the Karnali, which feeds into the Ganges (south); the Indus (north); the Sutlej (west) and the Brahmaputra (Yarlung Tsangpo, east).

Mt Kailash, at 6714m, is not the mightiest of the mountains in the region but, with its hulking shape – like the handle of a millstone, according to Tibetans – and its year-long snow-capped peak, it stands apart from the pack. Its four sheer walls match the cardinal points of the compass, and its southern face is famously marked by a long vertical cleft punctuated halfway down its traverse by a horizontal line of rock strata. This scarring resembles a swastika – a Buddhist symbol of spiritual strength – and is a feature that has contributed to Kailash's mythical status. The mountain is known in Tibetan as Kang Rinpoche, or 'Precious Jewel of Snow'.

Kailash has long been an object of worship for four major religions. For the Hindus, it is the domain of Shiva, the Destroyer and Transformer. To the Buddhist faithful, Kailash is the abode of Samvara (Tibetan: Demchok), a wrathful manifestation of Sakyamuni thought to be an equivalent of Hinduism's Shiva. The Jains of India also revere the mountain as the site at which the first of their saints was emancipated. And in the ancient Bön religion of Tibet, Kailash was the sacred nine storey Swastika Mountain, upon which the Bönpo founder Shenrab alighted from heaven.

Mt Kailash has been a lodestone to pilgrims and adventurous travellers for centuries but, until recently, very few set their eyes on the sacred mountain. Even when tourism was jump-started by the Chinese authorities in the mid-1980s, Kailash remained an inaccessible destination. This situation has begun to change in recent years, but tourist numbers are still thankfully low.

Mt Kailash Kora

The 53km Kailash circuit is the holiest of all Tibet's pilgrimages and the beacon which draws most travellers to Western Tibet. The kora is a three day circumambulation of the holy mountain, crossing the 5630m Drölma-la en route and taking in various sites of religious significance along the way. The festival of Saga Dawa on the full moon of the fourth Tibetan month is an excellent time to be at Kailash as the place is packed with Tibetan pilgrims from across the country.

Unlike their western counterparts, many Tibetan pilgrims complete the Kailash kora in one long day of walking. Generally they aim to complete three circuits of the sacred peak, though for the hardy and determined 13 is a particularly auspicious number. Ascetics with plenty of time on their hands sometimes go for the ultimate in circumambulatory glory: 108 circuits. It is said that a single lap erases the accumulated sins of a lifetime, while 108 are a one-way ticket straight to nirvana (don't forget to say goodbye to your folks before you leave if this is your plan).

To the Land of Shiva

While out in Western Tibet you may well find bands of shivering Indian pilgrims hauling themselves around Mt Kailash. An agreement between China and India allows several hundred Indian pilgrims a year to make the pilgrimage to Manasarovar and Kailash. Hindus believe Kailash to be the abode of Shiva and Manasarovar to be a mental creation of Brahma and the trip is so important to Hindus that the quota is oversubscribed and places have to be determined by a lottery.

The kora is not an easy trek and it is important that you are properly equipped and acclimatised before attempting it. Snow can fall on the passes during the daytime at the height of summer, the accommodation possibilities are very limited, food supplies are equally poor and there's a 5600m pass to get over. See the Kailash Kora section in the Trekking chapter for full details.

The kora begins in Darchen, the closest town to Kailash. This is the place to stock up on last-minute supplies, write your will and perhaps hire some porters and a few dozen yaks.

DARCHEN

Darchen (4560m) is a forgettable little village strewn, as usual, with broken beer bottles and dotted around the outskirts with pilgrim tents. Most travellers linger here long enough to organise their kora of Kailash and then get out. There is a small, shabby monastery just above the village while to the western side is the important **Tibetan Medical School**.

Day Walks from Darchen

If you've got extra time at Darchen, or want to spend a day or two acclimatising before setting out on the kora, there are some interesting short walks (see also the Mt Kailash Kora Trek map in the Trekking chapter). The ridge to the north of the village obscures Mt Kailash but an hour's walk up to the top of the ridge, following the trail running to the north-west, will offer fine views of the mountain. You can also look back south, over the twin lakes of Manasarovar and Rakshas Tal (Lhanag-tso).

If you have more time you can venture north of the ridge into the sanctuary to the south of the mountain's south face. Two hours walk to the north will take you to the **Gyangdrak Monastery**, largest of the Kailash monasteries and, like the others, rebuilt after the Cultural Revolution depredations. One of Mt Kailash's four Buddha footprints or *shabje* is at the monastery. To the west, a 1½ hour walk, is the **Selung Monastery** and a trail continues west from that monastery, climbing over the ridge to descend into the Lha Chu valley, close to the **Chuku Monastery**.

It's also possible to continue north all the way to the glacial moraines at the base of the mountain's south face. Taking this route to walk the *nangkor* or inner circuit is reserved for those who have already completed 13 Mt Kailash koras. The walk goes around the hill known to Hindu pilgrims as Nandi, after the Hindu god Shiva's 'vehicle', the bull which customarily kneels in front of Shiva temples. The nangkor route passes by the twin lakes collectively known as the **Kapala-tso**; Rakta is said to have black water while Durchi has white.

Places to Stay & Eat

You can't miss the *Darchen Guesthouse* because the road into the village leads straight to the guesthouse compound's central gate. Don't be confused by the sign beside the gate announcing that it's the Gangdishi Guesthouse. They will try to charge foreign groups Y120 per bed, an extravagant price for the grubby facilities. The compound's toilets are so disgusting they've simply closed and locked them up and the best advice is to take a long walk out into the surrounding desert. Most visitors in trekking groups opt to camp in the guesthouse compound although they even charge you for that dubious pleasure.

Just outside the compound, right across from the PSB office, is the *Kunga Guesthouse* with rather cleaner rooms although they don't even try to pretend they have any toilet facilities. Here they ask Y100 per bed for group tourists but will soon bring the price down to a slightly more realistic Y50.

At the height of the season there may be a tent in the hotel compound with food, drinks and even karaoke entertainment on offer. There are several small shops in town offering a limited range of food supplies including biscuits, powdered milk and the ubiquitous instant noodles. The place signposted, in English, *Shop & Eating* is the most popular of a handful of restaurant pos-

sibilities. Some supplies can also be found in the tent city just across the river.

Depressingly enough the village at the foot of sacred Kailash now has a Chinese brothel, it's across from the PSB and, since there's no electricity at Darchen for red lights, female underwear hanging outside is the signpost.

Getting There & Away

Darchen is 6km north of the main Ali-Paryang route and about 12km from Barkha, 107km north of Purang, 330km south-east of Ali and a lonely 1200km from Lhasa.

LAKE MANASAROVAR

About 30km to the south of Mt Kailash, Lake Manasarovar (4560m), or Mapham yum-tso (Victorious Lake) in Tibetan, is the most venerated of Tibet's many lakes. It is divided from another lake, Rakshas Tal (4515m), also known as Lhanag-tso, or Demon Lake, by a narrow isthmus. A channel links the two lakes, and when, on rare occasions, water flows via this channel from Manasarovar to Rakshas Tal it is said to augur well for the Tibetan people. It's been long dry, but water has indeed been flowing between the two lakes in recent years.

According to Hindu mythology, Manasarovar was formed in the mind of Brahma when his sons requested a place to bathe after having 'performed austerities' (whatever that means) on the slopes of Kailash. Accordingly, Indian pilgrims bathe in the waters of the lake and circumambulate its circumference. Tibetans, who are not so keen on the bathing bit, generally just walk around it. It's not unusual to see a naked westerner throwing himself into the lake to wash away the sins of a lifetime (and catch hypothermia afterwards).

The Hindu classical poet, Kalidasa, once wrote that the waters of Manasarovar are 'like pearls' and that to drink of them erases the 'sins of a hundred lifetimes'. Be warned, however, that the sins of a hundred lifetimes tend to make their hasty exit by way of the nearest toilet. Make sure that you thoroughly purify Manasarovar's sacred waters before you drink them, however sacrilegious that may sound!

Few western travellers undertake the 90km, four day kora of the lake. One of the main problems is the marshiness of the ground around the lake, but there are also many streams to ford, some of which become quite deep in the summer months. Most groups and individuals base themselves at picturesque Chiu Monastery, on the north-western shore of the lake, and use this small monastery as a base for day walks. For information on the Manasarovar kora and a map of the region see the Trekking chapter.

Chiu Monastery

Thirty-three kilometres south of Darchen and 8km south of the main highway, Chiu Monastery enjoys a fabulous location atop a craggy hill overlooking the sapphire blues of Lake Manasarovar. (See the Trekking chapter for a map of the area.) Climb up to the roof of the monastery for stunning views of the lake. The huge peak on the southern horizon is 7728m Mt Gurla Mandata, near the border with Nepal.

There is a hot spring behind the monastery, and a small stone compound for bathing close to the village. The water is extremely hot, and unless you are Japanese it is unlikely that you will be able to wallow in it. You may have to content yourself with washing in the water that spills out from the compound while all the children in the village watch on with fascination. The hot spring itself has been somewhat crudely fenced off to discourage free bathing.

There are two unmarked *guesthouses* at the foot of the monastery which offer dorm beds for around Y20. Thermoses of hot water are available and the owners can cook up bowls of thugpa given enough warning. There is food available in Barkha, to the north of the lake, and in the village at the foot of Chiu Monastery, but it would be sensible to come supplied with whatever essentials you need.

Getting There & Away There is no public transport and very little in the way of truck activity on the road between Darchen and the monastery. There may, however, occasionally be trucks on the main Ali-Purang road, which is around 6km south of Darchen – be prepared for a long wait if you are hitching. Between Darchen and the monastery only the straight line of telephone poles defines the way, drivers have fanned out across the flat plain creating a plethora of vehicle tracks.

PURANG

Purang (Taklakot to the Nepalese) is a large trading centre composed of a number of distinct settlements separated by the Humla Karnali River and tributaries. Nepalese traders come up from the south-east, from the Humla district of western Nepal, following the same route as western trekking groups and crossing the border to Sher in Tibet. Nepalese also come in from the south-west, from Darchula in the extreme west of Nepal. In Purang, they trade a variety of goods including rice carried up from Nepal in huge trains of goods-carrying goats. This Nepalese rice is traded on a one to three basis for Tibetan salt. Unhappily the demand for timber in wood starved Tibet is also met, illegally, by Nepalese traders, contributing to their country's drastic deforestation problems. Wool from the Tibetan plateau and Indian consumer goods are other important trading commodities.

Nepalese traders and western trekkers are not the only foreigners passing through Purang. This is also the arrival point in Tibet for the annual influx of Hindu pilgrims from India, intent on making a *parikrama* of Mt Kailash, the abode of Lord Shiva according to devout Hindus.

Purang is a weird mix of the ultramodern mixed in with traditional Tibetan, and it's very spread out. The hill on the north-west side of the town is the site of a huge army base, said to extend far into the mountain in a series of caves. It's even rumoured there are missiles here, aimed at New Delhi. There are hundreds of PLA soldiers in baggy green uniforms throughout the town.

Information

Purang has a bank which will change US dollars in cash but not travellers cheques. Nepalese rupees are accepted in Purang shops on an eight rupees to one yuan basis. There's an intermittently open post office with a direct dial phone from which it may be possible to make overseas calls. Permits are checked at the northern, Mt Kailash, end of town but Purang also has a police and PSB building. Shops are dotted along the main street or there are the town's two busy bazaars.

The Bazaars

Purang has two bazaars, catering to Nepalese traders. The riverside **Humla bazaar** has an extensive collection of shops dealing mainly in Chinese consumer goods such as clothes and household equipment. It takes its name from the Nepalese Humla region to

the south. Pool tables are dotted along the bazaar street, for trekkers arriving from Nepal this will probably be the first sight of what is clearly the Tibetan national sport.

The **Darchula bazaar**, a 15 minute walk to the west, has lines of mud-walled buildings, some of them roofed with white canvas. There's a large trade in Tibetan wool in this bazaar as well as tinned food, cloth and necessities such as rice, sugar and flour. The focus of trade is with the Darchula district of Nepal, several days walk to the south. Many goods from India also appear here but Indians are not allowed the same freedom as Nepalis to trade in Tibet, so Darchula people dominate this market.

In the hills above the trail between the bazaars are caves, one containing the **Go-kung Monastery** and others which are used as houses. Many of the caves have doors and windows and have been made into substantial dwellings.

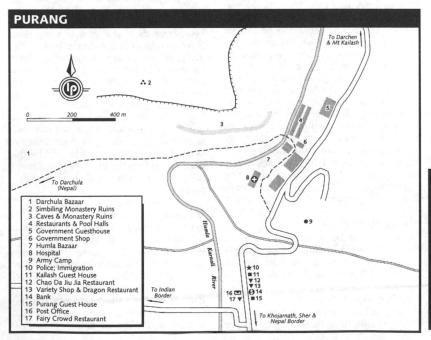

PURANG

To Darchen & Mt Kailash

0   200   400 m

To Darchula (Nepal)

1 Darchula Bazaar
2 Simbiling Monastery Ruins
3 Caves & Monastery Ruins
4 Restaurants & Pool Halls
5 Government Guesthouse
6 Government Shop
7 Humla Bazaar
8 Hospital
9 Army Camp
10 Police; Immigration
11 Kailash Guest House
12 Chao Da Jiu Jia Restaurant
13 Variety Shop & Dragon Restaurant
14 Bank
15 Purang Guest House
16 Post Office
17 Fairy Crowd Restaurant

Humla Karnali River

To Indian Border

To Khojarnath, Sher & Nepal Border

★10
■11
▼12
▼13
🏠14
■15
16 📮
17 ▼

WESTERN TIBET

Simbiling Monastery

Towering over Purang from its hilltop position at the north of the town is the ruined Simbiling Monastery.

In 1949 Swami Pranavananda described this monastery, housing 170 monks, as the biggest monastery in the region. The Chinese shelled the monastery during the Cultural Revolution and nothing remains apart from the crumbling walls. It's a steep and treacherous climb up to the monastery from the Darchula bazaar but there are fantastic views from the ridge, south over Purang and to the mountains beyond and north-east to mighty Gurla Mandata (7728m). Although it's an easier descent on the north side of the monastery ridge and a trail runs from there back towards the Humla bazaar, the route terminates in a sheer drop at the cliff face above the river. There is a point where you can fairly easily climb down the cliff but finding it without local knowledge is not easy.

Places to Stay

The *Purang Guest House* on the south side of town is bare, scruffy and, at the Y140 per bed they try to charge western group visitors, very overpriced. There is no running water, erratic electricity and the toilets at the rear of the compound are horrible to smell, see or use. The beer bottles piled in the toilet do not indicate that somebody has been holding a drinking party in these less than salubrious surroundings. They've been used to carry water to the toilets by toilet paper eschewing Indian pilgrims!

Just to the north is the *Kailash Guest House* which will try to persuade group tourists to pay Y120 per bed. A more realistic price is probably Y30 to Y40.

Places to Eat

There are a number of restaurants around the guesthouses including the engagingly named *Fairy Crowd Restaurant* and the busy little *Chao Da Jiu Jia Restaurant*.

Getting There & Away

Western trekkers arriving in Purang from Nepal usually arrange to be met at the border town of Sher for the 28km drive to the town. From Purang it's 74km north to Chiu Monastery on the shores of Lake Manasarovar and another 33km from there to Darchen, starting point for the Mt Kailash kora. The road from Purang passes Toyo, where the Sikh invader Zorawar Singh was killed in 1841, before passing a number of small Tibetan settlements and fording several rivers en route to the Gurla-la (4590m). Just beyond the pass Rakshas Tal lake and, on a clear day, Mt Kailash come into view. Two side roads lead east to the shore of Lake Manasarovar, one to a *guesthouse* and the other to Chiu Monastery.

TIRTHAPURI HOT SPRINGS

On the banks of the Sutlej River and only a few hours drive north-west of Darchen the Tirthapuri Hot Springs enjoy associations with Guru Rinpoche and pilgrims traditionally bathe here after the Kailash kora.

It only takes about an hour to walk Tirthapuri's own short **kora**, along the valley side overlooking the river. Starting from the hot springs the trail climbs to a cremation point, an oval of fire-blackened rocks. From this point an alternative longer route climbs up to the very top of the ridge. The regular kora trail continues past a hole where pilgrims dig 'sour' earth for medicinal purposes. Further along there's a 'sweet' earth hole. The trail reaches a miniature version of the Kailash kora's Drölma-la, marked with mani stones and a large collection of yak horns and skulls. Below prayer flags hang right across the gorge and a series of rocky pinnacles are revered as *ranjung*, or 'self manifesting' chörtens.

The trail passes the Guru Rinpoche Monastery and where the trail doubles back to enter the monastery a rock with a hole in it provides a handy karma self testing station. Reach in the hole and pull out two stones, both white and your karma is excellent, white and black and its OK, both black and you have serious karma problems. Perhaps another Kailash kora would help?

The monastery *dukhang* (assembly hall) is entered through an antechamber with vivid paintings of the Four Guardian Kings. A collection of comical looking statues, the one of Milarepa is particularly bad, overlook the altar while to the right side are stone footprints of Guru Rinpoche and his consort Yeshe Tsogyel. At one time the monastery was connected with the important Hemis Monastery in neighbouring Ladakh.

Outside the monastery a large circle of mani stones marks the spot where the gods danced in joy when Guru Rinpoche was enshrined at Tirthapuri. Beside it is a mani wall over 200m long, the end result of a demon firing an arrow at the guru. He stopped the arrow's flight and transformed it into this wall. Finally the kora path drops back down to the riverside, passing a large collection of assorted sized mani walls on the way.

There are no facilities at the hot springs so you must be self sufficient. Don't plan to wash away the dust of Western Tibet's roads either, the springs simply gush down to the river although pilgrims have dug a couple of very public bathing holes en route.

Getting There & Away

There is no public transport to Tirthapuri, the hot springs are 9km south of Moincer (Mensi) which in turn is 65km west of Darchen along the main road to Ali. Moincer is the dormitory town for the coal mines 20km to the north-east.

ZANDA & THÖLING MONASTERY

Thöling and neighbouring Tsaparang (see the following section) are the ruined former capitals of the ancient Guge Kingdom of Western Tibet. Thöling is now merely an adjunct to the modern Chinese town of Zanda (Thsada or Zhada) but Tsaparang, 21km further down the Sutlej River to the west, is a truly amazing sight, in part because it is so little known.

There is no public transport to Zanda so unless you have a rented Land Cruiser getting there can involve some tough hitching. Even with your own vehicle access is not easy, the roads to Zanda from the Darchen-Ali road are rough and go over some very high passes. Apart from the monasteries, chörtens and

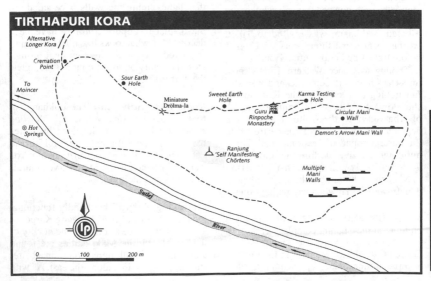

TIRTHAPURI KORA

Alternative Longer Kora

Cremation Point

To Moincer

Hot Springs

Sour Earth Hole

Miniature Drölma-la

Sweeet Earth Hole

Guru Rinpoche Monastery

Ranjung 'Self Manifesting' Chörtens

Karma Testing Hole

Circular Mani Wall

Demon's Arrow Mani Wall

Multiple Mani Walls

Sutlej

River

0   100   200 m

palaces at Thöling and Tsaparang the whole area is remarkable for its amazingly eroded scenery, cut through by the Sutlej River on its way to the subcontinent.

Zanda

Perched high above the Sutlej River the modern town is a major Chinese army post and, like many other towns in Tibet, is the centre for frenetic building construction. Unfortunately the associated ancient centre of Thöling is the centre for some equally frenetic restoration which is being conducted with amazing insensitivity and amateurism. The town has a post and telephone office from where you can, with luck, even make overseas phone calls.

Thöling Monastery

The monastic complex at Thöling was founded by Rinchen Zangpo, a monk who, under the patronage of the Guge king, Yeshe Ö, spent some 17 years studying in India in the late 10th century. Rinchen Zangpo returned to become one of Tibet's greatest translators of Sanskrit texts and a key figure in the revival of Buddhism across the Tibetan plateau. It was partly at his behest that Atisha, a renowned Bengali scholar and another pivotal character in the revival of Tibetan Buddhism, was invited to Tibet. Atisha spent some three years in Thöling before travelling on to central Tibet.

Thöling was once Western Tibet's most important monastic complex, and was still functioning in 1966 when the Red Guards shut down operations. Unfortunately much of what survived the Cultural Revolution depredations looks likely to be destroyed in the current round of 'restorations.' Three buildings survive within the monastery walls. Officially visitors need a Y100 permit to visit these buildings although independent travellers may get away without one.

Yeshe Ö's Mandala Chapel The main building in the Thöling complex, Yeshe Ö's Mandala Chapel, was also known as the Golden Chapel and was built in the form of a three dimensional representation of a

Tibetan mandala. Pre-destruction the square main hall had four secondary chapels at the centre of each wall. Figures of the deities were arrayed around the wall facing in towards a central image atop a lotus pedestal. All the images were destroyed during the vandalism of the Cultural Revolution although many of the wall murals survived.

Around this main hall is an open corridor with shrines and chapels facing in towards the centre. Again the images in these rooms were all destroyed in the 1960s. The four corners of the outer wall are topped by unusual Indian-style chörtens, their slender style making the building instantly recognisable. This is the only place in Tibet where these minaret-like chörtens are still found.

Externally the building may have survived but what is going on inside is a very different and very sad story. For many years only the walls remained of the original chapel but now a new roof has been slapped on top with a complete disregard for what the original might have been like. The position of the columns supporting this roof, for example, clearly bear no relation to the original configuration. In many places they actually go right through the positions where the statues lining the walls once stood. To complete the desecration the ceiling and its out-of-place support columns have been decorated in what looks like a Tibetan painting parody. Appalling looking light fittings, tacked roughly on to the columns, complete the horror story.

Main Assembly Hall The dukhang, or Red Chapel, has fine wall murals showing strong Kashmiri and Nepalese influence from either the 13th and 14th or 15th and 16th centuries. Bring a powerful light if you want to inspect these well preserved murals of deities and their consorts.

Lhakhang Karpo The blandly functional looking exterior of the Lhakhang Karpo, or White Chapel, doesn't hint at the quality of the murals within. Male deities are found along the west wall, female ones, in a better state of preservation, along the east. As with

Yeshe Ö's Mandala Chapel, a great deal of restoration is taking place.

Outside the Monastery Walls A few steps to the east of the monastery compound is the recently restored Serkhang chörten. An external stairway ascends the three levels of the chörten, it's unclear what relation this bears to the original Serkhang which was totally destroyed. A similar chörten stands in total isolation just to the west of the town. Standing as a background to this chörten, the canyon walls overlooking Thöling from a short distance along the road westward to Tsaparang are honeycombed with monastic cave hermitages. To the north, between the monastic compound and the cliff face, falling away to the Sutlej River below, are two long lines of miniature chörtens.

Places to Stay & Eat

The *Guge Hotel* has well kept rooms, by Tibetan standards, in the newer block. They even have TVs although the outside toilets are the usual Tibetan horror story and there's no running water except in a shower room and even there the water probably won't be running and/or the room may be locked up. The TVs can be used to provide illumination if your room lights aren't working. The official price per bed for foreign visitors is Y95.

Alternatively there's the *Army Hotel* with rather more basic rooms, a possibly slightly less horrible version of the Tibetan toilet-from-hell and no hope of running water except for a tap in the courtyard. Here the official price per bed is Y60.

The Guge Hotel has a *restaurant* downstairs while on the main street there's the *Jian Nan Restaurant* with reasonable food and a number of places to get a drink including the *Guge Tearoom*, *Your Best Friend Bar* and the *Guge Cold Beverage Drinking Room*. They like signs in English in Thöling.

Getting There & Away

To/From Darchen It's 65km from Darchen to Moincer, the turn-off to Tirthapuri, and

another 56km from there to the army base at Songsha. From there a road leaves the main Ali route and climbs to a pass after 15km then over the next 80km zigzags down into a series of gorges and climbs up the other side before eventually making a long, winding and very rough descent down a fantastically eroded gully where the hills on both sides are worn into incredible shapes. Eventually this side valley debouches into the wider Sutlej valley and after crossing a bridge the road finally reaches the oasis like town of Zanda, six or seven hours and 122km from Songsha.

The town appears like an apparition, a patch of vivid green in the unrelentingly barren surroundings. There are even real trees, the first in hundreds of kilometres.

To/From Ali Coming from Ali, or departing Thöling in that direction, the road is equally tough going. There are two routes from Ali to Namru (Nabuzh), in the Gar

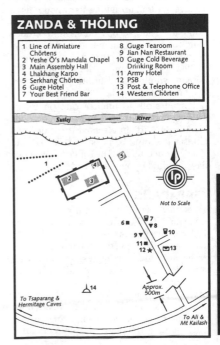

ZANDA & THÖLING

1	Line of Miniature Chörtens	8	Guge Tearoom
2	Yeshe Ö's Mandala Chapel	9	Jian Nan Restaurant
3	Main Assembly Hall	10	Guge Cold Beverage Drinking Room
4	Lhakhang Karpo	11	Army Hotel
5	Serkhang Chörten	12	PSB
6	Guge Hotel	13	Post & Telephone Office
7	Your Best Friend Bar	14	Western Chörten

Sutlej River

Not to Scale

Approx. 500m

To Tsaparang & Hermitage Caves

To Ali & Mt Kailash

WESTERN TIBET

valley, where the road turns off to Zanda (Thöling). One route follows the Indus out of Ali, running 40km west to the Gar River valley and then 95km south-east down that valley on the west side of the river via Gar to Namru. The other, much shorter, route, runs south-west for 30km across flat desert and over a pass to the valley and then 52km down the valley on the east side of the Gar River to Namru, crossing the river just a few kilometres north of Namru. This crossing may be impossible if the river is running high, necessitating taking the longer route down the west side of the river. The wide, flat valley is edged by high snow-capped mountains to the west, lower hills to the east. There are many villages dotted down this fertile valley.

From Namru, a forlorn little settlement of half a dozen low standing mud brick hovels and a few tents, the road branches west and climbs a long ravine from the plain and then up and over a series of low passes and wide valleys before zigzagging its way up to the very high 5610m Ayi-la. From this high point the route drops down into a deep valley and crosses a number of other valleys before reaching the eerily eroded mud-walled valleys approaching Zanda. It's 130km, winding and arduous kilometres, from Namru to Zanda.

It's possible to hitch a ride on trucks running directly from Ali to Zanda or to the Namru turn-off. In a rented truck or Land Cruiser it should be possible to make it to Zanda from either Ali or Kailash in a single day, providing you get an early start.

TSAPARANG

Tsaparang has been gracefully falling into ruin since its slide from prominence in the 17th century (see the Western Tibet History section earlier in this chapter) and is perhaps of greatest interest to those with some knowledge of early Buddhist art. The ruins, which seem to grow organically out of the hills, make for a photogenically surreal landscape, but there are restrictions on photographs of Tsaparang's foremost attraction: its early Tantric-inspired murals.

The ruins climb up the ridge through three distinct areas. At the bottom of the hill is the monastic area with the four best preserved buildings. From there the trail to the top climbs through the residential quarters with monks' cells dug into the clay hillside. This area is mainly in ruins. Finally the route dives straight into the hill and through a tunnel before emerging in the palace complex at the very top of the hill.

Although smaller and less impressive than the buildings at the bottom of the hill some of the palace buildings are also in rea-

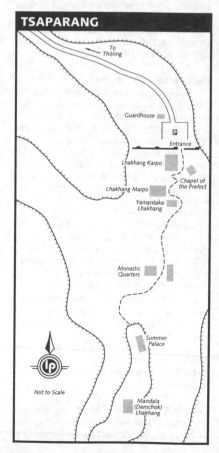

TSAPARANG

sonable repair and the views are fantastic. Because Tsaparang was already partially abandoned at the time of the Cultural Revolution the Chinese did not attack it with quite the same vandalistic fury they vented upon other religious complexes in Tibet. Surprisingly, however, when a little more survives it only makes it even more sadly evident how much was destroyed.

Permits

Having done their best to destroy Tsaparang the Chinese now charge western visitors a ridiculous Y300 to see what escaped their ravages. The permits are not always checked very effectively or enthusiastically. It might be worth checking the latest situation in Ali or Lhasa before you set out as part of the fee, theoretically, is supposed to be paid in Lhasa, another part of it at either the Ali or Darchen PSB and yet another part of it at Thöling!

Chapel of the Prefect

Just inside the complex entrance is the small building which was a private shrine for Tsaparang's prefect or regent. The wall murals date from the 16th century when the artistic inspiration seen in the other Tsaparang buildings was in decline. The main mural on the back wall shows Sakyamuni flanked by Atisha and Tsongkhapa in the pointed head coverings typical of the period. Small figures of the Buddha's disciples stand beside his throne and many other miniature images crowd between the three large ones.

Lhakhang Karpo

Slightly above the entrance the large Lhakhang Karpo, or White Chapel, has the oldest paintings at Tsaparang and is probably the most important chapel in Western Tibet. The murals of the chapel are of debated antiquity, but probably date back to the 15th or 16th centuries. Their influences, however, extend back to 10th century Kashmiri Buddhist art, and for this reason are of particular interest to scholars of Buddhist art. With the exception of here in Tsapa-

rang, very little material evidence of early Kashmiri art remains.

The ceiling is beautifully painted as are the many thin columns which support it. The carvings and paintings of the Sakyamuni figures which top each column are particularly noteworthy and the paintings around the skylight are vivid. At one time 22 life size statues lined the walls and although six of them have disappeared completely and the remaining 16 are damaged, this chapel has fared better than most temples attacked during the Cultural Revolution. In addition the doors are flanked by two 5m guardian figures, red Hayagriva and blue Vajrapani. Again both are damaged but in their armless anger they hint at the lost marvels of the chapel.

The huge figure of Sakyamuni which once stood in the recess, the Jowo Khang, at the back of the hall has gone while on the side walls at the back there were once row after row of smaller figures of deities, each perched on its own small shelf. A few of these figures on the higher levels have survived intact.

Fortunately the destruction of the statues must have distracted attention from the chapel's magnificent murals which have survived in excellent condition.

Lhakhang Marpo

Above the Lhakhang Karpo stands the equally large Lhakhang Marpo, or Red Chapel, which was built around 1470, perhaps 30 years earlier than the Lhakhang Karpo. The murals in this chapel were repainted around 1630, shortly before the fall of the Guge Kingdom, so they are actually younger than those in the Lhakhang Karpo.

The original door to the chapel, with its series of concentric frames, has survived and is worth close inspection. Inside, many thin columns support the chapel roof, like the neighbouring Lhakhang Marpo, and although the wall murals have been damaged by vandalism and water leakage they remain so remarkably brilliant it's hard to contemplate that they are actually over three and a half centuries old.

The statues which once stood in the chapel were placed towards the centre of the hall, not around the edges, and although only the bases and damaged fragments remain, the crowded feel to the space, the intense colours and the eerie silence combine to give the chapel the feel of a Hollywood movie set. You almost expect Indiana Jones to come striding out from behind the wreckage. At the back of the hall there were once many small statues on individual shelves, a handful of them still have bodies but all the heads have gone.

Yamantaka Lhakhang

The murals in this smaller chapel, a few steps above the Lhakhang Marpo and also painted red, are almost solely devoted to wrathful deities. Like the Chapel of the Prefect near the entrance gate the paintings are of later origin and lower quality than the earlier paintings in the larger chapels. All the statues that once stood here were destroyed.

The Palace

From the four chapels at the base of the hill the path to the top climbs up through the monastic quarters and then ascends to the palace citadel atop the hill via a tunnel. The Summer Palace at the northern end of the hilltop is well preserved with a balcony offering wonderful views over Tsaparang and out across the marvellously eroded valleys around the site. The wide Sutlej valley is just to the north while across the smaller valley just to the north-east is the ruined Lotang Lhakhang chapel.

The most interesting of the palace buildings is the small but well preserved Mandala (Demchok) Lhakhang, the red painted building in the centre of the hilltop ridge. The centrepiece of this small chapel was a wonderful three-dimensional mandala, only the base of which survived the desecrations of the Cultural Revolution.

Getting There & Away

Tsaparang is just 21km west of Zanda (Thöling) and unless you're very lucky with

Prehistoric Petroglyphs

In 1985 prehistoric rock carvings or petroglyphs were found at several sites in Rutok County. This was the first time such a find had been made in Tibet although subsequently similar finds have been made at numerous other sites. Two of these sites are easily found; one of them is actually right by the roadside between Rutok and Ali while the other is just south of the old Rutok settlement. For more information on these carvings and many others in Tibet look for the book *Art of Tibetan Rock Paintings* by Li Yongxian and Huo Wei (Sichuan People's Publishing House, 1993). Unfortunately the book has no map showing the location of the sites.

Rumudong The extensive collection of rock carvings at Rumudong are right beside the road about 30km south of the old Rutok turn-off or about 75km north of Ali. There are km markers every 5km along this road, travelling north from Ali start looking on the east side of the road at km marker 970, the petroglyphs would be at around 968. There are two distinct groups on the rock face right beside the road, just before the road crosses a bridge to travel along a causeway over the marshy valley floor of the Maga Zangbu Chu.

The first, and more extensive, group also features a number of more recent carvings, some of them right over their ancient predecessors. The most impressive of the rock carvings features four extravagantly antlered deer racing across the rock and looking back at three leopards in close pursuit. Other animals include eagles, yaks, camels, goats, tigers, wild boars and human figures.

hitching a ride the only way you will be able to get there is with a rented vehicle or by walking. The road follows the south side of the fantastically eroded Sutlej valley all the way from Zanda to Tsaparang. Many maps incorrectly show both centres on the north side of the river.

DUNGKAR

Caves with extensive wall paintings were discovered at this remote site in the early 1990s. The paintings of the Buddha are possibly the oldest in Western Tibet. Dungkar is approximately 40km north of Zanda (Thöling), near the road to Namru.

RUTOK

The new Chinese town of Rutok Xian is about 120km north of Ali and just 10km south of Lake Palgon, on the Ali-Kashgar road. It's a checkpoint on this important road and a busy army post with a number of new buildings in the bizarre modern Chinese architecture popping up all over Tibet.

North of Rutok Xian the road runs around the eastern end of Lake Palgon before reaching a junction from where the Kashgar road continues north while another road turns off east to meet the northern route to Lhasa at Yanhu-tso. Soon after you reach Lake Palgon there's a small cluster of lakeside fishing boats beside the *Shaou Tue* (Small Restaurant). You can buy very fresh, ie still alive, fish here.

The old town of Rutok is about 10km off the main road from a turn-off about 5km south of Rutok Xian. This white-painted and authentically traditional Tibetan village huddles at the base of a hillock, topped by the extensive ruins of an ancient dzong and a series of monasteries. Atop the hill is the red **Lhakhang Monastery**, flanked at both ends of the hill by the crumbling but still impressive ruins of **Rutok Dzong**. Clearly at one time the whole eastern face of the hill was covered in buildings, now all fallen into decay.

Rutok is surrounded by extensively irrigated fields and the prevalence of farm

Prehistoric Petroglyphs

Lurulangkar This collection is just a couple of kilometres south-west of the old town of Rutok (for details of the location see the Ancient Petroglyphs entry on the following page). The carvings are relatively primitive compared to those at Rumudong. They are found right beside the road, on the west-facing rock face, from one metre above the base of the cliffs. They show a variety of animals including eagles, dogs, yaks, deer and goats. Human figures are shown standing in isolation or riding on horses. There are a number of hunting scenes showing dogs pursuing deer or hunters shooting at them with bows and arrows.

TONY WHEELER

WESTERN TIBET

machinery in the area confirms that this is one of the few areas of intensive agriculture in Western Tibet. If you walk off to the north from Rutok you'll eventually reach a shallow lake noted for its seasonal migratory birdlife including the black-necked cranes which summer here and in the marshes beside the road to Ali. Off to the west of the lake are two picturesquely situated chörtens on a small, isolated saddle.

There's no accommodation or any other facilities at Rutok but there is a pleasant grassy area to camp behind the hills, on the banks of the Kargye-tso.

Lhakhang Monastery

At one time this ancient Gelugpa order monastery housed 160 monks. It was destroyed during the Cultural Revolution, rebuilt in 1983-84 and now has just six monks. *Thangkas* showing the Four Guardian Kings flank the entrance foyer to the dukhang. Inside, the dimly lit hall is dominated by a massive five to six metre high seated Buddha image. On the altar in front of the large image is a seated image of Tsongkhapa, founder of the Gelugpa order, flanked by two of his disciples. To the right

of this altar a glass-fronted cabinet is full of small Buddha images and images of other deities. The right wall is stacked with Tibetan books while on the wall to the left of the altar is a metal Garuda image.

In a small mustard yellow building on the village side of the monastery there's a big prayer wheel, while the walls are decorated with many brightly painted bas-reliefs of Buddhas and other figures.

Ancient Petrogylphs

A couple of kilometres south-west of Rutok, a small ruined monastery or watchtower crowns the lower end of a ridge. Just 100m or so round the ridge, right above the roadside, are the primitive scratchings depicting animals and symbols of Lurulangkar, closely connected to the prehistoric illustrations beside the Ali-Rutok road at Rumudong. See the boxed text 'Prehistoric Petroglyphs' for more on these ancient rock carvings.

Getting There & Away

It's about 130km from Ali to the new town of Rutok Xian. The turn-off to old Rutok is about 5km south of the new town. Lake Palgon is about 10km beyond Rutok Xian.

Trekking

A country as vast and mountainous as Tibet offers almost unlimited potential for walkers. From the frigid high northern plains to the steamy jungles of the south-east Tibet is a land of rich cultural and ecological contrasts. The remoteness of Tibet combined with its climatic extremes poses special challenges for trekkers, as well as unique rewards. There are few places left in the world where you can walk for days, witnessing an ancient and sophisticated culture, without having the experience marred once by the dross of modern civilisation.

Most trekking is conducted in the centre of the country in the vicinity of the major towns and highways. Cities such as Lhasa and Shigatse provide bases from which to equip and launch treks. The trailheads of four out of the seven treks covered in this section can be reached by public transport.

About Trekking

HISTORY
In the 17th century Jesuit priests intent on spreading Christianity trekked over the mountains of Western Tibet. In the late 19th and early 20th centuries a slew of spies, explorers and scholars, often in caravans, covered great distances on foot in their attempts to reach the holy city of Lhasa.

Most never made it, and some paid for their Tibetan adventure with their lives. One such unfortunate person was Dutreiul de Rhins, the leader of a French expedition, who in 1891, after being refused permission to enter Lhasa, was murdered by brigands. One of the greatest treks was made by George Roerich's Central Asiatic Expedition in the 1920s. During their archaeological explorations they traversed a great swathe of Tibet's northern plains

Still, there were many places that the earlier explorers didn't reach and there are still new frontiers in Tibet beckoning the explorer and experienced trekker.

GEOGRAPHY
For all its attractions, Tibet is a formidable place where even day walks involve survival skills and generous portions of determination. As it's situated on the highest plateau on earth and crisscrossed by the world's highest mountains, nothing comes easy and careful preparation is all important. Even on the most popular treks, which can involve several days of travel without any outside help, high passes up to 5300m are crossed.

Eastern and much of central Tibet are laced with large mountain ranges, towering passes and deep valleys and gorges. Western and northern Tibet are even higher, but between the mountains are expansive valleys

---

Trekking Disclaimer

Although the authors and publisher have done their utmost to ensure the accuracy of all information in this guide, they cannot accept any responsibility for any loss, injury or inconvenience sustained by people using this book. They cannot guarantee that the tracks and routes described here have not become impassable for any reason in the interval between research and publication.

The fact that a trip or area is described in this guidebook does not mean that it is safe for you and your trekking party. You are ultimately responsible for judging your own capabilities in the light of the conditions you encounter.

and plains that can take days to traverse. Travel in south-east Tibet, on the other hand, involves negotiating precipitous slopes to which lush subtropical vegetation clings.

CLIMATE

Trekkers must be prepared for extremes in climate even in the middle of the summer. A hot sunny day can turn cold and miserable in a matter of minutes, especially at higher elevations. Night temperatures at 4500m and above routinely fall below freezing even in July and August! At other times of the year it gets colder. In midwinter, in north-western Tibet, minimum temperatures reach -40°C. Yet Tibet is a study in contrasts and in the summer months a scorching sun and hot blustery winds can make even the hardiest walker scurry for any available shade. Between the two extremes the Tibetan climate is ideal for walking – cool and dry – but always be prepared for the worst.

ECOLOGY & ENVIRONMENT

Trekking responsibly in Tibet is a matter for special consideration. The beautiful but fragile alpine biomes of the upland regions of Tibet deserve the utmost respect. For instance, a fire can scar the landscape for centuries. In recent years, the environment of Tibet has suffered tremendously. Forests are being decimated, wildlife eradicated and economically important plants depleted. In such a context it is imperative that trekkers go out of their way to tread lightly and leave nothing but the proverbial footprints behind. Stay off fragile slopes and try not to tread on plants. Follow the Tibetan ethos, killing not even the smallest of insects. In the long run this approach will buy trekkers respect from the Tibetans and will help guarantee that successive groups of visitors enjoy the most pristine environment possible.

In the arid climate of much of Tibet water takes on a special significance and is highly regarded in Tibetan traditional beliefs. The *lu* (water spirits) are believed to guard the wellbeing of the community and are thought to be very dangerous if transgressed. For these reasons Tibetans tend to treat water reverently. Their traditional practices resemble those adopted by the ecotrek movement. For example, toilets are never constructed where they could contaminate water sources and the washing of clothes in rivers and streams is restricted. However we see it, in traditional or modern terms, the objective is the same: not to introduce foreign substances into water sources.

FLORA & FAUNA

The mountain slopes of Tibet are home to many dozens of plants and flowers but resist the temptation to pick them. There really is no need as many of the most useful plants are readily available as medicines, incense and condiments in the city markets. If you have an overpowering desire to drink the scenery plan a visit to the Tibetan Traditional Hospital in Lhasa, where some of the plants you see trekking go into medicines. If you are interested in identifying Tibetan medicinal plants check out *Tibetan Medical Thangkas Of The Four Medical Tantras*, a lavish coffee-table book available in most Lhasa bookshops. Also see Oleg Polunin's and Adam Stainton's *Flowers of the Himalaya* for some examples of Tibetan flora.

The more remote valleys and mountains of Tibet are home to a rich variety of wildlife (for more information see the Flora & Fauna section in the Facts about Tibet chapter). If you are lucky you might see the Himalayan black bear or perhaps the giant Tibetan brown bear searching for food in the alpine meadows. Snow leopards in the craggy heights and the common spotted leopard in eastern Tibet are occasionally spotted by alert trekkers.

Less daunting but no less spectacular are the ungulates of Tibet including several species of deer, antelope, goat and sheep. Smaller mammals, a panoply of birds, as well as numerous reptiles, fish and amphibians can be seen trekking. Generally, large predatory animals are not attracted to campsites and stay well away from humans. Still, do not court trouble by discarding food scraps near your camp – you would be extending a welcome to the local rodent population.

PEOPLE & SOCIETY

Although Tibetans are a devoutly religious people they are fun loving by nature. With a little effort and goodwill it should be possible to break down cultural barriers and make friends. In most out-of-the-way places trekkers can quickly become the centre of attention. This can be turned to your advantage, sometimes with just a smile, and may lead to dinner invitations and offers of places to stay. If you really detest being the star of the show don't camp in villages, and if you do, don't expect western notions of privacy to prevail. If you want to be alone camp out of sight of people – usually not too difficult in a country as large as Tibet.

As in much of Asia, nudity and open displays of affection are frowned upon. Try to dress modestly, which is pretty easy in such a rugged environment. Remember, you are better off to cover up in the intense solar radiation of Tibet with light-coloured, lightweight clothing. Be especially vigilant at monasteries – these are no places for immodest western fashions. As a rule, don't wear shorts or short dresses, especially in villages and at religious sites. For more information on cultural considerations see the Society & Conduct section in the Facts about Tibet chapter.

Tibetans tend to be very informal but with elders and religious figures a certain amount of deference is called for. And don't forget a good joke, even if it's at your own expense. As is the case in adjoining countries, if you ask directions be prepared to be sent in the direction you are walking no matter where you are trying to go. To avoid this age-old travellers' trap be prepared to patiently and repeatedly explain what your travel goals are and, if in doubt, ask someone else.

If you have any religious sentiments your trek probably qualifies as a pilgrimage, in which case, you will usually receive better treatment than if you are just going somewhere. Another helpful hint: if all else fails try a song and dance. Even the most amateur of efforts are met with great approval – just stay clear of risqué numbers.

Facts for the Trekker

PLANNING
Maps

There are many commercially available maps covering Tibet but very few are detailed enough to be more than a general guide for trekkers. The Chinese government produces small scale topographical and administrative maps but these are not for sale to the general public. The Xinhua Bookstore near the Lhasa Hotel sells road and administrative maps of the TAR. The US Defense Mapping Agency, St Louis, Missouri, produces series of aeronautical charts covering Tibet in the 1:1,000,000, 1:500,000 and 1:250,000 scale (though the latter can be hard to find). See Maps in the Planning section in the Facts for the Visitor chapter for information on where to get these.

The most useful 1:500,000 references for trekking in Tibet are:

H-10A – Lhasa region, Ganden to Samye, Tsurphu to Yangpachen
H-9A – Kailash and Manasarovar
H-9B – Shigatse region, Shalu to Nartang, Everest region

What to Bring

There is a great deal to see while trekking and you will be revitalised by the natural surroundings, but you must be prepared for extremes in weather and terrain. The time of year you choose to walk will obviously dictate the equipment you will need.

Clothing & Footwear As a minimum, you will need basic warm clothing including a hat, scarf, gloves, down jacket, long underwear, warm absorbent socks, all-weather shell and sun hat, in addition to comfortable well-made pants and shirts. Women may want to add a long skirt to their clothing list.

If you attempt winter trekking you will need more substantial mountaineering clothing. Many people opt for synthetic pile clothing, but also consider wool, which has proven itself in the mountains of Tibet for centuries. One of your most important assets is a pair of strong, well fitting hiking boots. And remember to break them in before starting the trek!

Equipment Three essential items are a tent, a sleeping bag and a backpacking stove. There are no restaurants in remote areas of Tibet and provisions are hard to come by, so you will probably end up cooking all your own food. Count on camping because, except in certain villages on the main trekking routes, it can be difficult to find places to sleep. Invest in a good tent that can handle big storms and heavy winds. A warm sleeping bag is a must. Manufacturers tend to over rate the effectiveness of their bags so always buy a warmer one than you think you'll need – you can always unzip it if you get too hot.

You will also need a strong, comfortable backpack large enough to carry all your gear and supplies. To save a lot of misery test the backpack on day hikes to be certain it fits and is properly adjusted.

What you bring is clearly a personal choice: some may want a walkman or journal, others elaborate camera gear. Basics, however, must include water containers with at least a 2L capacity, a system for water purification, a torch (flashlight), compass, pocket knife, first-aid kit, waterproof matches, sewing kit, cup, shrill whistle and walking stick or ski pole. This last item acts as a walking aid and most importantly, for defence in case of dog attack. Tibetan dogs can be particularly large and brutal and roam at will in nearly every village and herders' camp. Bring your walking stick or pole with you from home, otherwise you can purchase a shovel handle in Lhasa. They can be found at hardware stores on Lingkhor Chang Lam.

Buying & Hiring Locally In Lhasa a wide range of warm clothing is sold. For cheap but fairly effective stuff check out the Chinese army surplus shops concentrated on Dekyi Shar Lam between Tashi I restaurant and the Potala. Around the Barkhor, better looking Tibetan-style clothing can be bought for a reasonable price. The woollen and fleece *chuba* (traditional coat) is especially effective in the mountains but takes time to master wearing.

Around the corner from Tashi I, on Dekyi Shar Lam, is the Mount Green Trekking shop, specialising in selling and renting trekking gear made in Nepal. It has backpacks, wool hats and socks, pile jackets, parka shells and some down coats for sale. It rents out sleeping bags (Y25 per day), stoves (Y10), tents (Y35) and clothing but the equipment compromises on quality. Yeti Mountaineering Shop & Trekking Equipment, across from the Potala, stocks mid-range Chinese-made gear adequate for most trekking needs. Its prices are as expensive as in the west. It carries trekking and mountaineering boots, backpacks, sleeping bags and jackets, pile clothing, tents, ski poles and basic mountaineering equipment.

Petrol for camping stoves is widely available in towns and cities but it is of fairly poor quality. To prevent your stove from getting gummed up you will have to clean it regularly. Kerosene (*méiyóu* in Chinese) can also be obtained in cities. In Lhasa, you will find the kerosene vendors on Dekyi Shar Lam opposite the road to Ramoche.

Physical Preparation
Before embarking on a trek make sure you are up to the challenge of high altitude walking through rugged country. Test your capabilities by going on day walks in the hills around Lhasa and Shigatse. Try a hike to the top of a small mountain such as Bumpa Ri, on the other side of the Kyi Chu from Lhasa.

TREKKING AGENCIES
There is now a plethora of tourist agencies in Lhasa, some of which can arrange treks. Let the buyer beware, for the standard of

service fluctuates wildly and may bear no correspondence with the amount you pay. In general, standards of service are much lower than in Kathmandu. Shop around carefully and compare the services and attitudes of at least several agencies. Kickbacks and shady dealings are part of everyday business but with some luck they won't ruin your trip.

The main advantage of going with an agency is that they take care of all the red tape and deal with the officials. Most of them offer a full package trek including transport to and from the trailhead, guide, cook, yaks or burros to carry the equipment, mess tent and cooking equipment. The package will probably not include tents to sleep in, at least ones up to the task of trekking in Tibet. Make sure the agency spells out exactly what is included in the price they are quoting you and be prepared to provide all your personal equipment.

None of the agencies selected below can be unconditionally recommended due to the general conditions prevailing in China but all have run at least some successful treks. Prices vary according to group size and location but none are cheap. Costs per person tend to be lower in bigger groups. For treks in remote and border areas expect to wait at least three days for the permits to be sorted out.

Tibetan Agencies – Budget
Shigatse Travels
(☎ 633 0489, fax 633 04821) In the Yak Hotel and managed by Dorje Tashi who works closely with the only foreign tour operators based in Lhasa. They have lots of tours but limited trekking experience. Prices run at about US$70 per person per day.
Tibet Nyingchi Tour Corporation
(☎ 633 3871) On Dekyi Shar Lam, around the corner from Tashi I restaurant and managed by David Mingmar, a Tibetan. This agency specialises in trips to the Kongpo region of south-eastern Tibet but can arrange treks to many parts of the country. Full package treks cost from US$60 to US$70 per day.

Tibetan Agencies – Top End
Tibet International Sports Travel
(☎ 633 1421, fax 633 4855) In the Himalaya Hotel compound in Lhasa, it is the oldest agency specialising in trekking. Under the able

management of Dawa it is a contractor for several international travel companies.
Tibet International Worker Travel Service
(☎ 681 4304, fax 683 4472) 215 Dekyi Nub Lam, Lhasa, two blocks west of the Lhasa Hotel and just east of the Xinhua Bookstore. Another long-established company, it is managed by the congenial Thupten Gendun and arranges treks just about anywhere.
Tibet Wind-Horse Adventure
(☎ 683 3009, fax 683 6793) In Room 1120 of the Lhasa Hotel. The manager, Chungdar, seems willing to please. Trekkers in 1998 who signed up with this outfit reported having a good trip and were impressed with the company's service and efficiency. Full-package treks cost US$100 to US$120 per person per day.

Kathmandu Agencies
If you want to organise your Tibet trek from Kathmandu here's a list of some of the most qualified agencies:

Arniko Travels
(☎ 421684, fax 414594, email arnikotv@ccsl .com.np) PO 4695, Baluwatar
Great Escapes
(☎ 418951, fax 411533, email grt@greatpc.mos .com.np) PO 9523, Baluwatar
Malla Treks
(☎ 410089, fax 423143, email tsedo@mallatrk .mos.com.np) PO 5227, Lekhnath Marg.
Mountain Travel Nepal
(☎ 411225, fax 414075, email info@tiger mountain.com.np) PO 170, Lazimpat
Shiva Treks & Expeditions
(☎ 414899, fax 419704, email shiva@kailash .wlink.com.np) PO Box 5385, Baluwatar

Western Agencies
A few western companies offer fixed departure treks in Tibet. Tours can be joined in your home country or abroad, usually in Kathmandu. Prices are higher than treks organised in Tibet or even Kathmandu and way beyond most travellers' budgets, but they take the hassle out of organising a trek and are useful if you have the money but only a couple of weeks.

A standard trek organised at home will include a western leader, a local leader, porters, a cook and so on. All your practical needs will be taken care of and you will be free to enjoy the trekking itself.

TREKKING

For a list of some western companies that can organise treks in Tibet see the Getting There & Away chapter.

DOCUMENTS

Officially, individuals are not permitted to trek in Tibet and must join an organised group. To trek, as with all trips apart from the tour of a small handful of cities, requires a travel permit (for more information see Permits in the Facts for the Visitor chapter).

That said, a number of trekkers opt to go it alone, in the true spirit of independent travel, and most succeed. If you are caught by the cops without the right documents be friendly but firm in your conviction that you did not know any better. You will probably be let off with a small fine unless either you or your tormentors loses their cool. It is unusual to be asked for any documentation while on a trek.

Trekkers headed from Ganden to Samye without a travel permit will face a problem after their trek is finished when they take the ferry over to the Tsetang side. Trekkers in the Kailash region face the same permit regulations as other travellers (see the Western Tibet chapter for details). At the time of research Shigatse PSB was issuing travel permits good for Samye (sometimes), Shalu and Everest Base Camp. Make sure you get these if you are trekking in the Everest region or doing the Ganden to Samye trek. If you get stopped at least you'll have something to show. At the time of research there were no permit checks anywhere on the Tsurphu-Yangpachen or Shalu-Nartang treks or at the trailheads. Travel permits were not needed for Ganden, Tingri, Everest Base Camp, Tsurphu, Yangpachen or Shalu.

HEALTH

To maintain your health in such a difficult high elevation environment you need to take special precautions. With a little preparation and good sense your trekking experience will be one of the highlights of your trip to Tibet. You will want to bring a first-aid kit with all the basics and perhaps some extras as well (see Health in the Facts for the Visitor chapter). Tibet is not the place to wander alone – always trek with companions. If anything goes wrong you will need people to depend on. For detailed information see *Medicine For Mountaineering* published by The Mountaineers.

The single most common trekking health problem is sunburn. Sunburn, which in serious instances (when accompanied by heat exhaustion) can require hospitalisation, is fortunately preventable. Wear loose-fitting clothes that cover your arms, legs and neck, and choose a wide-brimmed hat like the ones Tibetans wear. There are many fancy and expensive sunscreen lotions on the market but the most effective and cheapest is zinc oxide ointment. But bring it from home because you probably won't find it in Tibet.

Subfreezing temperatures mean that there is a risk of hypothermia even in summer. Make sure you have the right clothing and an outer shell that protects against rain, snow and wind. Remember that exposed plains and ridges are prone to extremely high winds and that this significantly adds to the cold. For example, on a 5000m pass in Central Tibet in July, the absolute minimum temperature is roughly -4°C but regularly occurring 70km/h winds plunge the wind chill factor or apparent temperature to -20°C.

Trekkers are particularly at risk from altitude sickness (acute mountain syndrome). For information on this important subject see the Health section in the Facts for the Visitor chapter.

WOMEN & CHILDREN

Women do not face any special difficulties trekking so long as they dress and behave modestly. Assaults on women in Tibet are rare and, relative to many countries in Asia, women enjoy a fairly high social status. Women might, however, be excluded from visiting protector chapels at monasteries and forced to take a back seat in male-dominated events. It is not a good idea to take young children high-altitude trekking because they might not acclimatise well. Older children who are properly trained and acclimatised can make great trekking partners but don't get demoralised when you see that the kids are faster than you.

GUIDES & PACK ANIMALS

The rugged terrain, long distances and high elevations of Tibet make most people rethink carrying their own gear. In villages and herder camps along the main trekking routes it is often possible to hire burros or yaks to do the dirty work for you. Even on less travelled routes you might find help.

You will need to know some Tibetan to negotiate what you want and how much you are willing to pay. Be prepared for a good session of bargaining, and don't set out until you and the Tibetans working for you are perfectly clear on what's in the bargain. Spell out the amount of time you expect from your helpers and the exact amount you intend to pay to avoid misunderstandings. Your mule skinner or yak driver will also serve as your guide, an important asset on the unmarked trails of Tibet. Consider just hiring a guide if you don't want or can't get pack animals – this could save you a lot of frustrating hours looking for the route.

RESPONSIBLE TREKKING

Tibet is one of the great unspoiled wildernesses left on earth. Please consider the following tips when trekking and help preserve the unique ecology and beauty of this fragile region.

Fires & Cooking

Building fires is not an option. Wood is nonexistent in much of Tibet and where there are trees and bushes they are often scarce resources needed by locals. Cook on a lightweight kerosene, petrol, alcohol or Shellite (white gas) stove and avoid those powered by disposable butane gas canisters.

If you are trekking with a guide and porters, supply stoves for the whole team. In alpine areas, ensure that all members are outfitted with enough clothing so that fires are not needed for warmth.

Rubbish

Carry out all your rubbish. If you've carried it in you can carry it out. Don't overlook those easily forgotten items, such as silver paper, orange peel, cigarette butts and plastic wrappers. Empty packaging weighs very little anyway and should be stored in a dedicated rubbish bag. Gain good karma by carrying out rubbish left by others.

Never bury your rubbish: digging disturbs soil and groundcover and encourages erosion. Buried rubbish will more than likely be dug up by animals, who may be injured or poisoned by it. Moreover, it may take years to decompose, especially at Tibet's high altitudes.

Minimise the waste you must carry out by taking minimal packaging and taking no more than you will need. If you can't buy in bulk, unpack small-portion packages and combine their contents in one container before your trek. Take reuseable containers, zip-loc bags or stuff sacks.

In Tibet it is not a good idea to burn plastics and other garbage as this is believed to irritate mountain spirits and affronts the sensibilities of the more traditional Tibetans.

Sanitary napkins, tampons and condoms should also be carried out despite the inconvenience. They burn and decompose poorly.

Toilets

Where there is a toilet, please use it. Where there is none, human waste should be left on the surface of the ground away from trails and habitations to decompose. The aridity, cold and high ultraviolet exposure renders wastes into innocuous compounds relatively quickly.

If you are in a large trekking group dig a privy pit. Be sure to build it far from any water source or marshy ground and carefully rehabilitate the area when you leave camp. Pieces of turf, rocks and soil removed from the hole can be used to cap it. Also be certain that the latrine is not located near mani walls, shrines or any other sacred structures. Encourage all party members, including porters, to use the site.

Washing

Don't use detergents or toothpaste in or near watercourses, even if they are biodegradable. For personal washing, use biodegradable soap and a water container (or even a lightweight, portable basin) at least 50m away from the watercourse. Widely disperse the waste water to allow the soil to filter it fully before it finally makes it back to the watercourse.

Wash cooking utensils 50m from watercourses using a scourer, sand or snow instead of detergent.

Erosion

Hillsides and mountain slopes, especially at high altitudes, are prone to erosion. It is important to stick to existing tracks and avoid short cuts that bypass a switchback. If you blaze a new trail straight down a slope it will turn into a watercourse with the next heavy rainfall and eventually cause soil loss and deep scarring.

If a well used track passes through a mud patch, walk through the mud: walking around the edge will increase the size of the patch.

Avoid removing the plant life that keeps topsoil in place.

Cultural Considerations

Seek permission to camp from landowners. They will usually be happy if asked, but may be confrontational if not. For more on this subject see Society & Conduct in the Facts about Tibet chapter.

Wildlife Conservation

Do not engage in or encourage hunting. This extends to not buying items made from endangered species.

FOOD

You should be self-sufficient in food because there isn't much to eat on the trail. In most villages there is little or no food surplus and thus probably nothing to buy. But don't worry: in Lhasa there are now literally thousands of stalls and stores selling a huge variety of foodstuffs making tasty, well balanced meals possible on the trail. Even in Shigatse and the smaller cities there are many foods suitable for trekking.

Vacuum packed red meat and poultry, and packaged dried meat and fish are readily found in Lhasa. Numerous kinds of packaged and bulk dried fruits are sold throughout the city. The newest and tastiest varieties are figs and pineapples which make a great trail mix when combined with peanuts and walnuts. You can even find almonds and pistachio nuts imported from America.

Soybean and dairy milk powders can be used with several kinds of prepackaged cereals available. Pickled and dried vegetables are good for dressing up soups and stir fries. On the Barkhor are stalls selling Indian pickles and curry powders. Lightweight vegetables such as bok choy can do wonders for instant noodles and macaroni, both of which are readily available.

Cooking mediums include butter, margarine, refined vegetable oil and sesame oil. Butter can be preserved for long treks or old butter made more palatable by turning it into ghee. Boil and strain the butter for about 20 minutes. For those with a sweet tooth all kinds of biscuits and candies are sold in Lhasa and the larger towns. Snickers bars are available in Lhasa.

DRINKS

As wonderfully cold and clear as much of the water is in Tibet it should not be assumed that it's safe to drink. Livestock contaminate many water sources and Tibetans do not always live up to their cultural ideals. Giardia is common in Tibet and can slow your trek down to a crawl.

To protect your health you should treat all water before drinking by using chemical or filtration methods, or by boiling it for at least 10 minutes. For added protection more than one method can be used in tandem. If you plan to rely on chemical purification bring your supply from home so that you know how to use it. For further information see the Health section in the Facts for the Visitor chapter.

PRAYER FLAGS

RICHARD I'ANSON

Strips of coloured cloth printed with Buddhist sutras are strung up at the top of passes and streams and houses to purify the air and pacify the gods. When the flags flutter prayers are thought to be released to the heavens. The colours are highly symbolic – red, green, yellow, blue and white represent the elements of fire, wood, earth, water and iron.

BRADLEY MAYHEW

Right & below left: Brightly coloured prayer flags are sold from stalls along Lhasa's Barkhor circuit.

Below right: Fluttering prayer flags adorn high passes, lakes and other significant points along pilgrimage circuits.

TONY WHEELER

GREG CAIRE

PRAYER WHEELS

RICHARD I'ANSON

Prayer wheels, which range from the hand-held variety to huge water-powered versions, are filled with up to a mile of prayers, which are 'recited' with each revolution of the wheel. Wheels can be the size of a fist or a small building and powered by hand, water, wind and even hot air (a cylinder made of paper and suspended over a hot flame).

Koras are lined with prayer wheels and circumambulating pilgrims spin the wheels to gain merit and to concentrate the mind on the mantras and prayers they are reciting.

RICHARD I'ANSON

Woman with prayer wheel circumambulating Sera Monastery, Lhasa.

Follow Tibetan tradition and eliminate the monotony of drinking plain water by downing as much tea as you can. You can buy Chinese green tea in virtually every city and town in Tibet.

Stay clear of Tibetan beer *(chang)* which is made with untreated water, but give yak butter tea a try. More like a soup than a tea, it helps fortify you against the cold and replenishes the body's salts. If you are offered tea, have it served in your own cup as per tradition – this eliminates the risk of drinking from used cups.

Trekking Routes

Detailed descriptions of seven popular treks are given here along with ideas for other treks. The treks featured offer fantastic walking, superb scenery and with the exception of Lake Manasarovar (Tibetan: Mapham

yum-tso) and Kailash are close to Lhasa or the highway to Nepal. Walking times given are just that; they don't include breaks, nature stops or any other off-your-feet activities. On average, plan to walk five or seven hours at most in a day interspersed with frequent short rests. You will also need time to set up camp, cook and just plain enjoy yourself.

Daily itineraries are suggestions only and are not intended to be strictly followed – remember to plan ahead to avoid spending the night at the highest point reached in the day.

Seriously consider hiring a local guide if at all possible. This will free you to enjoy the walk and not have to worry about finding the trail. Trails are not well marked in Tibet and in many locations they disappear altogether. A guide can also share his knowledge of the natural history and culture

Overview of Treks

trek	no of days	distance	passes	description
Ganden to Samye	four to five	80km	Shug-la (5250m), Chitu-la (5100m)	Difficult – the most popular trek in Tibet connecting two of Tibet's most important monasteries
Tsurphu to Yangpachen	three to four	55km	Lasar-la (5300m)	Difficult – gives a good insight into the lives of Tibet's semi-nomadic herders
Shalu to Nartang	two to three	40km	Showa-la (4200m), Char-la (4600m)	Moderate – easy access and relatively low passes make this a good beginner's trek
Trek to Everest Base Camp	three to four	105km	Geu-la (5170m) or Pang-la (5200m)	Difficult – but if you get tired you can always hitch part of the way
Everest Base Camp to Tingri	three to four	75km	Nam-la (5250m)	Difficult – an excellent way to trek in or out to Everest avoiding the road
Mt Kailash Kora	three	53km	Drölma-la (5630m)	Difficult – one of Tibet's holiest pilgrimage treks
Lake Manasarovar Kora	four to five	115km	4680m	Difficult – a most sacred and beautiful lake; the shore is dotted with monasteries

of the place, greatly adding to your experience. Even large trekking companies depend on local guides to make their trips work.

The directions 'right' and 'left' given in the route descriptions always correspond with the direction of travel.

GANDEN TO SAMYE
Duration: 4 to 5 days
This demanding trek crosses two passes over 5000m and begins less than 50km from Lhasa. A four or five day trek via the Shug-la and Chitu-la passes, it has emerged as the most popular in the Ü region.

Information
The best time for the walk is from the middle of May to the middle of October. The summer months can be wet but the mountains are at their greenest and wildflowers spangle the alpine meadows. Barring heavy snow, it is also possible for those with a lot of trekking experience and the right gear to do this walk in the colder months. If you are coming straight from Lhasa you will need to spend a couple of nights at Ganden Monastery (4500m) to acclimatise.

Getting to/from the Trek
Public buses run between Lhasa and Ganden and Lhasa and the Samye ferry crossing. See the Ganden Monastery and Samye Monastery sections of the Ü chapter for information.

The Trek
Day 1: Ganden to Hepu (3 hours) or to Yama Do (5 hours)
The trek begins from the parking lot at the base of the monastery, traversing south along the ridge to reach the first village, Hepu, after about three hours. Leave the parking lot and look for the well trodden trail heading south along the side of Angkor Ri, the highest point on the Ganden kora. The trail gradually ascends for 1½ hours before reaching a saddle. Near the saddle the trail comes close to the top of the ridge marked by cairns. The saddle itself is

marked by a cairn (*lapse* in Tibetan) 2m tall and 3m in diameter.

From the saddle look west down the Kyi Chu valley to Lhasa. Traversing the west side of the ridge from the saddle, the trail reaches a spur surmounted by a cairn after 30 minutes. The trail now descends towards Hepu village. Twenty minutes from the spur is a spring. From here it is a further 30 minutes to the village.

There are around 30 houses in **Hepu** and it is possible to *camp* or find *accommodation* here among the friendly locals.

If carrying your gear up the pass beyond Hepu is not a pleasant thought, you might be able to rent yaks to do the work for you. Villagers charge around Y30 per yak per day, plus the salary of the yak man, which is approximately Y50 per day. You will also have to pay half charges for the time it takes the yaks and herder to return home. Usually the yak man feeds himself and pro-

GANDEN TO SAMYE TREK

vides his own camping gear but make all
this clear before you set out. Intimately familiar with the environment, these people
know how to make themselves at home on
the trail. A yak can carry one or two backpacks depending on the weight. Yak drivers
will load the beasts lightly to maximise
their income and save wear and tear on the
animals.

Finding a person willing to accompany
your party all the way to Samye is not easy.
You may have to settle for the summit of the
first or second pass which is a big help. If
you don't get yaks all the way you might
find others further along at a herders' camp
but this not a sure bet. It you have no luck
hiring yaks in Hepu try down valley in the
nearby village of Trubshi.

From Hepu the trail climbs towards the
Shug-la 3½ hours away. Look for a red-
and-yellow masonry structure and white
incense hearths at the edge of the village.
This is the shrine of Hepu's *yul lha* (local
protecting deity), the Divine White Yak.
Go east from here and look for the bridge crossing the Tashi Chu Mig stream which runs
below the village. Outside of the summer
months you can also easily ford this stream
to the west bank. Head down valley for a
few minutes to the confluence with another
stream. Round the inner side of the confluence and head upstream along the east bank.
You are now following the watercourse
originating from the Shug-la. Near the confluence are good *campgrounds*.

One hour from Hepu you reach **Ani
Pagong**, a narrow, craggy bottleneck in the
valley. A small nunnery used to be located
above the trail. From Ani Pagong the trail
steadily climbs for one hour through marshy
meadows to **Yama Do**.

Yama Do offers extensive *campgrounds*
suitable for larger groups. Consider spending
the night here as it is still a long way to the
pass. Above Yama Do the valley's watercourse splits into three branches. Follow the
central or south branch, not the south-east or
south-west branches. The route leaves the
flank of the valley and follows the valley
bottom.

Beyond Yama Do the trail becomes in-
distinct but it is a straight shot upwards to
the pass. Thirty minutes from Yama Do are
two single tent *campsites*, the last good
ones until the other side of the pass and at
least five hours of hiking.

Day 2: Yama Do to Tsotup Chu valley (4 to 5 hours)

One hour past Yama Do leave the valley
floor and ascend a shelf on the east (left)
side of the valley to avoid a steep gully that
forms around the stream. In another 45
minutes you enter a wet, tussock grass
studded alpine basin. Because of the un-
suitable terrain you should only consider
camping here in an emergency.

The Shug-la is at least 1¼ hours from the
basin. Remain on the east side of the valley
as it bends to the left. You have to negotiate
boulders and lumpy ground along the final
steep climb to the pass. The **Shug-la** (5250m)
cannot be seen until you're virtually on top
of it. It is marked by a large cairn covered in
prayer flags and yak horns.

The route continues over the Shug-la and
descends sharply through a boulder field,
losing a couple of hundred metres of elevation. Be on the lookout for a clear and
cairned trail on the left side of the boulder
field. This trail traverses the ridge in a
south-easterly direction paralleling the
valley below. Do not head directly down to
the valley from the pass unless you have
good reason. It is a long steep descent and
once at the bottom you would have to go
back up the valley to complete the trek.
Retreat down the valley for a bolt hole back
to the Lhasa-Ganden Highway, a long day
of walking away.

The cairned trail gradually descends to
reach the valley floor 1½ hours from the
pass. Cross the large stream, the **Tsotup
Chu**, which flows through the valley. During
heavy summer rains take special care to find
a safe ford. The pastures in the area support
large herds of yaks, goats and sheep, and
during the trekking season herders are often
camped here. This is an ideal place to *camp*
and meet the herders (*drokpa* in Tibetan). It

is a two to 2½ hour walk from the stream ford to the second pass, the Chitu-la, and at least 1¼ more hours to the first camping place.

An alternative route to Ganden via the Gampa-la (5050m) follows the main branch of the Tsotup Chu past a couple of lakes to the pass. South of the Gampa-la the trail plunges into a gorge crisscrossing the stream that flows down from it. These fords may pose problems during summer rains or when completely frozen. See Gary McCue's *Trekking in Tibet – a traveler's guide* for details of this route.

Day 3: Tsotup Chu valley to herders' camps (5 hours)

From the Tsotup Chu ford, the main water course flows from the south-east and a minor tributary enters from the south-west. Follow this tributary, which quickly disappears underground, steeply upwards for 30 minutes until you reach a large basin. Stay on the west (right) side of the basin and turn into the first side valley opening on the right. Follow this broad valley which soon arcs south to the Chitu-la. The pass can be seen in the distance, a rocky rampart at the head of the valley. At first, stay on the west (right) side of the valley; there is a small trail. As you approach the pass the trail switches to the east side of the valley. If you miss the trail just look for the easiest route up. The terrain is not particularly difficult.

The **Chitu-la** (5100m) is topped by several cairns. Also on the summit is a small glacial cairn. Move to the west side of the pass to find the trail down and to circumvent a sheer rock wall on its south flank. A short but steep descent will bring you into a basin with three small lakes. The trail skirts the west side of the lakes. It takes 45 minutes to reach the south end of the basin. Drop down from the basin on the west side of the stream and you will hit the first place to set up *camp* in 30 minutes. Herders have carved out level places for their tents here.

Below the herders' highest camp the valley is squeezed in by vertical rock walls, forcing you to pick your way through the rock-strewn valley floor. There is no trail in this gorge and the descent is very steep. In about 20 minutes cross over to the west (right) side of the widening valley to recover the trail. In 10 more minutes you will come to a flat and a seasonal herders' camp on the east side of the valley, good for *camping*. At the lower end of the flat return to the west side of the valley. The trail again disappears as it enters a scrub willow and rosebush forest but there is only one way to go to get to Samye and that is downstream.

In 15 minutes, when a tributary valley enters from the right, cross to the east side of the valley. Fifteen minutes further, you will reach another seasonal herders' camp inhabited for only a short time each year. In another quarter of an hour beyond this camp hop back to the west bank to avoid a cliff hugging the opposite side of the stream. Pass through a large meadow and ford the stream back to the east bank. From this point the trail remains on the east side of the valley for several hours.

Camping places are now numerous, some of which are adequate for large groups. Soon the trail crosses the stream draining the valley coming from Gamba-la. During times of heavy summer rain you might not be able to ford this stream. If so, you will have no alternative but to wait for the water to subside.

Days 4 & 5: herders' camps to Samye Monastery (8 hours)

The trail is now wide and easy to follow as it traces a course down the east side of the valley. Walk through the thickening scrub forest for 45 minutes and you will come to another stream entering from the east side of the main valley. Look for a small wood-and-stone bridge a couple of hundred metres above the confluence. The valley now bends to the right and the trail enters the thickest and tallest part of the scrub forest. The right combination of elevation, moisture, and aspect create a verdant environment while just a few kilometres away desert conditions prevail.

The next two hour stretch of the trail is among the most delightful of the entire trek.

According to local woodcutters more than 15 types of trees and shrubs are found here, some growing 6m tall. Fragrant junipers grow on exposed southern slopes while rhododendrons prefer the shadier slopes. The rhododendrons begin blooming in early May and by the end of the month the forest is ablaze with pink and white blossoms.

The trail winds through a series of meadows. In 45 minutes look for a ruined stone structure at a place known as Gen Do. Nearby is a shrine to the protector of the area, the ancient goddess Dorje Yudronma. Just past the shrine cross a small tributary stream. In one hour the forest rapidly thins and the first permanent village since Hepu pops up, **Changtang**. Named after the northern plains of Tibet, its inhabitants are predominantly engaged in animal husbandry just like their northern counterparts. Although the villagers are friendly enough the village is infested with fierce dogs, which fortunately are usually tied up.

Look south to the distant mountains; this is the range on the far side of the Yarlung Tsangpo valley. Thirty-five minutes down the valley is the turn-off for the **Yamalung Hermitage**. Look for a field of small cairns to the right of the trail pointing towards a bridge over the valley stream. It is nearly a one hour steep climb to the hermitage. Members of parties not interested in making the climb can wait near the bridge with the group's gear. Yamalung (also called Emalung) is where Guru Rinpoche is said to have meditated and received empowerment from the long life deity Amitayus (Tibetan: Tsepame).

Consisting of several small temples, a few meditators live here. Below the temple complex is a sacred spring and an old relief carving in stone of Guru Rinpoche, King Trisong Detsen and the Indian pundit Shantarakshita, all of whom lived in the 8th century. The cave Guru Rinpoche meditated in is enshrined by the Drup Pug Mara Titsang temple. Inside are the footprint and handprint of the saint said to have been created when he magically expanded the size of the cave.

From the turn-off to Yamalung the trail becomes a motorable track and the valley much wider. In 15 minutes you will reach a bridge; the trail now remains on the west (right) side of the valley all the way to Samye, a 3½ hour walk away. Twenty minutes from the bridge you will come to the village of **Nyango** with its substantially built stone houses. A big tributary stream, entering from the north-west, joins the Samye valley here. The old trade route from Lhasa to Samye via the Gokar-la follows this valley. In the lower half of Nyango are four small shops selling soda, cigarettes and, maybe, basic food supplies like instant noodles. If you are looking for a place to doss down ask the shopkeepers; they might oblige you.

Half an hour past Nyango is the village of **Wango** and an hour beyond it, the hamlet of **Pisha**. En route there are several meadows in which you can set up *camp*.

From the lower end of Pisha, a hill can be seen in the middle of the mouth of the Samye valley. This is Hepo Ri, one of Tibet's most sacred mountains (see the Samye Monastery section of the Ü chapter). The entire lower Samye valley can be seen from Pisha: a tapestry of fields, woods and villages. Pisha is the last place that water can be conveniently drawn from the river. From here on in the trail only intersects irrigation ditches.

Fifteen minutes past Pisha a ridge spur called Dragmar meets the trail. On the summit is the partially rebuilt palace where King Trisong Detsen is said to have been born. Formerly a lavish temple it now stands empty. Below, just off the road, is a small red and white temple enshrining the stump of an ancient tree. Legend has it that a red and white sandalwood tree grew here, nourished by the buried placenta of King Trisong. In the Cultural Revolution the tree was chopped down.

Twenty minutes further down the trail is Sangbu village from where there are good views of the golden spires of Samye. The route follows the jeep track directly to Samye along the margin of woods and desert: it takes about one hour. Use the shiny temple roof as your beacon. The closer you get to Samye the hotter the valley can become; in May and June it can even be fiery hot. If the heat gets too much flee to the stands of willows and poplars not far from the road. The gilt roofs get ever brighter as you approach the monastery. You will reach Samye several minutes after passing inside its perimeter wall.

If you can't catch a lift it is about a two hour walk from Samye to the ferry crossing. One day's walk down the Tsangpo valley at Tsetang, or six hours upstream from Samye, are alternative ferry crossings using traditional Tibetan leather coracles. If you don't have a travel permit for Samye, authorities can be eluded at these other crossings but the route is through extremely harsh sand dune country. It is probably better to give them a miss unless your party is prepared for full-blown desert conditions.

TSURPHU TO YANGPACHEN

Duration: 3 to 4 days

The Tsurphu to Yangpachen trek is an excellent choice for those who want to get a close look at the Tibetan herders (drokpa) and their semi-nomadic lifestyle. Although they have permanent winter homes they spend much of the year camping with their animals.

Beginning at Tsurphu Monastery this rugged walk crosses several alpine valleys before emerging into the broad and windswept Yangpachen valley. This is a high elevation trek exceeding 4400m for the entire duration and a maximum elevation of 5300m at the Lasar-la. Combining alpine tundra and sweeping mountain panoramas with visits to monasteries and a nunnery, this trek nicely balances cultural and wilderness activities.

Information

The best time for this walk is from the middle of April to the middle of October. Summer months can be rainy but be prepared for snow at any time. Plan on at least three days for this walk. As you will be in nomad country, beware of vicious dogs,

some of which take a sadistic pride in chasing hapless foreigners. Fuel and food are not available so come prepared. There are few permanent settlements along the way and the inhabitants are often away from home so don't count on these places to provide accommodation. Your only option on this trek is to be fully self-sufficient.

Getting to/from the Trek

Minibuses leave the Barkhor every day at some time between 7 and 8 am for Tsurphu (four hours, Y18). Minibuses to Yangpachen (three hours, Y25) depart from the CAAC office in Lhasa. Lhasa-Naqu minibuses also pass through Yangpachen.

The Trek

Tshurpu Monastery at 4500m is a good place to spend a couple of nights acclimatising. Two kilometres downstream from Tsurphu, beside the Karmapa's summer palace, is a small copse which is ideal for *camping*. Some of the area's herders spend a lot of time at the monastery so this is a good place to start looking for guides and yaks. However, sometimes Tsurphu is crawling with police in which case you'd better get up valley before you let your plans be known.

Day 1: Tsurphu Monastery to Leten (3½ hours)

The trek begins at Tsurphu, heading west or up the valley. Follow the kora trail 15 minutes west to a walled copse of old trees with a brook. This garden-like wood is used by the monks in the summer so ask permission before you set up camp. The trees here will be the last you will see until after finishing the trek. Just above the copse, the valley splits: follow the north-west branch and remain on the north side of the stream.

Forty-five minutes of walking through a rocky chasm on a well graded trail brings you to Shupshading, a herders' camp on a shelf above the trail. If you are looking for yaks to carry your equipment try asking the herders here. The valley remains narrow above Shupshading and is often engulfed with ice left over from the winter. After 30 minutes cross a seasonal stream coming from the north-west (right). Soon the trail switches over to the south (left) side of the valley. Forty-five minutes onwards the trail forks. The left branch switchbacks up the ridge south of the valley and then traverses west into the drokpa settlement of **Leten** (5000m). Although you want to go here take the right fork which follows the valley floor – this is a more straightforward route to Leten, about one hour away.

Leten is divided by the stream running through it. Several families live here permanently, braving the severe climate with their livestock. Leten is the last chance to find yaks and a guide, both of which are highly recommended because the route to and from the Lasar-la is not easy to find. Locals will ask at least Y50 per yak per day plus a salary of around Y50 per day but you should be able to negotiate.

Spend one or preferably two days in Leten acclimatising.

Day 2: Leten to Bartso (5 hours)

It is about a three hour walk from Leten to the Lasar-la. Head for the northern half of the settlement (assuming you aren't already there). The route climbs steeply up the north side of the Leten valley, reaching the highest house. Bear north-west into a steep side valley. As you ascend, a reddish knob of rock looms up ahead. Angle to the north, or right, of this formation and leave the valley by climbing to the top of a spur marked by three cairns. It is a 45 minute walk to here from Leten. This spur, called **Damchen Nyingtri**, is holy to the god ruling the environs.

As per Buddhist tradition, stay to the left of the cairns crowning Damchen Nyingtri and descend sharply into a narrow valley. Once on the valley bottom, cross to the east (right) side of the stream and strike out north (up the valley). In 15 minutes the valley forks: follow the north (right branch). Cross back to the left side of the stream as the terrain here is easier to traipse over. Walk up the widening valley through arctic-like mounds of tundra for one hour following a

minor trail. Then, as the valley turns west, look for a cairn on the opposite bank of the stream.

Using this cairn as a marker bear north-west over an inclined plain. This plain parallels the valley floor before the two merge. Continue ascending as the plain opens wider in the direction of the pass. There is no clear trail but favour the west side of the plain; the east side spills down into another valley system. The **Lasar-la** (5300m) is a broad gap at the highest point in the plain and is heralded by cairns lining the final approach. Just before reaching the pass you'll see the Nyenchen Tanglha range come into view far to the north.

From the Lasar-la there is a steep descent into a north running valley. A trail can be found on the east (right) side of this valley. In a few minutes the grade levels out and the trail crosses the stream bed and continues down the west side of the valley. There are many possible *campsites* between the Lasar-la and Bartso.

As the trail descends you peer into the expansive Yangpachen valley, a broad plain laced with streams that opens up in front of

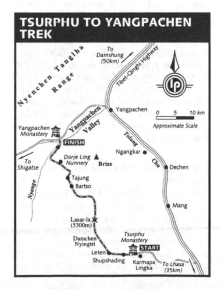

TSURPHU TO YANGPACHEN TREK

the Nyenchen Tanglha range. This range is part of the trans-Himalaya which circumscribes the plateau and divides southern Tibet from the Changtang.

The valley is covered in hummocks but there is a trail that avoids the ups and downs of these mounds of turf and earth. About one hour from the pass a break in the ridge running along the east side of the valley comes into view. The break coincides with a big west bend in the valley. As soon as you spot this interruption in the ridge line, ford the stream and traverse up to the right into a side valley. Heading north, the valley soon gives way to a plain paved with big plates of tundra.

There are superb views of the surrounding mountains along this stretch of the walk. In the north is Brize, a heavily glaciated peak enclosing the west side of the Yangpachen valley, and to the west is a distinctive pinnacle in the trans-Himalaya range called Tarze. Brize, meaning female-yak herder, and Tarze, horse keeper, are two of many topographical features in a mythical society ruled by the mountain god Nyenchen Tanglha. These two mountains make convenient landmarks as one goes against the grain by heading north over a series of east-west running drainage systems.

In one hour the trail intersects a east-west valley at the settlement of **Bartso**. This drokpa village of five homes with its permanent sources of water is a good place to *camp*. The slopes around the village are still covered in juniper bushes. In the 1960s and 70s huge amounts of this valuable resource were extracted from the region and trucked to Lhasa to feed the hearths of the new provincial city.

Day 3: Bartso to Djore Ling Nunnery (3½ hours)

Look north-west from Bartso to the opposite side of the valley. Clearly visible, a wide trail winds up from the valley to the top of the ridge. Ford the valley stream and make for this trail, a 20 minute walk over marshy ground from Bartso. It takes another 25 minutes to reach the summit of the ridge.

From the top you will see a saddle north of an intervening valley. On the far side of this saddle is the Dorje Ling Nunnery, still more than 2½ hours away.

Views of **Nyenchen Tanglha**, the 7111m mountain which gives its name to the range, is fantastic from here. This huge massif has a distinctive flat summit. Nyenchen Tanglha is the holiest mountain in central Tibet and is said to be inhabited by a god of the same name. Envisioned as a regal white warrior on a white horse, the god's half-smile, half grimace symbolises the benevolent and destructive sides of his personality.

From the saddle, drop down to the valley in 25 minutes to the village of **Tajung**. Stay to the left of the 14 whitewashed houses and ford the stream below it. Bear north-east into the parting in the ridge and after a few minutes cross a low saddle. Continue going north-east in the direction of Brize until a large dip appears in the hills to the west 40 minutes from Tajung. Leave the trail going towards Brize and head to the right of the dip cross-country. Traverse to the right of the low point in the ridge, remaining high enough to avoid the highest part of the east-west ridge looming up ahead. If you have gained enough height, you will see a group of white houses at the base of a hill to the north-west. The Dorje Ling Nunnery is just downstream of here.

A 25 minute traverse will bring you to a stream at the base of the ridge aligned east to west. A broad trail appears on the north bank of the stream. Follow it to the top of the ridge. From this point you'll have good views of the village just upstream of **Dorje Ling Nunnery**. The nunnery, which is out of view, sits at the bottom of a rock outcrop visible from the ridge top.

During the winter you can strike out across a swamp that fills the valley to go directly to Dorje Ling, reaching it in just 30 minutes. Otherwise you will have to take the long way around and skirt the north edge of the swamp to reach the north side of the Dorje Ling valley. This longer route requires at least one hour of hiking. There is a motorable road on the far side of the valley and the nunnery is only 10 minutes down from here.

The centrepiece of this friendly nunnery is a red lhakhang in the midst of a group of little white houses. The lhakhang is simply decorated, reflecting the modest means of the 52 nuns who call this place home. A concerted effort is underway to build a house for all of the nuns. The nuns are happy to show visitors around and donations are welcome. Good *camping* is found in the meadows around Dorje Ling.

Day 4: Djore Ling Nunnery to Yangpachen Monastery (3 hours)

From Dorje Ling follow the motorable road west, or downstream. In 15 minutes the road crosses to the south bank of the valley watercourse and soon forks. Take the right fork over the small concrete bridge and continue down the east bank of the stream along the track. Forty-five minutes from Dorje Ling the valley drains into the spacious Yangpachen valley. Stay on the same track which turns into a motorable road as it runs north paralleling the course of the Nyango Chu which drains the upper Yangpachen valley. The road stays close to the east bank of the river, skirting meadows that afford fantastic *camping* and encompassing views of the trans-Himalaya.

Once entering the Nyango drainage area it is an easy two hours walk to a steel bridge spanning the river. Cross the bridge to join the northern road to Shigatse. Walk north on the road for 15 minutes suddenly coming to **Yangpachen Monastery** at the end of a line of cliffs. Perched on top of a small hill on the left side of the road, the monastery overlooks a broad sweep of trans-Himalaya peaks. There are several trails leading from the road to the monastery but beware of the pack of dogs loitering around the grounds. The monastery was home to 115 monks, but many of them have fled to Rumtek Monastery in Sikkim. Yangpachen is headed by Shamar Rinpoche, a leading lama of the Kagyupa order, who is based in India. If you're interested in seeing what Nyenchen Tanglha looks like check out the mural in the inner vestibule of the main assembly hall. It depicts the god in several of his wrathful animal manifestations.

From Yangpachen Monastery it is a 15km road journey to Yangpachen. If your luck holds you should be able to hitch there. The hot springs complex at Yangpachen is great to ease your aching limbs. Entry costs around Y20. From here there are many minibuses back to Lhasa (three hours).

SHALU TO NARTANG

Duration: 2 to 3 days

This two or three day walk is a good opportunity to get a feel for trekking in Tibet. The two passes en route, Showa-la and Char-la, are not particularly high or difficult and the trailheads are easily accessible from Shigatse.

Information

The optimal walking season is from the beginning of April to the end of October. In the summer months (June, July and August) the trail can be sizzling hot, and in other months cold and windy, so be prepared! One advantage of hiking in the summer months is that this region gets less rainfall than the Ü region.

This trek begins at the historic Shalu Monastery (see the Tsang chapter for more information about this monastery) and traverses west over a couple of small ranges to Ngor Monastery. From Ngor it is a downhill slog to Nartang Monastery. The route passes through several villages as well as uninhabited dry canyons. It is about a 10 hour walk to Ngor from Shalu, which is best divided into two days, and another seven hours from there to Nartang. Finding guides and burros (yaks are not an option) to carry your gear is not easy but you can try in Shalu. If you can get local support go for it, because the route is not always easy to discern – in the canyons the trail tends to peter out.

Getting to/from the Trek

For getting to Shalu Monastery see the Shalu entry in the Tsang chapter. Lhatse-Shigatse minibuses travel the Friendship Highway and pass near Nartang.

The Trek

Day 1: Shalu Monastery to Upper Lungsang (5½ hours)

From Shalu Monastery walk the motorable road south (up the valley). It is about three hours to the first pass, Showa-la. Thirty minutes from Shalu you will pass by the **Ri-puk Hermitage** set on a hillside on the west side of the valley. If you wish to visit, cut across the fields and head directly up to the hermitage – the way is not difficult and there are several trails leading up to it. For more information see the Shalu Monastery entry in the Tsang chapter.

Forty-five minutes from Shalu the road forks: take the south (right) fork. In the south, a conical-shaped hill and a village at its base can be made out. If you struck out in Shalu, stay on the road to this village,

called **Phunup**, about one hour's walk away, to look for a guide and burros. Otherwise, there is a short cut that saves a couple of kilometres of walking. A few minutes from the fork in the road look for the base of a long red ridge. Leave the road and skirt the base of this ridge, going in a southerly direction. First cross a flood plain to reach a rectangular red shrine and beyond it enter a plain bounded in the south by the red ridge.

Gradually the trail climbs to a small white ridge blocking the route to the south. As you approach you will see white cairns marking its summit. Look for the trail that ascends to the cairns, a 45 minute walk from the fork in the road. From the ridge's summit Phunup village is to the left and the Showa-la to the west (left). The pass is the obvious low point in the range at least one hour away. The trail descends gradually to enter the stream bed coming from the

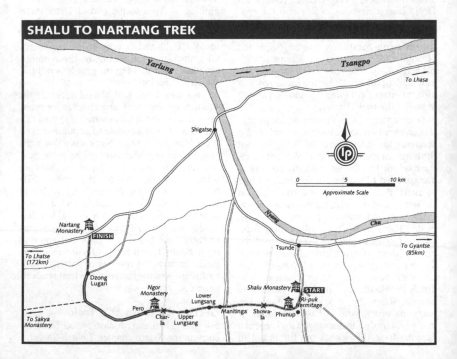

SHALU TO NARTANG TREK

Showa-la 30 minutes from the cairns. If you came via Phunup, your route will converge with the main trail here.

The climb to the pass and the descent on the other side are through heavily eroded, waterless ravines and slopes or badlands. So bring plenty of drinking water. From the stream bed the trail soon climbs back up the right side of the valley only to drop back in and out of the stream bed in quick succession. Don't make the mistake of walking up the stream bed for you would soon encounter ledges and other difficult terrain. After twice briefly dropping into the narrow stream bed be alert for a trail carving a route up the right slope. The trail climbs steeply to a group of ruins and then winds around to the pass in 20 minutes.

From the **Showa-la** (4200m) the second pass, Char-la, can be seen in the range of hills west of an intervening valley. It is the dip in the crest of the range. The easy-to-follow trail descends from the pass along the south (left) side of a ravine. In one hour you will reach the valley floor. Leave the trail when it crosses a small rise marked with cairns and continue west towards a distant group of trees. Cross over the sandy north-south running valley intersecting a road. Shigatse is about three hours north from here along this road.

The valley watercourse is dry except during summer flash floods. West of it is a poplar and willow copse, the only bit of shade in the area. Consider stopping here for lunch and a rest. From the copse you enter a side valley continuing in a westerly direction towards the Char-la. In a few minutes you will reach the village of **Mani-tinga**, on the southern margin of the valley, and pick up the main cart track going up the valley. The track passes through the village of **Lower Lungsang** and, one hour from the copse, crosses to the south side of the valley. You can glimpse the Char-la from here, which for most of the trek is hidden behind the folds in the mountains.

In 30 minutes you will reach **Upper Lungsang**. There is a fine old woods here ideal for camping and resting.

Day 2: Upper Lungsang to Ngor Monastery (3½ hours)

From Upper Lungsang cross back to the north side of the valley. The cart track does not extend past the village and the trail up to the pass may be difficult to find in places. If you are in doubt try to hire a local person to show you the way. It is at least 2½ hours from Upper Lungsang to the Char-la. At first, the trail skirts the edge of a gravel wash. However, in 15 minutes a series of livestock tracks climb out of the stream bed and onto an eroded shelf that forms above it.

The terrain becomes more rugged and a gorge forms below the trail. There is a side stream and small reservoir 45 minutes above Upper Lungsang. This is the last convenient place to collect water until over the pass. From the reservoir the trail descends back to the stream bed but quickly exits the opposite side of the valley.

Look for a series of switchbacks on the south (left) side of the gorge and follow them upwards. Fifteen minutes onwards the trail crosses a gully and then another gully in 15 more minutes. The final leg to the pass is cross country over a steep slope of raw expanses of rock. From the second gully the Char-la can be reached in 45 minutes of steep uphill walking. At one time this trail was well maintained and formed a main trade link between Shalu and Sakya monasteries but it has fallen into disrepair.

Eventually, cairns on the summit ridge come into focus. The pass is the obvious notch in the ridge line. From the **Char-la** (4600m), mountain ranges stretch west across the horizon and Ngor Monastery is visible below. Ngor is a 45 minute downhill ramble from the pass. The route from the Char-la descends the south (left) side of a ravine that forms below it. Several trails cross the stream that flows from the pass and access Ngor but the first trail is the quickest route – it climbs the right side of the ravine and traverses directly to the monastery. Consider *camping* near Ngor (ask the monastery for permission and the best place to camp) and save the last five hours of walking for the next day.

The Sakya master Ngorchen Kunga Sangpo founded Ngor Monastery in 1429, giving rise to the Ngorpa suborder, a distinctive school of Buddhist thought. Once an important centre of learning, Ngor boasted four monastic estates and 18 residential units inhabited by approximately 340 monks. Only a small fraction of the monastery has been rebuilt. The most eye-catching feature is a beautiful row of chörtens at the lower end of the complex dedicated to the eight victorious forms of the Buddha. The largest structure is the assembly hall called the Gonshung; the outer walls of its gallery are painted in vertical red, white and blue stripes, a characteristic decorative technique used by the Sakya order. The three colours represent the Rigsum Gonpo, the three most important bodhisattvas. The present head of Ngor, Luding Khenpo, resides in northern India.

Day 3: Ngor Monastery to Nartang Monastery (3½ hours)

From Ngor a motorable road runs down the valley. Fifteen minutes from the monastery is the sizeable village of **Pero**. Ninety minutes from Ngor the valley and road bend to the north while the old trade route to Sakya continues west over a saddle. Thirty minutes further there is a copse at the edge of the flood plain which is good for fair weather *camping*.

The road now swings to the west side of the wide alluvial valley and 30 minutes past the copse is the village of **Dzong Lugari**. The road exits the north side of the village and extends north-east for 10km before joining the Lhatse-Shigatse Highway 10km south-west of Shigatse. The trail to Nartang Monastery, however, splits from the road on the northern outskirts of Dzong Lugari and heads north. From Dzong Lugari it is a two hour hike across a broad valley to Nartang.

The trail to Nartang crosses a small stream and an electric utility line. The track tends to merge with a welter of agricultural trails and if you miss it simply continue walking north. Soon the massive ramparts that surrounded the **Nartang Monastery** come into view. Just before arriving, cross the Lhatse-Shigatse Highway 14km west of Shigatse. It should be pretty easy to hitch from here to Shigatse.

TREK TO EVEREST REGION
Duration: 3 to 4 days

With the attraction of the highest mountain in the world, the trek to the Everest Base Camp has become the most popular in Tibet – although in recent years increasing numbers of people are driving there instead of walking. Featuring spectacular views of the Himalaya from stark desert valleys, this is an unforgettable adventure for those who are not afraid to use their own two feet.

Information

This and the following trek are described walking in to Everest from Shegar and out of Everest to Tingri, but the direction can be reversed. One possible tiny advantage of doing it in reverse is that you may not have to pay the Y65 Qomolangma Nature Preserve entrance fee. It is also possible to hitch or hire a Land Cruiser in to Everest Base Camp and then trek out to Tingri. If you get tired of trekking in along the road you can always try to get a lift part of the way. Land Cruisers ply the route in summer and there are also plenty of pony carts if you want a brief respite from carrying your bag.

The trekking season in the Everest region extends from April through October. This is a difficult high elevation walk beginning at 4400m and attaining altitudes of nearly 5200m, so careful preparation and the right gear are imperative. Subfreezing temperatures occur even in the summer at higher elevations and, conversely, hot gusty winds in May and June can make walking a sweaty experience. For very well equipped and seasoned walkers, winter treks to Base Camp are often possible. Thanks to the rain shadow created by Mount Everest and its lofty neighbours even the monsoon months are relatively dry in the region.

It is a very good idea to travel with a tent and stove despite there being a couple of restaurants and lodges on the route. These facilities are few and far between and the

Détente

Since the 1980s persistent accounts of unfriendly villagers, petty theft and stone throwing have come out of the Everest region. Such incidents have soured relations between the local Tibetans and foreigners, and have led to a significant drop in the numbers of trekkers coming to this area. While there are no excuses for bad behaviour there are historical factors contributing to these antisocial episodes.

Under the Communists, the entire religious and civic infrastructure of the region was destroyed and never satisfactorily restored, creating many hardships in a high, dry and poor area. In the early 1980s travellers and climbers started appearing in ever greater numbers, and the majority of them spent little or no money locally. This marginalisation of the locals created ill will which continues to this day. While the locals are not anti-foreigner they are clamouring for a piece of the action. It can only be hoped that Qomolangma Nature Preserve with its grand promises of bettering lives will give the people of the area a piece of the economic pie, but as of yet there is little sign of this.

With some goodwill and understanding on your part you should be able to pull off a trip without any grief from the locals. A realisation is dawning among Tibetans that working with tourists rather than repelling them is the best long term strategy. Encourage this new attitude by patronising local services and businesses as much as possible.

John Bellezza

---

service rudimentary. The only way to ensure privacy and comfort and have the potential to trek out from Base Camp via an alternative route is to have your home and hearth in your pack.

Getting to/from the Trek

There is no public transport in the region but it shouldn't be too difficult to get a lift along the Friendship Highway to either the turn-off to Everest (km marker 5145) or Tingri. Hired Land Cruisers can go all the way to Everest Base Camp.

The Trek

The trek begins at the km marker 5145 on the highway to Nepal, 6km west of Shegar police checkpoint and 12km west of the nearest accommodation at the Shegar turn-off. The route to Base Camp leaves the highway and goes south to the village of Chay and then over the Geu-la into the Dzaka valley. Mount Everest is at the head of the monastery-filled Dzaka valley.

If you are coming directly from Nepal be ready to spend as much as one week at

4400m before attempting the trek. One possibility is to walk a couple of kilometres north of the highway and camp in the meadows on the banks of the Bum Chu for a couple of days. A fine spot directly north of the turn-off to Chay has chörtens and a ruined stone bridge, the only traces left of a village abandoned long ago.

Day 1: Kilometre marker 5145 to beyond the Geu-la (4½ hours)

Six kilometres west of the Shegar police checkpoint, a small, unmarked road heads south to the village of Chay. After one hour it reaches the Qomolangma Nature Preserve checkpoint on the outskirts of Chay. Individuals must pay Y65 to enter the preserve and are given a pass which has a set of regulations printed on it in English and Chinese. Visitors are appropriately instructed to behave modestly, not purchase cultural relics, leave plants and animals alone and not to litter. The money raised supposedly goes to management of the preserve.

There are no restaurants or lodges in Chay but it's pretty easy to find a local family willing to put you up for the night. Burros can be hired to carry your gear to the top of the Geu-la for around Y30 each. You might also find someone willing to haul your stuff all the way to Tashi Dzom in the Dzaka valley, a long day's walk, but expect to pay as much as Y100. Watch out for hidden charges – negotiate exactly what you will pay before setting out.

From Chay there are two passes that cross the range south of the village and drop into the Dzaka valley. The pass furthest west is the Pang-la and is the way the road goes. The shortest and nicest walk is via the eastern pass, the Geu-la. The two routes meet a couple of hours south of the crest.

Follow the road out of Chay for 10 minutes and turn right onto a wide trail. This trail climbs directly up the valley, avoiding the switchbacks in the road. The trail soon fades out across rocky ground but keep heading south towards the switchbacks etched in the side of the ridge. The route crosses the road twice and remains on the west (right) side of the valley. Steadily climb, paralleling the road which is visible traversing the ridge to the right. The route keeps to the valley floor, intersecting an older disused road several times. One hour from Chay you'll reach a small, seasonal herders' camp and the valley's small watercourse; this is the last reliable source of water until well over the other side of the pass.

From the camp angle over to the left side of the valley towards the series of switchbacks cut into the slope. Twenty minutes from the herders' camp is the base of the Geu-la. Look for the trail in a gully below the switchbacks and follow it up. The trail climbs steeply crossing over the road twice. If you want to walk via the Pang-la, pursue the road west (right). The route to the Geu-la ascends directly above the road, reaching the crest of the ridge 1¼ hours from the herders' camp. It is 30 minutes from here to the pass. Once on top, follow the crest south-west and look for a well defined trail posted with cairns that leaves the ridge line

Qomolangma Nature Preserve

The Qomolangma Nature Preserve (QNP) was established by the TAR in 1989 to conserve the natural and cultural heritage of the Mount Everest region. Covering over 34,000 sq km, the Preserve is designed to protect diverse habitats on the northern slopes of the Himalaya stretching east of Makalu all the way to Shisha Pangma. The QNP borders the Sagarmatha and Langtang national parks and the Makalu-Barun Conservation Project in Nepal, creating the only protected area straddling both sides of the Himalaya.

In addition to conserving biodiversity, the project promotes trans-border cooperation between Nepal and the TAR. Exchanges between park managers in the TAR and Nepal are planned to develop natural resource and tourist management strategies. The master plan also calls for local cultural, health and educational standards to be improved.

More than 7000 foreign tourists visit the QNP each year and the number is growing. The QNP's stated primary goal is to train local people in the skills needed so that they can earn a livelihood from tourism. The premise is that if the Tibetans get a piece of the action they will be more likely to protect their culture and environment. Park entrance fees are eventually supposed to be made available to local communities in the form of small loans to develop the tourist industry.

To learn more about the workings of the QNP contact The Mountain Institute, Dogwood and Main Street, PO Box 907, Franklin, West Virginia 26807, or email The Mountain Institute (wendy@lama.wlink.com.np) in Kathmandu.

John Bellezza

to traverse the south side of the slope over to the pass.

The **Geu-la** (5170m) is festooned with prayer flags and cairns and presides over a dramatic view of the Himalaya. Before you is a 150km cross section of the Great Himalayan arc. To the south is Makalu and the unmistakable black pyramidal form of Everest, and in the south-west is Cho Oyu, the big snowy massif, and Shisha Pangma in the far west. Barren brown and purple mountains in the foreground flank the Dzaka valley. In the neighbourhood of the Geu-la blue-white gentians bloom in late May and a little further down, purple irises enliven the windswept meadows.

From the pass you can reach the Dzaka valley in 4½ hours. At first the descent is steep but in 30 minutes you reach a high valley floor along a well trodden path. There is a stream and grassy *campsites* here.

Day 2: Base of the Geu-la to upper Dzaka valley (5½ hours)

Skip over the stream to the right side of the valley and continue downhill. The valley soon turns to the west (right) and in 50 minutes crosses back to the left bank of the stream. A five minute walk to the ford delivers you back to the road coming from the Pang-la. The road is now your constant companion all the way to Everest Base Camp.

Head downhill and in a few minutes you will see the first of three short cut trails at the top end of a slew of switchbacks. At the bottom of the switchbacks the valley squeezes through a gorge before opening back up to reveal the first village 45 minutes from the pass. Just before the village the road crosses over to the right side of the valley. Except during heavy summer rains the stream draining the valley is but a trickle. Thirty minutes further on another valley joins the road from the right. Near the confluence at the hamlet of **Ulung**, the road crosses to the right of the joined valleys.

In 15 minutes you will reach extensive ruins stretching a couple of kilometres down the valley. Called **Dzongkog Pongdro**, this is all that left of an ancient fortified settlement.

Below the ruins the road jumps over to the left side of the valley. In 30 minutes the big Gara valley enters from the west. Thirty more minutes of walking and the road joins the Dzaka valley at the town of **Tashi Dzom** (the name means Auspicious Meeting Place or Plentiful Good Luck), the headquarters of the local township or region. If you go left at the road junction or down the valley you will eventually reach Arun, Kharta and the east face of Everest. See Gary McCue's *Trekking in Tibet – a traveler's guide* for details of further treks in this region.

Right at the junction of the road from the pass and the Dzaka valley road is a small *shop* and *inn* which sells drinks, including beer and tea, and biscuits, as well as rice and noodle dishes. Beds in common rooms go for Y20 each. The bedding is reasonably clean and the proprietors seem helpful and willing to please, but there's little privacy as the two large rooms have no doors. There's also a hideously noisy video hall across the road – bring earplugs. There is little in the way of hospitality or foreign language skills taught locally, so don't expect anything but the basics.

If you are looking for yaks or burros to save your back, start at Tashi Dzom and work your way up the valley. Chances are you will receive offers but weigh your choices very carefully. Some locals might try to take advantage of you and quote exorbitant prices. Stick to your guns but expect to pay around Y50 per person per day. If you don't find animals and can't carry your pack, consider hitching rather then suffering.

The road to Everest goes up the valley from Tashi Dzom, a long two day walk away. Engulfed by the enormity of the valley, the road passes through barley, pea and mustard fields spreading out in all directions. Twenty minutes out of Tashi Dzom the road splits; take the left or main branch. The right branch serves the nearby villages of Lha Shing and Rephel. **Lha Shing** was named after sacred ancient trees that grew on the slopes above the village, the last of which died 30 or 40 years ago. Rephel hosts the small Rabshi Monastery.

The trail reaches the hamlet of **Pelding**, 30 minutes beyond Rephel, and in another 45 minutes, **Puna**. Fifteen minutes past Puna, a rocky spur juts into the valley, this is the site of **Chetetong**, the ruined pre-Communist centre of power in the region. Traditionally, the Dzaka valley upstream of Tashi Dzom was known as Phadrug and was affiliated with the fortress at Shegar.

Forty-five minutes up the valley the road cuts through **Pasum**, the administrative centre for the upper Dzaka valley. In the middle of the village is the *Passum Pembah*

Teahouse-Hotel run by a man who knows some English. This well run shop, restaurant and hotel approaches the quality of service found in the smaller trekking lodges of Nepal. The restaurant serves momos, local vegetables, eggs, mutton, rice and noodles for Y5 to Y10 per plate. The lodge has 15 beds priced at Y20 and Y25 each.

Day 3: Upper Dzaka valley to Chö Dzom (3 hours)

In the hill behind Pasum is the tiny monastery of **Dzabug** with a small handful of

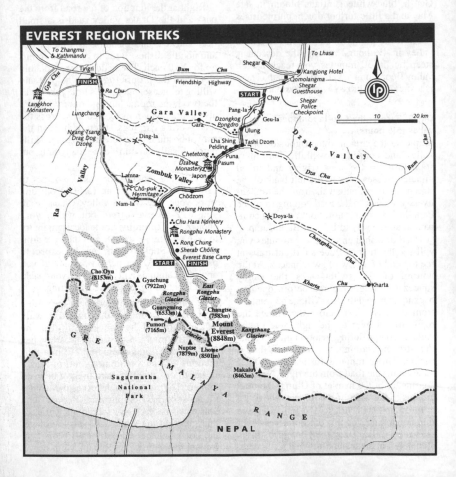

EVEREST REGION TREKS

The approach to Mt Everest Base Camp via Rongphu Monastery (middle) – inspirational scenery (bottom) and the awesome north face of the world's highest mountain (top).

Mt Kailash
Top: Kailash's dramatic north face. **Bottom left:** The west face viewed from the Mt Kailash kora.
Bottom right: The south face and the Tarboche flagpole.

STAN ARMINGTON

TONY WHEELER

TONY WHEELER

Everest Region
Top: The township of Tingri backed by Cho Oyu. **Middle:** Everest, Lhatse, Mokalau and Cho Oyu from Pang-la. **Bottom:** A common feature at high mountain passes – the mani stone.

Top: Prayer flags recite to the breeze off Lake Manasarovar. **Middle right:** Unburdening the beast, Mt Kailash kora. **Bottom right:** Monastery overlooking Lake Manasarovar. **Left:** Beautifully barren Nam-tso flanked by the majestic Tanglha Shan.

TONY WHEELER

TONY WHEELER

BRADLEY MAYHEW

GARRY WEARE

monks. Twenty minutes further the valley completes a big bend to the south. On the road, a small concrete bridge spans a stream coming from a valley in the west. This valley leads towards Tingri via the Ding-la, two days of walking away.

In 45 minutes the road passes the mouth of a valley leading east. Up this side valley via the Doya-la is a three or four day route to Kharta. Thirty minutes past this confluence you reach the village of **Japon**. Fifteen minutes further a recently built concrete bridge crosses to the east (left) side of the Dza Chu (also known in its upper reaches as the Rongphu Chu).

The valley now arcs to the west and is carpeted in lush meadows. One hour from the bridge is the uppermost agricultural village in the Dzaka valley, **Chö Dzom**. Operating out of the local school grounds is a *lodge*, *teahouse* and small shop. Beds here cost Y20. If you are camping move up the valley at least 30 minutes to skip being the village's feature entertainment for the evening. It is still a long day's walk from Chö Dzom to Everest Base Camp.

Out of Chö Dzom the road ascends a small slope and a trail diverges to the left. While the road remains in the valley bottom the trail crosses an inclined plain, reuniting with the road in 1¾ hours. The trail, a shorter walk, follows a south-west trajectory, turning south where it meets the road. Ninety minutes from Chö look right, up the mouth of the Zombuk valley – the pass at its head, the Lamna-la, leads to Tingri. Also on the west side of the Dzaka valley, 20 minutes onwards, is the remnants of the **Chö-puk Hermitage** nestled in an escarpment.

Day 4: Chö Dzom to Rongphu Monastery (3 hours) and Everest Base Camp (5 hours)

After the trail merges with the road, sheer rock slopes close in around the valley. After a few minutes walk, the valley leading to the Nam-la, the southernmost route to the plains of Tingri, is visible. In 20 minutes a bridge crosses over the Dza Chu, accessing the valleys to the passes. Just above the

bridge, a big tributary originating from the Gyachung massif flows into the Dza Chu.

It is still about 2½ hours to Rongphu and 4½ hours to Everest Base Camp. Twenty minutes further is a small spring and place to *camp* on the left side of the road. Another 30 minutes upstream, perched in a side valley to the left of the road, are the ruins of **Kyelung Hermitage**. Beyond here a wide, cairn-studded pilgrim's trail splits off the road, a less dusty walking option.

A stone stupa called the Khumbu Chörten is 30 minutes up the trail. Forty-five minutes further and the exquisite form of **Mt Everest** comes into view for the first time since you surmounted the Geu-la. The trail continues to ascend for 20 minutes and then drops into a deep stream bed. East of the trail, where the stream emerges from the defile, are the crumbling walls of the remains of the **Chu Hara Nunnery**. Up from the stream, the trail meets the road and wends its way through a cluster of morainal hills reaching the **Rongphu Monastery** in 30 minutes. At the last bend in the road the monastery suddenly comes into view with Everest as the all-encompassing backdrop.

For information on Rongphu Monastery and the two hour hike to Everest Base Camp see the Tsang chapter.

For highly fit and prepared groups it is possible to trek as far as Camp III. Including time for acclimatisation, allow one week for this trek. The route skirts the Rongphu Glacier until Camp I and then meets the East Rongphu Glacier at Camp II. This glacier must be crossed in order to reach Camp III (6340m). For more information on reaching the advanced camps see Gary McCue's *Trekking in Tibet – a traveler's guide*.

From Everest Base Camp you can either walk or hitch back to the Shegar-Nepal Highway. See the next trek for details on how to walk to Tingri.

EVEREST BASE CAMP TO TINGRI

Duration: 3 to 4 days
If you walked into Everest Base Camp from the highway near Shegar and are looking

for an alternative exit route consider the trek to Tingri. This is a three or four day walk through remote country where it is essential to be absolutely self-sufficient. (You may be able to buy some basic foodstuffs at the small shop at the Rongphu Monastery.)

Information

The route passes through an isolated valley on the way up to the pass of Nam-la and enters a region used by the herders and their livestock. Following the Ra Chu valley, the route swings north to the plains of Tingri. It is possible to do this trek in the opposite direction.

The trek via the Nam-la is the fastest route from Base Camp to Tingri, but if you are short on supplies or not so well equipped consider one of the alternative passes covered in Gary McCue's *Trekking in Tibet – a traveler's guide*. The longer routes may be preferable because they follow more of the main road, reaching villages where supplies might be bought – but don't count on finding much. Once you leave Rongphu Monastery there are no permanent settlements until well in reach of Tingri, three days away. Such an untravelled route is great for those who are up to a wilderness experience but is best missed by everyone else. Don't chance this trip unless you are really ready.

Getting to/from the Trek

See the previous trek to Everest Base Camp for information.

The Trek

Day 1: Rongphu Monastery to beyond the Nam-la (8½ hours)

The route to the Nam-la retraces the route taken to reach Everest Base Camp as far as the bridge over the Dza Chu two or more hours down the valley from the Rongphu Monastery. A trail angles down a steep embankment from the road to the bridge. Cross the bridge and look for the trail along the west bank of the river. Soon the trail ascends the embankment and emerges onto a shelf above the Dza Chu. In a few minutes the trail climbs further and traverses around

the base of a slope into the mouth of a side valley. You'll reach the mouth of this valley in 30 minutes from the bridge.

While the majority of the Dzaka valley is dry and barren this side valley is relatively luxuriant, hosting a variety of plants and shrubs and plenty of fresh water. This is a nice place to *camp* or take a long lunch break. The valley bends to the left as the trail to Nam-la leaves the valley floor and climbs past a corral onto a plain abutting the north (right) side of the valley. The route to the pass now bears west all the way to the summit, paralleling the valley floor. It is at least a 3½ hour hike to the pass.

As you begin your ascent towards the pass there is a saddle in the ridge bounding the north side of the valley – this is the most direct route to the Zombuk valley. Walk close to the ridge enclosing the north side of the valley. Past the corral there is no trail. The route clambers over rock-strewn shrubby terrain and then over big plates of tundra that fit together like a giant jigsaw puzzle. One hour from the corral, a steep slope blocks the view to the west. It takes 10 minutes to climb over this onto another broad tundra-covered pitch. In 10 more minutes you can see the head of the valley; however, the Nam-la is out of sight, tucked behind the folds in the ridge.

The route gradually levels out and in 15 minutes descends into a marshy side valley. There is a small stream in this valley, the last place you can count on for water until well beyond the pass. Look for a small corral on the far side of the side valley and bear to the left of it. Continue walking up for 10 minutes before gradually descending into the main valley floor in another 15 minutes.

Remain on the right side of the valley, taking the trail that steeply climbs towards the pass. The trail remains clear for 40 minutes until it is absorbed by the tussock-grass-studded valley floor. The pass is near where the ridge south of the valley bends around to the west. It is still 40 minutes from here to the Nam-la over alpine meadows, but the terrain is now much more open and the gradient less steep.

Proceeding west, looking out for the lowest point on the horizon. The **Nam-la** (5250m) is a very broad summit simply delineating the parting of drainage basins over a vast plain. There are a few small cairns on top, seen only when you are upon them. To the west, across a wide, wet downhill slope is a small valley bottom and the Ra Chu valley far beyond that. North of the Nam-la, with only a small summit in between, is the Lamna-la coming from the Zombuk valley.

Descend from the pass in a westerly direction over tussock grasses and tundra for one hour and cross the cart track coming from the Lamna-la. If the time is right you may see gazelles during your descent. From the cart track descend a precipitous slope into the valley floor. There are both springs and a stream in this swampy valley of grasses and wildflowers, a tributary of the Ra Chu. Great *campsites* are found on the drier margins of the valley. It is at least a five hour trek from here to the first village, Lungchang.

Day 2: Base of Nam-la to Lungchang (5 hours)

Do not follow the valley down and northward. It is easier to walk west to the ridge next to the valley and pick up the cart track. You can see the cart track cutting across the ridge from a group of corrals on the west side of the valley. The track goes all the way to Tingri, making route finding easy.

By tracing a north-west trajectory over the ridge the track avoids the swampy valley floor. Follow the cart track for 20 minutes, coming to a junction marked by a cairn. The foot trail to Lamna-la leaves the road here and goes east to intersect the valley. Leave the cart track and take the trail bearing north-west – this is a short cut which rejoins the main track in 15 minutes.

The short cut descends to cross the cart track and then merges with it after a switchback. Back in the valley bottom the track stays on the south (left) side of the valley, crossing a small stream coming from the south. This unbridged crossing may pose problems during heavy summer rains, in which case try to ford it in the early morning when the volume of water is lower.

The track angles across the middle of the stony valley and is very wide and straight, like a runway used by bush planes. In 30 minutes the track returns to the left side of the valley. Fifteen minutes further, it passes through a narrow constriction in the valley formed by a series of orange cliffs. Beyond the cliffs the valley turns north (right) and retains this bearing all the way to Tingri. A few minutes after emerging through the bottleneck look for a continuation of the track on the north bank of the stream. During summer rains carefully select a ford in the stream braids a little downstream of the track crossing.

The view to the north is now dominated by the blue or purple Tsebu Mountains. Tingri is in front of these mountains, south of the Bum Chu. The mostly sandy track unfolds along the east (right) bank of the stream for 45 minutes. It then ascends above the bank and traverses the side of a ridge with the stream running through a narrow channel directly below. Look south to see the glittering white Cho Oyu massif. In 30 minutes descend into the widening valley floor. In 10 more minutes cross a small side valley.

The track unrolls across a level shelf above the stream for 30 minutes before climbing over a small ridge that circumvents the gorge forming below. Just upstream of the gorge, the stream you've been following from the base of the pass flows into the much higher volume main branch of the Ra Chu which originates from the flanks of Cho Oyu. The summit of the ridge is marked with a cairn and prayer flags and takes 10 minutes to reach from the shelf.

From the summit the track descends to cross a side valley before ranging across a long, barren stretch of valley. In the distance you can see two rocky knobs at the end of the long east ridge line. It takes about one hour to reach the knobs. On top of them are the disintegrating walls of the long-abandoned fort **Ngang Tsang Drag Dog Dzong**. Thirty minutes after passing beneath the ramparts of the ancient fort you reach **Lungchang**, the first permanent settlement since Rongphu.

The cubicle two-story houses of Lungchang are impeccably whitewashed and decorated with red, blue and white stripes near their roof lines. Blocks of dung are neatly stacked on the roof between prayer flag masts. At the north end of the village, in one of the houses, is a small lodge and shop marked by a sign in English that reads *Leg Jang*. Simple meals and beds are usually available here or with other families in the village. It is still 3½ hours from Lungchang to Tingri and the highway.

Day 3: Lungchang to Tingri (3 hours)

From Lungchang, you can see several low-lying hills in the mouth of the Ra Chu valley – Tingri is at the foot of the northernmost of these. From Lungchang the track moves towards the middle of the valley, following a bluff along the edge of the Ra Chu. In 1½ hours it reaches the outskirts of the village **Ra Chu**. Before the village, at a white shrine, the track splits; the right, or main, branch goes to Tingri via Ra Chu village while the left fork jogs west and then north over wide pastures to Tingri. The left fork is the shorter route to Tingri and a more pleasant walk. The lower part of the Ra Chu valley is green during the warmer half of the year; extensive meadows support numerous flocks of goats and sheep. The homes of the shepherds dot the edges of the huge expanse of turf.

Fifteen minutes south of Ra Chu village you will pass ruins on the slopes bounding the east side of the valley – look back to see Everest pop up from behind the anterior ranges. The two tracks that split near Ra Chu village are reunited 45 minutes beyond the village.

Thirty minutes further, reach a bridge over the Ra Chu, which allows you to access the south side of Tingri. You can cross the Ra Chu here and pass through the village to the highway or remain on the right bank and cross the new highway bridge. It is only 15 minutes to the highway. If you stay on the right bank there is an irrigation ditch to cross below the shoulder of the highway.

For information on Tingri see the Tsang chapter. If you decide to trek into Everest from Tingri by reversing the direction in this trek description it is usually possible to hire yaks, guides and even pony carts in Tingri, though if you want to keep a low profile it might be better to organise this in Ra Chu.

MT KAILASH KORA
Duration: 3 days

The 53km circuit or kora of Mt Kora is one of the most important pilgrimages in Asia. See the Western Tibet chapter for an introduction to Mt Kailash and the kora as well as for further information on Darchen, the shabby little town which serves as a starting and finishing point for the walk. The usual Kailash trekking season runs from mid-May through mid-October but trekkers should be prepared for cold and changeable weather at any time. Snow may be encountered on the Drölma-la pass at any time of year and the temperature will often drop below freezing at night. The pass tends to be snowed in from early November to early April every year.

Information

Darchen PSB requires all foreigners to buy a permit for Y50 for the Kailash/Manasarovar region, possibly even if you already have one from Lhasa! Some travellers have apparently been fined for spending the night at Manasarovar before heading to Darchen to buy the permit. Check with your tour agency or Darchen or Ali PSB. Having paid Y50 to start the Kailash kora there's a checkpoint at the end where you have to pay another Y50 to finish it!

If you have a heavy backpack it is worth considering hiring a porter or yaks; the Darchen guesthouses can help makes arrangements and store gear while you are on the kora. Porters are usually friendly young guys who know the circuit well and typically cost about Y50 per day, perhaps less if you arrange it yourself in the village. If you hire yaks and yak drivers count on about Y25 per yak and another Y25 for each handler, yaks are skittish creatures which require expert management. Allow a couple of days to arrange for the yaks.

Instant noodles and a very limited range of other supplies are available at the shops in Darchen. A wider range of supplies are available in Ali to the north or Purang to the south.

If you do not have a tent the accommodation possibilities on the kora are very limited. There are primitive guesthouses associated with the Dira-puk and Zutul-puk monasteries, but they only have a half a dozen rooms each. During the Indian pilgrimage season tents are erected for the pilgrims near the two monasteries and it may be possible to get a bed in these tents. Very limited food may also be available at the guesthouses. If at all possible you should bring a tent since there is no guarantee you will find a room free or a bed available in a pilgrim tent. If you are equipped for camping, however, there are wonderful grassy campsites all around the kora and there is certainly no shortage of water. Fuel for cooking, however, is another matter. There is no wood and even yak dung is in short supply.

Getting to/from the Trek

For information on getting to/from Mt Kailash see the Western Tibet chapter.

The Trek

Day 1: Darchen to Dira-puk Monastery (6 hours)

The Kailash kora trail quickly leaves grubby Darchen behind, heading west along the base of the east-west ridge which blocks off views of the holy mountain. The vast Barkha plain spreads out to the south, Gurla Mandata (7728m) rises off to the south-east, Api and other peaks in Nepal to the south and the twin, sharp humps of Kamet (7756m) in India off to the south-west. Only a few km from Darchen the trail climbs up over the south-west end of the ridge to reach a cairn at 4730m after about an hour's walk. It's bedecked with prayer flags and marks the first views of the mountain's southern or sapphire face and a *chaktsal gang*, the first of the kora's four prostration

points. From here the more rounded profile of Nanda Devi (7816m) in India can also be seen, to the east of Kamet.

From this point the trail bends round to the north and enters the Lha Chu valley where the tall **Tarboche flagpole** soon comes into view. It's about an hour's walk to the flagpole at 4750m. The flagpole is replaced each year at the major festival of Saga Dawa marking Buddha's enlightenment on the full moon day of the fourth Tibetan month, falling in May-June on our calendar. How the flagpole stands when it is re-erected is of enormous importance. If it stands absolutely vertical all is well but if it leans towards Kailash things are not good, if it leans away, however, things are even worse.

Just to the west of the Tarboche is the 'two legged' **Chörten Kangnyi**, it's an auspicious act for pilgrims to walk through the small chörten's archway. The kora trail continues along the eastern bank of the Lha Chu but a

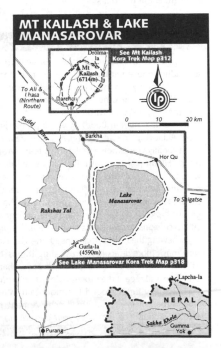

MT KAILASH & LAKE MANASAROVAR

short climb above the Tarboche is the **Sky Burial Site of the 84 Mahasiddhas**, revered as it was once reserved for monks and lamas. This eerie site is marked by numerous small rock cairns draped with clothing, shoes and locks of hair but visitors are unlikely to be welcome if a sky burial is underway. The first of the kora's three *shabje* or Buddha footprints is here but it's hard to find.

You can continue across this small plateau and descend back down to the kora trail and the river in the area known as Sershong. The valley narrows dramatically at Sershong with majestic hills falling down to the swift flowing Lha Chu and Mt Kailash appearing impressively above the eastern ridge. The trail passes a series of ruined chörtens and a number of long mani walls before arriving at a small bridge across the Lha Chu at 4710m. The bridge is less than an hour's walk from Tarboche or about three hours from Darchen and directly below the Chuku Monastery.

The **Chuku Monastery**, perched high above the valley floor at 4820m on the hillside to the west, blends secretively into its rocky background. All the Kailash monasteries were wrecked during the Cultural Revolution and the Chuku (or Nyenri) Monastery was the first to be rebuilt. It takes about 20 minutes to climb from the river bank up to the hillside monastery which was founded in the 13th century by Gotsangpa Gompo Pel, a Kgyupa order devotee. In the monastery's assembly hall, or *dukhang*, look up to the skylight for the mirror angled to perfectly frame a fine view of Mt Kailash. In a glass case over the altar there's a highly revered marble statue called Chuku Opame (originally from India and reputed to talk!) and a conch shell inlaid with silver. Beside the altar there's a copper pot and elephant tusks, as found in temples in Bhutan.

From the Chuku bridge there are alternative trails along the east and west banks of the river. The trail along the east bank is the

Which Direction, How Many Days, How Many Times, How Many Rivers?

These are the important questions for walking the 53km circuit – a kora if your pilgrimage is a Buddhist one, a parikrama if you're on a Hindu circuit – of Asia's most holy mountain. Buddhist or Hindu you should be walking the mountain in a clockwise direction, but if you meet walkers coming the other, counter-clockwise, way don't be surprised, they're followers of Bön, the ancient pre-Buddhist religion of Tibet.

If you're a Tibetan Buddhist you'll probably plan to complete the circuit in one hard day slog. Achieving this feat requires a pre-dawn start and a late evening return to Darchen. Occasionally westerners emulate this feat – Austrian Reinhold Messner recorded a time of 12 hours. Hindu pilgrims, with the odd ritual immersion in an icy cold lake to endure along the way, typically take three days, overnighting in encampments set up for them close to the Dirapuk and Zutul-puk monasteries. Independent western visitors usually aim for a three day circuit as well, staying at the gompa guesthouses at the same locations. Western trekking groups typically do the circuit in three or four days, a longer circuit allows time for side trips and excursions such as visits to the Kailash north-face glaciers.

Eschewing the normal high-speed one-day circuit, some very enthusiastic Tibetans make the walk much more difficult by prostrating themselves the entire way. They lie down at full length with their arms stretched over their heads, then stand up, place their feet where their hands ended up and repeat the process. Count on around three weeks to complete a prostration kora.

How many times around the mountain? Well at least once to wipe out the sins of a lifetime, although even that small achievement requires the right attitude pre-departure and perhaps a couple of checks of your current sin status at the 'sin testing stones' on the ascent

regular pilgrim route but the west side trail offers better views of the west face of Mt Kailash. Either way it's about another three hours to the Dira-puk Monastery. Trekking groups generally take the west side trail since there are some fine grassy *campsites* on the river banks at **Damding Donkhang** (4890m), about an hour before the monastery. The west or ruby face of Kailash makes a dramatic backdrop to this campsite and in the early morning Tibetan pilgrims will be seen striding resolutely past on the other side of the river, already well into their one-day circuit.

At points along the trail the west and north faces of the mountain can be seen together. The steep hillsides on both sides of the valley make this one of the most impressive stretches of the walk. Golden marmots, *piya* in Tibetan, regularly pop up out of their holes to peer worriedly at passing walkers. Many of the formations along this stretch have mythical connec-

tions, a number of them related to Tibet's legendary hero Gesar of Ling. The second prostration point is also encountered on the east side of the valley and the second Buddha footprint.

The **Dira-puk Monastery**, rebuilt in 1985, looks across to the north or gold face of Kailash from the hillside north of the Lha Chu. Walkers who have followed the Lha Chu's east bank trail will have to cross the river to reach the gompa and its guesthouse, at the base of the hill below. West bank walkers may also get their feet wet since they have to cross the Belung Chu and Dunglung Chu, tributaries of the Lha Chu, before they reach the monastery. The monastery takes its name from the female yak horn *(dira)* cave *(puk)* where Götsangpa meditated. It was Götsangpa who first discovered the kora route around Mt Kailash and he was led here by a yak which turned out to be the lion-faced dakini goddess who guards the Khando Sanglam-la. The main

Which Direction, How Many Days, How Many Times, How Many Rivers?

to the Drölma-la. Tibetans look upon three circuits as a much more satisfactory starting point and 13 as the real minimum. Like gold status for frequent fliers, completing 13 circuits also allows access to high status detours like the short cut over the Khando Sanglam-la pass or a visit to an inner kora or *nangkor* on the south side of the mountain. Real walkers should aim for 108 circuits which guarantees instant nirvana and a clean sin slate for all your lifetimes. Economisers should note that koras completed during a full moon are better than ordinary ones, ditto for koras during the Tibetan Year of the Horse (the next occasion is 2002).

And the rivers? Well it's a geographic quirk that four of the subcontinent's most important rivers all have their birth close to the base of Mt Kailash. The mighty Indus flows off to the west through Ladakh and the Pakistani held portion of Kashmir before turning south and flowing through the whole length of Pakistan and eventually emptying into the Arabian Sea to the east of Karachi. The Sutlej River also heads off to the west, flowing through the Indian states of Himachal Pradesh and Punjab then turning south-west into Pakistan and finally joining the Indus near Multan. Meanwhile, the Humla Karnali heads straight off to the south, cutting its way right across the Himalaya through western Nepal then turning east and, as the Ghaghara or Gogra, joining the mighty Ganges River just before Patna. Finally, the Yarlung Tsangpo flows eastward all the way across Tibet before bending south around the eastern-most end of the Himalaya and, as the Brahmaputra River, flowing through India and down into Bangladesh. The Ganges and Brahmaputra both empty into the Bay of Bengal in an extensive delta system between Calcutta and Dhaka, 2500 km east of the Indus' arrival into the Arabian Sea.

image in the dukhang is of Avalokiteshvara, flanked by images of the Buddha and a fearsome deity.

From the monastery there are superb views of the impressive north face of Mt Kailash. Three lesser mountains are arrayed in front of Kailash: Chana Dorje (Sanskrit: Vajrapani) to the west, Jampelyang (Manjushri) to the east and Chenresig (Avalokiteshvara) in the centre. The Kangkyam Glacier descends from the north face of Mt Kailash between Chana Dorje and Chenresig and it takes a couple of hours round trip to walk up to the

glacier. Hindu pilgrims usually camp near the monastery while independent walkers often overnight in the monastery's rather basic **guesthouse**, where a grubby mattress on the dirt floor will cost Y20.

Day 2: Dira-puk Monastery to Zutul-puk Monastery (6 hours)

The Lha Chu flows down the valley running north from Dira-puk, and Swami Pranavananda followed this valley up to the source of the Indus River, a two to three day

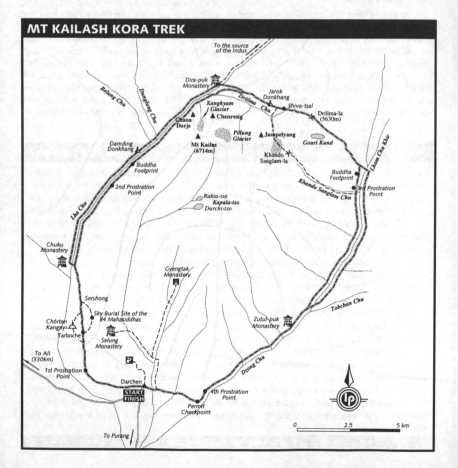

MT KAILASH KORA TREK

To the source of the Indus

Belung Chu

Dunglung Chu

Dira-puk Monastery

Drölma Chu

Jarok Donkhang

Shiva-tsal

Drölma-la (5630m)

Kangkyam Glacier

Chenresig

Chana Dorje

Pölung Glacier

Jampelyang

Gouri Kund

Lham Chu Khir

Damding Donkhang

Mt Kailas (6714m)

Khando Sanglam-la

Buddha Footprint

2nd Prostration Point

Rakta-tso
Kapala-tso
Durchi-tso

Khando Sanglam Chu

Buddha Footprint

3rd Prostration Point

Lha Chu

Chuku Monastery

Gyengtak Monastery

Sershong

Tobchan Chu

Sky Burial Site of the 84 Mahasiddhas

Zutul-puk Monastery

Chörten Kangnyi

Tarboche

Selung Monastery

To Ali (330km)

1st Prostration Point

Darchen

START FINISH

Dzong Chu

4th Prostration Point

Permit Checkpoint

To Purang

0   2.5   5 km

walk. Kora walkers, on the other hand, head off to the east, crossing the Lha Chu by a bridge and starting the long ascent up the Drölma Chu valley that will eventually lead to the Drölma-la pass. The route climbs on to a moraine and soon meets the trail from the east bank of the Lha Chu.

Less than an hour along this route some trekking groups *camp* on the meadow at **Jarok Donkhang** (5210m). Camping here makes the ascent to the Drölma-la on the following day a much easier task. It is not wise to camp any higher than Jarok Donkhang because of the risk of acclimatisation problems.

Another **glacier** descends from the eastern ridge off the north face of Mt Kailash, down the Pölung valley between Chenresig and Jampelyang. This glacier can also be reached in a couple of hours round trip from this campsite. You can follow the glacial stream which runs down the middle of the valley to merge with the Drölma Chu or avoid losing altitude from the campsite by terracing around the side of Jampelyang.

From here to the Drölma-la there is a constant parade of interesting points along the trail. Only a short distance above Jarok

Donkhang is **Shiva-tsal** (5330m), a rocky expanse dotted with stone cairns draped with items of clothing. Pilgrims are supposed to undergo a symbolic death at this point, leaving their old life behind along with an item of clothing to represent it. A drop of blood or a lock of hair might be even better. If you really do decide to drop dead at this point this is a very meritorious place to die. Right by the trail at the end of the Siva-tsal is a red footprint of Milarepa.

Nearby a trail branches off to the southeast, leading over the snow-covered **Khando Sanglam-la** pass, a shortcut to the east side of Mt Kailash which bypasses the normal route over the Drölma-la. Don't be tempted to take this route, only on your auspicious 13th kora is the pass open to you and intruders are likely to find themselves face to face with the pass's protector, the fearsome lion-faced dakini goddess.

Climbing beyond Siva-tsal the trail reaches the sin testing stone of **Bardo Trang**. A narrow passages squeezes beneath the flat stone and pilgrims are supposed to measure their sinfulness by wriggling under the stone. Fat or thin you may find yourself stuck under the rock if your sin quota is too high, in that

The Faces & Rivers of Kailash

It's easy to confuse the mystical Mt Kailash, the Mt Meru of legend reaching from the lowest hell to the highest heaven, with the real one. From the legendary Kailash a river flows into the legendary Manasarovar (Mapham yum-tso), from which flow four legendary rivers in the four cardinal directions. In reality there may not be any rivers flowing from Manasarovar but four real rivers do flow off in, more or less, the cardinal directions. And Kailash really does have four distinct faces.

direction	face	mythical river	real river
south	Sapphire (or Lapis Lazuli)	Mabja Kambab (River from the Peacock Mouth)	Karnali
west	Ruby	Langchan Kambab (River from the Elephant Mouth)	Sutlej
north	Gold	Seng-ge Kambab (River from the Lion Mouth)	Indus
east	Crystal	Tamchog Kambab (River from the Horse Mouth)	Yarlung Tsangpo (Brahmaputra)

case the sin washing powers of a Kailash kora may not be sufficient to clean up your karma. A little further along the much more convoluted passage under the **Dikpa Karnak** awaits those in need of a second opinion. Other points of interest along this stretch include a stack of stones marking where Milarepa and Naro Bönchung engaged in one of their contests of saintly one-upmanship. Naturally Milarepa's stone tops the pile.

Finally the trail turns to the east for the final 200m ascent to the 5630m **Drölma-la**, look south for your last glimpse of the north face of Mt Kailash. A small glacial trickle half way up presents your last sin washing opportunity before the top. Allow about an hour for the 200m climb to the wide and rocky pass, festooned with an enormous numbers of prayer flags strung from the **Drölma Do**, Drölma's Rock. Pilgrims perform a circumambulation, pasting money on to the rock with butter, stooping to pass under the lines of prayer flags and chanting the Tibetan pass-crossing mantra *ki ki so so, la gyalo* (ki ki so so – long life and happiness invocation, la gyalo – 'the gods are victorious') as they go. Naturally there's a tale associated with the pass's revered rock.

When Götsangpa, the Kailash kora's original discoverer, wandered into the lion-faced dakini's valley he was led back to the correct route by 21 wolves who were, of course, merely 21 emanations of Drölma, the goddess of mercy and protectress of the pass. Reaching the pass the 21 wolves merged into one and then merged into the great boulder. To this day Drölma helps pilgrims on the difficult ascent – it did seem easier than you expected didn't it? Drölma is another name for the goddess Tara, who in turn appears in white and green variations.

Weather permitting pilgrims and trekkers usually pause at the pass for a rest and refreshments before starting the steep descent. Almost immediately **Gouri Kund** lake (5608m; one of its Tibetan names translates as the Lake of Compassion) comes into view below. Hindu pilgrims are supposed to immerse themselves in the lake's green waters, breaking the ice if necessary. Tibetans, as is well known, have no truck with this bathing nonsense. It takes about an hour to make the long 400m descent across generally barren and rocky ground before reaching the grassy banks of the **Lham Chukhir** river. There's the remains of a stone hut where the trail meets the river, leaning up against a huge rock topped by the kora's third Buddha footprint.

As in the Lha Chu valley, on the western side of Mt Kailash, there are once again routes along both sides of the river. The east bank trail presents better views and follows firmer, less marshy, ground, but requires

Milarepa vs Naro Bönchung

All around the Kailash kora there's evidence of the long running contest for supremacy between Milarepa, the Buddhist poet-saint, and Naro Bönchung, the Bön master. In every encounter it was Milarepa who came out the victor, but despite this he still agreed to a final, winner-takes-all duel, a straightforward race to the top of the mountain. Mounting his magic drum Naro Bönchung immediately set out to fly to the summit, but despite his acolytes' urgings Milarepa didn't even bother getting out of bed. Finally, as the first rays of dawn revealed that Naro Bönchung was about to reach the top, Milarepa rose from his bed and was carried by a ray of light directly to the top. Shocked by this ultimate defeat his opponent tumbled off his drum, which skittered down the south face of the mountain, gouging the long slash marking Mt Kailash to this day. Hindu pilgrims call it the 'stairway to heaven'. Gracious in victory Milarepa decreed that Bön followers could continue to make their customary counter-clockwise circuits of Mt Kailash and also awarded nearby Bönri as their own holy mountain.

wading back across the river at some point. If you opt for that side keep an eye on the river level, which may become uncomfortably deep further south during the wetter months. Not far south a valley comes down from the Khando Sanglam-la to join the main trail. This valley provides the only glimpse of Mt Kailash's eastern or crystal face and the kora's third prostration point is at the valley mouth.

Trekking groups may decide to camp on the grassy west banks of the river somewhere along this stretch but walkers without tents will probably press on to the guest house at the **Zutul-puk Monastery** (4790m). The monastery is about two hour's walk along the valley. By this point the river has changed name to the Dzong Chu or 'Fortress River,' after the Tobchan Chu comes in from the east.

The miracle *(zutul)* cave *(puk)* which gives the monastery its name is at the back of the main hall. Milarepa is said to have

Kailash & Manasarovar Books

There are numerous books about Mt Kailash, Lake Manasarovar and the surrounding area but the gold star for Kailash enthusiasm has to go to the Indian author Swami Pranavananda. His numerous stays in the region between 1928 and 1947 normally lasted two to six months but included two visits which lasted a year. Not only did he complete 23 parikramas (circuits of the holy mountain), he also did 25 circuits of Lake Manasarovar, including seven when it was completely frozen over, and visited the source of all four holy rivers. He also sailed on the holy lake, made many scientific measurements and in 1949 published his findings in *Kailas Manasarovar*. It was reprinted in India in 1983 and you may be able to find a copy in a Kathmandu bookshop. Clearly Kailash trekking has become much easier in the past 50 or 60 years. Under the heading 'Highway Robbers, Firearms and Guides' the Swami suggests firing two or three blank shots into the air after sunset to frighten off 'any robber lurking in the neighbourhood'. The Kailash chapters in Lama Anagarika Govinda's *The Way of the White Clouds* (Rider, London, 1966) includes a classic account of the pilgrimage during a trip to Tibet in 1948.

Each year several hundred Indian pilgrims are allowed to visit Mt Kailash and the Indian government selects the lucky candidates by a lottery. Since the Chinese charge US$500 per person the pilgrimage is only open to wealthy Indians but they have plenty of guidebook possibilities. Kathmandu bookshops will probably have several titles on their shelves including *Kailash-Manasarovar – A Travelogue & Yatra Guide* by Dipti Sharad (Dipta Publications, Chennai, 1998). The author advises on everything from suitable supplies to how to ride a yak and even wags a warning finger at Indian gentlemen who may 'suffer from the wrong notion that the women in the group should be responsible for the cooking'.

Kathmandu bookshops may also have Sven Hedin's three volume *Transhimalaya: Discoveries & Adventures in Tibet* (London, 1909-13). Volumes II and III cover his time in the Kailash region. Charles Allen's *A Mountain in Tibet* investigates the hunt for the sources of the Kailash region's four great rivers. *The Sacred Mountain* by John Snelling reports on not only the early western explorers but also the colourful list of characters who turned up in the early 1980s, when the door to China and Tibet first creaked narrowly open. *Kailas – On Pilgrimage to the Sacred Mountain of Tibet* by Kerry Moran with photos by Russell Johnson is a beautifully photographed essay on Mt Kailash, Lake Manasarovar and the region's colourful pilgrims. *Walking to the Mountain* by Wendy Teasdill is a delightfully laid back account of the author's lengthy pilgrimage to Kailash, a far from easy task when she went there in 1988.

Prostrations Points & Footprints

Really serious pilgrims may make the kora in continuous prostrations but even the least dedicated will prostrate themselves at the four major prostration points or *chaktsal gang*. If you want to join them quickly touch your joined hands to forehead, mouth and heart then stretch full length with your arms extended. The kora is also dotted with important footprints and *shabje*. The Buddha's are the most important of course, but you may also come across indications that Milarepa and other notables have set foot on the trail.

meditated in this cave, which was also the site of yet another confrontation between the Buddhist poet-saint and his Bön opponent. Needing shelter from the rain they agreed to jointly construct a cave but when Milarepa casually put the roof in place, without waiting for Naro Bönchung to make the walls, it was yet another easy victory for Buddhism. Milarepa then decided the roof was too high and went outside and pressed it down with his foot, leaving a footprint. Back inside he realised he'd pushed it too far, but some more shoving from below adjusted things to his satisfaction. His hand and head prints can be seen on the cave ceiling but the gompa roof covers the footprint atop the cave.

The monastery *guesthouse* is primitive, but probably in slightly better shape than the one at Dira-puk. Cost per bed is typically Y20.

Day 3: Zutul-puk Monastery to Darchen (2-3 hours)

The final day's walk only takes two to three hours and starts with the easy stroll down to where the river emerges on to the Barkha plain. The valley narrows and at times the sere valley sides look like something from the American southwest or Australian outback, were it not for the prayer flags fluttering across the river.

Where the trail emerges on to the plains, close to the fourth prostration point (4610m), there's a permit checkpoint where westerners are charged another Y50 for their kora. Gurla Mandata once more provides a backdrop to the lake Rakshas Tal (Lhanag-

tso). There's a rough road from here back to Darchen but it's less than an hour's walk, passing many mani walls embellished with yak skulls en route.

LAKE MANASAROVAR KORA

Duration: 4 to 5 days

Tucked away in the extreme south-west corner of Tibet near Mount Kailash, Lake Manasarovar (Tibetan: Mapham yum-tso; 4560m) is one of the country's most sacred and beautiful lakes. Just 20km from Kailash across the Barkha plain, Manasarovar can be circumambulated in four or five days. Five of the original eight monasteries have been partially rebuilt.

Information

Don't expect to find many supplies locally – bring everything you need. May, June and September are the best months to visit. July and August are also good months but in some years they are very wet. A tent and stove are required on this trek and be prepared for any kind of weather any time. Strong winds often hit in the afternoons so plan on doing most of your walking in the morning.

The kora trek, save for a spell on the north side, follows the shores of the lake. The route alternates between sandy, gravelly and marshy ground. Manasarovar is often a gem-like cobalt blue colour but during storms it can turn into a churning black sea. High elevation lends it a radiance unmatched by lower lakes and its fresh waters are as clear as can be.

According to ancient Hindu and Buddhist cosmology the four great rivers of the Indian

Subcontinent, the Indus, Ganges, Sutlej and Brahmaputra, arise from Manasarovar. In reality, only the Sutlej River originates at the lake, though the headwaters of the other great rivers are in close proximity.

Manasarovar is linked to the smaller lake Rakshas Tal (also known as Lhanag-tso) by a channel called Ganga Chu: these two bodies of water are associated with the conjoined sun and moon, a powerful symbol of tantric Buddhism. Sadly the sacred landscape of the lake has lately been disturbed by the construction of a large mine dug by bulldozers on the isthmus between the two lakes.

Manasarovar has been circumambulated by Indian pilgrims at least since being extolled in the sacred Sanskrit literature called the *Puranas* written around 1700 years ago. According to one Hindu interpretation, Manas refers to the mind of the supreme god Brahma, the lake being its outward manifestation. This helps explain the lake's popularity among Indian saints and sages. Legend has it that the mother of the Buddha, Queen Maya, was bathed at Manasarovar by the gods before giving birth to her son.

At the end of the 10th century the founder of the west Tibet Guge Dynasty, Nyima Gön, subjugated the indigenous *lhadre* spirits here, paving the way for the founding of his kingdom. In the first half of the 20th century the great Indian saint Swami Pranavananda made more than one dozen trips to Manasarovar, befriending lamas, bandits and commoners alike. His book *Kailas Manasarovar* is still one of the most authoritative accounts of this region and, with detailed route descriptions, it is of special interest to trekkers.

Getting to/from the Trek

There is no public transport throughout Western Tibet. You will have made it this far either by hitching or by hiring a Land Cruiser. If you are hitching you should be aware of the permit restrictions in this region. See the Western Tibet chapter for more details.

The Trek

The best place to start the Manasarovar circuit is at the north-west corner near **Chiu Monastery**. The road from Kailash comes within a kilometre of here. Chiu (Little Bird) Monastery sits astride a crag overlooking the lake and enshrines a cave said to have been used by Guru Rinpoche at the end of his life.

The fantastic view from the top of the monastery helps put the trek in perspective – there are not many treks of this duration where the entire route is visible from the start point. At the base of the monastery are two *shops* selling basic foodstuffs. Nearby, at the edge of the Ganga Chu, are hot springs great for washing. Some of the eroded stone walls in the vicinity are part of a pre-Buddhist archaeological site.

Day 1: Chiu Monastery to Hor Qu (7½ hours)

As per Buddhist tradition, head in a clockwise direction from Chiu, travelling east along the north shore. You will pass mani stones nearly 2m tall. The trail soon leaves the waterline and ascends over the top of a red escarpment for two hours. The cliffs below are sprinkled with caves used by religious practitioners for centuries. Some of these caves have been converted into permanent homes. From the grass capped, rolling top of the escarpment the route descends into a small vale where you can see the ruins of **Cherkip Monastery**; at this point you're a little over two hours from Chiu Monastery.

From Cherkip it is faster to follow the trail east over the headlands to **Langbona Monastery**, a 90 minute walk. There is also a lake shore route past more caves and cliffs. When the escarpment ends look for the trail going north along the Gyuma valley to Langbona on the west bank of the Gyama Chu.

East of Langbona the route traverses a marshy plain to the settlement of Hor Qu four hours away. There are *campsites* along the watercourses before Hor Qu so this does not have to be a long day.

Look for a series of tracks heading towards the distant margin of the plain. Under no circumstances return to the edge of the lake from Langbona. The swamps along this part of the lake shore give way to several lakes which flow into Manasarovar, effectively blocking the route to all but birds and fish.

Hor Qu is the administrative centre of the area and there are a couple of *shops* here that sell beer, soda, instant noodles and other basics. There is a *guesthouse* in Hor Qu used by Indian pilgrims; beds here cost Y20 each.

Day 2: Hor Qu to Seralung Monastery (3 hours)

The trail from Hor Qu leaves the settlement in a south-westerly direction, avoiding the extensive swamps abutting the lake. A little south of Hor Qu you cross the bridge over the **Samui Chu** – the main road east initially follows this valley. South of the swampy

tracts, the trail rejoins the lake shore along a stone beach. Look out for white-and-black polished stones, sacred to both Buddhists and Hindus.

The route is squeezed between the water and a cliff before a side valley and the **Seralung Monastery** appear. Rebuilt in the mid-1980s, Seralung (Hailstone Valley) Monastery is run by an able-bodied householder monk. Some of the monastery's religious property thrown into Manasarovar during the Cultural Revolution has been recovered. The valley here is a good place to *camp*.

Day 3: Seralung Monastery to Trugo Monastery (7 hours)

At first the route south of Seralung stays near the lake shore but in about one hour the mountains retreat and a plain forms next to Manasarovar. The trail moves inland about

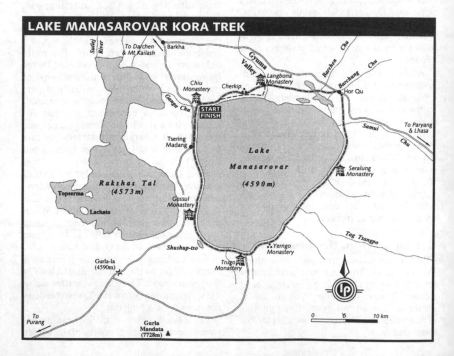

LAKE MANASAROVAR KORA TREK

1km and crosses the bridge over the **Tag Tsangpo** about three hours from Seralung. Up this valley are extensive hot springs and geysers as well as ancient Bön and Buddhist sites.

About three hours from the Tag Tsangpo bridge you will round the south side of Manasarovar and reach the ruined **Yerngo Monastery** situated in a broad plain. This is spacious country ideal for those looking for secluded *campsites*. South of the plain the massive flanks of the **Gurla Mandata** (7728m) massif rise up to a heavily glaciated summit. In Buddhist tradition Gurla Mandata (called Menmo Nanyi in Tibetan) is the dwelling place of the goddess of wisdom, Saraswati. However, in the older Bön tradition the mountain is the home of the Queen of the Dralha, an important class of ancient warrior deities.

You will reach **Trugo Monastery** after another hour. Trugo is the only monastery at either Kailash or Manasarovar belonging to the Gelugpa order. Trugo (Bathing Head) is so named because of its importance as a place for ritual bathing. Kailash seems to embrace the lake from this angle, lending credence to ancient myths which speak of the two representing a god and goddess in union. Large by local standards, Trugo has both a *shop* and *hostel* and is a fine place to take a day or two off to enjoy the atmosphere. You can get a bed here for about Y20.

Days 4 & 5: Trugo Monastery to Chiu Monastery (9 hours)

From Trugo a motorable track shoots over the range of hills south-west of the lake to join the Purang-Darchen road, but the kora route stays near the lake shore. Eventually swampy ground gives way to sandy expanses near the south-west corner of Manasarovar. The trail passes between the lake and the much smaller Shushup-tso along a narrow sand and gravel bridge. Two hours from Trugo you'll round the west side of the lake two hours from Trugo; continue walking along the beach for two more hours to Gossul Monastery.

Gossul Monastery sits on top of a cliff and is best known as the place where the

great Kargyud saint Gotsangpa meditated. On the lake shore below the monastery are a couple of caves used by pilgrims to camp. Retreat caves are found on the circuit around the monastery. The kora follows the lake shore to the Tsering Madang valley three hours away. You can crash out in the *guesthouse* here unless the authorities have been coming down particularly hard on individual travellers. From here it is two more hours back to Chiu along the beach.

OTHER TREKS IN TIBET

In a country as wild as Tibet there is no shortage of treks. If you've done the more popular ones and want to move on to something else have a look at Keith Dowman's *The Power Places of Central Tibet* and Victor Chan's *Tibet Handbook – a pilgrimage guide*. These books are loaded with interesting places suited for trekking. If you decide to venture far afield carefully select your trekking partners and try to hire a local guide. A good guide can show you things you would probably never find otherwise.

When visiting more remote and sacred places in Tibet put extra thought and time into respecting the land and its people – this way the next batch of trekkers finds a warm welcome. Authorities and the tourist agencies will tell you that the only way to go is with them, but in the spirit of true adventure try it without them. This is a tougher option but, then again, real benefits don't often come cheaply.

Here are just a couple more walks beckoning trekkers.

Nam-tso

Nam-tso, the 2000 sq km lake north of Lhasa, offers interesting possibilities for well equipped walkers. Reposing on the north slope of the trans-Himalaya, Nam-tso occupies the south-east corner of the Changtang, the almost endless northern plains of Tibet. Trekking anywhere on the Changtang demands special preparation as this is the coldest, most windswept and unpredictable part of Tibet. Blizzards can even hit in the middle of the summer, so watch it!

The easiest trek to Nam-tso is by way of the Largen-la (5150m), following the road up from Damxung. It takes about two days to reach the south shore of the lake at Tashi Do. Tashi Do, the site of a Buddhist hermitage, was a Bönpo stronghold until it was conquered by the monks of Taglung Monastery 700 years ago.

Another way to Nam-tso from the Damxung valley is via the Kong-la (5240m). This excellent circuit of about one week takes in both the Kong-la and Largen-la. This is a demanding and remote route over the trans-Himalaya and is best done with a guide. There is a circuit around Nam-tso, a journey of 18 or more days, but this is a long and difficult trip which should only be attempted by highly experienced trekkers who also have the right language skills. Going around the lake is not possible during heavy summer rains – streams coming from the flanks of the trans-Himalaya turn into impassable torrents at this time.

For those who want highly detailed information on Nam-tso see *Divine Dyads: Ancient Civilisations in Tibet* (Library of Tibetan Works and Archives, Dharmsala) by John V Bellezza.

Language

The two principal languages of Tibet are Tibetan and (Mandarin) Chinese. The importance of Chinese is an unfortunate reality in Tibet, and all Tibetans undertaking higher studies do so in Chinese. In fact, in urban Tibet – the countryside is another matter – almost all Tibetans speak Chinese. Nevertheless, even if you have studied or picked up some Chinese in China, it is worth trying to get a few phrases of Tibetan together. It will be much appreciated by Tibetans you encounter on your travels.

Chinese and Tibetan have little in common linguistically. They use different sentence structures, and the tonal element in Tibetan is far less crucial to conveying meaning than it is in Chinese. Also, unlike the dialects of China (and Japanese, Korean and Vietnamese), Tibetan does not and never has used Chinese characters for its written language.

Tibetan

Tibetan is classed as belonging to the Tibeto-Burman family of languages. It differs in many ways from Chinese, having a different written language, a different grammar and being non-tonal. Lhasa dialect, which is the standard form of Tibetan, does employ a system of rising and falling tones, but the differences are subtle and meaning is made clear by context. Beginners need not worry about it.

Grammar

Like Chinese, Tibetan has no articles (a/the) and doesn't use plurals. Here the similarity ends, however. Tibetan differs from European and Chinese languages in employing a subject-object-verb sentence structure. Thus, where in English we would say *I* (subject) *see* (verb) *John* (object), in Tibetan the sentence is rendered *nga*, 'I' (subject) *John* (object) *thong gi duk*, 'see' (verb). In another marked difference with Chinese, Tibetan also has tenses and conjugates its verbs with particles. There's also a fairly complicated system of prepositions (in, on, at etc) in Tibetan.

If all this makes Tibetan sound extremely difficult to pick up on the road, don't fret; providing you relax a little, it's fairly easy to get together a basic repertoire of phrases that will win you friends and help to get things done.

Written Language

The Tibetan script was developed during the reign of Songtsen Gampo in the 7th century. It was founded on Indian models and comprises 30 basic letters (each of which may be written in three different styles depending on the context in which a text is to be used), including the vowel 'a', and four extra vowel signs for 'e', 'i', 'o' and 'u'. This 7th century Tibetan script was based on the language that was spoken in Tibet at the time, and spellings have never been revised since. This means that, due to significant changes in spoken Tibetan over the last 12 centuries, written Tibetan and spoken Tibetan are very different, making the development of a transliteration system for speakers of European languages a formidable task.

Romanisation

There is no commonly accepted romanisation system for Tibetan. Some academic texts use a romanisation system that is based on written Tibetan, but for those who have not studied the written language of Tibet the results are usually unintelligible. Some examples of this system include: Drepung (Monastery), which is rendered as *bras spungs*; Gyantse, which is rendered as *rgyal rtse*; and Shigatse, which is rendered as *gzhis ka rtse*. It's the kind of system that works best in the cloistered halls of academia and simply won't do in the real world.

The alternative, then, to basing romanised Tibetan on the written language is to base it on contemporary Lhasa dialect as it is spoken. This is what most writers on the subject of Tibet generally do, and already certain standards have begun to emerge. Most guides and histories, for example, use the same spellings for cities and towns (Lhasa, Shigatse, Gyantse etc) and for major geographical features. In the case of less well known Tibetan place names, however, there's a lot of disagreement in English sources.

In this book we have tried not to introduce new complexities to the various spellings available and have generally chosen the most widely used term. In cases where there is wide disagreement, we have chosen the spelling that's easiest to pronounce.

Phrasebooks

Naturally, the best way to approach these difficulties is to work through a phrasebook with a native speaker or with a tape. Lonely Planet publishes a useful *Tibetan Phrasebook* which includes sections on trekking, visiting temples and handicrafts. The *Tibetan Phrasebook* (Snow Lion 1987) is another excellent phrasebook which comes with a tape. In Lhasa's Barkhor Square look out for an orange paperback *Say it in Tibetan*, which also comes with a tape.

Pronunciation

Like all foreign languages Tibetan has its fair share of tricky sounds. There are quite a few consonant clusters, and Tibetan is a language (like Korean and Thai) that makes an important distinction between aspirated and non-aspirated consonants.

Vowels

The following pronunciation guide is based on standard British pronunciation – North Americans beware.

a	as the 'a' in 'father'
ay	as the 'ay' in 'play'
e	as the 'e' in 'met'
ee	as the 'ee' in 'meet'
i	as the 'i' in 'begin'

o	as the 'o' in 'slow'
oo	as the 'oo' in 'soon'
ö	as in German, like the 'u' in 'put'
u	as the 'oo' in 'woo'
ü	as in German, like the 'u' in 'flute'

Consonants

With the exception of the consonants listed below, Tibetan consonants should be pronounced as in English. Where consonants are followed by an 'h', it means that the consonant is aspirated (accompanied by a puff of air). An English example might be 'kettle', where the 'k' is aspirated and the 'tt' is non-aspirated. The distinction is fairly important, but in simple Tibetan the context should make it clear what you are talking about even if you get the sounds muddled up a bit.

ky	as the 'kie' in 'Kiev'
ng	as the 'ng' in 'sing'
r	like a slight trilled Spanish 'r'
ts	as the 'ts' in 'bits'

Pronouns

I	*nga*
you	*kerang*
he, she	*khong*
we	*nga-tso*
you all	*kerang-tso*
they	*khong-tso*

Useful Phrases

Hello.
   tashi dele   བཀྲ་ཤིས་བདེ་ལེགས
Goodbye.
(when staying)
   kale phe   ག་ལེ་ཕེབས
Goodbye.
(when leaving)
   kale shoo   ག་ལེ་བཞུགས
Thank you.
   thoo jaychay   ཐུགས་རྗེ་ཆེ
Yes, OK.
   la ong   ལགས་འོང
Sorry.
   gonda   དགོངས་དག
I want ...
   nga la ... go   ང་ལ ... དགོས

I don't understand.
ha ko ma song ཧ་གོ་མ་སོང་
Do you understand?
ha ko song-ngey? ཧ་གོ་སོང་ངས་
I understand.
ha ko song ཧ་གོ་སོང་
How much?
ka tsö ray? ག་ཚོད་རེད་
It's expensive.
gong chenpo ray གོང་ཆེན་པོ་རེད་

What's your name?
kerang gi ming la karey zer gi yö?
ཁྱེད་རང་གི་མིང་ལ་ག་རེ་ཟེར་གྱི་ཡོད་
My name is ... and you?
ngai ming-la ... sa, a- ni kerang-gi ming-la karey zer gi yö?
ངའི་མིང་ལ་...ཟ། ཨ་ནི། ཁྱེད་རང་གི་མིང་ལ་ག་རེ་ཟེར་གྱི་ཡོད་
Do you speak English?
injeeke shing gi yö pe?
དབྱིན་ཇི་སྐད་ཤེས་ཀྱི་ཡོད་པས་
Is it OK to take a photo?
par gyabna digiy-rebay?
པར་བརྒྱབ་ན་འགྲིག་གི་རེད་པས་

Where are you from?
kerang lung-pa ka-ne yin?
ཁྱེད་རང་ལུང་པ་ག་ནས་ཡིན་
I'm from ...
nga ... ne yin
ང་...གྲ་ནས་ཡིན་
Australia
Ausitaliya
ཨོསི་ཊ་ལི་ཡ་
Canada
Canada
ཁེ་ནཌ་
France
farensi
ཕ་རན་སི་
Germany
jarman
འཇར་མན་
New Zealand
shinshilen
ཞི་ནུ་རྫོ་ལནྡ་

UK
injee lungpa
དབྱིན་ཇི་ལུང་པ་
USA
amerika
ཨ་མེ་རི་ཀ།

Accommodation

Where is ...?
... kaba du?
... ག་པར་འདུག
a guesthouse/inn
dhön khang
མགྲོན་ཁང་
a hotel
dru-khang/fandian
འགྲུལ་ཁང་
Do you have a room?
kang mi yöpe?
ཁང་མི་ཡོད་པས་
How much is it for one night?
tsen chik la katsö ray?
མཚན་གཅིག་ལ་ག་ཚོད་རེད་
I'd like to stay with a Tibetan family.
nga phöbe mi-tsang nyamdo dendö yö
ང་བོད་པའི་མི་ཚང་མཉམ་དུ་བསྡད་འདོད་ཡོད་
I need some hot water.
nga la chu tsapo go
ང་ལ་ཆུ་ཚ་པོ་དགོས་
boiling water
chu körma
ཆུ་འཁོལ་མ་

Getting Around

Where is the bus going?
(mota diy) kaba drugiy ray?
མོ་ཊ་འདི་ག་པར་འགྲོ་གི་རེད་
Will it go to ...?
diy...-la drugiy rebay?
འདི་...ལ་འགྲོ་གི་རེད་པས་
Is this bus going to (Ganden monastery)?
mota di (ganden gompa) drugiy rebay?
མོ་ཊ་འདི་(དགའ་ལྡན་དགོན་པ་) འགྲོ་གི་རེད་པས་

I want to go to...
nga ... la drondö yö
ང ... ལ་འགྲོ་འདོད་ཡོད
Can I get there on foot?
phagay gompa gyab-nay leb thub-kiy rebay?
ཕ་གིར་གོམ་པ་བརྒྱབ་ནས་སླེབས་ཐུབ་ཀྱི་རེད་པས
I'm getting off.
nga phap-gi yin
ང་འབབ་ཀྱི་ཡིན
What time do we leave?
ngatso chutsö katsö la dro-gi yin?
ང་ཚོ་ཆུ་ཚོད་ག་ཚོད་ལ་འགྲོ་གྱི་ཡིན
What time do we arrive?
ngatso chutsö katsö la lep-gi ray?
ང་ཚོ་ཆུ་ཚོད་ག་ཚོད་ལ་སླེབ་ཀྱི་རེད
What time is the ... bus?
mota ... chutsö katsay-la drogiy ray?
མོ་ཊ ... ཆུ་ཚོད་ག་ཚོད་ལ་འགྲོ་གི་རེད

next
jema-te རྗེས་མ་དེ་
first
tangpo-te དང་པོ་དེ་
last
thama-te མཐའ་མ་དེ་

airport
nam-tang གནམ་ཐང་
bus
basay/ འབའ་ས་/
mota/ མོ་ཊ་/
lamkhor ལྷངས་འཁོར་
bicycle
kanggari ཀང་སྒ་རི་ལ

Where can I get a bicycle?
kanggari kaba ragi ray?
ཀང་སྒ་རི་ལ་གཡར་ས་ག་པར་ཡོད་རེད
How much per day?
nyima chik-la gong katsö ray?
ཉིན་མ་གཅིག་ལ་གོང་ག་ཚོད་རེད
I'm lost.
nga lam khag lag song
ང་ལམ་ག་བརླགས་སོང

Signs

DANGER
nyen-ka ཉེན་ཁ
ENTRANCE
zu-sa འཛུལ་ས་
EXIT
donsa དོན་ས་
STOP
kah kag ཁ་བཀག
OPEN
ko-chay སྒོ་ཕྱེ
CLOSED
ko-gyab སྒོ་བརྒྱབ
NO PHOTOGRAPHS
pa gyab michok པར་བརྒྱབ་མི་ཆོག
NO SMOKING
tama ten michok ཐ་མག་འཐེན་མི་ཆོག
TOILETS
sang cho གསང་སྤྱོད་

Where is the ...?
... kaba yo ray? ... ག་པར་ཡོད་རེད

right
yeba གཡས་པ
left
yönba གཡོན་པ
straight ahead
shar gya ཤར་ཀྱག
north/south
chang/lo བྱང་/ལྷོ
east/west
shar/noop ཤར་ /ནུབ
porter
dopo khur khen དོ་པོ་ཁུར་མཁན
pack animals
kel semchen/ ཁལ་སེམས་ཅན་/
kelma ཁལ་མ
yak
ya གཡག

Geographical Terms

road/trail
  lam ལམ་
mountain
  ree རི་
cave
  puk/trapoo ཕུག་ཕུག
pass
  la ལ
river
  chu/tsangpo ཆུ་/གཙང་པོ
valley
  loong shon ལུང་གཤོང་
lake
  tso མཚོ
hot spring
  chu-tsen ཆུ་ཚན

Health

I'm sick.
  nga bedo mindu
  ང་བདེ་པོ་མིན་འདུག
Please call a doctor.
  amjee ke tangronang
  ཨེམ་རྗེ་ཞིག་སྐད་གཏོང་རོགས་གནང་།

hospital
  menkang སྨན་ཁང་
diarrhoea
  troko she-wa གྲོད་ཁོག་བཤལ་བ
fever
  tsawa ཚ་བ

Time

What's the time?
  chutsö katsö ray?
  ཆུ་ཚོད་ག་ཚོད་རེད།
... hour ... minute
  ... chutsö ... karma
  ... ཆུ་ཚོད་ ...སྐར་མ
When?
  kadü? ག་དུས
now
  thanda ད་ལྟ

today
  thiring དེ་རིང་
tomorrow
  sangnyi སང་ཉིན

yesterday
  kesa ཁ་སང
morning
  shogay ཞོགས་སྐད
afternoon
  nying gung gyab la ཕྱི་དྲོ་/ཉིན་དགུང་རྒྱབ་ལ
evening/night
  gonta དགོང་དག

Numbers

1	*chik*	གཅིག
2	*nyi*	གཉིས
3	*sum*	གསུམ
4	*shi*	བཞི་
5	*nga*	ལྔ
6	*troo*	དྲུག
7	*dün*	བདུན
8	*gye*	བརྒྱད
9	*gu*	དགུ
10	*chu*	བཅུ
11	*chu chik*	བཅུ་གཅིག
15	*cho nga*	བཅོ་ལྔ
18	*chob gye*	བཅོ་བརྒྱད
20	*nyi shu (tsa)*	ཉི་ཤུ་ (ཚ)
21	*nyi shu tsa chik*	ཉི་ཤུ་ཚ་གཅིག
30	*sum shu (so)*	སུམ་བཅུ་ (སོ)
40	*shi chu (zhe) chig*	བཞི་བཅུ་ (ཞེ)
50	*nga chu (nga)*	ལྔ་བཅུ་ (ང)
60	*troo chu (ray)*	དྲུག་བཅུ་ (རེ)
70	*dun chu (don)*	བདུན་བཅུ་ (དོན)
80	*gye chu (gya)*	བརྒྱད་བཅུ་ (གྱ)
90	*gu chu (go)*	དགུ་བཅུ་ (གོ)
100	*chik gya*	གཅིག་བརྒྱ
200	*ngi gya*	ཉིས་བརྒྱ
1000	*chik tong*	ཆིག་སྟོང

one million *saya-chig/* སཡ་གཅིག་/
  bum chu འབུམ་བཅུ

Chinese

The official language of China is Mandarin, which in Chinese is usually referred to as *pǔtōnghuà*. This term means literally 'common speech' and is taught throughout China as a linguistic standard for the many dialect and minority-language speakers of China. It is based on, though by no means the same as, the dialect spoken in Beijing and much of northern China.

Dialect speakers of Chinese have a huge head start in learning Mandarin over speakers of non-Chinese languages such as Tibetans. For a start, all Chinese dialects (and some are as different as Dutch and German) share the same written language. Many Westerners understandably find this puzzling. It has to do with the simplicity of Chinese grammar and the fact that all Chinese words are represented not by a phonetic script but by ideographs, or characters. While a character contains a single idea it might be read in various ways: thus the characters for American in Mandarin read *meiguoren*, in Cantonese *meigwokyan*, and in Hokkienese *bigoklang*. In terms that make more sense to westerners, think of the numbers from one to 10; now think of them again in French or German. The Arabic numerals we use operate in much the same way for us that characters do for the Chinese.

Dialect speakers have other advantages in learning Mandarin of course. All Chinese dialects are tonal and share many grammatical characteristics. Speakers of non-Chinese languages who choose (or in the case of Tibetans are forced) to learn Chinese are confronted with a language in which they have to master a difficult tonal system and get several thousand characters under their belt if they want to be literate.

Grammar

This is the easy bit. If Chinese were a non-tonal language it would be as easy to put together a travel vocabulary for China as it is for Indonesia. There are no articles (a, the), no tenses and no plurals. In fact, once you cotton on to the idea that constructing a Chinese sentence is simply a matter of stringing words together, you can make a lot of progress very quickly.

The important thing to bear in mind is that Chinese, like English, follows a subject-verb-object sentence structure. Thus Chinese constructs the sentence 'I (subject) go (verb) to the shop' (object) the same way as English but without the preposition (to) and the article (the): *wô* (subject) *qù* (verb) *shāngdiàn* (object).

Those travelling from China into Tibet or from Tibet onwards into China are well advised to pick up a Chinese phrasebook such as Lonely Planet's *Mandarin Chinese Phrasebook*. It should help you through most of your travel needs, both in Tibet and China.

Tones

As already mentioned, the dialects of China are tonal. In other words, every Chinese morpheme (the basic building blocks of meaning) has a tonal value. In Mandarin there are four of these tones. Other dialects generally have more; Cantonese, for example, has six or nine depending on how zealously you count.

Tones are a real mental block for many students of Chinese. Yet all of the tones of Mandarin are used in English as an emotive overlay to our daily speech – for emphasis or for querying. The difference in Chinese is that the tones make a difference to meaning.

The standard example given for learning Chinese tones is *ma*, which can variously mean 'mother', 'hemp' (yeah, as in 'dope'), 'horse' or 'scold' (see the 'Mandarin Tones' boxed text below).

Note In the phraselist included in this guide no tone marks are indicated for some

---

Mandarin Tones

high tone	*mā*	mother
rising tone	*má*	hemp
falling-rising tone	*mǎ*	horse
falling tone	*mà*	scold

words. This is because certain Mandarin words comprise two characters in which the second has a 'neutral' tone. Don't be too concerned about it.

Pinyin

The standard form of romanisation for Mandarin adopted by the PRC is known as *pinyin*. It means literally 'spell the sounds', and once you get used to the idiosyncracies of its spellings it is a very accurate way of representing the sounds of Mandarin. The pronunciation of pinyin spellings are by no means obvious to speakers of European languages, however, and need to be memorised. There's no way of knowing, for example, that a pinyin **x** is pronounced like an English 's' or that **zh** is pronounced like a 'j'.

Pronunciation

If you really want to use a Mandarin phrasebook effectively, you need to internalise the pronunciation of pinyin. The best way is naturally to learn pinyin with a native speaker or with a tape. Failing this, the following guidelines should help get you started.

The pronunciation given in this section is for standard Mandarin as spoken in northern China. Unfortunately you are unlikely to meet many northern Chinese in Tibet. Most of the Han Chinese settlers, businesspeople and officials in Tibet are from Sichuan province, where a southern form of Mandarin is spoken. Even for students of Chinese who have studied for many years, the Sichuan accent can be baffling. Deng Xiaoping was from Sichuan, and many northern Chinese complained that his speeches, delivered in thick Sichuanese, were incomprehensible. Perseverance is recommended – with time pronunciation will gradually become clearer.

Vowels

Mandarin vowel sounds can be fairly tricky for English speakers. In some cases they change depending on the consonant that precedes them, and in other cases they are sounds that are not used in English.

The following vowel sounds follow standard British pronunciation – North Americans beware.

a	as in 'father'
ai	as the 'y' in 'fly'
ao	as the 'ow' in 'cow'
e	as the 'ur' in 'blur'
ei	as the 'ay' in 'way'
i	as the 'ee' in 'meet' when preceded by **j**, **q**, **x** or **y**
i	as the 'e' in 'her' when preceded by other consonants
ian	as in 'yen'
iao	as in the exclamation 'yow!'
ie	as the 'ere' in 'here'
o	as in 'or'
ou	as the 'oa' in 'boat'
u	as in 'flute' after **j**, **q**, **x** or **y**
u	as the 'oo' in 'woo' when preceded by other consonants
ü	as in German or as the 'u' in 'flute'
ui	as in 'way'
uo	as in 'war'

Consonants

Don't assume that consonants are pronounced as they are in English or in other European languages.

One point worth noting briefly is that some consonants have the same pronunciation. This is not a redundancy. While **q** and **c**, for example, have the same pronunciation, the value of the following vowel changes depending on which is used. Thus **ci** is pronounced 'tser', while **qi** is pronounced 'tsee'. There are three such pairs of consonants: **c** and **q**, **j** and **z**, and **s** and **x**.

c	as the 'ts' in 'bits'
ch	as the 'ch' in 'church'
j	as the 'ds' in 'suds'
h	as the guttural 'ch' in Scottish *loch*
q	as the 'ts' in 'bits'
r	somewhere between an English 'r' and the 's' in 'pleasure'
s	as in 'sock'
sh	as in 'shack'
x	as the 's' in 'sock'
z	as the 'ds' in 'suds'
zh	as the 'j' in 'judge'

Pronouns

I
  wǒ　　　　　　我
you
  nǐ　　　　　　你
he, she, it
  tā　　　　　　他/她/它
we, us
  wǒmen　　　　我们
you (plural)
  nǐmen　　　　你们
they, them
  tāmen　　　　他们

Greetings & Civilities

Hello.
  nǐ hǎo　　　　你好
Goodbye.
  zàijiàn　　　　再见
Thank you.
  xièxie　　　　谢谢
You're welcome.
  búkèqi　　　　不客气
I'm sorry.
  duìbùqǐ　　　　对不起

Small Talk

No. (don't have)
  méi yǒu　　　　没有
No. (not so)
  búshì　　　　不是
I'm a foreign student.
  wǒ shì liúxuéshēng　我是留学生
What's to be done now?
  zěnme bàn?　　　怎么办?
It doesn't matter.
  méishì　　　　没事
I want ...
  wǒ yào ...　　　我要 ...
No, I don't want it.
  búyào　　　　不要
Where are you from?
  nǐ shì cōng　　　你是从
  nǎr láide?　　　哪儿来的?
I'm from ...
  wǒ shì cōng ... láide　我是从 ... 来的
Australia
  àodàlìyà　　　澳大利亚
Canada
  jiānádà　　　加拿大

France
  fǎguó　　　　法国
Germany
  déguó　　　　德国
New Zealand
  xīnxīlán　　　新西兰
Spain
  xībānyá　　　西班牙
Sweden
  ruìdiǎn　　　瑞典
Switzerland
  ruìshì　　　　瑞士
UK
  yīngguó　　　英国
USA
  měiguó　　　美国

Language Difficulties

I understand.
  wǒ tīngdedǒng　我听得懂
I don't understand.
  wǒ tīngbudǒng　我听不懂
Do you understand?
  dǒng ma?　　　懂吗?
Could you speak more slowly please?
  qǐng nǐ shuō màn　请你说慢一点,
  yìdiǎn, hǎo ma?　好吗?

Visas & Documents

passport
  hùzhào　　　护照
visa
  qiānzhèng　　签证
visa extension
  yáncháng qiānzhèng　延长签证
Public Security Bureau
  gōng'ān jú　　公安局
Foreign Affairs Branch
  wài shì kē　　外事科

Money

How much is it?
  duōshǎo qián?　多少钱?
Is there anything cheaper?
  yǒu piányi yìdiǎn　有便宜一点
  de ma?　　　的吗?
That's too expensive.
  tài guìle　　　太贵了

Bank of China
   zhōngguó yínháng   中国银行
change money
   huàn qián   换钱

Directions
Where is the ...?
   ... zài nǎlǐ?   ... 在哪里?
I'm lost.
   wǒ mílùle   我迷路了
Turn right.
   yòu zhuǎn   右转
Turn left.
   zuǒ zhuǎn   左转
Go straight ahead.
   yìzhí zǒu   一直走
Turn around.
   wàng huí zǒu   往回走
map
   dìtú   地图
road
   lù   路

Getting Around
I want to go to ...
   wǒ yào qù ...   我要去 ...
I want to get off.
   wǒ yào xiàchē   我要下车
What time does it
depart/arrive?
   jǐdiǎn kāi/dào?   几点开/到?
How long does the
trip take?
   zhècì lǚxíng yào huā   这次旅行要花
   duōcháng shíjiān?   多长时间?

buy a ticket
   mǎi piào   买票
one ticket
   yìzhāng piào   一张票
two tickets
   liǎngzhāng piào   两张票
microbus taxi
   miànbāo chē, miàndī   面包车, 面的

airport
   fēijīchǎng   飞机场
CAAC ticket office
   zhōngguó mínháng   中国民航
   shòupiào chù   售票处

one way ticket
   dānchéng piào   单程票
return ticket
   láihuí piào   来回票
bus
   gōnggòng qìchē   公共汽车
When is the first bus?
   tóubān qìchē jǐdiǎn kāi?
   头班汽车几点开?
When is the last bus?
   mòbān qìchē jǐdiǎn kāi?
   末班汽车几点开?
When is the next bus?
   xià yìbān qìchē jǐdiǎn kāi?
   下一班汽车几点开?

bicycle
   zìxíngchē
   自行车
I want to hire a bicycle.
   wǒ yào zū yíliàng zìxíngchē.
   我要租一辆自行车
How much is it per day?
   yìtiān duōshǎo qián?
   一天多少钱?
How much is it per hour?
   yíge xiǎoshí duōshǎo qián?
   一个小时多少钱?

Accommodation
hotel
   lǚguǎn   旅馆
hostel
   zhāodàisuǒ/lǚshè
   招待所/旅社
tourist hotel
   bīnguǎn/fàndiàn/   宾馆/饭店/
   jiǔdiàn   酒店

dormitory
   duōrénfáng   多人房
single room
   dānrénfáng   单人房
twin room
   shuāngrénfáng   双人房
bed
   chuángwèi   床位
toilet (restroom)
   cèsuǒ   厕所

toilet paper
  wèishēng zhǐ   卫生纸
bathroom (washroom)
  xǐshǒu jiān   洗手间
Men/Women   男/女

Geographical Terms

hot spring
  wēnquán   温泉
lake
  hú   湖
mountain
  shān   山
mountain path
  shānlù   山路
river
  hé   河
road/trail
  lù   路
valley
  shāngǔ   山谷
waterfall
  pùbù   瀑布

Post & Telecommunications

post office
  yóujú   邮局
letter
  xìn   信
envelope
  xìnfēng   信封
package
  bāoguǒ   包裹
air mail
  hángkōng xìn   航空信
surface mail
  píngyóu   平邮
stamps
  yóupiào   邮票
postcard
  míngxìnpiàn   明信片
poste restante
  cúnjú hòulǐnglán   存局候领栏

telephone
  diànhuà   电话
telephone card
  diànhuà kǎ   电话卡
international call
  guójì diànhuà   国际电话

direct-dial call
  zhíbō diànhuà   直拨电话
fax
  chuánzhēn   传真

Time

What's the time?
  jǐ diǎn?   几点?
... hour ... minute
  ... diǎn ... fēn   ... 点 ... 分
3.05
  sān diǎn wǔ fēn   3点5分
now
  xiànzài   现在
today
  jīntiān   今天
tomorrow
  míngtiān   明天
day after tomorrow
  hòutiān   后天
yesterday
  zuótiān   昨天
Wait a moment.
  děng yī xià   等一下

Health

hospital
  yīyuàn   医院
pharmacy
  yàodiàn   药店
diarrhoea
  lādùzi   拉肚子
fever
  fāshāo   发烧
giardia
  āmǐbā fùxiè   阿米巴腹泻
hepatitis
  gānyán   肝炎
rabies
  kuángquǎnbìng   狂犬病
tetanus
  pòshāngfēng   破伤风
flu
  liúgǎn   流感
anti-diarrhoea
medicine
  zhǐxièyào   止泻药
aspirin
  āsīpǐlín   阿司匹林

antibiotics
  kàngjùnsù 抗菌素
condom
  bìyùn tào 避孕套
tampon
  wèishēng mián tiáo 卫生棉条
sanitary napkin (Kotex)
  wèishēng mián 卫生棉
sunscreen (UV) lotion
  fáng shài yóu 防晒油
mosquito coils
  wénxiāng 蚊香

Numbers

0	*líng*	零	
1	*yī, yāo*	一	幺
2	*èr, liǎng*	二	两
3	*sān*	三	
4	*sì*	四	
5	*wǔ*	五	
6	*liù*	六	
7	*qī*	七	
8	*bā*	八	
9	*jiǔ*	九	
10	*shí*	十	
11	*shíyī*	十一	
12	*shí'èr*	十二	
20	*èrshí*	二十	
21	*èrshíyī*	二十一	
100	*yìbǎi*	一百	
200	*liǎngbǎi*	两百	
1000	*yìqiān*	一千	
2000	*liǎngqiān*	两千	
10,000	*yíwàn*	一万	
20,000	*liǎngwàn*	两万	
100,000	*shíwàn*	十万	
200,000	*èrshíwàn*	二十万	
one million	*yìbǎiwàn*	一百万	

Emergencies

I'm sick.
  wǒ shēng bìng le 我生病了
I'm injured.
  wǒ shòushāng le 我受伤了
Fire!
  huǒ zāi! 火灾
Help!
  jiùmìng a! 救命啊
Thief!
  xiǎo tōu! 小偷

emergency
  jǐnjí qíngkuàng 紧急情况
hospital
  yīyuàn 医院
emergency room
  jízhěn shì 急诊室
police
  jǐngchá 警察
foreign affairs police
  wàishì jǐngchá 外事警察
rapist
  qiángjiānzhě 强奸者

CHINESE FOOD
At the Restaurant
I don't want MSG.
  wó bú yào wèijīng 我不要味精
I'm vegetarian.
  wǒ chī sù 我吃素
not too spicy
  bú yào tài là 不要太辣
(cooked) together
  yíkuàir 一块儿

Dishes

steamed white rice
  mǐfàn 米饭
steamed meat buns
  bāozi 包子
boiled dumplings
  jiǎozi 饺子
fried rice & vegetables
  shūcài chǎofàn 蔬菜炒饭
fried rice with beef
  niúròusī chǎofàn 牛肉丝炒饭
fried rice with egg
  jīdàn chǎofàn 鸡蛋炒饭
fried noodles with
vegetables
  shūcài chǎomiàn 蔬菜炒面
beef noodle soup
  niúròu miàn 牛肉面
spicy chicken with
peanuts
  gōngbào jīdīng 宫爆鸡丁
sweet & sour
pork fillets
  tángcù lǐjī 糖醋里脊
double-cooked pork
  huíguō ròu 回锅肉

'wooden ear'
mushrooms & pork
   mùěr ròu   木耳肉
'fish-tasting' aubergine
   yúxiāng qiézi 鱼香茄子
red cooked aubergine
   hóngshāo qiézi 红烧茄子
fried green beans
   chǎo biǎndòu 炒扁豆
fried vegetables
   sùchǎo sùcài 素炒素菜
fried tomatoes & eggs
   fānqié chǎodàn 番茄炒蛋
spicy tofu
   málà dòufu 麻辣豆腐
egg soup
   dànhuā tāng 蛋花汤
wanton soup
   húndùn tāng 馄饨汤

Muslim Food

Muslim noodles
   lāmiàn   拉面
Muslim noodles &
beef
   gànbàn miàn 干拌面
noodles, tofu &
vegetables in soup
   dàlǔmiàn 大鲁面
fried noodle squares
   chǎopàozhàng 炒泡涨

DRINKS

beer
   píjiǔ   啤酒
milk
   niúnǎi   牛奶
mineral water
   kuàng quán shuǐ 矿泉水
water (boiled)
   kāi shuǐ 开水
tea
   chá   茶
Muslim tea
(in Muslim restaurants)
   bābǎo wǎnzi 八宝碗子
hot
   rède   热的
ice cold
   bīngde   冰的

Gazetteer

Ali (Shiquanhe)
   ཨ་པེ་   狮泉河(阿里)
Chamdo
   ཆབ་མདོ་   昌都
Chongye
   འཕྱོངས་རྒྱས་   阱结
Chumbi Valley
   རྒྱམ་པེ་
Chusul
   ཆུ་ཤུལ་   曲水
Damxung
   འདམ་གཞུང་   当雄
Drepung Monastery
   འབྲས་སྤུང་   哲蚌寺
Drigung
   འབྲི་གུང་
Everest, Mt (Jomo Langri)
   ཇོ་མོ་གླང་རི་   珠峰
Ganden Monastery
   དགའ་ལྡན་   甘丹寺
Gegye
   དགེ་རྒྱས་   革吉
Gertse
   སྒེར་རྩེ་   改则
Golmud
         格尔木
Gongkar
   གོང་དཀར་   贡嘎
Gongkar Airport
         贡嘎机场
Gyantse
   རྒྱལ་རྩེ་   江孜
Gyatsa
         加查
Hor Qu
         霍尔区
Jokhang
   ཇོ་ཁང་   大昭寺
Kailash, Mt (Gang-ka Tesi/Gang Rinpoche)
   (གངས་དཀར་ཏེ་སེ་/   神山
   གངས་རིན་པོ་ཆེ་)   (冈仁坡齐峰)

Kangding
康定

Kashgar
喀什

Lhasa
ལྷ་ས
拉萨

Lhatse
ལྷ་རྩེ
拉孜

Lhundrub
ལྷུན་གྲུབ
林周

Litang
ལི་ཐང
理塘

Manasarovar, Lake
མཚོ་མ་ཕམ
圣湖(玛旁雍错)

Markam
སྨར་ཁམས
芒康

Medro Gungkar
བསམ་ཡིད་དགོན་པ
墨竹工卡

Mindroling Monastery
སྨིན་གྲོལ་གླིང་དགོན་པ
敏珠林寺

Nam-tso
གནམ་མཚོ
纳木错

Nangartse
浪卡子

Naqu
ནག་ཆུ
那曲

Norbulingka, the
ནོར་བུ་གླིང་ཁ
罗布林卡

Nyalam
གཉའ་ལམ
聂拉木

Nyingchi
林芝

Paryang
帕羊

Pongba
雄巴

Potala
པོ་ཏ་ལ
布达拉宫

Purang
སྤུ་ཧྲེང
普兰

Rongphu Monastery
绒布寺

Sakya
ས་སྐྱ
萨迦

Samding Monastery
བསམ་སྡིང་དགོན་པ
桑顶寺

Samye Monastery
བསམ་ཡས་ཡེ་དགོན་པ
桑耶寺

Sangsang
桑桑

Sera Monastery
སེ་ར་དགོན་པ
色拉寺

Shegar
ཤེལ་དཀར
新定日

Shigatse
གཞིས་ཀ་རྩེ
日喀则

Tingri
དིང་རི
定日

Trandruk Monastery
昌珠寺

Tsang
གཙང

Tsaparang
རྩ་ཧྲེང
札达

Tsetang
རྩེ་ཐང
泽当

Tsochen
མཚོ་ཆེན
措勤

Tsomei
མཚོ་སྨད
指美

Tsona
མཚོ་སྣ
错那

Tsurphu Monastery
མཚུར་ཕུ་དགོན་པ

Ü
དབུས

Yamdrok-tso
ཡར་འབྲོག་མཚོ
羊卓雍错

Yatung
ཡར་དུང
亚东

Yumbulagang
ཡུམ་བུ་བླ་སྒང
雍布拉康

Zhangmu
གཞམ་མོ
樟木

Zhongba
仲巴

Glossary

Many of the terms in this chapter are of Sanskrit origin. Italicised entries in parentheses indicate their Tibetan equivalents. For detailed information and illustrations of important figures in Tibetan Buddhism, see the colour iconographical guide earlier in the book.

Akshobhya – *(Mikyöba)* the Buddha of the state of Perfected Consciousness, or Perfect Cognition; literally 'Unchanging', the 'Immutable One'

Amban – Chinese representatives of the Manchu Qing Dynasty posted in Lhasa from the early 19th century until the Chinese Republican overthrow of the Qing in 1911

Amdo – one of the three traditional provinces of Tibet, now Qinghai province. The other two provinces are *Kham* (Sichuan) and *Ütsang*, which includes central and Western Tibet.

Amitabha – *(Öpagme)* the Buddha of Perfected Perception; literally 'Boundless Light'

Amitayus – *(Tsepame)* a meditational deity associated with longevity; literally 'Limitless Life'. Amitayus is often featured in a trinity with White *Tara* and Vijaya.

AMS – acute mountain sickness

ani – Tibetan for 'nun', as in ani gompa, 'nunnery'

apsara – a Sanskrit term meaning 'angel'

arhat – literally 'worthy one', the arhat is neither a *Buddha* nor a *bodhisattva*, but is one who has become free of the *Wheel of Life* and is free of hatred and all delusions

Atisha – *(Jowo-je*; 982-1054) Buddhist scholar from contemporary Bengal. His arrival in Tibet at the invitation of the king of Guge, in Western Tibet, was a catalyst in the 11th century revival of Buddhism on the high plateau.

Avalokiteshvara – *(Chenresig)* an embodiment of compassionate bodhisattvahood and the patron saint of Tibet. The *Dalai Lamas* are considered to be manifestations of this deity.

Bardo – as detailed in the *Tibetan Book of the Dead*, this term refers to the intermediate stages between death and rebirth

Barkhor – an intermediate circumambulation circuit, or *kora*, but most often specifically the intermediate circuit around the *Jokhang* temple of Lhasa

Bhrikuti – the Nepalese consort of King Songtsen Gampo, an early Tibetan king

Black Hat – strictly speaking, this refers to the black hat embellished with gold that was presented to the second *Karmapa* of the *Karma Kagyupa* order of Tsurphu Monastery by a Mongol prince, and worn ceremoniously by all subsequent incarnations of the Karmapa; by extension the black hat represents the Karma Kagyupa order.

Bodhgaya – the place in contemporary Bihar, India, where *Sakyamuni*, the Historical Buddha, attained enlightenment

bodhisattva – literally 'enlightenment hero', the bodhisattva voluntarily does not take the step to *nirvana*, motivated by compassion for all sentient beings to stay within the *Wheel of Life*

Bö – the Tibetan name for their own land; sometimes written Bod or Po

Bön – the indigenous religion of Tibet prior to the introduction of Buddhism; a shamanistic faith associated with spirits, demons and exorcisms among other things

Bönpo – a practitioner of *Bön*

Buddha – literally 'Awakened One', a being who through spiritual training has broken free of all illusion and karmic consequences and is 'enlightened'; most often specifically the Historical Buddha, *Sakyamuni*

Büton – sub-order of Tibetan Buddhism based on the teachings of Büton Rinchen Drup, the 14th century collator of the major Buddhist texts. Associated with Shalu Monastery, near Shigatse.

cairn – *(lapse)* a mound of stones erected as a marker

Chaktsal – Tibetan for the ritual of 'prostration'

Chaktsal Gang – prostration point

Cham – a ritual dance carried out by monks and *lamas* usually at festivals; with the exception of the central lama, all participants are masked

Chan – Chinese for a branch of Buddhism more famously known in the west by its Japanese name, Zen

Chana Dorje – see *Vajrapani*

chang – Tibetan barley beer

Changtang – vast plains of northern Tibet extending into Xinjiang and Qinghai; the largest and highest plateau in the world

Chenresig – see *Avalokiteshvara*

chömay – butter lamp

chörten – Tibetan for 'stupa'; usually used as reliquaries for the cremated remains of important *lamas*

chu – river, stream, brook etc

chuba – long-sleeved sheepskin cloak

CITS – China International Travel Service

CTS – China Travel Service

Dakini – literally 'Sky Dancer', a fierce, lower-ranking *Tantric* goddess, often depicted as red

Dalai Lama – one of 14 (so far) manifestations of *Avalokiteshvara* who, as spiritual heads of the *Gelugpa* order, ruled over Tibet from 1642 until 1959. The honorific title means 'Ocean of Wisdom' and was bestowed by the Mongolian Altyn Khan. The present 14th Dalai Lama resides in Dharamsala, India.

dharma – *(chö)* sometimes translated as 'law', this very broad term covers the truths expounded by *Sakyamuni*, the Buddhist teachings, the Buddhist path and the Buddhist goal, *nirvana*; in effect it is the 'law' that must be understood, followed and achieved in order to be a Buddhist

dorje – literally 'diamond' or 'thunderbolt' this is a metaphor for the indestructible, indivisible nature of Buddhahood; also a *Tantric* hand-held sceptre symbolising 'skilful means'

dri – female yak

drokpa – Tibetan for 'nomad'

Drölma – see *Tara*

Dromtönpa – 11th century disciple of *Atisha* who founded the *Kadampa* order

dukhang – Tibetan for 'assembly hall'

dukkha – Sanskrit for 'suffering', the essential condition of all life

dungchen – long, ceremonial Tibetan trumpet

dürtro – sky burial site, see also *sky burial*

Dusum Khyenpa – founder of Tsurphu Monastery and first *Karmapa*

dzo – domesticated cross between a bull and a female yak

Dzogchen – the Great Perfection teachings associated with the *Nyingmapa* order

dzong – Tibetan for 'fort'

Eightfold Path – one of the *Four Holy Truths* taught by *Sakyamuni*, this term refers to the path that must be taken to achieve enlightenment and liberation from the *Wheel of Life*

Ekajati – deity associated with the *Dzogchen* movement

Four Holy Truths – the first speech given by *Sakyamuni* after he achieved enlightenment: they are the truth that all life is suffering; the truth that suffering originates in desire; the truth that desire may be extinguished; and the truth that there is a path to this end

Ganden – the Pure Land of *Maitreya*, the Future Buddha, and the seat of the *Gelugpa* order (Ganden Monastery, *Ü*). The Sanskrit term is Tushita.

Garuda – mythological bird associated with Hinduism; in Tibetan *Tantric* Buddhism it is seen as a wrathful force that transforms malevolent influences

gau – an amulet or 'portable shrine' worn around the neck; contains the image of an important spiritual figure – usually the *Dalai Lama*

gelong – the full indoctrinal vows of monkhood only achieved after many years of study and not necessarily by all monks

Gelugpa – major order of Tibetan Buddhism, associated with the *Dalai Lamas*,

Panchen Lamas and Drepung, Sera, Ganden and Tashilhunpo monasteries; founded by *Tsongkhapa* in the 14th century; also known as the Yellow Hats

Genden Drup – the first *Dalai Lama*

Genden Gyatso – the second *Dalai Lama*

genyen – one of the lesser ordination vows for monks

Gesar – a legendary king and the name of an epic concerning his fabulous exploits; the king's empire is known as Ling, and thus the stories, usually sung and told by professional bards, are also known as the *Stories of Ling*

geshe – awarded on completion of the highest level of study, something like a doctorate, that monks may undertake after completing their *gelong* vows; usually associated with the Gelugpa order

getsul – one of the lesser ordination vows for monks

gompa – Tibetan for 'monastery'

gönkhang – protector chapel

Guge – a 9th century kingdom of Western Tibet

guru – Sanskrit term for 'spiritual teacher'; literally 'heavy'; the Tibetan equivalent is *lama*

Guru Rinpoche – known in Sanskrit as Padmasambhava, Guru Rinpoche is credited with having suppressed demons and other malevolent forces in order to introduce Buddhism into Tibet during the 8th century; in the *Nyingmapa* order he is revered as the 'Second Buddha'

Gyeltsab Je – one of *Tsongkhapa's* chief disciples and the first Ganden Tripa, or abbot

Hayagriva – *(Tamdrin)* literally 'Horse Necked', a wrathful meditational deity and manifestation of *Avalokiteshvara*; associated usually with the *Nyingmapa* order

Hinayana – also called Theravada, this is a major school of Buddhism which follows the original teachings of the Historical Buddha, *Sakyamuni*, and places less importance on the compassionate *bodhisattva* ideal and more on individual enlightenment; see also *Mahayana*

Jainism – an ancient Indian faith that, like Buddhism, believes in the cyclic nature of life

Jamchen Chöde – disciple of *Tsongkhapa* and founder of Sera Monastery, also known as Sakya Yeshe

Jampa – see *Maitreya*

Jamyang Chöde – founder of Drepung Monastery

Je Rinpoche – an honorific title used for *Tsongkhapa*, founder of the *Gelugpa* order

Jokhang – *(Tsuglhakhang)* the most sacred and one of the most ancient of Tibet's temples; in Lhasa

Jowo-je – see *Atisha*

Jowo Sakyamuni – the most revered image of *Sakyamuni* in Tibet; it depicts the Historical Buddha at the age of 12 and is kept in the Jokhang

Kadampa – order of Tibetan Buddhism based on the teachings of the Indian scholar *Atisha*; the school was a major influence on the *Gelugpa* order

Kagyupa – order of Tibetan Buddhism that traces its lineage back through *Milarepa*, *Marpa* and eventually to the Indian *mahasiddhas*; it is divided into numerous sub-orders, the most famous of which is the *Karma Kagyupa*, or the *Karmapa*

Kalachakra – depicting the 'Wheel of Time', Kalachakra is the most complex of all supreme yoga *Tantra* deities

kangling – a ceremonial human thigh-bone trumpet

kangtsang – monastic residential quarters

Kangyur – the Tibetan Buddhist canon; its complement is the *Tengyur*

karma – action and its consequences, the psychic 'imprint' action leaves on the mind and which continues into further rebirths; a term found in both Hinduism and Buddhism, and which may be likened to the law of cause and effect

Karma Kagyupa – sub-order of the Kagyupa order, established by Gampopa and Dusum Khyenpa in the 12th century

Karmapa – a lineage of spiritual leaders of the *Karma Kagyupa*; also known as the Black Hats, there have been 17 so far

Kashag – Tibetan for the Cabinet of the *Gelugpa* Lamaist Government

kathak – prayer scarf; used as a ritual offering or as a gift

Kham – traditional eastern Tibetan province; much of it is now part of Sichuan

Khampa – a person from the province of *Kham*

khenpo – Tibetan term for 'abbot'

kora – ritual circumambulation circuit

kumbum – literally '100,000 images', this is a *chörten* that contains statuary and paintings; most famous in Tibet is the Gyantse Kumbum in *Tsang*

la – Tibetan for 'mountain pass'

lama – literally 'unsurpassed', this is the Tibetan equivalent of *guru* and is a title bestowed on monks of particularly high spiritual attainment

lamaism – term used by early western writers on the subject of Tibet to describe Tibetan Buddhism; also used by the Chinese in the term *lamajiao*, literally 'lama religion'

Lamrim – the 'Stages on the Path to Enlightenment', a graduated approach to enlightenment as expounded by *Tsongkhapa*; associated with the *Gelugpa* order

Langdharma – the 9th century Tibetan king accused of having persecuted Buddhism

lapse – see *cairn*

Lha – Tibetan term for 'life spirit'; it may also be present in inanimate objects such as lakes, mountains and trees

lhadne – ancient class of Tibetan spirits which inhabit the underworld as well as the sky

lhakhang – Tibetan term for 'chapel'

ling – Tibetan term usually associated with lesser, outlying temples

lingkhor – an outer pilgrimage circuit; famously, the outer pilgrimage of Lhasa

Lokpalas – the Four Guardian Kings

Losar – Tibetan New Year

lu – 'road' in Chinese; see also *naga*

lungta – prayer flag

mahasiddha – *(drubchen)* literally 'of great spiritual accomplishment', the mahasiddha is a *Tantric* practitioner who has reached a

high level of awareness; there are 84 famous mahasiddhas

Mahayana – the other major school of Buddhism along with *Hinayana*, Mahayana emphasises compassion and the altruism of the bodhisattva who remains on the *Wheel of Life* for the sake of all sentient beings

Maitreya – *(Jampa)* the Buddha of Loving Kindness; also the Future Buddha, the 5th of the 1000 Buddhas who will descend to earth (*Sakyamuni* was the 4th)

mandal – stones piled as offerings

mandala – *(kyilkhor)* a circular representation of the three-dimensional world of a meditational deity, and used as a meditational device

mani – prayer

mani lhakhang – small chapel housing a single large prayer wheel

mani stone – stone with the mantra *om mani padme hum* carved on it

mani wall – wall made with *mani stones*

Manjushri – *(Jampelyang)* the Buddha of Discriminative Awareness, who is usually depicted holding a sword, which symbolises discriminative awareness, in one hand and a book, which symbolises his mastery of all knowledge, in the other

mantra – literally 'protection of the mind', this is one of the *Tantric* devices used to achieve identity with a meditational deity and break through the world of illusion; a series of syllables which are recited as the pure sound made by an enlightened being

mara – literally 'evil influences'; mara stands between us and enlightenment

Marpa – an ascetic of the 11th century whose disciple, *Milarepa*, founded the *Kagyupa* order

meditational deity – a deified manifestation of the enlightened mind with which, according to *Tantric* ritual, the adept seeks union and thus experience of enlightenment

Meru, Mt – the sacred mountain at the centre of the universe; also known as Sumeru

Mikyöba – see *Akshobhya*

Milarepa – 11th century disciple of *Marpa* and founder of the *Kagyupa* order; renowned for his songs

momo – Tibetan dumplings

Mönlam – a major Lhasa festival established by *Tsongkhapa*

naga – *(lu)* water spirits who may take the form of serpents or semi-humans; the latter can be seen in images of the Naga kings

Namri Songtsen – 6th century Tibetan king, father of *Songtsen Gampo*

nangkhor – inner circumambulation circuit, usually within the interior of a temple or monastic assembly hall, and taking in various chapels en route

Nechung – protector deity of Tibet and the *Dalai Lamas*; Nechung is manifested in the State Oracle, who is traditionally installed at Nechung Monastery, near Drepung, Lhasa

Newari – the people of the Nepalese Buddhist kingdoms in the Kathmandu Valley

Ngari – ancient name for the province of Western Tibet; later incorporated into *Ütsang*

nirvana – literally 'beyond sorrow', nirvana is an end to desire and suffering, and an end to the never-ending cycle of rebirth

Norbulingka – the Summer Palace of the *Dalai Lamas* in Lhasa

Nyentri Tsenpo – legendary first king of Tibet

Nyingmapa – the earliest order of Tibetan Buddhism, based largely on the Buddhism brought to Tibet by *Guru Rinpoche*

Oracle – in Tibetan Buddhism an oracle serves as a medium for protective deities, as in the State Oracle of Nechung Monastery near Drepung, Lhasa. The State Oracle was consulted on all important matters of state

om mani padme hum – this mantra means 'hail to the jewel in the lotus' and is associated with *Avalokiteshvara*, patron deity of Tibet

Öpagme – see *Amitabha*

Padmasambhava – see *Guru Rinpoche*

Palden Lhamo – see *Shri Devi*

Panchen Lama – literally 'Guru and Great Teacher'; the Panchen Lama lineage is associated with Tashilhunpo Monastery, Shigatse, and goes back to the 17th century; the Panchen Lama is a manifestation of *Amitabha*

Pandita – a title conferred on great scholars of Buddhism, as in the Sakya Pandita

parikrama – the Hindu equivalent of a *kora*

Pehar – oracle and protector of the Buddhist state

PLA – People's Liberation Army (Chinese army)

PRC – People's Republic of China

protector deity – deities who can manifest themselves in either male or female forms and serve to protect Buddhist teachings and followers; they may be either wrathful aspects of enlightened beings or worldly powers who have been tamed by *Tantric* masters

PSB – Public Security Bureau (*gonganju* in Chinese)

puk – Tibetan for 'cave'

Pure Lands – otherworldly realms that are the domains of Buddhas; they are realms completely free of suffering, and in the popular Buddhist imagination are probably something like the Christian heaven

Qiang – proto-Tibetan tribes that troubled the borders of the Chinese Empire

Qomolangma – Tibetan name for Mt Everest as transliterated by the Chinese; also spelt 'Chomolangma'

Qu – Chinese term for an administrative district, as in Shannan Qu (around Tsetang)

Ralpachen – 9th century king whose assassination marked the end of the Yarlung Dynasty

ranjung – self-manifesting; for example a rock spire could be a ranjung *chörten*

rebirth – a condition of the *Wheel of Life*; the rebirths of all beings are limitless until they achieve enlightenment

regent – a representative of an incarnate *lama*, who presides over a monastic community during the lama's minority; regents came to play an important political role in the *Gelugpa* Lamaist Government

ri – Tibetan for 'mountain'

Rinpoche – literally 'high in esteem', a title bestowed on highly revered lamas; they are usually incarnate, but need not be

RMB – acronym for Renminbi or 'People's Money', the currency of China

rogyapas – the 'body-breakers' who prepare bodies for *sky burial*

rongpa – non-nomadic farmers of Tibet's valleys

sadhu – an Indian ascetic who has renounced all attachments

Saga Dawa – festival held at the full moon of the fourth lunar month to celebrate Sakyamuni's enlightenment

Sakyamuni – *(Sakya Thukpa)* literally the 'Sage of Sakka', the founder of Buddhism, the Historical Buddha; see also *Buddha*

Sakyapa – Tibetan Buddhist order associated with Sakya Monastery and founded in the 11th century; also known as the Red Hats

samsara – the cycle of birth, death and rebirth

Samvara – a wrathful manifestation of *Sakyamuni*

Samye – the first Buddhist monastery in Tibet, founded by King Trisong Detsen in the 8th century

sang – incense

Sangha – community of Buddhist monks or nuns

sangkang – pot-bellied incense burners

Sanskrit – ancient language of India, has a complex grammar and rich vocabulary; a classical mode of expression with the status that Latin had in earlier western society

shabje – footprint

Shambhala – the mythical great northern paradise, near the Kunlun Mountains. The modern era consists of 32 Kings of Shambhala. We are in the reign of the 29th king at present. There will be a terrible war in the reign of the 32nd king, followed by a great period of piece and enlightenment.

Shangshung – ancient kingdom of Western Tibet and origin of the *Bön* faith

Shantarakshita – Indian scholar of the 8th century and first abbot of Samye Monastery

Shenrab – mythical founder of the *Bön* faith

Shötun – the Yoghurt festival of Lhasa

Shri Devi – *(Palden Lhamo)* special protector of Lhasa, the *Dalai Lama* and the

Gelugpa order, Shri Devi is the female counterpart of Nagpo Chenpo

Siddhartha Gautama – the personal name of the Historical Buddha; see also *Sakyamuni*

Sinmo – a demoness

sky burial – Tibetan funerary practice of chopping up the corpses of their dead in designated high places *(dürto)* and leaving them for the birds

Songtsen Gampo – the 7th century king associated with the first introduction of Buddhism to Tibet

stupa – see *chörten*

sutra – Buddhist scriptures which record the teachings of the Historical Buddha, *Sakyamuni*

Tamdrin – see *Hayagriva*

Tantra – scriptures and oral lineages associated with *Tantric Buddhism*

Tantric – of Tantric Buddhism; a movement combining mysticism with Buddhist scripture

TAR – Tibetan Autonomous Region

Tara – *(Drölma)* a female meditational deity who is a manifestation of the enlightened mind of all Buddhas; sometimes referred to as the mother of all Buddhas; she has many aspects but is most often seen as the Green Tara or White Tara

Tengyur – a Tibetan Buddhist canonical text that collects together commentaries on the teachings of *Sakyamuni*

Tenzin Gyatso – the 14th and current *Dalai Lama*

terma – 'discovered' or 'revealed' teachings; teachings that have been hidden until the world is ready to receive them

terton – discoverer of *terma*

thamzing – 'struggle sessions', a misconceived Chinese tool for changing the ideological orientation of individuals; ultimately a coercive tool that encouraged deceit under the threat of torture

thangka – a Tibetan religious painting usually framed by a silk brocade

Theravada – see *Hinayana*

thugpa – traditional Tibetan noodle dish

torma – offerings of sculptured *tsampa* cakes

trapa – Tibetan for 'monk'

tratsang – monastic college

Tripa – the post of abbot at Ganden Monastery; head of the *Gelugpa* order

Trisong Detsen – 8th century Tibetan king; founder of Samye Monastery

trulku – incarnate *lama*

tsampa – roast barley flour, traditional staple of the Tibetan people

Tsang – traditional province to the west of *Ü* which has Shigatse as its capital

tsangpo – large river

Tsepame – see *Amitayus*

tso – Tibetan for 'lake'

Tsongkhapa – 14th century founder of the *Gelugpa* order and Ganden Monastery

tsuglhakhang – 'grand temple', but often specifically the *Jokhang* of Lhasa

Ü – traditional province to the east of *Tsang* which has Lhasa as its capital

Ütsang – the provinces of *Ü* and *Tsang*, also incorporating *Ngari*, or Western Tibet; effectively central Tibet, or political Tibet

Vairocana – Buddha of Enlightened Consciousness

Vaishravana – the Guardian of the North, one of the *Lokpalas* or Four Guardian Kings

Vajrapani – *(Chana Dorje)* the wrathful *bodhisattva* of Energy whose name means 'Thunderbolt in Hand'

Vajrayana – literally the 'Diamond Vehicle', a branch of *Mahayana* Buddhism that finds a more direct route to bodhisattvahood

through identification with meditational deities

Wencheng – Chinese consort of King Songtsen Gampo

Wheel of Life – often pictured in monasteries, the Wheel of Life depicts the cyclic nature of existence and the six realms where rebirth take place

yabyum – *Tantric* sexual union, symbolising the mental union of female insight and male compassion. Fierce deities are often depicted in yabyum with their consorts.

Yama – Lord of Death, who resides in *sky burial* sites

Yamantaka – *(Dorje Jigje)* a meditational deity; Yamantaka comes in various aspects; the Red and Black aspects are probably most common

yidam – see *meditational deity*; may also have the function of being a personal protector deity that looks over an individual or family

yogin – yoga in Sanskrit refers to a 'union' with the fundamental nature of reality; for Tibetan Buddhists this can be achieved through meditative techniques and through identification with a meditational deity; a yogin is an adept of such techniques

yuan – unit of Chinese currency

zhaodaisuo – Chinese for 'guesthouse', usually a basic hostel

Acknowledgments

THANKS

Many thanks to the travellers who used the last edition and wrote to us with helpful hints, useful advice and interesting anecdotes:

Ms A Alexander, G DeLois Anders, Neil Anderson, John Atkinson, Oded Barer, Jeff Bell, Jeremy Bernstein, Jan Beukema, Michael Boehm, John Bower, Claire Brondex, James Buchanan-Dunlop, LE Butler, C Butzlaff, Dwight Call, EA Carswell, Anne Carter, Max G Chapman, Melanie Cheng, Dudu Cohen, Nick Conway, G De Lois Anders, Barbara Dombrowski, Eshed Doni, Gudrun Droop, B Dubois, James Dunn, Troy Etulain, Brooks Evans, Ferdinand Fellinger, Jim & Linda Franklin, Margaret Gardner, Frank de Groot, Rolf Gross, Jez Gunnell, Jacob Hak, Ron Harding, Stephanie Harrison, James Hatcher, Bob Hoffman, Raimo Huebner, Sally Ingleton, Sarah Jenkins, Derek Jennings, Robert Kelman, Dudi Kenig, Kerstin Knopf, Lt Col Nilesh Korgaokar, Edward J Kormondy, Sibylle Latza, J Lester, Lonny, Connie McGuire, Jim McHugh, Csaba Mikusi, Phil Miller, Ryo Miyanami, Dieter Neujahr, Nilesh, Uri & Nomi Nir, David Owen, Paul Oxenham, Manibrata Paul, Julio Penalva-Puig, Pelle Petersson, Bernard Phelps, Juan Carlos Picena, Wolfgang Rabitsch, Raimo, Helen Ranger, Michelle Renbaum, Claus Rislin, Susanne Ritz, David Robertson, Bryan Roche, Jan Willem Roks, S Latza, Lori Panther, Alan Savage, Kelvin Schafli, Brett Schuppan, Andrew Sewell, Dan Shingleton, Diana Silbergeld, Zsolt Sipeki, Donald Smith, Lea Stogdale, Johanna Surla, Tibet Foundation, Stephen Van Wyck, Daniel Vetter, Ricard Vilata, Frederic Wehowski, Jan Willem Roks, Kirsten Wilson, Richard & Arianne de Zwart.

LONELY PLANET

Phrasebooks

L onely Planet phrasebooks are packed with essential words and phrases to help travellers communicate with the locals. With colour tabs for quick reference, an extensive vocabulary and use of script, these handy pocket-sized language guides cover day-to-day travel situations.

- handy pocket-sized books
- easy to understand Pronunciation chapter
- clear & comprehensive Grammar chapter
- romanisation alongside script to allow ease of pronunciation
- script throughout so users can point to phrases for every situation
- full of cultural information and tips for the traveller

'...vital for a real DIY spirit and attitude in language learning'
– Backpacker

'the phrasebooks have good cultural backgrounders and offer solid advice for challenging situations in remote locations'
– San Francisco Examiner

Arabic (Egyptian) • Arabic (Moroccan) • Australian *(Australian English, Aboriginal and Torres Strait languages)* • Baltic States *(Estonian, Latvian, Lithuanian)* • Bengali • Brazilian • Burmese • Cantonese • Central Asia • Central Europe *(Czech, French, German, Hungarian, Italian, Slovak)* • Eastern Europe *(Bulgarian, Czech, Hungarian, Polish, Romanian, Slovak)* • Ethiopian (Amharic) • Fijian • French • German • Greek • Hill Tribes • Hindi/Urdu • Indonesian • Italian • Japanese • Korean • Lao • Latin American Spanish • Malay • Mandarin • Mediterranean Europe *(Albanian, Croatian, Greek, Italian, Macedonian, Maltese, Serbian, Slovene)* • Mongolian • Nepali • Papua New Guinea • Pilipino (Tagalog) • Quechua • Russian • Scandinavian Europe *(Danish, Finnish, Icelandic, Norwegian, Swedish)* • South-East Asia *(Burmese, Indonesian, Khmer, Lao, Malay, Tagalog Pilipino, Thai, Vietnamese)* • Spanish (Castilian) *(also includes Catalan, Galician and Basque)* • Sri Lanka • Swahili • Thai • Tibetan • Turkish • Ukrainian • USA *(US English, Vernacular, Native American languages, Hawaiian)* • Vietnamese • Western Europe *(Basque, Catalan, Dutch, French, German, Greek, Irish)*

LONELY PLANET

FREE Lonely Planet Newsletters

We love hearing from you and think you'd like to hear from us.

Planet Talk

Our FREE quarterly printed newsletter is full of tips from travellers and anecdotes from Lonely Planet guidebook authors. Every issue is packed with up-to-date travel news and advice, and includes:

- a postcard from Lonely Planet co-founder Tony Wheeler
- a swag of mail from travellers
- a look at life on the road through the eyes of a Lonely Planet author
- topical health advice
- prizes for the best travel yarn
- news about forthcoming Lonely Planet events
- a complete list of Lonely Planet books and other titles

To join our mailing list, residents of the UK, Europe and Africa can email us at go@lonelyplanet.co.uk; residents of North and South America can email us at info@lonelyplanet.com; the rest of the world can email us at talk2us@lonelyplanet.com.au, or contact any Lonely Planet office.

Comet

Our FREE monthly email newsletter brings you all the latest travel news, features, interviews, competitions, destination ideas, travellers' tips & tales, Q&As, raging debates and related links. Find out what's new on the Lonely Planet Web site and which books are about to hit the shelves.

Subscribe from your desktop: www.lonelyplanet.com/comet

LONELY PLANET

Guides by Region

Lonely Planet is known worldwide for publishing practical, reliable and no-nonsense travel information in our guides and on our Web site. The Lonely Planet list covers just about every accessible part of the world. Currently there are nine series: travel guides, shoestring guides, walking guides, city guides, phrasebooks, audio packs, travel atlases, diving and snorkeling guides and travel literature.

AFRICA Africa – the South • Africa on a shoestring • Arabic (Egyptian) phrasebook • Arabic (Moroccan) phrasebook • Cairo • Cape Town • Central Africa • East Africa • Egypt • Egypt travel atlas • Ethiopian (Amharic) phrasebook • The Gambia & Senegal • Kenya • Kenya travel atlas • Malawi, Mozambique & Zambia • Morocco • North Africa • South Africa, Lesotho & Swaziland • South Africa, Lesotho & Swaziland travel atlas • Swahili phrasebook • Trekking in East Africa • Tunisia • West Africa • Zimbabwe, Botswana & Namibia • Zimbabwe, Botswana & Namibia travel atlas
Travel Literature: The Rainbird: A Central African Journey • Songs to an African Sunset: A Zimbabwean Story • Mali Blues: Traveling to an African Beat

AUSTRALIA & THE PACIFIC Australia • Australian phrasebook • Bushwalking in Australia • Bushwalking in Papua New Guinea • Fiji • Fijian phrasebook • Islands of Australia's Great Barrier Reef • Melbourne • Micronesia • New Caledonia • New South Wales & the ACT • New Zealand • Northern Territory • Outback Australia • Papua New Guinea • Papua New Guinea (Pidgin) phrasebook • Queensland • Rarotonga & the Cook Islands • Samoa • Solomon Islands • South Australia • Sydney • Tahiti & French Polynesia • Tasmania • Tonga • Tramping in New Zealand • Vanuatu • Victoria • Western Australia
Travel Literature: Islands in the Clouds • Sean & David's Long Drive

CENTRAL AMERICA & THE CARIBBEAN Bahamas and Turks & Caicos • Bermuda • Central America on a shoestring • Costa Rica • Cuba • Eastern Caribbean • Guatemala, Belize & Yucatán: La Ruta Maya • Jamaica • Mexico • Mexico City • Panama
Travel Literature: Green Dreams: Travels in Central America

EUROPE Amsterdam • Andalucía • Austria • Baltic States phrasebook • Berlin • Britain • Central Europe • Central Europe phrasebook • Czech & Slovak Republics • Denmark • Dublin • Eastern Europe • Eastern Europe phrasebook • Edinburgh • Estonia, Latvia & Lithuania • Europe • Finland • France • French phrasebook • Germany • German phrasebook • Greece • Greek phrasebook • Hungary • Iceland, Greenland & the Faroe Islands • Ireland • Italian phrasebook • Italy • Lisbon • London • Mediterranean Europe • Mediterranean Europe phrasebook • Paris • Poland • Portugal • Portugal travel atlas • Prague • Romania & Moldova • Russia, Ukraine & Belarus • Russian phrasebook • Scandinavian & Baltic Europe • Scandinavian Europe phrasebook • Scotland • Slovenia • Spain • Spanish phrasebook • St Petersburg • Switzerland • Trekking in Spain • Ukrainian phrasebook • Vienna • Walking in Britain • Walking in Italy • Walking in Switzerland • Western Europe • Western Europe phrasebook
Travel Literature: The Olive Grove: Travels in Greece

INDIAN SUBCONTINENT Bangladesh • Bengali phrasebook • Bhutan • Delhi • Goa • Hindi/Urdu phrasebook • India • India & Bangladesh travel atlas • Indian Himalaya • Karakoram Highway • Nepal • Nepali phrasebook • Pakistan • Rajasthan • South India • Sri Lanka • Sri Lanka phrasebook • Trekking in the Indian Himalaya • Trekking in the Karakoram & Hindukush • Trekking in the Nepal Himalaya
Travel Literature: In Rajasthan • Shopping for Buddhas

LONELY PLANET

Mail Order

L onely Planet products are distributed worldwide. They are also available by mail order from Lonely Planet, so if you have difficulty finding a title please write to us. North and South American residents should write to 150 Linden St, Oakland, CA 94607, USA; European and African residents should write to 10a Spring Place, London NW5 3BH, UK; and residents of other countries to PO Box 617, Hawthorn, Victoria 3122, Australia.

ISLANDS OF THE INDIAN OCEAN Madagascar & Comoros • Maldives • Mauritius, Réunion & Seychelles

MIDDLE EAST & CENTRAL ASIA Arab Gulf States • Central Asia • Central Asia phrasebook • Iran • Israel & the Palestinian Territories • Israel & the Palestinian Territories travel atlas • Istanbul • Jerusalem • Jordan & Syria • Jordan, Syria & Lebanon travel atlas • Lebanon • Middle East on a shoestring • Turkey • Turkish phrasebook • Turkey travel atlas • Yemen
Travel Literature: The Gates of Damascus • Kingdom of the Film Stars: Journey into Jordan

NORTH AMERICA Alaska • Backpacking in Alaska • Baja California • California & Nevada • Canada • Florida • Hawaii • Honolulu • Los Angeles • Miami • New England USA • New Orleans • New York City • New York, New Jersey & Pennsylvania • Pacific Northwest USA • Rocky Mountain States • San Francisco • Seattle • Southwest USA • USA phrasebook • Washington, DC & the Capital Region
Travel Literature: Drive Thru America

NORTH-EAST ASIA Beijing • Cantonese phrasebook • China • Hong Kong • Hong Kong, Macau & Guangzhou • Japan • Japanese phrasebook • Japanese audio pack • Korea • Korean phrasebook • Kyoto • Mandarin phrasebook • Mongolia • Mongolian phrasebook • North-East Asia on a shoestring • Seoul • South-West China • Taiwan • Tibet • Tibetan phrasebook • Tokyo
Travel Literature: Lost Japan

SOUTH AMERICA Argentina, Uruguay & Paraguay • Bolivia • Brazil • Brazilian phrasebook • Buenos Aires • Chile & Easter Island • Chile & Easter Island travel atlas • Colombia • Ecuador & the Galapagos Islands • Latin American Spanish phrasebook • Peru • Quechua phrasebook • Rio de Janeiro • South America on a shoestring • Trekking in the Patagonian Andes • Venezuela
Travel Literature: Full Circle: A South American Journey

SOUTH-EAST ASIA Bali & Lombok • Bangkok • Burmese phrasebook • Cambodia • Hill Tribes phrasebook • Ho Chi Minh City • Indonesia • Indonesian phrasebook • Indonesian audio pack • Jakarta • Java • Laos • Lao phrasebook • Laos travel atlas • Malay phrasebook • Malaysia, Singapore & Brunei • Myanmar (Burma) • Philippines • Pilipino (Tagalog) phrasebook • Singapore • South-East Asia on a shoestring • South-East Asia phrasebook • Thailand • Thailand's Islands & Beaches • Thailand travel atlas • Thai phrasebook • Thai audio pack • Vietnam • Vietnamese phrasebook • Vietnam travel atlas

ALSO AVAILABLE: Antarctica • Brief Encounters: Stories of Love, Sex & Travel • Chasing Rickshaws • Not the Only Planet: Travel Stories from Science Fiction • Travel with Children • Traveller's Tales

Index

Text

Bold indicates maps.
Italics indicates boxed text.

Bold indicates maps.
Italics indicates boxed text.